Teaching ADOLESCENTS with LEARNING DISABILITIES

SECOND EDITION

STRATEGIES AND METHODS

Donald D. Deshler
University of Kansas

Edwin S. Ellis
University of Alabama

B. Keith Lenz
University of Kansas

LOVE PUBLISHING COMPANY®
Denver • London • Sydney

Published by Love Publishing Company
Denver, Colorado 80222

The first edition was titled, *Teaching the Learning Disabled Adolescent: Strategies and Methods,*
copyright © 1979 by Love Publishing Company, and authored by Gordon Alley and Donald Deshler.

Library of Congress Catalog Card Number 95-075399

Copyright © 1996 Love Publishing Company
Printed in the U.S.A.
ISBN 0-89108-241-7

PREFACE

When the first edition of this textbook appeared in 1979, the field of learning disabilities was different than it is today. Our understanding of how adolescents with learning disabilities gain knowledge was slowly expanding and being shaped. Indeed, many of the programs developed for adolescents with learning disabilities were extensions of elementary school programs and were ill conceived and frequently ineffective. Therefore, the first edition of this text focused on proposing a different way of thinking about instruction for adolescents with learning disabilities. This new approach was called learning strategies instruction and focused on defining learning strategies, making a case for learning strategies instruction, and describing how learning strategies instruction might be applied in different skill areas.

However, today we must go beyond the challenge of simply making a case for using learning strategies instruction. Programs for adolescents are vastly different than they were twenty years ago when the first edition of this text was created. Researchers and practitioners now agree that the task of altering the patterns of failure is complicated and time consuming. The full benefits of effective programming in the secondary school setting are only realized when a variety of strategies, methods, and components are organized and implemented thoroughly and consistently over a period of years. Learning strategies instruction alone is not enough; we must develop strategies programs.

We also now know more about how changes in teacher practices occur. It is clear that many teacher educators do not have opportunities to model the types of instruction that they expect novice and experienced teachers to use when they begin teaching in academically diverse classes. Powerful educational practices often are taught superficially and, as a result, the beginning teacher does not internalize or generalize them. It is also clear that many staff developers in school districts do not provide the support, follow-up, and time needed for more experienced teachers to incorporate new strategies and methods into their teaching routines. Therefore, textbooks must not understate the professional challenge that teachers face in a changing practice.

The first edition of this text has been well received. Like the first book, this text is built around contributions from solid research and the best practices in adolescent education and psychology. Surprisingly, many of the principles and practices on which the earlier text was based have found their way into this edition. Although, they now may have a different look and appear in more elaborated forms.

Most of the chapters in this second edition are authored by individuals currently conducting intervention research. Therefore, the information is current and well-grounded. New topics have been introduced and new issues raised. However, some issues and questions regarding adolescents with learning disabilities still need to be addressed by researchers. These issues continue to pose dilemmas for teachers who are required to respond to student needs on a daily basis (e.g., sexual responsibility, suicide, drug abuse, prejudice and discrimination, gang involvement, etc.). Hopefully, researchers will develop new perspectives, research programs and interventions to help teachers address these issues.

Finally, in reviewing what is known about teaching adolescents with learning disabilities, it is clear that the challenges of building secondary programs that effectively meet the needs of all adolescents is an ongoing process. Therefore, we see this edition as a work in progress, to be sculpted in future editions by continuing research and fresh perspectives on practice. We welcome your comments and suggestions for future editions of this classic text.

Acknowledgment

Much of the content of this text is the product of years of research and product development conducted by a group of colleagues who currently work at or have previously been affiliated with the University of Kansas Center for Research on Learning (formally the Institute for Research in Learning Disabilities). For well over 15 years, the Center for Research on Learning has promoted collaborative efforts among numerous researchers, teachers, and teacher trainers who are committed to improving the academic and social success of adolescents with learning disabilities. As a result of these joint efforts, a great deal has been learned about the complexities of learning and development among adolescents as well as what is required for students to successfully respond to the realities presented to students in secondary schools. Without the collective wisdom and insights of all who have participated in this work over the years, especially those who teach and work with students on a daily basis, this book would have much less to offer.

In particular, we wish to acknowledge the tremendous contributions of our colleague and friend, Dr. Jean B. Schumaker. Jean's knowledge of adolescents, the school process, and what is required to improve the academic success and life adjustments of students who are at risk has been invaluable to us in shaping this book. While her support and wisdom has been highly significant in influencing our thinking and work with adolescents with learning disabilities, her friendship and personal support has been an even greater influence.

We also wish to acknowledge Dr. Gordon Alley. Gordon not only co-authored the first edition of this text, his ideas, humor, and commitment to research have touched us all in profound ways.

Finally, we wish to express our appreciation to Martha Larkin, who provided invaluable editing assistance in earlier drafts of this manuscript.

D. D. D.   E. S. E.   B. K. L.

To Carol, Reed, Jill, Todd, and Chad

Ann, Linda, Kana, and Aman

Peter, Andrew, and Danny

Contents

FIGURES

TABLES

MEET THE EDITORS

DONALD DESHLER, Ph.D., is the Director of the University of Kansas Center for Research on Learning and is a Professor in the Department of Special Education. As the Director of the Center for Research on Learning, he provides leadership and direction for the research activities related to learning disabilities in adolescents and young adults. Dr. Deshler is internationally recognized for contributions to the field of learning disabilities through the many articles and books published as the result of research conducted under his leadership. His major research interests include the development of learning strategies interventions, as represented in the development of the Strategies Intervention Model, the infusion of learning strategies and more strategic teaching into regular classroom settings, and promoting school reform through the translations of research into practice.

EDWIN ELLIS, Ph.D., is a Professor and Program Coordinator of Interdisciplinary Programs in Teacher Education at the University of Alabama. His research interests are in cognitive based intervention for facilitating self-reliance and empowerment of students and teachers. He emphasizes strategies and methods that "water-up" the curriculum to make "thought-full classrooms" for all students.

B. KEITH LENZ, Ph.D., is a Senior Research Scientist at the University of Kansas Center for Research on Learning. His research has focused on procedures for developing learning and social skills strategies, content area teaching routines, planning routines for inclusive teaching, adult literacy programs, and teacher education reform.

MEET THE AUTHORS

JANIS BULGREN, Ph.D., is an Associate Research Scientist at the University of Kansas Center for Research on Learning. Her research has focused on the development and implementation of teaching routines designed for mainstream secondary content teachers to use in classes that contain students with learning disabilities. In these studies, she has worked with teachers to enhance student understanding of critical concepts and use of higher order thinking in secondary content classes.

GALE COLVERT is currently a doctoral candidate at the University of Alabama, Tuscaloosa, in the area of learning disabilities where she works with the Multiple Abilities Program (MAP). The MAP is an experimental special education/general education teacher preparation program. Her research interests include developing teaching techniques for multiple ability classrooms and the development of thoughtful questioning practices to enhance learning, particularly for students with learning disabilities.

LINDA K. ELKSNIN, Ph.D., earned her doctorate in special education from the University of Virginia. She is currently a Professor and Coordinator of Graduate Special Education Programs at The Citadel. Dr. Elksnin has taught preschoolers, children, and adolescents with learning disabilities, behavior disorders, and mental retardation. Areas of research interest include career and vocational assessment and education, social skills assessment and instruction, and collaboration with professionals and parents.

NICK ELKSNIN, Ph.D., earned his doctorate in school psychology from the University of Georgia and completed postdoctoral training at the Medical University of South Carolina. He has twenty years of experience as a school psychologist, special education administrator, and consultant. His research interests include issues relating to infant, toddler, preschool assessment and intervention, and career, vocational, and transition services for adolescents and adults with disabilities.

CHARLES HUGHES, Ph.D., is an Associate Professor of Special Education at Pennsylvania State University. He is also Professor-in-Charge of the Special Education Program at Penn State and an Adjunct Associate Scientist with the University of Kansas Center for Research on Learning. His research interests include teaching adolescents and young adults to self-manage social and academic behaviors needed for success in educational settings.

E. ANN KNACKENDOFFEL, Ph.D., is an Assistant Professor in the Department of Special Education at Kansas State University. Her publication and research interests include collaborative teaming, structures and strategies for inclusive settings, cooperative learning, and children with attention deficit disorder.

DARYL MELLARD, Ph.D., is a principal investigator at the University of Kansas Center for Research on Learning. He works on several research projects concerning assessment and interventions of adults with learning disabilities in adult education and postsecondary settings.

SUSAN PETERSON MILLER, Ph.D., is an Associate Professor in the Department of Special Education at the University of Nevada, Las Vegas. She is a Strategy Intervention Model preservice trainer and co-author of the Strategic Math Series. Her research interests involve math interventions for students with learning difficulties and teacher training procedures.

M. LEWIS PUTNAM, Ph.D., is a researcher at Washington Research Institute in Seattle. His research has focused on inclusion, adult literacy programs, learning strategies, and crisis interventions for adolescents with mild disabilities.

DAVID J. SCANLON, Ph.D., is an Assistant Research Scientist at the University of Kansas Center for Research on Learning and Courtesy Assistant Professor of Special Education at the University of Kansas. His research has addressed social construction of knowledge and strategic approaches to education for students with LD. He works primarily with teachers and students at the secondary and adult levels.

SHARON KAY SURITSKY, Ph.D., is the Educational Supervisor at the Wesley Highland School, Pittsburgh. Her research interests include instructional and behavioral strategies for adolescents with disabilities and the effects of experiential/adventure based programming on students' academic and social skills development.

Learning Disabilities in Adolescents: A Perspective

DONALD D. DESHLER AND M. LEWIS PUTNAM

Over the past 20 years the lives of individuals with disabilities and their families have changed dramatically. At the heart of these changes are policies enacted by the U.S. Congress and state legislatures, requiring that, like their nonhandicapped peers, all children and adolescents with disabilities be provided a free and appropriate public education.

Beyond creating a vision, these policies have opened the door for individuals with disabilities and their families to the types of educational opportunities to which all citizens should have access. The farsighted and ambitious nature of the policy goals embodied in these legislative initiatives have challenged program developers and researchers to produce knowledge, interventions, and practices that schools and the wider community need in meeting and implementing both the letter and the spirit of these policies.

For example, the research and development enterprise in special education has produced an impressive array of "pedagogical technologies," which have led to marked improvement in the overall quality of supports available to individuals with disabilities. Without the innovations that result from the research and development process, practitioners would have to rely upon unvalidated instructional procedures and material—an untenable situation in light of the extremely complex and challenging conditions presented by individuals with disabilities, including adolescents with learning disabilities (LD).

Indeed, adolescents with LD are among the prime benefactors of recent research and development efforts. Prior to enactment of the legislation described above, adolescents with LD either were ignored or were treated like their primary- or elementary-aged counterparts without regard for the their unique needs and circumstances. More recently, however, numerous research and development efforts have targeted this age group specifically. For example, since 1978, the University of Kansas Center for Research on Learning (the parent organization for the Institute for Research in Learning Disabilities) has had as its primary research mission the design and validation of interventions for adolescents and young adults with LD. In this organization alone, more than $20 million of contracted research has been completed on this age group of individuals with LD. Work by other researchers and program developers has added significantly to the existing knowledge base as well.

Even though the number of validated innovations now available to those working with adolescents with LD has increased markedly, surprisingly few of these innovations have found their way into teacher training programs or classroom practice. One of the purposes of this text is to present some of the instructional methods and practices that have emerged through these recent research and development efforts in the hope of bridging the gap between development and practice.

PROGRAMMING FOR ADOLESCENTS WITH LEARNING DISABILITIES

The collective research and development efforts of professionals in both the public school and the research arena have established several factors as central to the improved performance of adolescents with LD. Among these factors, the following six have been found to be foundational to quality programming for adolescents with LD.

1. *Adolescence is one of the most difficult and challenging of all developmental stages.* The struggle inherent in moving toward independence and establishing a new identity among peers is a significant challenge for any adolescent. For adolescents with learning disabilities, the struggle is doubly difficult. Indeed, coping with the demands of secondary schools, trying to establish independence from one's parents, and gaining acceptance from peers often become overwhelming when also faced with the effects of a learning disability such as a lack of fluency in language and comprehension, difficulties in detecting and relating to the nuances of a social situation, and so on.

2. *Quality programming decisions for adolescents with LD must be based on an understanding of the exact nature of the difficulty(ies) with which they contend.* Historically, the field of special education has focused mainly on analyzing the characteristics that define the student's deficits. The search for the root of the problem(s) generally has been confined to studying the attributes *inherent in* the adolescent. Although understanding an adolescent's learning deficits is important, it is not sufficient. Equally important is to understand the demands of the setting that contribute to the student's problems. For example, the academic and social demands of secondary schools are markedly different from those encountered in elementary school. Therefore, the effects of these escalated demands on students' performance must be considered to arrive at a more complete picture of why a student is functioning in a dysfunctional manner. In short, an adolescent's behavior is understood best when viewed as the result of an *interaction between* the characteristics of the learner and the characteristics of the setting or environment.

3. *Adolescents must be involved in all aspects of planning and implementing their instructional program—including assessment; program specification; goal setting; monitoring and evaluation; and program modification.* Adolescents with LD represent a rich source of information and insight that must be tapped on an ongoing basis. Consequently, they should be viewed as highly valued and capable partners in the educational process. To the extent that adolescents with LD are expected and permitted to take an active role

in helping to define the nature of their difficulties as well as have a voice in determining the scope and composition of their intervention program, their motivation to be active participants in the learning process will improve, as will the overall quality of the outcomes.

4. *How teachers define their role in relation to the adolescent with LD greatly affects the nature and quality of the at-risk student's education.* Quality programming for adolescents with LD requires that teachers work together as a well orchestrated team. Content teachers and support teachers (e.g., resource room and remedial teachers) represent different perspectives and strengths and, therefore, should bring different emphases to the educational arena on behalf of the adolescent with LD.

Specifically, the primary role of the support teacher should be to teach adolescents with LD specific skills and strategies to enhance their effectiveness as learners and enable them to cope with the specific demands they are facing in their various content classes. Support teachers sometimes get caught in the trap of "tutoring" adolescents with LD in the subject matter in some of their classes. This can be a costly error, because it is generally done at the expense of teaching valuable strategies that will enable students to function independently in the content classroom. Thus, in the absence of this type of instruction, students with LD will not change as learners. Although they may "get by" and even be promoted socially, they will leave the educational system grossly underprepared to face the harsh demands of the postsecondary world. Instead, by focusing most of their time on teaching students *how* to learn and perform, support teachers will empower students to benefit independently from the instruction offered in the content classroom.

On the other hand, the role of content teachers, with their subject matter expertise, should be to carefully select the information they consider essential for all students to learn (the process of selecting critical information is one of the most important things content teachers do because they do not have time to teach everything they would like; thus, what they do teach must be of utmost importance) and transform and organize this information so as to make it easier for all students to learn. They also should use well conceived instructional routines to present that information in a participatory fashion with students in the class.

In addition, content teachers are in a perfect position to prompt students to use strategies their support teacher(s) have taught them. Further, they may point out and model for all students in their class different strategies that they personally have found helpful in learning the subject matter. Through such discussion and demonstration, students get additional instruction in how to learn, and thus improve their overall effectiveness as learners.

5. *What teachers teach to adolescents with LD will have a profound influence on the extent to which these students become independent learners and performers.* To enable students with LD to respond effectively to the complex demands typical in secondary schools, especially the almost overwhelming flow of information they must process, often independently, they must be armed with a broad array of academic strategies. Unless they are taught "how to learn," adolescents with LD will leave school ill prepared to

make satisfactory life adjustments. In addition to academic strategies, they should be taught different social strategies that will enable them to interact and work effectively with others, as well as strategies for setting goals, self-advocacy, and making meaningful transitions to postsecondary settings.

Because the instructional time available to work with adolescents with LD is so limited, teachers have to choose carefully and deliberately how to spend those precious instructional minutes. Research has demonstrated clearly that when the instructional emphasis is concentrated on teaching students important learning, social, and transition strategies, remarkable gains accrue. We contend, therefore, that the majority of a support teacher's time (and a significant portion of the content teacher's time) should be spent in these areas to empower adolescents with LD to compete with their peers in the content classroom and in the world of work.

6. *How teachers teach strategies to adolescents with LD is paramount.* Students' performance improves dramatically if they are taught strategies systematically. The most effective strategy instruction is characterized by:

— thorough description of the alternative strategy to be learned
— a clear model of the new strategy, in which the teacher thinks aloud so the student can better understand how good learners think as they solve problems
— multiple opportunities for practice with the new strategy
— well designed feedback
— opportunities to generalize and adapt the strategy to a variety of situations and settings

In addition to thorough and systematic instruction of the strategy by one teacher, a master plan of action must be in place among several of a given student's key teachers so the strategies taught in one setting get cued and reinforced in other settings. Similarly, it has been found to be important that teachers coordinate their efforts across school years and across school sites (e.g., high school teachers coordinate with teachers from the feeder middle schools) to build a logical scope and sequence of skill and strategy instruction. In the absence of coordinated and sustained efforts, instruction will be sporadic and unfocused, resulting in little if any student gains. In short, to the extent that strategy instruction is both *intensive* (i.e., *systematic* and *intense*) during a given instructional setting and *extensive* (i.e., presented or prompted in multiple settings and by multiple teachers over time), students with LD will improve markedly as learners and performers.

AN OVERVIEW

This book describes an alternative instructional approach to educating adolescents with LD. Philosophically, it represents a specific direction in which the roles of the teacher and the student converge on teaching a broad array of strategies to empower students with LD to compete successfully in the content classroom, in postsecondary education, and in the world of work. The instructional ideas and recommendations presented in this text have been refined through years of collaborative work by researchers and teachers and have been designed to correspond closely with the major academic, social, and transitional demands that adolescents with LD encounter in secondary and postsecondary settings. When the key factors are followed closely, students' performance improves. This is not to say that the approach introduced in this text is a panacea. It is not! If the methods are systematically taught using the instructional principles of strategy acquisition and generalization, however, students will improve.

2

Perspectives on Instruction in Learning Strategies

EDWIN S. ELLIS AND B. KEITH LENZ

QUESTIONS TO KEEP IN MIND

- What is it about the cognitive characteristics of adolescents with LD that make learning strategy instruction desirable?

- Why do learning strategies work?

- What are the characteristics of effective learning strategies?

- In what ways do the three approaches to teaching learning strategies differ? In what ways are they similar?

- What is the difference between learning strategy instruction and instruction in study skills?

- Of the various instruction principles addressed in this chapter, which are the most important? Why?

ADVANCE ORGANIZER

This chapter provides a closer look at learning strategies and how they can be taught effectively to adolescents with learning disabilities. After reading this chapter, you should understand the following concepts.

- Why learning strategies instruction is appropriate for adolescents with learning disabilities
- Rationale for taking a functionalist approach to learning strategies instruction
- How a strategies instructional approach differs from basic skills and study skills instruction
- Features of an effective strategy
- Principles on which effective strategy instruction is based
- Features of each stage of effective strategy instruction.

Figure 2.1 shows the organization of this chapter.

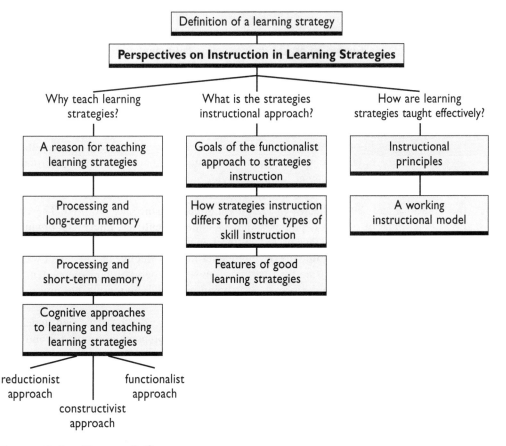

FIGURE 2.1 CHAPTER 2 ORGANIZATION

An individual's approach to a task is called a strategy. Strategies include how a person thinks and acts when planning, executing, and evaluating performance on a task and its subsequent outcomes (Deshler & Lenz, 1989). An approach includes both cognitive (what goes on in a person's head) and behavioral (what a person does) elements that guide student performance and evaluation of a task.

This chapter is designed to help you understand the strategies instructional approach. After discussing the goals of this approach and reviewing how strategy instruction differs from basic skill or study skill instruction, we take an in-depth look at the specific features of effective strategies. In the last half of this chapter, we address the critical features of effective strategies instruction.

THE REASON FOR LEARNING STRATEGIES INSTRUCTION

Instruction in learning strategies is based on a cognitive approach to teaching. Advocates of this approach believe that what happens to the learner internally deserves as much attention as what happens externally during the learning process. A cognitive approach to teaching is based on providing instruction consistent with how a student thinks in the context of learning tasks. Many cognitivists also believe that learning is best thought of as a constructive process. The learner makes learning occur, and materials, teachers, and other external influences are important only if they provide experiences that enable the learner to construct new meanings.

The major implication of the cognitive approach for teachers is that instruction must be developed based on an understanding of the interaction taking place between the individual and the environment. The teacher must understand not only the environment and how the environment may influence behavior but also how the student perceives and interprets the environment. This includes the instructional process, the materials, and the situations and settings in which learning and performance are required. Therefore, the teacher must be able to hypothesize how a student identifies, interprets, organizes, and applies information, and then provide instruction that will guide the student in learning. Instruction must either promote the development of more effective and efficient ways of learning, or it must compensate for a perceived mismatch between how the student processes information and how information is being presented by the teacher and the instructional materials.

The work of most cognitive psychologists in America can be classified under the information-processing paradigm (Gagne, 1985). To comprehend this approach and how it applies to a student's ability to learn, we have to understand the overall system of how an individual processes information.

Information-processing theory focuses on *what* and *how* information is acquired. Information-processing theorists examine how people select, extract, maintain, and use information in the environment. Although cognitive psychologists may disagree on how information actually is processed, there is general agreement that information processing is *thinking*. To understand thinking, we must explore: (a) the nature of the information an individual must process, (b) the process the individual uses to transform the information, and (c) memory limits that restrict the amount of information that can be processed (Siegler, 1986). Siegler argued that:

> The quality of children's thinking, at any age, depends on what information they represent in a particular situation, how they operate on the information to achieve their particular goal, and how much information they can keep in mind at one time. (p. 63)

Many aspects of the information-processing system have been studied in association with learning disabilities. Aspects of the information-processing system most relevant to understanding the needs of adolescents with learning disabilities relate to the processes of storing and retrieving the types of knowledge that we seem to hold in long-term memory and to the integrative processing that takes place in short-term memory.

PROCESSING AND LONG-TERM MEMORY

The processes associated with long-term memory are composed of the search strategies that are used to retrieve information that has been learned already. This information can be thought of as *acquired knowledge*. In general, if the individual has organized the information effectively, the search and retrieval process will be more efficient. The knowledge, however, must be available for retrieval. Some studies have indicated that students with LD differ from students without LD in the knowledge stored in long-term memory (Swanson, 1986).

Cognitive psychologists have proposed that there are three types of knowledge: (a) declarative knowledge, (b) procedural knowledge, and (c) conditional knowledge. *Declarative knowledge* (sometimes called semantic knowledge) describes the information we commonly think of as concepts and facts. It is the knowledge we memorize for tests, contribute in a conversation, and retrieve to answer questions and solve problems. *Procedural knowledge* describes the steps involved in how we carry out activities or perform tasks. Procedural knowledge is often hard to discuss because it includes the fluent operations involved with activities such as decoding a word, kicking a soccer ball, tying a shoe, and making an outline. Once we understand the procedure we are applying and can describe it, however, it is considered to be both declarative and procedural knowledge. *Conditional knowledge* can be thought of as the information regarding integration of procedural and declarative knowledge in the learning process. Mayer (1987) also has called this *strategic knowledge*.

Metacognitive or executive strategies can be considered aspects of conditional knowledge as well as a feedback mechanism related to how things are going in the learning process. Self-monitoring is one example of the feedback mechanism. The terms *feedback, executive processes,* and *metacognition* often are used synonymously. Some researchers apply the term *executive* to capture the idea of top-level coordination of cognitive resources, much like the role an executive assumes in a company. Other researchers have used the term *metacognition* to express the processes that transcend (meta) other thought processes (cognition).

All these terms attempt to convey the idea that the learner uses these processes primarily to provide themselves with feedback on learning. These processes enable the student to focus, select an appropriate task, predict, stay on task, check progress, monitor performance, and evaluate work. Educationally, we usually think of these processes as the ability to self-question (e.g., What do I need to do? How did I do that?). These processes are considered vital to information processing because they seem to play a central role in helping to direct learning and feelings of competence (Meichenbaum, 1977). Flavell (1976) noted:

> "Metacognition" refers to one's knowledge concerning one's own cognitive processes and products or anything related to them, e.g., the learning relevant properties of information or data. For example, I am engaging in metacognition....if I notice that I am having more trouble learning A than B; if it strikes me that I should double-check C before accepting it as fact; if it occurs to me that I had better scrutinize each and every alternative in any multiple-choice type task situation before deciding which is the best one....Metacognition refers, among other things, to the active monitoring and consequent regulation and orchestration of these processes. (p. 232)

Declarative, procedural, and conditional knowledges are stored in long-term memory. Long-term memory also can be described as background knowledge or prior knowledge. When presented with a demand, the individual must retrieve information concerning the task (declarative knowledge), evaluate the critical features of the task, in terms of time and purpose, to make decisions about the best approach to the task (conditional knowledge), and then complete the task in a planful and fluent manner (procedural knowledge). Therefore, the better the organization of knowledge, the more efficient is the learner. If knowledge is organized so the student can access the appropriate information, the processing demands are likely to be minimized, allowing for more effective and efficient processing.

The ways in which an individual organizes information are called *schemata*. Some cognitive psychologists believe that individuals store relevant or associated information together in schemas. Therefore, related declarative, procedural, and conditional knowledge might be thought of as "packaged" together. Thus, when the topic of soccer is discussed, a person most likely will think of knowledge associated with soccer such as rules, concepts, skills, and experiences rather than knowledge an individual associates with chess.

Schemas also exist within schemas. For example, soccer may exist within the schema of sports. Within soccer may be schemas associated with players, specific games, equipment, rules, tournaments, and so on. Within each of these schemas exist additional schemas, and so on. How well an individual can access this knowledge is an important concept in cognitive approaches to instruction. The teacher searches for the perfect example, experience, or analogy that will help the student magically connect new information in the lesson with stored information or experiences.

PROCESSING AND SHORT-TERM MEMORY

Once information is retrieved from long-term memory, it has to be held so it can be manipulated and worked. This "holding tank" is called *short-term memory*, and it supports integrative processing. Some psychologists do not make a distinction between integrative processing and short-term memory (Gagne, 1985). The term *working strategies* can be used to convey both ideas.

Once the information in long-term memory has been retrieved and placed in short-term memory, the individual uses this information to construct a plan or plans. These plans are composed of the working strategies the student has learned and remembered. An individual's approach to a task integrates various types of declarative, procedural, and conditional knowledge, as well as other unconscious thought processes. In the field of education, this stage of processing is associated most closely with the term *learning strategies*. The processing that takes place in the integrative processing stage, however, requires the learner to retrieve and use multiple cognitive strategies in developing an approach to a task. In addition, the strategies that could be generated might relate to the social and motivational dimensions of a task as well as the purely academic aspects.

This stage of information processing often is referred to as *higher-order processing*. Much attention has been given to the strategies that learners employ at this stage because opportunities for teaching students how to approach specific tasks in a strategic manner (e.g., how to read a story for better comprehension, listen and take notes from a lecture, write an interesting story) are more prevalent. For example, students might be taught how to construct acronyms or other mnemonics to aid in remembering information as a response to a studying task.

Some educators have concerns regarding isolated training in specific strategies. They argue that isolated training requires students to integrate the strategy independently into their information-processing system, which requires them to know when, where, and how to use the strategy. An example of isolated learning strategy training is to teach students a strategy for skimming for main ideas in a textbook chapter in a "study skills class" and then tell the students to use the strategy whenever they need to get information from a textbook. Some studies indicate, however, that students with learning disabilities are unwilling or are not able to generalize strategies to other tasks or settings (Ellis, Lenz, & Sabornie, 1987) once they have been taught a strategy in isolation.

Some researchers have tried to address the problem of isolated strategy training by conceptualizing the learning process as a system of integrated strategies. Swanson (1987a) has argued against a focus on isolated strategies as part of information-processing oriented instruction: "Intelligent performance requires a student to integrate several kinds of mental capabilities rather than merely access an appropriate strategy" (p. 5). From this perspective, the learner's approach to a task must include all of the knowledge, strategies, and substrategies that are required for the learner to respond in an effective and efficient manner *for generalized learning to occur*. This concept of strategies instruction is reflected in the broad strategy-system definition proposed by Deshler and Lenz (1989). The definition they have suggested for conceptualizing training is based on the idea that the term strategy should be used to describe an individual's global approach to a task. They define a strategy as "an individual's approach to a task including how a person thinks and acts when planning, executing, and evaluating performance on a task and its outcomes" (p. 205).

A CONTEXT FOR USING LEARNING STRATEGIES

Information-processing models acknowledge the environmental influences on the learner. That is, learning and performance demands placed on the student enhance information processing. The learner must evaluate what learning tasks require across various learning situations (i.e., school, work, home, and in the community) to know how to process the information and form the expected response within the context of the situation and setting. Sometimes the expected response is to answer "yes" or "no." At other times the required response may be to read a passage, write a paragraph, point, repeat, and so on. Therefore, the learning task often defines the types of strategies that may be appropriate for a task.

LEARNING STRATEGIES AND LEARNING DISABILITIES

Individuals with learning disabilities who seem to have difficulty completing tasks are often considered to be inactive, strategy-deficient, or insufficiently strategy-oriented learners (Torgesen, 1977a, 1977b). Some research indicates that many students with learning disabilities have trouble with this level of information processing. For example, in some studies children with learning disabilities and those who are immature did not seem to use *active* strategies for learning or problem solving (Hall, 1980; Lloyd, 1980; Loper, 1980). Several authorities (Hall, 1980; Lloyd, 1980; McKinney & Haskins, 1980) believe this failure results, in part, from an inability to generalize a previously learned problem-solving strategy to a new problem. Havertape and Kass (1978) examined the strategies of adolescents with learning disabilities and those who were normally achieving. The students' self-directions were recorded while they attempted to solve problems. From the analysis of these tapes, the researchers concluded that the students with learning disabilities lacked strategies to apply to the problem. According to the data, 40 percent of the responses (as opposed to 6 percent for the control group) consisted of random answers without any relationship to the tasks.

Efforts to train students with learning disabilities to use specific cognitive strategies to improve learning have been successful (e.g., Torgesen & Houck, 1980; Wong, 1978, 1979; Wong & Jones, 1982; Wong, Wong, Perry, & Sawaktsky, 1986). Training paradigms have encountered the most success when the training has consisted of both cognitive and metacognitive aspects of the strategy. This means that not only training in a strategy was provided, but also how the students could generate feedback to themselves through self-evaluation, self-monitoring, and goal setting (e.g., Palincsar & Brown, 1984). Debate continues, however, over how strategies that promote successful information processing should be taught.

The idea of "information-processing sensitive instruction" (Lenz, Bulgren, & Hudson, 1990) refers to instruction that:

— is fashioned and delivered differentially based on the teacher's knowledge of the range of students' information-processing and communication abilities (e.g., Deshler, Alley, Warner, & Schumaker, 1981).
— promotes student attention or reception of incoming information (e.g., Lenz, Alley, & Schumaker, 1987; Mayer, 1975, 1984, 1987).

— promotes the activation of strategies that enable the student to access and integrate prior knowledge with to-be-learned information (e.g., Ausubel, 1960; Lenz, Alley, & Schumaker, 1987; Mayer, 1983).

— promotes the activation of strategies that enable the student to build logical or structural connections between and among incoming ideas and ideas already in memory (e.g., Bulgren, Schumaker, & Deshler, 1988; Mayer, 1987).

— promotes the active participation of the student in the learning process as a planner, implementer, and evaluator (e.g., Brown, 1978; Hughes, Schumaker, Deshler, & Mercer, 1988; Van Reusen, Bos, Schumaker, & Deshler, 1987).

— instructs the student in the "why, when, and where" aspects of information related to the use of knowledge (e.g., Brown, Day, & Jones, 1983; Lenz & Hughes, 1990).

— informs the student of progress and provides appropriate feedback in a manner that improves learning (e.g., Kline, 1989; Palincsar & Brown, 1984).

— leads the student in the learning process through expert scaffolding and proleptic teaching (e.g., Deshler & Schumaker, 1988; Vygotsky, 1978; Wertsch & Stone, 1979).

— takes advantage of the developmental and social contexts of learning by gradually moving from adult guidance and modeling to peer and student guidance and modeling (Allington, 1984; Palincsar & Brown, 1984; Lenz, Schumaker, Deshler, & Beals, 1984; Vygotsky, 1978).

— plans for and promotes the acquisition and integration of semantic, procedural, and strategic knowledge throughout all phases and types of instruction (Mayer, 1987).

Identification of the teaching methods that are sensitive to an information-processing perspective requires a practical interpretation of information-processing theory. Ideally, the interpretation would set the stage for the teacher to monitor and adjust the teaching process as necessary. That is, a teacher's instructional procedures must be designed to interrupt an existing information-processing sequence, if necessary, and then to guide externally or prompt the student's strategic processing of information more effectively and efficiently than would be possible if the learner were to proceed alone. As a result, while the learner processes information, the teacher attempts to *hypothesize* how the learner processes information. This, in turn, can lead to the modification of instruction in an attempt to alter how the learner is learning and performing.

To accomplish this, the complex nature of information-processing theory must be reduced to a simpler framework and still retain the essential and powerful elements of the information-processing model. Lenz, Bulgren, and Hudson (1990) have argued that pedagogy accomplishes this when three conditions are met that deal with (a) the student's awareness that learning is about to occur, (b) the student's active and personal involvement in the learning process, and (c) the student's willingness to use this new knowledge.

1. The learner must orient himself or herself to the instructional situation by:
   a. becoming aware that a learning situation or opportunity exists
   b. attending to the new information

     c. drawing upon appropriate prior knowledge to contextualize or make logical associations with the new information

2. The learner begins to understand the information by:
   a. identifying concepts
   b. identifying similarities between different examples that indicate that they belong or do not belong to the same concept class
   c. making appropriate associations with prior knowledge regarding these concepts
   d. distinguishing between important and unimportant pieces of information in the reconstruction of his or her knowledge base

3. The learner must start acting on the new information by:
   a. testing knowledge and the impact of this knowledge in the real world
   b. exploring the various dimensions of knowledge across situations, settings, and conditions
   c. applying knowledge to solve problems
   d. ensuring that the knowledge is available for later access through self-practice and memorization activities.

APPROACHES TO TEACHING LEARNING STRATEGIES

Many educators agree that students with learning disabilities may need to become more strategic in learning, but they disagree how strategies should be taught. Three general paradigms have developed for promoting more strategic learning: reductionism, constructivism, and functionalism. Instructional methods currently being implemented can be placed on a continuum according to these three paradigms. An understanding of these paradigms is pivotal to understanding how cognitive strategy approaches currently are being implemented in programs for students with learning disabilities.

REDUCTIONIST APPROACH

The reductionist approach is based on the idea that to understand or explain something complex, it must be analyzed and divided or reduced into simpler, smaller, or more understandable components. In science, a reductionist research paradigm has led to understanding of cell biology, neurology, atomic energy, and the nature and cure of diseases. Similarly, reductionism has been applied to the study of human cognition and behavior. For example, behavioral approaches are based on the reductionist principle of behavioral task analysis. That is, understanding what the individual must do observably will enable the teacher to teach the student how to do the task. A content analysis involves identifying the component concepts and information that must be acquired in a task. A cognitive task analysis involves identifying the mental steps and states that may have to be present for an individual to complete a task. These different types of analyses are based on a reductionistic approach to teaching and learning.

    A reductionist approach is a central tenet of behavioral approaches. Reductionist approaches also have been embraced by those with a cognitive orientation. From a reductionist viewpoint, cognition is reduced to the major components, principles, processes, and structures that might govern learning. The earlier discussion of information-processing theory rests largely on a reductionist paradigm. Identification of strategies and knowledge types is an attempt to organize cognition into some components that can be discussed and understood. The strategy training program that Lloyd (1980) described as "attack strategy training" is one example of strategy training that might fit within this paradigm.

Cognitive behavior modification (CBM) is another example of a reductionist approach to cognitive training. CBM combines behavior modification techniques with self-training methods (e.g., monitoring instruction, evaluation, and verbalization). The basic tenet of this approach is that cognitions (of which inner speech is one) influence behavior and by modifying cognitions, behavior can be changed (Meichenbaum, 1977, 1979). Essentially, inner speech is viewed as behavior that is subject to the same learning principles as overt behavior. Keogh and Glover (1980) discuss the respective roles of cognitive and behavior therapy:

> It is *behavioral* in that it is structured, utilizes reinforcement techniques, is usually focused on particular problems or complaints, and is not concerned with antecedents or etiology of the problem. It is *cognitive* in that its goal is to produce change in the individual by modifying his thinking. (p. 5)

Meichenbaum (1975), the pioneer of cognitive behavior modification, describes the steps of a self-instructional program in the following way:

1. An adult model performed a task while talking to himself out loud (cognitive modeling);
2. The child performed the same task under the directions of the model's instruction (overt self-guidance);
3. The child whispered the instructions to himself as he went through the task (faded, overt self-guidance); and finally
4. The child performed the task while guiding his performance via private speech (covert self-instruction). (pp. 16–17)

Because of the cognitive deficits of students with learning disabilities, cognitive behavior modification seems to be highly compatible with their needs because it is multidimensional and includes a variety of strategies, techniques, and programs. Research reviews pinpoint two factors that are essential in successful self-instruction: (a) training should use the academic materials themselves, and (b) self-instructions have to be highly specific (Hallahan et al., 1985). To date, most of the work with students with learning disabilities has focused on self-monitoring (Rooney & Hallahan, 1985), which involves the components of self-evaluation and self-recording. For example, in a self-monitoring intervention the student keeps a record of his or her behavior and periodically monitors his or her progress toward established goals.

Hallahan (1980) and his colleagues at the University of Virginia have conducted much of the research on this approach to teaching students with learning disabilities. Hallahan and Kauffman (1986) found it useful because it stresses self-initiative and helps the student overcome passivity in learning, offers specific methods for solving problems, and applies to treating poor attentiveness and impulsivity. Research suggests that cognitive behavior modification can be used successfully to improve handwriting performance (Kosiewicz, Hallahan, & Lloyd, 1981), attention to task (Kneedler & Hallahan, 1981), reading comprehension (Swanson, 1981; Wong, 1980), and arithmetic productivity (Hallahan, Lloyd, Kosiewicz, & Kneedler, 1979).

Cognitive behavior modification techniques have been well documented to improve specific behaviors of students with LD in certain situations. Hresko and Reid (1981) reported that critics of the CBM theory question the generality and durability of the training. Rooney and Hallahan (1985) noted that generalization using cognitive behavior modification has not been established. They reported that little evidence suggests that cognitive change is occurring. As Karoly (1984) stated, "A telling criticism of published work to date in self-control and self-regulation training is the possibility that investigators may have provided children with clothes they will not likely wear outside the treatment context" (p. 98). These findings concerning generalization are not surprising because investigators focused only on influencing behaviors on specific tasks or in specific situations (Rooney & Hallahan, 1985). In short, generalization and cognitive changes have not been stressed.

The potential impact of cognitive behavior modification is not likely to be recognized in learning disabilities until a broader intervention focus is developed and studied (Meichenbaum, 1980). Because of the large number of cognitive behavior modification techniques, Rooney and Hallahan (1985) called for a curriculum-oriented view of cognitive behavior modification in which specific interventions are matched to learner needs.

CONSTRUCTIVIST APPROACH

The constructivist approach to understanding learning is what might be considered the closest approximation to a pure cognitive approach. Constructivism has been embraced in both science and psychology as a way of explaining complex or traditionally unexplainable phenomena. Researchers posit that some phenomena in biology and physics cannot be studied or explained according to a reductionist paradigm. Likewise, cognitive psychologists argue that learning is too complex to reduce to simple constructs, that learners construct knowledge in their own ways. This construction is based on the person's active involvement with new experiences in the context of previous experiences, values, needs, beliefs, and other factors that remain unknown to observers.

Schema theory was proposed as a way of expressing the dynamic relationship between the learner and the environment. Although, as discussed earlier, schemas represent how we organize knowledge, to the constructivist the important aspect of schema is that they are generalized, active, and always changing. Therefore, they cannot be reduced to simpler elements. Though schema theory emerged as a constructivist response to reductionist methods, the basis for organizing and discussing these structures has often relied on reductionist tactics. The difference is that the constructivist is satisfied with organizing understanding of learning into broad and complex structures and working within this understanding to promote learning, whereas the reductionist would not be satisfied until these structures were reduced to much simpler elements. A whole-language approach to teaching is an example of a constructivist approach to teaching language arts.

The instructional model that probably best articulates the basic principles of a constructivist approach to teaching is called reciprocal teaching. In most instances reciprocal teaching has been associated with reading instruction. The instructional principles that serve as the foundation of this approach, however, have been used as the basis for representing the constructivist approach to teaching. According to the descriptions provided by Palincsar and Brown (1984, 1986), this approach can be characterized by the following dimensions:

1. Instruction is viewed as a dialogue between the teacher and the students.
2. Instruction is characterized by much ongoing interaction between the teacher and students and among students.
3. Instruction is *scaffolded*. The teacher begins instruction in a strategy at the point where instruction is required to support the student in the next step to complete a task and then fades the support so the student is challenged to use the strategy.
4. Teacher judgment and timing are critical in the process of guiding students successfully to reflect on their performance and learning.
5. The student's skill level should not affect participation.
6. The purpose of teaching strategies is to answer questions; the goal of instruction is not to learn to use strategies.

The steps described by Palincsar and Brown (1984, 1986) indicated the importance of adhering to the following set of procedures for effective instruction:

1. Initiate instruction by discussing why a task may be difficult, about the importance of strategies, and the conditions for using strategies to help in learning.
2. Introduce each strategy, define it, and discuss it with rationales.
3. Provide practice in the strategy under controlled conditions using familiar and everyday situations.
4. Before the dialogue begins, check students' use of key aspects of the strategy to ensure minimal competence in using the strategy.
5. Ask students to apply the strategy in increasingly difficult aspects of the task and support them in their attempts to use the strategy.
6. Lead a dialogue with students, and model the use of strategies to use by thinking aloud.
7. Prompt students to comment on the teacher's model; clarify, make predictions, and answer questions that the teacher might have posed about the task.
8. Shift the responsibility for the dialogue from the teacher to the student through guided practice.
9. Monitor students' performance by praising their attempts to use strategies and, when necessary, provide additional instruction and modeling in the use of the strategy.

Studies on reciprocal teaching have indicated that reciprocal teaching can be effective with some students who have learning disabilities (e.g., Brown & Palincsar, 1982; Palincsar, 1982). Whereas few studies have been implemented with students identified as having learning disabilities, improvement in the performance of students classified as poor readers indicates that this approach may be appropriate for some students with learning disabilities (e.g., Palincsar & Brown, 1986). Palincsar and Brown reported that students generalized the use of the strategies over time and across setting (Palincsar & Brown, 1984; Brown & Palincsar, 1987). They reported that students continued to use the strategies in test situations 8 weeks after the training had ended and observed generalization of the trained strategies to similar tasks and to regular classrooms. Questions related to long-term use of the strategies by students with learning disabilities and the degree of expertise required of the teacher in implementing the procedures with students with learning disabilities have not been addressed yet in the research.

FUNCTIONALIST APPROACH

The functionalist approach to understanding learning is based on the idea that learning and our approaches to promoting learning depend on the individual, the place, and the time. Effective instruction evolves by attempting to understand the learner at various stages in the acquisition of information and then by determining when information must be reduced to a simpler form for comprehension. The teacher also must determine when the student must be given the opportunity to explore and construct meaning from experience. The functionalist tries to identify the critical strategies important for meeting a variety of demands, seeks to identify instructional methods that try to achieve a balance between the role of the teacher and of the student at various stages required for acquisition and generalization of strategies and the targeted content/information, and tries to create an instructional environment that guides and supports students' use of strategies across situations and settings. To accomplish this, curriculum, instruction, and the environment may have to be analyzed, evaluated, and reduced to simple elements to understand them. Subsequently, these components must be integrated and students must be emersed in tasks that will require them to apply and generalize strategies naturally and to develop belief systems about learning and how to learn.

From the functionalist's viewpoint, neither the reductionist nor the constructivist model can be used as the sole basis for determining instructional practice. The functionalist believes that learning consists of both reductionist and constructivist qualities and that both paradigms are useful in understanding learning and developing instructional programs. Under certain conditions adhering exclusively to a constructivist or a reductionist approach may be inappropriate for conceptualizing instruction, and such dogmatism may even be harmful to students. Both paradigms, however, are seen as contributing to the development of instructional practice.

STRATEGIES INTERVENTION MODEL

Although a number of efforts based on the functionalist approach to cognitive instruction are being developed, the most fully developed practices representing a blend of reductionist and constructivist principles are embodied in the *strategies instructional approach* (Deshler & Lenz, 1989), which serves as the basis for the strategies intervention model developed by Donald Deshler and Jean Schumaker and their colleagues at the University of Kansas Center for Research on Learning.

The strategies instructional approach was used first as the basis for development of the strategies intervention model, which was designed for developing a broad range of programs for adolescents with learning disabilities. Since then, many aspects of the strategies instructional approach have been used broadly as the basis for strategy training with younger and older students alike.

Many of the features of the strategies instructional approach are based on research from both behavioral and cognitive psychology. Many of the features manifested in cognitive behavior modification and reciprocal teaching also are included directly or are encouraged as part of the model. According to Deshler and Lenz (1989), the approach is based on the idea that teachers must fully develop three instructional areas for effective instruction.

1. A range of general strategies that can be applied to all content areas, as well as specific strategies for learning targeted content, must be identified (e.g., strategies for learning content and strategies for learning social studies content). The teacher must know the strategies that are most related to success, must understand their critical features, and must be able to articulate them in meaningful ways to students. These strategies may relate to student motivation, social interactions, or academic performance.
2. The teacher must know how to present information in a way that will induce students to learn when students do not have effective and efficient strategies for acquiring information. This means that the acquisition and generalization of strategies for learning content requires explicit instruction that is both intensive and extensive to ensure that the time spent teaching strategies to help students learn is not wasted.
3. The environment in which learning and instruction take place must facilitate and enhance strategic learning, performance, and competence across all educational settings and interactions.

Instruction in a learning strategy is seen as a means to more effective and efficient learning and performance. Initial instruction in some strategies, however, may require the teacher to reduce the demands of learning the content so as to direct the student's attention to key aspects of the strategy (e.g., practice the strategy on a shorter segment of the content or in materials that may be of high interest to the learner). Once the student understands the key dimensions of the strategy, the instructional emphasis immediately shifts to applying the strategy to naturally occurring tasks related to learning in the student's environment (e.g., notetaking on mainstream class lectures, applying test-taking strategies to approach mainstream class tests more efficiently). Since 1978, more than 80 studies involving more than 1,000 students have demonstrated the appropriateness of various applications of this instructional approach and the benefits that can be achieved for many students with learning disabilities. In addition, ongoing research has continued to refine and develop the instructional dimensions of the approach, and current research efforts promise to expand its applications. This book focuses on explaining learning strategy instruction from the perspective of the functionalist and uses the research on the strategies intervention model as a framework for describing effective practice in this area.

GOALS OF THE STRATEGIES APPROACH

Different individuals employ different strategies when completing similar tasks. Unfortunately, some approaches clearly do not always lead to success. Thus, some strategies are effective, and others are not. The goal of a strategies instructional approach is to identify strategies that are optimally effective. These strategies will help the student meet the demands of current as well as future tasks. The strategies also should be efficient in that they will help students meet the demands of a task in a manner that is appropriate, timely, judicious, and resourceful.

To illustrate this concept, consider four students studying for a biology test: Kana, Aman, Sally, and Fran. Each used different strategies to study for this test. As a result, Kana and Aman each received "A's" on their test, and both Sally and Fran received "F's." Thus, the strategies Kana and Aman employed were effective and, of course, the strategies Sally and Fran used were not. In terms of efficiency of their strategies, Kana studied 6 hours for the test, and Aman studied only 1 1/2 hours. Both, then, used effective strategies, but only Aman used a strategy that was both effective and efficient.

To summarize, the goal of strategies instruction is to teach strategies in a manner that is effective so the student learns and generalizes them. The instruction also has to be efficient. It must result in optimal learning with a minimal amount of effort by both the teacher and the student.

COMPARISON TO BASIC SKILLS OR STUDY SKILLS APPROACH

Some people view strategies as basic skills or study skills. We see them as something considerably more. Typically, a basic skill is viewed as a component of a larger domain of functioning. The basic skill of "knowledge of prefixes," for instance, is part of a larger domain of reading. Basic skills typically are operationalized and taught through the specification of behavioral task analysis. If a student has not mastered a basic knowledge of prefixes, for example, this knowledge is targeted for instruction. Under basic skills instruction students typically learn to read isolated prefixes (e.g., pre, pro, non, be, in), then learn to make words by combining prefixes with root words (e.g., pre + view = preview), then read the words in sentences, and so forth. Strategy instruction, in contrast, tends to focus more on the problem-solving aspects of using knowledge. For example, knowledge of prefixes is emphasized in terms of how to use this knowledge when encountering words that require decoding when reading for meaning (e.g., "Here's a word I don't know. Does it have a prefix? Maybe I can figure it out by isolating the prefix."). Figure 2.2 illustrates how the steps direct problem-solving behaviors, part of which is to employ one's background knowledge of prefixes.

A strategy is a form of plan, but a plan is not necessarily a strategy. For example, the procedure of performing long division and the procedure for completing an outline are both composed of sets of steps, but neither is considered a strategy. To be an effective learner or problem solver, students have to make critical decisions about which skills and procedures to use in a given situation. A strategy is a plan that not only specifies the sequence of needed actions but also consists of critical guidelines and rules related to making effective decisions during a problem-solving process. The guidelines often attempt to enable students to make decisions about using known skills or procedures.

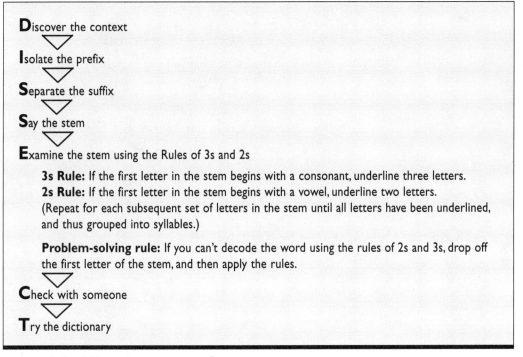

Discover the context

Isolate the prefix

Separate the suffix

Say the stem

Examine the stem using the Rules of 3s and 2s

3s Rule: If the first letter in the stem begins with a consonant, underline three letters.
2s Rule: If the first letter in the stem begins with a vowel, underline two letters.
(Repeat for each subsequent set of letters in the stem until all letters have been underlined, and thus grouped into syllables.)

Problem-solving rule: If you can't decode the word using the rules of 2s and 3s, drop off the first letter of the stem, and then apply the rules.

Check with someone

Try the dictionary

FIGURE 2.2   WORD IDENTIFICATION STRATEGY

Source: From *Learning Strategies Curriculum: The Word Identification Strategy,* by B. K. Lenz, J. B. Schumaker, D. D. Deshler, and V. L. Beals, 1984, Lawrence, University of Kansas.

An effective strategy addresses other critical dimensions of learning and performing as well. For example, many strategies contain steps that cue students specifically to engage self-motivation and emphasize control tactics. They also may contain steps that cue students to monitor the problem-solving process and evaluate their own progress.

To illustrate this concept, consider the plan for completing an outline illustrated below:

Step 1: Find out the part of the chapter that has to be outlined.
Step 2: Read the chapter.
Step 3: Outline the main ideas and details.
Step 4: Put your outline safely in your notebook.

This plan is viewed most appropriately as a study skill rather than a strategy because the steps contain little guidance with regard to facilitating effective thinking behaviors (e.g., decision making, self-motivation, monitoring). Alternatively, the plan below might be considered considerably more strategic because it provides cues for planning, executing, and evaluating performance as well as using self-motivation and self-control procedures.

THINK AHEAD	Clarify the assignment.
	Check to see if you have all materials ready.
	Psych yourself up to do excellent work; set goals.
THINK DURING	Select a section of the chapter to be analyzed.
	Look for "clue words" that indicate type of information (compare/contrast, cause/effect, description, etc.).
	List details in abbreviated form.
	Decide a main idea that best captures what the details are about.
THINK BACK	Make sure each section of chapter has its own outline.
	Explain your outlines to someone else to see if they make sense.
	See if you met your goals.

FEATURES OF GOOD LEARNING STRATEGIES

As noted earlier, some strategies are effective and efficient, and others are not. Those that are both effective and efficient share characteristics that fall into three categories: content features, design features, and usefulness features. The *content* of the strategy refers to its steps and what they are designed to facilitate during the learning process. The *design* features refer to how the steps are packaged to facilitate learning and subsequent use of the strategy. The *usefulness* feature refers to the potential transferability of the strategy to everyday needs in a variety of settings. Ellis and Lenz (1987) identified a number of critical features across these dimensions. They are presented in Table 2.1 and described below.

CONTENT FEATURES

The content features of the strategy relate to how well the process of meeting a common setting demand has been specified in terms of both mental and physical actions. The critical features that must be considered generally relate to the extent to which the strategy has incorporated principles of learning and have been found to facilitate a more effective and efficient response to meeting a demand. Although a strategy intervention may not contain all of these features, the intervention is more likely to be strategic if the following features are included in the intervention:

1. *Effective learning strategies contain a set of steps that lead to a specific and successful outcome.* A strategy is not a collection of suggestions and guidelines that result in separate outcomes. Rather, it is a set of steps that organizes the approach to the task and results in successful completion of the task. Although individual units of performance may be evaluated (e.g., "How well is the student performing the second step in the test-taking strategy?"), one outcome always is used to judge the ultimate success of the strategy (e.g., "Did the strategy help the student pass the test?"). The student then can examine the result of his or her effort and begin to evaluate the effectiveness of the strategy.

TABLE 2.1   EFFECTIVE AND EFFICIENT STRATEGIES

Features	Characteristics
Content	Lead to a specific and successful outcome.
	Are sequenced in a manner that leads to an efficient approach to the task.
	Cue students to use specific cognitive strategies.
	Cue students to use metacognition.
	Cue the students to select and use appropriate procedures, skills, or rules.
	Cue the student to take some type of overt action.
	Can be performed by the student in a limited amount of time.
	Are essential and do not include unnecessary steps or explanations.
Design	Use a remembering system.
	Use simple and brief wording.
	Begin with "action words."
	Use seven or fewer steps.
	Use words that are uncomplicated and familiar to students.
Usefulness	Address a common but important existing problem that students are encountering in their settings.
	Address demands that are encountered frequently over an extended time.
	Can be applied across a variety of settings, situations, and contexts.

2. *The steps of an effective strategy are sequenced in a manner that leads to an efficient approach to the task.* A strategy is not a collection of good ideas organized into a set of steps. A strategy that simply leads to completion of the task is not enough. A strategy taught to students must be a collection of "best" ideas organized in the "best" sequence that leads to the "best" mental and physical actions for the task.

The approach that is "best" for adults is not necessarily "best" for youth. For example, whereas adults often stop to check comprehension after chunks of reading passages consisting of multiple paragraphs, adolescents with learning disabilities who are struggling to improve their comprehension often must stop at the end of much smaller chunks to induce comprehension (e.g., at the end of each paragraph or several times within a paragraph). Such frequent stops to check comprehension actually may feel unnatural and inefficient to adults but nevertheless may be the "best" approach for immature readers.

3. *The steps of an effective strategy cue students to use specific cognitive strategies.* Effective learning strategies often are "strategy systems" incorporating many cognitive strategies such as activating background knowledge, generating questions, summarizing, imaging, and so forth. A number of powerful cognitive strategies can be used to

enhance learning and performance. Some of these strategies are used primarily for motivational purposes; others are used for processing information effectively. Cognitive strategies for motivation include:

— establishing a purpose
— setting goals
— using self-affirmation statements
— using self-coping statements
— using self-reinforcement
— monitoring progress toward goals

Some cognitive strategies for processing information are:

— activating background knowledge
— predicting
— self-questioning
— visualizing
— paraphrasing/summarizing
— monitoring comprehension
— prioritizing
— comparing/linking new information to background knowledge
— creating analogies
— looking for patterns of information
— organizing information into patterns

If the strategy does not include cues to use cognitive strategies and the instruction does not include explanations related to using the cognitive strategies, the strategy likely is simply a procedure with few strategic qualities. A variety of cognitive strategies are cued in the PASS reading comprehension strategy illustrated in Figure 2.3.

4. *The steps of an effective strategy cue students to use metacognition.* Reflection on and evaluation of the way a task is being approached and accomplished are important components of the problem-solving process. Therefore, these behaviors (e.g., self-questioning, goal setting, checking, reviewing, self-monitoring) should be included in the steps of the strategy when they are important in completing a task. An effective strategy cues students to use these behaviors at optimal times, and effective strategy instruction explains them to students.

5. *The steps of an effective strategy cue students to select and use appropriate procedures, skills, or rules.* Strategies guide students in selecting procedures, skills, or rules that are most appropriate for meeting the demands of a task. An effective strategy provides a guide for students as to which resources to apply and where. The strategy should name the appropriate procedure or skill and cue students to employ it at the optimal time during the problem-solving process. The word-attack strategy that was illustrated in Figure 2.2, for example, cues students to use prefix skills to decode the word only after the student has attempted first to solve the problem using context analysis (using the context of the sentence to try to guess what the word is).

Preview, review, and predict
Preview by reading the heading and one or two sentences.
Review what you know already about this topic.
Predict what you think the text will be about.

Ask and answer questions

Content-Focused Questions	*Monitoring Questions*	*Problem-Solving Questions*
Who? What? When? Where? Why? How?	Is my prediction correct? How is this different from what I thought it was going to be about? Does this make sense?	Is it important that it make sense? Do I need to reread part of it? Can I visualize the information? Do I need to read it more slowly? Does it have too many unknown words? Do I need to pay more attention? Should I get help?
How does this relate to what I already know?		

Summarize
Say what the short passage was about.

Synthesize
Say how the short passage fits in with the whole passage.
Say how what you learned fits with what you knew.

FIGURE 2.3   PASS READING COMPREHENSION STRATEGY

6. *The steps of an effective strategy cue students to take some type of overt action.* A strategy must cue both mental and physical actions. An absence of physical actions will make it difficult to evaluate application of the strategy and to monitor progress toward meeting the setting demand. When teaching the strategy, you need to ensure that all physical actions are supported by a clear explanation of the associated mental actions that need to take place. Information about the mental actions provide guidance related to decisions about the best way to meet the demand. For example, if a step in a paragraph writing strategy you are teaching cues students to outline their ideas before writing their first draft, then you will need to provide guidance on how to make decisions about what information should be included in the outline.

7. *Students can use all the steps of an effective strategy in a limited amount of time.* A strategy must be performed in a relatively short time. Otherwise the self-instruction process involved in performing the strategy will be undermined, rendering the process

ineffective. Strategies designed to address tasks that extend over a period of time (e.g., 1 or 2 days) tend to suffer from insufficient analysis of the task or demand. Strategies that attempt to address such tasks (e.g., homework completion) must take into consideration that many strategies probably are involved, not just one.

8. *An effective strategy does not contain unnecessary steps or explanations.* The number of steps and the amount of explanation in the strategy should be no more than what is needed to enable the student to learn the strategy and meet the setting demand. Unnecessary steps or trivial information increases the amount of information to be learned and remembered about a strategy. Thus, steps such as "open your book" should not be included in an effective strategy.

To summarize, the content of an effective strategy provides guidelines for *how to think and act when planning, executing, and evaluating performance on a task and its outcomes.* It should guide the student's approach to a task while promoting flexibility that will enable the student to meet unexpected circumstances and situations that may be associated with the task at any given time.

Content features of the strategy are related to how well the process of meeting a common setting demand has been specified in terms of both mental and physical actions. Critical features that must be considered under this dimension generally relate to the extent to which the strategy has incorporated principles of learning and has been found to facilitate a more effective and efficient response to meeting a demand. Although a strategy intervention may not contain all of these features, the intervention is more likely to be strategic if the following design features are included in the intervention.

DESIGN FEATURES

The design features of the strategy concern the way the strategy is packaged for presentation to the student. An effective strategy design organizes and arranges the content of the strategy for the student's optimal learning and use. Although an effective strategy may not share all of the design features listed below, we have found that students with LD tend to more readily learn and use strategies that incorporate more of these design features.

1. *The steps of an effective strategy are encapsulated with a remembering system.* Each step in a strategy always has two aspects. The first aspect concerns the actions the step is designed to facilitate or the content of the strategy. When teaching the strategy, this first aspect is addressed through full explanation of all the guidelines, cues, rationales, procedures, rules, processes, and exceptions, that are important to performing the strategy successfully. To use the strategy successfully, students must remember this information. The second aspect of each step consists of key action words learned in association with the step. These action words serve as the remembering system of the strategy because they trigger the appropriate associations or explanations related to successful performance of the strategy. Because the content of the strategy can be quite extensive and many individuals need assistance in learning and remembering information, the design of the strategy must facilitate the memorization process. The content of an effective strategy is organized to facilitate ease of remembering, and many strategies utilize a

mnemonic device to facilitate memorization and recall of the strategy steps.

When a first-letter mnemonic device is used as a remembering system, effective strategies use a mnemonic word whose meaning closely parallels the overall strategic process the strategy is designed to address. The first letters of the word-attack strategy, D-I-S-S-E-C-T, illustrated in Figure 2.2, illustrate this concept. They spell the word *dissect*, as in to dissect a word to decode it. Although students with LD have developed and successfully used many strategies without this consideration, this feature can make the mnemonic easier to learn and remember for many students.

2. *The wording of each step in the remembering system is simple and brief.* The steps in an effective strategy do not contain unnecessary words. Each step contains only a few action words to facilitate a direct association to the cognitive and physical actions that are necessary to perform the step and that have been presented to the individual already as part of the full explanation of that strategy. The steps to the reading comprehension strategy illustrated in Figure 2.3 illustrate this concept.

3. *Each step of the remembering system begins with an "action word."* To promote an active approach to the task, the action word is usually a verb or a key word related to the action the step is designed to cue. Words such as "if," "then," and "materials" have less power than verbs such as "preview," "ask," and "summarize."

4. *An effective strategy utilizes seven or fewer steps in the remembering system.* Naturally, as more steps are included in the strategy, the memory load on students increases. Conversely, too few steps can limit the effectiveness of the strategy, as more steps are needed to cue important actions. Effective remembering systems seek a balance between too many and too few steps. The remembering systems of effective strategies generally utilize seven or fewer steps.

Some tasks require a relatively sophisticated approach involving more than seven steps. The remembering systems of effective strategies address this by embedding a substrategy, or ministrategy, within a general set of steps. For example, a strategy may contain five steps. The second step, however, cues students to perform a short three-step substrategy before going on to the third step of the general strategy.

5. *The strategy steps are communicated using words that are uncomplicated and familiar to students.* Effective strategies are designed so the wording to convey the strategy steps is readily understandable to students. At times, however, a remembering system employs words that convey powerful actions that may be new to the student and for which no suitable, more familiar words can be substituted without making a strategy step excessively long. For example, the last step of the reading comprehension strategy illustrated in Figure 2.3, "Synthesize," cues the student to relate the short passage just read to the overall theme of the chapter. In such cases, instruction in these concepts and language prerequisites should be included during the instructional process.

USEFULNESS FEATURES

Naturally, a strategy should be useful in enabling students to realize personal goals that are relevant to their needs. The usefulness features generally relate the strategy's potential use and transferability across materials, settings, situations, and people. Most strategies that are effective meet the following criteria:

1. *The most effective strategies address a common but important existing problem that students are encountering in their settings.* Strategies that are useful immediately and whose benefits are apparent immediately tend to be learned and generalized more quickly than strategies that seem to have less utility from students' perspectives. Thus, the problem the strategy is designed to address and what students perceive as problems in their environments must match.

Some teachers target a strategy for instruction in anticipation of future problems their students will encounter. For example, although test-taking may not be a particularly pressing demand in some 6th-grade settings, some 6th-grade teachers might choose to introduce a test-taking strategy in anticipation of the testing demands their students will encounter in junior high school. Although preparing students for future problems may seem prudent, our experience has shown us that unless LD students perceive an immediate need for the strategy, their commitment to learn it, as well as their subsequent generalization of it, will be minimal.

In addition, effective learning of the strategy requires that students have ample opportunities to experiment with its utility on real problems. If these opportunities are not provided, the strategy often will have to be retaught when students enter settings where the strategy is needed.

2. *Effective strategies address demands that are encountered frequently over an extended time.* Because strategy instruction is necessarily intensive and extensive, the relative cost-benefit ratio plays an important role in the effectiveness of strategies. Teaching a strategy for meeting the setting demands that are encountered only infrequently (e.g., once-a-semester book reports) will have considerably less impact on students' overall success than instruction in strategies that target setting demands that students encounter frequently (e.g., daily or weekly).

Naturally, the more opportunities students have to apply the strategy, the more readily students will perceive its benefits, attribute success at the tasks to using a more effective strategy, and habitualize its use. Although the strategy has to meet current demands, it also should be powerful enough to have long-term utility and benefit the individual in the near future as well as into adulthood.

3. *Effective strategies can be applied across a variety of settings, situations, and contexts.* Strategies that are designed to meet highly unique and specific situations are often the most powerful in these specific contexts (e.g., a test-taking strategy to be used to address a specific teacher's highly unusual approach to giving tests). These types of strategies usually have limited value in other situations and settings. Thus, effective strategies are specific enough to enable students to meet task demands successfully, but also general enough to be generalizable across settings and situations. For example, an effective test-taking strategy is designed to be effective when used when taking the types of tests commonly encountered in science, social studies, geography, or health classes.

IMPORTANT INSTRUCTIONAL PRINCIPLES

Good strategies are composed of the essential processes for accomplishing a goal. Use of a good strategy consumes as few intellectual processes as necessary to do so (Pressley, Borkowski, & Schneider, 1989). Similarly, good strategy instruction incorporates procedures based on sound instructional principles that are powerful enough to enable students to acquire a new strategy as quickly and as efficiently as possible. Some basic principles that have been found to facilitate this type of strategy instruction are reviewed below.

TEACH PREREQUISITE SKILLS BEFORE STRATEGY INSTRUCTION BEGINS

Prior to beginning formal learning strategy instruction, students should be taught the necessary prerequisite skills. Because most learning strategies are designed to enable students to use skills in a problem-solving context, skills that are required for successful strategy use should be mastered *before* instruction in the actual strategy begins. To facilitate prerequisite skill instruction, students' skills must be assessed to determine whether they have mastered the skills necessary for successful application of a specific learning strategy. Some skills may require only a brief review. Others may require more intensive instruction. As a general rule, students should have mastered prerequisite skills well enough to apply them fluently. For example, instruction in the paraphrasing strategy (see Figure 2.4), in which students are expected to read and paraphrase the content of a paragraph, may have to be preceded by instruction in a related prerequisite skill area such as paraphrasing smaller information chunks (e.g., one sentence). Similarly, if students are to be taught the sentence writing strategy (Schumaker & Sheldon, 1985), instruction in the strategy is enhanced if students first learn how to identify subjects, verbs, and prepositions.

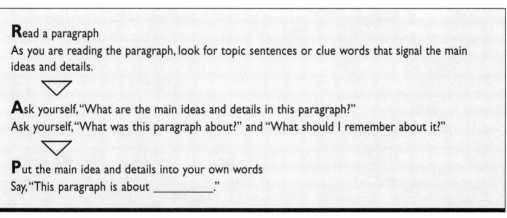

Read a paragraph
As you are reading the paragraph, look for topic sentences or clue words that signal the main ideas and details.

▽

Ask yourself, "What are the main ideas and details in this paragraph?"
Ask yourself, "What was this paragraph about?" and "What should I remember about it?"

▽

Put the main idea and details into your own words
Say, "This paragraph is about _____."

FIGURE 2.4   PARAPHRASING STRATEGY

Teaching the necessary prerequisite skills prior to strategy instruction has two main benefits. First, teachers will be working only with students who are prepared to benefit from instruction in the given strategy; hence, the necessary steps already have been taken to prevent students from failing. Second, instruction in the strategy will be more efficient because using instructional time to cover prerequisite skills in the middle of strategy instruction will not be necessary. This will allow students to travel a relatively straight and uninterrupted path between the initial introduction and description of the strategy and actual application of the strategy to classroom assignments. Such a path can enhance students' motivation to learn additional strategies.

TEACH REGULARLY AND INTENSIVELY

The second principle associated with strategy instruction is that learning strategies should be taught intensely and regularly. For students with learning disabilities to master complex learning strategies successfully to a point of fluency, these strategies have to be taught consistently. This means *daily* exposure to strategies instruction, if possible, with ample practice opportunities programmed into an instructional period. Thus, activities that prevent or interrupt daily instruction (e.g., assemblies, standardized tests, trips to the counselor's office) must be kept to a minimum. In addition, regular attendance must be required and encouraged.

A key to ensuring intensive instruction is for both teachers and students to set daily, weekly, and semester goals related to strategy acquisition and generalization. Students should set semester goals that specify the strategies they want to learn. The daily and weekly goals they set should specify the skills they want to acquire in the process of mastering the new learning strategy. In goal setting students have to consider two factors as they work on meeting a goal:

1. A *quantity factor* specifying how much work will be accomplished during a given period (e.g., "Today I will complete five word problems in math using the problem-solving strategy I am learning").
2. A *quality factor* specifying what kinds of behaviors or attitudes a student will try to incorporate during completion of a strategy practice exercise (e.g., "Before beginning any test or assignment, I will make a self-affirming statement").

Student goals should specify target dates for completing specific instructional components. These goals should be referred to regularly, and performance should be adjusted accordingly to meet them. In the absence of ambitious goals for strategy acquisition and generalization, students tend to prolong the time spent mastering a given strategy. Given the many deficits that most low-achieving students and students with learning disabilities exhibit, the limited instructional time available must be used optimally, and every effort must be made to prevent students from getting bogged down in learning a given strategy.

Teachers likewise should set goals regarding how much to accomplish with each student within a specified time. Without clearly defined goals, it is easy to fall a little behind schedule each week, resulting in significant slippage by the end of the semester. Well defined and ambitious goals tend to increase the intensity of instruction as well as students' overall progress. By sharing their goals with their students, teachers can model effectively for students how to set goals and express the personal value they have found in doing so regularly.

EMPHASIZE PERSONAL EFFORT

A third principle upon which learning strategy instruction is founded relates to the role that personal effort plays in the learning process. Students need to understand that successful problem solving, in the simplest terms, is related to choosing a strategy that effectively addresses the demand of the setting and then trying as hard as possible to use the strategy correctly. Teachers should remind students regularly that academic success results when students exert significant personal effort in applying an appropriate learning strategy to a problem they are facing. In short, they need to teach their students that the key elements in the formula for successful problem solving in an academic setting are:

Appropriately Chosen Learning Strategy + Personal Effort =
Successful Problem Solving

Frequent reference to this formula in discussing progress and providing feedback to students can enhance students' understanding that personal effort must be exerted to ensure success. Using this formula over a sustained time can increase students' understanding of the learning process.

REQUIRE MASTERY

An important principle underlying learning strategy instruction is to require student *mastery* of a learning strategy. Research has shown that students usually are unable to generalize a given learning strategy (the major instructional goal) until they can perform the strategy proficiently at the specified mastery levels (Schmidt, Deshler, Schumaker, & Alley, 1989). Specifically, two dimensions constitute mastery performance:

1. *Correct performance* of a given strategy.
2. *Fluent use* of the strategy.

Typically, the early phases of strategy instruction focus on students' acquiring and performing the correct strategy routines. After they have learned the routines in the correct order, the instructional emphasis must shift to increasing the speed and fluidity with which students use the strategy. The strategy must be integrated in their repertoire at the automatic level (Pressley, Johnson, & Symons, 1987). Older students often are required to acquire, store, or express large amounts of information quickly. If a learning strategy is to serve these students well, they must believe they are more efficient at tackling a task or assignment with the strategy than without it.

Establishing a mastery criterion that is appropriate for all students is difficult. A 10th-grade student who is reading at the 4th-grade level must first demonstrate mastery of a strategy on 4th-grade materials, but the instructional goal is to perform at a mastery level on 10th-grade materials. Unfortunately, the instructional time required to achieve the goal of mastery on 10th-grade materials may not justify the trade-offs with regard to other instructional activities. For some students, extending the time period over which mastery is achieved might be necessary. For example, if a student is having difficulty mastering the verbal expression of the different routines of a strategy, proceeding to a subsequent instructional stage and allowing the student to use a cue card when practicing with the strategy rather than relying on memory may be wise. The decision not only may enable mastery of the strategy more quickly and reduce student frustration, but it also may afford the student multiple opportunities for exposure to the steps of the strategy in other contexts and circumstances, helping to compensate for what was not mastered at an earlier instructional stage.

INTEGRATE INSTRUCTION

The instructional methodology discussed in the next section of this chapter is presented as a set of instructional stages that on the surface seem to be linear in nature. Although the stages are arranged in a logical order, beginning with a pretest of the student's skills and ending with specific generalization activities, strategy instruction seems to be most effective when several of the instructional methods are *integrated* throughout the entire series. For example, the generalization activities seem to be most effective if generalization is forecasted and emphasized in all the instructional stages (Ellis, Lenz, & Sabornie, 1987a, 1987b). Even as early as the pretest stage of the instructional methodology, students' attention can be focused on generalization by emphasizing how they will be able to use the given strategy in a broad array of settings and situations once they have mastered it.

Similarly, teachers continually can identify situations in which additional demonstration of the strategy or a substep of a strategy would be advantageous for students. For example, when giving feedback to a student on performance of the strategy, modeling might be helpful to show the student what to do on the next practice attempt. Teachers also can give students multiple opportunities to verbalize the steps of the strategy and the reasons for each step or substep of the strategy by asking them regularly to name and explain certain aspects of the strategy they are learning. This can be done even at times that typically are considered to be "noninstructional." For example, when students are being dismissed from class, they can "earn their way out of the room" by repeating a certain step of a strategy, by specifying why a step is useful, or by giving a situation in which the strategy can be used. Consistently expecting students to perform in this fashion can do much to help them achieve mastery. In short, teachers have to be sensitive to students who may need repeated exposure to an instructional technique (e.g., another model) or to those whose learning can be enhanced by recycling through an earlier stage.

EMPHASIZE COVERT PROCESSING

Throughout the instructional process teachers should deliberately discuss and demonstrate the covert processes involved in performing the strategy. Application of a learning strategy to meet a specific academic task demand often involves covert processes (e.g., cognitive strategies such as visual imagery, prioritizing, hypothesis generating, relating new information to prior knowledge, or paraphrasing; and metacognitive strategies such as problem analysis, decision making, goal setting, task analysis, and self-monitoring). Thus, instruction in a learning strategy should address the covert processes involved in applying the learning strategy. For example, when teaching a learning strategy that contains a step designed to cue the student to paraphrase the main idea of a paragraph, an effective teacher will *explain* and *demonstrate* the cognitive processes one might use to find and state the main idea. This teacher also would coach students to enable them to perform these cognitive processes effectively and efficiently. Roehler and Duffy (1984) have called instruction that emphasizes covert processing "direct explanation" (p. 265). In short, they argue that effective teachers focus not only on the mechanical aspects of learning and performing but also on teaching students directly to understand and use the covert processes involved in the task. A less effective teacher might simply instruct (with *no* explanation or demonstration) the student to perform the covert behavior and then provide feedback with regard to whether the desired outcome was attained (e.g., whether students generated the correct main idea).

EMPHASIZE GENERALIZATION IN THE BROADEST SENSE

Over time, the focus of instruction should shift from teaching students to use a task-specific learning strategy to meet the demands associated with a specific problem domain to a focus on how strategies can be used to address similar problems in other domains. Although a task-specific learning strategy typically is designed to target a problem that might be encountered in a specific academic domain (e.g., studying for a test), instruction in that strategy must impact the student beyond the scope of the original problem domain. Students have to learn to be flexible and to adapt the processes involved in the task-specific strategy to meet a variety of needs in other problem domains. For example, if students are being taught to organize and prioritize in the context of studying for tests, they also might be taught how to apply these skills in other problem-solving contexts.

Original instruction might emphasize how ideas can be depicted in a manner that clearly communicates relationships, as well as the processes used to prioritize what should be memorized first, second, third, and so on. Later, after students have mastered application of the skills within the context of studying for a test, these same skills might be addressed within the context of a paragraph-writing task or a notetaking task. Naturally, the more experience students have in learning the skills associated with categorizing and prioritizing in specific contexts, the more readily they will be able to apply them in contexts they have not encountered previously.

A WORKING INSTRUCTIONAL MODEL FOR TEACHING LEARNING STRATEGIES

The information presented in the previous sections provides the underpinnings of a working model for teaching learning strategies. This working model has been operationalized through specification of the eight instructional stages, listed in Table 2.2. We refer to them as the "stages of acquisition and generalization" (SAG). Specific instructional stages have been identified to denote different emphases in the instructional process. The procedures described for these stages have this emphasis and have been organized into specific phases

TABLE 2.2   STAGES OF ACQUISITION AND GENERALIZATION

Stage	Phase
1: Pretest and make commitments	1: Orientation and pretest 2: Awareness and commitment
2: Describe the strategy	1: Orientation and overview 2: Current strategy and remembering system
3: Model the strategy	1: Orientation 2: Presentation 3: Student enlistment
4: Verbal elaboration and rehearsal	1: Verbal elaboration 2: Verbal rehearsal
5: Controlled practice and feedback	1: Orientation and overview 2: Guided practice 3: Independent practice
6: Advanced practice and feedback	1: Orientation and overview 2: Guided practice 3: Independent practice
7: Confirm acquisition and make generalization commitments	1: Confirm and celebrate 2: Forecast and commit to generalization
8: Generalization	1: Orientation 2: Activation 3: Adaptation 4: Maintenance

of instruction. In addition, the procedures associated with the stages of instruction are employed over various time periods and are unique to each stage of instruction. The time frame can range from as short as one instructional period to as long as several weeks for a given instructional stage. Although the emphasis of instruction varies depending on the instructional stage, the structure of the daily lesson generally remains consistent regardless of the stage of instruction.

Two important instructional elements are incorporated into each instructional stage to promote learning and motivation: (a) the use of organizers and (b) principles of goal attainment. Because these elements are standard across the implementation of each instructional stage, only the aspects unique to a specific instructional stage will be addressed as each instructional stage is described below. First, each instructional stage uses advance, lesson, and post organizers to promote learning. Each lesson begins with an advance organizer. The purpose of this organizer is to help the teacher:

— gain the students' attention

— review any relevant prior learning

— make the connection between previous learning and the current instructional goals

— focus students' attention on the relationship between activities of the day's lesson with the overall goal of mastering the new strategy

— personalize learning

— communicate specific learning and performance expectations.

As each instructional stage is implemented, teachers should use lesson organizers to further cue organization, state expectations, prompt the integration of new information with information previously learned, and make relationships clear. Finally, a post organizer is provided that prompts students to review learning and evaluate whether expectations for learning and performance have been met.

Second, the process of setting and evaluating goals related to strategy learning are incorporated into each instructional stage. To accomplish this, students set their own performance goals for the lesson, and evaluate their performance at the end of the lesson. Progress is noted on a chart, and the student decides what must be accomplished in the next instructional period.

An overview of the key instructional behaviors associated with each stage of strategy acquisition and generalization is presented below. The instructional stages are described in terms of the major focus of instruction, expected outcomes, and critical components and processes associated with each stage.

STAGE 1: PRETEST AND MAKE COMMITMENTS

Consistent with the underlying principle that instruction should be driven by student goals, the major purpose of Stage 1 is to have students *want* to make a commitment to learn the strategy. The intent of this stage, therefore, is to motivate students to learn a new strategy by making them aware of: (a) a specific setting demand encountered in many of their classes, (b) how they are performing with regard to this demand, and (c) the existence of alternative approaches or strategies to meet this demand. They also are informed about the results obtained by other students with similar learning habits and entry-level skills who have learned the new strategy. In short, through a discussion with the teacher, students are led to the following conclusions: (a) certain setting demands are causing significant problems for them in school; (b) their failure is not innate but, instead, is a function of not knowing the best strategy for the task at hand; (c) alternative approaches can produce success once these routines (strategies) are learned and used through consistent effort on the students' part; and (d) other students with similar difficulties in school have been successful after using the new strategy.

Another purpose of this first instructional stage is to establish a baseline related to how each student is performing currently in meeting the targeted setting demand. By observing students carefully as they perform tasks related to the setting demand and by discussing with students how they approach specific tasks and how they feel when they are trying to respond to different task demands, teachers can determine students' current learning habits and anticipate the relative degree of instructional intensity required to teach the new strategy.

This stage has two phases of instruction: (a) an initial Orientation and Pretest, and (b) a phase in which students demonstrate Awareness and Commitment to learn. Upon completion of these two phases, a signed goal statement indicating a commitment to learn and apply the strategy and a record of the student's baseline performance should have been produced.

PHASE 1: ORIENTATION AND PRETEST

The purpose of the Orientation and Pretest phase is to introduce students to the importance of jointly (i.e., the teacher and the student) determining *how* students are approaching a specific curriculum demand (e.g., storing information from a lecture). Students need to understand at this point that the purpose of the probes or "tests" in this stage are not the same as those given in the general classroom. Here the purpose is to try to figure out what strategies the student uses effectively and what current strategies/learning habits should be modified or changed altogether. They need to know that how they score on the pretest will have no bearing on their grades in the course.

Students also need to understand that the deficits to be identified through the pretesting process are specific to the task or setting demand and are not indicative of generalized deficiencies or inadequacies in the student. Often, students with a long history of academic failure have difficulty separating their worth as individuals from difficulties they may have in completing a specific task. During this phase the teacher should:

— give students a rationale for this phase of the instructional process.
— provide an overview of the entire pretest stage, and point out how it is tied into the rest of the instructional process.
— discuss how decisions will be made regarding instruction on strategies in the area being assessed. Specifically, inform students that they will have a major voice, through the goal-setting process, in determining whether to work on a given strategy.
— assess how students perform relative to a specific setting demand. This assessment should include observations of students' strategic *processes* and *products*. The processes to be observed include the general approach students might use to accomplish the task and the specific behaviors they display while approaching the task (e.g., what students do when attempting to take notes). The result of these processes is a product (e.g., a record of how much of the critical information students were able to include in their notes, how well this information was organized, and so on).
— use materials and tasks from the regular classroom (i.e., the setting in which students ultimately must demonstrate mastery with the strategy) as the vehicles for the assessment process.
— score the student's products, compare each student's scores to the set mastery criteria, and determine whether the strategy is appropriate for each student who took the pretest.

PHASE 2: AWARENESS AND COMMITMENT

One purpose of this phase is to make students aware of what was learned about them as learners as they were observed performing tasks and through the analysis of the products that they produced. In essence, this information represents their current habits in coping with setting demands. A second purpose is to give students a general idea of the strategy they can choose to learn as an alternative to their current approach to the task. Finally, students make commitments related to learning the new strategy, and the teacher makes a commitment to students to teach the strategy in a manner that will promote understanding and remembering. As a part of this phase, the teacher should:

— review results of the pretest. Evaluate the student's performance according to *categories* of strengths and weaknesses. By characterizing strengths and weaknesses in relation to categories, students will more easily understand their performance and the areas in which improvement is needed. As a result, they will be able to focus their goal setting and effort on these areas.
— briefly describe the alternative strategy for meeting the specified demand, including the potential benefits of using the strategy to increase success at school, home, and work.
— describe what is required (in terms of time, energy, and commitment) to learn the new strategy.
— describe the results other students have achieved after learning the strategy.
— After enlightening the student on the requirements to acquire this new strategy, ask the student if he or she is willing to make a commitment to learn the new strategy.
— explain the commitment the teacher is willing to make to teach the strategy effectively.

STAGE 2: DESCRIBE THE STRATEGY

The purpose of this instructional stage is to describe the new strategy so students can: (a) become aware of the overt *and* covert processes involved in performing the new strategy, (b) become aware of how the steps of the strategy are used to approach academic tasks and solve problems and how self-instruction is used to regulate use of the steps, (c) clearly see how this new strategy is different from their current habits of problem solving, and (d) become motivated to learn and apply the new strategy. In short, the teacher attempts to clearly "paint a picture" of what the new strategy is all about and how it will alter learning and performing.

During the Describe stage of strategy acquisition and generalization, two phases of instruction are utilized. *First,* students receive an Orientation and Overview of the strategy and how they can use the strategy to meet specific setting demands. *Second,* they are made aware of the Current Strategy and Remembering System.

PHASE 1: ORIENTATION AND OVERVIEW

The purpose of the first phase of the Describe stage is to orient students to different reasons for adopting the new strategy as an alternative to problem solving. Students also are made aware of where and when the strategy is used appropriately and when not to use it. In addition, teachers should stress the importance of students' active listening and comparing the new strategy with how they typically approach tasks. During this phase the teacher should:

— ensure that students understand the rationale for learning the strategy and how the strategy can affect success across a wide number of settings.

— describe the general characteristics of situations in which the strategy can be used. Discuss examples of those situations, and emphasize the strategy's relevance to school, home, work, and leisure activities.

PHASE 2: CURRENT STRATEGY AND REMEMBERING SYSTEM

During this instructional phase students are exposed to the overall intent of the strategy as well as to the nature and purpose of each of the instructional steps. Instruction should emphasize the overt and covert processes involved in using the strategy effectively. As a part of this phase of instruction, the teacher should:

— describe the strategic processes involved in using the overall strategy. For example, students should be told that a given strategy is effective because it helps them *transform* (e.g., cluster, organize, paraphrase) material into a form that is easier to understand and remember.

— describe, explain, and guide students to understand the overt and covert processes involved in each of the steps. This explanation should underscore for students the importance of self-instruction when performing a strategy. Students should realize that they should understand the steps well enough to be able to talk their way through implementation of the strategy to guide and monitor its successful application. Thus, the focus initially is *not* to learn to perform the steps of the strategy but, rather, on how one must use self-instruction to regulate use of the strategy steps.

— explain to students how to remember the strategy by discussing the remembering system used with the strategy.

— ensure that students understand the relationship between the remembering system and what is involved in applying the learning strategy, placing particular emphasis on self-instruction.

— through an open discussion, encourage students to compare and contrast the new strategic approach to their old approaches. This instruction should focus on how self-instructional use of the strategy steps differs from what they typically do when attempting to meet the setting demand.

— guide students in setting individual goals for learning the strategy.

STAGE 3: MODEL THE STRATEGY

Research suggests that students with learning disabilities and other low-achieving students may not use self-talk effectively to guide their performance (Warner, Schumaker, Alley, & Deshler, 1989). Thus, teachers need to teach students these cognitive behaviors as well as the overt physical acts they need to perform a given task. The Model step of instruction is fundamental for teaching and demonstrating these cognitive behaviors. A mistake that is made frequently in the instructional process is to confuse the Describe stage of instruction with the Modeling stage. Teachers traditionally have not been trained to demonstrate their thought processes by thinking aloud. Once a student masters this instructional step, the teacher can enhance understanding of the strategy as well as the speed with which it is learned. This step is considered to be the "heart of strategy instruction" (Schumaker, 1989). The Modeling stage has four major phases.

PHASE 1: ORIENTATION

Orientation usually includes a *review of previous learning* covering the nature and purpose of the strategy steps and where and when the strategy can be applied. In addition, the teacher *personalizes the strategy* so students understand how its use will benefit them. This phase also includes a *definition of the lesson content,* in which the teacher provides an explanation of what a model is, how it can help students as learners, and a brief description of the activities in the lesson. Finally, the teacher states the *expectations* regarding student involvement during the lesson (e.g., instructions for students to watch the demonstration, pay particular attention to what the teacher says and does, and imitate what has been demonstrated).

PHASE 2: PRESENTATION

During this phase of the Model stage the teacher demonstrates the strategy. The demonstration includes all the elements of how to think and act while carrying out the strategy. The presentation has to be fluid and organized. Thus, preparation and practice are critical. Specifically, the demonstration emphasizes the cognitive acts required to perform the strategy through a thinking-aloud process. The teacher must take care to provide a balanced model that shows enough of the cognitive processes involved to enable the student to understand application of the strategy without bogging down the model in a manner that will make the strategy seem difficult and cumbersome. As a part of this phase, the teacher should:

— emphasize three types of cognitive processes while thinking aloud: (a) demonstrate *self-instruction* (e.g., model how to cue oneself to use the next step of the strategy—"Let's see, the next step is: "Insert a letter"); (b) model how to do *problem solving* (e.g., "Hmmm...I have a problem. There are nine items in this list, and I should only have seven. I know! I'll put four items together because they're all related to plants and the other five are all related to animals."); and (c) demonstrate the *monitoring* required while performing a strategy (e.g., "Let's see, where am I? I just finished checking for punctuation errors; next I need to check for spelling errors").

— Demonstrate how to *perform the task*. Merely describing a performance (telling what to do) does not provide a true model of the thinking processes and physical acts that students can imitate. The entire strategy must be demonstrated, and performance with regard to the whole task must be shown.

— Avoid making mental leaps between specific steps or actions. Students will have difficulty making correct decisions throughout a strategy if they do not see the major thinking processes involved in a strategy.

PHASE 3: STUDENT ENLISTMENT

During this phase students are *prompted* to gradually perform more and more of the required thought processes and physical acts themselves. They become the demonstrators. Initially students can be prompted to name the next step. Once that is mastered, they should be prompted to say what they would say as they: (a) check their progress, (b) evaluate their performance, (c) make adjustments, and (d) problem-solve. By involving students, the teacher can check their understanding of the strategy steps and the processes involved in performing them. Frequently students will not be able to explain the covert processes involved in a strategy during the formal Model stage of instruction. Students often find it difficult to "talk out loud" about the strategic processes until they begin to understand how to apply the strategy. This level of understanding gradually emerges as instruction proceeds. Forcing students to "think out loud" before they are ready can inhibit instruction and make the strategy difficult. Therefore, enlisting students at a level appropriate to prompt maximum involvement and to guarantee success is important. Furthermore, students enlisted in the modeling process will be more fully a part of the practice and feedback stages of instruction. As a part of this phase of instruction, the teacher should:

— require students to use the actual words they would say to themselves in using the strategy
— provide feedback including correction and expansion of student responses during the exercise
— prompt as much self-talk as possible
— assign tasks that have a high likelihood of success
— draw students' attention to good performance models and emphasize the importance of imitating the processes they have seen and heard.

Stage 4: Verbal Elaboration and Rehearsal of the Strategy

The aim of this instructional stage is to ensure comprehension of the process involved in applying the new strategy. To use self-instructional processes effectively while performing a strategy, students have to be able to use their own language structures to communicate with themselves about the strategic process. Thus, the instructional emphasis during this stage is on facilitating students' mediation or elaboration of the key information presented to them so they will be able to restructure the new material in terms of their prior knowledge. This instructional stage has two major phases: verbal elaboration and verbal rehearsal.

Phase 1: Verbal Elaboration

The purpose of Verbal Elaboration is to facilitate explanation of key information associated with the strategy in the students' own words. At first the focus of instruction is on facilitating students' ability to elaborate on what the overall strategic process is designed to accomplish and generally what the process involves. Students must understand clearly the goal of the overall strategy before they are able to elaborate on the processes of a strategy. Once students are able to describe the "big picture" in their own words, instruction shifts to facilitating student elaboration of the specific strategy steps. Here, while looking at the list of the strategy steps, students describe what each step is designed to do and *why* it is important to the overall strategic process. Once students can describe the strategy steps accurately, they should be asked to elaborate on the role of self-instruction with regard to performing the strategy.

PHASE 2: VERBAL REHEARSAL

Before students can be asked to use a given strategy, they must be able to name the strategy steps automatically. Thus, students are expected to commit the strategy steps to memory via rote rehearsal. Steps are memorized to fluent 100% mastery levels, so the steps can serve readily as self-instructional cues for what to do as the strategy is performed. A procedure called "rapid-fire practice" promotes memorization of the strategy steps. Using this method, the teacher points to each student in succession and requires performance of the next step of the strategy. This exercise begins slowly, and students are called on in a predictable order. As they become more familiar with the steps of the strategy, the speed of practice is increased and students are called on randomly. Students' verbal mastery of the steps is checked individually until they reach the mastery criterion.

STAGE 5: CONTROLLED PRACTICE AND FEEDBACK

Several instructional goals are associated with Controlled Practice and Feedback stage of instruction. One goal is to give students ample opportunity to practice using the new strategy with materials or in situations largely devoid of many of the demands found in regular class settings. A second goal is to build the students' confidence and fluency in using the strategy. Third, controlled practice will help students gradually take over (from teachers) the responsibility of mediating effective use of the strategy.

Three major dimensions control practice of the strategy: (a) the type of instructional materials used, (b) the context within which the strategy is practiced, and (c) the amount of teacher/peer mediation employed. Each of these dimensions must be considered regularly and carefully if students are to progress successfully through this instructional stage. At the end of this stage, students should be ready to transfer their mastery of the strategy to more difficult materials, approximating those found in a regular class setting.

The first dimension that must be taken under consideration to implement the Controlled Practice and Feedback stage concerns the appropriate use of instructional materials. As students begin practicing the strategy, the stimulus materials used should be devoid of many of the demands of the regular class setting (e.g., complex vocabulary and concepts, lengthy reading selections) so the students can focus their attention on learning the technique and can build confidence and fluency in performing the steps of the strategy. As students become fluent in applying the strategy to these easier materials, the teacher should provide increasingly complex materials to promote mastery of the strategy. Thus, students learn to use the strategy when interacting with materials that gradually approximate the difficulty of those in their regular educational settings. For example, when practicing the Paraphrasing strategy, students might begin applying the strategy to reading materials well below their instructional levels that address topics of high interest. Then, once students are able to perform the strategy when reading these easier materials, they are asked to apply the strategy to more challenging reading selections.

When implementing this stage, the second dimension that must be taken into consideration concerns the context or conditions under which the students practice the strategy. During initial practice attempts, some students have benefited from working with the strategy in a *different* and *less complex* context. Many of the cognitive processes associated with performing a specific learning strategy can (and should) be practiced under conditions that do not require higher-order skills. For example, when learning the Paraphrasing strategy in which students (a) read a paragraph, (b) stop and ask themselves what the main ideas and details are, and then (c) put the main idea and details into their own words, students might first learn to do the last two steps using the strategy in a reading-free context. The teacher might read the paragraph to the students and then ask students to perform the cognitive processes associated with identifying and paraphrasing main ideas and details. Later they might practice performing the whole strategy in a reading context. Therefore, the practice session is controlled not only by the materials that are used, but the conditions under which the student must perform may be controlled also to enhance strategy learning.

The third important dimension of this stage of strategy instruction relates to the amount of teacher/peer mediation that might be employed. The degree of assistance provided by the teacher as students attempt to use the new procedure should also be carefully controlled. Initially, when students first practice using the strategy, the teacher provides *ample* cues and prompts to assure that students are performing the strategy steps appropriately and learning to use self-instruction. Then, as students become proficient at performing the strategy steps, teacher prompts are gradually faded until the students can perform the strategy on controlled materials without assistance.

Like fading the use of prompts and cues, the teacher's role in providing feedback also shifts as students become proficient at using the new strategy. Initially, feedback is totally teacher-directed. The students are informed explicitly not only about what they are doing effectively but also how to improve their performance. Later, the nature of the teacher's feedback shifts. The teacher simply cues students or gives them partial information with the expectation that they will be able to participate in the mediation of their learning. Rather than providing all of the corrective feedback and reinforcement, the teacher cues students to analyze their own performance and give themselves corrective feedback and reinforcement. In short, the teacher deliberately and gradually passes to the student the responsibility to learn and perform. Through cooperative group structures or other peer tutoring arrangements (Johnson & Johnson, 1986; Kagan, 1989; Slavin, 1989), peers also can play a key role in mediating the learning process.

The quality of feedback teachers provide affects the gains that students experience during controlled practice. Kline (1989) found "elaborated feedback" to be much more effective than feedback that merely provided students with "knowledge of results." Elaborated feedback entails categorizing the types of errors and provides students with specific information that is both positive and corrective in nature. If necessary, it also can include the description and demonstration of a mini-strategy that may help the student avoid the same type of error in the future. The overriding purposes of elaborated feedback are to (a) have students understand the types of problems they are encountering in dealing with tasks, (b) translate the information by the teacher into a plan to solve the problem, and (c) implement the plan to alter and improve performance.

The three dimensions described above are implemented into the three phases of the Controlled Practice and Feedback stage. This stage may continue for many days, and the three phases are repeated each time a practice session is held. First, the teacher orients the students to the practice session. Second, the teacher carefully guides the entire group of students through practice trials, ensuring that the strategy is being applied correctly and that the students understand the practice activities. Third, the teacher prompts independent student practice and monitors individual performance.

PHASE 1: ORIENTATION AND OVERVIEW

As the Controlled Practice and Feedback stage moves gradually from teacher-mediated to student-mediated instruction, the students have to be oriented to the purpose of the specific practice activity and informed of their progress in this stage of instruction. In addition, the teacher should review critical components of the strategy as needed and, before the practice session begins, direct student attention to the most common types of errors they are making. This orientation period provides a good opportunity to discuss specific day-to-day instances in which application of the strategy might be beneficial. During this phase of instruction, the teacher should:

— review the steps of the strategy before each practice session and have students elaborate on what each step means. The frequency of these reviews should fade gradually as students become proficient in describing the strategy steps.
— prompt students to review the results of previous practices and identify the areas that require improvement.
— identify and discuss group progress and errors. If necessary, review and re-explain applications of the strategy to avoid incorrect performance.
— prompt students to describe how they would use or are currently using the strategy across different situations or settings.

PHASE 2: GUIDED PRACTICE

In the Guided Practice phase the teacher is concerned with ensuring that students are performing the strategy correctly. Because the instructional materials, the context, and the level of teacher or peer mediation may be shifting throughout this stage, the teacher may have to lead students through some of the practice activities before allowing them to work independently. During this phase of instruction, the teacher should:

— provide specific directions on how to complete the practice activity.
— model how to apply the strategy to the practice materials. During the initial stages of practice, the model may be detailed and explicit. As the daily practice sessions progress, the teacher model can be shortened and the students can be enlisted in performing the model.
— provide a model that approximates the behaviors discussed in the Model stage of instruction.
— prompt students to complete the practice activity as the teacher models application of the strategy on the practice materials.
— prompt students to gradually assume more responsibility for completing the practice activity independently.
— provide clear and explicit instructions for arranging peer-mediated practice sessions. To determine the best groupings and conditions for arranging future peer-mediated practice sessions, the teacher has to monitor practice activities and evaluate progress.

PHASE 3: INDEPENDENT PRACTICE

In this phase of instruction, the teacher must allow the student to complete the practice activity independently. The teacher, however, should monitor performance and look for opportunities to provide individualized and direct instruction to students on specific aspects of the strategy. During this phase of the instructional process, the teacher should:

— inform students to work independently.
— monitor performance by walking around the room to ensure that students are proceeding correctly.
— provide additional information to students on an individual basis and prompt correct application of the strategy and performance of the task whenever possible. If a student is having difficulty performing the strategy, the teacher can provide a model of the strategy, using the practice activity as a basis.
— prompt the students to "think aloud" as they complete the practice activity. This will enable the teacher to evaluate how the student is thinking about and using the strategy under different conditions.
— on the progress chart differentiate practice trials with substantial assistance from the teacher from ones completed independently.

STAGE 6: ADVANCED PRACTICE AND FEEDBACK

The real test of students' mastery of a strategy is their ability to apply it to advanced assignments and materials that approximate those found in "criterion settings" (settings where they were unable to cope originally, such as the regular classroom or the workplace). This stage of instruction marks an important turning point in the overall learning process. Learning shifts from learning how to perform the strategy to learning how to apply the strategy to meet the various *real* demands typically found in the criterion environment. During this stage of instruction, students learn to apply the strategy to these real-life tasks while still in a setting (e.g., a remedial class) that can offer support as needed. Thus, students learn how to proficiently use and adapt, if necessary, the strategy, to a wide variety of materials and assignments and to discriminate when the strategy is appropriate for meeting specific types of problems. As in the Controlled Practice and Feedback stage, the amount and type of teacher mediation in the learning process should be faded gradually over time. A deliberate change from teacher-mediated to student-mediated feedback must occur. As a part of this stage, then, the teacher should:

— provide a wide variety of grade-appropriate stimulus materials from a problem domain. For example, if reading comprehension is the problem domain that the new strategy is designed to target, students should practice applying the new strategy to a wide variety of reading materials (e.g., health and history textbooks, newspapers and news magazines).
— structure assignments that require students to adapt the strategy to meet different characteristics of instructional materials. For example, students learn a textbook reading strategy designed to enable them to use textbook cues. Some textbooks require students to focus primarily on one form of cue (e.g., visual aids). Others

might require students to focus on organizational cues (e.g., introductions, summaries, headings).

— structure assignments that allow students to practice in poorly designed materials (or situations). Using the reading comprehension example, students should be asked to use the strategy in poorly designed textbooks (e.g., those in which visual aids and organizational cues are present, but they provide relatively useless information).

— fade the instructional prompts and cues so students become responsible for taking the initiative in using and evaluating the strategy in a variety of contexts. This involves having students ask themselves questions about their responses, enabling them to analyze their performance and the appropriateness of the strategy application.

The instructional phases that guide daily implementation of the Advanced Practice and Feedback stage are the same as those described in the Controlled Practice and Feedback stage. In the *Orientation and Overview phase* the teacher should review progress, discussing the strategy as it is applied to advanced materials and identifying critical errors that have emerged from applying the strategy to more difficult materials and circumstances. In the *Guided Practice phase* the teacher should help students see how the materials are becoming more difficult and how to discriminate cues that signal use of the strategy. Finally, during the *Independent Practice phase* the teacher should monitor the independent and correct application of the strategy in the advanced materials.

STAGE 7: CONFIRM ACQUISITION AND MAKE GENERALIZATION COMMITMENTS

The purpose of this stage in the strategy-acquisition process is to document students' mastery of the strategy and to design a rationale involving students in promoting self-generalization of the strategy across settings. Whereas earlier stages of the instructional process are critical to the learning process, this stage is critical to the application process. Unfortunately, many teachers who are successful at promoting the acquisition of a strategy have difficulty promoting generalization. Many teachers completely disregard generalization or attempt to address generalization merely through supplemental worksheets to be completed at the end of other lessons. As a result, many strategy-training efforts have failed to result in significant levels of generalization outside of the training setting because of the lack of teacher attention to the transition from acquisition to generalization. If the full benefits of strategy instruction are to be realized, significant instructional attention must be given to this transition.

This stage of instruction has two phases: The first phase affirms success by confirming that the strategy has been mastered. The second phase focuses on forecasting the generalization process and making commitments related to both the student's and the teacher's role in the generalization process.

PHASE 1: CONFIRM AND CELEBRATE

This phase of instruction provides an opportunity for the teacher and the student to confirm and document that the student has acquired the procedural and strategic processes involved in the strategy. In practice, the student probably has demonstrated this level already as part of the Advanced Practice and Feedback stage of the instructional process. Many teachers have reported that they simply use the last advanced practice attempt in which the student met the mastery requirements as the confirming posttest score. Nevertheless, once the student has met the expectations, requirements, and goals related to performance on routine and daily practice efforts involved in the Advanced Practice and Feedback stage, the student should have an opportunity to prepare for and confirm, to the best of his or her ability and with maximum motivation and effort, that he or she can perform the strategy and meet the demand. Therefore, the student is allowed to create a "trophy" that he or she can point to and that can be used as documentation on educational planning documents such as the IEP.

The activities implemented in this phase should prompt the student and the teacher to celebrate the results of their efforts and commitments. If the student has set goals related to acquiring and applying the strategy and then has worked hard to meet these goals, time should be devoted to affirming progress and reviewing what did and did not work along the way. Both the student and the teacher should reflect and discuss their efforts and be prompted to say, "I did great." To accomplish the goals associated with this phase, the teacher should:

— prompt each student to identify when he or she has met the mastery criteria associated with the Advanced Practice stage.
— arrange for final confirmation of mastery when a student informs the teacher that he or she has met the specified mastery criteria.
— inform the student that he or she will have an opportunity to perform the strategy to confirm mastery and to prepare by reviewing the strategy.
— provide the student with the appropriate task, and allow the student to complete the task under appropriate classroom conditions.
— provide encouragement and feedback and arrange for continued practice if the student does not meet the mastery criteria. If the student confirms mastery by meeting the mastery criteria, congratulate him or her.
— arrange for a special opportunity to talk to the student about his or her achievement, and review with the student all the effort and learning that contributed to his or her success.
— if acceptable to the student, identify different ways to make the student feel good about his or her success, and recognize the accomplishment.

PHASE 2: FORECAST AND COMMIT TO GENERALIZATION

Within this instructional phase the student and the teacher should make commitments related to ensuring that the student generalizes the strategy across settings, situations, and time. As part of this process, the teacher must adopt an instructional philosophy in which the success of strategy instruction is defined only by the degree to which the student uses the strategy to meet demands across regular classroom and other natural settings. In addition, this perspective must be transferred to students. Therefore, the teacher must:

— explain the general goals of the generalization process.

— identify specific consequences related to focusing versus not focusing attention on the generalization process.

— explain the four phases of the generalization process and what will be involved in each of the four phases.

— prompt the student to make a commitment to participate in and put forth maximum effort in the generalization process.

— explain the commitments of the support-class teacher and regular-class teachers in assisting students in the generalization process.

STAGE 8: GENERALIZATION

Students who have mastered specific strategies in the support-class setting often do not use these strategies automatically to facilitate learning across content settings (Ellis et al., 1987a, 1987b). For strategy instruction to be worthwhile, students must generalize the strategy to other settings. Successful generalization requires active, independent application and adaptation of the strategy across settings and tasks that vary in complexity and purpose. Students also must be able to recognize naturally occurring cues across settings that signal appropriate opportunities to apply the strategy. Therefore, the instructional processes for promoting generalization must be geared toward enabling the student to:

1. Discriminate when to use the strategy to meet everyday learning and performance demands.
2. Develop methods for remembering to use the strategy appropriately.
3. Experiment with how the strategy can be used across circumstances encountered across settings.
4. Receive and use feedback to develop goals and plans to improve performance.
5. Adapt the strategy to meet additional problems and demands.
6. Incorporate the strategy and various adaptations of the strategy into the student's permanent system for approaching problems across settings and time.

To facilitate application of these processes, the Generalization stage of the instructional process is divided into four phases: (a) Orientation, (b) Activation, (c) Adaptation, and (d) Maintenance. Each of these phases is described briefly in the following pages.

PHASE 1: ORIENTATION

The purpose of the Orientation phase of Generalization is to make the student aware of the necessity of applying the strategy in a purposeful manner to meet relevant setting demands. The teacher prompts the student to evaluate the pros and cons of using the new strategy and to begin to explore how the strategy might be used beyond the context in which it was taught (Ellis et al., 1987a, 1987b). During this phase of generalization, the teacher should prompt students to:

— identify rationales for using the strategy across settings.

— explain why specific attention to strategy transfer and generalization is necessary.

— identify which settings are most likely to require use of the strategy.

— discuss how they might remind themselves to use the strategy in different settings.

— construct cue cards on 3" x 5" cards and place the cards in books, notebooks, and other materials used in settings in which the strategy might be applied.

— specify cues that exist in specific settings and across settings that will signal use of the strategy.

— review different types of materials that they might encounter across settings, and discuss how the strategy might or might not be applied.

— evaluate materials to which the strategy should *not* be applied, and discuss reasons why the strategy is not appropriate.

— discuss which aspects of the strategy seem to be most helpful and least helpful, and then discuss how this information can be used to increase performance.

— generate ways to improve or adjust the strategy to make the strategy more responsive to setting demands.

— identify other strategies and procedures that might be combined with this strategy to make the strategy more effective and improve overall performance.

PHASE 2: ACTIVATION

The purpose of the Activation phase of Generalization is to prompt the student to use the strategy purposefully, monitor the student's application of the strategy across a wide variety of materials, situations, and settings, and prompt appropriate application of the strategy when generalization does not occur. To accomplish this, the responsibility for promoting generalization, heretofore generally left to the support-class teacher and the student, must be shared by other individuals, such as the general classroom teacher, with whom the student comes in contact across a variety of settings. Therefore, the activities in this phase of the Generalization process entail a variety of interactions that must take place among the support-class teacher, the student, and the general classroom teachers. Initially the support-class teacher should prompt students to:

— apply the strategy to a specific assignment related to another class, and afterward demonstrate and describe how the strategy was used to complete the assignment.

— apply the strategy to a variety of assignments that must be done at home or in the general classroom setting, and demonstrate and describe how the strategy was used to complete these assignments.

— set daily and weekly goals related to increasing the use of the strategy to a variety of settings and situations and to improving performance.

— develop a plan related to how to increase application of the strategy to meet these goals.

— monitor implementation of the plan and the effects of using the strategy across different settings and situations.

— enlist the help of the support-class teacher or the regular-class teacher, or both, to solve problems related to applying the strategy.

— request feedback from general class teachers related to improved performance in the areas the strategy addresses specifically.

— develop a chart and record progress related to applying the strategy and its results on related measures of classroom performance.

— reinforce progress and success in the form of self-congratulatory statements and, if necessary, extrinsic rewards.

Although part of the responsibility for ensuring generalization of strategies rests with the support-class teacher, the general classroom teacher, who teaches subjects such as social studies, language arts, or science, also must assume responsibility for facilitating generalization. The major instructional goals related to promoting strategy generalization in the general classroom are to: (a) help the student see the relationship between the demands of the setting and appropriate strategies, and (b) guide the student to the automatic and independent identification and application of strategies to meet setting demands successfully (Lenz & Bulgren, in press). Therefore, the key to facilitating strategy generalization rests in the ability of teachers to ensure that sufficient opportunities are available to the student to apply the strategy and to experience success in meeting setting demands.

As a result, the content teacher should be in communication with the support-class teacher to inform him or her of the demands the student is not meeting. Although the degree of involvement of the content teacher in the intervention process may vary at this point, the content teacher must be informed of the types of strategies that the student will acquire and what skills are involved in performing each strategy. Afterward the support-class teacher and the content teacher should communicate regularly to determine the student's progress with regard to generalization of the pertinent strategy, provide feedback to the student on his or her progress in the generalization process, and help the student set and plan for long-term application of the strategy across settings. Each general classroom teacher should be prompted to observe if the strategies being used are meeting the specific learning demands presented in or characteristic of his or her content area.

A number of systems have been discussed and developed in an attempt to accomplish these goals (e.g., Ellis et al., 1987a, 1987b; Deshler, Schumaker, & Lenz, 1984; Schumaker, Deshler, & McKnight, 1991; Lenz, Schumaker, Deshler, & Beals, 1984). Lenz and Bulgren (in press) presented the following synthesis of procedures based on research related to promoting generalization of strategies across settings. In general, the general classroom teacher should be prompted to:

— obtain from the support-class teacher a short description of the strategy that has been taught to the student, the conditions or criteria for correct and successful application, and what the student has been taught with regard to applying the strategy in content lessons.

— determine if the student has been taught to identify specific cues to indicate when a strategy or part of a strategy is to be used.

— evaluate teaching materials, presentation routines, and classroom activities to ensure that sufficient cues are available for the student to be able to identify when to use a specific strategy.

— determine which situations and activities in the content classroom lend themselves best to direct monitoring of strategy generalization.

— initiate direct monitoring of generalization by simply *checking* to see if the strategy is being used. If this cannot be determined by direct observation or review of permanent products, the general class teacher should ask the student if the strategy was used and have the student explain how he or she used the strategy.

— *cue* use of the strategy if the student has not started to use the strategy after several checks. As part of generalization instruction the support-class teacher provides, the student should have a 3" x 5" cue card with a list of the strategy steps written on it. The general classroom teacher can check to see if the student has implemented this cueing system. If not, this teacher should prompt the student to design his or her own cue card. More direct ways for cueing strategy use include: (a) telling the student discreetly to use a specific strategy; (b) informing the whole class to use a given strategy; (c) writing the name of the strategy on the chalkboard or bulletin board; and (d) prompting peers who know the strategy to cue students who are just beginning to learn and apply the strategy.

— *prompt* the student to begin using the strategy. If the student does not respond to cues after a short time, ask the student to list the steps of the strategy and ask how the first step would be accomplished. Then watch the student as he or she performs the first step.

— if the student does not respond to a prompt, determine if the student can perceive the relationship between the strategy and the specific demands of a class. If he or she cannot, *model* how the strategy can be applied to meet the content learning demand.

— once the student is applying the strategy, provide *feedback* to the student on the outcomes related to use of the strategy, what the student is doing right, what the student is doing wrong, and how to improve performance. A written or verbal system should be developed for providing specific feedback to students. Then the teachers should work collaboratively with students to try to reduce specific problems or errors.

PHASE 3: ADAPTATION

The purpose of the Adaptation phase of Generalization is to prompt students to explore the strategy by identifying the various cognitive strategies in which they are engaging as the strategy is performed and to begin to change and integrate the elements of the strategy to meet new and different setting demands. As part of this phase of Generalization, the teacher should:

— prompt students to describe the strategy and all of its parts as the teacher writes the features of the strategy on the chalkboard.

— prompt students to discuss what they are actually doing and thinking about as they apply each step of the strategy.

— have students identify, with teacher guidance, the various cognitive strategies embedded in the strategy (e.g., self-questioning, clustering, categorizing, monitoring, checking, predicting, summarizing, paraphrasing).

— have the students describe, with teacher assistance, what cognitive processes are involved in each of these strategies.

— discuss with the students how and where these cognitive process/strategies are required across different settings.

— help the students identify how to modify the strategy to meet additional setting demands (e.g., "How can we modify the Paraphrasing strategy to help in notetaking? How could we make it work in the social skill of carrying on a conversation?").

— have the students write down the strategy modifications and how they can be used.

— ask the students to repeat the necessary orientation and activation activities that might be necessary to apply the modifications.

PHASE 4: MAINTENANCE

The purpose of the Maintenance phase of Generalization is to ensure that students continue to use the strategy across time and contexts. In this phase of Generalization, the student and teacher jointly develop plans related to promoting long-term use of the strategy. During this phase the teacher should:

— discuss with the students the rationales related to long-term use of the strategy.

— have the students identify habits and barriers that might prevent them from continuing to use the strategy.

— prompt the students to determine how they might monitor long-term application of the strategy.

— discuss with the students ways that the teacher can help to monitor long-term application and successful use of the strategy.

— ask the students to set goals related to monitoring long-term application of the strategy.

— ask the students to determine how many times a week the teacher should check use of the strategy.

— have the students determine how this check will be conducted and if other teachers or students will be involved (e.g., peer checks, classroom products or assignments).

— have the students specify, with guidance from the teacher, the criteria for successful performance of the strategy at the various checkpoints.

— prompt the students to plan, with teacher guidance, the procedures that will be used to improve performance if the students are not applying the strategy effectively or efficiently.

— have the students determine the length of time during which weekly maintenance checks will be required before implementing biweekly maintenance checks.

— discuss and identify with the students when the strategy can be considered a permanent part of their approach to meeting setting demands and when maintenance checks will be needed no longer.

— have the students develop a chart and record results of efforts to maintain use of the strategy.

— ask the students to identify self-reinforcers or self-rewards that can be used in conjunction with successful maintenance of the strategy.

SUMMARY

The impact of a strategies instructional approach on adolescents with LD depends on the effectiveness of the strategy system being taught, as well as the instructional delivery system. A strategies instructional approach differs from basic skill approaches and study skill approaches primarily in its emphasis on thinking processes, self-regulation, and problem solving. Skill instruction tends to focus on mastery of specific operations, whereas strategy instruction centers on how to use these skills optimally to solve problems.

The features of an effective strategy fall into three areas: content, design, and usefulness. *Strategy-content* refers to the composition of the strategy, or how the steps of the strategy are designed to facilitate the learning process. Essentially, an effective strategy is an efficient approach to a task utilizing steps designed to cue specific covert or overt actions that lead to specific and successful outcomes. The *strategy-design* features concern packaging of the strategy steps. Effective strategies utilize a remembering system to communicate the strategy steps. These remembering systems are designed specifically to accommodate the needs of students who have problems with memory and retrieval of information. The wording is in a language familiar to students and is designed to facilitate action. *Strategy-usefulness* refers to how well the strategy works to solve a problem that students encounter commonly and whether the strategy is transferable to other settings, contexts, and situations.

An effectively designed strategy will have little impact on students with LD if it is taught poorly. Because the learning problems of students with LD are very real, strategy instruction is necessarily intensive and extensive. Careful attention to the principles of strategy instruction is essential. Because a strategy is basically a plan for using skills in an optimal manner, students need to know the prerequisite skills before the strategy is taught. When strategy instruction begins, it should be treated earnestly. The strategies should be taught regularly and intensely, with a mastery orientation to instruction. The covert processes associated with self-regulation of cognitive strategies, goal setting, and monitoring should be emphasized. Students need to be taught that a strategy is not an inflexible algorithm but, rather, a plan that is employed flexibly. Generalization of the strategy should be emphasized throughout the instructional process.

Because students with LD have difficulty learning and tend to be particularly deficit in their knowledge and ability to use strategies, strategy instruction is apt to be difficult. Students must be committed to learn the strategy, and teachers must be committed to stick with it. Teachers have to recognize that strategy instruction must be viewed as a long-term intervention rather than as a "quick fix." We recommend that teachers approach the instructional process as a series of stages that build students' competence and confidence gradually using the new strategy.

REFERENCES

Allington, R. L. (1984). So what is the problem? Whose problem is it? *Topics in Learning and Learning Disabilities, 3*(4), 91–99.

Ausubel, D. P. (1960). The use of advance organizers in the learning and retention of meaningful verbal material. *Journal of Educational Psychology, 51*, 267–272.

Brown, A. L., & Palincsar, A. S. (1982). Inducing strategic learning from texts by means of informed self-control training. In B. Y. L. Wong (Ed.), Metacognition and learning disabilities. *Topics in Learning and Learning Disabilities, 2*(1), 1–18.

Brown, A. L. (1978). Knowing when, where, and how to remember: A problem of metacognition. In R. Glaser

(Ed.), *Advances in instructional psychology*. Hillsdale, NJ: Lawrence Erlbaum.

Brown, A. A., & Campione, J. C. (1986). Psychological theory and the study of learning disabilities. *American Psychologist, 14*, 1059–1068.

Brown, A. L., & Palincsar, A. S. (1987). Reciprocal teaching of comprehension strategies: A natural history of one program for enhancing learning. In J. Borkowski & J. D. Day (Eds.), *Intelligence and cognition in special children: Comparative studies of giftedness, mental retardation, and learning disabilities*. New York: Ablex.

Brown, A. L., Day, J. D., & Jones, R. S. (1983). The development of plans for summarizing texts. *Child Development, 54*, 968–979.

Bulgren, J. A., Schumaker, J. B., & Deshler, D. D. (1988). Effectiveness of a concept teaching routine in enhancing the performance of LD students in secondary-level mainstream classes. *Learning Disability Quarterly, 11*, 3–17.

Deshler, D. D., Alley, G. R., Warner, M. M., & Schumaker, J. B. (1981). Instructional practices for promoting skill acquisition and generalization in severely learning disabled adolescents. *Learning Disability Quarterly, 4*(4), 415–421.

Deshler, D. D., & Lenz, B. K. (1989). The strategies instructional approach. *International Journal of Disability, Development, and Education, 36*(3), 203–224.

Deshler, D. D., & Schumaker, J. B. (1988). An instructional model for teaching students how to learn. In J. L. Graden, J. E. Zins, & M. J. Curtis (Eds.), *Alternative educational delivery systems: Enhancing instructional options for all students*. Washington, DC: National Association of School Psychologists.

Deshler, D. D., Schumaker, J. B., & Lenz, B. K. (1984). Academic and cognitive interventions for LD adolescents: Part 1. *Journal of Learning Disabilities, 17*(2), 108–117.

Ellis, E. S., & Lenz, B. K. (1987). A component analysis of effective learning strategies for LD students. *Learning Disabilities Focus, 2*(2), 94–107.

Ellis, E. S., Lenz, B. K., & Sabornie, E. J. (1987a). Generalization and adaptation of learning strategies to natural environments: Part 1–Critical agents. *Remedial and Special Education, 8*(1), 6–21.

Ellis, E. S., Lenz, B. K., & Sabornie, E. J. (1987b). Generalization and adaptation of learning strategies to natural environments: Part 2–Research into practice. *Remedial and Special Education, 8*(2), 6–24.

Flavell, J. H. (1976). Metacognitive aspects of problem solving. In L. B. Resnick (Ed.), *The nature of intelligence*. Hillsdale, NJ: Lawrence Erlbaum.

Gagne, E. D. (1985). *The cognitive psychology of school learning*. Boston: Little, Brown, & Company.

Hall, R. J. (1980). Information processing and cognitive training in learning disabled children: An executive level meeting. *Exceptional Educational Quarterly, 1*, 9–15.

Hallahan, D. P., (Ed.). (1980). Teaching exceptional children to use cognitive strategies. *Exceptional Education Quarterly, 1*, 1–102.

Hallahan, D. P., & Kauffman, J. M. (1975). Research on the education of distractible and hyperactive children. In W. M. Cruickshank & D. P. Hallahan (Eds.), *Perceptual and learning disabilities in children* (Vol. 2). *Research and theory* (pp. 221–256). Syracuse, NY: Syracuse University Press.

Hallahan, D. P., & Kauffman, J. M. (1986). *Exceptional children: Introduction to special education* (3d ed.). Englewood Cliffs, NJ: Prentice Hall.

Hallahan, D. P., Kauffman, J. M., & Lloyd, J. W. (1985). *Introduction to learning disabilities* (2d ed.). Englewood Cliffs, NJ: Prentice Hall.

Hallahan, D. P., Lloyd, J., Kosiewicz, M. M., & Kneedler, R. D. (1979). *A comparison of the effects of self-recording and self-assessment on the on-task behavior and academic productivity of a learning disabled boy* (Technical Report No. 13). Charlottesville: University of Virginia Learning Disabilities Research Institute.

Havertape, J. F., & Kass, C. E. (1978). Examination of problem solving in learning disabled adolescents through verbalized self-instructions. *Learning Disability Quarterly, 1*(4), 94–100.

Hresko, W. P., & Reid, D. K. (1981). Five faces of cognition: Theoretical influences on approaches to learning disabilities. *Learning Disability Quarterly, 4*(3), 238–243.

Hughes, C. A., Schumaker, J. B., Deshler, D. D., & Mercer, C. M. (1988). *The learning strategies curriculum: The test-taking strategy*. Lawrence, KS: Edge Enterprises.

Johnson, D. W., & Johnson, R. T. (1986). Mainstreaming and cooperative learning strategies. *Exceptional Children, 52*(6), 553–561.

Kagan, S. (1989). The structural approach to cooperative learning. *Educational Leadership, 47*(4), 12–16.

Karoly, P. (1984). Self management problems in children. In E. J. Mash & L. G. Terdal (Eds.), *Behavioral assessment of childhood disorders*. New York: Guilford Press.

Keogh, B. K., & Glover, A. T. (1980). The generality and durability of cognitive training. *Exceptional Education Quarterly, 1*, 75–82.

Kline, F. (1989). *The development and validation of feedback routines for use in special education settings*. Unpublished dissertation, University of Kansas, Lawrence.

Kneedler, R. D., & Hallahan, D. P. (1981). Self-monitoring of on-task behavior with learning-disabled children: Current studies and directions. *Exceptional Education Quarterly, 2*(3), 73–82.

Kneedler, R. D., & Hallahan, D. P. (1984). Self-monitoring as an attentional strategy for academic tasks with learning disabled children. In B. Gholson & T. Rosenthal (Eds.), *Applications of cognitive development theory*. New York: Academic Press.

Kosiewicz, M. M., Hallahan, D. P., & Lloyd, J. (1981). The effects of an LD student's treatment choice on handwriting performance. *Learning Disability Quarterly, 4*(3), 133–139.

Lenz, B. K., Alley, G. R., & Schumaker, J. B. (1987). Activating the inactive learner: Advance organizers in the secondary content classroom. *Learning Disability Quarterly, 10*(1), 53–67.

Lenz, B. K., Bulgren, J., & Hudson, P. (1990). Content enhancement: A model for promoting the acquisition of content by individuals with learning disabilities. In T. E. Scruggs & B. Y. L. Wong (Eds.), *Intervention research in learning disabilities* (pp. 122–165). New York: Springer-Verlag.

Lenz, B. K., & Hughes, C. A. (1990). A word identification strategy for adolescents with learning disabilities. *Journal of Learning Disabilities, 23*(3), 149–158).

Lenz, B. K., Schumaker, J. B., Deshler, D. D., & Beals, V. L. (1984). *The learning strategies curriculum: The word identification strategy*. Lawrence: University of Kansas Institute for Research in Learning Disabilities.

Lloyd, J. (1980). Academic instruction and cognitive techniques: The need for attack strategy training. *Exceptional Education Quarterly*, 53–63.

Loper, A. B. (1980). Metacognitive development: Implications for cognitive training of exceptional children. *Exceptional Education Quarterly, 1*, 1–8.

Mayer, R. E. (1975). Information processing variables in learning to solve problems. *Review of Educational Research, 45*, 525–541.

Mayer, R. E. (1983). *Thinking, problem solving, cognition*. New York: Freeman.

Mayer, R. E. (1984). Aids to prose comprehension. *Educational Psychologist, 19*, 89–130.

Mayer, R. E. (1987). *Educational psychology: A cognitive approach*. Boston: Little, Brown.

McKinney, J. D., & Haskins, R. (1980). Cognitive training and the development of problem solving strategies. *Exceptional Education Quarterly, 1*, 41–51.

Meichenbaum, D. (1975, June). *Cognitive factors as determinants of learning disabilities. A cognitive-functional approach*. Paper presented at NATO conference on "The Neuropsychology of Learning Disorders: Theoretical Approaches," Korsor, Denmark.

Meichenbaum, D. (1977). *Cognitive-behavior modification*. New York: Plenum Press.

Meichenbaum, D. (1979). Teaching children self-control. In B. B. Lahey & A. E. Kazden (Eds.), *Advances in clinical child psychology* (Vol. 2). New York: Plenum Press.

Meichenbaum, D. (1980). Cognitive behavior modification with exceptional children: A promise yet unfulfilled. *Exceptional Education Quarterly, 1*, 83–88.

Palincsar, A. (1986). The role of dialogue in providing scaffolded instruction. *Educational Psychologist, 21*, 73–98.

Palincsar, A. S. (1982). *Improving reading comprehension of junior high school students through reciprocal teaching of comprehension-monitoring strategies*. Unpublished doctoral dissertation, University of Illinois, Urbana.

Palincsar, A. S., & Brown, A. L. (1984). Reciprocal teaching of comprehension fostering and comprehension monitoring activities. *Cognition and Instruction, 1*(2), 117–175.

Palincsar, A. S., & Brown, A. L. (1986). Interactive teaching to promote independent reading from text. *Reading Teacher, 39*(8), 771–777.

Pressley, M., Borkowski, J. G., & Schneider, W. (1989). Good information processing: What it is and what education can do to promote it. *International Journal of Educational Research, 13*, 857–867.

Pressley, M., Johnson, C. J., & Symons, S. (1987). Elaborating to learn and learning to elaborate. *Journal of Learning Disabilities, 20*, 76–91.

Reid, D. K. (1988). *Teaching the learning disabled: A cognitive developmental approach.* Boston: Allyn and Bacon.

Reid, D. K. (1978). Genevan theory and the education of exceptional children. In J. M. Gallagher & J. A. Easley (Eds.), *Knowledge and development* (Vol. 2: *Piaget and education*). New York: Plenum.

Roehler, L. R., & Duffy, G. G. (1984). Direct explanation of comprehension processes. In G. G. Duffy, L. R. Roehler, & J. Mason (Eds.), *Comprehension instruction: Perspectives and suggestions* (pp. 265–280). New York: Longman.

Rooney, K. J., & Hallahan, D. P. (1985). Future directions for cognitive behavior modification research: The quest for cognitive change. *Remedial and Special Education, 6*(2), 46–51.

Schmidt, J. L., Deshler, D. D., Schumaker, J. B., & Alley, G. R. (1989). Effects of generalization instruction on the written language performance of adolescents with learning disabilities in the mainstream classroom. *Journal of Reading, Writing, and Learning Disabilities, 4*(4), 291–311.

Schumaker, J. B. (1989). The heart of strategy instruction. *Strategram, 1*(4). Lawrence, KS: Center for Research on Learning, 1–3.

Schumaker, J. B., Deshler, D. D., & McKnight, P. C. (1991). Teaching routines for content areas at the secondary level. In G. Stover, M. R. Shinn, & H. M. Walker (Eds.), *Interventions for Achievement and Behavior Problems*, pp. 473–494. Washington, DC: National Association for School Psychologists.

Schumaker, J. B., & Sheldon, J. (1985). *The sentence writing strategy.* Lawrence: The University of Kansas.

Siegler, R. S. (1986). *Children's thinking.* Englewood Cliffs, NY: Prentice Hall.

Slavin, R. E. (1989). Research on cooperative learning: Consensus and controversy. *Educational Leadership, 47*(4), 52–56.

Swanson, H. L. (1981). Modification of comprehension deficits in learning disabled children. *Learning Disability Quarterly, 4*, 189–201.

Swanson, H. L. (1987). Information-processing theory and learning disabilities: An overview. *Journal of Learning Disabilities, 20*, 3–7.

Torgesen, J. K. (1977a). Memorization processes in reading-disabled children. *Journal of Educational Psychology, 79*, 571–578.

Torgesen, J. K. (1977b). The role of nonspecific factors in the task performance of learning disabled children: A theoretical assessment. *Journal of Learning Disabilities, 10*, 27–34.

Torgesen, J. K., & Houck, G. (1980). Processing deficiencies in learning disabled children who perform poorly on the digit span test. *Journal of Educational Psychology, 72*, 141–160.

Van Reusen, A. K., Bos, C. S., Schumaker, J. B., & Deshler, D. D. (1987). *The learning strategies curriculum: The educational planning strategy.* Lawrence, KS: Edge Enterprises.

Vygotsky, L. S. (1978). *Mind in society: The development of higher psychological processes.* Cambridge: Harvard University Press.

Warner, M. M., Schumaker, J. B., Alley, G. R., & Deshler, D. D. (1989). The role of executive control: An epidemiological study of school-identified learning disabled and low achieving adolescents on a serial recall task. *Learning Disabilities Research, 4*(2), 107–118.

Wertsch, J. V., & Stone, C. A. (1979, February). *A social international analysis of learning disabilities remediation.* Paper presented at international conference of Association for Children with Learning Disabilities, San Francisco.

Wong, B. Y. L. (1978). The effects of directive cues on the organization of memory and recall in good and poor readers. *Journal of Educational Research, 72*, 32–38.

Wong, B. Y. L. (1979). Increasing retention of main ideas through questioning strategies. *Learning Disability Quarterly, 2*(2), 42–47.

Wong, B. Y. L., & Jones, W. (1982). Increasing comprehension in learning disabled and normally achieving students through self-questioning training. *Learning Disability Quarterly, 5*, 228–240.

Wong, B. Y. L., Wong, R., Perry, N., & Sawaktsky, D. (1986). The efficacy of a self-questioning summarization strategy for use by underachievers and learning disabled adolescents in social studies. *Learning Disabilities Focus, 2*, 20–35.

Wong, B. Y. L. (1980). Activating the inactive learner. Use of questions/prompts to enhance comprehension and retention of implied information in learning disabled children. *Learning Disability Quarterly, 3*, 29–37.

Ysseldyke, J. E. (1973). Diagnostic-prescriptive teaching: The search for attitude-treatment interactions. In L. Mann & D. Sabatino (Eds.), *The first review of special education* (Vol. 1). Philadelphia: Journal of Special Education Press.

3

Reading Strategy Instruction

EDWIN S. ELLIS

QUESTIONS TO KEEP IN MIND

- Does reading literacy imply more than being able to decode words and comprehend text?

- How has understanding of the process of reading changed during the last decade?

- How do good readers differ from poor readers?

- What are some key cognitive processes associated with reading? Why are they important?

- What are the similarities and differences among models for teaching strategic reading processes? Which model makes the most sense to you? Why?

- What are the similarities among recommended ways to teach learning strategies for reading comprehension, unknown word problem solving, and understanding visual aids? How do they differ?

- Why should students have to learn to recognize semantic structures and organizational patterns in information? How can use of graphic organizers facilitate these skills?

- What are some of the problems with using adaptive textbooks? Why do they represent a problem?

- What is the relationship between "knowledge of the world" and reading comprehension?

ADVANCE ORGANIZER

During the past decade the work of cognitive scientists on the relationship between cognitive processes and learning tasks such as reading has resulted in a significant shift in traditional paradigms of instruction. Prior to this paradigm shift reading was viewed largely as a composite of discrete skills, each of which required mastering to produce literate readers. The assumption was that effective reading instructors need target only the skills that were "deficit" and provide intensive instruction in these specific skills until they were mastered. The result would be a competent reader.

Although not discounting important knowledges and skills involved in reading, this new paradigm of literacy views reading and reading instruction from a much broader perspective. We now view literacy as not just mastery of various skills involved in reading but also knowledge of how to orchestrate self-regulation of these skills and various cognitive processes in relation to knowledge of oneself and the task demands. Reading literacy, in essence, is the ability to organize and transform information, make decisions about its importance, link new information with background knowledge, and remember. It is also the ability to call upon and effectively and efficiently use a host of known reading strategies to meet the demands of a task. Thus, although we provide you with various strategies for teaching discrete reading skills in this chapter, we will focus primarily on the teaching of reading strategies. In this chapter, you will learn about:

- The role of self-regulation in the reading process in relation to characteristics of adolescents with reading disabilities and setting demands
- Facilitating use of metacognitive knowledge and cognitive strategies when reading
  - key metacognitive and cognitive processes and strategies for increasing reading comprehension
  - models for teaching self-regulated reading
    - strategies intervention model
    - reciprocal teaching model
- Facilitating knowledge and use of strategies for performing reading tasks
  - strategy instruction for increasing reading comprehension
  - strategy instruction for problem-solving unknown words
  - strategy instruction for text chapter perusal
  - strategy instruction for interpreting visual aids
- Facilitating knowledge of text structures and organizational patterns
- Selecting appropriate textbooks for students with LD
- Teaching strategy interrelations and integrations

Because a large majority of adolescents with LD have reached at least 4th to 5th grade reading levels, we will target reading instruction appropriate for students with similar skills.

Figure 3.1 shows how the chapter has been organized.

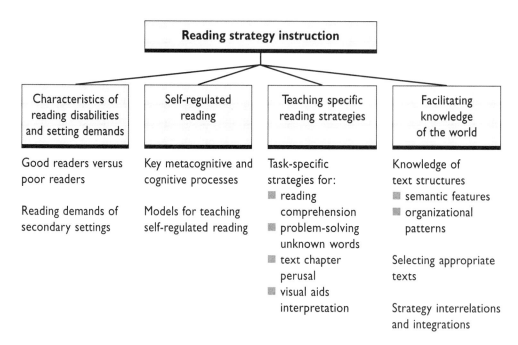

FIGURE 3.1   CHAPTER 3 ORGANIZATION

INTRODUCTION

Reading is a complex process. It entails more than merely decoding printed symbols. It embraces all types of thinking, including evaluating, judging, imagining, reasoning, and problem solving. The relationship between reading and cognition is clear: The product of reading and cognition is achievement.

We have made considerable advances in the past decade in our understanding of the reading process, particularly in relation to teaching reading as a *thinking* process. In this chapter we present several approaches to teaching reading. Some of these are quite different from traditional perspectives on reading instruction. We believe they are effective with many adolescents with LD. For example, educators traditionally have viewed reading as a developmental process. Mastering various subskills in reading (e.g., knowledge of prefixes and suffixes, consonant blends) was believed to be important before beginning instruction in higher-order thinking skills for reading. Even though many educators still embrace this notion, no research supports the idea (for a review, see Harris & Pressley, 1991). We know now that even poor readers can be taught relatively sophisticated thinking skills and strategies for reading.

Likewise, traditional views of remedial reading instruction have strongly reflected a diagnostic-prescriptive orientation, adhering to the notion that reading is composed of a set of discrete skills. The traditional role of the LD teacher was to test the student to identify skills the student had not yet mastered, begin teaching the deficit skills that are lowest on the developmental hierarchy, and continue instruction until the student had mastered all skills along the hierarchy. Presumably, mastering these discrete skills produced a competent reader. Although this view does have merit, research has demonstrated some severe limitations. Many adolescents with LD do not use the skills they have been taught.

Too often teachers have taught discrete skills at the expense of teaching students how to use these skills strategically to meet their goals. For example, many students with LD have mastered basic word-attack tactics such as sounding out words, using sentence contextual clue tactics (guessing what the word means based on the context of the sentence), and using word structural cue tactics (e.g., using knowledge of prefixes, suffixes, root words), yet they rarely employ these tactics when they encounter words they cannot read. More often than not, they skip the unknown word and hope it does not matter. What often is missing from their knowledge is a strategy for employing these various tactics systematically in a strategic manner and for making decisions about when to use which tactic and the motivation to do so.

Likewise, many adolescents with LD perform beautifully on various reading tasks designed to facilitate practice at specific comprehension skills (e.g., drawing inferences from short passages, finding the main idea of paragraphs), yet continue to have severe comprehension problems when reading. Again, what is missing is often knowledge of effective reading comprehension strategies for putting skills such as drawing inferences and locating main ideas to work on real reading problems and the ability to *self-regulate* these processes.

A common mistake that many educators make is to confuse mastery of what traditionally have been called "basic skills" with literacy. Because of this, measures of literacy (e.g., graduation examinations, minimal competency tests) often measure discrete reading skills on the assumption that if the student has learned these skills, he or she has attained reading literacy. Literacy, however, is a great deal more than knowledge of word-attack skills and being able to select from among several phrases the one that best describes the main idea of a passage. Palincsar and her colleagues (1993) described literacy as, "the ability to engage in intentional self-regulated learning with an awareness of the variables that influence learning and an ability to take control of one's activity as a learner" (p. 248).

CHARACTERISTICS OF ADOLESCENTS WITH LD WITH READING DISABILITIES

GOOD VERSUS POOR READERS

Literate readers have the motivation to expend mental energy to perform the cognitive processes necessary to gain meaning from text combined with a good working knowledge of these processes. This includes the flexible use of strategies for completing tasks successfully and effective use of metacognition (awareness of own characteristics and of the task demands needed to select, employ, monitor, and evaluate strategy use, knowledge of information structures, and knowledge of the world (Pressley, Borkowski, & Schneider, 1989). The background knowledge the reader brings to the task is a critical variable in the reading process. Johnston and Pearson (1982) concluded that prior knowledge can account for more variation in reading performance than either IQ or measured reading achievement. Research has indicated consistently that students who possess relevant prior knowledge comprehend text significantly better than students who lack the pertinent knowledge base.

The dimensions of self-regulated reading, illustrated in Figure 3.2, are interdependent. For example, students who have extensive world knowledge likely will encounter reading difficulties if they do not also have extensive knowledge of strategies for completing tasks or metacognitive awareness of what is involved in the task. Conversely, readers who have extensive strategic knowledge still will encounter difficulties when attempting to read text that addresses information about which they have little or no world knowledge, or when they lack knowledge of word meanings or of information structures. Although these knowledges are interdependent in a negative sense (weaknesses in one form of knowledge undermine use of other knowledges), they also can be interdependent in a positive sense. Good readers will recognize weaknesses in one aspect of their knowledge base and compensate for them by using their other knowledges. Consider the sentence below:

> The role of macrobits in the formation of hyperborean semiconductors has three functions. First...

While you realize that you do not understand the sentence fully, you also realize that part of the reason is your lack of background knowledge about semiconductors ("I've heard of these before, but I don't really know much about them") and your lack of knowledge of specific word meanings ("What is a 'macrobit'? What does 'hyperborean' mean?"). You also may realize that the sentence signals an upcoming text structure that you can use to help you comprehend upcoming information. (*"It's going to tell about the three functions. Maybe I can figure out what a macrobit is based on these functions"*).

Regrettably, many students with LD are not savvy at using what they know to comprehend better. Table 3.1 summarizes some of the basic differences between capable readers and immature or poor readers. A number of recent findings from research are pertinent to understanding the reading problems of LD adolescents. These include the following:

- Students with higher levels of metacognitive awareness have higher levels of reading comprehension. Good readers are aware of variables that interact in reading; poor readers are less aware of these variables.
- Good readers are able to identify key ideas from text and discriminate their relative importance; poor readers have considerable difficulty in this area.
- Good readers are sensitive to text features (e.g., headings, subheadings, organization) whereas poor readers are considerably less sensitive to these features.
- Good readers monitor their comprehension of text, whereas poor readers tend to do poorly at comprehension monitoring. Good readers stop and attempt to repair comprehension breakdown (e.g., rereading passages that do not make sense), whereas poor readers keep moving on to new text even though previous text did not make sense.

Good reading =

Metacognitive knowledge	+ Knowledge of strategies for completing tasks	+ Knowledge of information structures	+ Knowledge of the world	+ Motivation
Knowledge of one's own characteristics *For example:* • Knowing how your current attitude affects your performance • Knowing what you can and cannot do well when reading Knowledge of task demands *For example:* • Knowing that you need to find the main ideas of each heading in a chapter • Knowing that you need to understand a character's intent in a story	Cognitive strategies *For example:* • Relating new information to background knowledge • Self-questioning • Summarizing • Imaging Self-regulation strategies *For example:* • Thinking ahead to plan and anticipate learning • Thinking during to execute and monitor learning • Thinking back to consolidate and extend learning Task-attack strategies *For example:* • How to peruse a textbook chapter • How to read for specific information • How to interpret visual aids Problem-solving strategies *For example:* • Monitoring comprehension • Comprehension repair strategies • Word-attack strategies	Knowledge of word structures *For example:* • Knowing morphographical components of words (prefixes, suffixes, etc.) Knowledge of information organizational structures *For example:* • General-to-specific • Compare/contrast • Cause/effect • Problem/solution	Knowledge of concepts and facts *For example:* • Knowing the characteristics of things • Knowing the relationships between things • Knowing the meaning of words Knowledge of processes *For example:* • Knowing why events happen • Knowing how things work	Motivation source *For example:* • Intrinsic motivation to read because the information is interesting • Extrinsic motivation to read to get some payoff from others Beliefs *For example:* • Beliefs about your ability to perform tasks successfully • Attributions for success or failure • Commitments to less effective strategies

FIGURE 3.2   DIMENSIONS OF SELF-REGULATED READING

TABLE 3.1   SELF-REGULATED BEHAVIORS OF GOOD AND POOR READERS

Mature/Good Readers	Immature/Poor Readers
Before reading:	
Activate prior knowledge Understand task and set purpose Combine intrinsic and extrinsic motivation Use positive, affirming self-statements Choose appropriate strategies	Start reading without preparation Begin reading without knowing why Use primarily extrinsic motivation Use negative, deprecating self-statements Read without considering how to approach the task
During reading:	

Focus attention
Monitor their comprehension by
  — knowing comprehension is occurring
  — knowing what is being understood
Anticipate and predict
Use fix-up strategies when they lack understanding
Use contextual analysis to understand new terms
Use text structure to assist comprehension
Organize and integrate new information
	Are easily distracted
	Do not know they do not understand
	Read to get done
	Do not know what to do when they lack understanding
	Do not recognize important vocabulary
	Do not see any organization
	Add on rather than integrate information

After reading:	
Reflect on what was read Summarize major ideas Seek additional information from outside sources Believe success is a result of effort	Stop reading and thinking Believe success is a result of luck

Source: Adapted from *Strategic Learning in the Content Areas*, by H. Grover, D. Cook, J. Benson, & A. Chandler, 1991, Madison: Wisconsin Department of Public Instruction.

■ Good readers have knowledge of and use a variety of reading strategies effectively, whereas poor readers' knowledge of strategies is limited and they do not effectively use strategies they do know.

■ Good readers tend to have greater world knowledge bases and thus are less likely to approach a new topic with misconceptions. When they do have misconceptions, they tend to adjust their understanding of the topic to fit new information about it, although this is a difficult task. In contrast, poor readers tend to have an extremely difficult time adjusting their prior knowledge to accommodate new information. Many students with LD attempt to reconstruct their understanding of new information so it will "fit" with their prior knowledge base or what they first thought a topic was about, rather than adjust their prior knowledge to accommodate the new information.

SETTING DEMANDS

Expectations regarding reading in secondary settings vary widely across different schools and even among secondary teachers within specific buildings. In some secondary content-area classes little or no reading is required. In others, extensive reading is expected. Likewise, a gap often exists between what teachers say are significant expectations (e.g., "To do well on my tests, my students *must* read and study the textbook chapter") and the reality of their situations (e.g., *students in this class can get high marks on tests without ever reading the textbook chapter*). Also, a significant gap often exists between what teachers believe are significant expectations in their classes and what students say are the demands of these classes.

Chances are great that when you were a secondary school student, much of the instruction you received was "textbook-driven." The curriculum was dictated largely by content found in the textbook used and the instructor's manual. Many educators recently have been engaged in school reform efforts that deemphasize textbook-driven approaches (at least more so at the elementary and middle school level), and these efforts may turn out to be advantageous to students with LD. These efforts are largely sporadic and do not represent what most teachers do. In short, textbook-driven approaches still are the vastly predominant mode of instruction. Despite the new teaching approaches, use of technology, and efforts at school reform over the last four decades, instruction in secondary classes arguably is nearly identical to that provided during the 1950s (Schlechty, 1993).

Textbook-driven approaches generally require students to (a) read a portion of text independently, (b) answer study guide questions and write definitions for new vocabulary terms, (c) use information gleaned from the text to engage in class discussions, and (d) locate and memorize significant concepts and details so they can answer test questions correctly. Although many secondary teachers may intend to facilitate "reading for understanding," the nature of the tasks teachers often require students to complete is more indicative of "read for school compliance" (e.g., read the text to locate specific pieces of information so they can complete a study guide question correctly).

On a more positive note, many of the more innovative teachers we have observed engage students in much more meaningful reading processes in which the primary purpose is reading for understanding and reading with a more authentic purpose. For example, rather than studying a textbook chapter to be able to complete end-of-the-chapter questions and score well on tests about the Civil War, students in these more innovative classes use the text, in addition to a variety of other sources, to glean information about the Civil War so they can write a play or construct a display for the library.

The traditional and the innovative expectations share a set of communalities related to two key tasks associated with reading:

1. Students are expected to comprehend what they read. Specifically, they are expected to recognize main ideas and significant details *and* understand how these interrelate.
2. Students are expected to engage in problem-solving processes associated with how to address unknown words they encounter when reading (as will be learned later in this chapter, this involves considerably more than decoding).

To engage successfully in these two tasks, students must utilize effectively the various supplemental aids often included with well written texts (e.g., visual aids and text structural cues such as headings and subheadings, text introductions and summaries, text questions, highlighted words). Finally, students must engage effectively in these processes while reading textbooks that often are poorly designed and written (Armbruster & Anderson, 1988), and when there is a mismatch between students' reading ability and that needed to address the textbooks assigned to them effectively (Schumaker & Deshler, 1984).

As a result of these expectations, this chapter features instruction in four key areas of reading: (a) strategies for reading comprehension, (b) strategies for problem-solving unknown words, (c) strategies for text perusal, and (d) strategies for interpreting visual aids. A relatively heavy emphasis is also placed on teaching students to recognize semantic structures and organizational patterns, as these skills can enhance the reading-for-understanding process greatly.

SELF-REGULATED READING

Differentiating cognitive strategies and task-specific strategies is important. *Cognitive* strategies are analogous to mental tools that can be used on a variety of tasks and problems. Examples of powerful cognitive strategies are predicting, self-questioning, visualizing, and summarizing. These information-processing tools can be applied when performing reading tasks (e.g., reading text, perusing text chapters, interpreting visual aids) and in nonreading tasks (e.g., listening and notetaking). *Task-specific* strategies are specific plans for incorporating cognitive strategies systematically on *specific tasks.*

During the past decade cognitive research has provided a wealth of information regarding mind operations (cf. Jones, Palincsar, Ogle, & Carr, 1987). These findings support a model of the mind that engages recursively in activating, online processing, and consolidating or extending processing. To activate thinking, the learner becomes cognizant of new information and then does something to activate prior knowledge so a sense of the new information is attained through comparison or association to similar, already known ideas. During this activation process, the learner focuses attention on the new information and its features, as well as appropriate strategies for understanding it, and also establishes a purpose for learning it, performing a task related to it, or solving a problem that involves it. Comparing the new information to prior knowledge results in forming hypotheses, predictions, and questions about the new data. As the hypotheses are formed, the mind shifts into online processes. In essence, previewing new information, reviewing related prior knowledge, and predicting what the new information is about are key cognitive strategies used during activation processes.

In online processes, the mind engages in two important cognitive operations:

1. The mind is busy interacting with the information. A variety of information strategies are used at this point to process it further. These involve mental tools such as self-questioning, visualizing the information, forecasting, looking back to verify, looking ahead to anticipate, and so on.
2. As these strategies are applied to the information, the hypotheses or predictions formed earlier during the activation process are tested against prior knowledge, and the stream of incoming new information and comprehension is monitored. Some hypotheses are confirmed and assimilated into an overall schema of understanding about a topic, and others are held in abeyance. New hypotheses, predictions, and questions are formed to "recycle" and make sense of the new information.

In essence, the process of asking and answering questions about the new information and one's own understanding of it are key processes associated with the online phase.

During the consolidating or extending processes, the mind is assimilating what was learned and understanding the information as a whole. Some of these processes involve extending what was learned, some involve synthesizing or connecting various new ideas as they stream in, and some involve summarizing and expressing what has been learned. In essence, summarizing and synthesizing are key components of the consolidation phase.

To summarize, the goal of literacy strategy instruction is (a) to make students aware of how to process information effectively; (b) to enable them to self-regulate these processes using cognitive tools or strategies for processing information; and (c) to enable them to use these processes effectively and efficiently when engaged in various academic and nonacademic tasks. In short, the objective is to make students literate about their thinking and how they can control it to attain goals. Students not only should be taught *how* to use these processes but also to know *what* they are.

MODELS FOR TEACHING SELF-REGULATED READING

Numerous models of self-regulated reading instruction emerged during the past decade. Each employs its own terminology to describe instructional processes reflected by the model. Close examination, however, indicates that they are *far* more similar than they are different (cf. Harris & Pressley, 1991). In this chapter, we will consider two of these models: the strategies intervention model developed by Deshler, Schumaker, and their colleagues, and the reciprocal teaching model developed by Palincsar and her colleagues. Scaffolded instruction (see discussion in chapter 2) is a common thread running through these models. Likewise, instruction in cognitive strategies related to activating prior knowledge, predicting, generating questions, imaging, summarizing, and monitoring comprehension are features of these three models, albeit in different ways. The models differ more in the manner and context in which the strategic processes are communicated initially to students and in how students are taught to generalize the processes to new problem domains.

STRATEGIES INTERVENTION MODEL

Instructional procedures throughout this book reflect a bias toward the strategies instructional model (SIM) approach for several reasons. First, this model has a strong empirical basis for both of the instructional tactics found within the stages of acquisition and generalization (see chapter 2 for an in-depth review). Also, the individual task-specific strategies have empirical validation with adolescents with LD and social validation with the teachers who use it (albeit the SIM model does have its limitations and weaknesses). In essence, the authors of SIM identified specific academic tasks that adolescents with LD encounter commonly in school settings and then developed individual task-specific strategies to enable students to complete the tasks or solve problems effectively and efficiently.

The paraphrasing strategy (Schumaker, Denton, & Deshler, 1984), shown in Figure 3.3, illustrates one of the SIM strategies targeted for facilitating reading comprehension. Another example of a SIM strategy for reading is the word identification strategy illustrated in Figure 3.4 (Lenz, Schumaker, Deshler, & Beals, 1984). Although many teachers have incorporated the SIM strategies informally into mainstream classes, these are designed to be taught primarily in resource settings where teachers can teach the strategies for at least 30 minutes a day on an ongoing basis.

The SIM model provides in-depth instruction in the strategic processes associated with the strategy steps. The mnemonic remembering device used to encapsulate these processes for students is *not* the strategy but, rather, is simply part of the overall strategy system used for a specific type of task. In this model the strategies are designed by experts, and then students are taught to use them in a flexible manner. The ultimate goal is for students to internalize the processes reflected in the strategy steps to a point at which the students use them automatically, fluidly, and recursively. Thus, although the steps of the SIM strategies reflect a linear process, students should be taught to use them recursively.

Also in this model students are expected to ultimately create their own understandings and variations of problem-solving strategies. The explicit, teacher-directed instruction and presentation of concrete strategy steps and remembering devices that occurs initially in the SIM instructional process serves as a foundation upon which students construct their own understandings. SIM strategies are decidedly more tactical in nature than the other model discussed next. That is, a primary focus of the SIM strategies is on how to orchestrate, using self-instruction, a set of tactics for "getting the job done."

Some of these tactics involve cognitive strategies, but the model does not place great emphasis on what these cognitive processes are (Ellis & Lenz, 1987). Many teachers are attracted to the SIM model because of its practical focus on enabling students with LD to perform successfully the academic tasks so often necessary for school survival (e.g., read texts, prepare for tests, take tests, write paragraphs) and view the cognitive training aspects of the SIM instruction as a desirable but secondary benefit.

RECIPROCAL TEACHING MODEL

The reciprocal teaching (RT) model, validated for use with adolescents with LD, is different from SIM in some ways. It is decidedly nontactically oriented, and a major purpose of the model is to teach students about specific cognitive strategies and how one self-regulates their use when reading. Absent from RT is a set of strategy steps that are communicated explicitly to students. Rather, students gain an understanding of the cognitive processes associated with self-regulation of these cognitive strategies via an ongo-

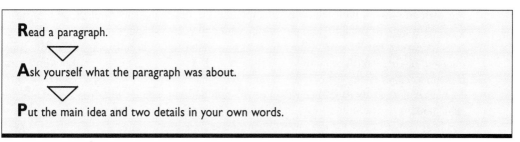

FIGURE 3.3 PARAPHRASING READING STRATEGY

Source: From *The Learning Strategies Curriculum: The Paraphrasing Strategy*, by J. B. Schumaker, D. D. Deshler, & P. Denton, 1984, Lawrence: University of Kansas.

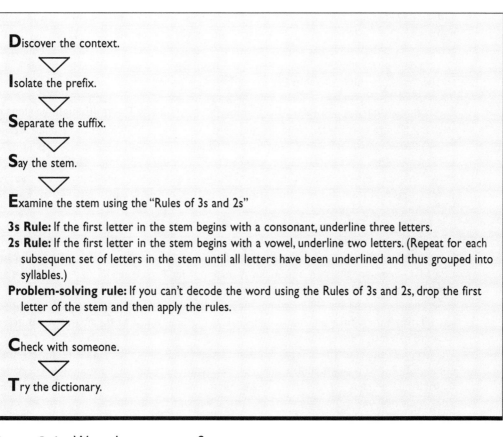

FIGURE 3.4 WORD IDENTIFICATION STRATEGY

Source: From *Learning Strategies Curriculum: The Word Identification Strategy*, by B. K. Lenz, J. B. Schumaker, D. D. Deshler, & V. L. Beals, 1984, Lawrence: University of Kansas.

ing dialogue that occurs between students and the teacher throughout the reading process. Also absent from RT is instruction in how to perform specific reading tasks (e.g., how to peruse text chapters, how to interpret visual aids, how to answer study guide questions). These skills are taught holistically within the ongoing context of reading comprehension instruction.

RT is composed of a general set of procedures that heavily incorporate features of scaffolded instruction. Palincsar and Brown (1984) described RT as a dialogue between teachers and students for the purpose of jointly constructing meaning from text. In RT, students are taught to use four cognitive strategies: (a) predicting future content, (b) question generating, (c) summarizing main content of a passage/paragraph, and (d) clarifying (determining when confusion or a problem exists and taking corrective action). This approach relies greatly upon the skills of the person conducting the instruction.

An RT reading lesson typically begins with a brief discussion to activate students' prior knowledge. Then students use this knowledge to make predictions about the passage. The teacher models or demonstrates *how* to predict, summarize, question, and clarify, and guides students eventually to perform these activities independently. The teacher models and provides assistance by (a) prompting, (b) instructing, and (c) modifying the activity. Ultimately, students "act as teachers" by engaging in the activities independently. During the initial phase of RT, when students are beginning to learn the process, the teacher assumes the leadership responsibility. As students develop the process skill, the teacher may assign a discussion leader to direct reciprocal activities.

Although RT is a promising instructional model, it has some limitations with regard to practical implementation in secondary settings. *First,* a high level of teacher competency is required for RT instruction to truly teach self-regulated learning. This consideration becomes particularly important in the secondary schools, where most teachers are content instructors rather than skill instructors. Few teachers are well versed in teaching reading, and most lack understanding of the cognitive dimension of information processing.

RT is similar in structure to the traditional "read and discuss" format common to many content-area classes. Thus, teachers attempting to use RT may slip back to old habits while operating under the illusion that they are teaching self-regulated reading. Likewise, because RT is so nonlinear, it does not lend itself easily to teacher manuals and other instructional aids that teachers are accustomed to using. As such, the saying "a little knowledge can be a dangerous thing" rings true when novice teachers attempt to use RT when they have little knowledge of its application or of the cognitive strategies they are using (cf. Hermann, 1990).

Second, much of the RT research has been targeted at traditional reading groups commonly found in elementary settings. Few secondary settings are conducive to this instructional format. At this time, it is unclear how secondary resource teachers should implement RT in light of the various setting demands with which students must cope, along with their other needs. Equally unclear is how content-focused classes (either remedial or traditional) should implement RT in large-group instruction.

Third, the amount of research directed at RT use with adolescents with LD is limited. Thus, teachers who use RT at the secondary level should be reflective about what they are doing and evaluate its effectiveness carefully.

Although the limitations of RT as applied to secondary students with LD reflect primarily the current state-of-the-art, it has high potential for impacting adolescents' lives. The concerns addressed above involve implementation for the most part, and as research continues in this area, many of these concerns likely will be dispelled as more is learned about how to use RT in secondary schools.

Which model of strategies instruction is best for students with LD? The two models described above fall along a continuum of cognitive training. On one side are models that are mainly "instructive" in nature. The "best practices" are identified by experts and then systematically taught to students using principles of teacher-directed instruction. The instruction is driven by a mastery learning orientation. On the other end of the continuum are models that are primarily "constructive" in nature. Here, though the teacher may have knowledge of "best practices," these are not communicated to students explicitly. Rather, students are offered opportunities for discovering these practices and constructing their own, personalized understandings of them. Mastery of specific criteria is not used in making decisions about instruction. Rather, the goal is to build greater and more sophisticated understanding and skills holistically.

Although the two models just discussed share both instructive and constructive elements, SIM is primarily instructive in nature and RT is primarily constructive. Many students with LD respond extremely well to models that are instructive and direct, and others respond extremely well to the more constructive-oriented models. In keeping with diagnostic-prescriptive models and notions of designing instruction to fit students' individual learning styles, it might seem reasonable to design a test that would reveal quickly which orientation a student is likely to respond to best. You should be extremely skeptical of overly simplistic notions, though. Research is sparse in this area, but one of the best predictors of the success of a given instructional model is the teacher. If instructive models seem to provide a better fit with how the teacher views learning and methods of teaching, he or she probably will have more success using reductionalistic models. Conversely, if more constructive models fit the teacher better, he or she likely will be more effective when using the holistic models.

TEACHING SPECIFIC READING STRATEGIES

STRATEGY INSTRUCTION FOR INCREASING READING COMPREHENSION

The paraphrasing strategy (Schumaker, Deshler, & Denton, 1984)* has been demonstrated to increase significantly the reading comprehension skills of adolescents with LD. Although the strategy contains only three major steps (read a paragraph, ask yourself questions about the main idea and details, put the main idea and details into your own words), and seems to be a simple strategy to teach, teachers need to know that it is deceptively

---

* For in-depth training in how to teach the paraphrasing reading strategy, teacher manuals, videotapes, and other instructional resources for this intervention, contact the University of Kansas Center for Research in Learning.

more complex than the three steps suggest. Instruction in the paraphrasing strategy should follow the stages of acquisition and generalization described in chapter 2. Here, how these stages should be applied when teaching this strategy will be highlighted briefly.

STAGE 1: PRETEST

To pretest the student, teachers collect two types of information in the form of permanent products: product measures and process measures. In addition, it is suggested that teachers read a few passages with the student while conducting a dialogue similar to RT.

Product measures concern the actual level of the student's comprehension of specific reading passages. Thus, product measures are attained by evaluating the student's comprehension of main ideas and details presented in the previously read passage. A rough estimate of comprehension can be attained by having students respond to a set of written comprehension questions that address the content read by the student.

Process measures concern how well students are able to follow the strategic process to be taught. Process measures of paraphrasing ability are determined in part by evaluating students' verbalizations about each paragraph in relation to performance criteria. The performance criteria for evaluating students' paraphrases developed by Schumaker, Deshler, and Denton (1984) are:

- Must be in the student's own words
- Must contain only one main idea per paragraph
- Must contain two details
- Information in paraphrase is meaningful
- Complete sentence
- Information is new

To attain this measure, students are asked to read text passages from mainstream textbooks written at their grade-placement level. Each passage should contain a minimum of five paragraphs. Students are asked to read one paragraph at a time silently, to turn on a tape recorder, then to tell the recorder what the main idea and two details were for the paragraph just read, and finally to turn off the recorder. This process is repeated for each subsequent paragraph in the passage. Later these statements can be analyzed and compared to the performance criteria to produce a "paraphrasing score."

Teachers should interpret both the product and process scores with caution. Being able to discriminate correctly among a set of possible main ideas on multiple-choice questions provides only the most rudimentary indicator of comprehension. Likewise, analyzing what students say during their paraphrases reveals only the result of their cognition and tells little about what students actually are thinking during the reading process. For example, it does not tell us how well students are able to activate and use their prior knowledge, to what extent they form predictions about their reading and modify them as they learn more about the passage, how well they monitor their comprehension, how well they are synthesizing the specific information with the overall topic of study, and so forth. These kinds of insights can come only from the dialogue between the student and adult associated with the RT model. Thus, teachers should also read with students and converse with them about their thinking to informally gain insight into this domain.

STAGE 2: DESCRIBE THE PARAPHRASING STRATEGY

During this stage the teacher describes the situations and setting students encounter in which being able to identify main ideas and important details from reading materials will help them attain their goals. Students have to understand *why* and *when* expending the mental energy to paraphrase main ideas is important, as well as when and under what circumstances a reader should not bother. After listing and describing situations and reading materials in which paraphrasing is desirable, students should be encouraged to identify and discuss others as well. The teacher also will describe the steps of the strategy, provide a rationale for the steps, and discuss how the steps are to be used to cue important thinking behaviors when reading. Thus, during this stage, the teacher already will have begun to discuss the parameters of generalization and the process of enabling students to understand what the strategy is and how it works. Although these discussions begin during the Describe stage, the teacher should continue to discuss and explore related ideas throughout the instructional sequence.

STAGE 3: MODEL THE PARAPHRASING STRATEGY

During this stage the teacher performs the paraphrasing strategy using think-aloud, dialectal, and scaffolding techniques. The teacher's initial modeling of the strategy should be simple and straightforward. It should focus mainly on the surface features of the strategy (e.g., self-cueing performance of the strategy steps). Subsequent modeling of the strategy will involve the students gradually (e.g., as the teacher reads a passage aloud, students tell him or her what to do, and the teacher does it) and gradually will reveal to students more sophisticated cognitive processes (e.g., activating prior knowledge, generating different types of questions, monitoring comprehension and initiating comprehension repair strategies, and so forth). Likewise, teacher modeling should become dialectal (done in collaboration with students). Even though the teacher's modeling of the strategy begins in this stage, the teacher should continue to model the strategy as necessary throughout the remainder of the instructional sequence. These models should focus increasingly on the cognitive processes associated with performing the strategy and less on the overt strategy steps.

STAGE 4: VERBALLY ELABORATE AND REHEARSE

This stage is intended to help students develop an in-depth understanding of the overt and covert features of the strategy. Having students use their own language to describe these processes facilitates understanding and comprehension. Elaboration activities such as asking students to compare steps or processes associated with the paraphrasing strategy to strategies or processes they use already will facilitate understanding. Likewise, the more students know what is expected of them, the more likely they will be to meet that expectation. Thus, students also should elaborate on the critical features of an effective paraphrase presented earlier.

STAGE 5: PRACTICE ACQUISITION

The main purpose of this stage is to enable students to acquire skills for paraphrasing main ideas and relevant details from paragraphs they have read. Because this form of reading requires most students to engage in different, unfamiliar ways of thinking during the reading process, the reading materials that students use are controlled for difficulty. Essentially, reading materials should be relatively easy for students to read. Ellis and Graves (1990) concluded that an ideal level to begin practicing the paraphrasing strategy would be material that students can read already at a rate of 100 to 135 words per minute while maintaining a 97% accuracy in decoding. Practically speaking, these materials usually are a grade level below their tested ability level.

During acquisition practice, scaffolded and dialogic instruction is used extensively and then is faded gradually as students become confident and competent at paraphrasing. As students master the skill on easier reading materials, they are presented gradually with ever more challenging text to read so the material begins to approximate the material that the students encounter normally in general classes.

As students begin reading materials that contain numerous words that cannot be decoded or have unknown meanings, the effectiveness of the paraphrasing strategy diminishes. Thus, the teacher's goal should be to enable students to paraphrase effectively and efficiently any reading material they can decode with relative ease.

STAGE 6: UNDERTAKE ADVANCE PRACTICE

Learning to apply the paraphrasing strategy to a host of different reading materials under conditions where instructional support is still available is the distinguishing feature of advanced practice. Scaffolded and dialogic instruction is used as needed when students attempt to use the strategy with a variety of information sources that have not been controlled for difficulty (e.g., mainstream textbooks, encyclopedias, magazines, newspapers). The teacher's role during this stage is to help students analyze reading materials to determine whether the strategy should be applied, to help students determine goals for reading the material, and to anticipate how the strategy can be used and modified to meet these goals. For example, the goals for textbook reading might be to answer study guide questions. Here the teacher's role is to help students understand how the paraphrasing strategy can be used to meet this requirement. At other times the goal might be to glean information from a magazine article to compose an oral social studies report. Here the teacher's role would be to help students understand how they can modify the strategy to meet this task requirement. Thus, during advanced practice, the teacher must provide students with a variety of reading tasks that simulate those that students encounter in their mainstream classes.

STAGE 7: POSTTEST AND CELEBRATE

The purpose of this stage is (a) to ensure that students can perform the strategy effectively and efficiently, and (b) to officially recognize attainment of a milestone in learning the strategy. The posttest can be designed similar to that used during the pretest. Students then can compare their skills prior to learning the strategy with their present levels. Likewise, students appreciate teachers' celebrating with them the completion of the first major phase of learning the strategy (acquisition). Last, teachers should note that efforts now will be directed toward generalizing the strategy in earnest.

STAGE 8: GENERALIZE

Although the focus of this stage is on facilitating generalization of the paraphrasing strategy, all of the previous instruction should have been couched in terms of generalization. Students should know from the first day of instruction that the goal of strategy instruction is generalization. Teachers should have been encouraging students to experiment with generalizing the strategy and sharing the results and their perceptions with the teacher and other students. Instruction during this stage differs only in that generalization now is targeted intensively and extensively.

To ensure generalization, the teacher should engage in four types of generalization activities: orientation, activation, adaptation, and maintenance. *Orientation* activities consist primarily of efforts to make students highly cognizant of the need to generalize the strategy, to communicate the expectation that they do so, and to ensure students are aware of the situations and circumstances in which the reading strategy can be used.

During *activation* activities the teacher should review with students situations where the strategy is applicable, discuss using the strategy flexibly, and discuss cues that may signal appropriate times to apply the strategy. The objective is to ensure that students begin engaging in generalization behaviors and that they receive feedback on their efforts to use the strategy independently. Students are given (a) specific assignments to use the strategy in settings other than the one in which the strategy was learned originally, and (b) nonspecific assignments in which they are required to recognize appropriate opportunities to use the reading strategy independently and apply it to meet personal goals. Following these assignments, the teacher should conduct debriefings with students to discuss how they used the strategy (e.g., difficulties encountered, decisions made about using it, any adaptations), to check their comprehension of the text to which the strategy was applied, and to provide them with feedback regarding their use of generalization.

Adaptation activities are designed to facilitate student adaptation of the strategy to other problem domains. For example, during these activities students might practice using the paraphrasing strategy as a class participation strategy to become more involved in discussions.

Maintenance activities are designed to ensure that students maintain their knowledge of what the strategy is, how it is performed, and when it should be used. Periodic review sessions (e.g., every 2 weeks) are recommended.

STRATEGY INSTRUCTION FOR PROBLEM-SOLVING UNKNOWN WORDS

The ability to identify unknown words independently is an important text-reading skill, and during adolescence and adulthood this ability is increasingly important for other reading formats (e.g., reading tests, instructions, application forms). Whereas young readers often come to rely on external sources (e.g., teachers, parents) to tell them unknown words, adolescents and young adults often encounter conditions that prohibit or impair the use of external resources. For example, determining unknown words on tests often must be done independently. Likewise, having to ask others what a word is may be embarrassing to many adolescents.

Many students prefer the consequences of failing to read important words over the risk of becoming embarrassed by revealing that they cannot read the word. Because many adolescents have much of the prerequisite knowledge related to problem-solving unknown words, teaching them a task-specific strategy for word attack has been demonstrated to be highly beneficial. In the following discussion the various problem-solving tactics involved when problem-solving an unknown word, along with a task-specific strategy that incorporates components of these processes into a systematic plan of attack is described.

PROBLEM-SOLVING TACTICS

When students encounter unknown words in reading, two scenarios are involved. The first involves encountering words that the reader does not recognize in text (e.g., the word is not in his or her sight vocabulary) but is familiar with in the context of aural language (the word is in his or her listening vocabulary). For example, a reader may not recognize the word "revolutionary" when reading but does understand its meaning when the word is spoken during a discussion.

The second scenario involves instances in which the meaning of the word simply is not known. For example, the reader does not recognize the word "paraprofessional" when reading, nor does he or she understand what it means when it is spoken during a discussion. Five tactics that can be employed in problem-solving unknown words are: (a) context analysis, (b) semantic analysis, (c) structural analysis, (d) morphological analysis, and (e) using external sources for help (e.g., other persons, dictionary).

Context analysis involves using the context in which the word appears to guess what the unknown word is or means. The major limitation is that it is content-specific. Conversely, a major limitation of using the dictionary is that the word may be accompanied by qualifying words that affect the meaning of the word in a specific context ("The area is hot, dry, and sparsely populated"). The qualifying word "sparsely," if not considered with the key word *"populated,"* will cause students to misinterpret the sentence even though they have the correct dictionary meaning of the key word.

Thomas and Robinson (1972, p. 38) devised guidelines for students with LD to help them distinguish circumstances for using either context cues or the dictionary to arrive at the meaning of the word. Table 3.2 presents these guidelines.

Semantic analysis is an extension of context analysis. It involves looking for familiar-looking words within the unknown word, thinking about the meaning of the familiar-looking word, and using this information along with the context of the sentence to determine what the word is or means.

Structural analysis involves analyzing the unknown word for its components (e.g., prefixes, suffixes) and then attempting to decipher it (e.g., breaking down the word into recognizable syllables). Structural analysis is useful for decoding unrecognized words that already are in the reader's listening vocabulary but provides little in the way of promoting understanding of unknown words. Special problems arise when students with LD have difficulty decoding polysyllabic words that require the use of not only simple sound-symbol phonics but also related syllabication skills. Polysyllabic words are of four types: (a) compound words (e.g., shellfish, shipmate, pullman); (b) known words to which a prefix or suffix has been added (e.g., adverb, embattle, federalize, feminism, incandescent, inbreeding); (c) words that can be divided into familiar syllables (e.g., incarnate, respiration, subsidiary); (d) words that only dictionaries can be used to decode (e.g., mnemosyne, zygapophisis) (Olsen & Ames, 1970). Olsen and Ames (1970, p. 135) offered the following three generalizations that LD students can use when approaching similar polysyllabic words:

TABLE 3.2   GUIDELINES FOR USING CONTEXT CLUES AND DICTIONARIES

Do Rely on Context Clues	Do Rely on your Dictionary (*Don't rely* on Context Clues)
1. When you have an "unmissable clue," a direct explanation 2. When you have highly revealing clues and the meaning you arrive at "clicks" with the rest of the passage 3. When, in view of your purpose for reading the selection, you need only a general sense of the meaning (previewing material or reading for the main idea)	1. When you require a precise meaning (e.g., It *almost always* takes the dictionary to pin down the meaning 2. When the word is a key word, one crucial to your understanding, and full comprehension is important to you 3. When the context clues suggest several meanings and you must know which 4. When you don't know the nearby words (watch this carefully for clarifying words) 5. When you have encountered a word a number of times, realize that it is a common, useful word that you will meet again and want to master it thoroughly (record it in your word file for future reading)

1. Prefixes and suffixes usually form separate syllables (e.g., *ad-verb*).
2. Syllables generally divide between two consonants or double consonants (e.g., *wel-come, poly-dac-tyl*).
3. Words ending in *le* usually take the consonant immediately before it and form the final syllable (e.g., *syl-la-ble*).

Morphological analysis is similar to structural analysis in that it also involves analyzing the unknown word for its components but is more appropriate for determining the meaning of unknown words. All words are composed of morphemes, units which have specific meaning (e.g., "pre" means "before"; "ing" means "in the process of doing an action"). When encountering a word to which the student does not know the meaning, morphological analysis is used, usually in conjunction with context analysis, to determine the meaning of the word.

Although the processes just described are technically different, their distinction is largely academic. Good readers do not use these as isolated skills. Rather, they use the skills integratively or in conjunction with each other.

TASK-SPECIFIC STRATEGY

Specific learning strategies for problem-solving unknown words are simply systematic plans for orchestrating the above tactics in a thoughtful and self-regulatory manner. The word identification strategy* illustrated in Figure 3.4 provides an example of how the

---

* For in-depth training in how to teach the word identification strategy, teacher manuals, and other instructional resources for this intervention, contact the University of Kansas Center for Research in Learning.

processes associated with problem-solving unknown words can be illustrated concretely. Although this strategy seems to consist of a set of linear steps, students should be taught to use these processes in a recursive, rather than a linear, "cook book" fashion. For example, the process of using background knowledge, making predictions about what the word means, and monitoring comprehension often recycles until the reader feels confident in understanding the word well enough to get closure and move on.

The strategy cues students to begin by using context analysis to decipher the word or its meaning. If this proves unsatisfactory, the strategy steps direct the student to use various structural analysis tactics (e.g., separate prefixes and suffixes from the word, look for root words and stem words). If the word still is unknown, the student is directed to check with someone or try the dictionary as a last resort.

Although most of the strategy steps simply organize various familiar problem-solving tactics into a more systematic plan for their use, the authors of the strategy introduced a novel tactic in the "examine the stem" step. This step is designed to enable students to use their knowledge of phonics to sound out the word. Many students become overwhelmed at the prospect of sounding out a long word. The "examine the stem" step is designed to enable students to recognize the syllables within the word, breaking the stem into smaller, more manageable parts that are more easily read. To perform this step, students are taught to apply the "rules of 3s and 2s:"

- **3s rule.** If the first letter is a consonant, underline the first three letters. Example:

  <u>jur</u>isprudence

- **2s rule.** If the first letter is a vowel, underline the first two letters. Example:

  <u>jur</u> <u>is</u> prudence

- Continue applying the 3s and 2s rules for the remaining letters until all words in the stem have been broken into syllables or you have run out of letters. Count vowel digraphs as one letter when applying the 3s and 2s rules. Example:

  <u>jur</u> <u>is</u> <u>pru</u> <u>den</u> ce

Students also are taught guidelines to apply when the 3s and 2s rule does not result in word recognition.

- **Problem solving using the 3s and 2s rules**. If you cannot make sense of the word, drop the first letter in the stem and then apply the 3s and 2s rules starting with the second letter.

Instruction in this strategy has been demonstrated to improve word-attack skills (Lenz & Hughes, 1990), but the authors do not recommend that students apply it to every word they cannot read. Its use should be reserved for those occasional words that seem particularly important (e.g., words in chapter headings, words that seem to be the main idea of a paragraph, etc.). The authors also recommend that students who will be taught the strategy have attained a minimum of a 3rd-grade reading level in their knowledge of phonics and word structures.

Strategy Instruction for Perusal of Text Chapter

Well written textbooks incorporate a number of components to help readers comprehend information within the chapter (e.g., headings, introduction, summary, italicized words, focusing questions, comprehension questions, graphics). Many students, however, do not utilize these features as tools to understand and study the text chapter (Schumaker, Deshler, Alley, Warner, & Denton, 1982). Some students do not recognize that these features can enhance their comprehension, nor do they understand *how* to use them to facilitate comprehension of text material.

Many students learn to resent some parts of the text because of the manner in which teachers have required students to address them (e.g., homework assignments requiring students to look up the definitions of the words in italics or to write answers to end-of-chapter questions). Fortuitously, explicit instruction in the information processes for using textual cues can produce significant increases in comprehension (Schumaker et al., 1982). Because up to 44% of the information for which students are responsible for learning is presented in textbooks but not discussed in class (Zigmond, Levin, & Laurie, 1985), facilitating full use of the chapter design is an important instructional technique to promote comprehension of text material.

Key Components of Information Processing

Analyzing chapter features effectively and efficiently requires that students know *why* these should be analyzed. Students must believe that the process will increase their understanding and memory of the text material. Students also must know *when* these parts should be studied and for *what* purpose, as well as *how* to analyze them. For example, these processes can be used in advance of reading a chapter (think ahead), while reading it (think during), and after reading it (think back). The most common use of these processes is *text perusal*, analyzing textual cues before reading the passage to get a sense of what the chapter is about.

These processes also can be used *while reading the text*, to help clarify the content and relate what is being learned to an overall schema of the chapter. The processes can be used further as a way to structure *reviews* of the text chapter. Students use the chapter features in a manner similar to using flashcards for studying. For example, students read a specific text heading, say to themselves what this section is about, and then scan the prose to self-check and determine if they are correct. (A more detailed explanation of these applications and how to teach them is provided below.)

When analyzing chapter features, some of the key cognitive strategies utilized include clarifying the purpose of the task, setting goals, making positive self-statements, activating knowledge, summarizing, predicting, relating, prioritizing, and generating questions. To analyze chapter features effectively, students use these processes systematically and flexibly in conjunction with monitoring processes to assure that they are reaching goals. Naturally, prior knowledge of the content to which these processes will be applied will impact the extent to which students are able to employ these processes successfully.

An Effective and Efficient Set of Strategic Processes

Processes that focus on self-motivation are essential to problem solving and should be employed early. Thus, clarifying the purpose of the task, setting goals related to this purpose, and using self-affirmation statements are particularly important to employ initially when analyzing text chapter components and also throughout the problem-solving process. Therefore, when analyzing text chapter parts, students might employ self-questioning techniques first to clarify the purpose of their efforts and then establish specific goals that relate directly to the purpose. Table 3.3 illustrates purposes of analyzing the text components and possible goals that might be established.

Following the establishment of goals, another effective process is to make a positive self-statement. For example:

This is a good trick. I'm good at this.

This is going to take some effort, but I can handle it.

Once self-motivation strategies are in place, processes for analyzing chapter components are initiated to glean specific information and gain an understanding of the overall chapter content. Although a number of strategies might be called into play at this time and the order in which they are employed may vary widely and still be effective, most students can learn and use the following sequence readily in a manner that results in significant advances in text comprehension.

At this point students interact with specific parts of the chapter to glean information. First they read the title and paraphrase it. This requires them to activate prior knowledge about the content reflected in the title and form predictions about the chapter content.

Next, students analyze the various headings (and subheadings) by elaborating on

TABLE 3.3   PURPOSES AND GOALS FOR ANALYZING TEXT CHAPTER FEATURES

Purpose	Goal
I am analyzing these text features because:	*My goal is to:*
This may help me understand what the whole chapter is about before I read it.	Understand this stuff as easily as possible.
It may help me clarify and understand a specific difficult part of the chapter before I read it.	Read this without having to reread it over and over to understand it.
It's a good way to get the gist of the chapter without reading the whole thing.	Be able to talk about these things in class because I don't have time to read the whole thing.
It may help me clarify and understand a difficult passage I just read.	See if I can make better sense of this section.
It's a good way to check and make sure that I understand or remember important information.	Knock'm dead on that test tomorrow.

the information they think the heading indicates, and predicting the content that accompanies the heading or translating headings into questions they believe the section under the heading will answer. Students also develop statements about the apparent relationship between various subheadings under a heading and how these subheadings relate to each other.

Analysis of the headings extends to the various graphics and visual aids in the chapter. Essentially, readers analyze these to determine the main idea of each and then relate this information to the apparent content of the chapter and other chapter components. Similar processes are applied to special terms that are highlighted in some way (e.g., boldface print, italics). After reading the sentence (or a few sentences, if necessary) surrounding the highlighted word, the reader elaborates on the apparent meaning of the word and how it relates to the section of the chapter in which it appears.

To analyze the chapter introduction, readers scan the section to identify signal words that might indicate key ideas to be presented in the chapter. If these are identified, the readers reflect on what they already know about this information (activates knowledge) and then form an elaboration on the information by paraphrasing the identified main ideas. If readers fail to identify specific signal words that indicate key points, they paraphrase the introduction. Similar processes are repeated when analyzing the summary. Because some summaries are long, students break them into manageable segments and paraphrase each separately.

Next students use the questions provided by the author to help understand and clarify information to be learned. These questions often are located at the end of the chapter or at the end of specific sections of the chapter. Many textbook publishers now place questions *at the beginning* of specific sections of the chapter and throughout the chapter in margins or insets. Thus, readers should examine the entire chapter to locate questions. An effective process is to paraphrase each question. For example, if a textbook question reads:

Water vapor comes out of the air at what temperature?

a student could paraphrase the question by saying:

They want me to know how hot the air has to be for water vapor to form.

In addition, the readers can generate personal questions they hope the chapter will address.

Once students have analyzed the various chapter components to get a sense of its content, they turn their attention to understanding how the chapter content relates to an overall schema of study. For example, self-questioning techniques can be used to determine how the chapter content relates to previous chapters studied and the unit in which the chapter appears. These processes can be facilitated if the student turns to the table of contents, where chapter and unit titles are listed and uses these as cues when forming the elaboration.

At this point students should reflect on what they perceive to be the content of the chapter and relate this to what they already know. The following semistructured sentence can facilitate this elaboration:

This chapter seems to be about _____. Some things I already know about this topic are _____.

Steps of the text perusal strategy (Ellis, 1994) are indicated in Figure 3.5.

TEACHING THE TEXT PERUSAL STRATEGY

The text perusal strategy is designed for explicit instruction associated with the SIM instructional sequence. Once students become familiar with the strategy steps and have begun practicing them, the teacher can introduce a variety of fun and interesting activities to facilitate deep understanding of the strategy and its processes. These are briefly described below.

Perform goal setting

    Clarify *why* you are analyzing the chapter parts.

    Identify a goal related to this reason.

    Make a positive self-statement.

Analyze little parts (title, headings, visuals, and words)

    Explain the information indicated by the part.

    Predict what the section under the part is about.

    Tie the parts together.

Review big parts (introduction and summary)

    Search for signal words that indicate main ideas.

    Decide what the author thinks is important.

    Relate new information to what you already know.

    Paraphrase the main messages.

Think of questions you hope will be answered

    Check questions provided by the chapter.

    Formulate your own questions.

State relationships

    How does the chapter relate to the unit?

    How does the chapter relate to what you already know?

FIGURE 3.5   TEXT PERUSAL STRATEGY

Source: From An Instructional Model for Integrating Content-Area Instruction with Cognitive Strategy Instruction, by E. S. Ellis, 1994, *Reading and Writing Quarterly: Overcoming Learning Difficulties, 10*(1), 63–90.

GROUP CRITIQUES OF CHAPTER PARTS   Perhaps one of the best ways to integrate use of the strategy with content-area instruction and provide opportunities for interactive instruction is to empower students to analyze chapter parts from the perspective of how well each part clarifies the content of the chapter. Students are taught (or given permission) to be critical consumers of chapter parts. When instruction is approached from a critical consumers' perspective, students tend to be more invested in the learning process. The approach also provides students with practice in making decisions about which of a chapter's components can be interpreted readily versus which have been designed so poorly that even use of the strategy does not make the chapter more comprehensible.

Use of "critical consumer" activities also helps students with long histories of failure to recognize that their failures are not always due to their own inadequacies. In other words, an inability to glean information from chapter parts may, in some instances, be due to the fact that the parts were poorly written and designed, and anyone, not just students with learning difficulties, will experience difficulty when encountering poorly designed chapter parts. Such activities also provide opportunities for students to learn less self-effacing beliefs about their role in the success or failure process.

From a motivational perspective, one of the goals of strategy instruction is to enable students to understand the dimensions of a formula for success (see Figure 3.6).

Dimension #1:   The *authors* did a good job of incorporating chapter features that provide effective hints as to what the chapter is about. The hints are relatively easy to understand and accurate.

The authors (a) made good decisions about whether to include a feature, and (b) used an effective and efficient strategy when designing the chapter components.

Dimension #2:   The *student* does a good job of analyzing the chapter components so the information therein is understood, related to the unit of study, and remembered.

The student (a) makes good decisions about whether a specific chapter feature should be analyzed, (b) uses an effective and efficient strategy for analyzing the chapter components, (c) makes wise decisions about when to use the strategy and how to use it flexibly when analyzing chapter components, and (d) makes a concerted effort to apply the strategy.

If the *authors* do a poor job of *designing* the chapter components, *then* student success is impaired.

If the *student* does a poor job of *analyzing* the chapter components, *then* student success is impaired.

Success is a function of the author being strategic *and* students being strategic.

FIGURE 3.6   FORMULA FOR SUCCESS APPLIED TO TEXT CHAPTER PERUSAL

Source: © 1993 E. S. Ellis, *SMART Strategy Associates*

Critical consumer activities are best conducted using cooperative learning formats. An example is to assign each group specific chapter features to critique and have them rate these across the dimensions illustrated in Figure 3.7. For example, if one group is assigned the task of rating headings from a text chapter, students assign each heading a set of scores indicating their perceptions of its relevance, usefulness, interpretability, stand-alone-ness, and essential-ness. These scores are summed to produce an overall score for that specific heading. After groups have rated the chapter features (e.g., one group

---

Relevance to text passage

has almost nothing to do with the text	relates directly to what the text passage is about
0	5

Usefulness

does not provide any information that is useful or important to remember	contains a good hint about what the chapter is about; contains important information that should be remembered
0	5

Interpretability

does not make any sense	is easy to understand and interpret
0	5

Stand-alone-ness

does not make sense without reading text passage underneath	makes a lot of sense even when text passage has not been read
0	5

Essentialism

is not essential to understand the text	only way to really understand the text is to understand the chapter
0	5

FIGURE 3.7   DIMENSIONS OF EFFECTIVE TEXT COMPONENTS

Source: From An Instructional Model for Integrating Content-Area Instruction with Cognitive Strategy Instruction, by E. S. Ellis, 1994, *Reading and Writing Quarterly: Overcoming Learning Difficulties, 10*(1), 63–90.

evaluates and rates the title and various headings and another group evaluates highlighted words), they then compare ratings and discuss their rationales for the ratings they assigned. Similarly, individuals within each group might rate the same set of chapter parts independently, and then members within the group can discuss their ratings.

To make it fun, an overall mean of scores can be computed reflecting group ratings of a subset of chapter components (e.g., headings) or the entire set of chapter components (e.g., title, headings, figures, highlighted words). Then a grade is assigned to the chapter *author*. A copy of the chapter can be put on the bulletin board, accompanied by the grade assigned to the author and students' comments regarding the clarity or usefulness of the chapter components. The display should contain both highly and poorly rated features.

GROUP PRACTICE ACTIVITIES   Peer-mediated cooperative learning practice activities enable students to learn how others think when performing the strategy. Two peer-mediated activities are recommended.

1. Assign each group the same chapter to analyze from the textbook. After stating the time limits in which the activity is to be completed, have members within each group apply the strategy *together*. Each group formulates a response to each of the chapter features. Then the groups compare their responses. Each group is to include not only its interpretation of the chapter parts but also the questions generated and how the information relates to past and future learning.
2. Assign each member of the group different roles related to performing the strategy (e.g., one student does the "Analyze the little parts" step, another group is responsible for the "Review the big parts" step, and so on. Although other members of the group should be allowed to make suggestions, each individual is responsible for forming a response to the step he or she has been assigned.

INTEGRATING USE OF THE TEXT PERUSAL STRATEGY WITH STUDY GUIDE QUESTIONS   Homework assignments can include specific cues to generalize the text perusal strategy. Teachers can evaluate students' ability to perform the strategy by analyzing students' responses. A sample study guide question that cues use of the strategy is:

> Use the strategy for analyzing chapter features to estimate what chapter 16 is about. Develop a short outline of the chapter that:
> (a) indicates what you think is the main idea of the chapter.
> (b) shows the organization of information presented in the chapter.
> (c) indicates the relationship between this chapter and past and future chapters.

STRATEGY INSTRUCTION FOR INTERPRETING VISUAL AIDS

INFORMATION PROCESSING INVOLVED IN ANALYZING VISUAL AIDS

When analyzing visual aids, students need to think ahead, think during, and think back during the problem-solving process. These processes include analyzing the task demands associated with gleaning knowledge from visual aids, clarifying the purpose of the task, regulating various cognitive strategies as the visual aid is interpreted, and monitoring the problem-solving process.

To analyze visual aids successfully, students first must value the task. They must recognize that analyzing visual aids will enable them to attain in part something they want (e.g., students may want to learn more about the subject matter addressed in the visual aid or score higher on an upcoming test). Conversely, students must recognize that failure to interpret the visual may prevent them in some circumstances from getting what they want. Many difficult-to-teach students do not seem to recognize the value of analyzing visual aids. They tend to view these features as supplemental to what is important (Ellis & Lenz, 1990). For example, when studying a textbook chapter, many of these students ignore the visuals presented in the chapter and instead attempt to gain knowledge by attending to only the chapter prose. Because analyzing visual aids is relatively difficult at times and requires sustained mental energy, students must set goals (e.g., What do I want to learn from this visual aid?) and monitor whether they are making sufficient progress toward attaining the goal and reinforcing themselves along the way.

Instruction in strategic processes for analyzing visual aids may be hampered somewhat by the failures that many students with LD have accumulated. In some circumstances students not only have to learn effective and efficient processes for analyzing visual aids but also may have to overcome counterproductive beliefs about themselves and their ability to perform successfully (Ellis, 1986; Ellis, Lenz, & Sabornie, 1987; Ellis, Deshler, Schumaker, Lenz, & Clark, 1993). Thus, effective instruction in strategic processes for analyzing visual aids should include instruction in closely related self-motivational processes (e.g., setting goals, using affirmation and self-coping statements, using self-reinforcement).

The main cognitive strategies utilized when analyzing visual aids include generating questions, activating knowledge, predicting, clarifying, relating, prioritizing, and summarizing. To analyze visual aids effectively, students use these processes systematically and flexibly in an effective and efficient manner to glean information from visual aids and think about the information in a manner that will enable them to understand and remember it. Figure 3.8 illustrates the strategy for analyzing visual aids designed to cue students to engage in these processes.

THINK-AHEAD PROCESS   Metacognitive processes relating to understanding the purpose of the task and the inherent goal-setting processes involved in performing the set of strategic processes, or strategy, is the *first* information-processing skill students use when analyzing a visual aid. Therefore, to perform the strategy, students first look at the visual aid and ask a question to clarify the purpose of their efforts. Sample questions include:

> Am I analyzing this visual because it may help me understand what the passage I am *about to read* will be about?
>
> Am I analyzing this visual because it may help me clarify and understand a difficult passage I *just read*?
>
> Am I analyzing this visual because it's a good way to get the gist of the chapter without reading the whole thing?
>
> Am I analyzing this visual to identify things I need to learn for the test?

Next students generate questions they hope will be answered by analyzing the visual. If they cannot generate their own questions, they identify the type of visual and use it as a cue to ask a specific question. These structured questions provide students with a guide

Start with questions and predictions

> Question to clarify *why* you are analyzing the visual.
> Question to find out what is important to understand and remember about the visual.
> If you can't think of your own question, let the type of the visual be a signal for a good question.
>> **Picture** = What is it a picture of? Is it something important to remember?
>> **Graph/chart** = What is being compared? How?
>> **Map** = What key areas are important to see? Why are they key areas?
>> **Timeline** = Shows the history of what? From when to when?
> Using what you already know about the information in the visual, predict what you think the visual will be about.

$\bigtriangledown$

Note what you can learn from the hints

> Look for hints that signal answers to your question, and then identify what they tell you.
>> **Title** says the visual is about...
>> **Print** says...
>> **Lines** are used to show...
>> **Numbers** are used to show...
>> **Color** is used as decoration? or to show...
>> **Other** hints indicate...?

$\bigtriangledown$

Identify what is important

> What is the main idea that should be remembered about the visual?
> What are some important facts that can be identified from the visual? Which facts should be remembered?

$\bigtriangledown$

Plug it into the chapter

> Think about what the chapter is about.
> How does the visual relate to the chapter?
> How does the visual relate to what this section of the chapter is about?

$\bigtriangledown$

See if you can explain the visual to someone

> Find someone to whom you can explain the visual (explain it to yourself if nobody else is available).
> Tell *what* you think the visual is about and *how* you think it relates to what the chapter is about.
> Identify what you think are the best hints on the visual and tell *why* they are good hints.

FIGURE 3.8   STRATEGY FOR ANALYZING VISUAL AIDS

Source: From An Instructional Model for Integrating Content-Area Instruction with Cognitive Strategy Instruction, by E. S. Ellis, 1994, *Reading and Writing Quarterly: Overcoming Learning Difficulties, 10*(1), 63–90.

for what type of information they should be attempting to glean from the visual aid.

If the visual aid is a picture, students must determine whether the picture has been included in the chapter for decorative purposes to make the material more interesting to the reader or whether it has been included because it contains important information that should be remembered. Therefore, if the visual aid is a picture, students might ask themselves questions such as: "What is it a picture of? Is it something important to remember?"

Because charts and graphs are used to compare or show the relationship between concepts, students should be cued by the chart or graph to ask questions such as, "What things are being compared?" Comparisons can take many forms (e.g., comparing proportions, durations, frequencies, critical features) and employ many formats (e.g., pie charts, compare/contrast charts, bar graphs, line graphs). Therefore, students also should ask questions to help them clarify the purpose of the visual (e.g., "How are they being compared?").

If the visual aid is a map, students should ask clarifying questions such as, "What key areas are important to see? Why are they key areas?"

Because timelines always illustrate the history of something, students should ask clarifying questions such as, "What does this timeline show the history of?" Students also should ask questions that help them relate the timeline to personal knowledge: "From when to when? What other events that I know about happened close to this time?"

After students have clarified the purpose of the task and generated clarifying questions for which they intend to seek answers, they complete the think-ahead process by reflecting on what they already know about the topic the visual addresses and then predict what they think the visual will be about.

THINK-DURING PROCESS   Students now begin the think-during process of analyzing the visual to glean information that will lead to their identifying the main idea and pertinent details of the visual. Students first analyze the more salient hints or cues provided by most visual aids. These include the title of the visual, captioned print, numbers, and color.

Students read the title of the visual, then paraphrase it. This process may require students to think about the topic of the chapter (or section within the chapter) and relate what they think the chapter is about to what they think the title of the visual is telling them. Students also paraphrase the prose found in the caption for the visual.

Some visual aids contain numbers that indicate a variety of different types of information (e.g., years, weights, percentages). Students analyze the visual to determine whether the numbers are being used and, if so, what they represent. Students not only must indicate the nature of the notation (e.g., "These look like they show the *years*") but also must indicate the relationship between what the numerals indicate and the topic of the visual aid (e.g., "These look like they show the years *that different types of mammals live*").

Another hint that can signal important information on the visual is color. Authors sometimes use color to highlight important information, and other times they use it simply to make the visual more attractive. If color is used in the visual, students determine how it is being used. If it is used to indicate important information, the students indicate what information is being highlighted.

After analyzing the most common hints in visual aids, students peruse the material to determine if other, less common, hints (e.g., unusual features, exaggerated attributes) are present.

Some visual aids contain general information that serves only to supplement the text of the chapter. Others are for decorative purposes only. Some visual aids, however, contain specific information that is vital to understand and remember. An important function that students should perform is to relate the purpose of the visual to a summary of the information gleaned from it and to decide whether further, more in-depth study is required. Therefore, after analyzing the visual to determine what it is about, students make a precise elaboration concerning its content. Students identify the main idea of the visual and pertinent facts that could be interpreted from the visual. In addition, they decide whether it contains vital information that should be remembered. The elaboration process tends to enhance students' memory of the information. It also promotes students' use of monitoring comprehension processes. Inability to summarize the main idea signals students of a breakdown in comprehension.

THINK-BACK PROCESS Once students have determined the content of the visual, they begin the think-back stage of the process. This requires students to relate the content of the visual aid to the overall topic of the chapter *and* to the section of the chapter in which the visual appears. Although most students automatically relate information gleaned from the visual aids to existing knowledge throughout the analyzing process, this process also is performed explicitly during the think-back stage to *assure* that students view the information in the visual as part of an overall schema rather than a set of isolated, disconnected pieces of information.

Finally, students explain the content of the visual to someone else (or themselves, if no one is available). Here students make a precise elaboration of the visual, noting how the main idea and pertinent details of the visual enhance their understanding of the chapter text. They also explain how they used the features of the visual aid to draw their conclusions.

TEACHING THE STRATEGY

Explicit, direct explanation instructional techniques such as those associated with the SIM instructional model should be employed when teaching the strategy of interpreting visual aids. Additional instructional ideas are provided below.

ENLISTING THE STUDENTS AS COLLABORATIVE INSTRUCTORS Many educators are aware of the benefits of enlisting students as peer-tutors and involving them in cooperative learning processes. Enlisting students as collaborative instructors (as in collaborating with teachers) also can be an effective way to maintain students' investment in the learning process and their interest in the content-area subject. In enlisting students as collaborative instructors, teachers seek out students' opinions about instructional activities and assistance in making decisions critical to the instructional process. For example, instead of presenting a visual aid as a means to convey important to-be-learned information and then simply teaching the subject matter, the teacher presents the visual *while* enlisting students as instructional collaborators. The goal is to empower students with permission to help the teacher become more effective and to make them feel like *partners* in the teaching process. In so doing, students more readily learn the content subject matter.

The brief scripts below illustrate this concept:

Example #1: While presenting a visual aid during an American history lesson, the teacher might say:

> Here's a map that shows the sequence of critical battles of the Vietnam war. Help me figure out whether I should use this map to teach this or whether I should try to find some other visual that might do a better job.

Example #2: While presenting a visual aid during a biology lesson, the teacher might say:

> Today we've been taking a close look at how a cow's intestinal tract works. I think some of the students in one of my afternoon classes will have difficulty understanding this process. What would be a good way to explain this chart to them?

Many of the instructional techniques recommended for use with the text perusal strategy can be adapted when teaching the interpreting visual aids strategy. Some of these are briefly described next.

GROUPS CRITIQUING VISUAL AIDS   This activity allows students to practice making decisions in regard to visuals to which the strategy can be readily applied versus visuals that have been designed so poorly that use of the strategy cannot make them comprehensible. Activities might involve assigning each group a specific visual to critique and having the groups rate the visual across the similar dimensions shown in Figure 3.7. After the groups have rated the visuals, they compare their ratings and discuss their rationales for conferring those ratings. A variation on this activity is to have individuals within each group rate the same visual independently and then to have members within the group discuss their ratings.

GROUPS CREATING VISUAL AIDS   As students become proficient in analyzing visual aids, group projects that require them to create visual aids can be an effective way of integrating what they learned about how to think about visuals. After students have created their visual aids, they present them to the class formally. As they do so, group members relate the analyzing visuals process step by step. The rating scales presented in Figure 3.7 can be adapted as a guide for evaluating the visuals.

Variations on this activity include:

- Assign students a specific text passage and ask them to create a visual aid that would make the passage easier to understand.
- Assign students a specific topic (e.g., preventing AIDS), and ask them to research the topic and design a visual aid encapsulating what they learned.
- Ask students to redesign an existing visual aid (e.g., "Look at the visual aid on page 234. Although it addresses some important information, I don't think it does a good job of helping students understand it. I want you to redesign this visual so it will be clearer.").

INTEGRATING USE OF THE STRATEGY WITH STUDY GUIDE QUESTIONS   Homework assignments can include specific cues to generalize the strategy. Teachers can evaluate students' comprehension of the visual from their written responses. As an example of a study guide question that cues use of the strategy:

Use the SNIPS strategy to analyze the visual on page 137. Write a short paragraph that explains the main idea and important details in the visual. Be sure to state how the visual relates to the theme of the chapter.

INTEGRATING USE OF THE STRATEGY INTO CONTENT-AREA QUIZZES AND TESTS   A test can include a copy of a visual aid, and specific questions can be written that require students to analyze it. Test instructions remind students that they know an effective strategy they can use.

PROVIDING GROUP PRACTICE ACTIVITIES   Recommended peer-mediated activities include the following:

- Assign each group the identical visual to analyze from the textbook. After stating the time limits in which the activity is to be completed, have members within each group apply the strategy *together* and formulate a group response. Then have different groups compare their responses.
- Assign each member of the group different roles related to performing the strategy (One student performs the "Start with questions and predictions" step, another is responsible for the "Note what you can learn from the hints" step, and so on.). Although other members of the group should be allowed to make suggestions, each individual is responsible for forming a response to the step he or she has been assigned.
- Assign each member of the group a *different* visual aid from the text and have the members analyze the visual. Although they may seek assistance from others, each student is responsible for analyzing his or her own visual. At the end of the activity, the students "teach" the visual to other group members by performing the last step of the strategy, "See if you can explain the visual aid to somebody."

ASSESSING STUDENTS' ABILITY TO ANALYZE VISUAL AIDS

With regard to assessment, the teacher should be concerned with two dimensions of student competence. The first concerns assessing various components related to information-processing knowledge and skills. The second dimension concerns assessing the result of using these information processes.

ATTAINING PROCESS MEASURES   *Process measures* are taken to get a general indication of students' metacognitive knowledge in relation to the processes associated with analyzing visual aids (how much does the student know about *why* visual aids should be analyzed and *how* to go about interpreting them?). Process measures should address students' (a) knowledge of the cognitive processes associated with analyzing visual aids (recognizing the need to analyze visuals, activating knowledge, predicting, clarifying), (b) knowledge of procedures for using these processes (e.g., steps to the strategy), and (c) knowledge of the variables that may influence one's ability to use these processes and procedures effectively and efficiently (e.g., graphics, motivation, motivational beliefs).

Paper-and-pencil tests are *poor* devices for attaining process measures and should be avoided. To get a more accurate picture of what students know about the information processes related to analyzing graphics, you can provide students with a graphic and ask them to explain what they are doing as they interpret it. After this process you can conduct a dialogue with the student using a structured interview format. Here you would interview the student to find out what he or she knows about analyzing visuals. A set of questions can be followed generally during the interview, but you should feel free to stray from the sequence and pursue a line of thinking a student is expressing.

When having a dialogue with a student to assess process knowledge, the teacher should begin with global-general questions to determine what students know without being prompted to remember specific techniques they have been taught. By starting with global-general questions, you will more likely attain a true picture of what students think about the process of analyzing graphics. If you begin by asking detail-specific questions about specific processes students have been taught, students will more likely provide responses that reflect what they think teachers want them to say than what they more likely believe or value about the processes. Later, more detail-specific questions can be asked to determine what students know about *specific* components of information processing. A set of questions that might be used during a structured interview for assessing process knowledge is provided below.

Some sample global-general questions are:

What do you think are some important things people should know about graphics?

What should a student do to figure out what a graphic is about? Why are those good things to do? How will students benefit if they do those things? Which of those things do you think are the most important to do?

What sorts of things can be learned from graphics?

What are the types of information that graphics tell you? Do certain types of graphics tell you one type of information and other types of graphics tell you something else?

Should students with LD analyze graphics carefully, or is that really necessary? How do you know when you need to analyze a visual carefully and when you shouldn't bother?

What sorts of things make a graphic really good or useful? What sorts of things make a graphic really poor or not useful?

What should you do if the graphic seems like it's important but you can't figure it out?

What are some good things to think about as you are getting ready to analyze a graphic? What are some good things to do as you begin to analyze it?

What are some good things to think about as you are analyzing it? What are some good things to do as you are analyzing it?

Once you think you know what the graphic is about, what are some good things to think about or do?

What are some things that probably are a bad idea to do as you begin analyzing a graphic? While analyzing the graphic? After you have figured out what is important about the graphic?

What thoughts or beliefs might you have that could keep you from going to the trouble of analyzing an important visual?

Where can this strategy be used? Besides using it when analyzing graphics in the textbook for this class, where else could the strategy be used? What are some opportunities to use the strategy outside of school?

Besides using the strategy on textbook graphics, how can it be modified so it can be used when I am teaching something using a graphic?

Some sample detail-specific questions are:

What does "activating knowledge" mean? Why would somebody do that when analyzing graphics?

The first step of the strategy says, "Start with questions and predictions." Why start with questions? What sorts of questions would you ask? If you can't think of your own questions, what can you do? If the graphic is a picture, what would be a good question to ask? If it's a chart, what would be a good question? Map? Timeline?

Why bother with predictions? How does generating questions and making predictions early in the process of analyzing graphics help somebody understand the graphic?

What sorts of hints do graphics provide that you should look for to help you understand the graphic? How do you use the hints?

What does the step "Identify what is important" mean? What should you do to identify what is important? Why is it important to say the main idea of the visual in your own words? Why should you identify dates that should be remembered?

Why should you say how the visual is related to what the chapter or unit of study is about?

How does explaining the graphic to somebody else help you understand and remember the graphic?

Because traditional paper-and-pencil tests are poor indicators of process knowledge, conducting a structured interview for each student in a large class usually is not feasible. The interview can, however, be conducted with selected students with whom the teacher is particularly concerned.

ATTAINING PRODUCT MEASURES *Product measures* can be taken to determine how well students comprehend content information from visual aids. Again, although these measures can be attained using paper-and-pencil tests, probably the best approach to assessing comprehension of visuals is to dialogue with individual students. If dialoguing is to be used to attain product measures, you identify a graphic and then ask the student to explain it. Specifically, you should be assessing whether the students can:

— identify the main idea of the graphic.
— identify whether the graphic contains detailed information that should be remembered.
— can relate the graphic to the schema or unit of study.

FACILITATING KNOWLEDGE OF THE WORLD

As discussed earlier in this chapter, success in reading is related in large part to familiarity of the material being read. Thus, the power of students' reading comprehension strategies will be affected considerably by their background knowledge of what they are reading. In short, increasing knowledge of the world around them will have a significant impact on the ability of adolescents with LD to gain meaning from text. Chapter 9: *Strategy Instruction in the Content Areas*, provides a detailed discussion on ways teachers can broaden students' knowledge of the world.

One of the more specific forms of world knowledge, vocabulary, is crucial to success in reading. Although instruction in new vocabulary should be intensive and exten-

Q & A

TEACHING COGNITIVE STRATEGIES VERSUS MORE RAPID READING

Q: *Which is more important, teaching students to read more slowly and thoughtfully using cognitive strategies or teaching students to increase their reading rate?*

A: This question has no right/wrong answer, but some insight is offered below.

■   Some reading theorists (Snider & Tarver, 1987) favor emphasis on teaching decoding fluency (reading quickly). At the risk of oversimplifying their theories, they essentially believe that students have finite cognitive processing capabilities. As long as students are using a lot of "cognitive energies" to decipher words, few cognitive resources will remain to focus on regulating higher-order thinking skills such as using cognitive strategies.

■   Some reading theorists advocate a technique referred to as *repeated readings* to enhance decoding fluency and allow students to develop reading comprehension skills (for a review, see Rashotte & Torgesen, 1985). The technique essentially calls for students to read the same passage repeatedly so that new vocabulary and difficult-to-decode words do not interfere with comprehension processes. In many cases effective comprehension of the material occurs in as little as three readings (O'Shea, Sindelar, & O'Shea, 1987).

■   Although there is little research available to support the notion that instruction in higher-order thinking skills should be delayed until more basic skills have been mastered (Harris & Pressley, 1991), the relationship between *fluency* of basic skills in specific areas (e.g., reading) and the efficiency of strategy instruction in those specific areas has been explored only minimally. Ellis and Graves (1990), however, reported that teaching students to use cognitive strategies for reading (e.g., paraphrasing) had significantly superior effects on the comprehension of the reading materials.

   Moreover, in conditions where instruction in a paraphrasing strategy was paired with RR, students fared no better than those who received the strategy instruction only. Results of this study suggest that teaching students to use reading strategies requiring elaboration of main ideas and important details was considerably more empowering than RR. Other studies (e.g., Schumaker, Denton, & Deshler, 1984) demonstrated that instruction in a paraphrasing strategy increases students' ability to comprehend more difficult reading material. Thus, although RR procedures may increase comprehension of the special materials that are read repeatedly, its use as a technique for increasing students' innate reading comprehension ability remains in question.

■   Many students with LD place too great an emphasis on completing a task quickly rather than on engaging meaningfully in learning, and too few students with LD think reflectively about their thinking and their reading.

■   The ultimate goal of reading strategy instruction is for students to employ the reading strategies automatically with ease.

Thus, though the importance of promoting fluent reading is recognized, teaching students to slow down, reflect, and engage in thoughtful analysis of the information presented in text and to learn to engage in thoughtful reading in a fluent manner may be much more important than teaching them to read rapidly.

sive (as discussed in other chapters), teachers can impact students' knowledge of the world, including vocabulary, by using a technique called *sustained silent reading* (SSR) (Cline & Kretke, 1980; Minton, 1980). Here students are encouraged to make their own selections from the reading materials provided and read them for a set period each day without interruption. The purpose is to build reading fluency and more positive attitudes about reading. Students are neither questioned about nor tested over the material read. SSR should *not* be used as a substitute for reading instruction but, rather, should accompany it.

FACILITATING KNOWLEDGE OF TEXT STRUCTURES

TEACHING STUDENTS WITH LD TO RECOGNIZE SEMANTIC FEATURES

To understand the idea of "semantic features," consider this example: *Fossils* is an abstract concept that has a set of distinctive features: *petrified remains of plants and animals*. These distinctive features comprise a class (e.g., *remains*) and features that set it apart from other concepts in the same class (e.g., *petrified, plants, animals*). In most cases concepts can be organized into superordinate and subordinate relationships. Thus, *rocks* might be considered a supraordinate concept, *fossils* one of its subordinate concepts, and *petrified wood* and *skeletal imprints* two concepts subordinate to fossils.

Each subordinate concept takes a set of distinctive features from its superordinate concept (e.g., petrified wood is in part the petrified remains of something that once lived) and also possesses distinctive features that set it apart from other subordinate concepts (petrified wood is always a self-contained object. It once was wood from a plant that was permeated with minerals to a point at which it became stone. Skeletal imprints, on the other hand, are not self-contained but, rather, are a pattern imposed on another object that subsequently turned to stone).

To summarize, an abstract concept usually is composed of a class, or superordinate concept, and a set of critical features that distinguish it from other classes. These features sometimes can be grouped into subsets, or subordinate concepts. Although all subordinate concepts in a class share the same set of critical features as those associated with the superordinate class, individual subordinate concepts may have additional distinguishing features that set them apart from other subordinate concepts of the same class.

Typically, information presented in textbooks (and lectures) is rich with superordinate and subordinate concepts, but students with LD often have difficulty perceiving the relationships between them. The teacher can help them comprehend their text and understand concepts presented in it by using a technique called *semantic features analysis* (Bos & Anders, 1987; Bos, Anders, Filip, & Jaffe, 1989). The steps in this procedure are listed below.

PREPARATION FOR SEMANTIC FEATURES ANALYSIS

1. Peruse the text chapter and identify the supraordinate concepts that students should be expected to know and understand (Note: A text chapter often contains many of the superordinate concepts, some of which are not essential for students to learn. Use your judgment and decide which are *essential* concepts for understanding the chapter as a whole and eliminate those that are not essential).

2. Identify the critical features of the superordinate concepts.
3. Identify subordinate concepts and their critical features.
4. Identify examples of subordinate concepts, and generate a list of nonexamples or other concepts that share some but not all of the critical features of the subordinating concept. (The fossilized remains of a saber-tooth tiger is an example; a nonexample would be a tiger that performs in a circus today.)
5. Create a chart depicting the superordinate and subordinate concepts and features. As an example, requirements for a paraphrase include the following subordinate and superordinate concepts (Schumaker, Deshler, & Denton, 1984):
   a. Must contain a complete thought (subject, verb).
   b. Must be totally accurate.
   c. Must have new information.
   d. Must make sense.
   e. Must contain useful information.
   f. Must be in your own words.
   g. Only one general statement per paragraph is allowed.
6. Prepare a set of questions that students should be able to answer about the content by the end of this instructional sequence.

PRESENTATION OF SEMANTIC FEATURES ANALYSIS

1. Provide students with copies of the chart.
2. Introduce superordinate and subordinate concepts and facilitate a discussion so students will relate their background knowledge of the concepts.
3. Facilitate prediction making. Here the goal is to have students form predictions about whether specific examples and nonexamples are associated with various concepts. Collaborate with students as specific examples and nonexamples of the concepts presented on the chart are evaluated with regard to the semantic features of the concepts. This collaboration can take place via dialogue as you and your students share understandings. Predictions about relationships can be indicated on the chart by having students record +, –, ?, or 0 (no relationship) next to the examples. These should be done in pencil because they may have to be changed after more is learned about the concept (see next step). Figure 3.9 provides an example of this chart.
4. Facilitate confirmation making. Now students read the text material to confirm or disconfirm their predictions. Students should make changes in the chart as appropriate. Among the several ways to facilitate this activity are the following:
   a. Read portions of the text collaboratively with your students, dialoguing with them about what was read and then making changes in the chart by mutual agreement.
   b. Employ a modified version of the "jig-saw" (Kagan, 1989) cooperative learning technique. Assign small teams of students to specific portions of the chart to evaluate. Have them read and discuss portions of the text related to the concepts and then make changes in the chart by mutual agreement. After all the teams have finished, reorganize the teams so that new teams will each have members who collectively represent all of the topics investigated on the

	believed in one god	believed in 10 command-ments	very strict set of religious laws to live life by	believed in prophets sent by God	believed Jesus was prophet sent by God	believed Jesus was the son of God	believed in sacrificing animals to please God	believed you went to heaven by believing in Jesus' sacrifice	believed you went to heaven by doing good or special deeds
Ancient Greeks	−	−	+	+	−	−	+	−	+
Early Judaism	+	+	+	+	+	−	+	−	+
Early Christianity	+	+	−	+	−	+	−	+	−
Early Muslim	+	−	+	+	+	−	−	−	+

FIGURE 3.9   SEMANTICS FEATURES CHART

chart. Each member then shares and discusses the results of findings of the original team on specific chart items.

   c. Have students independently read the text to confirm or disconfirm predictions on the chart. Once everyone has finished, the class discusses any changes made and the reasons why.

5. Require students to express their knowledge and demonstrate learning by answering specific questions about the concepts (e.g., "Trilobites were a type of _____ life that lived in _____ and _____."). Students also might be required to write short essays addressing the concepts.

TEACHING STUDENTS WITH LD TO RECOGNIZE ORGANIZATIONAL PATTERNS

Authors usually signal the main idea of a passage in two ways. First, authors use signal words such as "important," "basic," "key," and so forth (see Table 3.4). These often (but not always) occur in the first sentence of a paragraph. Teaching students to be alert to words that may signal the importance of ideas can help students locate and identify main ideas of a passage.

Second, main ideas often are the central focus of an overall pattern of information. These patterns commonly take the form of enumerative (e.g., list-and-describe), compare-contrast, sequential, cause-effect, and problem-solution. Thus, the ability of students with LD to recognize organizational patterns in paragraphs will greatly assist them in recognizing the important ideas presented by the writer. Of the number of categories of organizational patterns, seven of the most common are (a) enumerative order, (b) sequential order, (c) comparison and contrast relationships, (d) cause-and-effect relationships (Jones, Palincsar, Ogle, & Carr, 1987), (e) problem-solution (combination) format, (f) story grammar, and (g) structural connectives. When facilitating students' abil-

TABLE 3.4 SELECTED CUE WORDS THAT MAY SIGNAL INFORMATION STRUCTURES

Information Structure	Cue Words
Importance	prominent significant superior inferior negative important critical principle main major serious urgent key required funda- mental
Enumerative	*list-and-describe, general-to-specific, specific-to-general* many several charac- features related a number ordinal words charac- elements teristics traits parts ("three") (e.g., first, teristics factors advant- numbers second) uses ages or letters in paren- theses (1), (2); (a), (b)
Compare/ Contrast	*similarities (shared characteristics) and differences* similar- differ- same contrast negative but, on the other hand ities ences analogy like as if versus positive parallel
Sequential	*time-order* steps series next until arrange ordinal words (first, second) stages levels then finally before numbers/letters in parenthesis (1), (2); (a), (b)
Cause/Effect	*general-to-specific, specific-to-general* causes effects results conse- because If... then... connection although quence so that consequence link analyze
Problem/ Solution	*general-to-specific, specific-to-general* advant- resolve problem solution difficulty conflict results need explain ages alterna- identify decision solve brain- negotiate compro- deter- tives storm mise mine

ity to recognize organizational patterns, teaching enumerative and sequential patterns before the more conceptually challenging patterns such as compare/contrast and cause/effect is suggested. Story grammar is not nearly as conceptually demanding and can be taught any time.

ENUMERATIVE FORMATS   In the enumerative order format facts of similar importance are presented, and each is elaborated upon. This is termed the *list-and-describe* pattern when teaching it to students with LD. Facts are presented from general to specific (e.g., "Many scientists think the two main reasons for global warming are the excessive amounts of carbon dioxide and the reduction in the amount of oxygen resulting from our current lifestyles. Carbon dioxide is produced by...."). Enumerative order patterns also can be from specific to general (e.g., "Excessive amounts of carbon dioxide and the reduction in large quantities of oxygen once produced by rain forests are two of the reasons for global warming"). Teachers can help students recognize enumerative patterns when reading by sensitizing them to cue words that indicate these patterns (see Table 3.4 for sample enumerative cue words).

Teachers can increase students' ability to recognize organizational patterns by (a) defining the patterns, (b) providing examples and nonexamples, and (c) modeling how a reader thinks when reading and encountering a pattern. Teachers then can (d) provide students with practice recognizing cues that signal the pattern and then (e) provide practice picking out key information as well as (f) practice writing paragraphs using the patterns when students communicate information using the patterns. The steps below illustrate a type of activity teachers can use to make students more aware of these organizational patterns.

1. Describe the list-and-describe pattern to students.
   a. Explain the pattern.
   b. Show students examples of various texts that utilize this pattern (e.g., social studies textbook, encyclopedia, *Time* magazine).
   c. Discuss the advantages of recognizing the pattern (e.g., increases comprehension, helps you focus on what's important).
2. Present examples and nonexamples.
   a. Show students example phases indicating list-and-describe formats (e.g., "There are many parts to..." "Three reasons why...").
   b. Show students examples and nonexamples of cue words for list-and-describe formats (example: "Three unfortunate events led to General "Stonewall" Jackson being shot by his own men" versus nonexample: "General "Stonewall" Jackson was shot late that night by his own men"). Cue students to discriminate between them.
3. Describe order in which list-and-describe formats may occur (general-to-specific, specific-to-general) and provide examples.
4. Practice identifying list-and-describe cue words, general topics, and specific details from text passages; indicate on a graphic organizer.
   a. Provide students with copies of the same text passage containing multiple paragraphs. Use think-aloud techniques as you read the first paragraph, looking for cue words that signal a list-and-describe format. Model the process of

constructing a graphic that depicts the organizational pattern.
b. Guide students as the whole class reads the second paragraph; collaborate with them to identify cue words, general topic, and details. Repeat with new paragraphs as necessary, gradually fading cues as students perform task.
c. Have students form pairs. Have each pair analyze text passages to identify cue words, general topic, and details.
5. Write short essays using list-and-describe cue words.
a. Provide a short list of general topics for each pair of students.
b. Model the process of selecting a topic, identifying specifics, and writing a short essay.
c. Have students write short essays and share them with other pairs of students. The other pair must identify the cue words used, general topic, and specifics.

Enumerative organizational patterns can be illustrated graphically using a variety of formats. Figure 3.10 illustrates how these can be illustrated using a "web." Here the student identifies the central theme of a reading passage as the center of the web. Main ideas of the passage are illustrated as outgrowths of the central theme, and important details emulate from each main idea. Graphic frames such as the one illustrated in Figure 3.11 can be useful in facilitating comprehension as well. These frames are designed to cue students to look for the central theme of the passage (e.g., "What is this whole thing about?"), then look for main ideas, and finally, to identify important details.

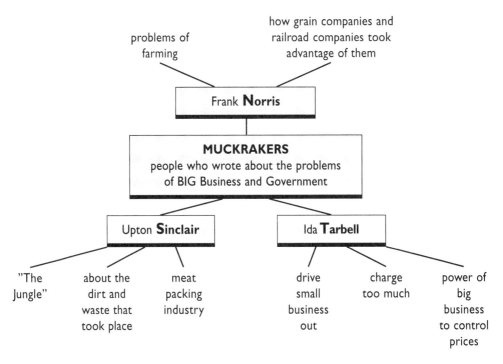

FIGURE 3.10 EXAMPLE OF "WEB" ENUMERATIVE FORMAT

Form

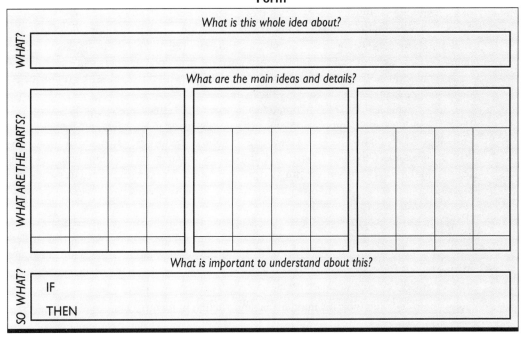

Completed Example

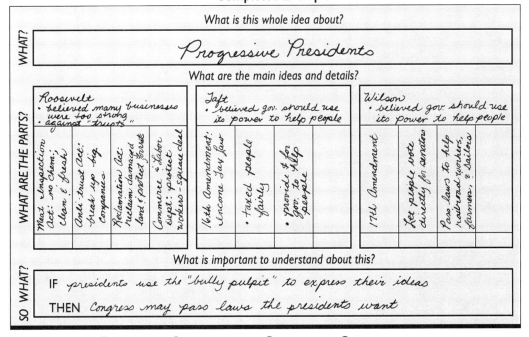

FIGURE 3.11   ENUMERATIVE ORGANIZATIONAL PATTERN FOR COMPREHENSION

SEQUENTIAL ORDER FORMATS   The chronological order of history is a good example of sequential order (e.g., "After the death of Lincoln, Andrew Johnson assumed the presidency"). Following a sequence is important in reading, especially in prevocational and vocational subjects such as home economics and business. Table 3.4 illustrates cue words many writers use to signal time-order formatted information. Teachers can adapt the instructional sequence described to familiarize students with this format. A graphic organizer similar to the one in Figure 3.12 may be used.

Some sequences of information are not linear but, rather, are cyclic or reciprocal. Figure 3.13 illustrates a graphic organizer that can be used to help students frame important main ideas and details associated with a cyclic or reciprocal sequence of ideas.

COMPARE-AND-CONTRAST FORMATS   Compare-and-contrast relationships typically compare factual information concerning two general topics. Good writers use cue words that signal comparison or contrast text structure (e.g., "There are many *differences* between Presidents Reagan and Bush").

Each of the general topics has a set of characteristics. Some are shared characteristics (e.g., similarities); others are unique to each general topic. In many cases characteristics can be grouped into categories, or main ideas. In some text the main ideas are made explicit for readers, but this is not always the case. In the latter instance the information processing demands are greater. Consider these samples.

An example in which main ideas of comparison are explicit:

> There were many differences between Presidents Reagan and Bush. *On foreign policy* Reagan's approach was to organize meetings with foreign leaders and get television reporters to cover them to get a lot of publicity. He then would use the publicity to pressure other countries to do what he wanted. Bush, on the other hand, liked to work quietly behind the scenes, and he tried to avoid publicity when he could. *On national policy* Reagan actively tried to reduce the size of the federal government by reorganizing some departments and by removing many government regulations. Bush took a different approach. He vetoed almost every bill the Congress passed, and he....

An example where main ideas of comparison are implied:

> There were many differences between Presidents Reagan and Bush. Reagan liked to organize meetings with foreign leaders and get television reporters to cover them to get a lot of publicity. He then would use the publicity to pressure other countries to do what he wanted. Reagan also tried to reduce the size of the federal government by reorganizing some departments and by removing many government regulations. President Bush was different. He liked to work quietly behind the scenes, and he tried to avoid publicity when he could. He also....

The teacher can facilitate student recognition of compare/contrast relationships using an instructional sequence similar to that described above. Use of the compare/contrast graphic organizer illustrated in Figure 3.14 is suggested. When students begin practicing recognition of the key information, teachers initially should identify for students the main-idea categories of comparison instead of expecting them to generate the main-idea categories. This is especially important in instances when the main ideas are not explicit. Thus, the teacher should read text passages ahead of time, decide what the main ideas are, and identify them for students. The teacher then cues students to search for

Form

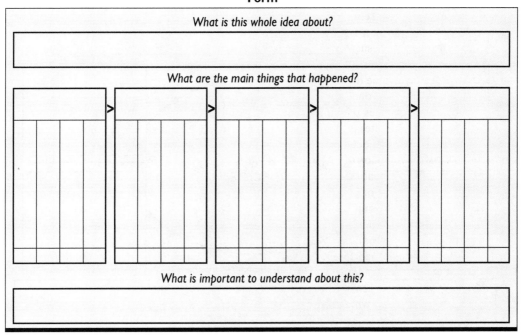

Completed Example

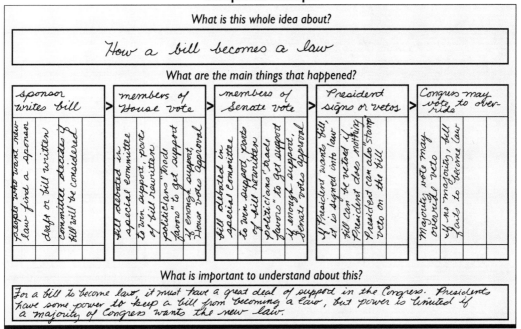

FIGURE 3.12 GRAPHIC ORGANIZER FOR TIME-ORDERED INFORMATION

Form

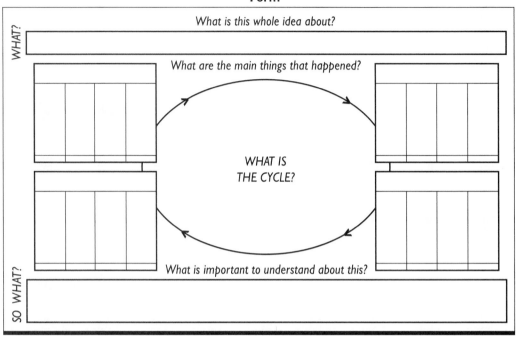

Completed Example

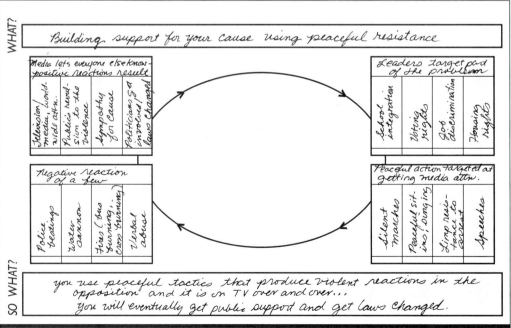

FIGURE 3.13   GRAPHIC ORGANIZER FOR RECIPROCAL SEQUENCE OF IDEAS

Form

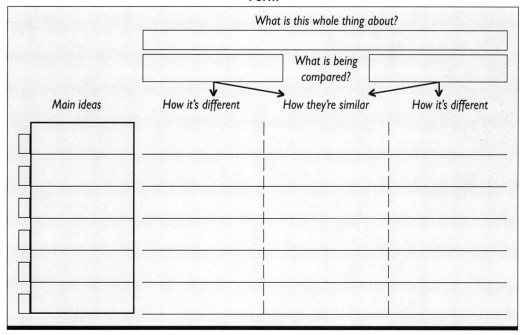

Completed Example

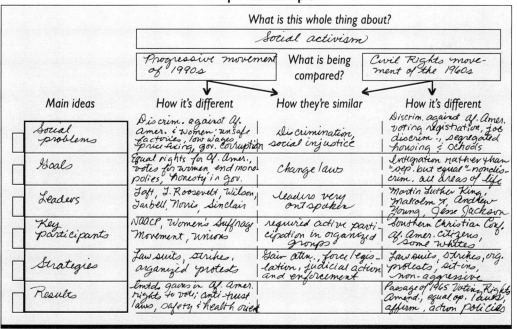

FIGURE 3.14   GRAPHIC ORGANIZER FOR COMPARE/CONTRAST FORMAT

key information related to each main idea. Once students demonstrate competence at this level, the teacher guides them in performing the more difficult task of recognizing main ideas of comparison when they are made explicit and, later, when the writer does not cue main ideas explicitly.

CAUSE-AND-EFFECT FORMATS Implicit in the idea of cause-and-effect relationships is *change.* Something changes as a result of the occurrence of another factor. What makes this concept particularly difficult for adolescents with LD is that sometimes the change relationship is made explicit to the reader via the use of signal words (e.g., "*If* _____ happens, *then* _____ is likely to result"), and sometimes authors discuss cause-and-effect relationships but never alert readers explicitly to the text structure using cue words. Moreover, sometimes authors write about cause/effect relationships that *have* happened (e.g., "The abolitionists' pressure on Lincoln, in conjunction with the fact that the war was not going well, caused him to write the Emancipation Proclamation before he really wanted to"). Other times authors write about *potential* cause-effect relationships (e.g., "If the President cannot convince voters that he has an effective plan to improve the economy, then he probably will lose the election").

Information structures for cause-and-effect formats are similar to enumerative formats in some ways. Three patterns of cause-effect information formats are common. The first (and easiest to recognize and understand) follows a general-to-specific format. Effective writers will clearly state a cause-effect relationship and then elaborate and explain details and other factors associated with the relationship. For example:

> If candidates believe they are losing the election and are running out of time, then they tend to make promises they do not intend to keep. For example, the President said many times that less federal money should be spent on special-interest groups and that we should protect our environment. In the last election, however, the President was far behind in the polls with only a month before the election. As he traveled around the country and stopped to make speeches, he started making promises to spend federal money on whatever he thought people in that community wanted. For example, in Florida people wanted to have an Air Force base, so he promised he would make sure it was built. In Iowa farmers wanted the government to pay them more money for crops they couldn't sell, so the President promised that he would make sure this happened. In Oregon many people wanted the right to cut giant trees on the government-owned land, so the President promised that they would be given permission to cut the virgin forests.

The second approach (more conceptually challenging for readers) follows a specific-to-general format. Here authors present various ideas that lead to a clearly stated conclusion about a cause-effect relationship.

> The President said many times that less federal money should be spent on special-interest groups and that we should protect our environment. In the last election, however, the President was far behind in the polls with only a month before the election. As he traveled around the country and stopped to make speeches, he started making promises to spend federal money on whatever he thought people in that community wanted. For example, in Florida people wanted to have an Air Force base, so he promised he would make sure it was built. In Iowa farmers wanted the government to pay them more money for crops they couldn't sell, so the President promised that he would make sure this happened. In Oregon many people wanted the right to cut giant trees on the govern-

ment-owned land, so the President promised that they would be given permission to cut the virgin forests. If candidates believe they are losing the election and are running out of time, they tend to make promises they do not want to keep.

In the third common (and most difficult) approach, cause-effect relationships are implied, rather than being identified specifically.

> The President said many times that less federal money should be spent on special-interest groups and that we should protect our environment. In the last election, however, the President was far behind in the polls with only a month before the election. In Florida people wanted to have an Air Force base, so he promised he would make sure it was built. In Iowa farmers wanted the government to pay them more money for crops they couldn't sell, so the President promised that he would make sure this happened. In Oregon many people wanted the right to cut giant trees on the government-owned land, so the President promised that they would be given permission to cut the virgin forests.

Teachers can teach students to recognize cause-effect relationships by adapting the instructional sequence described earlier. When teaching the formats, students should be taught first to recognize these structures when they are cued explicitly at the beginning of the message (general-to-specific), then when the cues fall at the end of the message (specific-to-general), and finally when the structure is implied. The cause-effect graphic organizer illustrated in Figure 3.15 can facilitate their understanding.

PROBLEM-SOLUTION FORMAT Problem-solution formats often reflect a combination of enumerative, sequential, and cause-effect formats. Generally, a problem is composed of a set of critical features, or main elements of the problem. Good authors first signal the reader that a problem is being explained and indicate the number of elements contained in the problem. As each element is explained, good authors carefully signal them as well. Thus, the first part of a problem-solution format often resembles either a general-to-specific or a specific-to-general enumerative information structure. Sometimes problem elements build upon each; thus, they are presented using a sequential format. After the elements of the problem have been explained, good authors often signal that the solution to the problem now is being presented, and they may discuss solutions using formats similar to cause-effect. The paragraph below illustrates this.

> Things weren't going well in the classroom, and Mr. McDuffy knew he had a problem. First he noticed that both Pridgeon and Lyle were becoming the targets of ridicule from other students. Last week it was more subtle. For example, he was aware that the other students were making fun of these students covertly by whispering jokes about them. He hoped that by not making it an issue, the students would tire of it, but that did not happen. Now the ridicule was more brazen, with out-loud name-calling and teasing in the classroom. Second, all of the students were becoming increasingly more competitive with each other. Not only were they less willing to help one another, but they also were becoming downright hostile toward each other. Snide remarks, tattling, and accusations seemed to rule the day. Attempts to punish the offenders only seemed to make things worse. In desperation, Mr. Pridgeon decided to forego traditional instruction and have a class meeting to solve the problems. First he asked the students to push the desks out of the way and sit in a circle on the floor with him. This eliminated the formality of the class setting so students would be more willing to discuss openly what had been happening. Next, he....

Form

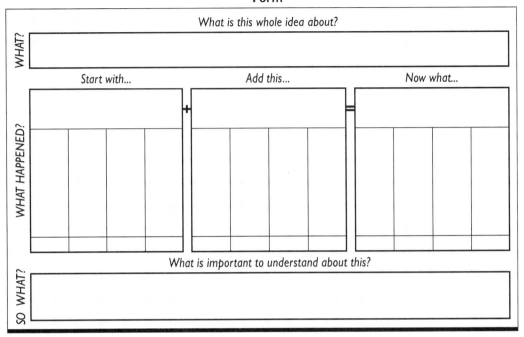

Completed Example

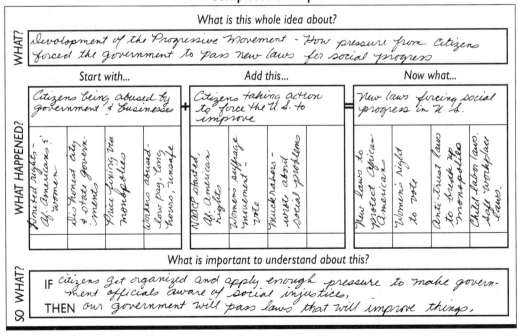

FIGURE 3.15   GRAPHIC ORGANIZER FOR CAUSE–EFFECT FORMAT

Like other common information structures, good authors use cue words to signal use of the formats (Table 3.4), but this does not always happen. When teaching students about problem-solution formats, the graphic organizer illustrated in Figure 3.16 may be useful.

STORY GRAMMAR   In language arts classes and, to a more limited extent, in other content-area classes, students are expected to read and comprehend both fictional and biographical stories. Stories are almost always structured so that they contain a set of generic components (e.g., setting, characters, a problem, a goal, an action-sequence, and an outcome). Comprehension of stories can be enhanced considerably for students with LD if you teach them about the components of stories and how to identify them (Idol & Croll, 1987). Figure 3.17 illustrates a story-mapping graphic organizer .

STRUCTURAL CONNECTIVES   The final organizational pattern uses structural connectives. Paulsen and Lamar (1966) cite four categories of connectives that relate to organizational patterns. They are (a) word order, (b) punctuation, (c) word shifts, and (d) structural cues. Word order is related to the syntax of the sentences in a paragraph. The closer the syntax comes to subject-verb-object order, the easier it is to read and to determine organization. Punctuation also is important in determining the organization. Probably the most difficult paragraph to organize is the one in which the author uses many word shifts. Consider, for example, how the sentence "When the engine would not start, we hitchhiked to town" compares with a sentence with the word shift, "We hitchhiked to town when the engine would not run"). Structural cues often take the form of subordinating conjunctions, (see Table 3.4).

SELECTING APPROPRIATE TEXTBOOKS

Because reading difficulty is such a common problem in adolescents with LD, using adaptive textbooks for content-area classes might seem like a logical compensation. Characteristics of adaptive textbooks include the following:

- Require 3rd to 4th grade equivalent decoding and word recognition skills.
- Short paragraphs focusing on essential information.
- Short chapters (2–3 pages).
- Ample use of pictures and other visual aids.
- Ample use of color.

The advantages of using adaptive texts may be deceiving and problematic, however. Among the many considerations involved in making textbook selection decisions are two key factors: (a) *readability* (as computed by various readability formulas and length of chapters) and (b) *attractiveness* (as indicated by extensive use of color and pictures). Some research indicates that these texts may not facilitate student learning but, rather, *impair learning.*

For example, the methods used to control the readability levels of textbooks yield a number of problems. Popular readability formulas, which often guide the development of controlled texts, tend to emphasize word length, sentence length, word familiarity, and sentence complexity (Dupuis & Askov, 1982). Lovitt, Horton, and Bergerud (1987) noted that different readability formulas do not produce similar scores on the same text

Form

What is this whole idea about?

What is the problem?   What is the solution?

What are the main elements of the problem?

What are the main elements of the solution?

Completed Example

What is this whole idea about?   *Enormous U. S. budget deficit*

What is the problem?   What is the solution?

Unnecessary spending   *Responsible spending*

What are the main elements of the problem?

"Pork-barrel" spending
Congress spends $$ get re-elected
Prof. lobbyists - "wine & dine"

Military defense
Excessive "military might"
Industrial/military complex

Entitlements
Automatically go up
Don't represent the nation's needs

What are the main elements of the solution?

Better legislative "checks/balances"
Presidential "line item" veto
Limited terms for Congress

Downsize military
Close unnecessary military bases
Better monitoring of contracts

Creat control mechanisms
Eliminate "most $$ for least good"
Every increase subject to votes

FIGURE 3.16   GRAPHIC ORGANIZER FOR PROBLEM–SOLUTION FORMAT

My Story Map

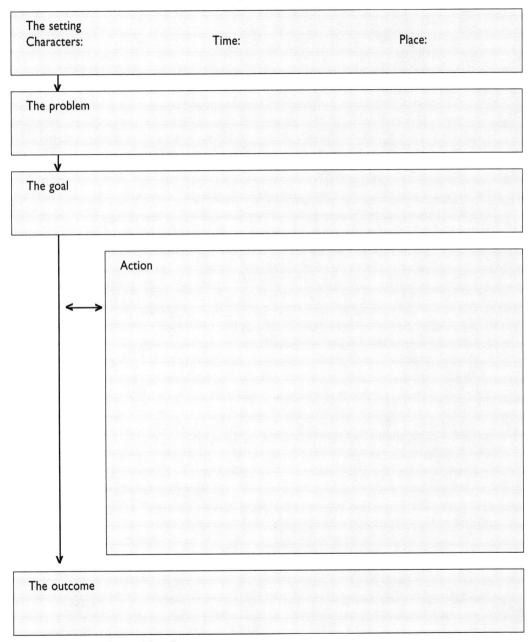

FIGURE 3.17 STORY MAP FORM

Source: From "Group Story Mapping: A Comprehension Strategy for Both Skilled and Unskilled Readers" by L. Idol, 1987, *Journal of Learning Disabilities, 20*, p. 199. Copyright 1987 by *Journal of Learning Disabilities*. Reprinted by permission.

and a student's reading achievement scores on different standardized tests typically are inconsistent. Moreover, two texts can yield the same readability scores but be markedly different in their comprehensibility because of the nature of their organization, use of visual aids, sentence structure, and so forth. If texts are modified based on the application of reading formulas, the elements that indicate important relationships may be eliminated in the process of achieving formula compatibility. The readability of a textbook may involve considerably more than what readability formulas measure.

Anderson, Armbruster, and Kantor (1980) suggested that the readability of text should be based on structural coherence, unity, and audience appropriateness. These elements cue the learner as to the various relationships between ideas in the text and those of the learner. The question of contextual relationship also emerges when larger topics or chapters are subdivided into a variety of shorter chapters. Whether these types of chapter configurations facilitate or inhibit content acquisition is unclear.

Another feature often incorporated into controlled textbooks is the more extensive use of visuals—either in number or in size, or both. Some researchers have challenged this practice, finding that illustrations make text *more difficult* for some naive readers (Harber, 1983). Lenz, Alley, Beals, Schumaker, and Deshler (1981) found that visuals (pictures, graphs, charts, maps) in controlled textbooks were harder for adolescents with learning disabilities to interpret for meaning than visuals in grade-level textbooks. Adolescents with LD were able to generate more statements relevant to the surrounding text from the visuals in grade-level texts than from those in controlled texts. An analysis of the visuals in the two types of texts indicated that the visuals in the controlled textbooks tended to be used more for motivational or decorative purposes than to inform. The visuals also tended to supplant text rather than complement text, forcing students to make their own contextual generalizations. This finding is in contrast to research findings indicating that visuals are most helpful to readers when they are tied directly to the text in specific ways (Schallert, 1980).

Because textbooks play a major role in delivering content-area information to students, selection of texts should be based on the degree to which the book incorporates features that provide prompts and cues similar to those provided by a teacher when mediating learning. Adjunct questions, objectives, advance organizers, summaries, pointer words, and textual highlighting are examples of textual mediators that have been found to be effective with students who have comprehension problems (Meyer, 1981). In an analysis of elementary- and intermediate-level textbooks, Armbruster and Anderson (1988) reported that most textbooks were deficient in structure (the manner in which ideas and relationships are organized in the text), coherence (the logical flow of ideas presented in text), and audience appropriateness (the match between the text and the reader's level of knowledge and skills). Common problems with text structure tended to center on the texts' failure to employ organizational signals (e.g., introductory statements, pointer words such as first, second, third, and textual cues such as boldface print words). In addition, the structure the textbooks employed was often illogical. Rather than having a book that employed structures that mediated students' selection of critical information and facilitated its organization into a coherent concept, students' books often presented information that required readers to "simply encode information as an unstructured list of ideas" (Armbruster & Anderson, 1988, p. 48).

Q & A

TAPE-RECORDING TEXTS

Q: *Because adolescents with LD tend to be poor readers, why not tape-record their textbooks?*

A: Providing tape-recordings of textbooks for students who are poor readers may seem like a logical and simple solution to a difficult problem. Researchers, however, have demonstrated that this practice may not be desirable. Why not?

1. Tape-recorded textbooks often are monotonous and boring.
2. The thinking skills involved in listening comprehension and remembering auditorily presented information often are the identical information-processing skills involved in reading (e.g., activating background knowledge, forming predictions, generating questions, monitoring comprehension, imaging, summarizing). Many students who do not use these processes when reading do not use them effectively in other learning contexts either (e.g., when listening) (Ellis & Lenz, 1990).
3. Torgesen, Dalhem, and Greenstein (1987) found that recordings of original text accompanied by verbatim printed text where important portions were marked had little effect on the recall of most students in the study.
4. The positive benefits of tape-recording texts are likely to accrue *only* when the texts *and* the recordings have been adapted so students are cued specifically to think strategically about the material (e.g., tape-cue students to preview text chapter by reading and paraphrasing important parts such as titles and headings; stop and summarize a paragraph just read to them on the tape; read a different paragraph in the text verbatim; stop and answer a specific study guide question). When such adaptations were constructed, according to Schumaker, Deshler, and Denton (1984), students' performance on tests covering the text increased an average 51% to 84%. When developing tape-recordings of texts, they suggest that the teacher:

   ■ Preread the text chapter and mark the portions of the text that should be read verbatim, those that can be explained or paraphrased for students, and those that can be skipped altogether.
   ■ Match text sections with corresponding study guide or end-of-the-chapter questions.
   ■ Determine actions in which students will be cued to engage throughout the text passage (e.g., "Stop and answer study guide question #2"; "Turn off the tape recorder and write what you think was the most important idea just discussed").
   ■ Prepare students with a copy of the text chapter that has been marked and an accompanying study guide. The first page of the study guide should be an outline of the chapter. Chapter marking should indicate sections that will be read verbatim, those that will be paraphrased only, and those that will be skipped. Marks also should provide signals for students to engage in specific activities.
   ■ On the tape recording cue students to preview the chapter and make responses (e.g., "The title of this chapter is "The Last Days." The unit we are studying is about the Civil War, so what do you think this chapter will be about? Turn off the recorder and write, in your own words, a paraphrase of this title").
   ■ Read sections of the text that are important, and paraphrase other sections that are not. Throughout the presentation cue students to engage in specific learning activities. Use a natural tone of voice and a comfortable rate.
   ■ Summarize the key information. Adequate recordings of textbooks require a great deal of preparation.

With regard to coherence, Armbruster and Anderson (1988) reported that textbooks often presented information in a "list-like format which failed to convey the relationship inherent in the text" (p. 49). Transitions between topics often were sudden, and sequences presented in the text frequently were presented out of chonological order or occurrence in real time. Linguistic cohesive ties that help carry the meaning across phrases, clauses, and sentences tended to be a major shortcoming. To produce lower readability scores on textbooks, publishers seemed to shorten sentences by transforming compound and complex sentences into simple independent clauses by removing coordinating and subordinating conjunctions that served as cohesive ties. The result was material written in short, choppy sentences not well connected and thus more incomprehensible. Consider the two passages below as examples. The first contains two sentences, and ideas have been connected using subordinating conjunctions. The second, an "adapted" version of the first passage, has much lower "readability" because the sentences are shorter and the information has been made less complex. Look what happens to the message, though.

Paragraph #1

Although Columbus is often viewed as a hero because he "discovered" America, many people do not realize that he also was a villain who tried to enslave the Native Americans he met on the islands. He also murdered thousands of these natives as well as several of his own men. He murdered natives because they would not bring him the gold he thought they were hiding from him. He murdered some of his own men because they refused to kill the natives when ordered to.

Paragraph #2

Columbus is a hero. He "discovered" America. Many people do not know that he was bad. He tried to make people into slaves. He also killed many people. They would not do what he wanted.

With regard to audience appropriateness, Armbruster and Anderson noted that many textbooks failed to account for the readers' limited amount of knowledge about the topic addressed by the text. Texts would "mention topics superficially" (p. 50) rather than provide sufficient explanation. Texts also tended to use words or phrases that failed to define important terms and used terms that were too vague to be of much use (e.g., "the *stuff* cells are made of..."). Figure 3.18 is an assimilation and adaptation of textbook evaluation guidelines and checklists provided by several experts (Armbruster & Anderson, 1988; Irwin & Davis, 1980; Lovitt et al., 1987).

TEACHING STRATEGY INTERRELATIONS AND INTEGRATIONS

Clearly, an interrelationship exists between teaching students to recognize cue words and organizational patterns when reading and teaching them to express information using cue words and organizational patterns when writing. In the discussion of writing strategy instruction (chapter 4), it is suggested that teachers teach students to plan their writing using graphic organizers similar to those presented above. Likewise, in chapter 4, it is suggested that teachers teach students a sentence writing strategy. Students' sentences become considerably more sophisticated as a result of instruction in how to use various sentence structures, and an added benefit is students' understanding of the vari-

Title: _____   Author: _____

Publisher: _____   Copyright date: _____

Use this scale to rate the text features	1	2	3	4	5
	Poor				**Very Good**
	Inconsiderate				**Considerate**

Look at the whole book

Appearance

_____ Is it interesting looking? Will students want to open it? Keep it open?

_____ Does it make ample use of space? Have large margins? Do pages appear crowded?

_____ Does it make effective use of color? (colored visuals, headings, etc.)

_____ Is print size appropriate (too small—cramped look; difficult to read; too large—babyish, may embarrass students)?

Content

_____ Does the overall content reflect what you believe are important concepts?

_____ Can you identify easily what the book is about by reading chapter concepts?

_____ Is the content up-to-date and relevant to needs of your students?

Organizational features

_____ Is the content of chapters organized logically?

_____ Can you identify easily what the book is about by reading chapter titles?

_____ Do the chapter titles reflect a logical organization of the content of the book?

_____ Does the book contain helpful table of contents, index, glossary, and appendixes?

Look at the way the book was written

Language

_____ Is the language clear and readable?

_____ Do ideas flow together well, or are they presented in a choppy, list-like format?

_____ Is level of vocabulary appropriate for the background of your students?

_____ Is level of sentence complexity appropriate for your students?

_____ Is length of paragraphs appropriate for your students?

_____ Does the text clearly link pronouns to referents and place subjects and verbs near the beginnings of sentences?

_____ Does the text stick to the topic and avoid irrelevant details?

Level of knowledge

_____ Are the assumptions about prior knowledge of the content appropriate for your students?

_____ Is new vocabulary introduced using direct definitions, examples, and nonexamples?

_____ Is the vocabulary density (% of difficult words) appropriate for your students?

_____ Are new concepts explained clearly using concrete examples that link the concepts to what students already know?

Metacognitive dimension

_____ Does the chapter provide cues for the reader to activate background knowledge?

_____ Does prose contain "strategy cues" (cues to visualize, predict, link to background knowledge, summarize, generate questions, etc.)?

_____ Does the prose contain "meta-discourse," or cues to think ahead, during, and back?

Personalizing

_____ Does the text use active verbs and personal pronouns such as *you, we,* and *us* to involve the students in the content?

_____ Does the text relate the content to students' lives?

_____ Does the text provide positive models for both sexes and for different ethnic or cultural groups?

(continued)

FIGURE 3.18   CHECKLIST FOR EVALUATING TEXTBOOKS

Look at each chapter

Organization features

____ Can you easily identify what the chapter is about by its title?
____ Can you easily identify what each section is about by its heading?
____ Is there a clearly recognizable overall organizational pattern to each chapter?
____ Is a helpful introduction provided at the beginning of each chapter?
____ Does the introduction link new topic of chapter to previous chapters and unit of study?
____ Is sufficient background knowledge provided so that students can link new knowledge with information previously learned?
____ Are there summaries that clarify the organization?
____ Do the questions encourage thoughtful responses rather than simply the identification of factual information?

Information structures

____ Are signal words used to help the reader recognize information structures? (enumerative, compare contrast, cause-effect, etc.).
____ Is the information structure signaled by headings, transition words, bold print, italics, or other indicators?

Visual aids

____ Are the pictures and graphic aids easy to understand? Will they require supplemental instruction?
____ Do the pictures, graphic aids, and supplementary information clearly relate to the important concepts of the chapter?
____ Does the prose "tie in" (refer to and discuss) pictures, graphic aids, and supplementary information with the ongoing text?

Questions and activities

____ Are questions dispersed through the chapter (i.e., in text and in margins), just at the end, or both?
____ Does the prose cue readers to question?
____ Do the questions and activities draw attention to the organizational pattern of the chapter?
____ Do questions and activities draw attention to information structures?
____ Do the questions and activities draw attention to the visual aids and require readers to assimilate information with that presented in the prose and prior knowledge?
____ Does the text suggest activities for students to practice using new concepts?
____ Do the questions and activities require students to engage strategies? (e.g., link new information to prior knowledge or experience, form predictions, generate questions, monitor comprehension, summarize, synthesize)

Look at the teacher's manual

____ Does the teacher's manual provide introductory activities that build on students' background and motivate them to read?
____ Does the teacher's manual provide guidance in helping students recognize organizational patterns?
____ Does the teacher's manual provide follow-up activities that help students integrate new knowledge into existing frameworks?
____ Does the teacher's manual provide guidance in helping students engage in metacognitive activities and use cognitive strategies?

Look at supplementary materials

____ Do supplementary materials, such as texts, worksheets, or computer programs, support the main concepts presented in the text?
____ Are supplementary materials motivating and interesting?
____ Do test questions require students to engage in higher order thinking skills (tell why or how, synthesize, explain within a larger context, etc.) rather than regurgitate factual information?
____ Do test questions provide students with opportunities to express their knowledge in various formats (e.g., draw graphic organizers, essay questions, etc.) rather than traditional subjective (multiple-choice, true-false, matching) recognition and discrimination tasks?

Weaknesses and strengths

On which items was the book rated lowest? Highest?
What are the weaknesses of this text? Strengths?
What can you do in class to compensate for the weaknesses of this text? To take advantage of the strengths of this text?

FIGURE 3.18   CONTINUED

ous structures. Thus, when students learn how to write complex sentences in which the dependent clause precedes the independent clause (e.g., "Although I like to play in the snow, I still hate winter"), they also are more likely to become more competent in understanding word shifts in sentences they encounter when reading text.

One of the more challenging aspects of teaching students with LD in special education settings is organizing instruction in a manner that interrelates and integrates various skills and strategies and at the same time provides sufficiently explicit and intensive instruction in specific areas. To the extent possible, teachers should couple instruction in reading strategies loosely with instruction in writing strategies. For example, if you teach in 50-minute blocks in a resource room setting, it could be divided into two main segments, one for reading strategy instruction and the other for writing strategy instruction, emphasizing overlapping concepts. For example, during the first half of the period, you might teach students how to recognize compare-and-contrast formats when reading and to take notes using compare-and-contrast graphic organizers. During the second half of the period, you would teach students a strategy for planning and executing compare-and-contrast paragraph writing. Another example would be to teach students how to write complex sentences involving word shifts during the first part of the period (the sentence writing strategy) and then how to recognize these sentence structures when reading during the second half of the period.

Summary

Six "big ideas" about teaching reading strategies to adolescents with LD are critical for teachers to understand.

Big Idea #1:

Because reading requires thinking and problem solving, reading instruction for adolescents with LD should focus on how to think and problem-solve when reading. Key cognitive processes associated with reading include organizing and transforming information, making decisions about the importance of the information gleaned from text, linking new information with background knowledge, and remembering. To be effective, readers need to call upon effectively and use efficiently a host of reading strategies, and they need to know which strategies are most important for which types of reading tasks. In short, reading requires active thinking. Because many adolescents with LD are ineffective at using these cognitive processes, they often are characterized as "inactive" or "passive" learners.

Research in facilitating reading ability suggests that some of the most important cognitive strategies to teach adolescents with LD deal with enabling them to become more effective at elaborating information. Elaboration strategies, in essence, require students to interact with the new information and relate it to background knowledge. Specific elaboration strategies include summarizing and paraphrasing, predicting and hypothesizing, generating questions, and imaging. In addition to elaboration strategies, teaching strategies for monitoring comprehension also produces promising results.

BIG IDEA #2:

Teachers should remember that teaching various cognitive processes for reading as decontextualized, stand-alone tactics rarely produces sustained reading improvement. Facilitating practice in specific cognitive tactics (e.g., just practicing visualization techniques or just practicing summarizing) generally is not an effective way to promote literacy. Thus, teachers should be wary of the plethora of commercial remedial reading materials designed to promote this type of practice (e.g., stories in which students practice "finding the main idea" and other stories in which students practice "finding the facts"). On the other hand, teaching students how to orchestrate these thinking processes and use them as strategies holds promise for many students.

BIG IDEA #3:

Although many of the learning strategies for reading reviewed in this chapter seem to present cognitive processes as a series of linear steps, teachers should remember that reading is not a linear process but, rather, is recursive. Success in meeting the various reading setting demands can be enhanced greatly if students are taught task-specific strategies for (a) comprehending text passages, (b) perusing text chapters, (c) integrating visual aids, and (d) problem-solving unknown words.

BIG IDEA #4:

Cognitive disabilities of some students account for many of their reading problems. The effectiveness of instruction in various reading strategies is further limited by these students' background knowledge of the world. If students do not already have some knowledge of the topic about which they are reading, effective strategies for paraphrasing, visualizing, and so forth will have only limited utility. Unfortunately, many traditional elementary special education practices reduce opportunities to accumulate knowledge about the world because students with LD often miss instruction in content areas such as social studies and science and instead attend resource programs to work on basic skills. Thus, reading comprehension can be enhanced if teachers preteach information about which students subsequently read. Unfortunately, the opposite often occurs; teachers assign reading as a homework assignment and then teach that information in class the following day or do not address it at all in class.

BIG IDEA #5:

Because so many students with LD have reading difficulties and seem unable to use grade-level textbooks, many teachers seek to provide these students with alternative "easier to read," "watered-down" textbooks that reflect limited vocabulary, short sentences, and fewer multisyllabic words. Unfortunately, these texts often are more difficult for students to comprehend because they are written so poorly. Teachers should be judicious when selecting these kinds of texts for their students. We need to be "watering up" the curriculum for adolescents with LD to make it more meaningful, not watering it down to make it easier to memorize.

BIG IDEA #6:

Facilitating students' knowledge of text structures can greatly increase their ability to understand and remember what has been read in many cases. Although authors rarely present information using only a single structure, creating tasks in which students search for structure can be productive and provide a purpose for reading and understanding the text. Likewise, teaching students to recognize cues that signal text structure can be helpful. Text structures include semantic features, organizational patterns, story grammar, and structural connectives.

Reading is only part of literacy. Many of the strategies for facilitating reading comprehension can be integrated with writing instruction as well. As will be seen in the following chapter about writing strategies, many of the same graphic organizers used for enhancing reading comprehension can be utilized to enhance the organization and quality of students' writing.

REFERENCES

Anderson, T. H., & Armbruster, B. B. (1984). Studying. In P. D. Pearson (Ed.), *Handbook of reading research*. New York: Longman.

Armbruster, B. B., & Anderson, T. H. (1988). On selecting "considerate" content area textbooks. *Remedial and Special Education, 9*, 4–52.

Anderson, T. H., Armbruster, B. B., & Kantor, R. N. (1980). *How clearly written are children's textbooks? or, of bladderworks and alfa* (Reading Education Report No. 16). Urbana: University of Illinois, Center for the Study of Reading.

Bos, C. S., & Anders, P. L. (1987). Semantic feature analysis: An interactive teaching strategy for facilitating learning from text. *Learning Disabilities Focus, 3*, 55–59.

Bos, C. S., Anders, P. L., Filip, D., & Jaffe, L. E. (1989). The effects of an interactional instructional strategy for enhancing reading comprehension and content area learning for students with learning disabilities. *Journal of Learning Disabilities, 22*, 384–390.

Cline, R. K. J., & Kretke, G. L. (1980). An evaluation of long-term SSR in the junior high school. *Journal of Reading, 23*, 503–506.

Dupuis, N. M., & Askov, E. N. (1982). *Content area reading*. Englewood Cliffs, NJ: Prentice Hall.

Ellis, E. S. (1986). The role of motivation and pedagogy on the generalization of cognitive strategy training. *Journal of Learning Disabilities, 19*(2), 66–70.

Ellis, E. S. (1989a). A metacognitive intervention for increasing class participation. *Learning Disabilities Focus, 5*(1), 36–46.

Ellis, E. S. (1989b). A model for assessing cognitive reading strategies. *Academic Therapy, 24*(4), 407–424.

Ellis, E. S. (1994). An instructional model for integrating content-area instruction with cognitive strategy instruction. *Reading and Writing Quarterly: Overcoming Learning Difficulties, 1*, 63–90.

Ellis, E. S., Deshler, D. D., Schumaker, J. B., Lenz, B. K., & Clark, F. L. (1993). An instructional model for teaching learning strategies. In E. Meyen, G. A. Vergason, & R. J. Whelan (Eds.), *Educating students with mild disabilities* (pp. 151–187). Denver: Love Publishing.

Ellis, E. S., & Graves, A. (1990). Teaching rural students with learning disabilities a paraphrasing strategy to increase comprehension of main ideas. *Rural Special Education Quarterly, 10*(2), 2–10.

Ellis, E. S., & Lenz, B. K. (1987). An analysis of the critical features of effective learning strategies. *Focus on Learning Disabilities, 2*(2), 94–107.

Ellis, E. S., & Lenz, B. K. (1990). Techniques for mediating content-area learning: Issues and research. *Focus on Exceptional Children, 22*(9), 1–16.

Ellis, E. S., & Lenz, B. K. (in preparation). *The development of learning strategy interventions*. Lawrence, KS: Edge Enterprises.

Ellis, E. S., Lenz, B. K., & Sabornie, E. J. (1987). Generalization and adaptation of learning strategies to natural environments: Part 2. Research into practice. *Remedial and Special Education, 8*(2), 6–23.

Harber, J. (1983). The effects of illustrations on the reading performance of learning disabled and normal children. *Learning Disability Quarterly, 6*, 55–60.

Harris, K., & Pressley, M. (1991). The nature of cognitive strategy instruction: Interactive strategy construction. *Exceptional Children, 57*, 392–404.

Hermann, B. A. (1990). Teaching preservice teachers how to model thought processes: Issues, problems, and procedures. *Teacher Education and Special Education, 13*, 73–81.

Idol, L., & Croll, V. J. (1987). Story-mapping training as a means of improving reading comprehension. *Learning Disability Quarterly, 10*, 216.

Irwin, J. W., & Davis, C. A. (1980). Assessing readability: The checklist approach. *Journal of Reading, 24*, 129–130.

Johnston, P., & Pearson, P. D. (1982). *Prior knowledge, connectivity, and the assessment of reading comprehension*. Technical report 245: Center for the Study of Reading. Urbana: University of Illinois.

Jones, B. F., Palincsar, A. M., Ogle, D. S., & Carr, E. G. (1987). *Strategic teaching and learning: Cognitive instruction in the content areas*. Alexandria, VA: Association for Supervision and Curriculum Development.

Kagan, S. (1989). The structural approach to cooperative learning. *Educational Leadership, 47*(4), 12–16.

Lenz, B. K., Alley, G. R., Beals, V. C., Schumaker, J. B., & Deshler, D. D. (1981). *Teaching LD adolescents a strategy for interpreting visual aids*. Unpublished manuscript, University of Kansas, Lawrence.

Lenz, B. K., & Hughes, C. A. (1990). A word identification strategy for adolescents with learning disabilities. *Journal of Learning Disabilities, 23*(3), 149–158, 163.

Lenz, B. K., Schumaker, J. B., Deshler, D. D., & Beals, V. L. (1984). *Learning strategies curriculum: The word identification strategy*. Lawrence: University of Kansas.

Lovitt, T. C., Horton, S. V., & Bergerud, D. (1987). Matching students with textbooks: An alternative to readability formulas and standardized tests. *British Columbia Journal of Special Education, 11*(1), 49–55.

Meyer, B. J. F. (1981). Basic research on prose comprehension: A critical review. In D. F. Fisher & C. W. Peters (Eds.), *Comprehension and the competent reader: Interspeciality perspective*. New York: Praeger.

Minton, M. J. (1980). The effect of sustained silent reading upon comprehension and attitudes among 9th graders. *Journal of Reading, 23*, 498–502.

Olson, A. V., & Ames, W. S. (1972). *Teaching reading skills in secondary schools*. Scranton, PA: Intext Educational Publisher.

O'Shea, L. J., Sindelar, P. T., & O'Shea, D. J. (1987). The effects of repeated readings and attentional cues on the reading fluency and comprehension of learning disabled readers. *Learning Disabilities Research, 2*, 103–109.

Palincsar, A. M., & Brown, A. L. (1984). Reciprocal teaching of comprehension fostering and monitoring activities. *Cognition and Instruction, 1*, 117–175.

Palincsar, A. S., Winn, J., David, Y., Snyder, B., & Stevens, D. (1993). Approaches to reading instruction reflecting different assumptions regarding teaching and learning. In L. J. Meltzer (Ed.), *Strategy assessment and instruction for students with learning disabilities*. Austin: Pro Ed.

Paulsen, L., & Lamar, N. (1966). Using writing to help the poor reader. In H. A. Robinson & S. J. Rauch (Eds.), *Corrective reading in the high school classroom*. Newark, DE: International Reading Association.

Pressley, M., Borkowski, J. G., & Schneider, W. (1989). Good information processing: What it is and what education can do to promote it. *International Journal of Educational Research, 13*, 857–867.

Rashotte, C. A., & Torgesen, J. K. (1985). Repeated reading and reading fluency in learning disabled children. *Reading Research Quarterly, 20*, 180–188.

Schallert, D. L. (1980). The role of illustrations in reading comprehension. In R. J. Spiro, B. C. Bruce, & W. F. Brewer (Eds.), *Theoretical issues in reading comprehension: Perspectives from cognitive psychology, linguistics, artificial intelligence, and education* (pp. 503-524). Hillsdale, NJ: Lawrence Erlbaum.

Schumaker, J. B., Deshler, D. D., Alley, G. R., & Denton, P. (1982). Multipass: A learning strategy for improving reading comprehension. *Learning Disabilitiy Quarterly, 5*(3), 295–304.

Schumaker, J. B., Deshler, D. D., & Denton, P. (1984). *The learning strategies curriculum: The paraphrasing strategy*. Lawrence: University of Kansas.

Schumaker, J. B., & Deshler, D. D. (1984). Setting demand variables: A major factor in program planning for LD adolescents. *Topics in Language Disorders Journal, 4*, 22–44.

Schlechty, P. C. (1993). *Schools in the twenty-first century.* Paper presented at James T. Curtis Lecture Series, University of Alabama, Birmingham.

Snider, V. E., & Tarver, S. G. (1987). The effect of early reading failure on acquisition of knowledge among students with learning disabilities. *Journal of Learning Disabilities, 20*, 351–356, 373.

Thomas, E. L., & Robinson, H. A. (1972). *Improving reading in every class.* Boston: Allyn & Bacon.

Torgesen, J. K., Dahlem, W. E., & Greenstein, J. (1987). Using verbatim text recordings to enhance reading comprehension in learning disabled adolescents. *Learning Disabilities Focus, 3*(1), 30–38.

Zigmond, N., Levin, E., & Laurie, T. (1985). Managing the mainstream: An analysis of teacher attitudes and student performance in mainstream high school programs. *Journal of Learning Disabilities, 18*, 535–541.

4

Writing Strategy Instruction

Edwin S. Ellis and Gale Colvert

QUESTIONS TO KEEP IN MIND

- What kinds of difficulties do adolescents with LD have in the writing domain? Why?

- What can be assessed when evaluating the writing skills of students with LD? How?

- How can students with LD acquire confidence in taking ownership of their writing?

- What writing strategies can be used to facilitate writing skills?

- How can students be empowered to write well-developed sentences? Paragraphs? Essays?

- How can students take control of the revision process?

- How can students be motivated to generalize the strategies taught and use them independently?

Advance Organizer

During the elementary school years instruction in writing generally is directed at the creative writing process (e.g., storytelling). In the secondary school the demands on writing often are quite different. For example, the secondary school curriculum typically expects students to take notes from lectures, complete essay examinations, and write reports and themes. Thus, after just the short time of a summer vacation, students entering secondary schools experience a whole new ball game with regard to meeting the writing demands of school. Adolescents with LD often are seriously unprepared to meet these demands, and therefore face a wide range of failure experiences in school.

These students often leave school unable to complete written tasks successfully and are thrust into new situations in which the demands for good writing skills are equally high. For example, young adults must exhibit proficient writing when applying for a job or college entrance, as part of actual work assignments, and in meeting personal needs such as letter writing. Deficits in written expression can be particularly devastating because the product is so visible and permanent. Likewise, students with writing problems frequently have developed extremely negative attitudes about writing and are reluctant to engage in writing instruction or activities.

Fortunately, significant progress has been made in recent years in understanding the processes involved in developing written language competencies, and much of this work has centered on the cognitive processes involved in writing and how to teach them. Methods for developing competent writers could easily comprise a whole book. In this chapter, however, we focus on key areas that research suggests are especially powerful methods that target some of the most common writing deficits of adolescents with LD. Figure 4.1 shows the topics addressed by this chapter and how they are organized.

Introduction

Writing tasks can be ordered in a continuum from early childhood through adulthood (Chalfant & Scheffelin, 1969). This developmental hierarchy presents the following sequence of steps involved in the writing act:

1. Scribbling
2. Tracing
   a. connected letters and figures
   b. disconnected letters and figures
3. Copying
   a. from a model
   b. from memory
   c. symbolic and nonsymbolic
4. Completion tasks
   a. figure completion

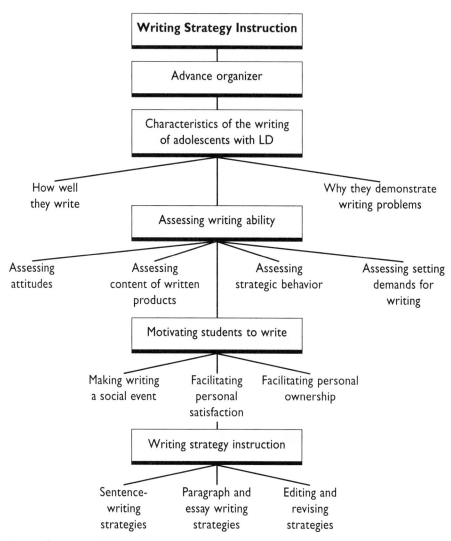

FIGURE 4.1   CHAPTER 4 ORGANIZATION

    b. word completion—supplying missing letters
       (1) multiple-choice
       (2) recall
    c. sentence completion—supplying the missing word
  5. Writing from dictation
    a. writing letters as they are spoken
    b. writing words or sentences
    c. supplying missing word
    d. supplying missing sentence
  6. Propositional writing

Students already are functioning somewhere along this continuum. This chapter presents methods of instructing adolescents with LD who are competent in skills 1–4 but have written expression deficits in skills 5 and 6. Students who have severe learning disabilities and deficits in skills 1 through 4 probably will require extensive clinical approaches to improve their writing skills.

The Chalfant and Scheffelin (1969) writing hierarchy reflects the observable behaviors associated with development of writing skills. Missing from this outline but of paramount importance is the development of students' understandings and perceptions about the writing process. *"Do I have to do this?"* followed by *"So how long does it have to be?"* often are the first questions that adolescents with LD ask when they encounter writing tasks. These questions reflect an orientation that writing is something to avoid at all costs, and something others impose on them. The writing behaviors of these students suggest that they write as little as possible to meet minimal requirements of assignments necessary to make a good grade rather than view writing as a key means of communication.

In contrast, skilled writers are concerned more with the communication process. They consider what they want to communicate and how to communicate it successfully to others. As Graham, Harris, MacArthur, and Schwartz (1991) noted, we write to communicate ideas, experiences, and feelings, and we write to make things happen—to make requests or persuade others to take action. When composing, for example, skilled writers say things to themselves such as, "Who will be reading this?" "What am I trying to say here?" "Will this sentence make sense when they read it?" Skilled writers have developed an understanding of the importance of tailoring their language and content to their communication goals and the needs of their audience (Flowers & Haynes, 1980).

Another important understanding of skilled writers is that writing is a process that involves planning, text production, and revising (Flowers & Haynes, 1980). Skilled writers understand that, although these processes have a general sequence, they are not necessarily linear but, rather, are recursive. Good writers often switch from planning to composing, to revising, to planning again throughout the writing task. Nevertheless, they do spend sufficient time planning their writing before composing their text, and after they have written a first draft, they spend a considerable amount of time editing what they have written.

Table 4.1 illustrates some of the components of the writing process. To implement these processes effectively, skilled writers use a combination of these components systematically. Table 4.2 illustrates components of knowledge that are essential. The skilled writer develops a variety of understandings and applies them to the writing task. A fundamental principle is that writing occurs in a social context. We write to communicate to others. Thus, the writer must work constantly to balance the intended message with how to communicate it best in a written manner that others will understand readily.

WRITING CHARACTERISTICS OF ADOLESCENTS WITH LD

Adolescents with mild to moderate learning disabilities usually demonstrate competence on writing tasks through the fourth step in the Chalfant and Scheffelin (1969) develop-

TABLE 4.1   COMPONENTS OF THE WRITING PROCESS

Planning process

Setting goals	Reflecting on who will comprise the audience, what to communicate to the audience, and how the audience will react to the message
Generating content	Searching memory and external sources to extract relevant information
Organizing content	Using goals or a purpose for writing and understanding the content to determine possible text structures for organizing the information to be communicated

Text production process

Physical production of writing letters and words	Coordinating muscles when writing script or typing
Production of meaningful and correct sentences	Writing complete sentences that communicate ideas effectively
	Adhering to the mechanical conventions of print (capitalization, punctuation, spelling, etc.)

Reviewing and revising

Evaluating text already written	Revising text structures and incorporating other text structures into writing as understanding of the content and goals change when writing
	Evaluating sentences for meaning and clarity in relation to goals; revising as needed
	Evaluating for conventions of print errors and making corrections (e.g., correcting incomplete sentences, spelling errors)
Evaluating and revising goals	Revising goals as result of changes in knowledge and understanding of the topic when gathering information or thinking about the topic during writing
Evaluating ideas not yet written	Determining whether (and where) a new idea fits into the written text and how it should be expressed best

TABLE 4.2   KNOWLEDGE COMPONENTS OF WRITING

Audiences

Audience's level of language competencies	Adjusting the level of language used in the text to the level of the writer's audience. (Skilled writers possess knowledge of their audience's language skills. For example, if they believe complex sentence structures will be confusing to their audience, they avoid using them.)
Audience's goals and expectations	Anticipating the audience's motivation for reading the text and attempting to accommodate these goals; anticipating and attempting to accommodate the audience's expectations, ensuring that work is free of errors and is neat and attractive in circumstances that have an expectation of these qualities.
Audience's level of content knowledge	Anticipating what the audience knows about a topic and adjusting writing accordingly; avoiding vocabulary that will be unfamiliar to the audience.

Text structures

Knowledge of different text structures	Being aware of and using various text structures (e.g., cause/effect, compare/contrast) so ideas can be expressed in a manner that helps the reader understand.
Knowledge of structural clue words	Incorporating various words into the writing to cue audience to the type of information being communicated (e.g., writers who are in the process of comparing ideas may use structural cues such as "similarly," "likewise," and "resemblance"); having knowledge of different text structures and also possessing a broad vocabulary of signal words that are used appropriately with specific text structures.
Knowledge of sentence structures	Constructing a variety of sentence structures (e.g., compound sentences, complex sentences, sentences containing adverbial clauses, prepositional phrases, etc.); using correct syntax; and using the different structures as tools for communicating the message effectively.
Knowledge of paragraph structures	Understanding that paragraphs are used to separate ideas to reduce confusion in the message; being knowledgeable of the internal structures of paragraphs as well and using a variety of structures as tools to communicate the message; being knowledgeable of transition from one paragraph to another.

(continued)

TABLE 4.2   CONTINUED

	Conventions of print
Grammatical rules Punctuation rules Spelling Neatness	Having knowledge of the conventions of print and when goals and audience dictate their use; recognizing lack of specific knowledge required to adhere to these conventions (e.g., do not know how to spell a word) and taking action to rectify the problem (e.g., use dictionary or ask someone).
Strategy knowledge	
Task-specific strategies	Employing task-specific strategies or loosely structured plans when engaging in the planning, production, and reviewing phases of writing (e.g., a strategy for planning writing might be to first clarify goals and identify intended audience, next create a list of ideas, and then organize them in graphic form); possessing knowledge of a host of different task-specific strategies (e.g., strategies for planning, strategies for editing) and using them fluently .
Cognitive strategies	Using "mental tools" (e.g., summarizing, visualizing, self-questioning, self-speech) to guide the problem-solving process; recognizing when different tools are needed; using them fluently and automatically monitoring their effectiveness; and readily switching to another as the need arises.
Content	
Content knowledge in memory	Having knowledge about the writing topic (e.g., the more we know about a topic, the easier it is to write about it; the more we have to rely on extracting information from external sources such as textbooks to gain knowledge about the topic, the greater is the information-processing demand placed on the writing process).
Knowledge of strategies for extracting content from external sources	Extracting information from external sources (e.g., newspapers, television, books) effectively, leaving more time to think about expressing the content rather than locating the content.

mental hierarchy. They probably had difficulty in earlier stages of language development, however, in listening, speaking, and reading. They achieved their current level of performance more slowly than their grade-level peers, and their current performance tends to be characterized by poor handwriting, poor organization, a limited word pool, poor sentence structure, a high frequency of mechanical errors (e.g., spelling, capitalization, punctuation), and limited monitoring of written errors (Graham & Harris, 1993b; Moran, Schumaker, & Vetter, 1981; Welsh & Link, 1992).

How Well Do Adolescents with LD Write?

Adolescents with LD typically have limited skill in the planning, production, and reviewing phases of the writing process. Many of these students have limited perspective-taking skills. Thus, they tend to consider the characteristics of their audiences inadequately as a guide to their writing. In addition, they often have limited command of the strategies to use throughout the writing process. Many of these students are particularly deficit in using the cognitive processes associated with skilled writing identified in Table 4.1. For example, they demonstrate difficulty generating content about which to write from memory or from external sources. They tend to have knowledge deficits in all the categories listed in Table 4.2 (for reviews, see Graham and Harris, 1993b) and have poorly developed content knowledge to use in developing their message. The result often is writing that is unorganized and replete with incomplete ideas and technical errors. Many of these students are unfamiliar with text, paragraph, and sentence structures. When given the chance to review and improve their writing, they express few skills in identifying and correcting their errors adequately.

Adolescents with LD usually do not know effective writing strategies, nor do they necessarily employ the strategies they do know. The writing sample illustrated in Figure 4.2 is typical of the writing skills of many adolescents with LD. Not only does the work lack visual appeal (e.g., poor handwriting, crooked margins, writing off the lines) and is inordinately short, but the content also reflects short, disjointed sentences that are poorly organized. The writing sample suggests that the student writes whatever comes to mind and lacks ideation. Important parts such as a premise or closure are missing. This sample also illustrates a common behavior found in students with LD. When given writing as-

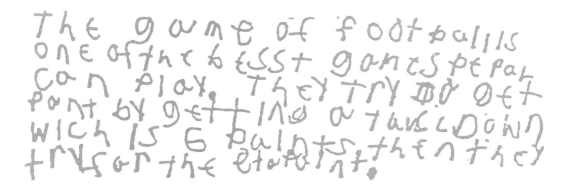

Figure 4.2   Sample Writing Skills of LD Adolescent

signments, they tend to convert the assignment into a question-answer format and then provide only minimal information (Graham & Harris, 1993a).

The writing strategies that students with LD employ reflect a lack of sophistication and knowledge of the writing process. For example, after writing initial drafts, many students do not bother to edit their work. When they do, they tend to use simplistic editing strategies that center on finding and correcting mechanical errors (e.g., capitalization, punctuation) rather than on making changes that improve the likelihood that their audience will understand their message fully (MacArthur & Graham, 1987). Deshler (1978) found that high school students with LD have a monitoring deficit on academic tasks that requires their detection of self-generated and externally generated errors. On a creative writing task, for example, students with LD detected only one-third of the errors they committed. The control group detected more than twice as many errors on the same task. The repercussions of such performance in academic and future employment situations should be obvious.

The inability to write complete and sophisticated sentences is a common problem in the population of students with LD (Schmidt, Deshler, Schumaker, & Alley, 1989). As noted above, their sentences tend to be short and choppy, devoid of phrases and clauses that provide meaningful elaboration. Consider these two sentences:

The boy went in the store.
After playing baseball, the boy went in the store to buy a drink because he was hot and thirsty.

The first one is typical of the type of sentences that students with LD write. We want students to be able to elaborate on their ideas, creating more meaningful sentences such as the second one.

In a study conducted with students in remedial classes in community college settings, Higgens (1975) investigated the composition of individual sentence and grammatical relations in essays written by college freshmen. A summary of errors with the highest frequency is provided in Table 4.3.

WHY DO ADOLESCENTS WITH LD DEMONSTRATE WRITING PROBLEMS?

Graham and Harris (1993) theorized that writing problems of students with LD stem from three key areas:

1. Difficulties transcribing ideas into printed words may be interfering with the ability to employ other important writing processes such as generating ideas.
2. Limited knowledge of the writing process or inability to access this knowledge may be interfering with their ability to use various cognitive processes essential to effective writing.
3. Limited knowledge of effective writing strategies may be restricting their ability to begin or move through the writing process.

The learner's innate characteristics are only part of the problem. Although a wide range of factors may contribute, the learner's cognitive and affective characteristics probably

TABLE 4.3   ERRORS OF HIGHEST FREQUENCY OCCURRING AND RECURRING IN COLLEGE
FRESHMAN ESSAYS

Fault	Percentage of all papers in which fault occurred	Percentage of all papers in which fault recurred
Misspelling (excluding homonyms)	83	64
Inappropriate contraction	78	55
Inappropriate use of verb *get*	69	50
Missing commas around parenthetical (including non-restrictive) element	65	34
Redundancy	64	36
Missing possessive apostrophe	62	21
Misspelling of homonym	57	30
Missing needed comma following introductory element	57	27
Poor subordination or coordination	53	26
Pronoun-antecedent nonagreement or general shift in number	53	16
Inappropriate use of noun *thing*	52	30
Vague pronoun reference	52	11
Run-together sentence (with or without comma)	50	27
Missing needed comma before coordinate conjunction	48	16
Sentence fragment	45	20
Shift in person	45	20
Miscellaneous superfluous comma	44	27
Wrong meaning of word	39	18
Nonparallel structure	38	8
Miscellaneous inappropriate colloquialism	37	13
Word substitution (usually inadvertent; e.g., "He hid it *is* the closet," for *in*)	37	10
Subject-verb nonagreement	36	15
Wrong or missing ending on regular verb form	35	20
Miscellaneous omission of word	35	10
Unidiomatic preposition	33	7
Wrongly included or omitted noun ending (excluding possessive)	31	13

interact with external factors to produce the writing deficits manifested in adolescents with LD. With regard to the affective domain, a multitude of failures, compounded by low academic self-concept, clearly can cause students to be reluctant to engage in even minimal writing tasks. The brevity of their writing may result in part from their desire to avoid mistakes (e.g., fewer words written equals fewer opportunities to misspell words) to circumvent opportunities for embarrassment.

The manner in which writing sometimes is taught in school also may result in students' failure to develop effective writing strategies. Christenson, Thurlow, Ysseldyke, and McVicar (1989) conducted a study of the type of writing instruction students with LD received in school. Their study revealed a striking contrast between general and special education classrooms in time allocated for instruction, time allocated for instruction of writing mechanics, and actual time spent writing. The researchers concluded that the students most in need of quality writing instruction were receiving the least. Too often, extensive instruction is provided in studying grammar (e.g., parts of speech, diagramming sentences) at the expense of teaching students how to actually write and instruction in writing may not be explicit enough to enable students with LD to develop effective writing strategies. In the former case, extensive data strongly indicate that studying the components of language (e.g., grammar) has little effect on the quality of students' writing (for a review, see Graham, 1982).

The key component of effective communication is organizing information for the reader. Van Nostrand, Knoblauch, McGuire, and Pettigrew (1978) suggested that nonsensical sentences, disjointed paragraphs, and wandering structure, *not* poor grammar, are the major characteristics of ineffective writing.

Perhaps as a reaction in part to a segmented grammatical approach, various whole-language approaches to instruction have risen in popularity in recent years. These programs are based on holistic and content-centered approaches, but the manner in which some teachers implement them is too discovery-learning oriented to be an effective instructional model for many adolescents with LD (for a review, see Ellis, 1994b). Although less explicit instructional models for teaching writing strategies may prove effective for use with some adolescents with LD, little research has demonstrated this. In contrast, there is ample data that supports using explicit instruction in the use of writing strategies (e.g., Graham, & Harris, 1993a; MacArthur & Stoddard, 1990; Moran, Schumaker, & Vetter, 1981).

To summarize, the quality of writing that many adolescents with LD produce is poor, and in terms of quantity, they produce very little. Both quality and quantity of their writing can be improved significantly through explicit instruction in effective and efficient writing strategies. These adolescents should be taught planning, production, and monitoring writing strategies. Later in this chapter we describe three task-specific strategies targeting some of the most common problems of adolescents with LD: writing sophisticated sentences, writing paragraphs and essays, and editing and revising.

ASSESSING WRITING ABILITY

The goal of language arts instruction in writing is to prepare students to be effective communicators of ideas. During the elementary years the early steps of writing instruction usually entail students' dictating stories to teachers, as well as instruction in the mechanics of writing (e.g., spelling, punctuation, handwriting). By about the 5th grade most students are able to write well-structured paragraphs. If adolescents with LD have failed to reach this skill level, their written language should be assessed to ascertain specific areas of difficulty. Formal and informal measures both can be used to assess students' performance on these writing skills, but these two approaches generally serve different goals. Standardized tests are used primarily for facilitating programmatic decisions (e.g., whether a student qualifies for special education services), whereas informal measures are used primarily for making ongoing instructional decisions. Commonly used formal measures of writing skills are reviewed below. Most of the focus of this section, however, is on informal ways to assess writing.

FORMAL ASSESSMENT OF WRITING

Standardized written language assessments can be useful for comparing a student's written performance on selected tasks to the performance of a norm group. Various standardized assessment instruments are available to examine written language skills. These can serve the purpose of identifying general strengths and deficits and can be part of the assessment used for qualifying a student for special education services. These tests are administered individually and provide an overall level of written language function. Generally, the tests either deal with direct assessment of student-generated text or indirect assessment measuring knowledge of writing mechanics (e.g., grammar, English usage, punctuation). Some, such as the TOWL–2, offer a combined format. Other standardized test instruments have a written language subtest or composite subtest score. Table 4.4 lists several standardized written language assessment tools.

Although standardized test instruments can provide important information about how students compare with their peers, the kind of information these instruments provide has limited utility when planning interventions for students with writing deficits. Sometimes they are useful for highlighting general areas of strengths and weaknesses. A variety of informal, curriculum-based measures are needed when designing interventions and measuring progress.

As the student moves into the secondary setting, the demand for writing increases, and a variety of knowledge and subskills are necessary to successfully meet the demands of the secondary curriculum. Tables 4.1 and 4.2 illustrated some of the key knowledge that should be considered when assessing students. An outline adapted from Hennings and Grant (1974) depicts various subskills for assessment consideration. Three main categories include: (a) attitude toward writing, (b) ability to generate and deal with ideas on the content, and (c) ability to deal with the mechanical aspects or the craft of written expression. The outline is presented in Table 4.5.

Because the development of written language skills is interdependent with other language skills such as reading and speaking, the process of conveying thoughts in writing is complex. Adolescents with LD who have poorly developed language skills in general are likely to become frustrated and anxious and even give up when they are expected repeatedly to complete complex writing assignments such as themes, essay examinations, research reports, and class notes. Consequently, the first consideration when beginning work with these students must be to deal with the attitudes of students toward writing. Progress in writing will be minimal unless anxieties and fears about writing assignments are addressed and students are motivated to write.

For example, Steve, an 8th-grade student with a learning disability, had an IQ of 120. He showed good comprehension during class discussion, and he was creative in

(continued)

TABLE 4.4   FORMAL WRITING ASSESSMENT INSTRUMENTS

Test	Range	Description	Authors	Publisher
Test of Adolescent and Adult Language (TOAL–3)	6th grade to adults age 24	*Direct and Indirect Assessment.* Separate composite scores are calculated in each of 10 language areas: listening, speaking, reading, writing, spoken language, written language, vocabulary, grammar, receptive language, and expressive language. Subtest scores are combined into an Overall Language Ability Quotient. All reliability coefficients exceed .80.	Hammill, P., Brown, V. L., Larsen, J. C., & Wiederholt, J. L. (1994)	Pro-Ed
Written Language Assessment (WLA)	Ages 8–18	*Direct Assessment.* Qualitative score derived for rhetorical skill evidenced in three pieces written over 5 days for legibility and overall quality. These scores are summed to yield an overall General Writing Ability score. Quantitative scoring component calculates productivity with word count, complexity with calculation of syllables, and a readability score using an adaptation of the Fry Readability Scale. Reliability is .90.	Grill, J. J., & Kerwin, M. M. (1989)	Academic Therapy Publications
Test of Written Language–2 (TOWL–2)	Ages 7–0 to 17–11	*Direct and Indirect Assessment.* Each of 10 subtests are designed to assess writing conventions (e.g., punctuation, capitalization, spelling), linguistic elements (e.g., syntax, morphology, semantics, or conceptual aspects pertaining to expression of ideas). A "contrived" writing quotient and a "spontaneous" writing quotient are calculated, and the 10 subtest scores are summed to produce an Overall Written Language Quotient.	Hammill, D. D., & Larsen, S. C. (1988)	Pro-Ed

TABLE 4.4 CONTINUED

Individual Achievement Tests with Writing Components

Test	Range	Description	Author	Publisher
Peabody Individual Achievement Test–Revised (PIAT–R)	Ages 5–18	*Direct and Indirect.* Written Expression Subtest consists of rating students' compositions on content, mechanics, and organization using an analytic scoring scale. A Total Written Expression score is obtained by combining raw scores on Written Expression and Spelling subtests. Reliability ranges from .91 to .44.	Markwardt, F. C., Jr. (1989)	American Guidance Services
Wechsler Individual Achievement Test (WIAT)	Grades K–12	*Direct and Indirect.* Using analytic and holistic scoring methods, student written piece is scored on ideas, development, organization, unity, coherence, vocabulary, sentence structure and variety, grammar and usage, and capitalization and punctuation. Writing Composite Score is a sum of spelling and writing subtest. Reliability is .80 to .90.	Roid, G. (Senior Project Director) (1992)	Psychological Corp.
Woodcock-Johnson Psycho-Educational Battery (WJ–R)	24 months to 95 years	*Direct and Indirect.* Battery includes dictation requiring written response measuring spelling, punctuation, and capitalization, and written samples requiring students to write sentences that are evaluated on quality of expression. Both subtest scores are combined for a composite Written Expression Score. Reliability is .48 to .63.	Woodcock, R. W., & Johnson, W. B. (1989)	DLM Teaching Resources

TABLE 4.5   WRITTEN EXPRESSION SKILLS REQUIRING ASSESSMENT AND INTERVENTION FOR LD STUDENTS

I. Attitude toward writing
    A. Emotional blocks
    B. Motivation to write
II. Content
    A. Reflection of the world
        1. Description
        2. Reports of happenings
        3. Procedures
        4. Retelling
        5. Summaries
    B. Conception of relationships
        1. Comparison and contrast
        2. Classification
        3. Qualitative analysis
        4. Sequential analysis
        5. Cause and effect
        6. Explanation in terms of
            supporting principles
    C. Projection of explanatory schemes
        and designs
        1. Hypothesis
        2. Conceptual schemes
        3. Design: Plan of action
    D. Expression of personal view
        1. Feelings
        2. Preferences
        3. Opinions
        4. Judgment

III. Craft
    A. Structuring paragraphs and themes
        1. Organizing ideas
        2. Sequencing ideas
    B. Vocabulary development
        1. Choosing words to express
            experiences
        2. Synonyms
    C. Sentence writing
        1. Building sentences
        2. Generating a variety of sentence
            patterns
    D. Writing questions
    E. Notetaking
        1. From lectures
        2. From texts
    F. Summaries and paraphrases
    G. Mechanical factors
        1. Punctuation
        2. Capitalization
        3. Neatness
        4. Spelling
    H. Monitoring written expression
        1. Habits of checking for errors
        2. Ability to detect errors
        3. Ability to correct errors
    I. Written test-taking

developing and verbally relating short stories. Whenever Steve was asked to show his ideas in writing, however, he exhibited what Drake and Cavanaugh (1970) called "paralysis of effort." The answers or stories he could convey verbally to the teacher disappeared when he tried to express them in writing. In some classes his anxiety and fear over trying to put his thoughts into written form were so high that he started to perspire and sometimes hyperventilated.

Irmscher (1972) noted that student attitudes toward writing are of fundamental importance. Because writing is primarily a psychological act and not a mechanical skill, students' feelings must be a major and first consideration. Attitudes about writing can be assessed via surveys and informal interviews.

ATTITUDE SURVEY

The Writing Attitudes Survey (Ellis, 1993) in Figure 4.3 is an example of a survey that the student can complete. After students have indicated their perceptions of various dimensions of their writing, the survey can be used as a basis for having students explain their responses. Students might complete the surveys first individually and then discuss their responses in a group. The session can enlighten students with regard to others' perceptions of similar problems, and it can bring negative feelings into the open so they can be addressed. The surveys can be administered again after the writing intervention, and pre- and post-scores can be compared to document progress in improvement in attitude.

THE METACOGNITIVE INTERVIEW

Before beginning instruction in various writing strategies, you may want to learn more about what students know, or think they know, about the writing process and various tactics for writing. A metacognitive interview is a series of loosely structured questions to assess students' understanding of the writing process and factors that facilitate or impede their success. At first the questions would be global in nature. This allows you to ascertain a student's thoughts and perceptions without "leading the witness" too much. These questions should give way gradually to direct and more specific questions. Sample questions that might be asked in the interview are:

1. *Beginning of Interview: Global Questions*
   When you have a writing assignment, how do you usually go about completing it? What else do you do?
   What do good writers do when they write? Which of these techniques are most important? Why?
   Do you like to write? Why or why not?
   How good is your writing?

2. *Middle of Interview: Direct Questions*
   What are some things you think about before you write? What else do you think about? Why?
   What are some things you do before you write? Why?
   When you're actually writing, what are some things you do and think about?
   Once you've written your assignment, what do you usually do? Why?

3. *Conclusion of Interview: Specific Questions*
   Some writers take time to plan their writing by making an outline or framing their ideas with a web. Do you ever do this? Why?
   What do you usually do?
   Do good writers do this? Why or why not?
   How do you edit? Do you fix errors as you write, or do you go back and try to find them after you have written?
   What problems do you usually look for when you are checking your work?
   Do you ever recopy your paper? When?

Instructions: The questions below ask you to indicate how you feel about different aspects of writing. For each question, circle the number that best shows what you really feel.

| 1 = Strongly agree | 2 = Mostly agree | 3 = Unsure | 4 = Mostly Disagree | 5 = Strongly Disagree |

1 2 3 4 5   1. I think writing about a topic helps you learn about it.

1 2 3 4 5   2. It really does not matter how you go about writing as long as you finish the job.

1 2 3 4 5   3. Writing is a waste of time.

1 2 3 4 5   4. Setting goals before you start writing is important.

1 2 3 4 5   5. Thinking about who will be reading your writing and what the reader already knows about your topic is an important thing to consider when writing.

1 2 3 4 5   6. I like to write.

1 2 3 4 5   7. The approach I'm using for writing now is a lot better than the approach I was using last year.

1 2 3 4 5   8. I am a good writer.

---

1 2 3 4 5   9. Before you actually start writing, creating an outline that shows the organization of the main points you will write about is important.

☐ I *almost never* make an outline before writing because:

☐ I *usually don't* make an outline before writing because:

☐ I *usually do* make an outline before writing, but when I don't, it's because:

(check all that apply to you)

___ I know the writing will be so short that an outline is not needed.
___ I'm not sure how to create outlines.
___ Outlining is too much trouble.
___ I usually forget to outline.
___ Outlining won't make a difference on my grade.

___ I can never think of ideas to note on the outline.
___ I'm not very good at outlining ideas before writing.
___ I usually don't have time to outline.
___ Nobody important will read what I have written.
___ I never end up following the outline anyway.

Other reason? _____

---

1 2 3 4 5   10. I think that editing and revising writing assignments are important.

☐ I *almost never* edit and revise my writing because:

☐ I *usually don't* edit and revise my writing because:

☐ I *usually do* edit and revise my writing, but when I don't, it's because:

(check all that apply to you)

___ I rarely need to edit and revise anything I write.
___ I'm not very good at editing or revising.
___ I usually don't have time to edit and revise.
___ I usually forget to edit and revise.
___ Editing and revising won't make a difference on my grade.

___ I'm not sure how to edit and revise.
___ Editing and revising are too much trouble.
___ Small writing mistakes don't matter.
___ Nobody important will read what I have written.
___ I usually catch mistakes and correct them as I write.

Other reason? _____

FIGURE 4.3   WRITING ATTITUDES SURVEY

Teachers can examine students' current level of content production with an informal assessment of an actual writing sample. They might obtain representative writing samples from the students by asking them to write a story about something that is interesting and motivating to them. For example, students may be shown an intriguing picture to write about or asked to write an account of an event they witnessed or in which they participated. The teacher also might provide students with a list of interesting topics and have them choose one about which to write. The following topics are suggested:

- How important is the amount of money you would make when selecting a career?
- Women should not be allowed to join the military service. Agree or disagree?
- Are insurance companies fair to charge more when the driver is a teenager?
- How old is too old to live with your parents?
- Members of the Rolling Stones are too old to be making rock albums. Agree or disagree?
- Which is a better age, 16 or 21?
- A person should have a job before getting married. Agree or disagree?
- Should couples who have children be allowed to get a divorce?
- During a date, should the guy pay for everything?
- Where is the best place to go on a first date?
- Should we allow other states to dump nuclear waste in our state?
- Should this state have stricter pollution laws?
- Do teachers get paid enough for their jobs? Why or why not?
- Computers eventually will take over everybody's jobs. Agree or disagree?
- Because many people don't bother to vote during elections, should we stop having elections for a while?
- Should we have fought the Vietnam War?
- You should turn in your parents to the police if they are using illegal drugs. Agree or disagree?
- Do you think teenagers should be allowed to see any movie they wish?
- If someone lies to you, should he/she be trusted ever again?
- Which is more important, the way somebody dresses or the way the person acts? Why?
- Should teenage couples be allowed to kiss at school?
- Should teachers be allowed to search your locker without your permission?
- Is it okay for a girl to ask a boy out on a date?
- Should students be required to pass a test to get a high school diploma?
- Divorce should be harder for parents to get. Agree or disagree?
- Anybody convicted of selling drugs should be put to death in the electric chair. Agree or disagree?
- Should teenagers who sell drugs be sent to prison?
- Should parents decide which television shows you are allowed to watch?
- Teenagers should have their own telephone. Agree or disagree.
- Is it fair for parents to give older brothers or sisters more money?
- Do you think that teaching students to "just say no" is a good solution to the drug problem?

- Parents should buy their teenager a car if he or she has a driver's license.
- Should parents decide how much television you are allowed to watch? Why or why not?
- Should 11-year-olds be allowed to babysit infants?

Students with LD should be allowed the time they need to complete the assignment.

Of equal importance is to obtain samples of students' writing from their other classes. The quantity and quality of students' writing may be quite different on assignments that have been structured to be highly motivating and interesting (e.g., During a date, should the guy have to pay?) than on tasks that have a more traditional academic focus (e.g., term paper). Also, the writing expectations vary greatly from school to school and even from class to class. Applebee (1986) noted that, although teachers often think in terms of teaching students how to write extended themes, the writing assignments in many schools tend to be a page or less. The assignments usually serve an evaluation purpose. Instruction in writing will be most effective if the type of writing being taught matches the type of writing that students are expected to produce (Putnam, Deshler, & Schumaker, 1993).

Engaging students in writing activities that closely match real-life purposes is an important point to consider. As discussed at the beginning of this chapter, students with LD often are grossly unprepared to deal with the writing demands of high school and later in the *real world*. Therefore, the more the teacher can use or create real writing situations the students encounter or will encounter in their daily activities, the more meaningful the assessment will be. An example of *authentic assessment* is to use actual themes the students have written in social studies or letters they have written and intend to send. In contrast, assignments for assessment purposes that are contrived and do not relate to students' real-life experiences may not reflect skills they can use independently.

Although students' written language can be assessed informally in many ways, three key methods are noted: (a) the writing profile, (b) holistic scoring used to evaluate the content of writing, and (c) component analysis to evaluate mechanical skills used in writing. All of these methods should be used in conjunction with *writing portfolios*, a systematic method of viewing students' progress over time. Together these methods can provide accurate evaluation of a student's writing and make assessment an ongoing part of the writing curriculum.

WRITING PROFILE

The profile form in Figure 4.4 has been developed to use in the informal assessment of groups of students or individuals. This profile enables the teacher to isolate students' specific writing problems and gain direction for more in-depth analysis of specific deficit areas.

Wallace and Larsen (1978) pointed out that the more mechanical components of written language (e.g., punctuation, capitalization, and spelling) lend themselves to objective assessment, but the more abstract components of written expression (e.g., content, organization) must be evaluated in relation to the student's experiential background and motivation to communicate.

Comments	Designator	Skill Area	
		Emotional blocks Motivation to write	ATTITUDE
		Description writing Relationship writing Explanatory writing Personal views	CONTENT
		Organizing ideas Vocabulary Building sentences Writing questions Notetaking Summaries Punctuation Capitalization Spelling Neatness Monitoring performance	CRAFT
		Test-taking skills	OTHER

Pupil's Name

Designators: A—performance on grade level
B—performance below grade level, but not critical
C—critical deficit area

FIGURE 4.4 PROFILE FORM FOR INFORMAL ASSESSMENT OF STUDENT WRITING SKILLS

The writing profile presents an overall rating of the attitude, content, and craft the student employs while writing. Although this is a general reflection of a student's level of functioning, the writing profile can be used to compile other assessment instruments to gain an overall perspective of the student's writing ability.

HOLISTIC SCORING USING ANCHOR SCORING METHOD

The anchor scoring method does not focus on quantifying specific error types but, rather, provides a more qualitative index of writing (Myers, 1980). The method can be used to provide an overall qualitative indicator, and to provide qualitative indices across specific dimensions of writing (e.g., ideas, style, organization, neatness, spelling, mechanics, sentence structure). Each dimension is exemplified by sets of descriptive statements called anchors, representing a range of 1 ("very poor") to 5 ("excellent") writing. Table 4.6 presents sets of descriptors used to evaluate the writing of middle school students with LD (Ellis, 1994a). An advantage of this approach is its flexibility. Descriptors can be developed for specific types of writing. For example, if evaluating students' book reports, the teacher can develop specific descriptors reflecting key elements of book reports as one of the dimensions to be evaluated. Teachers compare performance to the descriptors.

The writing profile and holistic scoring can be adapted in providing explicit writing strategy instruction. When beginning instruction in a specific strategy such as the ones suggested later in this chapter, teachers have to assess students' knowledge and use of the strategy. Evidence of strategic behaviors can be attained through:

1. *Direct observations.* Carefully observe students during the planning, producing, and editing process. Do students plan their writing by outlining ideas ahead of time? Do they revise sentences and correct errors as they write? After they have written a first draft, do they glance rapidly over their work, or do they appear to be more systematic in editing their work? Does any evidence indicate that they are attempting to edit their work for meaning? Evidence of editing for specific types of conventions-of-print errors?
2. *Analyzing students' work.* Look for evidence on the rough draft that students have found and corrected errors. Compare their current corrections to previous corrections on other samples.
3. *Interviews.* Ask students about what they did during the writing process, and ask them to tell what they were thinking as they were working. Dialogue must exist between students and teachers. It not only becomes a stimulus for idea generation and provides motivation, but it also gives teachers insight into the students' developing thought process.

COMPONENT ANALYSIS

The component analysis method (Schumaker, Nolan, & Deshler, 1985) allows teachers to evaluate specific types of written language errors and is used best for evaluating the craft or mechanical components of writing (see Figure 4.5). The method provides both quantitative scores for specific types of errors and an overall score reflecting the general

TABLE 4.6 SAMPLE ANCHOR SCORING CRITERIA

Characteristics	Scale				
	1	2	3	4	5
Ideas	• lacks coherency • rambling • ideas not well developed • lacks foundation, poor establishment of reader's background knowledge	• literal translation of topic • seems to have copied multiple sentences from another source • nothing seems to happen • ideas presented in list-like format (may be in a single sentence)	• imaginative ideas begin to emerge • main idea is carried through • ideas stated generally with little elaboration (e.g., one idea per sentence) • seems to have copied directly from another source (limited)	• well-developed, cohesive ideas • creative spark • consistent point of view • some idea elaboration, but inconsistent • "other source" ideas paraphrased	• well-developed, cohesive ideas • "other source" ideas paraphrased • obviously creative/researched • ideas presented in own words • ideas elaborated upon extensively • consistent point of view
Style	• limited vocabulary • general lack of adjectives • short, choppy sentences	• generally lacks attempts to go beyond common words	• attempts to use expanded vocabulary • some use of adjectives • stronger verb selections	• use of adjectives and adverbs • use of transitional words and phrases to help flow of writing • use of signal words (e.g., 1st, 2nd in comparison) to help reader comprehend message	• extensive use of adjectives and adverbs • use of transitional words and phrases to help flow of writing • use of signal words (e.g., 1st, 2nd in comparison) to help reader comprehend message • effective paragraph transitions
Organization	• lacks indention/paragraphing • lacks sequence	• has multiple paragraphs • generally indents	• lacks thesis statement • inconsistent use of explicit main idea statements	• thesis statement in first paragraph • main ideas usually stated clearly	• thesis paragraph • main ideas usually stated clearly *(continued)*

Table 4.6 (Continued)

Characteristics	Scale				
	1	2	3	4	5
	▪ lacks main ideas and supporting details	▪ lacks progression of ideas	▪ some main ideas inconsistent with overall implied thesis ▪ some supporting statements	▪ topic sentences follow thesis statement ▪ supporting details follow topic sentences	▪ topic sentences follow thesis statement ▪ supporting details follow topic sentences
Handwriting/ Neatness	▪ many words unreadable ▪ poor spacing ▪ messy	▪ generally not neat ▪ poor spacing ▪ inconsistencies in letter size, formation, and alignment ▪ shows disregard for margins ▪ some words unreadable	▪ no scratch-outs ▪ occasional spacing problem ▪ some erasure marks ▪ inconsistent margin	▪ generally neat ▪ sticks to margins ▪ spacing okay ▪ neat handwriting	▪ very clean paper ▪ very good handwriting ▪ very attractive work
Spelling	▪ many words unintelligible ▪ most words misspelled ▪ lacks sound symbol correspondence ▪ omits vowels	▪ misspells common words ▪ phonetic approach to spelling most words	▪ misspells common words occasionally ▪ attempts to spell difficult words are phonetic	▪ misspells few words ▪ generally successful attempts at spelling difficult words	▪ no words misspelled
Mechanical Conventions	▪ misuse of capitals ▪ lacks capitalization of proper nouns ▪ frequent capitals in middle of words ▪ lack of punctuation	▪ capitals at beginning of sentences ▪ inconsistent capitalization and end punctuation	▪ capitals at beginning of sentences ▪ occasional capital in middle of words or beginning of words in middle of sentences ▪ end marks used correctly	▪ uses a variety of mechanics well ▪ uses end marks other than periods ▪ uses commas in series	▪ few errors in mechanics ▪ generally proper use of commas for sophisticated sentences

(continued)

TABLE 4.6   (CONTINUED)

Characteristics	Scale				
	1	2	3	4	5
Grammar and Usage	▪ incorrect tense ▪ shift tense within composition ▪ frequent word omissions	▪ subject-verb agreement evident but inconsistent	▪ satisfactory subject-verb agreement (generally consistent) ▪ tense inconsistent	▪ good subject-verb agreement (generally consistent) ▪ tense generally consistent ▪ possessives used correctly	▪ few grammatical errors
Sentence Structure	▪ extensive sentence fragments and run-ons	▪ some awareness of sentence structure ▪ some sentence fragments ▪ little variance in sentence patterns	▪ some variance in sentence patterns ▪ most sentences declarative ▪ limited use of phrases ▪ no dependent clauses	▪ varied sentence patterns ▪ no sentence fragments or run-ons ▪ varied use of phrases and dependent clauses ▪ evidence of compound/complex sentences	▪ no sentence errors ▪ use of compound/complex sentences ▪ frequent use of sophisticated sentence structures

quality of the written product. The steps for using the component analysis method are:

COMPILING COMPONENT ANALYSIS

STEP 1   Decide which components of writing will be evaluated (e.g., sentences, punctuation, capitalization, spelling, appearance).

STEP 2   Construct a grid similar to the one illustrated in Figure 4.6. Indicate the areas to be targeted for evaluation on the left side of the grid. In our example we targeted paragraphs, sentences, punctuation, spelling, capitalization, and appearance. These or different skills may be targeted.

STEP 3   Collect a writing sample from students.

a. Provide students with a choice of topics about which to write (e.g., "Does the school have the right to search students' lockers?") and ask them to write, using a pencil, a minimum of a six-sentence paragraph about the topic. Ask them to do "as good a job as possible," but do not cue them specifically to search for and correct errors. Provide a dictionary, but do not cue them to use it to look up the spellings of words.

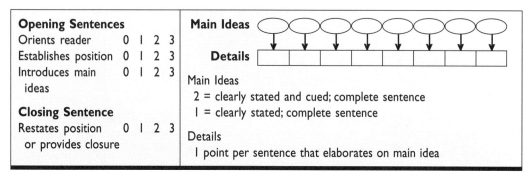

FIGURE 4.5   SAMPLE STRUCTURAL COMPONENTS SCORING FORM

	1	2	3	4	5	6	7	8	9	10	11	12	13	14	15	16	17	18	19	20	21	22	23	24	25	Totals
Paragraph																										
Sentence																										
Punctuation																										
Spelling																										
Capitalization																										
Appearance																										

FIGURE 4.6   SAMPLE WRITING MECHANICS SCORING FORM

Source: Adapted from *The Error Monitoring Strategy*, by J. B. Schumaker, S. M. Nolan, & D. D. Deshler, 1985, Lawrence: University of Kansas.

Note: As an alternative source for writing samples, collect copies of the students' actual written work from their content-area classes (e.g., science lab reports; social studies, language arts book reports). If you use these, make sure the student wrote the products independently and did not receive assistance in planning, producing, and editing the product.

b. After students have finished writing, give them a pen that marks in blue (or some color different from that used to write the sample), and ask them to use it to correct their work. *Without* identifying the specific types of errors they are to monitor and correct (e.g., capitalization, punctuation), encourage students to find and correct as many errors as they can. To gain some insight into how they go about the editing process, observe students as they edit. Tell students that you are not allowed to help them with the editing.

Note: Students use the colored ink pen so you can determine the types of errors students identify after they have been cued specifically to edit their work versus those they have failed to identify, even when cued to edit.

c. After they have finished editing, ask students to recopy their work as neatly as possible to produce a final draft. Have students turn in both the edited rough draft and the final draft.

Step 4 Collect the writing sample (both first draft and final copy), and then number the lines (not sentences) of writing (see Figure 4.7) on the final draft. The numbers on the top of the grid will correspond to the line numbers of the written product. Thus, column 1 on the grid will reflect any errors indicated in line #1 of the writing.

Note: Resist marking errors on the student's writing. The numbers you place next to the lines will be the only marks you make on the writing samples. This will allow you to follow up by having the student find and correct errors in each line of writing.

Step 5 Read the paper for meaning. Evaluate the student's flow of ideas, including how well ideas have been expressed and elaborated upon, and the logic by which they have been presented.

Step 6 On a line-by-line basis, evaluate the student's writing. Figure 4.7 illustrates our evaluation of the writing sample. Because the student misspelled one word in line #1, one spelling error is indicated.

Step 7 Total the scores of each type of error, and then add these scores together to calculate an overall total of errors.

Note: The scores of error types can be useful later when providing students with feedback regarding their performance. The errors are recorded on the grid, so there is no need to mark errors on the student's paper. Students can use the information on the grid to help them locate and correct their own errors. For example, using the feedback provided by the grid, our sample student would realize that somewhere in line #1 he has misspelled a word. The student can locate and correct these without the debilitating effect of excessive red correction ink.

CALCULATING OVERALL SCORE

Step 1 Calculate the total number of words (without regard to errors) the student has written.

Step 2 Divide the total number of errors by the total number of words written and then multiply by 100. This will produce a percentage score reflecting the student's overall performance relative to the areas evaluated.

Note: The overall performance score is not generated to produce a grade score but, rather, provide feedback. Students might plot their attained score on a graph indicating the desired level of performance, or "mastery." They then can judge how close their written performance is to the desired level of performance.

Note: Scores of specific error types also can be used to facilitate goal-setting activities. For example, if the student scored nine misspelled words, a goal of reducing this score to only four misspelled words might be set for the next written product.

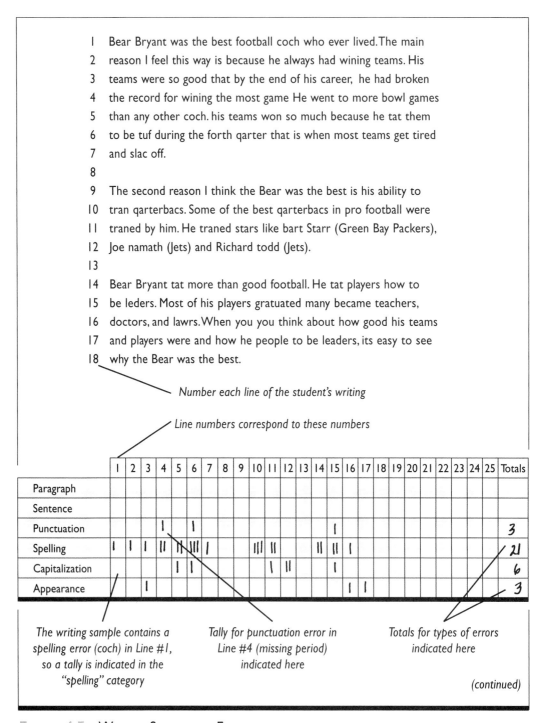

1   Bear Bryant was the best football coch who ever lived. The main
2   reason I feel this way is because he always had wining teams. His
3   teams were so good that by the end of his career, he had broken
4   the record for wining the most game He went to more bowl games
5   than any other coch. his teams won so much because he tat them
6   to be tuf during the forth qarter that is when most teams get tired
7   and slac off.
8
9   The second reason I think the Bear was the best is his ability to
10   tran qarterbacs. Some of the best qarterbacs in pro football were
11   traned by him. He traned stars like bart Starr (Green Bay Packers),
12   Joe namath (Jets) and Richard todd (Jets).
13
14   Bear Bryant tat more than good football. He tat players how to
15   be leders. Most of his players gratuated many became teachers,
16   doctors, and lawrs. When you you think about how good his teams
17   and players were and how he people to be leaders, its easy to see
18   why the Bear was the best.

Number each line of the student's writing

Line numbers correspond to these numbers

	1	2	3	4	5	6	7	8	9	10	11	12	13	14	15	16	17	18	19	20	21	22	23	24	25	Totals
Paragraph																										
Sentence																										
Punctuation				I		I								I												3
Spelling	I	I	I	II	III	IIII	I			III	II			II	II	I										21
Capitalization				I	I					I	II				I											6
Appearance			I														I	I								3

The writing sample contains a spelling error (coch) in Line #1, so a tally is indicated in the "spelling" category

Tally for punctuation error in Line #4 (missing period) indicated here

Totals for types of errors indicated here

(continued)

FIGURE 4.7   WRITING SAMPLE AND EVALUATION

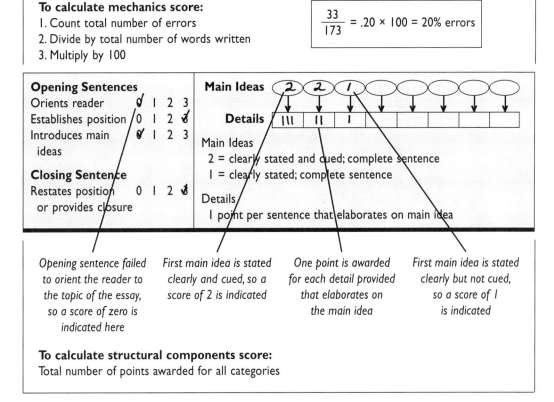

To calculate mechanics score:
1. Count total number of errors
2. Divide by total number of words written
3. Multiply by 100

$$\frac{33}{173} = .20 \times 100 = 20\% \text{ errors}$$

Opening Sentences
Orients reader   0̸ 1 2 3
Establishes position 0 1 2 3̸
Introduces main   0̸ 1 2 3
ideas

Closing Sentence
Restates position   0 1 2 3̸
or provides closure

Main Ideas   2 2 1

Details ||| || |

Main Ideas
  2 = clearly stated and cued; complete sentence
  1 = clearly stated; complete sentence

Details
  1 point per sentence that elaborates on main idea

Opening sentence failed to orient the reader to the topic of the essay, so a score of zero is indicated here

First main idea is stated clearly and cued, so a score of 2 is indicated

One point is awarded for each detail provided that elaborates on the main idea

First main idea is stated clearly but not cued, so a score of 1 is indicated

To calculate structural components score:
Total number of points awarded for all categories

FIGURE 4.7   CONTINUED

WRITING PORTFOLIOS

Assessment does not end with each writing sample. Assessment of the writing process should be viewed as an ongoing process continuing over weeks and months as an intricate part of the process. In addition to evaluating individual writing samples using the methods previously described, students' writing should be assessed as it evolves over time. An excellent method to gain this long-range perspective is to work with students to develop writing portfolios.

A writing portfolio is a *purposeful* collection of the student's writing (Graves & Sunstein, 1992). It contains pieces students select to represent their best work. Self-selection and the reflective process students use in making their selections are the core components of the writing portfolio. The end result should be a representative sampling of the writing skills the student has attained over time and the writing accomplishments the student judges to be significant. These portfolios may contain written products generated by the student in your class as well as those from other classes (e.g., social studies, language arts) as well. Because the portfolio is driven by individual choice, it changes throughout the year, becoming a dynamic collection. Students can learn a great deal about writing as they engage in compiling, reflecting upon, editing, and reassessing their writing when constructing their portfolios.

Some portfolio collections can be used for assessment purposes. Using the previously described assessment methods, each writing sample can be compared to a previous sample, and the teacher can observe changes in planning, text production, or editing components of the writing. In addition, each comparative sample can be judged according to the development and utilization of specific knowledge of the writing process. For example, growth might be documented in areas such as audience awareness, text structure, conventions of print, strategy use, and content knowledge.

The end result of the collection, selection, and reflection process is an individual portfolio that becomes a showcase of achievement for the student, similar to an artist's, photographer's, or stockbroker's portfolio. The writing portfolio should include a variety of writing samples, including all forms of writing required of the student in all his or her courses (e.g., notetaking, short answer, essays, reports, content area writing assignments). The portfolio will become a mirror of the writing curriculum.

The writing portfolio presents the student as writer, and it can take many forms. The portfolio can be compiled into a notebook with a table of contents, organized into file folders complete with revisions and reflections, or even displayed in video or audio forms. Whatever format the teacher and students choose to develop should reflect the care and effort involved in this long-term process. The portfolio becomes a document to celebrate. For the adolescent with LD, the portfolio becomes visible evidence of competence and growing writing skills.

Maintaining the long-term process of portfolio development affords many opportunities to increase dialogue among students, teachers, and peers. The verbal interaction in this reflective process is an important motivator for some students. They can become involved in self-reflection as they continually reassess their own work and also converse with others about the nature of the writing process itself (incorporating dialogue into the writing process will be addressed in more detail later in the chapter).

With students, establish your criteria for specific types of writing assignments in the portfolio. Having a criteria tends to raise the level of students' writing because it provides an effective goal-setting forum. One set of criteria for developing a writing portfolio was used by the Vermont Portfolio Project in 1991–92 (Abruscato, 1993). The following criteria were used to frame the writing portfolios for students in 4th and 8th grades. Teachers can expand or adapt the list to reflect the writing program.

The Vermont Portfolio includes two types of products: (a) a collection of six pieces of writing done by the student during the academic year; and (b) a "uniform writing assessment," a formal writing assignment given by all teachers to all students at the grade level.

Examining a student's writing portfolio reveals the following:

1. A table of contents
2. A "best piece"
3. A letter
4. A poem, short story, play, or personal narrative

5. A personal response to a cultural, media, or sports exhibit or event or to a book, current issue, math problem, or scientific phenomenon
6. One prose piece from any curriculum area other than English or language arts (for 4th-graders) and three prose pieces from any curriculum area other than English or language arts (for 8th-graders)
7. The piece produced in response to the uniform writing assessment, as well as related outlines, drafts, and so on

Students can include all revisions with the most recent draft of a writing project. Likewise, the teacher may ask the students to include any written communication between the teacher and the students. Some teachers have found that using mailing labels to document their comments to students is an excellent method of collecting a variety of comments for the portfolio efficiently without having to rewrite their notes. As teachers interact with individual students during conferences or informally, they date and record anecdotal comments on the mailing labels. The labels then are attached to specific pieces of writing or compiled on anecdotal record sheets for the portfolio. The teacher's written comments are useful in documenting growth and can serve as specific examples when discussing progress with students, their parents, and other teachers.

When teachers begin incorporating the writing portfolio into instruction, they may find it to be challenging and time-consuming. Once teachers have gained experience using this technique, they probably will find that it becomes much easier and that the benefits far outweigh the demands.

MOTIVATION AND THE WRITING PROCESS

Why do some students persevere when writing and others avoid writing any way they can? Many students seem to expend more energy trying to avoid writing than in completing the actual writing assignment. In this section several dimensions of motivation with particular attention to ways the environment may impede or facilitate motivation are discussed.

REWARDING STUDENTS FOR WRITING

Students may engage in a writing task when they anticipate receiving external rewards. For example, students often are more willing to expend effort when they anticipate receiving praise or other social rewards when others read the product.

In almost every secondary school the incentive to engage in writing is based on extrinsic rewards (i.e., grades), and, regrettably, many students with LD engage in writing primarily to avoid negative consequences that failing grades can produce. Although extrinsic rewards can be effective motivators for students with long histories of success, extrinsic reward structure may be counterproductive for some students with LD because these "incentives" actually may induce "failure-avoidance" (Ellis, 1986). Some students may not be willing to express their ideas and opinions in writing because they want to avoid receiving low grades for their lack of skill. By the time many students with LD have left elementary school, a clearly defined pattern of avoidance and passive engagement has developed (U.S. Department of Education, 1992). A variety of ways to facilitate motivation to write, other than by using grades, are discussed below.

MAKING WRITING A SOCIAL EVENT

The purpose of writing is inherently social—to communicate to others. The more like a social event the process of writing is (e.g., having students work together to plan and produce work, read drafts to each other, edit each other's work), the more likely students will perceive their writing as having an authentic audience and a real purpose. Having peers respond to the meaning of what they have written enables students to learn what works and what does not work in their writing (Graham et al., 1991). For example, when another student, rather than the teacher, indicates that a student's paragraph is clear or unclear, the impact upon the writer can be powerful. Peer review also emphasizes writing as a communication process in which the audience is important, rather than writing as an isolated task that one does only for a grade. At its best, peer response is conducted in an environment that encourages flexibility and communication about issues that are significant to the students.

DiPardo and Freeman (1988) conducted an extensive review of research on peer response groups in the writing classroom. Their findings indicate a clear difference between peer groups operating under teacher-mandated guidelines and those in which students were allowed to be empowered as decision makers. Peer response has to be more than teacher-controlled and teacher-initiated interactions. They suggested that peer interaction be conducted in an environment that is flexible to the spontaneous nature of students, one that fosters discussion about issues of true importance to them. To establish this type of class setting, the teacher becomes a guide, offering opportunities for students to solicit feedback from each other. The teacher's role becomes less intrusive and more focused on the dynamic interaction between peers that can produce a most powerful effect on the students as writers. The following sections present several other formats of writing instruction that utilize social interaction in the writing process.

USING WRITERS' CIRCLES AND WRITERS' CONFERENCES

Jochum (1991) described two methods of fostering social response in the writing process: writers' circles and writers' conferences. The formats of the two are similar, but they imply different contexts. Writers' circles could involve the whole class for "share meetings" in which several students share their writing with the class. The writer then calls on listeners for questions and other responses. Groups of writers' circles could be established, involving pairs or small groups who read each others' writing and respond either verbally or in writing.

Writers' conferences usually begin with the teacher and the student as the primary participants. These conferences are more formal and can be conducted as part of the prewriting instruction, revision, or part of a final sharing and response activity. The teacher and the writer reflect more on the ideas and purpose of the writing than on the mechanics. Conferences can be expanded to include other students. Regardless of the context, as teachers incorporate social response into their writing instruction, the key is to leave the writer in control of his or her work.

Using the "Compliment Sandwich"

Students do not know how to respond to each other's writing naturally. Therefore, Jochum (1991) developed a strategy for teaching students to respond to each other's writing. Responders use this strategy to construct a "compliment sandwich." The listener follows the response format to focus the writer on the message the piece intends to communicate. This strategy opens the door for continuing positive interaction between the writer and an audience.

The basic steps for the responder are: *learn, wonder,* and *like*. After either reading or listening to the written piece, responders first state what they learned through the writing. Second, the responders ask a question or concern they have about the writing. To close the process, the responders tell the writer something they liked or appreciated about the content, presentation, or organization of the writing. The goal is for students to learn to engage in constructive interaction instead of demoralizing criticism.

Using Peer Editors

Stoddard and MacArthur (1993) investigated the effectiveness of students' revisions of their writing as a result of integrating explicit strategy instruction, peer response, and word processing. Students were paired to help each other revise their writing. The strategy used consisted of two parts: (a) Students were asked to focus on the content and message of each other's writing; (b) The "peer editor" was given instructions to

— listen carefully while the writer read the written piece aloud,
— tell the writer what aspect he or she liked best about the piece,
— reread the piece on their own,
— ask the revision questions (listed below), and make notes on the draft,
— discuss his or her suggestions with the writer.

The basic procedure was reciprocal as each student took on the role of peer editor and then writer. The revision questions were:

■ *Parts?* Does it have a good beginning, middle, and end?
■ *Order?* Does it follow a logical sequence?
■ *Detail?* Where could more details be added?
■ *Clarity?* Is any part hard to understand?

After receiving the peer editors' feedback, the writers made revisions using a computer, then the pairs met again to edit each other's papers from a different perspective. The second part of the editing involved peer editors' evaluation of the mechanics of the writing (e.g., punctuation, spelling). Feedback again was given to the writers, and another revision followed. The students were given explicit instruction in the revision strategies. Peer interaction provided the appropriate social context for applying and practicing the strategies and also regulating use of the strategies. The teacher constructed the initial dialogue, but the students then used the internalized dialogue and presented it from their individual perspectives.

Using Cooperative Learning

Ellis and Feldman (1994) described a teaching model promoting "cognitive literacy" using the key elements of cooperative learning and cognitively based strategy instruction. The model used a writing strategy that guides students through the stages of prewriting (think ahead), production (think during), and revision (think back).

This strategy is used in conjunction with several different types of cooperative learning activities. Some cooperative learning formats focus on cultivating skills using the specific aspects of the strategy. Others are designed to facilitate understanding of complex ideas and concepts. Table 4.7 lists a variety of cooperative activities that correspond to the general instructional stages of orienting, framing, applying, and extending. (See Ellis & Feldman, 1994, for more detailed information about this combination of strategy instruction and cooperative learning.) The skillful selection of appropriate cooperative groupings for the lesson is essential to the success of this approach.

Incorporating all or some of these social interaction processes is likely to strengthen extrinsic motivation. Personal satisfaction (intrinsic motivation) is another essential aspect of motivation necessary for students to develop a sense of empowerment about writing.

Facilitating Personal Satisfaction

Enabling students to experience personal satisfaction from writing, to feel self-confident enough to write independently, should be one of the most important goals with regard to motivation (Spaulding, 1992). An example might be the student who becomes excited about poetry and begins to write and share personal poems written outside of class. This student has used certain skills independently to compose the poems and has then taken the initiative to share the results with others. One form of written expression common with adolescents but often disapproved of in school is writing and passing notes to other students, but this is an excellent example of students' intrinsic motivation. Despite the barriers or possible negative consequences, students write and pass notes skillfully and often ingeniously. When students engage in these types of tasks independently, they are expressing the self-confidence to use writing as a personal form of expression and communication.

Most writers with LD lack the confidence to engage in personally satisfying writing. As discussed previously, these students generally have limited knowledge of the process or components needed for successful writing, which produces a perceived sense of incompetence. Increasing their initial productivity, expanding their knowledge base, developing their vocabulary, and reinforcing their ownership of their writing can facilitate confidence to engage independently in the writing process.

Increasing Productivity via "Free-Writing"

For adolescents with LD who are hesitant to express their ideas in writing, the first goal is to increase productivity. Adolescents with LD should be encouraged to develop their ideas and not be concerned initially with the mechanical components of writing. Teachers can encourage students to make the content more important than the form in the beginning. Although correct capitalization, punctuation, and spelling are essential com-

TABLE 4.7 SUMMARY OF ISI INSTRUCTIONAL STAGES, GENERAL PURPOSE, AND EXAMPLES

Stage	Instructional Emphasis	General Purpose	Sample Cooperative Learning Activities
Orienting	Orienting students to ways of processing information. Teaching content strategically; providing an experiential base for key information processes/strategies, but not explicitly teaching these processes.	Teacher uses general-to-specific graphic organizer when addressing to-be-learned content information; students learn how information can be structured in general-to-specific format and how to construct these types of graphic organizers.	*Think-pair-share.* Students engage in dialogue to summarize key content information, prioritize in terms of relevance or importance. Modified *"jigsaw."* Students are given partially completed graphic organizer (main ideas listed); students conduct research and fill in details; team then teaches other members their findings.
Framing	Framing student's background knowledge of related information-processing tactics into a specific cognitive strategy.	Teacher describes the steps of the writing strategy, discusses rationale for its use, and suggests situations and settings in which it can be used. Teacher models the strategy steps using think-aloud techniques.	*Think-pair-share.* Identify various situations and settings where using the strategy would be beneficial; identify how the writing strategy ties in with knowledge of the graphic organizer used to learn content. *Modified group investigation.* Students engage in dialogue to identify components of the strategy that are similar and those that are different from what they usually do when writing.

(continued)

TABLE 4.7   CONTINUED

Stage	Instructional Emphasis	General Purpose	Sample Cooperative Learning Activities
Applying	Applying the strategy to meet task demands of content course. Integrating use of the strategy with ongoing instruction in content.	Teacher collaborates with students in writing tasks related to content of the course; designs learning activities that integrate use of graphic organizers and the writing strategy with acquiring an understanding of the content; integrates cues to use the writing strategy with writing tasks e.g., Draw a graphic organizer that illustrates three reasons why Columbus went home in chains on his last voyage. Include related facts. Explain these reasons using PASS.	*Team writing about content taught.* CL teams use completed organizers to write about content previously mediated by teacher. *Group investigation with writing assignment.* Teams investigate information related to specific topic; collaborate to create graphic organizer; use graphic organizer to share findings with class, and plan and write report.
Extending	Using what was learned about the cognitive strategy as a basis for understanding new applications; creating and using new strategies.	Teacher extends writing strategy and graphic organizer to use with other information formats—compare/contrast, cause/effect, etc. Teacher extends writing strategy to other problem domains by collaborating with students to create a new version of the cognitive literacy strategy; in this case, they work together to create an editing version of PASS.	*Group investigation: Research and evaluation.* CL teams engage in writing projects related to content of the class and experiment with editing version of the cognitive literacy strategy; engage in team editing of writing assignments; teams share results, refine strategy as needed.

Source: From "Creating 'Thought-Full' Classrooms: Fostering Cognitive Literacy via Cooperative Learning and Integrated Strategy Instruction," by E. S. Ellis and K. Feldman, 1994, in *Handbook of Cooperative Learning Methods* (pp. 157–176), New York: Praeger.

ponents of effective communication, they should be emphasized only after these adolescents feel comfortable with written assignments. Too frequently, adolescents with LD have had their greatest failures in trying to achieve perfection in the mechanics of writing at the expense of expressing their ideas.

Elbow (1973) suggested that students engage in "free-writing" exercises at least three times a week. In this method students are encouraged simply to write for 10 minutes. They are instructed to write as quickly as they can, never to stop and look back over their writing, never to correct the spelling of any word, or even to think about what they are doing. The objective is to have students put on paper whatever is in their mind. The only requirement is to never stop during the 10-minute period. Although some teachers have found that students enjoy keeping these papers as a journal of what is happening in their lives, Elbow maintained that the major advantage of free-writing is that it does not allow students to edit their work. He contended that compulsive and premature editing by students inhibits their ability to produce ideas.

Editing is introduced and required of students after they become at ease with putting down words on paper. Teachers have to remember, however, that even though free-writing exercises may help overcome writing anxiety and increase productivity, they do not necessarily improve writing along other dimensions (e.g., organization and flow of ideas, sentence structure, mechanics). Thus, free-writing should *not* become a substitute for writing instruction. Explicit instruction in writing strategies is necessary for most students with LD to develop true competence, but free-writing can be an initial activity used to stimulate reluctant writers.

INCREASING PRODUCTIVITY VIA TECHNOLOGY

Difficulty translating thoughts into printed words can be frustrating for students who are attempting to write. Using a tape recorder or computer with specialized software may be beneficial in generating ideas and producing spoken words that can be translated to printed form.

At first students can simply record their impressions using the tape recorder. Prompting them to talk like the report would sound if they were reading may be helpful. The teacher then types or writes these statements for students so they have a written record of their thoughts. On review, they can decide how to improve the flow, organization, and presentation of their ideas. Later, students can produce skeletal outlines and use these as they tape-record ideas under each heading.

Though expensive at this time, computer-assisted technology is available that will translate students' spoken words into written text. For example, DragonDictate-30K by Dragon Systems allows a student to input spoken words, and the computer then translates this speech into written text. The text then is edited using a word processing program with spell-checking and style-checking capabilities.

The computer has the potential of becoming an important writing tool for some adolescents with LD. Although the word-processing and publishing programs can produce attractive written pieces, the difficulty created by limited accessibility and students' command of adequate computer skills must be bridged before computers can be a help rather than a hindrance. Writing programs like the one described earlier (Stoddard & MacArthur,

1993), combining an explicit instructional program with the use of computers for composing final drafts, have been shown to be beneficial.

ENSURING A SUFFICIENT KNOWLEDGE BASE TO WRITE

Writing is a process best accomplished when specific strategies are used to develop the student's knowledge base before writing. If students think they have something to write about, they likely will be more motivated to do the assignment. Ensuring that students have sufficient knowledge of the subject matter about which they are going to write will help develop their self-confidence and enhance intrinsic motivation. This can be achieved by exposing students to a broad array of experiences to enlarge their pool of knowledge. The teacher can:

— provide students with firsthand experiences as a basis from which to develop writing ideas (e.g., field trips, resource materials).
— review information about the topic just prior to the writing assignment, and develop a visual representation to follow (e.g., graphic organizer, story web).
— allow students to express their ideas through nonverbal and dramatic activity (e.g., art, drama).
— provide students with ample opportunity to talk about their ideas before, during, and after writing.

ESTABLISHING A WRITING COMMUNITY

Bos (1988) recommended that teachers establish a "writing community" in the classroom that encourages ownership. This model was developed with older elementary students, but its components have implications for adolescents.

1. Provide opportunities for sustained writing.
   - Allow time to think, reflect, and write.
   - Make sure writing occurs regularly.
   - Allow written pieces to be developed over several class periods.
2. Establish a writing environment.
   - Create a sense of independence in your students.
   - Provide an environment rich with writing resources (e.g., dictionaries, books, magazines).
3. Establish a writing community.
   - Authorize individual students as "experts" in a given aspect of writing (e.g., idea generator, speller, plot master, listener, synonym finder).
   - Encourage students to use classroom "experts" as a writing resource.
4. Create a constructive atmosphere.
   - Promote listening, questioning, and observing.
   - Keep criticism out of evaluation.
5. Encourage students to take risks.
   - Allow students to experiment with different ways of expressing ideas.
   - Provide students with a variety of writing tools (e.g., colored pens, assorted paper, computer, typewriter).

This model provides opportunities for sustained writing activities by allowing longer periods to plan, draft, and revise. The classroom becomes a community composed of students with various areas of expertise. Some students take on the role of expert idea generator or expert speller. Others are encouraged to consult these student experts regarding specific writing needs. Establishing a writing community also creates an atmosphere in which students can take risks and experiment with their writing. As specific writing strategies are taught, students are encouraged to adapt them to their writing needs. Student ownership of the writing process evolves as more responsibility for controlling the writing process is afforded the students. Writers make their own decisions, with the input of others, by directing the writing process.

Using Instructional Scaffolding Approach

Another example of a writing program that supports student ownership of the writing process was described by Applebee and Langer (1983). Writing and reading skills competencies are taught in context using the support or scaffolding of more skilled writers. This support is withdrawn gradually as the student internalizes the skills. The criteria used to develop the appropriate instructional scaffold include five aspects of natural language learning:

1. *Intentionality:* The task has a clear overall purpose driving any separate activity that may contribute to the whole. Eventual evaluation of students' success can be cast in terms of what they intended to accomplish.
2. *Appropriateness*: Instructional tasks pose problems that can be solved with help but that students could not successfully complete on their own. The most appropriate tasks will be those that involve abilities that have not yet matured but are in the process of maturation.
3. *Structure:* Modeling and questioning activities are structured around a model of appropriate approaches to the task and lead to a natural sequence of thought and language.
4. *Collaboration:* The teacher's response to student work recasts and expands upon the students' efforts without rejecting what they have accomplished on their own. The teacher's primary role is collaborative rather than evaluative.
5. *Internalization:* External scaffolding for the activity is gradually withdrawn as the patterns are internalized by the students. (p. 170)

The first three principles address the development of competencies through instructional activities that have a clear overall purpose, are appropriate to the students' emerging skills, and provide structure through modeling and questioning activities. The last two principles of collaboration and internalization focus on students' developing ownership of the writing process.

Rather than give writing assignments that the students can complete independently, assignments are given that require support to complete. For example, a teacher might have a student read two different accounts of an historic event and then compare and contrast the two viewpoints. The student may not have the skills to complete a compare/contrast writing assignment independently, but with adequate support the student can complete the task. The following steps comprise this instructional approach:

1. The teacher models the writing process, using natural dialogue and questions to define the message the student wants to express.
   (The teacher's role is to prompt and ask questions to help the student think through the comparison and plan his or her writing, suggest words to use, and so on.)
2. The teacher expands upon the student's efforts without rejecting or correcting his or her work. (At this stage the student begins to take control of the process using what he or she determines is most appropriate.)
3. Last, as the student exhibits command of the process needed to write in a compare/contrast format, the teacher withdraws guidance gradually.

FACILITATING GOAL SETTING

Another component that can foster intrinsic motivation involves goal setting and self-determination. Graham et al. (1991) noted that the teacher can increase the possibility of students' viewing themselves as responsible for their writing when they are allowed to decide the topic and what and how much they have to say about it. These choices lead to higher levels of commitment and interest.

Facilitating goal setting can be a powerful tool for improving the writing performance of students (Johnson & Graham, 1990). Working with students to establish goals for their writing not only gives the student a focus for writing but also provides a measure for the student to use in evaluation as a target. You should focus on two types of goals: product and process. Product goals are directed to the end results (e.g., "I will write a two-page essay on the life of General George Patton" or "I will expand my report on General Patton to include his childhood." In contrast, process goals involve the processes the student goes through to achieve the product goal (e.g., "I will use a variety of sources as I collect information about General Patton" or "I intend to use an editing strategy during rewriting"). Teachers can incorporate goal setting as part of the teacher-student dialogue, peer discussion, or structured conferences. For example, during the prewriting stage, pairs of students could work together to establish goals for using a given strategy. During subsequent meetings the pairs can evaluate and discuss their use of the goals.

Writing instruction should begin with motivation and move on to skill development. Teachers should be sensitive to students' self-confidence, ownership, and social response. Motivating students to write is not something that happens only at the beginning but, rather, should be ongoing throughout the writing experience. Students with LD may appear confident with one writing task and then shift their attitude abruptly on a subsequent assignment. Therefore, specific activities may have to be used periodically to maintain students' motivation.

INSTRUCTION OF SPECIFIC WRITING STRATEGIES

Teaching explicit strategies and the self-regulation of those strategies is the heart of a successful writing program for adolescents with LD. Supporting the student in the writing process by teaching specific strategies that will address the students' needs is important. The remainder of this chapter is directed to writing strategy instruction in three key areas: (a) sentence writing, (b) paragraph and essay writing, and (c) editing and revising. These strategies are most successful when taught in conjunction with the assessment and motivational methods discussed previously.

Sentence-Writing Strategy: PENS

Instruction in sentence writing often is conducted by having students identify complete and incomplete sentences in textbook examples or by marking students' incomplete sentences in their written work. In both cases the assumption is that students will transfer their knowledge about sentences to the new sentences they construct in their writing.

Students need to recognize a complete thought and become comfortable analyzing their own writing. One of the simplest ways to help students when their sentences are illogical or worded poorly is for them to hear the sentences read aloud. The teacher can read back a passage to a student, or the student can read the passage into a tape recorder and then listen to it. When the student pauses at the end of a complete thought, the teacher can ask, "Why did you stop there?" This will give the student practice reflecting on why the thought was complete.

Simple, telegraphic-type sentences often do not constitute material that is read easily. Students who have only one sentence pattern (a simple sentence) should be taught how to combine sentences. An example is:

> Living things need energy.
> Energy comes directly from the sun.
> Energy comes indirectly from the sun.
>
> *combined to read:*
>
> The energy needed by all living things comes directly or indirectly from the sun.
> (Laurence, 1972, p. 72).

The purpose is not for the student to make the writing complex by writing longer sentences but, rather, to make it readable and to communicate ideas more effectively. In the above example the student has reworked and manipulated the short sentences to create a clearer, more readable statement for the reader. Ultimately, students with LD should understand and know sentence production strategies so well that they perform these automatically without conscience effort. To reach this point many students benefit from explicit instruction in a task-specific strategy for writing sentences. The strategy intervention should ensure that students gain an understanding of different ways to express ideas within the bounds of acceptable sentence structures.

Students need to construct a variety of sentences. Sentence formulas can establish a framework for constructing and evaluating different sentence constructs. In their sentence-writing strategy Schumaker and Sheldon (1985) developed a series of basic formulas for writing sentences. Students first learn the formulas for writing simple sentences or independent clauses (see Table 4.8). Once the student has mastered the ability to produce various types of independent clauses based on these formulas, this knowledge is expanded to address formulas for writing compound, complex, and compound-

TABLE 4.8   SENTENCE TYPES BASED ON KNOWLEDGE OF INDEPENDENT CLAUSES

Type of Sentence	Examples
Simple sentences—one independent clause*	*formula sample sentence* SV Jack was incredibly tired. SSV Sam and I could not believe his story. SVV Jack had run up the mountain and fallen off a cliff. SSVV The man and woman sat Jack up and gave him something to drink.
Compound sentences—two independent clauses joined by a coordinating conjunction	Jack was incredibly tired, *so* he went to bed. Sam and I could not believe his story, *and* he continued to lie about it. Jack had run up the mountain and fallen off a cliff, *but* he was not hurt. The man and woman sat Jack up and gave him something to drink, *and* he recovered quickly. (*so, and,* and *but* are coordinating conjunctions)
Complex sentences—one independent clause combined with a dependent clause**	Jack was incredibly tired *because* he had worked so hard. -or- *Because* he had worked so hard, Jack was incredibly tired. Sam and I could not believe his story, *although* he continued to tell it. -or- *Although* he continued to tell it, Sam and I could not believe his story. (*because* and *although* are subordinating conjunctions)
Compound-complex sentences—two independent clauses combined with a dependent clause	Sam and I could not believe his story, *so* we laughed at him. -or- *Although* he continued to tell it, Sam and I could not believe his story, *so* we laughed at him. *Because* he had worked so hard, Jack was incredibly tired, *and* he went to bed right away.

   * An independent clause has a subject and verb and makes a complete thought.
  ** A dependent clause is an independent clause with a subordinating conjunction in front of it.

complex sentences. In this intervention, students use their knowledge of these formulas and types of sentences in conjunction with the PENS sentence-writing strategy.

Although only a limited amount of research has been done on sentence-writing interventions for adolescents with LD, Schumaker and Sheldon (1985) demonstrated that teaching adolescents with LD the sentence-writing strategy improved both the technical correctness of students' sentences and the sophistication of sentence structures significantly. Before the intervention the students in the study typically wrote incomplete and simple subject-verb sentences. Following instruction in the sentence-writing strategy students produced a variety of simple, compound, complex, and compound-complex sentences in paragraph format. In addition, the students were more fluent. The sentences they produced often were more complex and technically correct than those of their same-age, normally achieving counterparts.

The sentence-writing strategy PENS follows two key steps.

1. Present understandings of sentence structure in a developmental fashion.
2. As these understandings become more sophisticated, teach students to apply their knowledge of sentence structure using the sentence-writing strategy to produce paragraphs.

Although research shows that traditional instruction in grammar usually does not improve writing skills, instruction in specific grammar knowledge (e.g., subject, verbs of sentences) *paired* with instruction in a strategy for using this knowledge can be effective. In the sentence-writing strategy, students first learn to write independent clauses or simple subject-verb sentences. Once they are able to write a variety of complete simple sentences in a paragraph-like format, instruction expands their knowledge of how independent clauses can be used to write more sophisticated sentences. They learn to join independent clauses to form compound sentences, then to create dependent clauses and join them with independent clauses to form complex sentences, and finally to use independent and dependent clauses to form compound-complex sentences. Finally, all types of sentences are combined to form paragraphs.

As students gain an understanding of each sentence structure, they learn to apply this knowledge using the strategy. The strategy steps illustrated at the top of Figure 4.8 were developed by Schumaker and Sheldon (1985). The steps presented at the bottom of this figure are an adapted version by Ellis. The adaptations are designed to be consistent with the Flowers and Haynes (1980) writing process of planning, producing, and reviewing. As students' knowledge of various sentence structures increases, they learn to apply the strategy at increasingly sophisticated levels.

Students' knowledge of sentence structure can be assessed using the assessment procedures described earlier in the chapter. You should teach the sentence-writing strategy if the following two conditions exist: (a) a student's writing consists primarily of short, choppy sentences, incomplete sentences, or run-on sentences; and (b) when cued to correct sentences, the student cannot do so without assistance. If students can correct sentences readily without help, the problem may be more related to motivation, monitoring, or editing than to a lack of sentence-writing knowledge. In these cases, instruction in an error-monitoring strategy may be more productive.

To begin teaching students the sentence-writing strategy, students' knowledge of subjects and verbs is reviewed thoroughly (or taught if necessary). Although instruction in other parts of speech is not necessarily advocated, basic knowledge of subjects and verbs is often a necessary prerequisite knowledge for subsequent sentence-writing instruction. Simple formulas are used to illustrate basic sentence structures. Essentially, students first learn how to write a simple sentence, or independent clause, containing a single subject and verb (e.g., "The boy went home"). Then they learn how to write simple sentences that contain compound subjects (e.g., "The boy and girl went home"), compound verbs (e.g., "The boy went home and washed his face"), or both compound subjects and verbs (e.g., "The boy and girl went home and washed their faces").

Original PENS steps

Pick a formula.

▽

Explore words to fit the formula.

▽

Note the words.

▽

Subject-verb identification.

   Look for the action or state-of-being word(s) to find the verb.
   Ask the "who or what question" to find the subject.

Source: From "The Sentence Writing Strategy: Instructor's Manual," by J. Schumaker & J. Sheldon, 1985, Lawrence: University of Kansas.

Ellis's suggested adaptation of PENS steps

Preview ideas

   Think about what you want to say.

▽

Explore words

   Identify the key words you will need in the sentence.

▽

Note words in complete sentence

   Write out the sentence.
   Be sure to capitalize the first word and punctuate the sentence.

▽

See if sentence is okay

   Make sure it makes sense.
   Select verb or verbs.
   Ask yourself who or what is doing verb/verbs.
   Check to see if sentence fits a formula.

FIGURE 4.8   PENS SENTENCE WRITING STRATEGY

INSTRUCTION IN SIMPLE SENTENCES

To enable students to produce different types of simple sentences, instruction should progress from discrimination activities to production activities. Discrimination activities are designed to enable the student to distinguish examples of simple sentences from nonexamples. They do not actually generate sentences but, rather, analyze sentences that someone else writes. Later, during production activities, students produce their own sentences. The five steps of this instructional sequence are listed below.

STEP 1   Students analyze simple sentences written by the teacher, mark the subjects and verbs, and write the formulas that represent each sentence's structure. For example:

Sentence (provided by teacher)	Formula (identified by student)
David and his brother went sailing.	*SSV*
The wind blew the boat over.	*SV*
The two boys swam to the beach and got help.	*SVV*

STEP 2   Students practice discriminating between simple sentences and nonsentences generated by the teacher. For example:

Sentence (or fragments written by teacher)	Formula (identified by student)
I was really tired last night.	*SV*
Woke up in the middle of the night.	*Nonsentence*
I drank some warm milk and went back to bed.	*SVV*
Slept until noon.	*Nonsentence*
Woke up feeling tired.	*Nonsentence*

STEP 3   Students are given a simple sentence structure formula and the beginning of a sentence. They then complete the sentence so it matches the given formula. For example:

Formula (provided by teacher)	Sentence (teacher-started, student-completed)
SV	John _made a tree house_.
SVV	Jill's father ran _and jumped in the water._
SSV	My best friend _and I hate girls_.

STEP 4   Students are given only sentence formulas. Students then write sentences that match the formula. For example:

Formula (provided by teacher)	Sentence (generated by student)
SSV	_Bob and Mary studied hard for the test_.
SVV	_Bob got nervous and panicked_.
SSVV	_Sam and Ed studied and still flunked the test_.

STEP 5   Up to this point teachers have been teaching prerequisite knowledge needed for application of the PENS strategy. Now instruction shifts from developing in the students a knowledge of sentence structure to how to use this knowledge when communicating to others in writing. You will have to describe the steps in PENS and model its use. In addition, you should promote student verbal elaboration of PENS. Finally, stu-

dents should practice writing short paragraphs that contain a variety of the four simple types of sentences. They should continue practicing writing these paragraphs until they can produce, without assistance, paragraphs that contain no sentence errors. For example:

> My best friend is from South America. Her name is Mandy. Mandy and I take walks and watch birds. She teases and laughs with me a lot. Mandy and I have a good time together. We have seen cardinals and blue jays. Mandy always flaps her arms like wings when we see a bird.

STEP 6   The purpose of this step is to begin to promote generalization of the PENS strategy, albeit limited to writing different types of simple sentences. Although instruction in generalizing the strategy will become more intense later, students should be encouraged to write different types of simple sentences when completing various written assignments from their other classes, and the teacher should provide them with feedback regarding how well they are using the strategy. Once students have mastered the four types of independent clauses thoroughly and can write short paragraphs using them, instruction shifts to teaching students to combine independent clauses and form compound sentences.

Essentially the same instructional procedure as that described below is utilized as students learn to write using increasingly more sophisticated sentence structures.* The teacher can employ a variety of tactics to promote generalization of the strategy. Three of the most important are (a) creating the expectation that the strategy will be generalized, (b) providing cues in the criterion environment to use the strategy, and (c) providing students with feedback regarding how well they are using the strategy in other settings (Schmidt, Deshler, Schumaker, & Alley, 1989). The recommendations below are adapted from Schumaker and Sheldon (1985).

1. Review situations and settings in which the strategy to write sophisticated sentences is applicable. Review cues that occur in these environments that may signal the need to use the strategy (e.g., the teacher signals the need for high quality writing by saying: "This week you'll be working on writing a letter to the editor of the town paper concerning the new policy about prohibiting dances at the City Hall Auditorium").
2. Have students create cue cards depicting the strategy steps and the various sentence-writing formulas, and insert them in their writing notebook. Use these to remind students that they possess a strategy for writing sophisticated sentences.
3. Target specific classes and assignments in which the sentence-writing strategy will be used. Have students create plans for using the strategy on these specific assignments. Schedule opportunities for students to report to their peers in their class how they used the strategy on specific assignments in other classes. In short, tell students to generalize the strategy.
4. Give students feedback concerning how well they are using the strategy. Although the teacher may wish to emphasize feedback concerning students' use of a vari-

---

* Teacher manuals and other instructional resources for this intervention are available from the University of Kansas Center for Research in Learning.

ety of sentence structures, the teacher should emphasize the logic, meaning, and flow of the students' sentences. During feedback sessions, the teacher should emphasize how well students communicate messages in their writing.

5. Schedule periodic maintenance review sessions. Check to see if students are using the sentence-writing strategy by giving them writing assignments *prior* to reviewing the strategy. If necessary, review the strategy steps and sentence-writing formulas.

PARAGRAPH WRITING AND ESSAY WRITING STRATEGY: DEFENDS

Explicit instruction in a paragraph and essay writing strategy can be beneficial for students whose writing demonstrates a disorganized flow of ideas and poor paragraph structure. It is beneficial particularly for students who do not know how to explain a position or point of view when writing.

The purpose of the writing strategy is to enable students to use an efficient, effective approach to expository writing and to facilitate students' use of self-regulation—self-motivation, self-reinforcement, and goal-directed self-speech—during the prewriting, production process, and revising. Because writing is thinking on paper, the student must manipulate and impose order on data according to logical methods of organization. The ultimate aim of writing should be to have students actively consider their reading audience and to choose the ways in which they impose order on the information they are dealing with so the information will make sense to others.

The strategy can be used to meet many common writing demands found in academic and nonacademic settings. The strategy is usable any time students are asked to express a point of view in writing (e.g., "Discuss the results of prohibition"). Also, it can be used to compose book reports for language arts classes, answer essay questions in history classes, write current event reports in social studies classes, and so on. Figure 4.9 shows the steps of DEFENDS, a writing strategy used in conjunction with various planning forms designed for adolescents with LD (Ellis, 1993a). Figure 4.10 illustrates a whole-to-part planning form that we have found beneficial to use with the DEFENDS strategy. The strategy and planning form is based, in part, on the earlier work of Schumaker (in preparation).

The steps of the DEFENDS strategy and the planning forms provide a framework that enables students with LD to look at specific situations, perceive key elements about which to write, and organize the major attributes. The planning forms guide students' observations and provide a basis from which to write.

A variety of organizer graphics can be used to structure students' thinking during the planning process. The planning forms in this chapter are particularly beneficial to adolescents with LD for three reasons.

1. The planning forms contain a set of questions that assist students in the thinking process. Students with LD tend to focus on various parts and pieces of information rather than on the "big picture" and main ideas. Questions such as "What is this whole thing about?" seem to be particularly beneficial in helping students

Decide on goals and theme.

Decide who will read this and what you hope will happen when they do.
Decide what kind of information you need to communicate.
Decide what your theme is.
Note the theme on your planning form.

▽

Estimate main ideas and details.

Think of at least two main ideas that will explain your theme.
Make sure the main ideas are different.
Note the main ideas on your planning form.
Note at least three details that can be used to explain each main idea.

▽

Figure best order of main ideas and details.

Decide which main idea to write about first, second, and so forth, and note on the planning form.
For each main idea, note on the planning form the best order for presenting the details.
Make sure the orders are logical.

▽

Express the theme in the first sentence.

State in the first sentence of your essay what the essay is about.

▽

Note each main idea and supporting points.

Note your first main idea using a complete sentence. Explain this main idea using the details you ordered earlier.
Tell yourself positive statements about your writing, and tell yourself to write more.
Repeat for each of the other main ideas.

▽

Drive home the message in the last sentence.

In the last sentence restate what your theme is about.
Make sure you use wording different from the first sentence.

▽

Search for errors and correct.

Look for different kinds of errors in your essay, and correct them.

▽

Set editing goals.
Examine your essay to see if it makes sense.
Ask yourself whether your message will be clear to others.
Reveal picky errors (capitalization, punctuation, spelling, etc.).
Copy over neatly.
Have a last look for errors.

FIGURE 4.9   DEFENDS WRITING STRATEGY

Source: From "The Adolescent with Learning Disabilities," by E. S. Ellis and P. Friend, 1991, in *Learning About Learning Disabilities* (pp. 506–561), edited by B. Y. K. Wong, Orlando, FL: Academic Press.

What? *What is this whole thing about?*

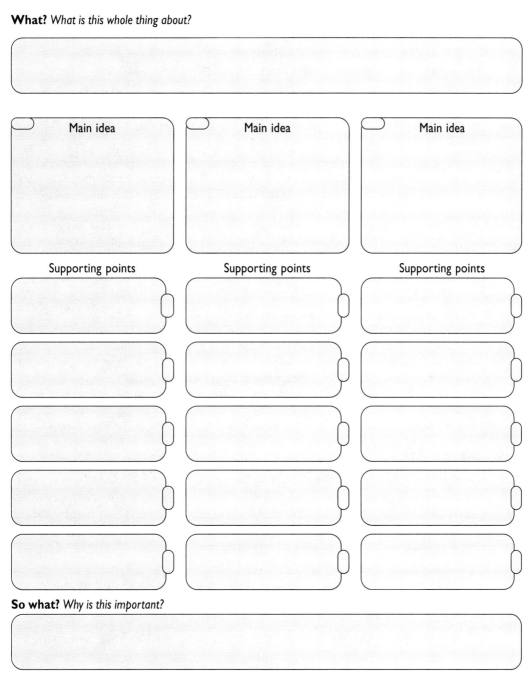

FIGURE 4.10 **WHOLE-TO-PART PLANNING FORM**

Source: From "Creating 'Thought-Full' Classrooms: Fostering Cognitive Literacy via Cooperative Learning and Integrated Strategy Instruction," by E. S. Ellis and K. Feldman, 1994, in *Handbook of Cooperative Learning Methods* (pp. 157–176), edited by S. Sharon, New York: Praeger.

keep their written message in perspective.

2. The forms are relatively simple to use.
3. The forms are readily adaptable for use when teaching content information.

THE PREWRITING PROCESS (STEPS D, E, AND F OF DEFENDS).

The earliest steps of the strategy are designed to facilitate prewriting activities. The student should realize that effective writing requires about as much time in thinking and organizing as in the actual act of writing. Time spent in prewriting activities is not wasted. Prewriting by analysis is a three-stage process:

1. Exploration through analysis means looking at a subject from as many viewpoints as possible to understand its complexity. This process reveals the necessity of limiting the topic. Students should carry on a dialogue with themselves (teachers should model this for students).
2. After exploring, students must limit the subject. In this prewriting phase students should continue to break down one aspect of the subject until they get it to a point at which they confidently grasp a pattern.
3. Formulating the thesis through an outline form suggests the specific direction of the writing activity.

Students conduct prewriting activities reflecting on their audience, setting goals, establishing a precise point of view, brainstorming to list a set of reasons they have taken this position, and then listing specific points they will use to explain each reason on a planning form. Students are to identify these without concern for the order in which they subsequently will be communicated when writing (see Figure 4.11).

After establishing a position and listing reasons and supporting points, students determine the best order for presenting reasons. The students place numbers by each reason to indicate the order in which they will be discussed. Next students determine the best order for presenting the supporting points for each reason and number these accordingly (see Figure 4.11).

THE PRODUCTION PROCESS (STEPS E, N, AND D OF DEFENDS).

In the production process students establish their position in the first sentence of the essay and then use the ordered reasons and supporting points previously listed to explain their position. The closing sentence confirms the students' positions (see Figure 4.12).

THE EDITING PROCESS (STEP S OF DEFENDS).

The final phase of the writing strategy involves editing. The specific editing strategy, SEARCH, presented in more detail later in this chapter, can be applied for finding and correcting content errors (the logic and organization of ideas) and conventions-of-print errors (e.g., sentence structure, capitalization, punctuation).

SKILLS TO TEACH BEFORE BEGINNING INSTRUCTION IN A WRITING STRATEGY

Before teaching the writing strategy, the teacher should ensure that the students can perform the following independently:

1. Write complete sentences.
2. Recognize and correct incomplete sentences or sentence fragments as well as run-on sentences.

What? *What is this whole thing about?*

Bald Eagle

Main idea

Hunting

Main idea

Baby

Main idea

In Danger

Supporting points

steals — 2

poor hunter — 1

eats fish — 3

dead animals — 4

Supporting points

6-8 weeks — 2

1 or 2 at a time — 1

it falls out — 4

brown head — 3

Supporting points

DDT - crops — 1

bugs — 2

water — 3

fish — 4

So what? *Why is this important?*

FIGURE 4.11   PLANNING FORM AS EXECUTED BY STUDENT

You probably know that the Bald Eagle is our national bird, and you have seen it on U.S. symbols and money. There are many interesting things about Bald Eagles. They usually lay only one or two eggs at a time. The eggs are white with blue spots. It takes about 6-8 weeks for them to hatch. Baby bald Eagles have brown heads. If the baby falls out of its nest, it dies.

Bald Eagles are poor hunters. They get their food by stealing from other birds. They eat fish and dead animals. Not many people know that our national bird is a thief!

Bald Eagles are in danger. Farmers put poison called DDT on their crops. Bugs eat the DDT. Fish eat the bugs. When the Bald Eagle eats the fish, DDT gets in them. The DDT causes egg shells to be too thin, so they break. Babies can not hatch.

FIGURE 4.12   ESSAY BASED ON IDEAS FROM THE WHOLE-TO-PART PLANNING FORM

3. Apply knowledge of conventions of print to identify and correct mechanical writing errors.
4. Possess sufficient knowledge about the subject in which they are expected to write.

INITIATING INSTRUCTION IN A REMEDIAL SETTING

Instruction in the writing strategy can take place in remedial settings (e.g., resource rooms), where teaching can be intensive and extensive, and it also can take place in traditional content-area classrooms (e.g., general education classrooms), albeit less intensively. Instructional procedures for using this strategy in a content-area classroom are discussed later. First and foremost, teaching the strategy until the students master it is suggested. Little benefit will accrue if the teacher tells students about the strategy steps, makes an attractive bulletin board depicting the steps, but practices it only occasionally. A suggested criterion for mastery is provided below.

MASTERY OF STRATEGIC BEHAVIORS   Student provides evidence of:
- Prewriting activities: outlining and organizing ideas showing use of two main ideas and supporting details.
- Writing activities: constructing at least one sentence for each idea listed on organization form.
- Postwriting activities: editing content and conventions of print.

MASTERY LEVELS FOR WRITTEN PRODUCTS   Minimal performance standards on a student's written products are as follows:
- First sentence of essay clearly establishes a point of view.
- Point of view remains consistent throughout the passage.
- Last sentence in passage reconfirms student's point of view.
- Passage contains a minimum of two different reasons explaining writer's point of view.

- Each reason is explained using a minimum of three sentences that elaborate on the reason.
- The passage contains no incomplete sentences or sentence fragments.
- The passage contains a maximum of one mechanical writing error per 20 words.

ASSESSING THE STUDENT'S PARAGRAPH WRITING ABILITY

Use of the component analysis or the holistic scoring assessment techniques described earlier in this chapter is suggested. Using more than one assessment method will provide a broader and more accurate picture of the student's writing.

MOTIVATING STUDENTS TO LEARN THE STRATEGY

Effective prelearning motivational activities include:

- Showing students pretest/posttest writing samples of students who learned the strategy previously.
- Showing students data reflecting pretest/posttest performances.
- Having students who mastered the DEFENDS strategy previously describe what learning the strategy was like and where they are using it currently.
- Providing students with samples of assignments in which the strategy would be beneficial.
- Having teachers from upper-grade classes tell how using the DEFENDS strategy could effect success in these classes.

PRESENTING THE DEFENDS STRATEGY TO THE STUDENTS

When describing the DEFENDS strategy, students must understand that effective writers engage in the major phases of planning, producing, and editing. Effective writers first engage in the planning stage of writing. Here, they plan and organize their ideas. Then they engage in a producing stage, in which they convert their ideas to written text. Finally they enter a stage involving editing and revising what they have written. Teachers should make sure that students understand that these processes are not exclusive to the stages. For example, although a major portion of their planning and organizing of ideas took place during the first stage of writing, good writers continue to plan, produce text, and even review and edit what they just wrote during the production stage. They also know that although they are editing in a limited way while they are writing, they will go back later and review and edit the entire text intensively.

When describing the strategy, you should explain what each step is designed to do and why it is important and also discuss the rationale for using the strategy and the setting demands the strategy is designed to address. In the remembering system, the first letter of each step in the strategy combine to spell the word "defends," as in defending a point of view.

When describing how to use the planning forms in the planning process, you point out the questions noted on the sheets. These questions are designed to help structure students' thinking. The teacher also emphasizes the need to engage in ongoing self-questioning activities. Table 4.9 lists the types of questions that effective writers ask themselves throughout the writing process. The teacher models use of these questions while completing the planning form. You should first model the planning process (e.g., D, E,

TABLE 4.9 SAMPLE QUESTIONS TO ASK YOURSELF DURING THE WRITING PROCESS

Prewriting	Who will be reading this? What do I want to happen when they do?
	What will the readers already know about this topic? What is their frame of reference?
	Do I have enough information to begin writing?
	What is the organizing idea (theme) of the paragraph?
	What are the main things I want to say?
	What can I say about each of these main things? What facts can I work into the paragraph?
	What kind of information is this?
	How can this information be organized best to communicate to the reader?
Production process	What else can I say?
	Does this sentence make sense?
Reviewing process	Did I tell the readers what I was going to tell them?
	Are the paragraphs purposeful?
	Are the paragraphs developed adequately?
	Are the paragraphs varied sufficiently?
	Are the paragraphs unified?
	Are the paragraphs coherent?
	Is each of the paragraphs needed?

and F steps of DEFENDS) and then discuss with students what you did when performing it. Next you model the production process (E, N, and D steps) and then model the editing process (S step).

Modeling should include the following thought processes:

- Positive self-statements.
- Analysis of writing assignment to determine whether DEFENDS is an appropriate strategy to use.
- Reflecting on characteristics of audience and setting demands.
- Self-cueing of the strategy steps.
- Reflecting on what one's point of view will be.
- Thinking about whether the student knows enough about this topic to write about it.
- Once reasons are established, monitoring to make sure reasons are different.
- Monitoring to make sure at least two reasons have been identified, as well as at least three supporting points for each reason.
- Monitoring for content and conventions of print errors.

FACILITATING VERBAL ELABORATION AND REHEARSAL OF THE STRATEGY

The students are to describe the overall strategic process in their own words. A student might say something like:

Well, basically, to use the writing strategy, you need to first plan what you want to say by doing things like brainstorming ideas and then organizing them on a planning form. Then you use this sheet to keep you organized when you write. After you have written what you wanted to say, you go back and look for errors and fix them. During the whole time, you're always thinking about what will make sense when somebody else reads it.

Next, students, while looking at the strategy steps if necessary, describe what each step is cueing them to do. Finally, each student memorizes the strategy steps.

GETTING STUDENTS TO PRACTICE THE PARAGRAPH-WRITING STRATEGY

During this phase of instruction, students are acquiring the skills necessary to use the strategy. They practice using the writing strategy under conditions that have been controlled for difficulty (writing about nonacademic topics about which they are familiar, e.g.,—"whether teenagers should be allowed to own a car"). Earlier a list of suggested topics about which students can write during the acquisition and practice stages of instruction was provided on page 145–146. Students now are given a shorter list from which to select one topic.

As students begin practicing the strategy, the teacher should provide ample assistance. Outlined below are some suggestions for different kinds of assistance. These are designed to gradually shift the responsibility for mediating use of the strategy onto students.

YOU DO IT   The teacher cues each step of the writing strategy and discourages students from moving ahead of the cueing. The feedback teachers provide is directive at first. Then the teacher begins to fade cues to perform specific aspects of the strategy, and cues primarily consist of cueing students to think in specific ways.

WE DO IT TOGETHER   Here the teacher performs the strategy *with* the students, providing guidance as needed. Students work in small cooperative learning groups. The entire group may be responsible for producing a single written product, or each individual might produce an essay. Group members assist individuals in the prewriting task of brainstorming and organizing ideas and the postwriting task of editing. Cooperative learning writing activities are used on several products for several days before shifting to the last phase, "They do it alone."

THEY DO IT ALONE   The students are now responsible for producing written essays independently. Feedback is meditative. Students continue with acquisition practice until they are able to perform the strategy independently at mastery levels on tasks similar to that found in the criterion environment.

Students practice applying the strategy in situations that simulate the requirements of their regular classes (e.g., they use the DEFENDS strategy to write a current events report, to answer an essay question on a mock test, to write a book report). At this point, they are learning to apply the strategy to meet real-life expectations. They repeat the practice phases of mediation as necessary. Below are some suggestions to integrate the strategy into content-area tasks and assignments, which can be adapted and used effectively in the resource room setting.

GENERALIZING AND MAINTAINING THE DEFENDS STRATEGY

Students review the natural environment to identify cues that signal a need to use the strategy, target specific real-life settings for applying the DEFENDS strategy, and establish generalization goals. By providing students with writing assignments that must be completed independently outside the setting in which the strategy training took place, the teacher is promoting generalization of the skill taught. Students must perform the skill at mastery levels a minimum of six times. Students also must recognize opportunities independently to use the DEFENDS strategy to meet actual demands of the general class setting.

General education teachers are asked to incorporate cues to use DEFENDS into routine content-area instruction by cueing students to use the strategy at opportunistic times (e.g., saying to the student while pointing at an essay test question, "Can you use the DEFENDS strategy to help you here?").

Teachers should have students periodically (every 2 weeks or so) review the benefits of the paragraph-writing strategy to meet real-life demands, identify specific instances in which the strategy has been applied independently to meet a setting demand, and take every opportunity to review the strategy steps as well as adaptations in the strategy. To maintain their skills, students must continue to write short essays and receive feedback.

Students' knowledge of the writing strategy can be extended in two basic ways. First, students learn to adapt the writing strategy for use in other information formats. Second, they learn to adapt the strategy to meet the demands of other problem areas that do not necessarily involve writing essays.

Using the DEFENDS Strategy with Other Writing Formats

An important extension of the DEFENDS strategy is to teach students how to use planning forms that represent formats other than the whole-to-part format discussed previously. Other common writing formats include personal view, descriptive, compare/contrast, procedure, and mixed formats. Here, instruction focuses on (a) how information structures differ (e.g., how compare/contrast differs from whole-to-part); (b) how to use the various planning forms; and (c) how to adapt the DEFENDS strategy to accommodate different information formats.

Students must be taught the essential skill of recognizing the needed format for a given task. For example, the essay history test question, "What did the U.S. Army learn from its experiences during the Vietnam war?" suggests a need to use a whole-to-part information format. The test question, "Compare the tactics used during World War II with those used in Vietnam" suggests a need for using a compare-and-contrast format to form a response. The teacher has to provide instruction designed to help students make these discriminations and to recognize the cues from their environment that signal different information formats. Table 4.10 lists sample statements that signal different information structures. The teacher can construct similar lists and have students practice deciding whether the writing tasks indicate whole-to-part, compare/contrast, cause/effect, or sequence.

Personal View Formats   In this format the writer expresses personal opinions and emotions. The writing of personal views utilizes both facts and opinions. Therefore, the writer has the responsibility for indicating to the reader which statements are facts and which are opinions. Four kinds of personal views are feelings, preferences, opinions, and judgments. To illustrate, personal opinions are discussed below.

TABLE 4.10   STATEMENTS REFLECTING DIFFERENT TYPES OF INFORMATION STRUCTURES

Type of Statement	Examples
Descriptive (whole-to-part)	*Illustration of statements within a set of instructions:* List the parts of an amoeba and describe the function of each. (biology) What was your impression of the President's campaign speech? (social studies) *Illustrations of statements to use when writing:* An amoeba has six main parts... For example... The second reason is...

Compare/ contrast	*Illustration of statements within a set of instructions:*
	Discuss the similarities and differences between America's Martin Luther King, Jr. and South Africa's Nelson Mandela. (social studies)
	In what ways is the reproductive cycle of a moth different from that of a housefly? (science)
	Compare the way rules are enforced in this school with the way laws are enforced in the courts. (social studies)
	
	Illustrations of statements to use when writing:
	On the other hand...
	Another difference/similarity...
	Both share some characteristics...
	
	Key structure vocabulary:
	To compare: similar to
	    like, alike
	    correspond to
	    resemble
	    common characteristics
	    at the same rate as
	    just as
	    in the same way
	    resemblance
	    similarly
	    likewise
	    correspondingly
	    to be parallel in _____
	    as
	    in like manner
	    to have _____ in common
	    almost the same as

(continued)

TABLE 4.10   CONTINUED

Type of Statement	Examples		
Compare/ contrast (cont.)	**To contrast:**	differ from otherwise nevertheless dissimilarly although unlike in opposition (to) on the opposite side different from faster than (etc.) however still even so at a different rate than while in contrast (to) on the contrary on the other hand less (more) than a larger percentage than	
Cause/effect	*Illustration of statements within a set of instructions:* How did John Brown's raid at Harper's Ferry affect people's attitudes about succession? (history) Why do high and low pressure fronts cause bad weather when they meet? (science) How did the salesman's death impact his family? (literature) Describe four ways to prevent AIDS. (health)		
	Illustrations of statements to use when writing: If you do not smoke, then... since...	As a result... because...	A reaction to this is... ...resulting in...
Sequence	*Illustration of statements within a set of instructions:* Describe the stages of aging. (health) Describe the steps whereby a bill becomes a law. (social studies)		
	Illustrations of statements to use when writing: First..., second..., third..., etc. Next... In the following stage...		

When students write personal opinions, they may support them with a single statement of reason: "I think we should do _____ because _____." Students with LD must be taught that their personal opinions are of value and should be stated. They must realize, however, that stating personal views carries with it the responsibility for identifying logical reasons to support their beliefs. The teacher can help students with LD develop the ability to state and support their personal views by encouraging them to state their opinions verbally on issues such as school regulations, busing, and drugs. The teacher always should ask the follow-up question: "Why?" At the same time, students should be encouraged to acquire the habit of asking themselves the question: "Why?" Students with LD have to be sensitive to the importance of identifying for the reader clearly what is opinion and what is fact.

The whole-to-part planning form (Figure 4.10) is an excellent device for helping students organize their ideas when preparing to discuss personal opinions. They might note their position on an issue at the top of the planning form and then write at least two reasons why they have this opinion. Under "supporting points" they list ideas they will use to explain each of the reasons.

Students should be taught to recognize and use some of the structure vocabulary associated with statements of personal opinion. For example:

" I think..."	"I disagree with..."	"I agree with..."
"seems to me..."	"it's my point of view..."	"I hesitate to say..."

To facilitate use of personal view statements, the teacher might write some of these on the board and review them just before students begin their writing.

Students also should be taught to recognize and use some of the structure vocabulary associated with cueing the reader to the organization of idea presentation. For example:

There are three reasons why I feel.... The first reason is...

There are two rules I disagree with. First, I think the rule concerning student use of the parking lot is unfair because...

DESCRIPTIVE FORMATS In the descriptive format students attempt to translate their impressions of objects, materials, and events into accurate representations in writing. People tend to observe what they expect and see what they are looking for. Consequently, teachers should instruct students in what to expect and what to look for. Students with LD often are passive observers and require structured guidelines and suggestions from the teacher to increase the productivity of their observations. Figure 4.13 illustrates how the whole-to-part planning form can be modified for use as an attribute guide for an object that is to be described in writing. Figure 4.14 illustrates a similar modification for describing the attributes of a person. Guides such as these structure students' observations and direct their attention to significant features. Teachers always should be concerned about the transfer of this skill from isolated activities or assignments to performance in the general education classroom. To ensure this transfer, teachers should require students to use the same guide in many settings until they have internalized the components of the guide for automatic and independent application. Obviously the type of framework may vary from one subject area to another and from student to student.

What is this whole thing about?

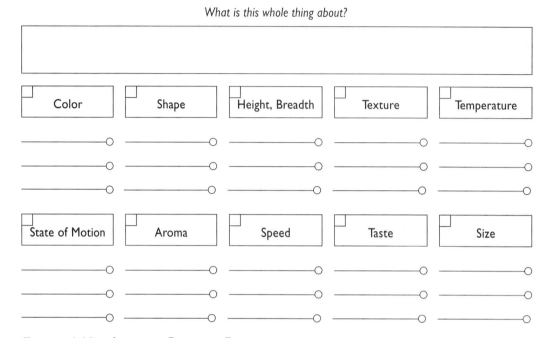

FIGURE 4.13   ATTRIBUTE PLANNING FORM

Source: From *Writing Strategies for Thought-Full Classrooms*, by E. S. Ellis, 1993, Tuscaloosa, AL: SMART Strategy Associates.

Students should acquire the habit of relying on such a framework as an aid in written expression.

COMPARE/CONTRAST FORMATS   Compare/contrast writing tasks require students to discuss the similarities and differences between two things. Comparison is a statement of likenesses and similarities, and contrast deals with differences. This type of writing requires the writer to compare *and* contrast, combining information from more than one source. To teach students to deal with likenesses and differences, the teacher must provide them with opportunities to recognize common features with differing items, ideas, and events.

Items (ideas, events, famous persons, story characters) being compared can be noted in the appropriate boxes of the planning form illustrated in Figure 4.15. The questions provided on the form can guide the planning process. The main ideas of comparison are listed in the boxes along the left side of the form. Differences between the two items with respect to each main idea are listed in the corresponding blanks, and the shared characteristics, or similarities between the items, are listed in the large box at the top of the planning form.

After listing the various similarities and differences, writers analyze the similarities, decide the order to present them in writing, and then indicate the order by numbering the small circles next to each item. The main ideas with regard to differences are treated in

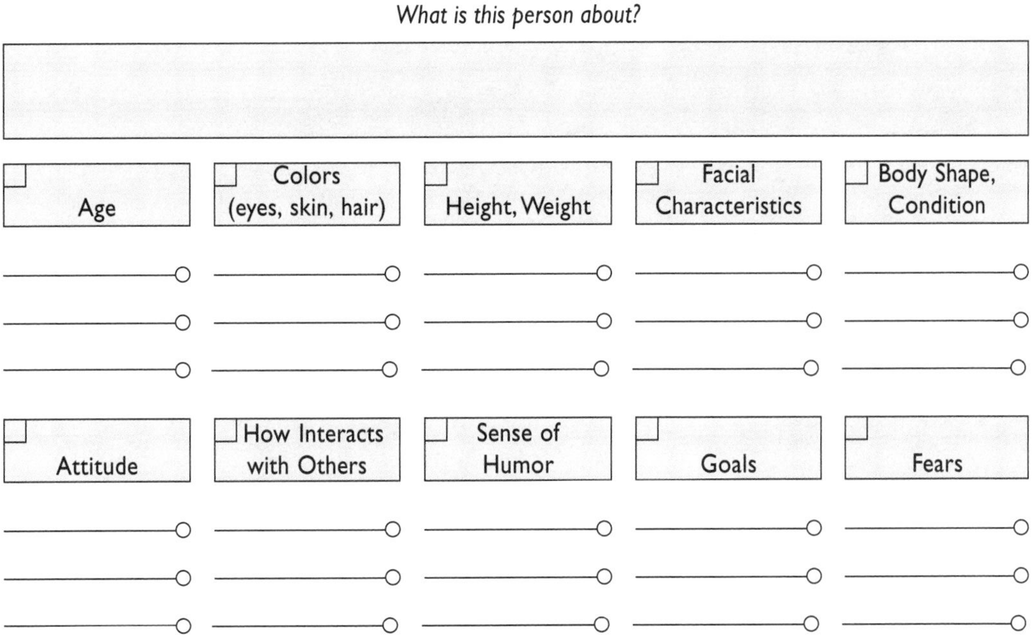

What is this person about?

FIGURE 4.14 PERSONAL ATTRIBUTES PLANNING FORM

Source: From *Writing Strategies for Thought-Full Classrooms*, by E. S. Ellis, 1993, Tuscaloosa, AL: SMART Strategy Associates.

the same manner. Figure 4.16 illustrates a completed compare/contrast planning form, and Figure 4.17 is a sample essay based on the points organized on the planning form.

Generally, students should master the whole-to-part information format before beginning instruction in compare/contrast essay writing. Then the teacher should:

1. Teach students to recognize and use statements that reflect comparison or contrast relationships. (Table 4.10 provides a list of these statements.)
2. Follow a similar instructional plan (describe, model, verbal elaboration, acquisition practice) when teaching compare/contrast essay writing. During the acquisition practice phase of instruction, students can practice comparing things in which they are generally familiar before writing about academic subjects.
3. Provide the main ideas for students in initial practice, as many adolescents with LD have trouble identifying the main ideas of compare-and-contrast relationships. To teach students how to generate main ideas, brainstorm with them and, on the chalkboard, list differences without regard to main ideas. Next, collaborate with students to identify main ideas from the list of details. Think aloud to model how you are identifying interrelationships between the details.
4. Ensure that students understand the "connectedness" of formats. The compare/contrast format is a logical extension of the descriptive format. In the descriptive format, writers describe the critical attributes of something. In the compare/con-

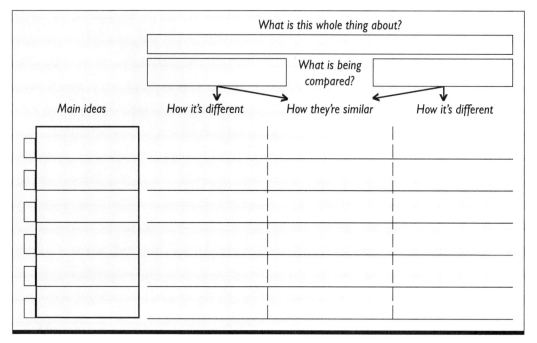

What is this whole thing about?

What is being compared?

Main ideas   How it's different   How they're similar   How it's different

FIGURE 4.15   COMPARE/CONTRAST PLANNING FORM

Source: From "Integrating Content with Writing Strategy Instruction: Part 1. Orienting Students to Organizational Devices," by E. S. Ellis, in *Intervention in the School and Clinic, 29*(3), 169–179.

trast format, writers discuss how the critical attributes of two or more things are similar or different. Thus, the compare/contrast format simply takes the descriptive format a step further.

PROCEDURE FORMATS   Various assignments in school require students to describe a sequence of actions or steps—for example, explaining how to carry out an experiment, how to bake a cake, or how to go from one location to another. The first step is for the student to identify the major events involved and the sequence of their happening. One effective way to communicate a given procedure is through a flow diagram. All writing need not be in paragraph form. Just as students with LD are taught to be flexible in their reading assignments, so they should be taught to use different writing styles for different writing assignments. The objective is clear communication.

The flow diagram is advantageous particularly with adolescents with LD for the following reasons:

1. It provides a simplified structure within which students can organize their thoughts.
2. The visual diagram serves as a memory aid to students who will use the information later.
3. It allows students to use shortened expressions (almost telegraphic expressions) and does not require transitions.

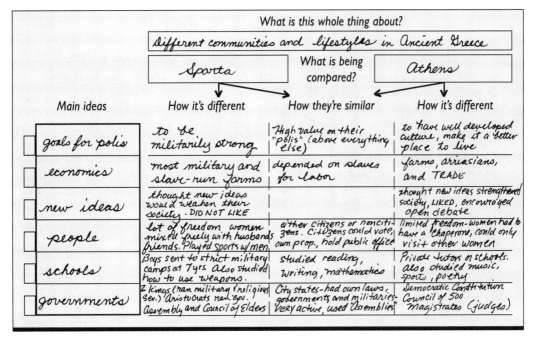

What is this whole thing about?

Different communities and lifestyles in Ancient Greece

Sparta	What is being compared?	*Athens*

Main ideas	How it's different	How they're similar	How it's different
goals for polis	to be militarily strong	High value on their "polis" (above everything else)	to have well developed culture, make it a better place to live
economics	most military and slave-run farms	depended on slaves for labor	farms, artisians, and TRADE
new ideas	thought new ideas would weaken their society. DID NOT LIKE		thought new ideas strengthened society, LIKED, encouraged open debate
people	lot of freedom women mixed freely with husbands friends. Played sports w/men.	either citizens or nonciti-zens. Citizens could vote, own prop., hold public office	limited freedom-women had to have a chaperone, could only visit other women
schools	Boys sent to strict military camps at 7 yrs. Also studied how to use weapons.	studied reading, writing, mathematics	Private tutors or schools. also studied music, sports, poetry
governments	2 kings (ran military & religious ser.) Aristocrats ran gov. Assembly and Council of Elders	City states-had own laws, governments and militaries. Very active, used Assemblies	Democratic Constitution Council of 500 magistrates (judges)

FIGURE 4.16 SAMPLE COMPARE/CONTRAST PLANNING FORM USED FOR SOCIAL STUDIES ESSAY

Source: From "Integrating Content with Writing Strategy Instruction: Part 1. Orienting Students to Organizational Devices," by E. S. Ellis, in *Intervention in the School and Clinic, 29*(3), 169–179.

Figure 4.18 provides an example of how a flow diagram can be used to describe a sequence of steps clearly and systematically.

Alternatively, the teacher may wish to teach students to use a planning form that has a step-by-step format. Figure 4.19 illustrates such a planning form (Ellis, 1993c). To use it, students first note what the whole essay is about and then list the major steps in a procedure (step 1, step 2, step 3, etc.). At times, students will realize they left out a step in the procedure after they have listed other steps. If this happens, they simply insert the step in any of the remaining boxes. Once all of the steps have been listed, students go back and indicate the order of the steps in the small circles of the boxes.

CAUSE/EFFECT FORMATS Cause-and-effect formats can be particularly difficult for adolescents with LD. Cause/effect formats, however, are a logical extension of procedural formats. Thus, if students master procedural formats first, cause/effect formats will be easier for them to learn.

"Cause" is the reason (or reasons) something happened, and "effect" refers to the results. This implies an "If - then" relationship. *IF* something happens, *THEN* something else is likely to occur. For example:

IF you frequently change the oil in your car, THEN your motor will last longer.

IF you don't wear a lifejacket when on a boat, THEN you may drown.

IF the president does not show more leadership, THEN he probably will not be reelected.

Lifestyles of Ancient Greeks

Two of the main communities in ancient Greece were Athens and Sparta. These communities were called City States because they were basically large cities that had their own governments and armies. Although Athens and Sparta were similar in many ways, they were also very different. The big difference was the goals they had for their communities. Although both highly valued their polis (city-state), Sparta's main goal was to be militarily strong so that no one would conquer them. On the other hand, Athens wanted a well developed culture so the polis would be a good place to live. Since Sparta was so militarily oriented, most of the jobs were in the army. They used slaves to run their farms. Athens also used slaves for labor, but they also had a lot more artists and merchants instead of army jobs.

In both city-states, you were either a citizen or a non-citizen. Citizens were allowed to hold own land and hold public office. Non-citizens were not. In terms of their governments, both Sparta and Athens had very active Assemblies which are similar to the U.S. Congress and a Council of Elders, which is sort of like the U.S. Senate. In Sparta, they had two kings. One king was in charge of the army, and the other king was in charge of religious services. Aristocrats ran the government, and they were not elected. On the other hand, Athens was more democratic. They had a Constitution that allowed citizens to be elected to what was called the "Council of 500." The Council made the laws, and Magistrates (judges) interpreted them.

In Sparta, new ideas were not welcome. They were afraid of new ideas because they thought new things would weaken their society. On the other hand, people in Athens loved new ideas. They thought new things would make them stronger. They like to have debates.

Surprise! Although Sparta did not like new ideas, people had a lot of freedom. For example, women mixed freely with their husband's friends and they played sports with men. In Athens, freedom was more limited. For example, women always had to have a chaperone, and they were only allowed to visit with other women.

Children studied reading, writing and math at school in both Sparta and Athens. Since Sparta was military, 7 year old boys were sent to strict military camps where they also learned how to fight with weapons. Since Athens was big on arts, music, sports and art was studied.

FIGURE 4.17   COMPARE/CONTRAST ESSAY, 8TH-GRADE LD CLASS

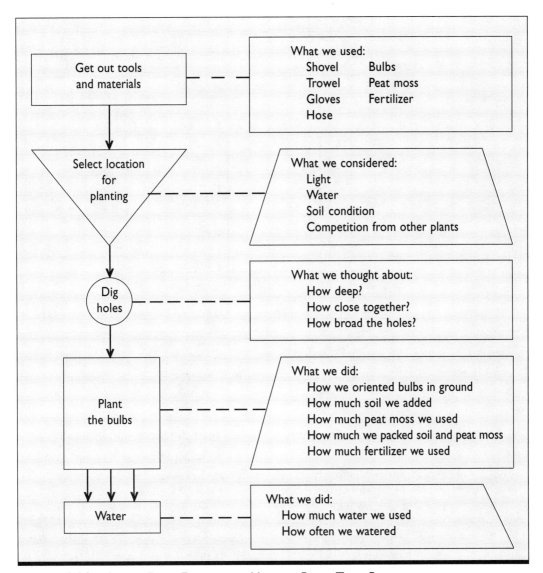

FIGURE 4.18   SAMPLE FLOW DIAGRAM OF HOW TO PLANT TULIP BULBS

Figure 4.20 illustrates a cause/effect planning form (Ellis, 1994b) that can be used to facilitate this form of writing. Figure 4.21 illustrates a set of ideas that have been organized for writing. To complete the cause/effect planning form, students should first answer the question, "What's this whole thing about?" When planning to discuss cause/effect relationships, students note idea-related factors to "start with," what was "added" to the situation, and "what happened" as a result. In the last part of the planning forms, students draw conclusions about the cause-and-effect relationship and note them in terms of "If - then" statements.

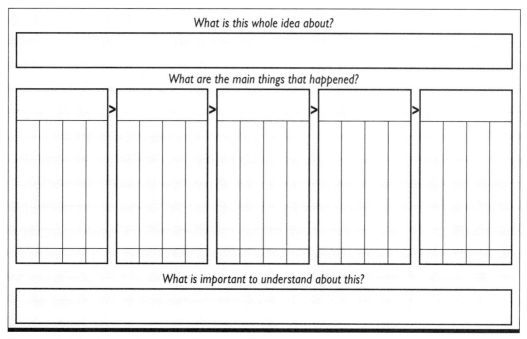

FIGURE 4.19   LINEAR SEQUENCE PLANNING FORM

Source: From *Writing Strategies for Thought-Full Classrooms*, by E. S. Ellis, 1993, Tuscaloosa, AL: SMART Strategy Associates.

Salient points concerning the cause/effect format can be summarized as follows:

- Generally, students should master the whole-to-part, compare/contrast, and procedural formats before beginning instruction in cause/effect essay writing.
- Following similar instructional plans when teaching all of these formats will enhance generalization.
- Students with LD tend to have the most difficulty composing relationship statements. In some cases, ample practice may be advisable, creating "If–then..." statements based on familiar experiences. For example:

    "If our football team has too many injuries, then...."

    "If I am late for work too often, then...."

    "If too many people dislike the president, then...."

MIXED FORMATS   Sophisticated writers can effectively mix writing formats (e.g., comparing and contrasting ideas while discussing cause/effect relationships simultaneously) and retain clarity in their writing. Although encouraging students to learn this skill is not recommended, encouraging less skilled writers to use different information formats within the same essay, albeit not simultaneously is a good idea. For example, one portion of a book report may discuss the social themes imbedded in the story (whole-to-part format),

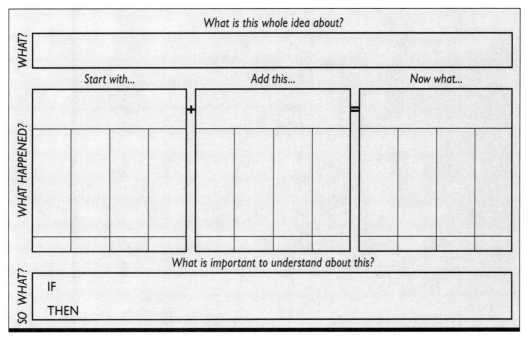

FIGURE 4.20   CAUSE/EFFECT PLANNING FORM

Source: From *Writing Strategies for Thought-Full Classrooms*, by E. S. Ellis, 1993, Tuscaloosa, AL: SMART Strategy Associates.

another portion might discuss two characters in the story (compare/contrast), and another portion of the book report can address the relationships between events in the story (cause/effect).

Students should master different information formats separately before beginning instruction in combining formats. You should encourage students to set goals for using different information formats when composing essays.

Students generate new strategies out of the DEFENDS strategy by identifying the internal cognitive processes involved in performing the strategy (e.g., planning ahead by brainstorming and organizing ideas, communicating the ideas in an organized fashion, checking to make sure that what they communicate is free of errors). After generating new strategies to meet other academic requirements, students practice using the new strategy and establish generalization goals. Specific academic requirements in which aspects of the strategy might be adapted include:

— Making oral reports and presentations.
— Participating in job interviews.
— Meeting nontraditional writing assignments (e.g., writing up lab experiments, writing school plays, writing news articles for school paper).
— Projects that require planning, producing, and monitoring quality (e.g., sewing projects from a home economics class, projects in an art or photography class, agricultural projects in a vocational education class).

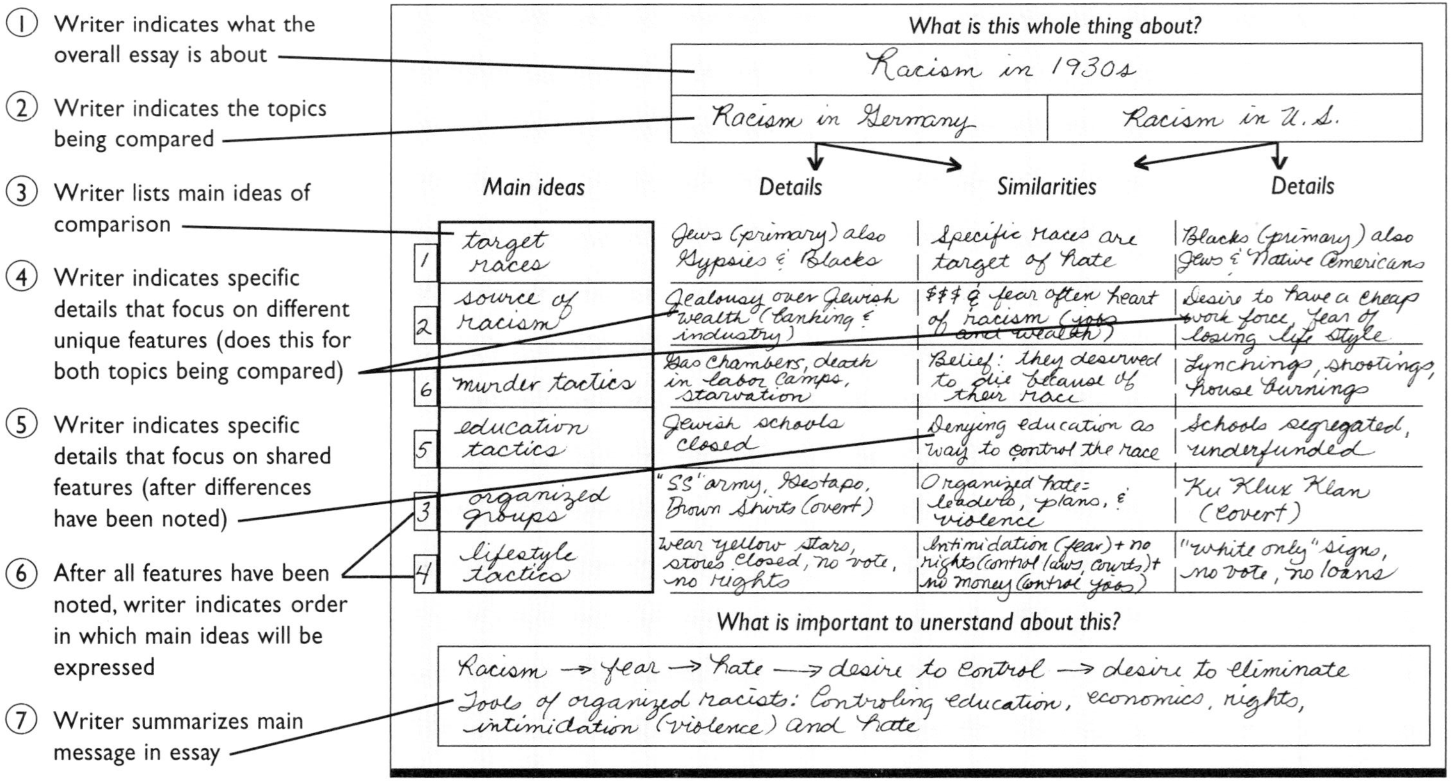

1. Writer indicates what the overall essay is about

2. Writer indicates the topics being compared

3. Writer lists main ideas of comparison

4. Writer indicates specific details that focus on different unique features (does this for both topics being compared)

5. Writer indicates specific details that focus on shared features (after differences have been noted)

6. After all features have been noted, writer indicates order in which main ideas will be expressed

7. Writer summarizes main message in essay

FIGURE 4.21 IDEAS ORGANIZED FOR WRITING

Source: From "Integrating Content with Writing Strategy Instruction: Part 2–Writing Processes," by E. S. Ellis, in *Intervention in the School and Clinic*, 29(4), 219–228.

Teachers who have taught DEFENDS have used a variety of techniques to make instruction fun, motivating, and interesting. Some ideas that teachers may wish to consider are listed below.

- Use charts to indicate progress. To attain a quality score that can be charted, assign a point value to each critical feature of the paragraph (e.g., an opening sentence that establishes a position = 3 points. Each different reason in the essay = 2 points. Each separate sentence that makes a point that supports the reason = 1 point, and so on). The chart should have a line indicating minimal mastery performance. For example, mastery on the quality might be established at 30 points.

  Charts also can be used to indicate quality of editing. To attain a score for editing, subtract the total number of conventions of print errors from the total number of words in the essay. Divide this figure by the total number of words in the essay and then multiply this number by 100. This will produce a % errors score. One error per 20 words = 5% errors. This goal also should be indicated on the chart (Schumaker, Nolan, & Deshler, 1985).

- Post each essay written by students, beginning with the pretest, in succession on the wall of the classroom. As the number of essays the students produce increases, a "ribbon" of essays begins to grow around the room. Students then can show visitors the growth they are making in writing by comparing pretest performance with performance in the most recent products. Leave the first essay and the last essay on the wall the following year. Looking at the "before" and "after" written products of upper-class students can be motivating to new students who will be learning the DEFENDS strategy in the upcoming year.

- As a fun, cooperative learning activity, have each student produce an outline for a prewriting activity and then pass the outline to a peer, who is responsible for producing the essay, using this outline. Pass this essay to a third peer, who is responsible for editing it.

- Another cooperative learning activity involves having each student use DEFENDS to write an essay. After the essay has been completed and as many errors as the author could find have been located and corrected, pass the essay to another student. For each error this student subsequently finds in the essay, award five points. Then pass the essay to a third person. Award each error this person finds 15 points. Finally, pass the essay to a fourth student, and award 40 points for each of any remaining errors. Have students maintain a record of accumulated editing points for fun. After the three peers have had an opportunity to find and correct any remaining errors, return the essay to the original author, who then recopies it and produces an error-free manuscript.

The types of trouble that students are likely to encounter when learning the DEFENDS strategy tend to occur in the following categories:

1. *Students do not know enough about a topic to write an essay.* To counter this problem, be sure to provide students a choice among four to five topics about which to write. Also, before noting ideas on a planning organizer, prompt students to discuss the topic orally. As they mention specific ideas relevant to the

writing assignment, note them on the board.

2. *Students do not know the difference between a reason and a supporting point.* In this case, ask the student to first tell you his or her point of view on the topic. Next, ask the student to tell you, in one sentence, one reason *why* he or she has taken that position. Then ask the student to offer a different reason. Now return to the original reason and ask the student to tell you what he or she means by the first reason. Repeat this question for the second reason.

3. *Students often write run-on or incomplete sentences.* If a student seems unable to distinguish between incorrect sentences and technically correct sentences, consider abandoning instruction in the DEFENDS strategy temporarily in lieu of teaching him or her a sentence-writing strategy. If a student is able to discriminate among these sentences but continues to use many sentence fragments in an essay, consider teaching an error-monitoring strategy.

4. *Students write minimalist sentences.* Minimalist sentence writing (e.g., "I like Cheers. The show is funny...."), devoid of adjectives, adverbs, and phrases, often can be corrected by telling the student to use more words in the sentence. In some cases charting the number of words the student writes is beneficial. By using the component analysis of assessment described earlier in this chapter, you can keep a comparative count of the number of words the student writes. In addition, though teaching students to identify adjectives, adverbs, and so on has little effect on writing ability, teaching them to use descriptive words that "decorate the sentence" can help considerably. If this suggestion proves inadequate, you may need to teach the sentence-writing strategy, PENS.

5. *Students make many mechanical writing errors.* If students lack knowledge of specific conventions of print, provide instruction in these with ongoing DEFENDS strategy instruction. If students seem to have a large void of knowledge in this area, consider abandoning DEFENDS strategy instruction and teach these skills directly. If students have this knowledge but fail to apply it when using DEFENDS, consider teaching them an error-monitoring strategy.

Editing and Revising Strategy: SEARCH

Students' written products often are laden with conventions-of-print errors. Although they may know basic rules of punctuation, grammar, and capitalization, they do not apply these rules routinely when writing. Moreover, passages often contain many misspelled words, although students can use dictionaries and other aids to locate correct spellings. Thus, many students with LD possess the necessary conventions-of-print knowledge, yet they do not often apply this knowledge systematically or strategically. In these cases instruction in an editing and revising strategy can be beneficial. For example, prior to instruction in an error-monitoring strategy, students with LD averaged one error in every four words they wrote. Following instruction in the strategy, students averaged only one error per 33 words they wrote (Schumaker, Nolan, & Deshler, 1985).

The purpose of teaching an editing and revising strategy is to enable students to use efficient and effective monitoring processes. Figure 4.22 illustrates an editing strategy (Ellis & Friend, 1991) designed to facilitate self-regulation behaviors related to self-

---

Set goals

Think about who you would like to read your work and the impression you would like to give them.

Set a quality goal.

Set a quantity goal (e.g., how many specific errors you will allow).

▽

Examine your paper to see if it makes sense

Read your paper out loud.

Does the overall passage make sense?

Make sure each sentence makes sense and that words have not been omitted.

Make sure each sentence expresses a complete thought.

Very long sentences should be broken into two or more sentences.

▽

Ask if you said what you wanted to say.

Make sure your ideas are clear and express what you mean.

Make sure the order of your ideas is logical.

▽

Reveal picky errors

Correct all the capitalization, punctuation, spelling, and grammar errors you can find.

Have someone else double check your work.

▽

Copy over neatly

As you copy over your work, make sure you don't make new errors.

▽

Have a last look for errors

Carefully look back over your work for any remaining errors.

Have someone else double check your work one last time.

Decide whether you met your goals.

FIGURE 4.22   THE SEARCH EDITING STRATEGY

Source: From *The Adolescent with Learning Disabilities*, by E. S. Ellis & P. Friend, 1991. In B. Y. K. Wong (Ed.), *Learning About Learning Disabilities*, pp. 506–561, Orlando, FL: Academic Press.

motivation, self-reinforcement, and goal-directed self-speech during the editing process. The SEARCH editing strategy can be used to meet many common writing demands in academic and nonacademic settings. The strategy is used any time students are expected to write passages that others will read and is especially important to use when addressing academic tasks (e.g., book reports for English classes, essay questions in history classes, current events reports in social studies classes).

Students apply the strategy following completion of their first draft of a composition. First, students reflect on their goals for editing their papers by identifying a person with whom they would like to impress favorably if this person were to read the composition. An overall quality goal is established (e.g., "This is an important piece. I want this composition to be medium-to-high quality/superior quality). Then students set specific numerical goals related to conventions-of-print errors (e.g., "When I'm finished editing, my goal is to have only one error I've overlooked per 20 words").

Once students have established their goals, they read the paper aloud for meaning. Their reading the paper to someone else can be effective. In doing so, students determine whether specific sentences make sense, whether they are sentence fragments or run-on sentences, and whether words have been omitted accidentally. In addition, students check to assure that they have expressed the message they intended to communicate.

After students have checked their papers for meaning, they search for and correct conventions-of-print errors, the "picky" errors teachers often mark on their papers. Students first identify as many of these as they can independently, and then they have someone else double-check their work.

During the last phase of the SEARCH editing strategy, students write a final draft of their work, making sure they include all corrections in the rough draft and undertaking a final "search for errors." Someone else can be enlisted to do a final double-check. Finally, students reflect on the quality of their work and determine whether they think they have met the goals established originally.

Students should be able to perform the following independently:

1. Write complete sentences.
2. Recognize and correct incomplete sentences and run-on sentences.
3. Possess basic knowledge of conventions of print to identify and correct mechanical writing errors (e.g., rules of capitalization, punctuation, basic grammar).
4. Recognize when a word probably has been misspelled and locate correct spellings of difficult-to-spell words.

Teachers should teach the strategy to mastery levels. Students must master the process, or strategic behaviors, of using the strategy, and their written products should reflect mastery levels of editing. Suggested mastery levels are as follows.

1. *Mastery of strategic behaviors.* Student provides evidence of:
   — completing both a rough draft and a final draft.
   — reading the document for meaning.
   — editing for conventions-of-print errors.
   — using someone to double-check the work *after* attempting to edit the work independently.
2. *Mastery of written products.* In students' written products, minimal performance standards require that the passage have the following characteristics:
   — maintaining a consistent point of view throughout the passage and a logical presentation of ideas.
   — containing no incomplete sentences or sentence fragments.
   — containing a maximum of one convention-of-print error per 20 words (95% error-free).

Before beginning instruction in the SEARCH editing strategy, the teacher should consider putting together three sets of writing samples.

1. The first set should represent writing tasks that traditionally are assigned to students in the classroom. These tasks should require students to use effective editing strategies to be successful (e.g., essay test questions, weekly current events reports, book reports, lab reports).
2. The second set should represent nonacademic writing tasks in which editing also is important (e.g., letters for job applications, letters to girlfriends, letters to parents asking for money).
3. The third set should represent writing tasks in which editing is *not* crucial for success (e.g., personal diaries, class notes, grocery lists).

The teacher should provide students with copies of the materials and have them work in pairs to analyze the products. Students have to analyze the task and the writing sample to determine whether effective editing strategies are important and whether the original writer seemed to use an effective editing strategy. Students then compare their findings.

This activity is used to introduce to students the importance of editing strategies and the concept that sometimes these strategies are necessary when performing academic tasks and sometimes they are not, and that the same holds true for nonacademic tasks. The teacher points out the frequency in which students are faced with these types of assignments. Then the teacher informs the students that they will be introduced to a strategy they can use to make the process of editing writing tasks a lot easier to tackle. This prelearning motivational activity can be enhanced further by:

- Showing students pretest/posttest writing samples of students who learned the strategy previously and having them analyze those writing samples in terms of quality of work and quantity of errors.
- Showing students data reflecting pretest/posttest performances (e.g., "Before learning the strategy, students averaged one error per every four words; after learning the strategy, they averaged one error per every 33 words").
- Having students who mastered the SEARCH strategy previously describe what learning it was like and where they are using it currently.
- Using humor by:
  — dressing up as "Ms. Messy" and using this as a basis for discussing the importance of appearance, eventually drawing the analogy that most people are concerned about how they look because of the impression it gives others, and many don't realize that the way their writing looks gives a similar impression.
  — using before-and-after "Glamour Photo" to stimulate discussion about the differences between the before and after. These can be compared to the process used in editing and revising.
  — showing students a "love letter" containing many conventions-of-print errors and discussing the impression the letter would make on the opposite sex. Point out errors that, if left uncorrected, would send the wrong message.

For strategy instruction in the classroom to be effective, teachers must take the time to describe and model the strategy using topics and assignments found traditionally in their various classes. They must model the covert processes as well as overt processes associated with the strategy. They also must allot some time for students to rehearse and elaborate on the strategy verbally. As a homework assignment, students could be asked to memorize the strategy steps. The teacher can provide a "bonus point" quiz on the strategy following the homework assignment.

In using the SEARCH strategy, students must understand that, although effective writers monitor for errors as they initially write their ideas, most of the editing takes place *after* they have generated a rough draft. More effective writers first think ahead to identify and organize their ideas, then write their ideas to produce a rough draft, and then edit, instead of doing these processes simultaneously. When presenting the remembering system, teachers should note that the first letter of each step in the strategy spells the word "search," as in "searching for errors and correcting them."

When modeling the SEARCH strategy, the teacher first prepares a 350–400 word rough draft of a composition that contains a few errors in logic (a sentence or two that doesn't fit in with the rest of the composition), as well as a variety of conventions-of-print errors. The teacher uses the "think-aloud" procedure to model critical thought processes and goal-directed self-speech when applying the SEARCH strategy (e.g., "Okay, let's see....Now I need to do the Examine step—read it out loud to see if it makes sense....").

In addition to modeling goal-directed speech related to cueing specific strategy steps, the teacher models the following thought processes:

- Analyzing the writing assignment to determine whether SEARCH is an appropriate strategy to use.
- Reflecting on personal goals related to the editing process.
- Making positive self-affirmation statements.
- Using self-reinforcement.

Students describe the overall strategic process in their own words, then, while looking at the strategy steps if necessary, describe what each step is cueing them to do. Finally, they commit the strategy steps to memory.

During acquisition practice activities, students are *acquiring* the skills necessary to perform the strategy independently. Teachers can use several instructional formats.

1. *"I wrote it; you fix it."* Before the practice activity, construct a 350–400 word passage that contains a variety of writing errors (approximately 20–25 errors). The content of these passages should address the subject area in which you are teaching (e.g., social studies, literature). Provide each student with a copy of the same passage, and then cue students to perform each step of the strategy while monitoring them to assure that they are performing the steps correctly. Be sure that each student has completed a specific step correctly before cueing all students to proceed to the next step. As students become familiar with the strategy steps, shift the nature of your cues from signaling students to perform explicit strategy steps (e.g., "Now you need to do the 'Copy over neatly step'") to cueing them to use goal-directed speech (e.g., "What do you need to tell yourself now?"). Repeat this activity using different error-laden passages you have constructed. As students take more responsibility for identifying and correcting errors, gradually fade your cues.

2. *"I wrote it; you guys fix it."* Once again, provide students with written passages about the content in which you are teaching that also have errors imbedded in them. Divide students into cooperative learning groups of four members each. Provide a copy for each member of the group, and then have the students work together to apply the SEARCH editing strategy. Sample alternative cooperative learning formats are as follows:

   a. When each team has a copy of the *same* composition:

      — A "team captain" directs the entire group to edit the work together, line-by-line. The "team recorder" notes all corrections on a master copy. Later, each team reports to the other teams the errors they identified and corrected.

      — The work is divided into four sections of approximately equal length. Each student is assigned one section and is responsible for editing that section. Once completed, each student reports corrections to the group, where they are transferred to a master copy, which subsequently is turned in to the teacher for evaluation and feedback.

   b. When each team has a copy of a *different* composition:

      Use the same procedures as those identified above, except that, once completed, the corrected master copies are exchanged between groups. This new group then applies the SEARCH strategy to the already edited composition. The second group is awarded five points for identifying each previously undetected error. The groups with the most points at the end win. Thus, the first group is highly motivated to identify all errors so the second group will not receive points. The second group also is more motivated to use the SEARCH strategy diligently to attain points, and so forth.

3. *"We wrote it; you guys fix it."* Have each group write a 350-400 word composition about the content subject matter. *Purposefully* include approximately 20 conventions-of-print errors. Have the groups exchange the compositions and subsequently apply the SEARCH editing strategy to the other groups' compositions. From this point the *"I wrote it; you guys fix it"* procedure described above can be applied.

4. *"We wrote it; we fix it; you guys double-check it."* Here, delegate to each group the responsibility for developing a composition *and* applying the SEARCH editing strategy. When completed, have the groups exchange their compositions. Each time the second group detects a previously undetected conventions-of-print error, award five points.

5. *"Student wrote it; student fixes it."* Make individual students responsible for writing a composition concerning the content subject matter, and then applying the SEARCH editing strategy.

For feedback to be maximally effective, it should focus explicitly on the types of correct behavior as well as the types of errors students make. In addition, it should reflect the effectiveness of strategic behaviors relative to established mastery criteria. Effective feedback also means facilitating students' elaboration on the feedback by having them use their own words to describe the feedback (Howell, 1986; Kea, 1987; Kline, 1989; Lenz, Ellis, & Scanlon, 1996). Intrinsic reinforcement should be facilitated as much as possible (Ellis, 1986; Ellis, Lenz, & Sabornie, 1987a, 1987b; Litcht, 1993; Litcht & Kistner, 1986). Specific activities to promote effective feedback and reinforcement include the following.

■ Create a checklist of the most common error types students make. Next to each error type, list the number of errors found and the line number in which it appeared. Then students will know how many of a specific type of error they need to continue to find and correct. For example:

Type of error	Number of this type of error
Capitalization	2
Punctuation	1
Spelling	5
Word Omission	0
Incomplete sentence	1
Run-on sentence	0
Grammar	2

■ To facilitate students' use of *self-reinforcement*, ask them to use the information on the error check sheet to identify and mark the type of conventions of print in which they are performing most successfully or the area of which they feel most confident and competent. Cue students to say something positive to themselves about their performance in this area.

■ Also to facilitate students' use of *self-reinforcement*, ask them to use the information on the error check sheet to identify and mark one error type for which they intend to set a self-improvement goal and to note the goal. Help students identify the nature of the error made. For example:

Type of error	Number of this type of error
Capitalization	2
Punctuation	1
Spelling	5

Goal: To reduce spelling error to one. Next time watch for "ed" endings on words.

■ If using a cooperative learning instructional format with small groups, consider:

— assigning one of the students to be the "feedback facilitator" to assure that all students in the group receive feedback on their use of the SEARCH strategy and reinforcement. A limited, structured approach should be employed. For example, the feedback facilitator assures that each member of the group has specific information about *one* category of error upon which to base future goals and also assures that each student is provided information about the category of performance in which he or she performed best. For example, the feedback facilitator might say: "Okay, Billy, let's see.... Your best area of performance was on editing sentences. You didn't have any run-on or incomplete sentences. Great. Now you need to take a look at areas that need work and set a goal for improvement."

— having each group make a report to the other groups in the classroom regarding the most effective areas of performance representative of the group as well as the most common types of errors made by the group. Group goals for improving one of the error categories can be reported as well. For example, the feedback facilitator might say: "Our group performed best in the area of capitalization. We did great. As a whole, what we are all going to work on is word omissions. We seem to keep leaving out words. Our goal for word omissions is to have only two in the whole group next time we write."

■ To provide extrinsic reinforcement, consider:

— using a grading system in which part of students' grades is based on effective use of the SEARCH strategy. For example:

20% or greater uncorrected error rate   = D
15%–19% uncorrected error rate   = C
8%–14% uncorrected error rate   = B
7% or less uncorrected error rate   = A

If a student's work is found to have an error rate of 6%, a grade of "A" is assigned for use of the SEARCH strategy.

— using a grading system in which part of students' grades is based on *improvement* in use of the SEARCH strategy. For example:

15 percentage points or better
   in improvement of error rate   = A
10–14 percentage points improvement   = B
6–9 percentage points improvement   = C
2–5 percentage points improvement   = D

If a student's previous work was found to have an error rate of 32% and the most recent work was found to have an error rate of 21% the student improved by 11 percentage points, which converts to a grade of "B" in use of the SEARCH strategy.

— providing students with extra credit for use of the SEARCH strategy any time the student independently recognizes an opportunity to use the strategy *without being reminded*.

Often, less effective learners seem to master a specific procedure or strategy following various practice activities but subsequently fail to utilize the strategy independently on everyday tasks. To avoid this, practice activities should be integrated thoroughly with real-life, or *applied*, assignments. The objective here is to require students to use the SEARCH strategy frequently to meet editing requirements typically found in the classroom. A technique that can be used is to provide explicit cues to use the SEARCH strategy. If teachers include explicit cues on using the strategy in content-area assignments, students will use the strategy much more frequently. Students can be cued to use the SEARCH strategy by:

— imbedding cues into written instructions or questions. For example, from a science class: "Describe two chemical changes that can occur in your body during the respiratory process. Use SEARCH to edit your work."

— providing written cues to remind students that they possess an effective strategy for performing the task. Following a study guide question from a geography class, the cue might be: "Why do farmers in the coastal plain of Texas have a difficult time? Use SEARCH to edit your work."

— providing verbal cues to remind students that they possess an effective strategy for performing the task. As an example from a basic science class: "Everybody look at question number three. It says, 'Describe an experiment that early scientists used to measure the impact of solar energy on our oceans.' What's a good strategy to use after you write the first draft of your answer?"

To generalize the SEARCH strategy, the teacher should review with the students the natural environmental cues that signal a need to use the strategy. Students should practice discriminating between writing tasks in which the strategy is important and those in which it is not. They should target specific assignments from other classes in which to apply the editing strategy and establish generalization goals.

The teacher also may want to provide students with writing assignments that they must complete independently outside the setting in which the strategy training takes place. Students must perform at mastery levels a minimum of six times to ensure that the strategy has been learned thoroughly and is used frequently. Students also must recognize opportunities independently and use the editing strategy to meet actual demands of the general classroom.

General education teachers should incorporate into their routine content-area instruction cues to use the editing strategy. They may have to be convinced of its benefits through examples of changes in the students' work. This is a good time to use the writing portfolio as a graphic example of changes over time.

SUMMARY

Research has demonstrated that writing is one of the most common deficits in students with LD and it is one of the more challenging areas to address. Students experience writing problems for a host of reasons. Some of the most common are: limited knowledge of subjects about which to write, limited expressive language skills, underdeveloped knowledge of writing processes and strategies, and negative attitudes about writing. The sources of these problems can be from within (e.g., poorly developed language skills, impulsive personalities), or they can originate from the external environment (negative experiences with nonauthentic writing tasks, intensive instruction in peripheral knowledge such as grammar, and so forth).

Motivation (or lack of it) is often a significant obstacle to meaningful instruction in writing strategies. Sometimes students' reluctance to write can rub off on the teacher, and as a result the student is not asked to write as much, to avoid negative reactions. Too often we teachers attempt to reinforce writing using artificial reward structures (e.g., grades, earning free time for good work). In this chapter a variety of alternative approaches to motivation that may have more lasting effects were reviewed. At the heart of these techniques are three key practices: making writing a social event, facilitating personal satisfaction, and promoting personal ownership. Together these practices suggest that the key to real motivation for empowered writing is to *make writing tasks authentic and to promote students' pride.*

When planning interventions teachers should consider assessing students' attitudes, the content of their written messages, their approach or strategies they typically use, and the demands of the setting or what is expected from them to be successful within the writing domain. The mechanics of writing (e.g., spelling, punctuation, capitalization) often are the easiest to assess and, thus, also are often the most frequently targeted for instruction. Although writing mechanics are important, the message or content of the writing is even more important. Fortunately, research has demonstrated that instruction in writing strategies can empower students significantly in their writing, and significant improvements often are demonstrated in the content of their writing as well as the technical manner in which it is expressed.

The writing strategies discussed in this chapter target three key areas: sentence writing, expository writing, and editing/revising. Teaching students strategies for organizing information via various graphic organizers can be particularly helpful. Although instruction in specific grammar may be appropriate in limited circumstances, grammar instruction rarely translates into more expressive, technically correct writing. Conversely, the efficacy of instruction in specific writing strategies has strong empirical support.

REFERENCES

Abruscato, J. (1993). Early results and tentative implications from the Vermont portfolio project. *Phi Delta Kappan, 74*, 474–477.

Applebee, A. (1986). Problems in process approaches: Toward a reconceptualization of process instruction. In A. Petrosky, D. Bartholomae, & K. Rehage (Eds.), *The teaching of writing: Eighty-fifth yearbook of the National Society for the Study of Education* (pp. 95–113). Chicago: University of Chicago Press.

Applebee, A. N., & Langer, J. A. (1983). Instructional scaffolding: Reading and writing as natural language activities. *Language Arts, 60*, 168–175.

Bos, C. S. (1988). Process-oriented writing: Instructional implications for mildly handicapped students. *Exceptional Children, 54*, 521–527.

Chalfant, J. C. & Scheffelin, M. A. (1969). *Central processing dysfunctions in children: A review of research* (monograph). Washington, DC: U.S. Printing Office.

Christenson, S., Thurlow, M., Ysseldyke, J., & McVicar, R. (1989). Written language instruction for students with mild handicaps: Is there enough quantity to ensure quality. *Learning Disabilities Quarterly, 12*, 219–229.

Deshler, D. D. (1978). Psychoeducational aspects of learning disabled adolescents. In L. Mann, L. Goodman, & J. L. Wiederholt (Eds.), *Teaching the learning disabled adolescent*. Boston: Houghton-Mifflin.

DiPardo, A., & Freeman, S. (1988). Peer response groups in the writing classroom: Theoretic foundations and new directions. *Review of Educational Research, 58*, 119–145.

Drake, C., & Cavanaugh, J. A. (1970). Teaching the high school dyslexic. In L. E. Anderson (Ed.), *Helping the adolescent with the hidden handicap*. Belmont, CA: Fearon.

Elbow, P. (1973). *Writing without teachers*. New York: Oxford University Press.

Ellis, E. S. (1986). The role of motivation and pedagogy on the generalization of cognitive strategy training.

Journal of Learning Disabilities, 19(2), 66–70.

Ellis, E. S. (1993a). A learning strategy for meeting the writing demands of secondary mainstream classrooms. *The Alabama Council for Exceptional Children Journal, 10*(1), 21–38.

Ellis, E. S. (1993b). Teaching strategy sameness using integrated formats. *Journal of Learning Disabilities, 26*(7), 448–482.

Ellis, E. S. (1993c). *Writing strategies for thought-full classrooms.* Tuscaloosa, AL: SMART Strategy Assoc.

Ellis, E. S. (1994a). An instructional model for integrating content-area instruction with cognitive strategy instruction. *Reading and Writing Quarterly: Overcoming Learning Difficulties, 10,* 63–90.

Ellis, E. S. (1994b). Integrating content with writing strategy instruction: Part 2–Writing processes. *Intervention in the School and Clinic, 29*(4), 219–228.

Ellis, E. S., & Feldman, K. (1994). Creating "thought-full" classrooms: Fostering cognitive literacy via cooperative learning and integrated strategy instruction. In S. Sharan (Ed.), *Handbook of cooperative learning methods.* New York: Preager.

Ellis, E. S., & Friend, P. (1991). The adolescent with learning disabilities. In B. Y. K. Wong (Ed.), *Learning about learning disabilities* (pp. 506–561). Orlando, FL: Academic Press.

Ellis, E. S., Lenz, B. K., & Sabornie, E. J. (1987a). Generalization and adaptation of learning strategies to natural environments: Part 1. Critical agents. *Remedial and Special Education, 8*(1), 6–21.

Ellis, E. S., Lenz, B. K., & Sabornie, E. J. (1987b). Generalization and adaptation of learning strategies to natural environments: Part II. Research into practice. *Remedial and Special Education, 8*(2) 6–23.

Flowers, L., & Haynes, J. (1980). The dynamics of composing: Making plans and juggling constraints. In L. Gregg & E. Steinberg (Eds.), *Cognitive process writing* (pp. 31–50). Hillsdale, NJ: Lawrence Erlbaum.

Graham, S. (1982). Composition research and practice: A unified approach. *Focus on Exceptional Children, 14,* 1–16.

Graham, S., & Harris, K. R. (1993a). Self-regulated strategy development: Helping students with learning problems develop as writers. *Elementary School Journal, 94,* (2) 169–181.

Graham, S., & Harris, K. R. (1993b). Teaching writing strategies to students with learning disabilities: Issues and recommendations. In L. Meltzer (Ed.), *Strategy assessment and instruction for students with learning disabilities* (pp. 271–292). Austin: Pro-Ed.

Graham, S., Harris, K. R., MacArthur, C., & Schwartz, S. (1991). Writing instruction. In B. Y. L. Wong (Ed.), *Learning about learning disabilities* (pp. 309–341). San Diego: Academic Press.

Graves, D. H., & Sunstein, B. S. (1992). *Portfolio portraits.* Portsmouth, NH: Heinemann.

Grill, J. J., & Kerwin, M. M. (1989). *Written language assessment.* Novato, CA: Academic Therapy Pulications.

Hammill, D. D., Brown, V. L., Larsen, S. C., & Wiederholt, J. L. (1994). *Test of adolescent and adult language.* Austin: Pro-Ed.

Hammill, D. D., & Larsen, S. C. (1989). *Test of written language,* Austin: Pro-Ed.

Harris, K. R., Graham, S., & Pressley, M. (in press). Cognitive strategies in reading and written language. In N. Singh & I. Beale (Eds.), *Current perspectives in learning disabilities: Nature, theory, and treatment.* New York: Springer-Verlag.

Hennings, D., & Grant, B. (1974). *Content and craft: Written expression in the elementary school.* Englewood Cliffs, NJ: Prentice Hall.

Higgens, J. A. (1975). Remedial teachers' needs versus emphasis in text-workbooks. *College Composition & Communication, 24,* 188–193.

Howell, K. W. (1986). Direct assessment of academic performance. *School Psychology Review, 15,* 324–335.

Irmscher, W. F. (1972). *The Holt guide to English.* New York: Holt, Rinehart & Winston.

Jochum, J. (1991). Responding to writing and to the writer. *Intervention in School and Clinic, 2,* 152–157.

Johnson, L. A., & Graham, S. (1990). Goal setting and its application with exceptional learners. *Preventing School Failure, 34,* 4–8.

Kea, C. D. (1987). *An analysis of critical teaching behaviors employed by teachers of students with learning disabilities.* Unpublished doctoral dissertation, University of Kansas, Lawrence.

Kline, F. M. (1989). *The development and validation of feedback routines for use in special education settings.* Unpublished doctoral dissertation, University of Kansas, Lawrence.

Laurence, M. (1972). *Writing as a thinking process.* Ann Arbor: University of Michigan Press.

Lenz, B. K., Ellis, E. S., & Scanlon, D. (1996). *Teaching learning strategies to adolescents and adults with learning disabilities*. Austin: Pro-Ed.

Litcht, B. (1993). Achievement related beliefs in children with learning disabilities: Impact on motivation and strategic learning. In L. Meltzer (Ed.), *Strategy assessment and instruction for students with learning disabilities* (pp. 195–220). Austin: Pro-Ed.

Litcht, B. C., & Kistner, J. A. (1986). Motivational problems of learning disabled children: Individual differences and their implications for treatment. In J. K. Torgesen & B. Y. K. Wong (Eds.), *Psychological and educational perspectives on learning disabilities*. New York: Academic Press.

MacArthur, C., & Graham, S. (1987). Learning disabled students' composing with three methods: Handwriting, dictation, and word processing. *The Journal of Special Education, 21*, 22–42.

MacArthur, C. A., & Stoddard, B. (1990). *Teaching LD students to revise: A peer editor strategy*. Paper presented at annual meeting of American Educational Research Association, Boston.

Markwardt, F. C. (1989). *Peabody individual achievement test–revised*. Circle Pines, MN: American Guidance Service.

Moran, M., Schumaker, J. B., & Vetter, A. (1981). *Teaching a paragraph organization strategy to learning disabled adolescents* (Research Rep. No. 54). Lawrence: University of Kansas Institute for Research in Learning Disabilities.

Myers, M. (1980). *A procedure for writing assessment and holistic scoring*. Urbana, IL: ERIC Clearinghouse on Reading and Communication Skills and National Council of Teachers of English.

Putnam, L., Deshler, D., & Schumaker, J. (1993). The investigation of setting demands: A missing link in strategy instruction. In L. Meltzer (Ed.), *Strategy assessment and instruction for students with learning disabilities* (pp. 325–354). Austin: Pro-Ed.

Roid, G. (1992). *Wechsler individual achievement test*. San Antonio: The Psychological Corporation.

Schmidt, J. L., Deshler, D. D., Schumaker, J. B., & Alley, G. R. (1989). Effects of generalization instruction on the written language performance of adolescents with learning disabilities in the mainstream classroom. *Journal of Reading, Writing, and Learning Disabilities, 4*(4), 291–311.

Schumaker, J. B. (in preparation). *TOWER: The essay writing strategy*. Lawrence: University of Kansas.

Schumaker, J. B., & Sheldon, J. (1985). *The sentence writing strategy*. Lawrence: University of Kansas.

Schumaker, J. B., Nolan, S. M., & Deshler, D. D. (1985). *The error monitoring strategy*. Lawrence: University of Kansas.

Spaulding, C. L. (1992). The motivation to read and write. In J. W. Irwin & M. A. Doyle (Eds.), *Reading and writing connection: Learning from research* (pp. 177–201). Newark, DE: International Reading Association.

Stoddard, B., & MacArthur, C. A. (1993). A peer editor strategy: Guiding learning-disabled students in response and revision. *Research in the Teaching of English, 27*, 76–103.

U.S. Department of Education. (1992). *Hard work and high expectations: Motivating students to learn*. Washington, DC: Office of Educational Research and Improvement.

Van Nostrand, A. D., Knoblauch, C. H., McGuire, P. J., & Pettigrew, J. (1978). *Functional writing*. Boston: Houghton-Mifflin.

Wallace, G., & Larsen, S. C. (1978). *Educational assessment of learning problems: Testing for teaching*. Needham Heights, MA: Allyn & Bacon.

Welsh, M., & Link, D. P. (1992). Informal assessment of paragraph composition. *Intervention in School and Clinic, 27*, 145–149.

Woodcock, R. W., & Johnson, W. B. (1989). *Woodcock-Johnson psychoeducational battery–revised*. Allen, TX: DLM Teaching Resources.

5

Memory and Test-Taking Strategies

CHARLES A. HUGHES

QUESTIONS TO KEEP IN MIND

- How is information-processing theory used to explain memory, and how has this theory led to specific interventions such as mnemonics?

- For what types of memory tasks are mnemonics useful or not useful?

- Who should be responsible for the development of mnemonic devices—the teacher or the student?

- Is spending time teaching students how to take tests important? Why or why not?

- Should teachers modify or change their testing procedures to accommodate adolescents with learning disabilities? If so, what kind of modifications should they make?

ADVANCE ORGANIZER

Many adolescents (as well as adults) would rather handle snakes than study for and take tests. Also, many professionals would argue that current classroom testing practices are not the best way to assess learning. Despite the aversion to taking tests and the criticisms about their efficacy, tests are used, and used frequently. Thus, students typically need to spend a significant amount of time trying to understand and remember information for the purpose of taking a test.

This chapter provides information about the memory and test-taking abilities of adolescents with LD as well as techniques and strategies to teach these skills. The chapter is divided into two major sections, one each for memory and test-taking. Figure 5.1 shows how the chapter has been organized.

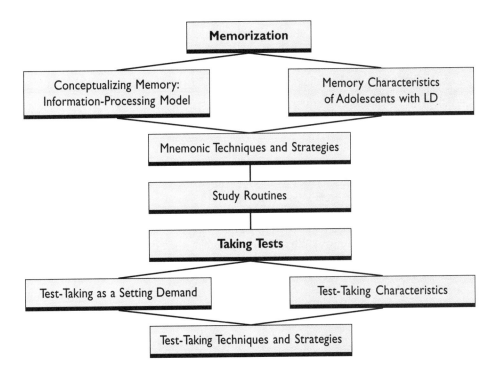

FIGURE 5.1   CHAPTER 5 ORGANIZATION

MEMORY

When was the last time you had to cram for a test? Do you remember much of the material now? Why are some things easy to remember and others hard to remember? These questions relate to memory. "Memory is the ability to encode, process and retrieve information that one is exposed to" (Swanson & Cooney, 1991, p. 104). Given this definition, memory and learning are inseparable, and severe problems in memory equate to severe problems in school (Brown, 1979). Memory is a constant and pervasive setting demand regardless of the academic content or skills taught. When memory is viewed as a process whereby information is attended to, processed and retrieved, it becomes more than something needed to take a test. Memory comes into play in many tasks in academic and nonacademic settings and throughout life (e.g., when listening to lectures, answering questions, following directions, reading, writing, and computing).

When students enter secondary school, the assumption is that they have stored in memory enough procedural and factual information to benefit from the more didactic and content-related instruction that takes place in that setting. Compared to students in elementary settings, students in secondary settings read more about more topics, listen to more lectures, write more about what they have learned, and take more tests designed to assess what they have retained. In addition to lacking memory skills needed to demonstrate understanding of presented content, students with memory problems come to this setting with less than adequate prior knowledge and vocabulary they need to benefit from instruction.

An overview of memory theory is presented first to provide a context for memory instruction and the memory characteristics of students with LD. Instructional issues and methods, too, are discussed and described.

MEMORY THEORY

What is a sensory register? Working memory? How does information get from short-term to long-term memory? Why do we remember some things but not others? What are the storage capacities and functions of the different components of memory? If you can answer these questions, your long-term memory, from courses in educational psychology, is working great. If you cannot answer all the questions, ask yourself why. Most likely, your answer was similar to one of the following: "It's been a long time since I read about it"; "I just studied this information for the test and haven't used it since"; or "I can't remember specifics, but it wouldn't take much reading to bring it all back." Keep these answers in mind as you read the discussion of memory.

Memory theory also helps explain where and why many adolescents with LD are having problems in understanding and retaining information. The area or type of memory difficulty has direct implications for which kinds of techniques and strategies may be most useful for students. Among the several explanatory models of memory, the *information processing model* is most commonly used.

Memory and Test-Taking Strategies

CONCEPTUALIZING MEMORY: INFORMATION-PROCESSING MODEL

Most of the information presented here is based on several sources (Eggen & Kauchak, 1992; Levine, 1987; Swanson & Cooney, 1991). This model is a hypothetical construct (our current best guess at describing something we cannot see) used to explain the components or stores of memory—how information is received, transformed, elaborated, stored, retrieved, and used. The stages or stores are presented graphically in Figure 5.2.

STIMULI AND THE SENSORY REGISTER

In school, students are presented with various stimuli, usually auditory or visual, to which they attend or do not attend. Thus, attention, though sometimes seen as separate from memory, is a vital part of the memory process, especially at the sensory-registration stage. Given documented attention problems of many adolescents with learning difficulties, teachers often institute procedures for increasing attention to important stimuli such as teaching students to self-monitor their attention or making the stimulus more apparent (e.g., voice emphasis, repeating important information, providing written directions along with verbal directions) to the student.

The sensory register is conceptualized as the place where a copy of the "attended to" material is held a few seconds (auditory stimuli are held longer than visual stimuli). Reading a sentence is an example of keeping information in the sensory register. If the memory traces of the first few words in the sentence are lost, the sentence has no meaning for the reader. Although the capacity of the sensory register is unlimited, care must be taken as to how many stimuli are presented. A common classroom example of this is when complex or multiple-step directions are given and students follow only the last step or two because the first parts of the directions have "faded away." This fading or decaying process occurs rapidly unless the information, if deemed important, is taken into the short-term or working memory.

SHORT-TERM AND WORKING MEMORY

This store is seen as a "temporary holding area" in which information is held for a brief time. This store serves two functions: a temporary, passive store (*short-term memory*), and a temporary, active store (*working memory*) in which mental calculations are performed. Information in the short-term store can be retained for up to 20 seconds in adults, at which point it is forgotten, retained a while longer through repetition or rehearsing, or transferred into long-term memory through extended rehearsal or elaboration. Thus, verbal rehearsal (saying something again and again) is the main cognitive strategy for enhancing short-term memory. For example, you use a verbal rehearsal strategy to remember a phone number you've looked up (or heard) so you can hold on to the information long

FIGURE 5.2   COMPONENTS OF THE INFORMATION PROCESSING MODEL

enough to dial the phone. If the line is busy (and you don't have a redial function on your phone), you may have to look up the number again because you've forgotten it already. Verbal rehearsal, therefore, is a relatively weak strategy for remembering.

As mentioned, working memory involves performing mental operations. Information is "held in mind," and previously learned facts or procedures (held in long-term memory) are recalled and used to solve a problem. A frequently used example of working memory is mental arithmetic. For example, solve this problem in your head: "Which is the better buy? 3 ounces of coffee for 67 cents or 9 ounces at $1.87?" To solve this problem, you have to hold some information in mind as you perform the operation (division). You also call upon information in long-term memory (e.g., knowledge of basic division facts, estimation) to help you.

Passive and active stores both have limited capacity and, as such, are susceptible to decay. Research has shown that only seven digits (plus or minus two digits) can be held in short-term memory. One method for increasing capacity and avoiding memory overload is to *chunk* material—to combine separate items into larger, meaningful units. For example, when given a phone number, many people will not try to remember each number by itself but instead will chunk and rehearse the number into two units consisting of the first three digits and the last four digits. In effect they have taken seven units/items and made them into two. When reading, we chunk automatically. For instance, when you read the word *chunk*, you do not see it as five letters or units, but, rather, as just one word. Other ways of dealing with information decay are to use *clustering* (organizing information into categories) or *mnemonics*. These methods will be discussed in more detail later in the chapter.

As mentioned earlier, working memory requires the retrieval and use of information already in long-term memory and thus has a unique capacity limitation. In the mental arithmetic example above, you are asked to keep in mind information (price of different quantities of coffee) and then retrieve your knowledge of math facts (division). If your recall of basic math facts was not automatic (fast, effortless), you would have had difficulty holding the derived prices in your working memory. Thus, automaticity in basic skills can affect the capacity and function of the working memory dramatically. This is seen often in adolescents who have not mastered basic or prerequisite skills. If most of the working memory is taken up with trying to remember the mechanics of writing, content and organization will suffer. The relationship of automaticity and memory will be discussed in more detail later, but teachers should keep problems with automatic retrieval and retention of basic skills in mind when deciding how much new information to present to students, and continually monitor comprehension of material by asking questions frequently. Students also benefit from receiving periodic summaries and time to consolidate information.

LONG-TERM MEMORY

When information is stored or manipulated in short-term or working memory, a decision usually is made to either forget the information or store it in long-term memory. Long-term memory is permanent storage with unlimited capacity (up to one billion bits or chunks of information). Memory in this store is classified as either episodic or semantic. *Episodic memories* typically are visual images of personal experiences (remember your first boyfriend or girlfriend?). *Semantic memory* consists of facts, concepts, or generalizations that are interconnected in some way. This type of memory is recalled as words, and the interconnections and relationships between this information, typically referred to as *schema* or *routines*, can be stored either verbally or visually. Later retrieval of semantic information is helped by these associations; the more meaningful the association, the better. Typically, students with LD have the most problems recalling the latter type of information.

To store information, it must be manipulated or encoded in some fashion. A common procedure for storing information in long-term memory is *multiple rehearsal* or *repetition*. As illustrated by the phone number example, however, this method is fairly inefficient when compared to deeper processing techniques such as elaborating and making associations with similar information already in long-term memory. Levin (1988) defined *elaboration* as meaningful enhancements, additions, constructions, or generations that improve memory. For example, in terms of later recall, requiring students to explain in their own words why a war started is more helpful than asking them to memorize a list of reasons.

In summary, information processing describes memory as hypothetical stores of information and procedures that facilitate the movement of information between stores. Selective attention to relevant stimuli and information entry into the sensory register are the first steps in the memory process. Small amounts of selected information in the sensory register are retained for additional processing in the short-term or working memory. The capacity (amount and duration) of working memory is affected directly by how automatic basic skills (e.g., math facts, word recognition) needed for solving the mental problem are, and whether the new information is rehearsed. Additional rehearsal transfers some of the information into long-term memory; however, more information is retained and available for retrieval in the long-term memory store if the information is encoded in ways that result in meaningful associations. Meaningfulness is enhanced through techniques such as organization, elaboration, and mnemonic devices (procedures used to make associations when they do not exist naturally). How a person controls these processes is called metamemory.

METAMEMORY AND EXECUTIVE FUNCTIONING

As mentioned throughout this book, executive functioning is the internal "director" that decides, among other things, which process or strategy will be performed, and monitors, evaluates, and adapts the strategy. This ability, as it relates to memory, is often referred to as *metamemory*. Metamemory is the awareness of memory strategies as well as the ability to use and monitor these strategies. It involves analyzing the memory task (e.g., study a list of vocabulary for a test, remember a phone number), considering one's memory abilities or limitations (e.g., knowing you need to write things down, knowing that memorizing lists is hard for you), selecting the appropriate strategy (e.g., write down the phone number, form a mnemonic for the list to be memorized), deciding how much effort (e.g., time) is needed to study the information, and evaluating the effectiveness of the strategy (Harris, Graham, & Freeman, 1988; Levin, 1983). This type of executive functioning begins to emerge in children in upper elementary and junior-high school, although poor metamemory is sometimes suggested to be characteristic of many adolescents with LD.

Memory Characteristics of Adolescents with Learning Disabilities

As with many other aspects of LD, much of the research conducted in the area of memory has been with elementary-aged students. Little is known about specific memory characteristics of adolescents with LD, so research findings on younger students must be extrapolated to older students. Although this is less than scientific, memory problems are not likely to disappear with the onset of adolescence. A further distortion is that much of the research on memory characteristics of students with LD takes place in clinical settings (nonclassrooms, experimenter with one student), and results are based on performance on tasks that are not required in classrooms (e.g., digit-span tasks). With these cautions in mind, a brief summary of findings about memory characteristics is presented in the next section. Based on the discussion about the components of memory, students may have problems in one or more memory functions including, the sensory register, short-term, working, and long-term (for both storage and retrieval) memory, and metamemory.

Sensory Register Characteristics

The little research that has been conducted on the sensory register of students with LD indicates that this store is intact; basic capacity is not deficient (Elbert, 1984; Lehman & Brady, 1982; Swanson & Cooney, 1991). Sensory registration of students with LD is enhanced, however, when information is presented at a reduced rate. Thus, even though the sensory register may be intact, rate of presentation may adversely affect the ability to register and store information. Also, attention problems may affect information processing at this store, although some researchers argue that the problem does not result from attention capability. Rather, the use (or nonuse) of this capability is what interferes with adequate registration of information. Levine (1987) argued that some students with LD have registration problems because they do not register information *intensely* enough. For example, a student might be sitting passively in biology class without taking notes or thinking about the content presented (this passivity may be because he hates biology, does not know how to take notes, or the lecturer is going too fast and is using terms the student does not understand). Whatever the reason, the problem is not with the student's sensory register but, instead, the degree to which he or she is paying attention. This superficial treatment of sensory information, combined with lack of attention to the important aspects of the information, results in "spotty" memory performance and lack of transfer into short-term memory.

In summary, sensory capability seems to be intact, but attention problems and lack of adequate processing inhibit memory performance at the sensory registration store. Content enhancement procedures such as those discussed in other parts of this text may increase student attention to critical aspects of information, which in turn will allow for deeper processing and entry of information to the short-term or working memory store.

Short-Term and Working Memory Characteristics

Students with LD seem to have problems with short-term and working memory (Bauer, 1979; Hagen & Barclay, 1982; Swanson, Cochran, & Ewers, 1990; Torgeson, 1977;

Torgeson & Goldman, 1977; Torgeson & Kail, 1980; Worden, 1983), and these problems do not stem from limited capacity of this register (Wong, 1980, 1982). Rather, the problems seem to be caused by inefficient processing/encoding. Students frequently do use rehearsal strategies, but the strategies are shallow (i.e., simple rehearsal) and therefore inefficient in terms of making the information permanent and accessible in the long-term store.

Many writers in this area characterize students with LD as lacking spontaneous use of elaborative memory strategies (extended rehearsal, chunking, organizing, and associating information to previously learned material). Older and relatively high-functioning individuals with LD do not use study or memory strategies efficiently. For example, Hughes (1991) interviewed university students with LD about how they studied for tests and what they considered the most difficult aspect of studying. A large percentage of the interviewed students said that memorizing information was the most difficult part of studying, and the strategy they reported most frequently was rereading the textbook—a relatively shallow and inefficient method for understanding and retaining information.

Swanson et al. (1990), who investigated the working memory of a group of students with LD, concluded that working memory tasks were difficult for these students. Using tasks similar to those in classrooms (requiring both processing and storage), they found that many of the students had difficulty suspending one set of information (keeping it in the back of the mind) while working on another set of information. The researchers concluded that part of the difficulty related to problems with automaticity (e.g., basic facts, word finding). Too much attention and memory were taken up with trying to recall and retain information, leaving little memory capacity for actually solving the problem (remember the 7-digit capacity of this store?).

Long-Term Memory Characteristics

When examining characteristics of adolescents with LD, two aspects of long-term memory are of concern: storage capacity and retrieval capability. Little research has been conducted on the long-term memory characteristics of children and adolescents with LD and it remains unclear whether the primary problem is capacity or retrieving or an interaction of the two (Swanson & Cooney, 1991). Too, retrieval likely is hindered by use of inefficient strategies at the short-term store where clear associations and connections have not been made, leaving a weak memory "trace" in the long-term store. This last contention is supported in part because when adolescents with LD have been taught to use elaborative techniques and strategies, their retrieval of information has been enhanced dramatically.

Levin (1988) provided a personal observation about retrieval characteristics of students with LD that, though not empirical, is a phenomenon that teachers often notice. He described students who do quite well when *they* select what to describe about a specific topic and seem quite knowledgeable and fluent about the topic. When *someone else* (e.g., the teacher) specifies the knowledge to be recalled (usually on a test), however, they have much more difficulty. Similarly, Hughes (1991) asked university students to rate the difficulty of various types of test items (i.e., essay, fill-in-the blank, short answer, multiple-choice, true-false, and matching). Fill-in-the-blank and short-answer items were rated as most difficult, and the most common difficulty related to these types of items was the ability to remember specific words. This is not surprising given that semantic memory is especially difficult for many students with LD.

METAMEMORY CHARACTERISTICS

As noted, metamemory involves knowledge about one's own memory abilities (e.g., capacity, strategies) as well as one's ability to regulate the memory process (allotting appropriate amounts of study time, selecting appropriate strategies, and monitoring progress). Several authors (e.g., Gelzheiser, Solar, Shepard, & Wozniak, 1983; Harris et al., 1988; Hughes, 1991; Torgeson, 1979; Trepanier & Casale, 1982) have suggested that numerous students with LD have difficulties with many of the components of metamemory. For example, many students have trouble with one or more of the following memory skills:

- knowing, selecting, and using appropriate strategies
- estimating their own memory capacity for specific tasks
- predicting accuracy on a memory task
- allotting appropriate time to study
- deciding when they have studied enough

Also, although some evidence indicates that adolescents with LD have better metamemory skills than younger students with LD, they still have more difficulty in this area than students without disabilities.

Currently, the relationship between measures of metamemory (usually interviews of students about how they solve memory tasks) and actual performance on memory tasks is minimal. The memory tasks used, however, are simple tasks and do not directly reflect tasks that occur in classrooms. Obviously, more work is needed to establish clearly the relationship between metamemory and actual task performance.

Based on the above analysis of memory and learning disabilities, many students with LD clearly have memory problems that hinder them, especially in secondary settings where memory demands increase and a large store of prior knowledge is assumed. Examination of memory characteristics in the context of the information-processing model indicates that the main problem is not necessarily one of capacity (although the volume and rate of presentation can affect the amount of information registered) but, rather, the lack of meaningful elaboration and organization of information. Many students do not spontaneously use appropriate memory strategies that facilitate both storage and retrieval, particularly for semantically related information.

Also, problems exist in overall, planful study behavior. Often students have difficulty allotting enough study time, as well as identifying which parts of the information to be learned merit the most attention.

GENERAL INSTRUCTIONAL IMPLICATIONS

Some general recommendations for instruction are supported by the above review. (Specific strategies are described later in the chapter.)

1. Orient student attention before presenting information, and stress important details (e.g., vocabulary, concepts) when they occur.

2. Ensure that students have the prior knowledge/prerequisite skills needed to understand, and make connections with, new material.
3. Be sensitive to how much information is presented and at what rate.
4. Provide practice in basic skills and procedures to promote automaticity (to help with working memory tasks and retrieval).
5. Give students time to rehearse and elaborate on new information.
6. Make connections to previously learned information whenever possible; encourage students to explain their connections in their own words.
7. Provide and encourage distributed practice of information.
8. Teach students to avoid "cramming," and encourage and provide time for them to review notes/readings immediately after the lecture. (If they wait, they will have to relearn material.)
9. Provide opportunities for students to practice material under different conditions and with different tasks to promote comprehension and transfer.

In addition, many of the strategies described in other chapters of this text will help facilitate retention and overall comprehension of information presented in secondary classrooms. For example, paraphrasing is an elaborative technique designed to increase understanding and retention of text information. Graphic organizers promote understanding of the "connectedness" of a group of related concepts. Also, components of notetaking strategies are designed to increase elaboration and consolidation of information presented through teacher lecture.

Before turning to more specific strategies and methods for increasing memory, some discussion of assessing memory is warranted. Teachers may have to identify students who most need this type of intervention, as well as the relevant memory interventions.

ASSESSMENT OF MEMORY

One existing source of information about memory characteristics of adolescents is their performance on memory tasks contained in intelligence tests. These tasks include repeating sentences and number sequences (both forward and backward), reproducing designs, and reconstructing the meaning of paragraphs and stories (Salvia & Ysseldyke, 1991). Other tests, such as the Developmental Test of Visual-Motor Integration (Beery, 1982), contain memory tasks (students copy designs from memory). This test and others like it also sample motor skills, thus limiting conclusions regarding memory. Although poor performance on memory-related subtests contained in intelligence and other psychological tests may signal possible problems, the tasks are often artifacts; they do not approximate the memory demands of the classroom. Therefore, more informal measures such as observations, academic task performance, and interviews should be used. Finding out where in the memory process problems occur is important, too.

At the sensory-register level sensory impairment as a possible problem has to be eliminated first, although by adolescence this probably has been done. Elimination of sensory impairments as the reason for registration problems typically is done through vision and hearing screenings. If sensory capabilities are intact, attention should be examined by directly observing student orientation to stimuli as well as "on-task behavior" during times when information is presented. The teacher also should try to present information both auditorily and visually to see if problems become apparent when one or the other modality is used. Further, the teacher can set up a situation such as presenting several task-related directions or facts about a topic and then ask the student to recall them. If the student seems to be attending but still has problems with retention and retrieval, two follow-up procedures may be warranted: referral for neurological testing and assessment of working and short-term memory.

Giving students tasks that require working memory can indicate whether they have trouble performing a task and remembering information at the same time (remember the mental computation task described earlier in the chapter?). One example of such a task is described by Levine (1987). In this task the teacher says a series of letters in random order (e.g., L, T, D) and asks the student to say the letters in alphabetical order. This requires the student to store the letters briefly and then refer to long-term memory to retrieve the alphabetical order.

The teacher also can provide tasks in a variety of content areas (e.g., math, reading, writing) to see if the memory problems are content-specific. This is a good time to assess fluency (speed and accuracy) of basic, prerequisite skills to see if problems with automaticity may be hindering performance on tasks requiring working memory. Basic skills to assess for fluency include computation of basic math facts, word recognition, spelling, and writing speed.

Finding out whether students are using efficient, elaborative strategies to transfer information from short-term to long-term memory typically is assessed by interview or observation or both. The teacher presents a memory task such as remembering a list of information (related, unrelated, or a combination) and directs the student to memorize the list. Then the teacher watches how the student performs the task and asks questions about what is being done at each point. Another variation of this task is to put the listed information on index cards and observe whether the student organizes the cards in some fashion (e.g., forms clusters, alphabetizes, forms mnemonics) or merely uses basic rehearsal strategies.

Hughes (1991) administered a structured interview to first- and second-year university students to sample how they would approach studying for a test. First a scenario was read to the students. The scenario went something like this:

> Your instructor tells your class that a test will be given one week from today. The test will include multiple-choice, true-false, and matching items, as well as one essay question. The instructor says the test will cover the last two chapters in the textbook, as well as important content from the last two weeks of lecture. Tell me in detail what steps you would take to get ready for this test.

Students were prompted with questions such as, "What will you do first? How will you study your text? Your notes? What will you do if you have questions about test content?" This interview and other interviews like it sample only whether students *know* about good memorization and study strategies, not whether they actually use them in real situations.

A final area of informal assessment is *retrieval*. The teacher examines how long a student takes to retrieve information that he or she already knows (sometimes known as "speed of processing"). Giving the students tasks or asking them questions about known information and judging the relative speed of retrieval may provide information about how "firm" this information is or whether the student is in need of strategies that provide better links through increased elaboration.

Before ending the discussion about assessing memory, we reiterate that most informal methods of assessing memory (such as the ones described above) have not been validated empirically, and little is known about their reliability and validity. Like many other areas of teaching, however, teachers sometimes are left to make professional judgments about their students and what they know or do not know. These informal measures should be used with some caution, and the teacher should not rely on just one form of memory assessment.

Once the teacher is fairly sure that one or more of the students have problems with memory and are in need of better memory and study strategies, the next step is to teach them. The following section contains information about techniques and strategies for memorization, specifically mnemonics.

Mnemonic Techniques and Strategies

Do you remember studying for tests for which you had to memorize lists, steps, terminology? Do you remember how you studied this information? Did you make sentences or words out of the first letters of related terms (e.g., the planets and their order in terms of distance from the sun)? If you did this or other related techniques, you were using mnemonics. Mnemonics are methods for improving memory, and the word *mnemonics* literally means "aids memory." Eggen and Kauchak (1992) stated that mnemonics "aid encoding by forming associations that do not exist naturally in the content" (p. 342). Mnemonics are used to recode, transform, or elaborate information by adding meaningful connections to seemingly unconnected information (Carney, Levin, & Levin, 1993; Weinstein, 1978). These elaborations and linkages assist transference of information into long-term memory and later retrieval. Given the memory characteristics of many students with LD (e.g., lack of spontaneous elaboration strategies and subsequent retrieval problems) and the value of creating meaningful links between new and existing information, many adolescents with LD can benefit from using mnemonic techniques. Indeed, a growing body of research supports this contention.

For the most part, the research has involved using mnemonics to remember facts and vocabulary. The focus on teaching factual information via mnemonics has raised some concern in the educational community. For example, teaching facts is seen as less important than the overall comprehension of conceptual information. Some critics might argue that mnemonics, with its focus on facts and vocabulary, is a form of "intellectual bulimia" in which students gorge themselves on bits of meaningless, unrelated information and then regurgitate it all when they take the test. Conversely, it can be argued that acquisition of factual knowledge and vocabulary is prerequisite to comprehension, and accurate, fluent recall of related facts and vocabulary enhances comprehension.

On a more practical level, methods promoting the retention of factual information are functional for adolescents with LD because, right or wrong and regardless of what may happen to school curricula in the future, students in today's classrooms are expected to learn large amounts of factual information, and their classroom tests reflect this (Putnam,

Deshler, & Schumaker, 1992). As a final note on this issue, mnemonics are not presented here as a substitute for teaching for understanding but, rather, are intended to *supplement* it. Among the several types of mnemonic techniques are the keyword method, pegword method, and acronyms and acrostics.

KEYWORD METHOD

The keyword method, introduced by Atkinson (1975) in the context of teaching students to remember foreign language vocabulary, is designed to increase retention of unfamiliar vocabulary. Following Atkinson's work, educational researchers such as Michael Pressley and Joel Levin conducted studies with nonhandicapped students and found the keyword method to be effective for acquiring and recalling a variety of academic content. In the early 1980s, research on the effectiveness of the keyword method with adolescents with LD was begun by Margo Mastropieri and Thomas Scruggs. Subsequently, they and their associates have published numerous articles on this topic. The following discussion and description of the keyword method is based primarily on their work (e.g., Fulk, Mastropieri, & Scruggs, 1992; Mastropieri, 1988; Mastropieri & Scruggs, 1989; Mastropieri & Scruggs, 1991; Mastropieri, Scruggs, Bakken, & Brigham, 1992; Mastropieri, Scruggs, & Fulk, 1990; Pressley, Scruggs, & Mastropieri, 1989; Scruggs & Mastropieri, 1989a, 1989b; Scruggs & Mastropieri, 1992a).

The keyword method is based on *reconstructive elaboration theory* (Levin, 1983, 1988). Levin defined elaboration as involving "meaning-enhancing additions, constructions or generations that improve one's memory" (p. 191). In essence, elaboration makes the content to be learned more meaningful and concrete to the learner by linking stimulus information (e.g., a word) with response information (e.g., the definition or meaning of the word). This linkage can be made by reconstructing the information pictorially, verbally, or through imagining. Whichever method is used, the elaboration should be meaningful, include information that the student already knows, and should make the to-be-associated information interactive. When applied to the keyword method, the elaboration process involves three components or steps (sometimes referred to as the 3 Rs): recoding, relating, and retrieving (Levin, 1988).

RECODING Sometimes referred to as reconstructing (Mastropieri & Scruggs, 1991), this component of the keyword method involves changing (reconstructing) the unfamiliar word-to-be-learned to a familiar and similar sounding word (keyword). This keyword should be concrete and easily pictured. For example, if students were learning the meaning of the word *allegro* in a music or foreign language class, good keywords would be *leg* and *row* because together they sound like *allegro*, students probably know their meanings, and the keywords can be pictured easily. Students practice saying the keywords and the stimulus word together until association is established.

RELATING Continuing with the example, the next step is to relate or integrate the words *leg* and *row* to the definition of *allegro*, which means "to move quickly." This relationship can be established by constructing a sentence, by forming a visual image, or by drawing a picture. Most of the research with adolescents with LD has involved pictures or illustrations. Therefore, the usefulness of internal visualization or making up sentences, both of which involve different processes than developing a pictorial relationship, has not been well established.

When drawing the picture, the keyword and the meaning of the vocabulary word must interact in some way. A good interactive image for the example might be a picture of a leg rowing a boat quickly. Pictures should be free of extraneous material and do not have to have great artistic merit. A simple line drawing is adequate if the objects and the interaction are apparent to the students. The picture typically is drawn on a large index card, along with the word, keyword, and key points of the definition. Often a box is drawn around the picture to separate it from the additional information. The keyword illustration for the word *allegro* is contained in Figure 5.3. Often only one keyword that sounds like part of the word is necessary (two are used in the allegro example). The word *alley*, for instance, might be selected as a word acoustically similar to allegro, with an illustration of a boy running "quickly" through an alley.

Variations such as creating a keyword for each of two paired words as well as the addition of dialog can also be used when creating illustrations. In a study by Mastropieri et al. (1992), students were taught to remember states and their capitals. Because both words had to be linked and could not be illustrated concretely, keywords were created for both words. For example, Madison and Wisconsin were given the keywords *maid* and *whisk broom*, and the illustration showed a maid dusting a table with a whisk broom. In the same study the authors decided that some illustrations required dialog to provide additional elaboration. For example, Albany and New York were linked in an illustration

FIGURE 5.3

depicting a woman asking a butcher, "Is this new pork?" (New York), and the butcher replying, "No, it's all baloney!" (Albany).

RETRIEVING Teaching students how to retrieve or recall a definition involves three basic steps.

1. Tell them that when they are asked to provide the definition of the target vocabulary word, they should think first of the keyword. Therefore, when presented with the example stimulus word *allegro*, students should think first of the keywords, *leg* and *row*.
2. Tell the students to think of the picture that illustrated the keywords and the definition and what was happening (the interaction).
3. Tell them to retrieve the definition from the information in the picture.

Thus, as Levin (1988) pointed out, a direct memory path is followed: stimulus (target word) —> keyword —> illustration —> response (definition of word).

Going back to the example, retrieving of the definition of *allegro* occurs when, presented with a question about the meaning of *allegro*, a student subvocalizes something like the following: "What's the definition of *allegro*? My keywords for allegro are *leg* and *row*, and I want to think of my picture. I can see the leg rowing the boat and the boy in back telling the leg to row quickly. Now I remember, the definition of *allegro* is 'moving quickly.'"

INITIAL INSTRUCTION Like any other skill, students must be *taught* to understand and use the keyword method. Teaching steps are typical of effective instructional procedures and include an advance organizer, description, model, and practice. Figure 5.4 contains a sample dialog (adapted from Mastropieri, 1988; Mastropieri & Scruggs, 1991) for teaching the keyword approach to learning the vocabulary word *allegro*.

PRACTICE To enhance fluent recall and maintenance, students must practice using the new vocabulary in a variety of situations and formats. Two basic formats can be used: selection and production. *Selection* practice formats require students to choose the correct response, and *production* formats require students to actually produce the word or definition. An example of a selection exercise is to present the student with a list of vocabulary words written horizontally across the top of a worksheet and definitions of the words written underneath. Students then select or match words with the correct definition. For example, at the beginning of the sentence, "_____ means to move quickly," students should write *allegro* in the blank. Production formats could include directing students to use the vocabulary words in sentences or paragraphs or instructing them to write synonyms or definitions for the vocabulary words.

Mastropieri and Scruggs (1991) also recommended that students complete worksheets with the column headings, "New Word," "Keyword(s)," "Definition," and "Picture" across the top. Blanks are provided under each heading (the number of blanks depends on the number of words practiced), and the teacher fills in one of the blanks for each word; students fill in the rest. For example, the teacher may fill in "leg" and "row" under the heading, "Keyword(s)," and the student fills in the rest of the blanks (writes the new vocabulary word *allegro*, the definition, and a short description of the picture). For the next vocabulary word, the teacher might fill in the blank under "Definition" and so on.

In addition to promoting acquisition and maintenance of vocabulary, varying the

Teacher: Let's begin the vocabulary lesson now. I need everybody's attention. Today we're going to continue working on vocabulary. Who can remember some of the words we've been working on?

Students: (Respond with examples)

Teacher: Who can remember the definition for the word (previously learned word). Remember to use your keyword method if you need to.

Students: (Respond with definitions)

Teacher: You all have done a good job of remembering those words. I'm impressed. Those are not easy words. Today we're going to learn five new and important words from the unit. Knowing what these words mean is going to help you understand the unit and do a lot better on the test. (OPTION: Ask students to identify rationales for learning vocabulary.) First, let's review the keyword method while we learn the first new word today, *allegro*. It means to "move quickly." When I say this word out loud, I hear two words I'm familiar with, *leg* and *row*. So I will use both of them as keywords. Why are they good keywords?

Students: (Respond with something like, "because when put together, they sound like allegro, and they can be drawn easily")

Teacher: Right. When asked what the keywords are for *allegro*, say *leg* and *row*. What are the keywords for allegro?

Students: (Respond with *leg* and *row*)

Teacher: Good. Now that you know the keywords, I'm going to show you a picture of a leg rowing a boat. (Show picture) What is the boy telling the leg to do?

Students: (Respond with something like "telling it to row quickly")

Teacher: Yes, he's telling it to row quickly. Now I'll show you how you can use this picture to help you remember the definition of the word *allegro*. Whenever you read or are asked about the word *allegro*, think of the keywords. What are the keywords for *allegro*?

Students: (Respond with words *leg* and *row*)

Teacher: Good. You remembered. After you think of the keywords *leg* and *row*, you need to think back to the picture and what was happening. What was happening in it?

Students: (Respond with something like, "A boy is telling a leg rowing a boat to row quickly")

Teacher: Excellent! So what is the definition of the word *allegro*?

Students: (Respond with "quickly" or "move quickly")

Teacher: That's right. Now let's learn the next word.

FIGURE 5.4 SAMPLE DIALOG FOR USING THE KEYWORD METHOD TO TEACH "ALLEGRO"

Source: Adapted from "Using the Keyword Method," by M. A. Mastropieri, 1988, in *Teaching Exceptional Children, 20*(2), 4–8; and *Teaching Students Ways to Remember: Strategies for Learning Mnemonically*, by M. A. Mastropieri and T. E. Scruggs, 1991, Cambridge, MA: Brookline.

practice formats has some further benefits. First, it provides for *backward retrieval* practice. One expressed concern about the keyword method is whether students who are taught to respond to the question, "What does *allegro* mean?" will be able to respond correctly to the question, "What is the musical term for *quickly*?" As you can see, the above formats provide practice in both forward and backward retrieval. Relatedly, practice in several formats will help in testing situations given the variety of response formats contained on classroom tests.

GENERALIZATION   In most of the studies on the keyword method, the teacher selects the keyword, draws the interactive illustration, and presents it to the students. Thus, whether adolescents with LD will be able to generalize this method in a strategic fashion is unclear. Recently some attempts have been made to teach students to generate keywords and illustrations (Fulk et al., 1992; King-Sears, Mercer, & Sindelar, 1992; Scruggs & Mastropieri, 1992a).

As part of transfer training study (Fulk et al., 1992), students were given cards with the vocabulary word, its meaning, and the written prompt, "Did you use the strategy?" In addition, they were given two cue cards. The first card contained three criteria for constructing an appropriate keyword: (a) should sound like the vocabulary word, (b) should be a real word you know, and (c) should be easy to draw. The second card cued the three steps used to develop the illustration: (a) choose the keyword, (b) think of something the keyword and definition can do together, and (c) draw the picture. Results in terms of generalization were tentative but encouraging. Some unprompted generalization of strategy use did occur but not consistently. Not surprisingly, student generation of keywords and illustrations takes significantly more classroom time than teacher generation of the materials. For example, Scruggs and Mastropieri (1992a) found that students covered only about a third of the vocabulary words when they were required to generate their own illustrations.

King-Sears et al. (1992) investigated whether adolescents with LD could use the keyword method independently while learning science vocabulary. As part of the study, they compared the efficacy of three conditions: (a) systematic teaching alone, (b) systematic teaching with teacher-generated keyword mnemonic, and (c) systematic teaching with student-generated keyword mnemonic. Students in the third condition were taught to use a keyword strategy called "IT FITS" to help them create keywords and illustrations. (Figure 5.5 presents the steps in the strategy.) Overall, students who were *provided* the keywords and illustrations outperformed the other two groups on recall and matching tasks. The group using the IT FITS strategy, however, consistently outperformed the systematic teaching-only group. Why the teacher-provided keyword group outperformed the student-generated keyword group is difficult to ascertain, because it was not reported whether students generated keywords and illustrations for all of the words, nor was quality discussed (e.g., acoustic similarity, degree of interaction in the illustration of strategy use).

Another variation of the keyword method is the LINCS strategy (Ellis, 1992). Designed to enable students to learn vocabulary words, LINCS is featured in Figure 5.6. In the first step, "list the parts," students determine which words and information are important to remember. They record this information on index cards by writing and circling the word on one side and the definition on the other side. Illustration 1 in Figure

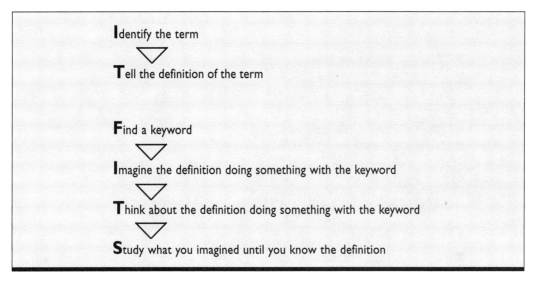

Identify the term

▽

Tell the definition of the term

Find a keyword

▽

Imagine the definition doing something with the keyword

▽

Think about the definition doing something with the keyword

▽

Study what you imagined until you know the definition

FIGURE 5.5   STEPS IN A KEYWORD MNEMONIC STRATEGY

5.7 shows how this is done for the vocabulary word *fief* and its definition. Once this information is on the card, students begin to use specific strategies to enhance their memory of the word and definition. In the second step, "imagine a picture," the students transform the information (word and definition) into a visual image and describe the image to themselves or to someone else. For example, a student creates a picture of a king and a knight and says, "I'm picturing a king giving a knight a large piece of land shown on a map. Then the knight is marching off to war in the King's army." Students then note a reminding word (this is basically a keyword) that is similar acoustically to the vocabulary word. For example, a word that rhymes with *fief* is *chief*. The reminding word then is written on the card (see illustration 2 in Figure 5.7).

In the fourth step, "construct a LINCing story," an association between the familiar word (chief) and the new word (fief) is created by generating a brief story or several sentences that links the two words in some way. The student in the example might think, "The knight receives his land for fighting for the king. When he gets back from fighting, he will be chief of his land." The student then notes his story on the card (see illustration 3 in Figure 5.7). Finally, in "self-test," students test their memory using backward and forward retrieval methods similar to those described earlier.

This strategy was used with students with learning disabilities enrolled in regular 6th-grade social studies classes. Results show that students with LD improved 24 percentage points after learning the LINCS strategy (Wedel, Deshler, Schumaker, & Ellis, in preparation).

In summary, students with LD seem to be capable of learning this type of memory strategy, and some will generalize its use. Also, based on the above studies, teacher-provided mnemonics seem to be more effective and efficient than student-generated mnemonics. Exactly why this is so remains unclear. If teachers are to hand over this

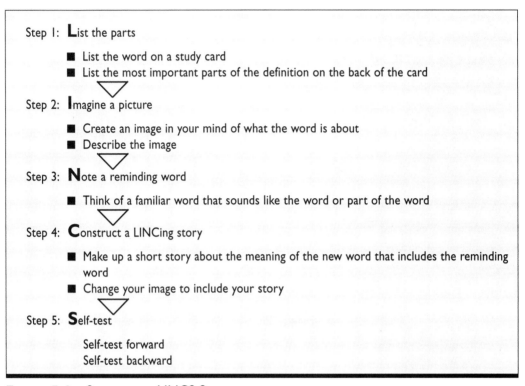

Step 1: **L**ist the parts

■ List the word on a study card
■ List the most important parts of the definition on the back of the card

Step 2: **I**magine a picture

■ Create an image in your mind of what the word is about
■ Describe the image

Step 3: **N**ote a reminding word

■ Think of a familiar word that sounds like the word or part of the word

Step 4: **C**onstruct a LINCing story

■ Make up a short story about the meaning of the new word that includes the reminding word
■ Change your image to include your story

Step 5: **S**elf-test

Self-test forward
Self-test backward

FIGURE 5.6   STEPS OF THE LINCS STRATEGY

method to students, more work has to be done regarding the nature and extent of instruction needed to ensure consistent and proficient generalization of this technique. This certainly is desirable from both a pedagogical and a logistical perspective. (See question box on next page for a discussion of the logistical concern.)

PEGWORD METHOD

Another mnemonic device employing visualization is the pegword method or system. This method is especially useful for remembering lists of items in order (e.g., the stages of metamorphosis leading to a butterfly), although it also can be used when sequential recall is not important. It is based on a rhyming system that links a number to a pegword. Typical number-pegword pairs are:

one	= bun	six	= sticks
two	= shoe	seven	= heaven
three	= tree	eight	= gate
four	= door	nine	= line
five	= hive	ten	= hen

Once students memorize these number-pegword relationships in the form of a rhyme, the number is associated to the item in a list through an interactive image. For example, if students need to remember that "butterfly" is the *third* stage of metamorphosis,

Q & A

MNEMONIC DEVICES

Q: *The procedures for developing mnemonic devices seem to be time-consuming. Are they worth all the trouble? Too, won't all these keywords and illustrations overwhelm or confuse my students?*

A: These are legitimate concerns. No one can argue about whether creating mnemonics is time-consuming: It is. Several factors, however, should be considered before discarding this approach to instruction on the grounds that it is too time-consuming. First, not *all* vocabulary has to be taught in this fashion, only critical vocabulary or concepts on which to focus—those that are important for overall understanding of the unit of content being presented and those that most students have difficulty remembering.

Too, as Mastropieri and Scruggs (1991) pointed out, in the long run mnemonic techniques such as the keyword method possibly can *save* time. Once you have developed the keywords and corresponding illustrations, you can use them for future students because much of the same content will be taught over time. Also, the illustrations do not have to be works of art. Line drawings are appropriate as long as the connections are apparent. Having artistic students at your school draw them also has been suggested (Mastropieri and Scruggs, 1991). I can't draw to save myself, so I asked my wife, Kathy Ruhl, to help me with Figure 5.3. I described what I wanted, and she drew it.

Ideally, you want your students to develop their own mnemonics, but generalization of strategy use has not been established firmly, and when students do apply the keyword strategies themselves, they do not create them as fast. You certainly want to try to promote independent strategy use whenever possible, but content and generalization coverage should be balanced. Scruggs and Mastropieri (1993) stated:

> In the future, teachers may have to compromise between strategy training and content instruction. For example, teachers...were able to train students to develop their own keyword strategies, but they proceeded through the content less than half as fast as they did when the strategies were directly provided by teachers. Teachers may wish to consider the relative importance of strategy training goals and content acquisition goals when planning instruction for particular academic units. (p. 394)

The other concern about the sheer number of keywords and illustrations overwhelming students also has been expressed about strategies instruction in general. For example, it has been conjectured that all those first-letter mnemonics for the variety of content-specific strategies (e.g., FIRST, PIRATES, DISSECT, RAP) will confuse kids. Although this concern seems logical, research and practice have not supported this contention. Most students do not have any trouble keeping them separate. Mnemonics help establish associations, thus providing easier access to stored information (i.e., retrieval).

---

they could visualize or create a picture of butterflies in a tree (pegword linked with the number 3).

In a study described by Mastropieri and Scruggs (1991), students in the experimental group were taught to remember nine possible reasons why dinosaurs became extinct. One of the reasons, "the climate became too cold," was associated with the number 1 and

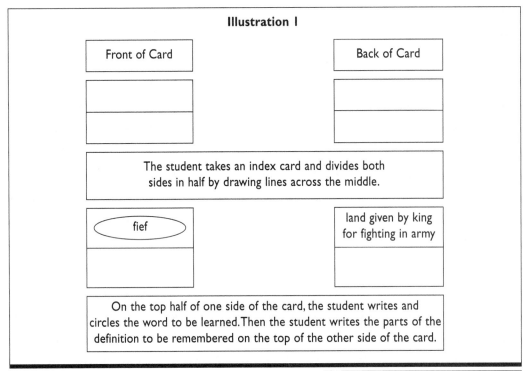

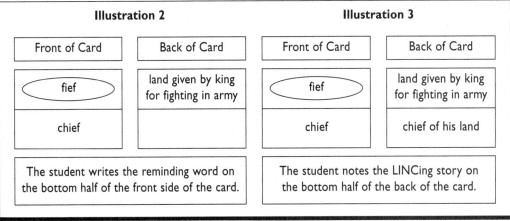

FIGURE 5.7   ILLUSTRATIONS OF USING THE LINCS STRATEGY

the pegword "bun." The image created was a cold dinosaur holding some frozen buns. Thus, the concept of "too cold" was pictured with the pegword "bun." When students were asked to recall information, they first thought of the number (e.g., 1), then the pegword (bun), then the image (dinosaur with frozen buns), and finally the word or concept (the weather became too cold). Students in the experimental group were twice as likely to recall information than students in the control group.

In another study (Elliott & Gentile, 1986), junior high students with LD were taught to use the pegword method to learn lists. Students who used the pegword method to study remembered significantly more of the lists than students with LD who did not. Too, this group of students performed the same as nondisabled students who did not use the pegword system.

ACRONYMS AND ACROSTICS

Acronyms and Acrostics, two methods sometimes referred to as embedded-letter or first-letter mnemonics, are used to remember related, listed information. When using these methods, the learner uses the first letters of listed information to form either a word (acronym) or a sentence (acrostic). These techniques help organize and retrieve information that is somewhat familiar to students. Thus, the minimal prompt of a letter is sufficient to recall the word associated with the letter. Acronyms and acrostics have long been used in schools: Many adults who do not read or play music still remember *FACE* and "*Every Good Boy Does Fine*," or the names of the Great Lakes using the acronym *HOMES*. Some acronyms are so much a part of everyday life that we sometimes forget that such words as *SCUBA*, *LASER*, and *RADAR* are acronyms, not words (Eggen & Kauchak, 1992).

An example of a strategy that teaches students to use acronyms and acrostics is the *FIRST-Letter Mnemonic Strategy* (Nagel, Schumaker, & Deshler, 1986). This strategy package contains two integrated strategies, one for designing a first-letter mnemonic device and one for making and memorizing lists. Figure 5.8 contains the steps for each strategy. These strategies are taught using the eight instructional stages described earlier in this book. Notice that the steps form the first-letter mnemonics *LISTS* and *FIRST*.

STEPS FOR DESIGNING A LIST   The first step of the FIRST strategy, "form a word," requires the student to write down, horizontally and in capitals, the first letters of each word in an identified list of words and ascertain whether it forms a recognizable word or

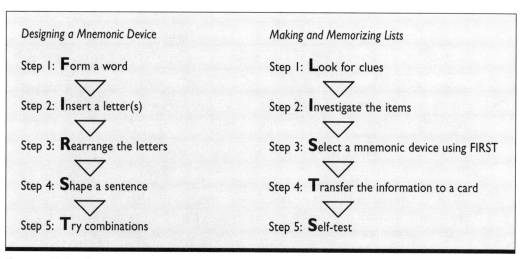

FIGURE 5.8   STEPS OF THE FIRST-LETTER MNEMONIC STRATEGY

a nonsense word that is easy to remember. For example, during a lecture a teacher presented five major types of societies in the following order: Democratic, Aristocratic, Republican, Tyrannical, and Socialist. The first letters form the word *DARTS*.

Because lists of information often do not occur in such a convenient order, students must manipulate the lists to help form a first-letter mnemonic. Thus, the second step instructs the student to "insert a letter(s)" into the horizontal list of letters to see if they can form a word. For example, if the student has written down the letters BAC (representing a list consisting of the words *B*lack holes, *A*ntimatter, and *C*osmic rays), inserting a lowercase "k" at the end of the letters would form the word *BACk*.

If insertion does not work, students can "rearrange the letters." For example, if students are attempting to learn the main parts of the eye (eyelid, iris, pupil, and sclera), they can rearrange the first letters to form the word *PIES*. If the first three steps did not work—which often is the case when the words all begin with a consonant—students try to "shape a sentence." For example, if students are learning the five basic senses—sight, hearing, smell, touch, and taste—they might make up a sentence such as "Sally Hated Sticky Toads and Tails." If students cannot form a mnemonic device using the first four steps, they "try combinations" of the other steps. Combinations include rearranging the letters and inserting a letter or rearranging the letters and trying to make a sentence of them. For example if students are trying to remember the three branches of the U.S. Government and the branches are presented in their text as Executive, Legislative, and Judicial, students could rearrange the letters as JEL and insert a lowercase "l" at the end and thus would remember the word *"JELl."* Rearranging, of course, should be used only when the order of the list is not important.

STEPS FOR MAKING AND MEMORIZING LISTS   Because listed information often is not provided directly to students, they must be able to identify important, listed information in their textbooks or class notes. When using the LISTS strategy, students first "look for clues." The most obvious clue is a series of items directly under a heading. In many textbooks, however, it is not that obvious. Therefore, students are taught to look for a variety of clues that may signal related, listed information. These clues include numbers (e.g., five or first, second) and words (e.g., several, parts, steps, examples, causes, categories, reasons). Other clues include headings, highlighted print, items separated by commas, the same word used as a second word (e.g., first-letter mnemonic, pegword mnemonic, keyword mnemonic). Students also are taught to identify "importance" clues such as the teacher telling class members that they must know this list for the test or writing the list on the board. End-of-chapter questions related to listed information also should signal importance. A more comprehensive list of the types of clues is presented in Figure 5.9.

Another part of this step involves devising a heading for a list deemed to be important. Guidelines for an appropriate heading include making sure the heading summarizes the list (i.e., is a general category) and is short, accurate, and limiting. For example, if students are memorizing the four major bones of the skull (temporal, occipital, parietal, and frontal), a heading of "Bones" is too general. A more limiting heading such as "Skull Bones" is more appropriate.

Once students have found a list clue and decided on a heading, they "investigate the items" to decide what should be included in the list. Once a decision is made as to the

Examples

Word Clues ——> many several kinds types parts elements
stages roles features ways jobs sources
causes reasons steps examples uses classes

Other Clues

Main headings ——> Branches of the Federal Government

Subheadings ——> Functions of the Executive Branch

Highlighted print ——> *italics*, **boldface print,** ALL CAPITAL LETTERS

Illustrations with labels ——> diagrams, maps, tables, charts

Words that seem similar ——> epidemic, endemic, pandemic

Items in a series separated ——> sight, hearing, smell, taste, touch
by commas

Numbers or letters in a ——> (1) sight, (2) hearing, (3) touch, (4) taste, etc.;
sequence followed by a word or (a) sight, (b) hearing, (c) touch, etc.

Importance Clues

Teacher says you must know ——> "You need to know the six parts of a woody stem for Friday's
information for the test test."

Teacher writes a list on the ——> temporal, occipital, parietal, frontal
board

Study guide questions ask ——> "What are the six parts of a woody stem?"
for a list

Questions at the end of a ——> "What are the parts of the respiratory system?"
chapter ask for a list

FIGURE 5.9   EXAMPLES OF CLUES THAT MAY SIGNAL LISTED INFORMATION

relatedness of an item to the heading and to the other items, students write down the list, making sure that each item is as short as possible and that the list itself is not too long (i.e., over seven items). Now that the list has been identified, students "select a mnemonic using FIRST." After the mnemonic has been formed, students "transfer the information to a card," using the following steps:

1. Write the heading on the middle of an index card.
2. Turn over the card and write the mnemonic device in the upper left corner.
3. Write the list items in the center of the card.

Once the card is completed, students study the information using the last step, "self-test." Students are instructed to look at the heading and try to recall the list by remembering the mnemonic and what it stands for. Students also practice the correct spelling of the words and, when appropriate, study the meanings of the words. For example, students probably would not be required to define *occipital* (although they may need to know the location of this bone), but most likely would need to know the definition of a cosmic ray. (See Figure 5.10 for an example of how the FIRST-letter mnemonic strategy could be applied.)

Students taught this strategy have improved test scores on reading and grade level materials by an average of 30 percentage points. In addition, some students have improved several letter grades on 9th-grade science tests.

COMBINATIONS OF MNEMONICS   In some cases different mnemonics can be used in concert. Scruggs and Mastropieri (1990) described two examples of combining acronyms with the type of visual elaboration used in the keyword method. In the first example, when using the HOMES acronym for learning the names of the Great Lakes, students also visualized a picture of several homes on some large lakes. In the second example, the acronym TAG was developed for the countries Turkey, Austria-Hungary, and Germany, Central Powers during World War I. To ensure that students associated these countries with the Central (versus Allied) Powers, an image of a game of TAG (first-letter mnemonic) being played in Central Park (the keyword for Central Powers) was generated.

The pegword method has been used in conjunction with the keyword method. In a study conducted by Mastropieri, Scruggs, and Levin (1985), students were taught to remember the hardness of minerals. For example, the mineral hornblende has a hardness level of 5 (on a particular scale). The illustration shown to students was a picture of a hive (pegword linked with the number 5) inside a horn (keyword for hornblende). When students were asked about the hardness level of hornblende they thought of horn, then the picture, then remembered that the hive in the picture stood for five (5 = hive), and then remembered that the hardness level of hornblende was 5.

Combining these two techniques can be helpful when the item or concept to be learned is abstract or hard to picture. Going back to the butterfly example used earlier, the stage before butterfly is "chrysalis." Many students find this word difficult to illustrate, so giving it a keyword such as "crystal" facilitates creation of an interactive image.

The *Paired Associates Strategy* (Bulgren, Schumaker, & Deshler, in press), designed to meet the demand for finding and remembering pairs of associated information (e.g., word and definition, person and associated accomplishment, date and event, place and event), contains several of the mnemonic procedures discussed earlier. When learning this strategy, students are taught to select from one of four mnemonic techniques to assist in recalling factual information. The four steps of the strategy form the first-letter mnemonic *CRAM* (see Figure 5.11). The first step, "create a mental image," is used for information that is imagined easily (e.g., concrete). Students are taught to "make a picture in your mind" of the associated information. For example, the fact that "Gold was discovered in the Black Hills" easily could be imagined as several black hills with gold nuggets shinning on the slopes. Students also are given the option of making quick sketches of their image.

The second step, "relate something," instructs students to relate the associated items to someone or something familiar if they cannot form a strong mental image. Bulgren,

Sample Text

On a more practical level, methods promoting the retention of factual information are functional for adolescents with LD because, right or wrong and regardless of what may happen to school curricula in the future, students in today's classrooms are expected to learn large amounts of factual information, and their classroom tests reflect this (Putnam, Deshler, & Schumaker, 1992). Mnemonics are not a substitute for teaching for understanding but, rather, are intended to *supplement* it. Among the several types of mnemonic techniques are the keyword method, pegword method, acronyms, and acrostics.

Step 1: Look for Clues

At the bottom of the paragraph, I see two clue words—"several" and "types"—which signal a list. In this case the list relates to types of mnemonic techniques.

Step 2: Investigate the Items

A careful investigation of the text shows me that the list has four related items. The items must be made as short as possible, so I will drop the word "method." A good title (short and inclusive) is "Types of Mnemonics." A final examination of the list shows me that all items are parallel and the list is not too long (fewer than seven items).

Step 3: Select a Mnemonic Using FIRST

The words, as they are presented in the text (keyword, pegword, acronyms, acrostics [KPAA]), do not *F*orm a word, so next I will *I*nsert a letter. Inserting letters does not form a word, so I will try *R*earranging the letters (e.g., KAPA, PAKA). That doesn't seem to work, so next I *S*hape a sentence. How about "Kings Punish Adulterous Aunts?" It might work, but maybe *T*rying combinations would be better. If I rearrange the list to KAPA and insert a lowercase "p" before the P, I come up with KApPA. That's good. A lot of fraternities and sororities have KAPPA in their name, and they are all Greek, and the word mnemonic is also Greek, so I can make that connection. KApPA it is!

Step 4: Transfer the Information to a Card

Now I get an index card and write the heading "Mnemonic Techniques" in the middle of one side of the card. I turn over the card, and in the upper left corner write my mnemonic KApPA. In the center of the card, I write the list of words, making sure they are in the same order as my FIRST-letter mnemonic. Finally, I double-check my spelling. It's okay.

Step 5: Self Test

Okay, let's see if I know this stuff. I look at the front of the card (heading), remember my mnemonic for the mnemonics, and see if I remember what the letters stand for. I also want to study their meanings after I have memorized my list. I'm fairly sure I will have to know how they are used in addition to their names. Maybe I can make acronyms for the steps of each type. Hey, it's already been done for the FIRST-letter (acronym) mnemonic strategy!

FIGURE 5.10   EXAMPLE OF FIRST-LETTER MNEMONIC STRATEGY

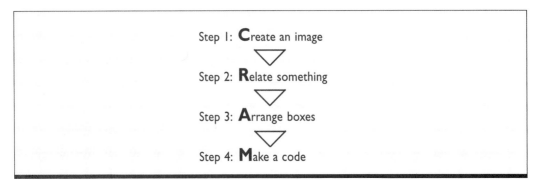

FIGURE 5.11   STEPS OF THE PAIRED-ASSOCIATES STRATEGY

Hock, Schumaker, and Deshler (1995) described how this step could be used with the fact "James Eastwood was a mountain climber." Because most students (and most of us, I suspect) do not know who James Eastwood is, he could be associated with a more familiar Eastwood named Clint.

Once students have "related," they can use the first step of the strategy to create a mental image of Clint Eastwood climbing a mountain. For remembering paired information that cannot be formed readily into a strong mental image or related to something familiar, students are told to "arrange boxes." This step, similar to the keyword mnemonic, instructs students to box-off a syllable in each of the paired facts. Bulgren et al. (1995) described how students could use this step to remember that "A. Petry wrote *Harriet Tubman*." Students box the keyword "pet" from Petry and the keyword "tub" from Tubman and then form an image of their pet in the bathtub.

Step four, "make a code," is used for memorizing information that includes a date as one of the items. Students learn to substitute letters for numbers (0–9) using the following code: 0 = B, 1 = C, 2 = D, 3 = F, 4 = G, 5 = H, 6 = J, 7 = K, 8 = L, 9 = M. The letters are used as the first letters of the first word in a sentence that says something about why the date is important. For example, Bulgren, Schumaker, and Deshler (in press) used the sentence "A *c*rashing *m*arket and *d*epression *m*ade trouble for America" to help students remember that the Great Depression occurred in 1929. When, as in this case, generated sentences contain more words than coded letters, the letters are used as the first four words (excluding articles) of the sentence. In addition to learning the CRAM steps, students learning the paired associates strategy also learn the list-making and studying strategy FIRST (described in the Acronym and Acrostics section). Bulgren et al. (1995) reported large increases (e.g., around 60 percentage points) on scores on recall tests for 12 high school students with LD who learned the paired associates strategy.

Finally, Bulgren, Deshler, and Schumaker (1994) used a variety of teacher-generated mnemonic procedures in a post-lecture review session to help students remember key facts presented in the lecture. Although the mnemonics (first-letter, visual imagery, and keyword) were not combined, each was used for different information. For example, first-letter techniques were used for listed information, mental imagery was used when a strong image was apparent, and the keyword method was used when reconstruction was needed. Adolescents with and without LD alike who were given the mnemonic review of lecture content outscored their counterparts who were provided a review in which the information was repeated and discussed.

GENERAL STUDY ROUTINES

As mentioned before, many adolescents with LD do not use specific memory strategies efficiently, nor do they implement overall study routines. Studying for the purpose of memorizing information for a test includes more than the use of one technique such as the keyword method. It is actually a relatively complex set of activities requiring planning, organization, implementation, and monitoring. Thus, teaching students mnemonic techniques in isolation is insufficient. Study routines and planning also must be taught, and taught to automaticity (Gelzheiser et al., 1983).

A task analysis of studying yields the following general steps or stages:

1. Being aware of an upcoming test.
2. Understanding the general content that will be covered and how it will be assessed (essay versus objective or combination).
3. Developing a plan for studying or memorizing (deciding *what* will be studied and *how* it will be studied).
4. Scheduling a sufficient amount of time to implement the plan.
5. Knowing when studying has been sufficient.

Although an emerging body of research exists for teaching students specific memorization techniques, the same cannot be said for teaching study routines. Therefore, many of the following suggestions, though logical, are not accompanied by supporting research.

AWARENESS OF AN UPCOMING TEST   Often students seem to "forget" that a test will be occurring in the near future. Whether this peculiar form of amnesia is a function of poor organizational skills, memory skills, or simply not wanting to think about it (or a combination of all three) is a matter of speculation. One method for helping students keep track of upcoming tests is to provide them with assignment books and teach them how to use them. Recording upcoming tests along with notes about what will be covered (e.g., which chapters in the book) and prompting students to check their book periodically may increase their awareness of impending tests.

GENERAL UNDERSTANDING OF TEST CONTENT   Frequently students do not have a good "feel" for what the teacher deems important (i.e., what will be on the test). In some instances this stems from lack of clarity on the instructor's part (either intentionally or unintentionally). In either case students should be taught that asking teachers to provide general information about the content that will be covered on the test is acceptable, and if information is given, they should write it down. They should also be informed that some teachers will be more helpful than others and regardless of the level of assistance provided, students should thank teachers for the help. Suggestions for deciding what teachers think is important with regard to lecture content are provided in chapter 6, on notetaking.

Knowledge of the test format also may guide the study plan. For example, students should find out (either ask the teacher or tap their own knowledge of how each teacher typically designs tests) what types of items will be on the test. If the test will be essay, students may decide to read for general understanding (and use corresponding comprehension strategies) rather than focus on memorizing specific lists or terminology using mnemonics such as those described earlier.

DEVELOPING A STUDY PLAN Once students are aware of an upcoming test and have a general idea of test content and format, they should develop a general plan for studying. This involves deciding, in detail, *what* should be studied and *how* it should be studied. When deciding what should be studied, students should list specific chapters to be read as well as which class notes to review.

Students then have to decide how they will go about learning and retaining the information. For example, they may decide that, to comprehend the content of a chapter, they should implement the following study sequence: (a) read the chapter and highlight the main points; (b) reread the chapter and paraphrase, in writing, the main ideas; and (c) reread and rehearse the main points over several study sessions. Again, study behaviors depend on the nature of the information and how it will be tested. For instance, if the student knows that an upcoming science test will cover recall of terminology, the above study plan may not be appropriate. The student instead should identify important terms and apply mnemonic methods such as the first-letter mnemonic strategy or the keyword method.

To teach this type of decision making, the teacher can provide study scenarios complete with information on the type of test and content covered (e.g., three chapters) and lead discussions concerning different ways to study. When discussing development of study plans with students, teachers should keep in mind that study strategies are to some extent idiosyncratic. Students may prefer one technique over another. This is acceptable as long as the student's current study strategies are considered relatively effective and efficient (e.g., not just rereading).

SCHEDULING STUDY SESSIONS Many students, including those with LD, often wait until the last minute to study. Research has shown that cramming is not as effective as several study sessions spread over time. One method for promoting distributed studying is to schedule study sessions. Scheduling involves two steps.

1. Students estimate how much time they will take to execute their study plan. For example, if part of the study plan is to read a chapter while taking notes, they should estimate how long this will take. They can practice this estimation skill by eliciting a study plan from students followed by a brainstorming session on how long they think it will take to carry out each step of the plan.
2. Once students have estimated how much time to allot for studying, they schedule when (time and day) they will study. This can be done on a typical calendar or in commercially available assignment notebooks.

Of course, having a plan does not necessarily mean it will be followed. To monitor studying is nearly impossible because most of it takes place outside the classroom. Teachers can encourage follow-through by prompting students to follow their plan and asking them to report on how their plan is progressing. Too, teachers can use self-monitoring and recording procedures by requiring students to plan study sessions on special forms.

For example, an assignment sheet similar to one developed by Hughes, Ruhl, Schumaker, and Deshler (1995) could be used (see Figure 5.12). This sheet is used to record out-of-class assignments including homework and studying for upcoming tests.

Name   *Hilary*

SUBJECT	Read _____	Partner *Larry*
	Answer _____	Phone *555 - 6943*
Eng.	(Write) *Bk. Report*	
	Other _____	

# of parts   *2*   # of study sessions   *6*

Due   *10/21*   Done _____

A
B
C
D
F

SUBJECT	Read _____	Partner *Marie*
	Answer *Study for Test*	Phone *555 - 9178*
Soc. Stud.	Write *Chap. 4+5 + Notes*	
	(Other) *Multi-Choice, T-F & / essay*	

# of parts   *3*   # of study sessions   *8*

Due   *10/22*   Done _____

A
B
C
D
F

SUBJECT	Read _____	Partner _____
	Answer _____	Phone _____
	Write _____	
	Other _____	

# of parts _____   # of study sessions _____

Due _____   Done _____

A
B
C
D
F

FIGURE 5.12   ASSIGNMENT SHEET

On the left side of the form, students record the subject (e.g., social studies, English) and the date and then write the assignment on the blank lines provided. Words in the vertical list (Read, Answer, Write, Other) are circled when appropriate. Two blanks (labeled Partner and Phone) are provided in the upper right corner, where the student writes the name and phone number of a "study buddy." This is a peer with whom the student will study or call if he or she has a problem with the homework. The two blanks labeled "# of parts" and "# of study sessions" are completed as part of estimating the amount of time and effort required to complete the assignment or to study for a test.

First the student breaks the assignment into general parts and records that number in the blank provided. For example, in the first assignment (English) the student (Hilary) decided that the assignment consisted of two parts, reading the book and writing the report. Then she estimated that she would take six one-half hour sessions to complete the assignment. These sessions are scheduled on a separate weekly study schedule form (Figure 5.13). When the assignment is complete, Hilary will write the date completed on the blank line next to the word "Done" on the assignment sheet. The student uses the vertical list of letters on the right side of the form to evaluate the quality of the assignment. Note that for social studies the assignment is to study for an upcoming test. Hilary wrote on the form that the test will cover certain chapters and class notes, that the test will consist of multiple-choice and true-false items as well as one essay question, and that the test will be administered on October 22. She decided that the study process can be broken into three major parts: (a) read the material, (b) read and take notes summarizing main points, and (c) rehearse the information. Accordingly, she wrote the number 3 in the "# of parts" blank. Hilary then estimated that she would need eight one-half hour sessions to study adequately. Finally she began to schedule these half-hour sessions on a separate scheduling sheet (Figure 5.13). Now all she has to do is follow through on her plan.

KNOWING WHEN STUDYING IS SUFFICIENT   The ultimate criterion for assessing when study is sufficient—a difficult skill—is performance on the test. Nevertheless, students should be encouraged to self-test themselves periodically or have a peer ask them questions. If possible, the teacher can provide practice tests to ascertain how well students have learned the content and if additional studying is necessary.

Carman and Adams (1972) developed a checklist to help students prepare for tests. Parts of this checklist that are most applicable for adolescents with LD are provided here.

The Week Before the Exam—"Go" Week
1. Find out exactly what is required for the exam by doing the following:
   (a) Ask your instructor what the exam will cover and what kinds of questions will
       be used.   _____
   (b) Ask your instructor what, if any, material will be omitted.   _____
   (c) Make a list of what things you must know, and rank them according
       to importance.   _____
   (d) Get copies of previous exams. Your instructor will often be willing
       to help with this.   _____
   (e) Talk to friends who have taken the course previously. Get their
       advice on what to study, what questions to expect, and what the
       test will emphasize.   _____

Name _Hilary_

PROJECT BEST Study Schedule for Week of _Oct. 17_

	DATE	10/16	10/17	10/18	10/19	10/20	10/21	10/22
	TIME	SAT.	SUN.	MON.	TUES.	WED.	THURS.	FRI.
	6:30							
	7:00							
	7:30							
	8:00							
	8:30							
	9:00							
	9:30							
	10:00							
	10:30							
	11:00							
	11:30							
	12:00							
	12:30							
Study Hall	1:00				Soc. Stud.	Eng.	Soc. Stud.	
	1:30				Soc. Stud.	Eng.	Soc. Stud.	
	2:00							
	2:30							
	3:00							
	3:30							
	4:00							
	4:30							
	5:00							
	5:30							
	6:00							
	6:30				Eng.			
	7:00			Eng.	Eng.	Soc. Stud.	Soc. Stud.	
	7:30			Eng.		Soc. Stud.		
	8:00			Soc. Stud.				
	8:30							
	9:00							
	9:30							
	10:00							

FIGURE 5.13 STUDY SCHEDULE

(f) Get together a "study group" of some serious students and fire
possible test questions at each other. Make certain the students
you select are really interested in studying.   _____
2. Organize yourself for maximum efficiency by doing the following:
   (a) Eat on schedule all week.   _____
   (b) Get a normal amount of sleep every day all week.   _____
   (c) Take time off from your out-of-school job or other activities.   _____
   (d) Set aside your usual daily activities (TV, dates, hobbies) for
      after the exam.   _____
   (e) Build up a positive mental attitude by reminding yourself of all
      the good consequences of succeeding on the exam and recalling
      past successes. Be positive.   _____
3. Learn what you need to know for the exam.
   (a) Read the material.   _____
   (b) Review it. On each successive review, skip those things you
      are most sure of.   _____
   (c) Recite. Buttonhole a friend or relative and tell him all about it.
      He'll think you're nuts, but do it anyway.   _____
   (d) Review the top priority items again at the last possible minute
      before entering the exam room. (pp. 201–202)   _____

When the day of the test arrives, the students are well prepared to demonstrate what they have learned. After the teacher lays the test on the desk, other student strategies come into play—those related to test-taking.

TEST-TAKING

Most adolescents with LD spend the majority of the school day in mainstream classes and are expected to cope with the academic demands of those classrooms. One frequent demand is to take tests for the purpose of demonstrating knowledge. Test performance, however, depends not only on how well students study but also, albeit to a lesser extent, on their "test-wiseness." Test-wiseness (TW) was defined by Millman, Bishop, and Ebel (1965) as "a subject's capacity to utilize the characteristics and formats of the test and/or the test-taking situation to receive a high score" (p. 707). Further, they presented TW to be "logically independent of the knowledge of the subject matter for which the items supposedly measure" (p. 707). TW, therefore, can be seen as a set of cognitive abilities, skills, or strategies that can be applied to a variety of tests regardless of their content (Hughes, 1987; Sarnacki, 1979).

Teaching TW to students is seen both as a measurement issue and a fairness issue. It is a measurement issue when TW is a source of measurement error (the lack of TW results in a less valid test score that does not reflect what the student truly knows). Relatedly, it becomes a fairness issue when one student scores higher than another solely because of TW. These two issues provide the basic rationale for teaching TW skills to adolescents with LD because, as will be seen later, many of these students lack TW and thus are at a disadvantage in taking tests.

Millman et al. (1965) analyzed TW and broke it down into strategies (a) independent of or (b) dependent on the test constructor. Figure 5.14, adapted from their analysis, provides an outline of many of these strategies. These strategies will be discussed in detail later in the chapter. Before describing these techniques, understanding test-taking as a setting demand, and what we know about the test-taking behaviors of adolescents with LD, will be useful.

TEST-TAKING AS A SETTING DEMAND

Variables important to understanding tests and test-taking as a critical setting demand include the frequency of tests, the impact of test scores on overall grades, and the content and format of the tests. Lewis Putnam and his associates at the University of Kansas Institute of Research on Learning Disabilities (e.g., Putnam, 1988; Putnam, 1992a & b; Putnam, Deshler, & Schumaker, 1993) examined these variables. Information about the testing practices of 7th- and 10th-grade classroom teachers was collected by interviewing 120 teachers (60 7th-grade teachers and 60 10th-grade teachers) from eight school

---

I. Elements *independent* of test constructor or purpose
  A. Time-usage strategies
     1. Begin working as soon as possible.
     2. Set up a schedule for progressing through the test.
     3. Skip items unsure of and mark them for later consideration.
  B. Error-avoidance strategies
     1. Pay careful attention to directions.
     2. Pay careful attention to items.
     3. If necessary (and permitted), ask for clarification.
  C. Guessing strategies
     1. Guess if correct answers only are scored.
     2. Guess if the penalty for guessing is less than for incorrects.
  D. Deductive reasoning strategies
     1. Eliminate obviously incorrect options, and choose from those remaining.
     2. Choose neither or both of two options that imply the correctness of each other.
     3. Use relevant information contained in other test items or options.
II. Elements *dependent* upon the test constructor or purpose
  A. Intent consideration strategies
     1. Interpret and answer questions based on knowledge of previous tests constructed by a particular teacher.
     2. Answer items as the test constructor intended.
  B. Cue-usage strategies
     1. Recognize and use cues that may distinguish the correct answer from incorrect options.

FIGURE 5.14   OUTLINE OF TEST-WISENESS PRINCIPLES AND STRATEGIES

districts in three states. The sample consisted of an equal number of social studies, English, science, and math teachers. In addition, each teacher provided three samples of unit or chapter tests typically used in their classes (total tests = 360). Analysis of the interviews and tests yielded the following general findings:

- Overall, about half of a student's grade was determined by test scores.
- Teachers created about half of the tests. The rest were publisher-provided (came with the textbook or curriculum material used in the class).
- An average of 11 tests per class was given in a 9-week period. When this number is extrapolated, students take at least 176 tests per school year.
- On the average, tests contained about 32 questions, divided into four sections usually based on the type of question/item (e.g., multiple-choice, true-false, essay, matching). Number of items increased from 7th to 10th grade.
- Overall, the most common item-type contained on tests was multiple-choice, followed by matching. This varied somewhat depending on the type of class (e.g., in math classes the most common type of item was computation).
- Based on Bloom's taxonomy, most of the questions required a response at the knowledge level, except English tests, which required higher levels of responses such as application.
- About half of the questions were recognition questions (i.e., selecting the correct answer from choices provided on the test). Recall/retrieval questions occurred about 10% of the time (i.e., fill-in the blank, short answer).
- Average readability of test directions was at a 7.6 and 8.4 grade equivalent for 7th- and 10th-grade tests, respectively, and readability of test items ranged from 7.1 on 7th-grade math tests to 10.7 on 10th-grade social studies tests.
- An analysis of Putnam's sample of tests (excluding the math tests) by Hughes and Clark (1993) indicated that essay questions were included on about 25% of the tests. Essay questions occurred about twice as much on 10th-grade tests than on 7th-grade tests. Surprisingly, most of the questions were at the lower cognitive level (e.g., list, describe, identify, explain, define) and few tapped application, analysis, or synthesis skills (e.g., compare and contrast, summarize, apply).
- The analysis by Hughes and Clark showed that, on the average, when essay questions were included on a test they were worth about 43% of the total available points. The percentage, however, ranged from 6 to 100%, indicating much variability between tests.

In summary, students seem to take tests frequently, tests are extremely important in deciding grades, and tests typically sample recall or recognition of factual information, usually in the form of multiple-choice or matching items. Now the question becomes: How well do many adolescents with LD meet the testing demands in their content classes?

TEST-TAKING CHARACTERISTICS OF ADOLESCENTS WITH LD

Scruggs and Mastropieri (1988) asked the question, "Are learning disabled students test-wise?" The answer, based on several research reports (Alley, Deshler, & Warner, 1979; Hughes, 1991; Hughes & Schumaker, 1991b; Scruggs, Bennion, & Lifson, 1985; Scruggs

& Marsing, 1985; Veit & Scruggs, 1986), is *no*. First, based on observational studies, many students attend to the wrong part of test directions, are misled by irrelevant and distracting information and are not persistent in searching for information. Too, they often do not read all options in a multiple-choice (MC) question before selecting their answer, do not use time wisely (e.g., do not start right away, skip over hard questions), and do not attempt to answer all the questions (you can't get it right if you don't answer it!).

Veit and Scruggs (1986) also found that many students had difficulty dealing with the format often used in standardized tests. Generally, they found that students had problems with reading a question and options on one page and marking the answer on a separate "bubble sheet." Students had difficulty staying inside the bubbles (a real problem when the computer/scanner scores them) and keeping track of the row in which to mark the answer. This format slowed them down considerably.

Other TW strategies examined were those related to deductive reasoning and use of cues. These skills were assessed using so-called test-wiseness tests. These tests, originated by Slakter, Koehler, and Hampton (1970), *appear* to be real tests sampling different content but contain fictitious terminology. Because important terms on the test are made-up, there is no right answer and students must use TW skills to decide how to answer the questions. The TW skills typically measured in this type of test include:

- *Eliminating similar options*. When two options in a MC question are so similar as to be the same, neither one should be considered because only one answer can be correct.
- *Eliminating absurd options*. The testee eliminates (ceases to consider) an answer that is obviously incorrect. This occurs when an option is "way out of the ballpark" or is an obvious attempt at humor by the teacher (college professors do this also).
- *Using stem-option agreement*. Sometimes teachers inadvertently provide a cue, typically dealing with grammatical construction. For example, if the stem of a MC item ends with the word "an" and several of the options begin with consonants, this may be a cue that they are wrong. Another variation (sometimes called stem-word in option) occurs when one option contains some of the same words as the stem.
- *Using length of option*. This cue occurs when one or more option in an MC item is obviously longer (by at least three or four words) than the other options. The best guessing strategy is to select this option as the correct answer.
- *Avoiding specific determiners*. Specific determiners are "absolute" words such as *always* or *never*. When these words are used in true-false items and guessing is required, the student should choose "false." When they are contained in MC options, those options should be avoided.

When given TW tests containing items assessing use of the above cues, many adolescents with LD do not make use of these cues, nor do they use the deductive reasoning strategies. Use of cues and deductive strategies, as well as specific items sampling these strategies, will be provided in the assessment and instruction sections.

Two studies utilized interviews to sample TW skills of students with LD (Hughes, 1991; Scruggs, Bennion, & Lifson, 1985). Scruggs et al. interviewed students with and without LD about the strategies they used when answering questions on standardized achievement tests. They reported that students with LD were less likely to use deductive reasoning strategies or closely attend to directions and items. Hughes found that most of the interviewed college students with LD reported having the most difficulty with essay questions and fill-in-the-blank items. The most frequently stated difficulties for answering essay questions dealt mainly with the writing process—organization, grammar, spelling, and writing fast enough. As mentioned earlier, fill-in-the-blank items are difficult because they require retrieval of specific words, and this was the reason given most often by the respondents for having difficulty with this type of item. About one-fourth of the respondents reported that multiple-choice items were extremely difficult. Interestingly, most of the stated reasons for difficulty with this type of item had to do with test construction. For example, confusing wording (e.g., including "all of the above" as an option and adding "which is not" to the stem), inadequate spacing between items, and horizontal ordering of options were given as reasons for their difficulty.

To assess TW skills, this group of university students was asked how they approach test-taking for objective and essay tests. Generally, they did not report using many TW behaviors. The only TW strategy reported as frequently used was skipping over difficult/unknown items. Few reported using the deductive and cue-usage strategies described above. When it came to answering essay questions, about half stated that they reread the question to ensure understanding as well as proofread their response. Few reported using any organizational strategies such as setting up an outline (these types of strategies are discussed in the section on test-taking strategy instruction).

In summary, many adolescents (even those who go on to college) do not apply an array of TW strategies systematically to improve their grades on tests. If teachers are concerned whether the lack of TW is stopping students from getting the highest possible grade on tests, teachers can conduct some informal assessments.

ASSESSING TEST-TAKING SKILLS AND STRATEGIES

One method of assessing TW is to develop and administer TW tests. Below are examples of items that assess the use of various TW strategies. Most of these items, similar to those created by Slakter et al. (1970), were developed by Hughes, Schumaker, Deshler, and Mercer (1988). Many of the key terms used are fictitious. Thus, students are forced to guess. When administering this type of test, the teacher should tell students that they will not know some of the answers and instruct them to make their best guess. Tests then can be examined for evidence of use of strategies and always should be followed up by interviewing students as to how they arrived at their answers. The interview process helps teachers decide whether a strategy was or was not used.

ELIMINATING SIMILAR OPTIONS

Architects stopped using argronimum in construction because

    a. it was too expensive
    b. it was too heavy
    c. it was not strong enough
    d. it weighed too much

In the above item, the student should select either **a** or **c** because **b** and **d** are essentially the same choice. Evidence of this strategy can be ascertained if the student has crossed off **b** and **d** as a way of noting that they are not viable answers and should be ignored during the answer selection process.

ELIMINATING ABSURD OPTIONS

Television and radio are

    a. inventions of the 18th century
    b. means of communication
    c. electrical appliances

Option **a** is absurd because most students know (we hope) that radio and television are more recent inventions. Evidence of strategy use would be crossing off this option as a possibility.

STEM OPTION AGREEMENT

The best possible example of a plinth is an

    a. creolate
    b. applax
    c. demidium

The best answer is **b** because both **a** and **c** begin with consonants and do not agree with the article *an*.

STEM WORD IN OPTION

The acidic properties of monoglymatic are similar to those of

    a. triglymatic acid
    b. selenic acid
    c. hydronic acid

The best choice is **a** because "glymatic" occurs in both the stem and this option.

LENGTH OF OPTION

The most common use of bason solutions is

    a. fermentation
    b. pigmentation
    c. as a cleaning compound
    d. as the organic catalyst found in oil solvents

The best choice is **d** because it is longer and more detailed than the other choices.

SPECIFIC DETERMINER

When the preservative monglate is added to food

    a. the food rarely spoils
    b. the food always changes color
    c. the food never changes color
    d. the food never spoils

The best guess in this item is **a** because the other options all contain "absolute" words. Assessment of this strategy also can be used for true-false items.

Using Relevant Information Contained in Other Test Items or Options

The Cadmos family fought with the Justins because they wanted

   a. their money back
   b. their land back
   c. their food back
   d. their house back

At this point a best guess is impossible. If the following true-false item occurs later in the test, however, it will provide a cue for making a guess about the nature of the Cadmos-Justin feud.

True or False? The Justins, who were land thieves, always got away with their thefts. Now there is a clue that the Justins were land thieves, making **b** the best guess for the previous item. This true-false item also contains a specific determiner, which means the best guess would be to mark it as **False**.

Interviewing

Another type of informal assessment procedure involves interviewing students using a scenario format similar to the one used earlier in regard to study strategies. This interview is to assess awareness of strategies, not their actual use. Hughes (1991) provided two scenarios, one for taking an objective test and one for an essay test. The following objective test scenario was read to college students with LD:

> You have just been handed a test made up of multiple-choice, true-false, and matching questions. Tell me in detail what you would do while taking this type of test.

A series of prompts was provided, including: "What is the very first thing you would do?" "What do you do when you come to a question you don't know the answer to?" "Do you guess?" "What clues or cues do you look for when you have to guess?" "What are some things you do to help you remember what you studied?"

For the essay test scenario, students are asked how they would go about answering essay questions, followed by these prompts: "What is the first thing you would do?" "Then what?" "Do you do anything before writing your response?" "After you have written your response, do you do anything?"

Another method of assessing test-taking behaviors is to examine actual classroom tests after administering them. Teachers can look for any evidence of TW and then follow up with an interview of the student. Evidence of TW to look for includes:

1. Allotment of time or ordering of sections (e.g., time notations, numbers at the top of each section).
2. Whether answers were marked in the appropriate place and manner.
3. Whether all questions were answered.
4. "Crossing off" marks (e.g., crossed off obviously incorrect options, or crossed off choices as they were used on matching items).
5. Any evidence (e.g., checkmark or X) indicating that the student skipped over difficult items and came back to them later.

Relatedly, actually watching students take the test may be useful to establish whether they start right away, skip over items, go over their test when finished, and so on. The observation, however, should be conducted in a manner that will not affect the student's performance.

Finally, Scruggs and Mastropieri (1992b) suggested assessing how well students can use separate answer sheets. Students are given a test (teacher-constructed) with the correct option indicated with an arrow. Students are told to identify the correct choice and fill in the bubble on the separate answer sheet as quickly as possible. The teacher then assesses speed, correctness, and how well the bubbles are filled in.

TEACHING TEST-TAKING STRATEGIES

Test-taking strategies can be taught and, in many cases, help students do better on tests (Hughes & Schumaker, 1991a, 1991b; Lee & Alley, 1981; Ritter & Idol-Maestas, 1986; Scruggs & Marsing, 1985). Before describing the "what" and "how" of test-taking instruction, two points should be stressed. First, test-taking skills do not replace adequate studying. Teachers should explain this clearly and often to their students. Although instruction in a variety of test-taking strategies can improve student test scores on classroom tests by about 10 to 13 percentage points, this gain clearly is insufficient to guarantee a passing score.

Hughes et al. (1988) suggested that when describing the expected benefits of learning a test-taking strategy to students, teachers write the following two sets of numbers on the board: 65% to 75% and 30% to 40%. They then explain to the students that the first set of numbers represents a 10% improvement in test scores based on the use of test-taking strategies, and point out that the grade went from a D to a C. Then they ask the students to examine the second set of figures and note that, although a 10% improvement occurred once again, the grade remained an F. This information may be presented graphically to students by writing the following on the board:

65% to 75%	30% to 40%
(D) (C)	(F) (F)

A second issue regarding instruction in test-taking skills centers on the advisability of teaching students to use cues based on poor test item construction (e.g., one option is longer than the others). Scruggs and Mastropieri (1992b) argued that students would be better off examining carefully the content of test items rather than depending on cues, and that guessing is better based on partial knowledge than on a presumed flaw in the test items. They also questioned the frequency of these types of cues, especially on standardized tests. These are important and valid points and should be considered when deciding which skills to include when teaching test-taking.

Accordingly, students should be told frequently that they should not use guessing strategies based on cues contained in flawed items until they have read the test item carefully and completely and have gone through the entire test (students should skip items they are unsure of and come back to them later). After students have attempted these procedures and still have *no idea* what the correct answer is, then and only then should they use a guessing strategy.

Scruggs and Mastropieri also are correct about standardized tests: They contain few if any cues of this nature. This finding is supported by their work. Based on an analysis of 100 randomly sampled classroom tests from Putnam's original sample, however, Hughes, Salvia, and Bott (1991) found that three-fourths of the tests contained one or more cues, most of which were in multiple-choice items. On the average, about 30% of the items on tests were flawed (contained possible cues). The most frequent cues were length of option and specific determiners. These two cues accounted for just over 80% of cues found on the tests. Further analysis showed that, if the cue was used as the sole basis for choosing the correct answer, a test-taker would be correct almost 75% of the time. Thus, teachers (and text publishers) often provide cues that can be used for guessing if all else fails.

Teachers of adolescents with LD have two basic choices at this point. They either can point out test-construction flaws to general education teachers at their school or go ahead and teach these types of strategies (and under what circumstances they should and should not be used) as a way of putting students with LD on equal footing with students who know these techniques already.

TEST-TAKING STRATEGY PACKAGES

Teachers can teach test-taking strategies and skills in isolation or together in the context of an overall strategy "package." Teaching skills in isolation or one at a time makes sense if the teacher knows which skills each student in the class has or does not have. If many of the students are deficient in several components of TW, teachers may wish to consider combining these strategies into one package. Three strategies designed for classroom tests are described next, two primarily for use with objective tests and one designed specifically for answering essay questions.

OBJECTIVE TESTS

A strategy package developed by Hughes et al. (1988) was designed primarily for use with objective test formats. It has been used successfully with adolescents with both learning and behavior problems (Hughes, Ruhl, Deshler, & Schumaker, 1993; Hughes & Schumaker, 1991a, 1991b). It includes most of the test-taking skills and strategies associated with TW and contains seven major steps. The first letter of each step forms the mnemonic PIRATES (see Figure 5.15).

The first step, "prepare to succeed," stresses time-usage strategies and is composed of four substeps that form the mnemonic PASS. The first step prompts students to *put* (write) their names (sometimes they forget) and the mnemonic PIRATES on their test. Writing the mnemonic helps cue strategy use.

Students then look over the test and make decisions about how much time they have and how much time they want to *allot* to each section of the test. They also indicate the order in which they want to complete the sections. This is a matter of preference. Some students like doing the easy items or sections first, and some like doing the hardest. Students then say self-affirmation statements such as, "I'm going to do well on this test." Finally, as part of this step, they make sure they *start* working on the test within 2 minutes.

Because many adolescents with LD do not attend well to directions regarding where and how to indicate answers, the second step focuses on this aspect of test-taking. The

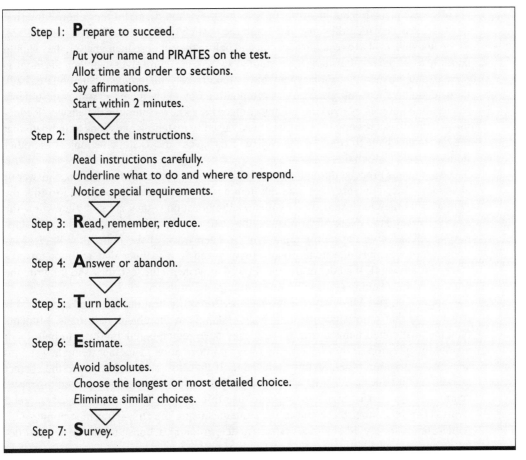

Step 1: **P**repare to succeed.

   Put your name and PIRATES on the test.
   Allot time and order to sections.
   Say affirmations.
   Start within 2 minutes.

Step 2: **I**nspect the instructions.

   Read instructions carefully.
   Underline what to do and where to respond.
   Notice special requirements.

Step 3: **R**ead, remember, reduce.

Step 4: **A**nswer or abandon.

Step 5: **T**urn back.

Step 6: **E**stimate.

   Avoid absolutes.
   Choose the longest or most detailed choice.
   Eliminate similar choices.

Step 7: **S**urvey.

FIGURE 5.15   STEPS AND SELECTED SUBSTEPS OF THE OBJECTIVE TEST-TAKING STRATEGY

step "inspect the instructions," is composed of three substeps that form the first-letter mnemonic RUN. Students are taught why and how to *read* directions and then to *underline* the key words (where and how to respond) as a way of focusing their attention on critical parts of the directions. Next, they *notice* special requirements related to directions. For example, the teacher might change the way answers are to be indicated (from "circle the correct letter" to "write the correct letter") or include a direction such as "indicate which answer is *not* correct."

The third step, "read, remember, and reduce," begins when students read the first item in a section. They are instructed to *read* the question carefully and all the way through. Some students are like eager contestants in a game show who blurt out the answer before the host states the entire question. Reading the whole item or question is important in multiple-choice items that read something like, "X, Y, and Z are examples of A. Which of the following is *not*?" Relatedly, students are taught to read *all* options in multiple-choice or matching items before making their selection. Students are taught that teachers often use plausible but incorrect options (as they should), and if they choose the first one that *seems* correct, they may not get to the best choice.

After students have read the question and before they choose their answer, they should pause to *remember* what they have studied by asking themselves whether the item is related to any lists or vocabulary they have memorized. The *reduce* substep relates back to the deductive reasoning strategy of eliminating obviously incorrect options. Students reduce their choices by marking off any choices they know cannot be the answer. Reducing also involves crossing off choices already used in matching questions to indicate that they no longer have to consider the choice. This saves time as students look at the other items to decide which ones match.

As students proceed through the section, they also utilize the fourth step, "answer or abandon." Once students have read the item and options carefully and tried to link the item to what they have studied, they *answer* the question if they are sure they know the answer. If they are unsure of the answer, they call upon the time-usage strategy of skipping or *abandoning* the item temporarily. To keep track of the items they have abandoned, students mark the items (unobtrusively and in a manner that will not mistake marks for answers). If students are not allowed to write on the test, they should write the number of the abandoned question on another piece of paper.

Steps 2, 3, and 4 are recycled for each section of the test until the end of the test is reached. At that point students "turn back" (step 5) to the abandoned items. Students read the abandoned items again to see if they have remembered anything to help them answer the question. If they have found relevant information in another item, they should answer the question based on this knowledge. If they still have no idea as to the correct answer and are taking a test in which guessing is not penalized, they proceed to step 6, "estimate." As part of this step, students use three guessing strategies based on cued items. They remember these cue-usage strategies using the first-letter mnemonic ACE, which stands for *A*void absolutes (specific determiners), *C*hoose the longest, most detailed option, and *E*liminate (cross off) similar options.

After they have examined and answered all abandoned items, students execute the final and seventh step, "survey." This step has two purposes: (a) to ensure that students have responded to all items, and (b) to make sure they responded to items the way they intended. This last purpose may involve changing answers. Students are told that changing answers is appropriate only if they are sure that the new choice is correct. If unsure, they should stay with the first choice.

This strategy is taught using the instructional stages described in chapter 2. Controlled practice consists of applying the strategy steps to a series of TW tests described in the test-taking assessment section. Once students master the strategy on these tests, specific generalization procedures are implemented. For example, flexibility is discussed in terms of when and where the strategy (or parts of it) can be used or not used. Part of this discussion focuses on not using the ACE steps when taking standardized tests. Students report to the teacher about how they have been using the strategy, what parts seem to be working for them, and how they may be adapting the strategy. For example, some students *despise* looking over the test before they take it. It does nothing but upset them, so they prefer not to do it.

To measure generalization the teacher can examine classroom tests for evidence of use of one or more strategies and sit down with students and discuss how they used the strategy on a given test. Periodic maintenance checks using test-wiseness tests also should be conducted.

Another test-taking strategy, developed by Carman and Adams (1972) and used successfully by Ritter and Idol-Maestas (1986) with middle school students is SCORER, a mnemonic for:

S = Schedule your time
C = Clue words
O = Omit difficult questions
R = Read carefully
E = Estimate your answers
R = Review your work

Many of the steps are similar to those in the PIRATES strategy, with some notable exceptions. First, the order of the PIRATES steps reflects the actual sequence of test-taking. For example, SCORER discusses "clue words" *before* "omit difficult questions" or "read (directions and items) carefully." Too, the "estimate" step in PIRATES instructs students to use "clue words" only after the abandoning/omitting process and only if students still have no idea about the correct answer. SCORER places the use of cues prior to omitting difficult questions and does not direct students to guess only if they "draw a blank." The O step in SCORER has more elaborate procedures than the "answer or abandon" step of PIRATES. Carman and Adams (1972) suggested following this procedure during the O step.

1. Move rapidly through the test.
2. When you find an easy question or one you are certain of, answer it.
3. Omit the difficult questions on this first pass.
4. When you skip a question, make a mark.
5. Keep moving. Never erase. Don't dawdle. Jot brief notes in the margin for later use if you need to.
6. When you have finished the easy questions, return to those with marks and try again.
7. Mark again the answers you are still not sure of.
8. In your review (the last R in SCORER), go over all the questions as time permits.

ESSAY QUESTIONS/TESTS

Although essay questions do not appear often on secondary classroom tests (Putnam, 1988), when they do, they make up a sizable portion of the test grade (Hughes & Clark, 1993). Some high school courses such as English and social studies use this form of assessment more often than other courses such as science.

This type of test item can be difficult for some adolescents with LD because it requires not only recall and comprehension but also many of the written expression skills discussed in chapter 4. Thus, teaching a systematic test-taking strategy to use with essay questions may be useful to many students. Such a strategy, developed to assist students in organizing better responses to essay questions, is called ANSWER (Hughes, Schumaker, & Deshler, in preparation).

This strategy, using the instructional stages described in chapter 2, was taught to college and high school students with LD, and preliminary results are encouraging. Students generated more complete and organized responses to essay questions. The strategy steps and substeps are presented in Figure 5.16.

In step 1, "analyze the situation," students instruct themselves to *R*ead the question carefully and *U*nderline key words (e.g., describe, compare, and contrast). Next they

Step 1: **A**nalyze the Situation

  *R*ead the question carefully
  *U*nderline key words
  *G*auge the time you need

▽

Step 2: **N**otice Requirements

  *S*can for and mark the parts of the question
  *A*sk and say what is required
  *T*ell yourself you will write a quality answer

▽

Step 3: **S**et Up an Outline

  *S*et up main ideas
  *A*ssess whether they match the question
  *M*ake changes if necessary

▽

Step 4: **W**ork in Details

  *R*emember what you learned
  *A*dd details to the main ideas using abbreviations
  *I*ndicate order
  *D*ecide if you are ready to write

▽

Step 5: **E**ngineer Your Answer

  *W*rite an introductory paragraph
  *R*efer to your outline
  *I*nclude topic sentences
  *T*ell about details for each topic sentence
  *E*mploy examples

▽

Step 6: **R**eview Your Answer

  *L*ook to see if you answered all parts of the question
  *I*nspect to see if you included all main ideas and details
  *T*ouch up your answer

FIGURE 5.16   STEPS AND SUBSTEPS OF THE ESSAY TEST-TAKING STRATEGY

Gauge the time needed to answer the question, using procedures similar to those in the PIRATES and SCORER strategies.

Step 2, "notice requirements," stresses behaviors needed to understand the question further and what kind of answer the teacher is looking for, along with a self-affirmation about the quality of the answer. Because many students have difficulty fashioning a cogent, organized response, they are instructed to spend several minutes to "set up an outline" of their response before actually writing it. In this third step, students *S*et up (list) the main ideas they wish to include in their answer, *A*ssess whether the main ideas match the requirements of the question, and *M*ake changes if necessary, based on the assessment.

Next, students "work in details." They *R*emember what they learned, *A*dd details to the outline under the appropriate main idea, *I*ndicate (number) the order in which they will address each main idea in their response, and then *D*ecide if they are ready to write. During this step students are taught to use abbreviations while constructing their outline to minimize the time spent in this process.

After writing the outline, students write their answer using the fifth step, "engineer your answer." Using the mnemonic WRITE, students *W*rite a short introductory paragraph stating what will be included in their answer, then *R*efer to the information in their outline to begin the rest of their response. Next, students *I*nclude a topic sentence for each paragraph (one for each main idea), then proceed to *T*ell about the details related to the topic sentence. Finally, students learn to *E*mploy examples (teachers often criticize essays for the lack of examples). The last step of the strategy, "review," requires students to *L*ook to see if they responded to all parts of the question, *I*nspect their writing to make sure that all main ideas and details in their outline were included in their answer, and *T*ouch up their answer (see if all words are legible, and so on).

Mini-instructional units are taught to ensure that students know how to execute certain imbedded skills. For example, to help students understand the requirements of a question (step 2), they are taught the meaning of "key" words used in essay questions, such as "discuss," "compare," "contrast," "identify," "justify," and "critique." During step 4, students are taught basic outlining skills, as well as four types of abbreviation skills: (a) use typical or standard abbreviations, (b) omit vowels, (c) use initials (e.g., BOG for branches of government), and (d) use the first two or three letters of a word (e.g., Eng for English). Figure 5.17 shows a sample question, outline, and student response along with comments on evaluating strategy use.

TEST-TAKING STRATEGIES USED WITH STANDARDIZED TESTS

Scruggs and Mastropieri (1992b) described a variety of general and specific strategies that can be used when adolescents with LD take standardized tests. These include the following.

- To help students keep their place on test pages and answer sheets and thus avoid marking answers on the wrong part of the answer sheet, have students fold test booklets and answer sheets so only one page shows at a time. This will decrease the likelihood of students' losing their place.
- To avoid turning two pages at the same time because they are stuck together, teach students to check page numbers whenever they turn a page.

Question: List the branches of government and describe at least two major functions of each. (10 points)

Outline: Executive branch (Pres)
   –declare war
   –veto legis
   Jud branch
   –decide if laws are const
   Legis branch (House of Rep & Senate)
   –pass legis
   –override Pres veto (2/3)

Answer: There are three branches of the federal government. These are the Executive, Legislative, and Judicial branches. Each of these branches is responsible for different functions.
   The Executive branch consists of the President of the United States. One of the President's most important functions is to declare war. Another thing the President can do is veto laws that are passed by the legislation. He does this if he thinks the law is not a good one.
   The Judicial Branch is the Supreme Court. These nine persons mainly decide if laws and court rulings are constitutional.
   The third branch, the legislative branch, which is made up of the House of Representatives and the Senate, is supposed to pass laws that affect the whole country.

Evaluation: The actual scoring guidelines for the ANSWER strategy are detailed and focus on organization, comprehensiveness, and clarity of response. Some of the major evaluation criteria include:
   (a) whether the student wrote the amount of time allotted for the question (which he didn't)
   (b) whether keywords were underlined and any parts of the question were underlined appropriately (which he did; key words were underlined once, and the words indicating the parts [list and describe] were underlined twice)
   (c) whether the student set up an outline listing main ideas (which he did) and added details (which he did to some extent, but he included only one detail under the main idea, Judicial Branch) and indicated in which order they would be presented in the response (which he did not do)
   (d) whether abbreviations were used (they were, but he could have used them more often and spent less time outlining)
   (e) whether an introductory paragraph was used (it was)
   (f) whether topic sentences were used, followed by detailed sentences (they were)
   (g) were all parts of the outline used in the response (they were all used except the detail about the legislative branch being able to override a Presidential veto with a 2/3 majority).

FIGURE 5.17   EXAMPLE ESSAY QUESTION, OUTLINE, STUDENT RESPONSE, AND EVALUATION GUIDELINES

- Tell students that answer sheets often have *two* sides and they should make sure they don't stop working after doing the first side.
- Teach students to always be sure that the item number matches the number (and subtest section) on the answer sheet.
- Teach students how to mark answers correctly (quickly and inside the bubble) and when they are finished to review the answer sheet.

Students should practice these strategies with close teacher monitoring and feedback using tests (sample or made up) similar in format to the actual standardized tests. For example, students should practice reading comprehension items, which usually require reading a passage, then answering a multiple-choice item about the passage content, or vocabulary subtests that typically present a word (in isolation or in a sentence) for which students are to select the correct synonym from several choices. Being familiar with these different test and item formats can increase students' confidence when taking the real thing. Many of the strategies suggested for classroom tests (use of time, avoiding errors, deductive reasoning) also are used when taking standardized tests, with the notable exception of using cues based on poor construction of test items.

Test Modifications and Accommodations

As stressed throughout this text, teaching adolescents strategies that will enable them to meet academic and social demands successfully and independently in much the same manner as their nondisabled peers is desirable. Sometimes, however, this is impossible because of the severity of the learning disability. If the disability precludes accurate assessment of what a student has learned or knows, modifying the test or testing procedure to accommodate that student's disability is appropriate. The question box on the next page further explores the issue of fairness in testing accommodations.

Whether an accommodation should or should not be allowed becomes arguable when the process of answering the question is as important as assessing the product (i.e., what the student knows). For example, if a teacher uses an essay question to assess both student knowledge and written expression, is an oral response to the question appropriate if the student has a disability related to written expression? Answers to issues like this are not clear-cut. Typically, consensus should be reached by negotiation among the concerned parties (e.g., classroom teacher, resource/support teacher, student, and parents).

Accommodations should be based on some form of documented need. Not all students who have a learning disability need testing modifications, and some students may need one type of modification but not another. Adolescents should be taught to self-advocate for appropriate testing accommodations. Appropriate self-advocacy is a *vital* skill for individuals with LD that will impact them throughout their lives.

Among the various testing modifications/accommodations that exist are the following:

- *Change in time allowed*. Because of problems with processing time, motor speed, and so on, many adolescents with LD need more time to complete the same amount of material than students without these problems. Time modifications probably are the most frequently requested accommodations for students with LD (Hughes,

Q & A

FAIRNESS IN TESTING

Q: *Why should we allow adolescents with LD to take tests in different ways than other students? Doesn't it give the students with LD an unfair advantage?*

A: Providing adolescents with testing accommodations such as extended time, reading the test to them, using alternate formats, and other strategies sometimes is seen as an unfair advantage. Let me offer a different perspective via some personal experiences.

I was speaking with a friend of mine about this very issue. My friend is a graduate student with a learning disability (he has had this label since he was 6 years old). He was telling me that during his undergraduate studies another student told him she thought it was unfair that he had more time to take his tests. His response was, "I can understand why you would feel that way but, believe me, I wish I didn't need the extra time."

The point is that many students with LD *need* the extra time because of a disability that sometimes manifests itself in slow processing. Many things, such as reading and understanding directions, retrieving information, and the actual act of writing, just take them longer. Providing more time doesn't mean they will get more of the test done. It just evens up things.

To take this argument one step further, would you expect a student with cerebral palsy to write the same length of response to an essay question in the same time as a person with no motor impairment? Would giving the person with cerebral palsy more time to write be unfair? In this case, most people would say, "No, of course not." So why is it different for individuals with LD? It may have to do with the "invisibility" of this type of disability. What do you think?

The second experience related to this topic happened to me in the summer of 1969. I was teaching a Red Cross life-saving class that students needed to pass to become lifeguards. In this class was a 16-year-old named Mike. Mike wanted very much to be a lifeguard and was the best in the class in performing the physical skills (saves, resuscitation, and so on). At the end of the course, a written, multiple-choice test was administered. The Red Cross required that the students pass both the performance and written tests to be certified. Mike failed this test badly. I then informed him that he could not be certified. He obviously was disappointed but said nothing.

A week later I received a phone call from a high school counselor, who asked me if I would meet with her. I did, and she explained that Mike was "learning disabled" (a term I had never heard of at that time) in the area of reading. She asked if I would give him the test orally. After receiving permission from the Red Cross, I readministered the test. Mike scored 100%.

Was that unfair to the rest of the class? Was the inability to pass the written test important to being a competent lifeguard? What do you think?

1991; Putnam et al., 1992). Recently, extended time has been granted (based on documentation) for tests such as the Scholastic Aptitude Test.

- *Change in test administration*. This accommodation typically is used with students with severe reading problems who have difficulty reading the test (these tests are written at up to the 10th-grade reading level). Directions and questions are read and repeated upon request. If asking for clarification about directions and items is permitted for *all* students in the class, the adolescent with LD also should be permitted to ask clarification questions.
- *Change in response format*. If the goal of the test is to assess knowledge (rather than the method of expression) and a student's writing disability is severe enough to preclude a comprehendible or complete response, verbal responses should be permitted.
- *Change in item format*. This accommodation allows students to be tested on the same content but involves altering the *type* of test item(s). For example, some students have problems with essay questions and may request assessment via objective items (or vice versa). One problem with this type of request is that two tests must be constructed. When this accommodation is used, the resource/support teacher, in consultation with the classroom teacher, often writes the second version.
- *Change in testing setting*. Often adolescents with LD are distractible to the extent that taking a test in a large-group setting may alter their performance. In response to this problem, they may be allowed to go to the resource room or another setting, where they can take the test under less distracting circumstances.
- *Change in grading procedures*. Sometimes classroom teachers are asked to alter their grading procedures. For example, teachers who normally "take off" for spelling errors can be requested to ignore spelling mistakes for a student with a disability in this area. Other procedures and issues involved in alternative grading options are discussed in the question box on the next page.

Requests for accommodations are not always allowed. To some extent, this is up to the teacher or instructor. Only about half of the university students with LD interviewed by Hughes (1991) stated that professors *always* granted their requests for testing accommodations. Putnam et al. (1992) noted that about 43% of the 7th- and 10th-grade teachers in their sample allowed testing modifications, and this number decreased from 7th to 10th grade. Although certain parts of public law (e.g., Section 504) require reasonable accommodations for disability, the term "reasonable" is ambiguous and not defined clearly in the legislation. Again, the student and those advocating for him or her are the ones who ultimately have to state clearly which accommodations are needed and provide sufficient documentation to support the request.

Test modifications and adaptations also have been made on minimum competency tests (MCT). In a sample consisting of 3rd-grade students with learning disabilities, Beattie, Grise, and Algozzine (1983) found improved performance on the Florida MCT when certain test modifications were made. The modifications were:

— ordering items from easy to hard
— placing answer bubbles on the answer sheet next to the corresponding item

Q & A

Fairness in Grading

Q: *Should students with LD be graded in the same way as peers without disabilities?*

A: Here is yet another sticky issue that drives both special education and content teachers to distraction. Before addressing this complex issue, delineating grading purposes may be helpful. Carpenter, Grantham, and Hardister (1983) identified four distinct (but not mutually exclusive) purposes of grades/grading:

1. Competence (mastery of skills, knowledge, etc.)
2. Progress (level of improvement from beginning to end of grading period)
3. Effort (how hard the student tried)
4. Comparison (ranking a student's performance in relationship to others)

Most often students are graded on competence. Thus, many students with severe learning difficulties do not fare well gradewise. Is this fair to students to whom learning does not come easy but who may be trying hard and making good (for them) progress? Would it be more "fair" to these students to evaluate them, at least partially, on the effort and progress they make? On the surface it makes sense that students should be rewarded if they try hard and make obvious progress. If a teacher grades solely on effort, however, a student who does not try hard but has complete mastery of the content conceivably might receive a failing grade. Is that fair (or even logical)?

Why not individualize grading procedures? That would mean grading nondisabled students in terms of competence and students with learning problems in terms of effort and progress. This seems like a happy compromise, but is it that simple? This type of grading may work okay in elementary school where grades "don't count." In secondary schools, however, grades do "count." Prospective employers and postsecondary schools use high school transcripts (and the diploma) to evaluate whether they will hire or accept students. If the grades and diploma are interpreted as documentation of competence but actually are based on effort or progress, how can employers or admissions directors make sense of them?

In response to this and other issues, some school districts have adopted a system of multiple diplomas or certificates. Some offer a regular diploma based on competence and others base the diploma on whether students with disabilities meet the objectives in their IEPs. Still others base diplomas on whether students show up to school on a regular basis (sometimes called a "certificate of attendance"). Certainly the goal for adolescents with LD is to obtain a regular diploma (in fact, this is the major reason for this textbook). For some students, however, other options may be better, and prospective employers should know what those options mean in terms of what students know.

— arranging multiple-choice options vertically
— not right-justifying tests, so words were not broken up
— shading passages used for reading comprehension items to highlight them
— including example items and responses on the test

These modifications related to test *construction* rather than changes in testing *procedures* such as those listed and discussed above.

Teachers should be aware that *how* they construct a test can affect the performance of adolescents with LD as well as the rest of the class. Therefore, teachers should be aware of best practices for constructing tests (detailed information on test construction can be found in several of the texts listed in the References). These practices, based on several sources (Miller & Erickson, 1985; Salend & Salend, 1985; Salvia & Hughes, 1990), include the following.

■ *Match the test to what is taught.* How many students (especially in college) have taken a test and found themselves wondering "where did this test item come from?" Relatedly, if a high percentage of instructional time is spent on certain topics, the test content should parallel this percentage closely.

■ *Match the test to how information is taught.* If much of the information is taught at the knowledge/factual level, administering a test in which most of the items measure application or comprehension is inappropriate.

■ *Allow a reasonable amount of time to take the test.* If students have 50 minutes to complete a test, the teacher should keep this in mind when deciding the number and type of items to include. One of the teachers in the Putnam et al. (1992) sample administered a 50-minute test with 130, free-recall, fill-in-the-blank items. What results can be expected?

■ *Test more on less.* More frequent tests on less information certainly benefit students with memory problems, and they provide teachers more useful information about the effectiveness of their instruction.

■ *Use "friendly" test formats.* Several relatively simple guidelines can be followed to make tests easier to read, understand, and answer. First, whenever possible, type tests. If typing is not possible, write the test in manuscript rather than cursive. Leave at least three horizontal spaces between items, provide plenty of space to write answers (especially on math tests), and do not continue an item on the next page. Write multiple-choice options vertically rather than horizontally. With matching questions, do not include more than eight items for each question.

CURRENT TRENDS IN TESTING AND ASSESSMENT

A major movement in schools today asks for more "authentic" assessment procedures. The term associated most frequently with authentic assessment is *performance-based assessment*. This movement is, to some measure, a result of dissatisfaction with paper-and-pencil formats often used with published, standardized tests and classroom tests, both of which rely heavily on objective formats to assess student knowledge. The current assessment practices, some believe, do not provide a complete picture of what a student knows or does not know, and these practices remove academic skills from their real purposes or contexts. They are not authentic.

Performance-based assessment (PBA) comes in many forms, including student projects, experiments, demonstrations, and portfolios. This last type, *portfolio assessment*, is one of the more frequently advocated forms of PBA. Portfolio assessment is not new. Visual artists, photographers, and writers have long used portfolios to illustrate the quality of their work. In an educational context, portfolios typically are collections of a student's best work in a variety of academic areas, which supposedly demonstrate academic growth or ability. Portfolios consist of a variety of products, including completed classroom assignments, short stories, art, interviews, and works in progress. In some instances students are required to write letters stating why they think each sample represents their "best." In sum, PBA comes in a variety of forms, and assessment of student performance is based, to a great extent, on the professional judgment of the person who does the evaluating (e.g., teacher, assessment specialist).

Although PBA has intuitive appeal as a more authentic way of assessing students, teachers should be aware that research to date has not provided much support for the reliability and validity of this approach (Lu & Suen, in press). Most likely the variety of formats, professional judgment, and concurrent lack of scoring/evaluation guidelines have given rise to problems in reaching high levels of technical adequacy. Further, little (if any) work has been conducted on the use of PBA with students who have disabilities. Regardless of the need for further empirical work in the area of PBA, its use is growing across the United States and many students with disabilities may be assessed in this fashion.

Because many of the test-taking skills and strategies described in this chapter are specific to traditional formats of assessment (objective tests), they are not applicable to PBA. Only some of the broader test-taking skills, such as making sure that students understand directions and checking to be sure that all aspects of the task have been addressed are relevant to this form of assessment. Teaching students to ask questions during the time they are working on the assessment task may further their understanding. This may be easier to do with PBA because it is more informal than the standardized procedures used with objective tests.

SUMMARY

This chapter covers two important and related skill areas: memory and test-taking. Research to date has shown that many children and adolescents with LD have problems retaining and recalling semantically related information. Although attention and motivation cannot be ignored as part of the memory problem equation, a large part of memory difficulties seem to result from the infrequent use of adequate elaboration strategies. The good news is that several methods can be used to improve the memory performance of adolescents with LD. Although these methods are somewhat different from each other, they have at least two things in common:

1. They involve manipulating to-be-learned information in a way that links it in a unique fashion to information that is already known. This linkage is what facilitates retrieval.

2. They are used primarily to facilitate factual recall rather than comprehension and retention of the "big picture."

Retention of basic facts, vocabulary, and concepts, however, is prerequisite to comprehension, analysis, and synthesis and, as such, is an important facet of instruction for adolescents with LD. Once students have fluent recall of these pieces of information, they can execute more readily global comprehension strategies such as paraphrasing and summarization. Too, teachers can help students tie it all together by following content-enhancement procedures such as graphic and verbal organizers (described elsewhere in this book). In addition to specific mnemonic procedures, teachers can assist students in mastering the overall process of studying. Instruction in study routines involves teaching executive strategies such as knowing what to study, how to study, and how much to study.

Adolescents frequently demonstrate what they understand and remember via classroom tests. Although adequate study behaviors probably have the largest impact on test scores, test-taking behaviors or strategies also can influence test grades positively. Teaching test-taking strategies to adolescents with LD who need them gives these students a plan. They proceed systematically through the test in a planful and efficient manner by using their time wisely, avoiding needless errors, and, when appropriate, applying effective guessing techniques.

Sometimes effective studying and test-taking behaviors are not enough for students to demonstrate their acquired knowledge adequately. If an aspect of the disability is severe enough, the method of assessment may have to be modified for these students to adequately show what they know. Because some teachers may be unwilling to provide these accommodations, students, through adequate instruction, must become adept at presenting a clear and persuasive rationale for teachers to provide accommodations.

REFERENCES

Alley, G. R., Deshler, D. D., & Warner, M. M. (1979). Identification of LD adolescents: A Bayesian approach. *Learning Disabilities Quarterly, 2*, 76–93.

Atkinson, R. C. (1975). Mnemotechnics in second-language learning. *American Psychologist, 30*, 821–828.

Bauer, R. (1979). Memory, acquisition, and category clustering in learning disabled children. *Journal of Experimental Child Psychology, 27*, 365–383.

Beattie, S., Grise, P., & Algozzine, B. (1983). Effects of test modifications on the minimum competency performance of learning disabled students. *Learning Disability Quarterly, 6*, 75–77.

Beery, K. E. (1982). *Revised administration, scoring, and teaching manual for the Developmental Test of Visual-Motor Integration.* Cleveland: Modern Curriculum Press.

Brown, A. L. (1979). The development of memory: Knowing, knowing about knowing, and knowing how to know. In H. W. Reese (Ed.), *Advances in child development and behavior.* New York: Academic Press.

Bulgren, J. A., Deshler, D. D., & Schumaker, J. B. (1994). The effects of a recall enhancement routine on the test performance of secondary students with and without learning disabilities. *Learning Disabilities Research and Practice, 9*, 2–11.

Bulgren, J. A., Hock, M., Schumaker, J. B., & Deshler, D. D. (1995). The effects of instruction in a paired associates strategy on the information mastery performance of students with learning disabilities. *Learning Disabilities Research and Practice, 10*, 22–37.

Bulgren, J. A., Schumaker, J. B., & Deshler, D. D. (in press). *The paired associates strategy*. Lawrence, KS: Edge Enterprises.

Carman, R. A., & Adams, W. R. (1972). *Study skills: A student's guide for survival*. New York: Wiley.

Carney, R. N., Levin, M. E., & Levin, J. R. (1993). Mnemonic strategies: Instructional techniques worth remembering. *Teaching Exceptional Children, 25*(4), 24–30.

Carpenter, D., Grantham, L. B., & Hardister, M. P. (1983). Grading mainstream handicapped pupils: What are the issues? *Journal of Special Education, 17*, 183–188.

Eggen, P. D., & Kauchak, D. (1992). *Educational psychology: Classroom connections*. New York: Macmillan.

Elbert, J. C. (1984). Short-term memory encoding and memory search in the word recognition of learning-disabled children. *Journal of Learning Disabilities, 17*, 342–345.

Elliott, J. L., & Gentile, J. R. (1986). The efficacy of a mnemonic technique for learning disabled and nondisabled adolescents. *Journal of Learning Disabilities, 19*, 237–241.

Ellis, E. (1992). *LINCS: A starter strategy for vocabulary learning*. Lawrence, KS: Edge Enterprises.

Fulk, B. J. M., Mastropieri, M. A., & Scruggs, T. E. (1992). Mnemonic generalization training with learning disabled adolescents. *Learning Disabilities Research and Practice, 7*, 2–10.

Gelzheiser, L. M., Solar, R. A., Shepard, M. J., & Wozniak, R. H. (1983). Teaching learning disabled children to memorize: A rationale for plans and practice. *Journal of Learning Disabilities, 16*, 421–425.

Hagen, J. W., & Barclay, C. R. (1982). The development of memory skills in children: Portraying learning disabilities in terms of strategy and knowledge deficiencies. In W. Cruickshank (Ed.), *Coming of age: The best of ACLD*. Syracuse, NY: Syracuse University Press.

Harris, K. R., Graham, S., & Freeman, S. (1988). Effects of strategy training on metamemory among learning disabled students. *Exceptional Children, 54*, 332–338.

Hughes, C. A. (1987). Test-taking skills for handicapped students. In C. R. Reynolds & L. Mann (Eds.), *Encyclopedia of special education: A reference for the education of the handicapped and other exceptional children and youth* (pp. 1040–1041). New York: Wiley.

Hughes, C. A. (1991). Studying for and taking tests: Self-reported difficulties and strategies of university students with learning disabilities. *Learning Disabilities, 2*, 65–71.

Hughes, C. A., & Clark, K. (1993). *An analysis of essay questions in seventh and tenth grade classroom tests*. Unpublished manuscript, Pennsylvania State University, University Park.

Hughes, C. A., & Schumaker, J. B. (1991a). Reflections on test-taking strategy instruction for adolescents with learning disabilities. *Exceptionality, 2*, 237–242.

Hughes, C. A., & Schumaker, J. B. (1991b). Test-taking strategy instruction for adolescents with learning disabilities. *Exceptionality, 2*, 205–221.

Hughes, C. A., Ruhl, K. L., Deshler, D. D., & Schumaker, J. B. (1993). Test-taking strategy instruction for adolescents with emotional and behavioral disorders. *Journal of Emotional and Behavioral Disorders, 1*, 189–198.

Hughes, C. A., Ruhl, K. L., Deshler, D. D., & Schumaker, J. B. (1995). *The assignment completion strategy*. Lawrence, KS: Edge Enterprises.

Hughes, C. A., Salvia, J., & Bott, D. (1991). The nature and extent of test-wiseness cues in seventh and tenth grade classroom tests. *Diagnostique, 16*, 153–163.

Hughes, C. A., Schumaker, J. B., & Deshler, D. D. (in preparation). *The essay test-taking strategy*.

Hughes, C. A., Schumaker, J. B., Deshler, D. D., & Mercer, C. D. (1988). *The test-taking strategy*. Lawrence, KS: Edge Enterprises.

King-Sears, M. E., Mercer, C. D., & Sindelar, P. T. (1992). Toward independence with keyword mnemonics: A strategy for science vocabulary instruction. *Remedial and Special Education, 13*, 22–33.

Lee, P., & Alley, G. R. (1981). *Training junior high school LD students to use a test-taking strategy* (Research Report No. 38). Lawrence: University of Kansas Institute for Research in Learning Disabilities.

Lehman, E. B., & Brady, K. M. (1982). Presentation modality and taxonomic category as encoding dimensions from good and poor readers. *Journal of Learning Disabilities, 15*, 103–105.

Levin, J. R. (1983). Pictorial strategies for school learning: Practical illustrations. In M. Pressley & J. R. Levin (Eds.), *Cognitive strategy research: Educational applications* (pp. 213–237). New York: Springer-Verlag.

Levin, J. R. (1988). Elaboration-based learning strategies: Powerful theory = powerful application. *Contemporary Educational Psychology, 13*, 191–205.

Levine, M. D. (1987). *Developmental variation and learning disorders*. Cambridge MA: Educators Publishing Service.

Lu, C., & Suen, H. K. (in press). Assessment approaches and cognitive styles. *Journal of Educational Measurement*.

Mastropieri, M. A. (1988). Using the keyword method. *Teaching Exceptional Children, 20*(2), 4–8.

Mastropieri, M. A., & Scruggs, T. E. (1989). Reconstructive elaborations: Strategies that facilitate content learning. *Learning Disabilities Focus, 4*, 73–77.

Mastropieri, M. A., & Scruggs, T. E. (1991). *Teaching students ways to remember: Strategies for learning mnemonically*. Cambridge, MA: Brookline.

Mastropieri, M. A., Scruggs, T. E., Bakken, J. P., & Brigham, F. J. (1992). A complex mnemonic strategy for teaching states and their capitals: Comparing forward and backward associations. *Learning Disabilities Research and Practice, 7*, 96–103.

Mastropieri, M. A., Scruggs, T. E., & Fulk, B. J. M. (1990). Teaching abstract vocabulary with the keyword method: Effects on recall and comprehension. *Journal of Learning Disabilities, 23*, 92–96.

Mastropieri, M. A., Scruggs, T. E., & Levin, J. R. (1985). Maximizing what exceptional students can learn: A review of research on the keyword method and related mnemonic techniques. *Remedial and Special Education, 6*(2), 39–45.

Miller, P. W., & Erickson, H. E. (1985). *Teacher-written students tests: A guide for planning, creating, administering, and assessing*. Washington, DC: National Education Association.

Millman, J., Bishop, C. H., & Ebel, R. (1965). An analysis of test-wiseness. *Educational and Psychological Measurement, 25*, 707–726.

Nagel, D. R., Schumaker, J. B., & Deshler, D. D. (1986). *The FIRST-letter mnemonic strategy*. Lawrence, KS: Edge Enterprises.

Pressley, M., Scruggs, T. E., & Mastropieri, M. A. (1989). Memory strategy instruction for learning disabilities: Present and future directions for research. *Learning Disabilities Research, 4*, 68–77.

Putnam, M. L. (1988). *An investigation of the curricular demands in secondary mainstream classrooms containing students with mild handicaps*. Unpublished dissertation, University of Kansas, Lawrence.

Putnam, M. L. (1992a). Characteristics of tests administered by mainstream secondary classroom teachers. *Learning Disabilities Research and Practice, 7*, 129–136.

Putnam, M. L. (1992b). Testing practices of mainstream secondary classroom teachers. *Remedial and Special Education, 13*(5), 11–21.

Putnam, M. L., Deshler, D. D., & Schumaker, J. B. (1992). The investigation of setting demands: A missing link in learning strategy instruction. In L. Meltzer (Ed.), *Strategy assessment and instruction for students with learning disabilities: From theory to practice*. Austin, TX: Pro-Ed.

Ritter, S., & Idol-Maestas, L. (1986). Teaching middle school students to use a test-taking strategy. *Journal of Educational Research, 79*, 350–357.

Salend, S., & Salend, S. J. (1985). Adapting teacher-made tests for mainstreamed students. *Journal of Learning Disabilities, 18*, 373–375.

Salvia, J., & Hughes, C. A. (1990). *Curriculum-based assessment: Testing what is taught*. New York: Macmillan.

Salvia, J., & Ysseldyke, J. E. (1991). *Assessment* (5th ed.). Boston: Houghton-Mifflin.

Sarnacki, R. E. (1979). An examination of test-wiseness in the cognitive domain. *Review of Educational Research, 49*, 252–279.

Scruggs, T. E., Bennion, K., & Lifson, S. (1985). Learning disabled student's spontaneous use of test-taking skills on reading achievement test. *Learning Disability Quarterly, 8*, 205–210.

Scruggs, T. E., & Marsing, L. (1985). Teaching test-taking skills to behaviorally disordered students. *Behavioral Disorders, 13*, 240–244.

Scruggs, T. E., & Mastropieri, M. A. (1988). Are learning disabled students "test-wise?": A review of recent research. *Learning Disabilities Focus, 3*, 87–97.

Scruggs, T. E., & Mastropieri, M. A. (1989a). Mnemonic instruction of learning disabled students: A field-based evaluation. *Learning Disability Quarterly, 12*, 119–125.

Scruggs, T. E., & Mastropieri, M. A. (1989b). Reconstructive elaborations: A model for content area learning. *American Educational Research Journal, 26*, 311–327.

Scruggs, T. E., & Mastropieri, M. A. (1990). The case for mnemonic instruction: From laboratory investigations to classroom applications. *Journal of Special Education, 24*, 7–32.

Scruggs, T. E., & Mastropieri, M. A. (1992a). Classroom applications of mnemonic instructions: Acquisition, maintenance, and generalization. *Exceptional Children, 58*, 219–229.

Scruggs, T. E., & Mastropieri, M. A. (1992b). *Teaching test-taking skills: Helping students show what they know.* Cambridge, MA: Brookline.

Scruggs, T. E., & Mastropieri, M. A. (1993). Special education for the twenty-first century: Integrating learning strategies and thinking skills. *Journal of Learning Disabilities, 26*, 392–398.

Slakter, M. J., Koehler, R. A., & Hampton, S. H. (1970). Learning test-wiseness by programmed texts. *Journal of Educational Measurement, 7*, 247–254.

Swanson, H. L, Cochran, K. F., & Ewers, C. A. (1990). Can learning disabilities be determined from working memory performance? *Journal of Learning Disabilities, 23*, 59–68.

Swanson, H. L., & Cooney, J. B. (1991). Learning disabilities and memory. In B. Wong (Ed.), *Learning about learning disabilities* (pp. 103–127). San Diego: Academic Press.

Torgeson, J. K. (1979). Factors related to poor performance on memory tasks in reading disabled children. *Learning Disabilities Quarterly, 2,* 17–23.

Torgeson, J. K., & Goldman, T. (1977). Rehearsal and short-term memory in reading disabled children. *Child Development, 48*, 56–60.

Torgeson, J. K., & Kail, R. J. (1980). Memory processes in exceptional children. In B. K. Keogh (Ed.), *Advances in special education: Basic constructs and theoretical orientations* (Vol. 1, pp. 55–99). Greenwich, CT: JAI Press.

Trepanier, M. L., & Casale, C. M. (1982). Metamemory development in learning disabled children. In W. M. Cruickshank & E. Tash (Eds.), *Academics and beyond.* New York: Syracuse University Press.

Veit, D. T., & Scruggs, T. E. (1986). Can LD students effectively use separate answer sheets? *Perceptual and Motor Skills, 63*, 155–160.

Wedel, M., Deshler, D. D., Schumaker, J. B., & Ellis, E. S. (in preparation). *Effects of instruction of a vocabulary strategy in a mainstream class.* Lawrence, KS: Institute for Research in Learning Disabilities.

Weinstein, C. E. (1978). Elaboration skills as a learning strategy. In H. R. O'Neil, Jr. (Ed.), *Learning strategies.* New York: Academic Press.

Wong, B. Y. L. (1980). Activating the inactive learner: Use of questions/prompts to enhance comprehension and retention of implied information in learning disabled children. *Learning Disabilities Quarterly, 3,* 29–37.

Wong, B. Y. L. (1982). Strategic behaviors in selecting retrieval cues in gifted, normal achieving, and learning disabled children. *Journal of Learning Disabilities, 15*, 33–37.

Worden, P. E. (1983). Memory strategy instruction with the learning disabled. In M. Pressley & J. R. Levin (Eds.), *Cognitive strategy research: Psychological foundations* (pp. 129–153). New York: Srpinger-Verlag.

6

Notetaking Strategy Instruction

SHARON K. SURITSKY AND CHARLES A. HUGHES

Questions to Keep in Mind

- What are the benefits of recording notes during a lecture? Why is notetaking better than other alternatives?

- How do the notes of LD adolescents compare to their nondisabled peers?

- What is the best instructional approach for teaching notetaking skills? Why?

- How can students engage in a deep level of cognitive processing during the lecture? What effect will this have on their retention of lecture ideas?

- What skills will enable a student to record the most effective notes?

- In what specific behaviors do good notetakers engage before, during, and after the lecture?

- Given the notetaking difficulties of adolescents with LD, should a teacher provide instruction in notetaking skills or alter the lecture so students do not have to record any notes? Why?

ADVANCE ORGANIZER

Can you recall sitting in your high school or college classes taking notes? Do you remember furiously trying to note all the key points and how much trouble you had retaining one idea long enough to jot it down while at the same time trying to listen to the next idea? And what about those teachers or professors who were great to listen to and interact with but impossible to take notes from because they kept jumping from one topic to another? Think about how difficult these situations must be for many students with learning disabilities.

This chapter provides information about the notetaking demands of high school and college classrooms and the notetaking characteristics of adolescents with LD. We discuss methods for assessing notetaking skills. In addition, we offer techniques and strategies to teach notetaking skills. Figure 6.1 outlines the organization of the chapter.

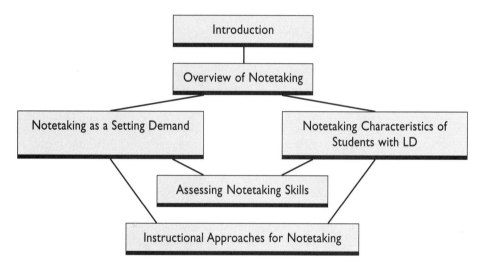

FIGURE 6.1 CHAPTER 6 ORGANIZATION

INTRODUCTION

In typical secondary and postsecondary classrooms students participate in many activities (e.g., lectures, reading, presentations by guest speakers, media, student-centered activities) that require listening and notetaking skills. More often than not teachers use lectures as the main instructional activity to disseminate important course content. Most students record notes during lectures to understand and remember lecture content later. Notetaking makes perfect sense as a strategy given that once a lecture is over, it cannot be recovered. Unless lectures have been preserved (e.g., tape-recorded), they cannot be listened to again. Without recorded notes students would have to rely strictly on memory to retain lecture information.

Despite the importance of notetaking, little attention has been paid to notetaking training for secondary or postsecondary students. For the most part, students are left to their own devices to record effective notes. Even without explicit training, many nondisabled students develop acceptable notetaking skills on their own not long after entering junior high school (Beirne-Smith, 1989). Many students with LD who characteristically experience difficulties with a variety of study skills, however, may not develop the same notetaking skills as their non-LD peers. This means that some students with LD and others who are poor notetakers are at a major disadvantage in terms of understanding and remembering lecture information. As a result, these students may not be as successful in classrooms that demand effective notetaking skills.

The first section of the chapter presents an overview of notetaking. The overview includes a discussion of the major components of notetaking, functions or benefits of recording notes, and factors that influence notetaking. Next we discuss the setting demands for notetaking, followed by a description of the notetaking characteristics of adolescents with LD. Finally, we describe in detail methods for assessing notetaking and instructional approaches.

OVERVIEW OF NOTETAKING

At one time or another most of us have recorded notes while listening to a lecture. Most secondary and postsecondary students are seasoned notetakers (in terms of frequency of use, not necessarily competence). Despite the frequency with which most students record notes every day in school, few individuals (yourself included) probably have really thought about the process of notetaking. Knowledge about the components of notetaking, as well as factors that influence a person's ability to take notes, should help teachers understand why adolescents with LD may have difficulties with notetaking. In addition, this information provides the foundation for assessing notetaking skills and, in turn, designing appropriate notetaking interventions. For example, how can one assess notetaking competence accurately if one cannot identify the precise skills involved in recording notes? The overview of notetaking here provides the necessary background information for later sections dealing with notetaking assessment and instructional approaches.

COMPONENTS OF NOTETAKING

Notetaking is a complex process consisting of four broad skills: (a) listening, (b) cognitive processing, (c) writing, and (d) reviewing noted information (LeBauer, 1984; Peck & Hannafin, 1983; Smith & Tompkins, 1988). Each of the four skills consists of several subskills.

LISTENING

Listening is defined traditionally as the translation of spoken words into meaning. It is not that simple, though, because listening, and thus the meaning of spoken words, is influenced through many channels of communication. Wilkinson, Stratta, and Dudley (1974) spoke of four channels of communication: (a) linguistic, (b) paralinguistic, (c) visual, and (d) kinesthetic.

Comprehension of information from the linguistic channel depends largely on the listener's vocabulary skills. This channel requires understanding the unique and multiple meanings of words in the context of different subject matter. For example, the words "frets," "string," and "notes" have different meanings when talking specifically about playing a guitar than when these words are spoken in everyday conversations. Paralinguistic communication comprises factors that run alongside (para-) the language and includes tone of voice, speed of speaking, and pauses in delivery. Visual communication feeds us information related to the speaker's appearance and often influences the listener's first impressions. Kinesthetic communication relies on the nonverbal components of communication such as posture, expressions, and gestures.

The skills required for listening range from simple to complex. Listening consists of three subskills: (a) hearing the information, (b) attending to the information—being selective about what words should receive attention and maintaining attention to the words over time, and (c) understanding the ideas by assigning meaning to what was heard (Bryan & Bryan, 1986; Lerner, 1993; Mandlebaum & Wilson, 1989; Wallace, Cohen & Polloway, 1987).

COGNITIVE PROCESSING

Cognitive processing requires students to distinguish between important and unimportant lecture ideas, predict future lecture information, remember previous lecture ideas, activate prior knowledge, associate previous ideas and new content, retain ideas in short-term memory, paraphrase lecture content, and/or elaborate lecture ideas (Anderson & Armbruster, 1986; DiVesta & Gray, 1972; Ladas, 1980a; Peper & Mayer, 1978, 1986).

WRITING

The broad skill of writing includes selecting and using a framework for recording notes, spelling known and unknown words, writing with sufficient speed and legibility, and using abbreviations (Vogel, 1982).

REVIEWING NOTED INFORMATION

When reviewing notes, students may read notes, extract meaning from notes after the lecture, delete or add information to notes, and apply appropriate memory strategies while studying notes.

During the lecture notetaking skills and subskills must be applied at the same time and at a rapid rate if the lecture is fast. The student must attend to a lecture idea, process the meaning of the idea by associating or integrating it with prior learning, extract the important information from the lecture idea, retain the meaning in memory, use a framework for recording notes, and write the idea using sufficient speed and abbreviations while simultaneously listening to additional lecture information.

Because all of these tasks have to be done together and done well, it is easy to understand why some students have problems with notetaking. Adding to possible notetaking difficulty is the fact that students do not control the speed of the task. In reading, for example, students can slow down if the material is difficult and reread sections they did not understand after the first pass-through. In contrast, the notetaker cannot slow down the lecturer (except for asking occasional questions) and the lecture cannot be replayed unless it has been tape-recorded. Also, tremendous pressure is involved because students have to acquire lecture information the first time around.

If notetaking is such a difficult skill, why do so many students take notes instead of using other strategies during the lecture? Think back to your own notetaking experiences in high school or college. Why did you record notes during class lectures? If you are like most other high school or college students, your reasons include: "What else would I do during the lecture if I didn't record notes?" "There's no way I could remember all of the information without writing anything down." "Taking notes makes me think about the material." "Teachers may say they use the book for tests, but I know they always make their tests from the lecture." If your responses match some of these reasons, you already are aware of some of the functions or benefits of notetaking.

FUNCTIONS OF NOTETAKING

Researchers (e.g., DiVesta & Gray, 1972; Peper & Mayer, 1978, 1986) suggested two general functions of notetaking: (a) a process or encoding function, and (b) a product or external storage function. The *encoding function* implies that just the simple act of recording notes has certain benefits.

1. Notetaking increases students' attention to the lecture material.
2. Notetaking, as opposed to just listening, requires the student to engage in a deeper level of cognitive processing. During notetaking, the student must make sense of the information and then write the ideas in a personally meaningful way. Thus, the student engages in active cognitive processing during the lecture.
3. The end result of all of this processing is the transfer of lecture ideas from short-term memory into long-term memory. Without a deep level of processing, this transfer is not likely to happen.

Notetaking also serves an *external storage* function. Notes are a permanent and transportable record of information that was presented verbally. Notes written in ink on paper in a notebook are permanent (to a certain degree) and also are portable. In addition, notes are the foundation for studying for tests for most students. The fact that students can add to or change their notes after a lecture means that notetaking actually provides two opportunities for learning lecture information. The first opportunity is while listening and recording notes, and the second comes while reviewing or studying notes for a later test (Anderson & Armbruster, 1986; DiVesta & Gray, 1972; Peper & Mayer, 1978, 1986).

Research supports the proposed benefits of notetaking. In general, notetaking seems to give students an advantage over simply listening during a lecture. In several reviews of the literature (Anderson & Armbruster, 1986; Hartley & Davies, 1978; Kiewra, 1985a; Ladas, 1980b), researchers found that the act of recording notes without later review was more beneficial than simply listening, except in situations in which the lecture was presented at a rapid rate or was full of complex and unfamiliar words and concepts. Also, reviewing notes after the lecture was beneficial.

Notetakers are likely to recall more lecture ideas than students who simply listen to a lecture. Students who record notes tend to recall far more of the information that appears in their notes (Aiken, Thomas, & Shennum, 1975; Einstein, Morris, & Smith, 1985; Kiewra & Fletcher, 1984). If information is not recorded in notes, it is not likely to be remembered later. Research shows that notetakers may recall different kinds of information than students who listen without recording notes. Notetakers recall more high-importance information than listeners do (Einstein et al., 1985). In a study conducted by Peper and Mayer (1978), college notetakers, in comparison to listeners, recalled more ideas that represented underlying concepts in the lecture and more information that was connected to other ideas.

FACTORS THAT INFLUENCE NOTETAKING

Notetaking is influenced by two broad categories: (a) factors related to the student (listener-related), and (b) factors related to the teacher (lecturer-related). The major student-related variables include, but are not limited to, the students' capacity for processing and writing, the amount of cognitive processing in which they engage during and after the lecture, and the students' purposes or goals for notetaking. The most important teacher-related factors include speed of presentation, density of content (amount of complex concepts per total number of words in the lecture), and verbal and nonverbal cues.

STUDENT-RELATED FACTORS

Students have a limited capacity for physically writing notes (Greene, 1928). Few students, if any, can write as fast as teachers can talk. As a result, students cannot expect to record exact words in the lecture. Fortunately, research finds that recording the most important lecture ideas is what makes notes beneficial. Based on several theories of processing (Craik & Lockhart, 1972; Ladas, 1980a), students should engage in a deep level of cognitive processing during the lecture. A deep level of processing means that students have associated new ideas from the lecture with ideas previously learned, paraphrased lecture content (put in "own words"), and elaborated on or added their own thoughts to lecture ideas. On the other hand, a shallow level of processing involves writing notes almost verbatim without really thinking about the information. Looking at a deeper level versus a shallow level of processing, logically deeper processing is likely to result in a greater amount of learning (understanding) of lecture content because lecture ideas will be transferred into long-term memory.

Students' purposes or goals for notetaking influence how much cognitive processing they engage in and how they record notes (what information they chose to record, how much information they chose to record) because the extent to which notes are complete is important. If students are not looking ahead to later tests or are not motivated to do well on these tests, this will affect the quality of their notes. Obviously, incomplete notes are less helpful when studying. Research results, however, are contradictory concerning how complete, in terms of total words, notes have to be to maximize learning. Some support exists for recording "efficient" notes (Howe, 1970; Maqsud, 1980). This means recording the maximum number of ideas in the fewest words. "Complete" notes, however, received positive support (highest number of total words) as well (Hartley & Marshall, 1974; Kiewra & Fletcher, 1984). Basically, important lecture ideas should be recorded as completely as possible (Kiewra, 1985a), and additional information may be added to notes after the lecture to achieve completeness.

TEACHER-RELATED FACTORS

The speed of the lecture impacts the time students have for recording notes and for processing lecture ideas cognitively. Not surprisingly, students recall less lecture information when lectures are presented rapidly (Aiken et al., 1975; Peters, 1972), because students cannot write fast enough to keep up with the lecture. Also, students do not have enough time for the deep processing of lecture information. Another factor reducing time for recording notes and processing information is a high level of *information density*. Information density is described as the number of lecture ideas or lecture information units (IUs) in the number of total lecture words (Aiken et al., 1975). "Dense" lectures (those that contain an unreasonably high number of lecture IUs) impact students' recall of lecture information negatively (Aiken et al., 1975). During rapidly presented lectures that are information-dense, notetaking seems to interfere with student learning.

Teachers can influence students' notetaking and subsequent recall positively by using a variety of verbal and nonverbal cues. Table 6.1 provides examples. Verbal cues include statements that stress important information (e.g., teacher spells a key word) and statements that provide some organizational framework for the notes (e.g., "Today we will talk about three important characteristics of a democracy: #1..., #2..., and #3..."). Nonverbal cues include gestures (e.g., writing information on the chalkboard) and pauses between ideas. Students are likely to note and remember information that is written on the board (Hartley & Cameron, 1967; Locke, 1977), as well as repeated points and dictated headings (Maddox & Hoole, 1975). Teacher cues can indicate the underlying organization of the lecture and focus students' attention by highlighting the most important lecture ideas that should be noted.

NOTETAKING AS A SETTING DEMAND

Effective listening and notetaking skills are critical for adolescents and young adults in academic, vocational, and even social settings. The demands for notetaking will be discussed across each of these three areas: academic, vocational, and social.

ACADEMIC

Students' listening and notetaking skills must progress with each grade level as learning demands increase. Listening demands are far more complex in secondary classrooms than elementary classrooms for several reasons. First, in a typical high school students must be able to follow oral directions and comprehend class lectures presented by as many as five or six different teachers (Robinson, Braxdale, & Colson, 1985). Second, the language environments of high schools become more complicated. Stories are longer; directions are more complex; subtle meanings are used more frequently; and the demands for critical listening and notetaking are greater. Finally, many secondary school classes are characterized by teachers' limited use of advance organizers, questions re-

TABLE 6.1   LECTURE CUES

Types of Cues	Examples
Organizational Cues	"Today we will discuss..."
	"The topic is..."
	"First of all,..."
	"Second [third, etc.],"
	"Then,"
	"Next,"
	"To review/summarize/recap/review/go back over"
Emphasis Cues	
Verbal	
	"You should remember that..."
	"You need to know/note/understand/remember/underline/think about..."
	"This is important/key/basic."
	"Listen carefully."
	"Let me emphasize/repeat/explain/make clear..."
	"What is it?"
Nonverbal	
	Teacher asks questions not meant to be answered by students.
	Teacher speaks more slowly or loudly.
	Teacher stresses certain words.
	Teacher spells words.
	Teacher repeats words or phrases.

quiring student responses, and feedback (Schumaker & Deshler, 1984; Schumaker, Sheldon-Wildgen, & Sherman, 1980).

In academic environments two recent trends underscore the need for secondary and postsecondary students with LD to have critical study skills including listening and notetaking. First, the emphasis on inclusion has resulted in recommendations to increase the number of students with LD who receive some instruction in general education classrooms. Students in inclusion settings must be able to meet the complex demands of those classroom environments. Second, college education has become a viable alternative for students with LD, and, not surprisingly, more students with LD are enrolled in colleges and universities (Beirne-Smith & Deck, 1989; Bursuck, Rose, Cowen, & Yahaya, 1989; McGuire, Norlander, & Shaw, 1990; Shaw & Norlander, 1986).

In general education high school classrooms curriculum demands place heavy requirements on students' ability to listen, comprehend, and retain oral information. Teachers value the importance of these skills. General education teachers were asked to rate their expectations for students in their classrooms (Knowlton, 1982, Link, 1982). They assigned a high level of importance to three specific listening skills: listening for meaning and retention, following oral and written directions, and taking notes from lectures. Based on their reported expectations, it is not surprising that teachers spend at least half of their class time presenting information through lectures (Putnam, Deshler, & Schumaker, 1993). Also, teachers rely on information presented in class discussion and lectures as the basis for a significant number of items on tests they prepare (Putnam et al., 1993). Therefore, the ability of students with LD to comprehend and retain lecture information is vital to success in inclusion classes.

As students with LD move from high school to college environments, they continue to need effective listening and notetaking skills. In college classrooms most professors rely heavily on lectures to disseminate course content (Carrier, Williams, & Dalgaard, 1988; Westendorf, Cape, & Skrtic, 1982), and notetaking is the primary method students use to understand and remember lecture information (Palmatier & Bennett, 1974). Thus, college success can be influenced greatly by students' ability to record effective notes.

VOCATIONAL

Effective listening skills can influence adolescents' and young adults' vocational success in many ways. Just getting a job requires good listening skills. Think about your last interview that resulted in getting a job or position you desired. Most likely, during this interview, you appeared to have good listening skills. You maintained eye contact, leaned forward to appear interested, and asked and responded to questions at appropriate times. Beyond these basics, you understood and responded accordingly to complex, often multipart questions, as few interviewers ask very many questions that require yes/no responses. In addition, you remembered information discussed earlier in the interview and used this information to formulate your own questions relevant to specifics the interviewer mentioned.

Once they acquire jobs, employees must often follow directives that a supervisor presents verbally. Consider job training situations. If you are lucky enough to have a manual, you can listen to a description of procedures without feeling totally pressured. You know you can refer to the manual and reread the steps as often as necessary. If you are not issued a manual, you will need to listen carefully to the verbal descriptions. If you are wise, you will note key parts to be remembered later. Throughout the explanations you can ask questions. You are likely to receive verbal answers, however. Thus, you will need to rely on your listening and notetaking skills to understand and remember the important information.

Beyond influencing your work with your supervisor, listening skills are likely to impact interactions with co-workers and possibly work output. The ability to listen effectively is important particularly in situations where you are required to work with others to complete job tasks.

SOCIAL

Social situations pose a tremendous demand for good listening skills. How can you keep friends if they always complain that you never listen to them? Adolescents and young adults spend a lot of time talking and listening to each other every day. Also, as members of the "TV generation," young people in general rely almost solely on television for information and entertainment. Even trying to learn the words to a favorite song on the radio requires good listening skills. Use of the telephone, the mode of choice with adolescents, relies totally on listening. The extent to which one is successful in group inter-action is a function of how well one receives verbal and nonverbal messages. Obviously, peer interactions in school and out of school are influenced by listening skills.

Notetaking Characteristics of Adolescents with LD

Researchers have devoted considerable attention to factors that influence the ability of adolescents without disabilities to record notes during lectures (see Anderson & Armbruster, 1986; Hartley, 1976; Hartley & Davies, 1978; Kiewra, 1985a; Kiewra, 1987; Ladas, 1980b for reviews of the notetaking literature). We know that rapid presentation rates and too much complex and unfamiliar content will impact negatively most, if not all, students' ability to record good notes. Little attention, however, has been paid to the notetaking *skills* of nondisabled students. Even more unfortunate, students with LD have been ig-nored for the most part. Little empirical information exists about the actual notetaking skills of high school students with LD. Another strike against notetaking research con-cerns study settings. Most notetaking research has been conducted in contrived, or arti-ficial, settings and imposes tasks that have no relevance to students' class performance. For example, in many studies students are asked to record notes while listening to a lecture pertaining to an obscure topic (e.g., The Many Uses of Quartz) that has no con-nection to class content or expectations. More research should be done in real, "live" classroom settings.

Research on the notetaking skills of adolescents with LD tends to be concentrated in three areas:

1. The difficulties students with LD have with notetaking components of listening, cognitive processing, writing, and reviewing.
2. Reported perceptions of students with LD on notetaking tasks and the strategies they use.
3. Comparisons of notes of students with and without disabilities.

The answers to these questions will be discussed in this section. Figure 6.2 summarizes the notetaking characteristics of adolescents with LD, and Figure 6.3 presents the com-ponents and functions of notetaking.

This section discusses specific difficulties associated with each of the four major notetaking components. These components are listening, cognitive processing, writing, and reviewing noted information.

Listening Difficulties

Adolescents with LD may have a variety of difficulties in attending to information when listening to a lecture. According to Bryan and Bryan (1986), three components of atten-tion are necessary to attend to information properly: (a) coming to attention—initially getting oriented to the listening task, (b) selective attention—the ability to pay attention

Difficulties with Notetaking Components	Self-Reported Notetaking Difficulties and Strategies	Comparison of LD Versus NLD Notetakers
▪ Listening —coming to attention —selective attention —vigilance ▪ Cognitive processing —auditory processing —active processing —organizing information —using mental elaborations ▪ Writing —speed of writing —legibility —spelling ▪ Reviewing —awareness of need to review —motivation —knowledge of effective strategies	▪ Problems writing fast enough ▪ Difficulty paying attention ▪ Cannot decide what information to note ▪ Difficulty making sense of notes after the lecture ▪ Limited use of abbreviations ▪ Limited application of comprehensive notetaking system	▪ Less complete notes ▪ Fewer total words abbreviated ▪ Fewer different words abbreviated ▪ Less key lecture ideas recorded

FIGURE 6.2   NOTETAKING CHARACTERISTICS OF ADOLESCENTS WITH LD

to important ideas while disregarding unimportant information, and (c) vigilance—the ability to sustain effort in listening in spite of internal or external factors. Internal factors include, among others, lack of sleep and boredom with the lecture topic. External factors include noise from outside the classroom, the buzzing sound of the air conditioner, and the loud talking from a student in the back row. Research (Hallahan & Reeve, 1980; Keogh & Margolis, 1976) shows that adolescents with LD have problems with skills similar to Bryan and Bryan's (1986) three attention components (initially focusing attention, selectively attending to auditory information, and maintaining attention).

COGNITIVE PROCESSING DIFFICULTIES

Students with LD report difficulties in understanding and processing auditory information (Whyte, 1984). Therefore, it is easy to understand why some adolescents with LD have difficulty assigning meaning to lecture ideas, a necessary skill for effective notetaking.

An effective notetaker processes lecture ideas actively (Peper & Mayer, 1978). For example, good notetakers selectively attend to the most important lecture ideas, as re-

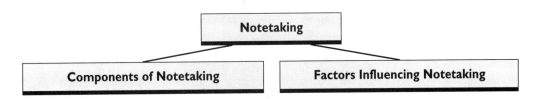

Listening	Cognitive Processing	Student Factors	Teacher Factors
■ Focus attention ■ Hear ■ Understand	■ Active prior knowledge ■ Associate new ideas and background knowledge ■ Distinguish between important and unimportant information ■ Retain ideas in short-term memory ■ Elaborate lecture information ■ Put content into one's notes	■ Limited capacity for writing ■ Student's goals ■ Ability to engage in deep processing	■ Lecture speed ■ Information density ■ Use/nonuse of areas
Writing	**Reviewing**		
■ Use organizational framework ■ Spelling ■ Write legibly ■ Write quickly ■ Use abbreviations	■ Read notes ■ Comprehend noted ideas ■ Modify (edit) notes ■ Apply effective study strategies		

FIGURE 6.3 COMPONENT SKILLS OF NOTETAKING AND FACTORS INFLUENCING STUDENTS' NOTETAKING

cording everything in notes would be impossible. This process requires discrimination between important and unimportant information. In addition, successful notetakers make associations between lecture content they hear and previous knowledge. In this way lecture ideas are more likely to be remembered because information moves from short-term memory into long-term memory when associations are made between new content and prerequisite knowledge.

Given the active processing necessary for successful notetaking, how would you expect adolescents with LD to fare as notetakers? Keep in mind that students with LD often are described as inactive or passive learners (Hallahan & Bryan, 1981; Torgesen, 1977; Wiens, 1983). Specifically, these students do not engage in active processing when completing various cognitive tasks (Hallahan & Bryan, 1981; Torgesen, 1977; Wiens, 1983). Even when students with LD do engage in some active processing, they still may not complete the necessary processing effectively (Swanson, 1985). Thus, during a lecture, you might expect adolescents with LD to attempt to record all information because they are unable to pick out the most important ideas. Also, several days or weeks after the lecture, you might expect adolescents with LD to have poor recall of lecture content because they failed to associate new lecture ideas with related content they had learned previously.

Also, students with LD often are not effective in organizing information and creating and using mental elaborations properly (Hall, 1980; Reid, 1988; Torgesen & Houck, 1980). Both of these deficiencies most likely will lead to a decrease in students' level of understanding and retention of lecture ideas. Based on the processing deficits of students with LD, this group does not seem to possess the characteristics for effective notetaking and recall of lecture information.

Writing Difficulties

Writing is an important component of notetaking because students must record notes legibly and completely enough to make sense of them after the lecture. Many adults with LD have difficulties with written language. Specifically, adolescents and young adults with LD have problems with handwriting in terms of speed of production and legibility (Bireley, Landers, Vernooy, & Schlaerth, 1986; Gajar, 1986; Hughes & Smith, 1990) and spelling (Hughes & Smith, 1990; Moran, 1981; Richards, 1985; Vogel, 1985). To compound the problem, illegible writing and incorrect spellings of unfamiliar and familiar words alike could negatively affect students' ability to make sense of notes after the lecture.

Suritsky (1990) demonstrated the production problems of many adolescents with LD by assessing the writing tool skill rates of a group of university students. A *writing tool skill rate* equals the number of legible letters written in a fixed amount of time. Students were told to write their name (first name only or full name) as many times as they could in 1 minute. Then the number of legible letters written by each student was counted. This number represented the students' individual writing tool skill rate (reported as letters per minute, LPM). Although the rates for students with and without LD did not differ significantly, a number of students with LD had tool rates far below their non-LD peers.

Difficulties Reviewing Noted Information

In general, adolescents with LD face four potential problems with regard to reviewing notes after the lecture. First, some adolescents with LD simply are not aware of the need to review their notes (a production deficiency stemming from a lack of knowledge); others simply are too lazy (a production deficiency resulting from lack of motivation). Second, notes must be fairly complete if they are to be useful during review. Given the difficulties of students with LD with notetaking, their notes typically are incomplete. Also, as mentioned earlier, problems with handwriting and spelling may produce problems during a review of the notes. If the notes cannot be deciphered, they cannot be a useful or strong foundation for studying. Third, chapter 5 addressed the memory problems of some adolescents with LD. Problems with short-term and long-term memory impact negatively students' ability to study and remember lecture information written in notes. Finally, many adolescents lack knowledge of effective review strategies. Many adolescents with LD simply reread their notes without making any elaborations or personal associations or filling in missing information.

Researchers have conducted interviews of college students with LD to determine the difficulties these students have with a variety of critical study skills, including notetaking, test taking, reading, and managing time. Based on the results of these surveys, college students with LD can recognize their own difficulties in recording effective notes. In one survey approximately three fourths of college students with LD were able to recognize and express a number of problems they experienced with recording adequate notes (Bireley, Landers, Vernooy, & Schlaerth, 1986). Further, college students with LD reported that one of their major notetaking difficulties was writing notes fast enough (Bireley et al., 1986; Cowen, 1988; Suritsky, 1992). When Suritsky (1992) asked 30 college students with LD to assign levels of difficulty to the major notetaking skills, the skills rated as most difficult were paying attention, deciding what information to write, and making sense of notes after the lecture. This is not surprising because adolescents with LD have difficulties with maintaining attention, selectively attending to relevant information, and spelling.

Suritsky (1992) also asked college students with LD to imagine themselves in a typical lecture where a lot of important information was being presented at a medium to fast rate. When asked to describe what strategies they would use if taking notes during this "pretend" lecture, most college students said they would try to simply "keep up with the lecture." Despite this response from students, no student indicated using personal or standard abbreviations to increase notetaking speed. Also, few students reported using a comprehensive notetaking system that would involve the key notetaking components either during or after the lecture.

The notetaking skills of college freshmen and sophomores with and without LD were compared in an investigation by Hughes and Suritsky (1994). In this study students were asked to take notes on a 20-minute videotaped lecture as they normally would in a required college class. The notes then were analyzed for two measures of effective notes: (a) completeness (percentage of cued lecture ideas, percentage of noncued lecture ideas, and total lecture ideas), and (b) abbreviations (number of different words abbreviated and number of total abbreviations).

The notes that students with LD recorded were less complete overall and contained fewer important lecture ideas. Actually, students with LD recorded an average of 20% fewer of the total lecture IUs. Also, students with LD used only half the number of total abbreviations and different words abbreviated as their non-LD peers did. Results further showed that students with LD did not recognize easily many of the lecture ideas that the speaker verbally cued as important and, therefore, the LD students recorded the cued ideas incompletely or not at all. Comparing the actual percentage of cued IUs recorded by both student groups, it is easy to see how much difficulty the LD students encountered when attempting to recognize the cued IUs. Students without disabilities recorded almost twice as many cued IUs.

ASSESSING NOTETAKING SKILLS

Assessment of notetaking performance is essential for gathering information about a student's specific notetaking strengths and weaknesses. In addition, information about notetaking performance is needed to guide teachers in developing and implementing the most appropriate notetaking interventions for students. For example, if assessment data indicate that a student does not record the most important lecture ideas in notes, the intervention should focus on improving the student's ability to differentiate important and unimportant information. Relatedly, if assessment indicates that a student writes slowly, the teacher should introduce techniques to increase writing speed—abbreviations or a telegraphic style (not writing complete sentences) for recording lecture information.

Because listening is an important component of notetaking, the first step in assessing the student's overall notetaking ability should be an evaluation of listening skills. Teachers may choose between formal and informal assessment methods to evaluate listening skills. Formal assessment involves standardized tests or subtests to measure listening skills. Burns and Richgels (1988) discussed five approaches used in most formal methods for measuring listening capacity: (a) rote recall, (b) following directions, (c) multiple-choice, (d) free recall, and (e) an informal reading inventory.

Although commercial tests are available to assess listening, many are not valid because they actually reflect intelligence, aptitude, or hearing rather than listening. Wilkinson et al. (1974) argued that students should be tested on their ability to listen to the type of material they would encounter naturally in a listening task rather than a written language passage that the teacher simply reads aloud. An additional criticism of formal methods for evaluating listening is that information is presented in isolation. Effective listening depends on the context within which the information is presented. Without the context the task of interpreting the information is much more difficult.

Because of the potential weaknesses of formal listening tests, a better choice may be to conduct informal assessment of listening skills. Figure 6.4 displays a checklist teachers can use to evaluate students' listening skills across different settings.

After assessing students' listening skills, teachers should evaluate students' specific notetaking skills. Because no formal tests of notetaking ability are available, informal measures will have to be used. Informal notetaking assessment should incorporate three components: (a) survey of students' notetaking difficulties and approaches for recording notes, (b) analysis of sample class notes, and (c) evaluation of student learning of lecture ideas.

Using Suritsky's (1992) interview procedure, teachers can determine what students perceive as their own notetaking difficulties and reasons for their difficulties. First, students are asked to use a 5-point scale to rate their level of difficulty with the following eight notetaking skills:

Listening Skills	Informal	Academic	Small Group	Large Group
1. Pays attention				
2. Discriminates environmental sounds				
3. Recognizes environmental sounds				
4. Attends to important auditory stimuli				
5. Pronounces common words correctly				
6. Follows oral directions				
7. Remembers concepts heard				
8. Recalls facts heard				
9. Properly answers questions asked orally				
10. Participates in conversations and discussions				

FIGURE 6.4   CHECKLIST TO EVALUATE LISTENING SKILLS

Source: Language Arts, by G. Wallace, S. B. Cohen, E. A. Poloway (Austin, TX: PRO-ED, 1987), p. 81.

1. Writing fast enough
2. Paying attention
3. Making sense of notes after the lecture
4. Deciding important information to note
5. Understanding the teacher
6. Seeing overheads/notes written on the board
7. Understanding overheads/notes written on the board
8. Hearing the teacher clearly.

After students have rated their level of notetaking difficulty, teachers meet with them individually or in small groups and ask them to describe two or three main reasons for each area of difficulty. Also, teachers ask students to describe their strategies for recording notes during a typical class lecture. Students are given a scenario similar to this to find out what they would do:

> You are in a lecture class where the teacher is giving a lot of new, technical information and is writing very little of the information on the board. You know that the material from this lecture will be important for you to know for your test next Friday. What will you do to make sure you get the information in your notes?

While the students are describing their notetaking approaches, the teacher can ask other questions such as, "How do you decide what information to note?" "What do you do if you can't keep up with the teacher?" "What do you do if you don't understand a lecture idea?" and so on.

Although the interview results provide information about students' perceived notetaking approaches and problems, this information does not reflect their actual notetaking performance. Students may be aware of the advantages of using personal and standard abbreviations but may fail to use these abbreviations during actual class lectures, for instance. Nonetheless, interview information may indicate certain areas of notetaking that should be analyzed more closely. Also, students' reasons for their difficulty may offer insight into ways that the teacher can present lectures better.

In addition to interviewing students about their notetaking approaches, the teacher should analyze a sample set of students' notes. The teacher may use several techniques or methods to obtain students' sample notes. For example, notes can be recorded and evaluated in the context of simulated environments (e.g., brief audiotaped or videotaped lectures created specifically for the assessment) or natural environments (e.g., "live" lectures in content area classes). An advantage of audiotapes or videotapes created specifically for assessment is that the teacher can control important lecture variables, such as speed, amount of technical content, number and type of cues, organization of the lecture, and clarity of content. During real class lectures, all lecture variables are not controlled and not all lectures provide easy notetaking opportunities.

You undoubtedly can remember class lectures during which teachers or professors rambled, got off the point to discuss a totally unrelated idea, or discussed information that was totally disorganized. Even though class lectures may not be well presented, a true assessment of students' notetaking ability must incorporate performance in real secondary school or college classes. Relatedly, assessment in these classes will provide the most useful information for intervention and training purposes.

Teachers should collect and analyze students' notes from different content-area classes. A student may be an effective notetaker in one class and poor in another. Students likely will record few notes or not very good notes during lectures they thought were boring or had no interest for them. Also, the teacher may have provided too much technical content, presented a disorganized lecture, or been vague when explaining new concepts.

Teachers will need a set of model notes to evaluate the quality of students' notes. Model notes can be thought of as "ideal" notes that contain all important lecture ideas (main ideas, definitions, names and dates, relevant supporting details). Model notes may be the teacher's own lecture notes or can be obtained from a nondisabled peer in the same class or from the content-area teacher. The teacher must read through the model notes and decide on a method of organizing the notes for scoring. Model notes can be organized into either lecture (IUs) or key words. A *lecture IU* describes each complete idea or piece of information that represents new information (i.e., information that has not been presented already during the lecture) (Bretzing, Kulhavy, & Caterino, 1987). Lecture IUs may be sentences or sentence clauses/phrases. *Key words* refer to single words in a statement that convey the most importance. For example, let's say you are giving a lecture on basketball and you state, "In 1993 the Chicago Bulls won the championship." Assuming this is an important idea in the lecture, you divide the idea into two lecture IUs: (1) Bulls won championship, and (2) 1993. Or you divide the idea into three key words: (a) 1993, (b) Bulls, and (c) championship.

All IUs or key words are listed on a sheet of paper. All lecture IUs or key words listed on the sheet then are marked as cued (C) or noncued (NC). As stated earlier, lecture ideas can be cued by doing things such as repeating an important point, spelling a word, using a dictated heading, or pausing after making an important point. The list of lecture IUs or key words is used to evaluate the quality of students' recorded notes by placing a checkmark next to the IU or key word if it has been recorded in students' notes. The number of checkmarks can be tallied to represent total IUs or key words in notes. The teacher can convert this number to a percentage by dividing the total number of IUs or key words in the lecture into the number of IUs or key words recorded in students' notes and multiplying by 100%. Figure 6.5 illustrates this scoring system applied to a set of notes.

Other key notetaking variables may influence note quality and therefore should be included in an analysis of students' sample notes. A checksheet of key variables to evaluate the quality of students' recorded notes is presented in Figure 6.6.

Lecture Excerpt
Pannus is a progressive corneal disease that affects a dog's eyes. It occurs most often in German shepherds. The cause is unknown, but the condition can be treated with eye ointments, radiation therapy, or surgical removal of the tissue.

Model Notes
  Pannus (1)
  progressive (2)   affects dogs (3)
  eye disease (4)—corneal
  occurs most in German shepherds (5)
  unknown cause (6)
  treatments (7)—can be treated
    —eye ointments (8)
    —radiation therapy (9)
    —surgical removal of tissue (10)

Student Sample Notes
  <u>Pannus</u>
    —<u>eye disease</u>
    —<u>German Sheps</u> get it
    —can <u>tret</u> it w/<u>eye cream</u>
    —tissue

Scoring
  5 key ideas in notes/10 total key ideas
  Total ideas recorded = 50%

Note: Each underline in student sample notes represents one key lecture idea from model notes.

FIGURE 6.5   NOTE-SCORING SAMPLE

Source: Lecture excerpts adapted from Pannus, by P. L. Walker, in *Dog Fancy*, 24:10 (1993), 80.

Important indicators of note quality include the following.

1. *Personal and standard abbreviations.* Examples of abbreviations include (a) symbols (e.g., + for *and*, # for *number*), (b) standard abbreviations (e.g., ave. for avenue), (c) using initials for words used frequently in a given lecture (TAP for "transfer appropriate processing"), (d) writing the first three or four letters of a long word, and (e) writing some words without vowels (e.g., tchr for teacher). Teachers should evaluate two indices of abbreviations: (a) total number of abbreviations, and (b) total number of different words abbreviated (Hughes & Suritsky, 1994). The two indices yield different student performance information. For example, a student may have abbreviated 15 times but abbreviated the same word 10 times. Thus, the total number of abbreviations equals 15, and the number of different words abbreviated equals only 6. This student needs to abbreviate more different lecture words.

2. *Highlights recorded during the lecture.* Effective notetakers use more markings during the lecture to highlight important lecture ideas (Hult, Cohn, & Potter, 1984). Students should mark (e.g., underline, use an asterisk, check) cued lecture ideas.

	# in Model Set of Notes	# in LD Student's Notes
I. During the lecture		
A. Note completeness		
Number or percent of cued lecture IUs or key words	_____	_____
Number or percent of noncued lecture IUs or key words	_____	_____
B. Standard and personal abbreviations		
Number of abbreviations	_____	_____
Number of different words abbreviated	_____	_____
C. Highlights		
Number of markings to signify cued lecture IUs	_____	_____
II. After the lecture		
A. Personal additions		
Number of personal details added in different color pen	_____	_____
B. Highlights		
Number of markings to identify points in need of clarification	_____	_____
C. Amount of integration		
Number of ideas added based on text content	_____	_____
Number of ideas added based on content from other outside sources (e.g., other classes, films)	_____	_____

FIGURE 6.6   CHECKSHEET FOR ASSESSING STUDENTS' RECORDED NOTES

3. *Personal details added after the lecture.* Notes are a tool for studying and should be made as complete and useful as possible after the lecture. Personal details include any information not from the lecture that is relevant to topics in the notes.
4. *Highlights marked after the lecture* to identify information that requires clarification. Markings may be a question mark, checkmark, asterisk, or some symbol indicating that a specific lecture idea requires further explanation. Students may use symbols to (a) denote key lecture ideas and (b) highlight points for further clarification. The teacher should ask students to name the symbols they use to highlight key ideas versus fuzzy ideas.
5. *Information integrated from other sources after the lecture.* Other sources include the textbook, films, outside readings, and other classes.

A possible criticism of using students' notes to evaluate note quality is that notes are a *personal* record of the students' thoughts. This means that students might not write all of the key ideas in their notes even though they fully understand these ideas. Let's go back to the example of the basketball lecture and the Chicago Bulls. The key words, again, are 1993, Bulls, and championship. If a student is a fan of the Bulls and has watched the championship series, he may not need to note this lecture idea at all. Or the student may choose other words to note this thought. He may write "3," knowing that it was their third consecutive championship. Instead of 3-Peat, he may write "MJ," as Michael Jordan was the MVP of the series, or "No destiny for Barkley" or "3 = more commercials," because the 3-Peat is likely to generate even more commercial appearances by Jordan.

The point is that if teachers use a list of key words or lecture IUs to evaluate the quality of notes, they might conclude that the notetaker had missed the most important lecture ideas. Obviously this conclusion is inaccurate. One way teachers can deal with the potential problem of scoring notes inaccurately is to make sure to conduct a follow-up assessment. This will indicate whether students really did understand and remember the important lecture ideas.

Teachers can test students' understanding of lecture information immediately after the lecture or later (e.g., one day after, two weeks after). The best assessment involves testing immediately after the lecture as well as later, recognizing that long-term retention and understanding of lecture ideas is most important. Two methods of testing students' learning of lecture ideas are free recall and objective test formats. Testing can incorporate free recall of lecture ideas. An example of a free recall test is to request the students to write as many ideas as they can remember from the lecture in 2 minutes. An example of an objective test is to have students respond to 10 multiple-choice questions.

INSTRUCTIONAL APPROACHES TO NOTETAKING

Research has not clarified whether intensive instruction in listening skills should precede instruction in notetaking skills or whether these skills should be addressed simultaneously. Conventional wisdom suggests that it might be best to teach listening first because listening is an important component of notetaking. We believe it may be best to begin teaching listening skills in circumstances in which notetaking is not required. This approach is logical because focusing on learning a skill may be easier than learning the skill while trying to execute various other skills simultaneously. For example, learning how to parallel-park in an isolated area should be easier than learning it on a busy city street where a driver needs to execute other skills such as maintaining a safe speed, being attentive to other drivers and pedestrians, and paying attention to and obeying traffic signals.

In addition, in many simple but relevant listening situations students are required to listen without having to record notes. Students must be able to understand and carry out brief directions given by the teacher, understand words and sentences stated by a friend, and interpret teacher questions and then state appropriate answers. In all of these tasks, as in notetaking, students must hear the information, maintain attention and selectively attend to the important ideas, and in turn get meaning from the words, although they would not necessarily have to record notes.

Unfortunately, listening has been neglected in many elementary and secondary classrooms and by many researchers in spite of the demands that academic, social, and job situations place on listening skills. Although educators typically are concerned about reading and speaking, they expect students to develop good listening skills without any systematic instruction (Lerner, 1993). Many students with LD have difficulties that directly affect listening. Therefore, teachers should provide specific, systematic instruction in listening skills.

When teaching listening skills, teachers may wish to use a prelistening, listening, and postlistening sequence. Although their suggestions are not empirically based, Mandlebaum and Wilson (1989) contended, and we concur, that these three stages provide a good basis for listening instruction. The three stages entail the following.

1. *Prelistening.* Teachers present expectations for good listening, provide motivation (e.g., use a model or picture), define or describe any new or difficult words and concepts, and instruct students to listen for a specific purpose and to target specific information.
2. *Listening.* During student listening teachers should ask appropriate literal and inferential questions, instruct students to process the information (e.g., require students to predict a future event), and focus students' listening on key information.
3. *Follow-up activities.* After each lesson students should be engaged in a variety of follow-up activities that build on concepts from the lesson. These activities may involve reading or writing, role playing, or art activities.

Another important consideration in creating effective listening instruction is the personal importance students place on listening skills. For this reason, teachers should use real-life activities that require students to practice effective listening skills. Wallace, Cohen, and Polloway (1987) suggested the following activities: listening to a favorite television show, talking to a friend, following a parent's directions, responding to the teacher's questions, listening to music, talking on the telephone, and interviewing for a job. Real-life situations reveal to students the personal relevance of learning and using good listening skills. This in turn should motivate students to learn.

Once students have started to develop basic listening skills needed for effective notetaking (e.g., identifying the most important information, putting the oral information into their own words), they are ready for specific notetaking interventions. Teachers may use one or more of the following four instructional approaches for notetaking: (a) provide notetaking accommodations, (b) use techniques that facilitate student notetaking, (c) teach notetaking skills in isolation or combination, and (d) teach notetaking strategies (Hughes & Suritsky, 1993). Table 6.2 suggests activities for each of the four approaches.

PROVIDING NOTETAKING ACCOMMODATIONS

Teachers who have students who are poor notetakers face a basic decision of whether to expend the time and energy necessary to alter their lectures and teach notetaking skills or whether to focus their energies on collaborating with other teachers to create accommodations. Because notetaking is such a complex skill and so difficult for many students, teachers might be tempted to provide notetaking accommodations that make notetaking unnecessary.

One accommodation is to provide peer notetakers or duplicate copies of notes recorded by a peer. Another option is to make model notes available to students. Also, teachers can allow and encourage students to tape-record lectures. Although tape-recording sounds appealing, teachers may have to teach their students how to use tape-recorded lectures.

TABLE 6.2   INSTRUCTIONAL APPROACHES FOR NOTETAKING

Approach	Activity
Providing notetaking accommodations	Provide peer notetakers of duplicate copies of notes Make lecture scripts of model notes available to students Encourage students to tape-record lectures
Using techniques that facilitate student notetaking	Change the rate of the lecture Provide visual aids Provide verbal and nonverbal cues Use advance organizers Insert questions into the lecture
Teach isolated notetaking skills or combinations of skills	Teach prelecture skills Teach concurrent lecture skills Teach postlecture skills
Teach notetaking strategies	Teach a listening/notetaking strategy (LINKS) Teach a notetaking strategy (AWARE)

Several problems may arise if teachers rely strictly on an accommodation approach to notetaking. If students are not required to take notes, they may lose some of the benefits inherent in recording their own notes. These benefits include increasing their attention to lecture information, increasing their memory of lecture content by writing the ideas in their own words, relating new ideas to information previously learned, and increasing the likelihood that they will relate and add personal details after the lecture.

Typically, notetaking accommodations are suggested as alternatives to teaching students how to record better notes. As such, they are intended to permit students to bypass notetaking. When deciding whether to teach notetaking to students or to emphasize accommodations, teachers might promote passivity in students with LD and provide little basis for improving their notetaking skills. In some situations, though, notetaking accommodations are warranted. For example, teachers certainly are justified in providing notetaking accommodations for students with severe aural or motor problems.

USING TECHNIQUES THAT FACILITATE STUDENT NOTETAKING

To facilitate students' notetaking, teachers can use a variety of techniques that involve, in some cases, only minor alterations. These include, but are not limited to (a) changing the rate of the lecture, (b) providing visual aids, (c) providing verbal and nonverbal cues that emphasize the importance of key points, (d) using advance and post organizers, and (e) inserting questions into the lecture.

CHANGING THE RATE OF THE LECTURE

To make notetaking easier for students, teachers can simply decrease the speed of their presentations (Peters, 1972). The slower rate enables students to record more information and possibly engage in a deeper level of cognitive processing. If decreasing the rate of delivery is not an option, a technique called the *pause procedure* (Rowe, 1976, 1980, 1983) allows teachers to build more processing time into the lecture while reducing the overall rate of the lecture only slightly. In the pause procedure the teacher stops talking briefly (2 to 3 minutes) at logical points. During these pauses students should be directed to discuss the lecture content with a classmate. The student and peer should fill in missing information, make corrections to information that has been noted, and note any personal details that arise during the discussion. The teacher does not have to provide any information or feedback during the pauses. The pause procedure has been shown to be effective with adolescents with LD at the junior high level (Hughes, Hendrickson, & Hudson, 1986).

PROVIDING VISUAL AIDS

Whenever possible teachers should use visual aids to supplement the lecture content. Visual aids include information written on the chalkboard or a transparency, diagrams/charts/tables, detailed handouts, and lecture outlines. Prior to the lecture teachers should write key ideas or details on the chalkboard or transparency. This solves students' problems with not being able to pick out the most important ideas or details in the lecture. In addition, students know in advance what information they should pay close attention to. Whenever possible teachers should supplement verbal content with pictures, diagrams, charts, or tables that illustrate key concepts in the lecture (see chapter 9 on teaching content-area subjects).

Two other visual aids—detailed handouts and lecture outlines—are useful for enhancing students' quality of notes and, most likely, their recall of lecture information. Before lectures in which students are expected to understand and remember a great detail of specific and complex information, teachers should provide detailed handouts. When lecturing on a new topic (e.g., the digestive system of the human body), teachers may want to give students a handout of key words and definitions before the lecture. Lecture outlines may be skeletal or detailed. Table 6.3 provides examples of both.

Skeletal outlines contain only the major ideas from the lecture and also provide space for student notetaking. Kiewra (1985b) described the purpose of skeletal outlines as "pre-

TABLE 6.3 EXAMPLES OF SKELETAL AND DETAILED OUTLINES

Type of Outline	Components of Notetaking
Skeletal Outline (space between topics)	Listening Cognitive processing Writing Reviewing noted information

Detailed Outline	Listening
	    hearing
	    understanding
	    paying attention
	
	Cognitive processing
	    put content in own words
	    make associations
	    distinguish between important versus unimportant information
	    elaborate ideas
	    activate prior knowledge
	
	Writing
	    spell
	    write quickly and legibly
	    use abbreviations
	    choose organizational system
	
	Reviewing noted information
	    read notes
	    comprehend ideas in notes
	    edit notes
	    study

senting the lecture's main ideas in an organized form with spaces for learners to detail or embellish those points throughout the lecture" (p. 35). *Detailed outlines* contain most of the ideas from the lecture with some space available for notetaking if students want to add any additional information.

Research has shown that students who use lecture outlines recall more lecture information than students who simply record their notes without the benefit of an outline (Hartley, 1976; Kiewra, 1985b). Research is somewhat contradictory concerning the amount of outline detail necessary for students to understand and remember the most important lecture information (Kiewra, 1985b). In general, skeletal outlines that require some student notetaking are more effective than outlines that supply almost complete information. Perhaps this is because skeletal outlines afford students opportunities to respond actively during instruction, whereas detailed outlines may foster passivity in the student. Interestingly, the amount of space an outline provides for notetaking directly influences the extent of students' notetaking. Even when the amount of detail in two different outlines is the same, students who are given an outline with more notetaking space will record more notes (Hartley, 1976).

Whether skeletal or detailed, lecture outlines may help students in several ways.

1. Outlines provide an advance organizer for notetaking. This reduces the strain on students to create their own structure or to spend time deciphering the unwritten structure of the lecture, particularly if the content is disorganized.
2. Outlines highlight key information (e.g., main ideas, important details).
3. Outlines guide the student to record necessary information.
4. Outlines supplement students' notes and give them a better product for reviewing.
5. Outlines may act as a cue for students' memory of notes written to explain the ideas.

Teachers may wish to try guided notes, a slight variation of lecture outlines that have been used effectively with students who have LD (Lazarus, 1991). *Guided notes* are defined as "a skeleton outline that lists main points of a verbal presentation and provides designated spaces for students to complete as the speaker elaborates on each main idea" (p. 33). Teachers can use their lecture notes to develop a set of guided notes. Basically, they extract each main idea and place these ideas in the guided notes, providing sufficient space for student notetaking after each main idea. In addition, teachers may include key terms and definitions. After developing the guided notes, they might develop a transparency that includes the information removed from the student version of the guided notes. During the lecture, teachers use the transparency and instruct students to record definitions and other information in the designated spaces. Figure 6.7 displays a student copy of guided notes and an example of the teacher's transparency with complete guided notes for the same lecture.

PROVIDING VERBAL AND NONVERBAL LECTURE CUES

Teachers may use verbal and nonverbal cues to highlight important information for notetaking. Cues would be inserted into the lecture to pinpoint the most important ideas and provide some organizational structure for notetaking. Teacher cues can alleviate students' difficulties in selecting what information to record.

Chapter 16
DRUGS

REVIEW TALLY

I. What is a drug?
   A. Definition
II. Source of Drugs
   A. Living Things
      1.
      2.
      3.
   B. Man-made in a lab
III. Drugs are used to treat
   A. Symptoms
   B. Diseases
IV. Drugs can be _____ or_____
   depending on
   A.
   B.
   C.
V. Drug labels include
   A.
   B.
   C.
   D.
   E.

I. What is a drug?
   A. Definition - *Any chemical that affects a living thing*
II. Source of Drugs
   A. Living Things
      1. *willow (aspirin)*
      2. *mold (penicillin)*
      3. *cow/pig glands (insulin)*
   B. Man-made in a lab
III. Drugs are used to treat
   A. Symptoms - *Body changes that occur because of a disease*
   B. Diseases
IV. Drugs can be *helpful* or *harmful*
   depending on
   A.
   B.
   C.
V. Drug labels include
   A. *Use*
   B. *How much*
   C. *How often*
   D. *When*
   E. *Warnings*

FIGURE 6.7   GUIDED NOTES AND GUIDED NOTES AND REVIEW 38

Source: "Guided Notes, Review, and Achievement of Secondary Students with Learning Disabilities in Mainstream Content Courses, by B. Lazarus, in *Education and Treatment of Children, 14* (1991), 112–127.

Teachers may use a variety of verbal and nonverbal cues during the lecture. They can employ the different types of organizational and accent cues discussed earlier.

USING ADVANCE AND POST ORGANIZERS

An advance organizer consists of either verbal or written information (or both) presented to students before the lecture. The purpose of advance organizers is to convey information about the lecture so students can gain some initial understanding of the content and become familiar with the organization of the lecture and the purposes for learning the information. Lenz, Alley, and Schumaker (1986) identified key components that should be included in an advance lecture organizer. These include information about topics and subtopics in the lecture, background information and concepts to be learned, and rationale and expected outcomes for learning.

INSERTING QUESTIONS INTO THE LECTURE

Teachers can facilitate student notetaking by asking questions during the presentation. Two specific types of questions are most helpful: (a) questions that require students to relate new lecture content to information previously learned, and (b) questions that test students' comprehension of key ideas that have just been presented (Bos & Vaughn, 1988). These suggestions are not entirely empirically supported but nonetheless make sense. Ideally, teachers should include comprehension questions that are parallel to questions to be used in follow-up tests. For example, if the test will involve basic recall of facts, the teacher should insert questions into the lecture that involve simple recall/recognition. If the test will incorporate essay responses, some lecture questions should require answers that demand higher levels of thinking, including analysis, evaluation, and comparison.

TEACHING ISOLATED NOTETAKING SKILLS OR COMBINATIONS OF SKILLS

Teachers may train students to utilize important notetaking components alone or in combination (Hughes & Suritsky, 1993). Teaching only individual or isolated notetaking skills, however, may not be enough to improve the notetaking performance of many students with LD because these students have difficulty with many different notetaking skills. For example, even if a teacher teaches students to identify cued lecture ideas, most likely they will be unable to record all of these ideas if the teacher does not also teach them to write faster by using abbreviations. Instruction in a combination of notetaking skills seems to be a better training option because an effective notetaker must perform a variety of notetaking skills simultaneously. In addition, researchers have not empirically validated an effective sequence for teaching isolated notetaking skills.

In general, when providing notetaking instruction, teachers should emphasize critical notetaking skills that students should use before, during, and after the lecture. Examples of these critical notetaking skills are:

1. Pre-lecture skills
   a. Be mentally prepared to record notes.
   b. Be physically prepared to record notes.
   c. Acquire the necessary vocabulary.

2. Concurrent lecture skills
   a. Pay attention to the lecturer.
   b. Recognize cues and record cued lecture ideas.
   c. Differentiate important and unimportant information.
   d. Highlight key words or cued lecture ideas.
   e. Paraphrase lecture ideas.
   f. Use a personalized system of abbreviations.
   g. Use an organizational framework for recording notes.
   h. Apply notetaking skills flexibly.
3. Post-lecture skills
   a. Read/review notes as soon as possible.
   b. Edit notes.
   c. Study notes.

Whether teaching isolated notetaking skills or a combination of skills, teachers should follow the instructional sequence outlined in chapter 2. They would begin by providing a rationale for learning a specific notetaking skill, describe the skill, model the skill using a videotaped or audiotaped lecture and a transparency, engage students in controlled practice, provide positive and corrective feedback, require mastery, and promote generalization to content-area classes.

BEFORE THE LECTURE

Students should be taught to use three key notetaking skills before the lecture: (a) being mentally prepared to listen, (b) being physically prepared to listen, and (c) acquiring the necessary vocabulary.

BEING MENTALLY PREPARED TO LISTEN

Students should prepare mentally for lectures by reviewing notes from previous lectures, relating text material to subjects to be discussed in class, and noting the content of the topic of discussion in relation to other topics discussed throughout the semester. In short, if students have a "set" for the information to be presented and are somewhat familiar with the topic, their learning should be more efficient and retention should be greater.

In addition to cognitive preparation, students should have a strong purpose for listening. Motivation adds considerably to understanding and retaining information. Teachers may stress each of these factors individually through specific pre-notetaking activities. For example, they can teach students how to quickly review notes and materials from previous lectures shortly before the new lecture by having them skim their notes and identify three to five main points or questions that they think the teacher stressed. Teachers can summarize these skills and put them into an abbreviated format for students for reference prior to each class period. These steps might be:

1. Review notes and materials from previous class.
2. Read material related to today's class.
3. Relate lecture topic to other topics.

Teachers should stress these skills until they become an automatic part of students' pre-notetaking repertoire.

BEING PHYSICALLY PREPARED TO LISTEN Teachers should emphasize the importance of being prepared to listen physically as well as mentally. As a starting point students should be taught to be selective in choosing a seat in the classroom. People find it easier to concentrate and maintain attention to the material being presented by sitting in the front of the room rather than the middle or back of the room, where the risk of being distracted is much higher. Also, a front-row seat enables interaction with the teacher both verbally and nonverbally.

Sitting in the back of the room may communicate the wrong message to the teacher. Teachers may assume that underachieving students who sit in the back of the classroom are saying (nonverbally) that they are not interested in the class or its activities. Therefore, choosing a seat near the front of the class not only tends to increase students' concentration during lectures but also communicates subtly to the teacher that "I do care about this class and what I can learn from it" (Ellis, 1989).

Being physically prepared to take notes also requires that students bring appropriate materials to each class session. Although this suggestion may sound trivial, it has to be pointed out because some students with LD have difficulties either remembering the materials or storing them in an organized, accessible fashion. Specifically, students should be instructed to always bring their textbooks and workbooks so they can check teachers' references to these materials. Teachers may refer to a diagram in the text or to a specific definition. Without a text to follow, the student can lose a great deal of information.

Students also should be prepared with pencils, pens, and notetaking materials. Teachers can develop a brief checklist for students to go through before reporting to each class to ensure that they have the necessary materials. Students might write this checklist on 3" X 5" cards and keep it in their pockets.

GAINING THE NECESSARY VOCABULARY When listening to a lecture on a new topic, students may not understand and retain the lecture ideas because of unfamiliar terminology. Therefore, as a pre-notetaking strategy, students should become familiar with the key vocabulary words that will be used in the upcoming lecture. New vocabulary should be taught before presenting the actual lecture. This will ensure that students understand key vocabulary words before having to record these ideas in their notes. In some cases key vocabulary words may be highlighted in students' textbook. Students with LD, however, are likely to require some instruction in learning these important vocabulary words prior to the lecture.

DURING THE LECTURE

Teachers should teach students to use a variety of specific notetaking skills during lectures. Eight skills have been recommended consistently. Although researchers have not validated these notetaking skills, conventional wisdom suggests that they most likely would improve students' notetaking.

PAYING ATTENTION TO THE LECTURER The student's ability to attend to the lecture is an important first step in notetaking. The student should have selected an appropriate seat, have materials ready for notetaking, and be prepared mentally to begin listening and taking notes. Throughout the lecture the student has to be able to maintain his or her attention to the teacher and any lecture aids.

RECOGNIZING CUES AND RECORDING CUED LECTURE IDEAS   Teachers often highlight certain important lecture points and convey information about the organization of the lecture by providing verbal and nonverbal cues. Students should be taught to recognize the cues their teachers use frequently, although this can be difficult because each teacher has his or her unique lecturing style and, thus, each will use lecture cues differently.

To begin teaching students to recognize cues, the skills can be practiced in a resource room setting. Students practice identifying verbal cues in simple listening situations only and then practice in situations that require notetaking. Teachers can use audiotaped or videotaped lecture segments or can simply read a brief passage containing verbal cues for simple practice sessions. As an initial listening activity the student may be asked to signal when a verbal cue is presented. Then the student can be requested to signal and state the cued lecture idea. After the students become proficient at recognizing verbal cues, they can do the same exercise in notetaking situations.

Two levels of difficulty are involved. First the student can be asked to record only the cued information. When students master this step, they can repeat the exercise while recording notes on all information (cued and noncued) in the lecture segment. Throughout these listening and notetaking exercises, the teacher should begin by using obvious verbal cues and then advance to using a higher number of less obvious cues. A sequence for providing verbal cues instruction is provided in Figure 6.8.

USING A PERSONALIZED SYSTEM OF ABBREVIATIONS   Effective notetakers, compared to ineffective notetakers, record more word abbreviations when taking notes during lectures (Hult, Cohn, & Potter, 1984). This makes sense because using standard and personalized abbreviations enables notetakers to increase notetaking speed and thus increase the amount of information they can record in their notes. In addition, by spending less time writing, students have more time for processing lecture information.

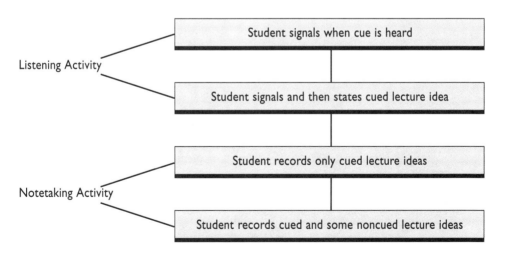

Note. Use audiotape, videotape, or brief oral passage.

FIGURE 6.8   **STEPS OF VERBAL CUES INSTRUCTION**

Students with LD should be taught to develop a personal system of using abbreviations. Examples are provided in Table 6.4. Abbreviations represent students' *personal* notations. Therefore, some variations in abbreviations should be expected. For example, if students are trying to record words without vowels, they may not use the exact no-vowel equivalent of a given word. Consider the word "points." The no-vowel equivalent is "pnts." Students, however, may write "pts." Variation is acceptable as long as the student knows the word.

Initially, teachers might want to simplify the process of learning to use abbreviations. They can require completion of worksheets in which students must practice writing personal and standard abbreviations. For example, a practice worksheet could require students to write words without vowels, one method for abbreviating words. After students have mastered the ability to generate abbreviations of written words, they then should practice generating and writing abbreviations for words in the context of a brief lecture.

TABLE 6.4   ABBREVIATIONS/PERSONAL SHORTHAND NOTATIONS

Classification	Examples
Words Without Vowels	reading = rdng common = cmmn student = stdnt personal = prsnl verbal = vrbl demand = dmnd
Standard Abbreviations/Symbols	street = st greater than = > without = w/o doctor = Dr. building = bldg incorporated = inc.
Word Initials	note quality = NQ information processing = IP external storage = ES lecture cues = LC
First Three or Four Letters of Word	frequency = freq instruction = instr. abundance = abun. literature = lit.

Students should be encouraged to use a variety of the different types of abbreviations and to use these abbreviations consistently throughout the lecture. When providing corrective feedback, teachers should tally and discuss students' total number of abbreviations used and total number of different words abbreviated (Hughes & Suritsky, 1993).

Teachers should inform students that abbreviations will vary depending on the subject area. Students should have a specific set of abbreviations corresponding to each content-area class. When reviewing their notes, students, especially those who are just beginning to use abbreviations, should make sure they recognize the whole-word equivalent of their noted abbreviations. During initial teaching of the skill, the teacher may wish to check students' accuracy in interpreting abbreviated words in their notes after the lecture. The teacher may find that many students can generate abbreviations but cannot interpret the abbreviation later. Also, teachers should stress that abbreviations should not be overused. If students attempt to abbreviate every word in notes, they may have trouble deciphering their notes after the lecture.

One issue teachers may face is how to treat "doodles" on students' notes. Doodles are any writings or drawings that have no relevance to the lecture topic. Should students be allowed to doodle while they are recording notes? If so, how should the teacher deal with a doodler who doodled so much that the notebook page was covered with irrelevant writing or drawing? Although we are not aware of any empirically based suggestions regarding doodling, one suggestion is to encourage the student to have two papers ready for notetaking—one to take notes on and the other to doodle on and discard. Teachers still will have to monitor students' notetaking success because excessive doodling may detract from attention to the lecture and, thus, reduce the effectiveness of notetaking.

USING AN ORGANIZATIONAL FRAMEWORK FOR RECORDING NOTES The physical organization of notes influences students' ability to understand noted information after the lecture. Organization of notes, therefore, affects how useful notes will be as a tool for studying. A variety of notetaking formats have been recommended; however, few studies have compared notetaking formats. For this reason teachers and students must, to some extent, use their own preferences. A number of organizational options exist, including (a) a system of simple indentation, (b) a traditional outline format, (c) a two-column format, and (d) various three-column formats.

One notetaking format, a system of simple indentation, might be best for students who have difficulty with a lot of notetaking components or students who have difficulty with organizational skills in general. Students begin at the left side of the paper and write a major point, then move to the next line and simply indent supporting details/ examples below the main point. Consider this brief example:

Colorado
    highest state
    ave. elevation = 6800 ft.

Denver
    capital
    Mile-high city
    in eastern foothills of Rockies

A second notetaking format, a traditional outline, indicates how each lecture idea is related to other ideas. This format, however, may be extremely difficult and inefficient to use during a lecture that the teacher has not organized. During highly organized lectures students may wish to use a traditional outline format. Teachers should provide training in using traditional outlines for recording notes, initially by providing prepared outlines that require students to fill in some of the outline information. Information on these outlines can be reduced gradually so students eventually have to create their own outlines while recording notes. If students are expected to use hierarchical outlines effectively, teachers may have to provide instruction in other skills, including how to use Roman numerals, cardinal numbers, and upper and lower case letters (Beirne-Smith, 1989).

Notetaking formats that divide students' paper or notebook page physically are recommended for students who have problems with notetaking. One two-column method requires students to divide their papers into two sections vertically, leaving more space on the right side of the paper. This method may be best for combining notes on lectures and written materials. The right side of the page may be used for notes from a lecture. Under each major section students should leave a large space in which to write notes later from texts covering the major subjects discussed in each section. On the left side students should write a label for each major subject. This will help them recall information, and it gives them easy access to the notes.

Three-column notetaking formats may be more difficult to learn than the two-column format. Two versions of a three-column format were suggested by Saski, Swicegood, and Carter (1983). Figure 6.9 provides examples of this format.

The numbers represent the approximate number of inches devoted to each column. In the first example, factual information from the lecture is written in the first column, and connections between previous content (e.g., lecture content, text information) and information in column one are combined in column two. In the third column students pinpoint noted ideas that require more explanation or clarification and highlight possible test information. In the second example, the teacher provides a topic sentence, written at the top of the students' notes. The student then uses three columns: basic ideas, background information, and questions.

Pauk (1974) recommended three-part formats incorporating the five Rs of notetaking: record, reduce, recite, reflect, and review. Examples are shown in Figure 6.10.

When selecting a notetaking format, teachers should encourage students to consider the characteristics of the lecture. Obviously, lecture organization is important to notetaking success. During lectures, if teachers do not stress the organization of the lecture, the student may waste valuable time trying to understand or figure out the lecture organization while missing important lecture ideas. The time could be spent more wisely on other critical notetaking behaviors during the lecture. Thus, students may fare better if they rank the importance of lecture ideas after the lecture (Anderson & Armbruster, 1986; Kiewra, 1985a; Saski et al., 1983).

IDENTIFYING IMPORTANT VERSUS UNIMPORTANT INFORMATION Students must be able to listen selectively and distinguish important from unimportant information. This task will be considerably easier for students if the teacher provides verbal and nonverbal cues to identify the most important information. If the teacher does not provide cues, students may be in the dark concerning main ideas. To prepare students for these situations, teachers

OLD INFORMATION	NEW INFORMATION	QUESTIONS
2"	5"	1"
	Basic notetaking column	Comments about notes that should be elaborated on or that are important for future assignments

BASIC IDEAS	BACKGROUND INFORMATION	QUESTIONS
5"	2"	1"
Basic notetaking column, stress on information for tests, reports, etc.	Related or interesting information	Comments about notes that have to be elaborated on or that are important for future assignments

FIGURE 6.9   **THREE-COLUMN NOTETAKING FORMAT**

Source: From "Notetaking Formats for Learning Disabled Adolescents," by J. Saski, P. Swicegood, & J. Carter, 1983, *Learning Disability Quarterly, 6*, 265–272.

should teach them strategies they can use instead of relying totally on teachers' use of cues to pinpoint the lecture's main ideas. The following activities may be used to help students find the main idea:

1. Have students listen to a short selection and suggest a title.
2. Tell a short story and have students summarize it in one sentence.
3. Give three statements, one containing a main idea and two containing subordinate ideas. Have students identify each statement.
4. Have students listen to a class presentation on videotape and identify the main ideas. In the beginning, students may be presented with a worksheet from which they can choose the main idea. Students should discuss why each of the other choices is not a main idea (too general, too specific, irrelevant, or inaccurate).

2"	5"	1"
Reduce to concise phrases as recite clues	Record main ideas and import details	Reflect putting here your own ideas

2"	6"
Reduce to concise phrases as recite	Lecture notes
2" Reflection and Synthesis	

FIGURE 6.10   THREE-PART NOTETAKING FORMATS INCORPORATING THE FIVE RS
Source: From *How to Study in College*, by W. Pauk, 1974, Boston: Houghton Mifflin.

HIGHLIGHTING KEY WORDS OR CUED LECTURE IDEAS   Effective notetakers use more highlights (e.g., checks, asterisks, underlines) when recording notes (Hult et al., 1984). Thus, students should be taught to highlight or mark (e.g., underline, place a checkmark next to) key lecture ideas. Key ideas may be implied and highlighted by the teacher's verbal and nonverbal cues. Students also may be taught to predict key ideas on the basis of judging how important lecture ideas sound and reflecting on previous test expectations (e.g., a teacher's emphasis on main ideas versus emphasis on specific details).

Teachers may instruct students to highlight key lecture information both during and after the lecture. The use of highlights during notetaking should produce a set of notes that are more organized and helpful for review purposes. Information also can be highlighted after the lecture. This encourages students to read through their lecture notes after the lecture to highlight key ideas.

PARAPHRASING LECTURE INFORMATION   As much as possible, students should be encouraged to record notes using their own words. Most of us tend to have better memory of information that we have transformed into our words and then put into storage. Also, students may be better able to relate new information to content previously learned if the new information is understood and has been written in their own words. Teachers should provide opportunities for students to practice paraphrasing sentences they read, then have students practice listening to individual sentences another person reads, and finally have students write the ideas in their own words.

APPLYING NOTETAKING SKILLS FLEXIBLY   To be successful notetakers, students must be flexible when applying notetaking skills and use the skill consistently across varied lecture characteristics. Teachers should stress the importance of considering lecture characteristics when applying notetaking skills. Ideally, students should record as complete notes as possible that include key lecture information. Depending on the lecture, however, this may not be possible because of the rapidity of the presentation. The best option in this case may be to record only key names and ideas and then attempt to use other sources to supplement the missing information (Anderson & Armbruster, 1986).

AFTER THE LECTURE

For the most part, suggestions for reviewing notes have not been empirically validated but nonetheless make sense. Generally, educators suggest three key skills that students should use after the lecture: (a) reading or reviewing notes as soon as possible, (b) editing notes, and (c) studying notes for a follow-up test. These skills can have a positive impact on students' recall of lecture information. The following discussion focuses on how students should adhere to these three behaviors.

READING/REVIEWING NOTES AS SOON AS POSSIBLE   The extent to which students remember information is influenced by the amount of review and the timing of review. Teachers need to teach students to read or review notes as soon as possible after the lecture, ideally right after the class period. If this is not possible, notes may be read during a study period, at the end of the school day, or later that evening. Teachers should stress the importance of students reading notes prior to recording further notes from the teacher's presentation in that subject area. Perhaps the best approach is for students, using their notes as a guide, to explain the information to another student. This requires much more active processing of the information. Reading the notes does not ensure that the student is thinking about the information while reading it.

One popular strategy for reviewing notes is to use a highlighter while reading. Although we are not aware of any notetaking research on this topic, a few strategies seem logical for improving students' effectiveness in using highlighters. But first a warning. Some adolescents with LD highlight nearly everything in their textbook or notes because they have difficulty selecting the most important information. We often have heard, "But all the information sounds like something I might be tested on."

Thus, a starting point for teaching highlighting skills is to provide clear instruction about what should be highlighted. Next you might teach students to use several colors in a highlighting system. For example, main ideas could be highlighted in blue, details highlighted in red, and information that has to be clarified highlighted in yellow.

Students with LD and other ineffective notetakers may record incomplete notes and thus depend on post-lecture notetaking activities to make their notes more complete. In addition to recording incomplete notes, students with LD are likely to have difficulties with organization and spelling, two areas that can be corrected or improved during initial review and edit of notes.

EDITING NOTES   Students should be taught to read through their notes several times, first without any attempt to add or delete information. Students should read their notes a second time with emphasis on editing noted information. Effective editing is accomplished by (a) filling in missing information, (b) adding personal details, (c) identifying areas that require clarification/explanation, (d) integrating relevant information from other sources (text, previous notes, media), and (e) comparing their notes to those recorded by an effective peer notetaker.

If notes are reviewed a short time (no more than 24 hours) after the lecture, students may be able to think of information they had heard but did not record in their notes initially. This information should be added to the existing notes. Students should write any personal details related to the noted information. For example, the student may be able to generate personal examples to illustrate a concept in the notes. Or the student may have read or viewed related information in an outside source (e.g., book, magazine, television documentary). Notes will be most useful for review if they are relevant to the student personally.

Another important part of review is to identify the specific pieces of notes that are confusing and require further explanation/clarification. The student should note these areas and formulate questions. Questions may be addressed to the teacher or to a successful peer, or the student may seek information in the textbook.

Immediately before the next class session, students should skim their notes once again as a prelistening/notetaking activity to prepare for the new information to be presented. This way they can relate the new information to the old information more readily.

STUDYING NOTES   When studying their notes, students should be taught to use the effective memory strategies discussed in chapter 5. The importance of transfer appropriate memory techniques should always be emphasized. Being able to recognize the correct answer in a group of four distracters is much different from being able to write an explanation to a question in a blank space. Teachers can assist students by making sure they know in advance what the testing expectations are and use this information to select the most appropriate strategies.

Although the post-lecture strategies presented in the above discussion may seem rather time-consuming and demanding, they are necessary for students with LD, who characteristically do not record effective notes or remember important information after the lecture. Only by reviewing notes actively can students with LD attain success in settings that require effective listening and notetaking skills.

TEACHING NOTETAKING STRATEGIES

Two comprehensive notetaking strategies have been developed for adolescents with LD. The first strategy, LINKS (Listening/Notetaking Strategy), teaches students to use teacher cues and record only the most important lecture ideas in their notes (Deshler, Schumaker, Alley, Clark, & Warner, 1981). The second strategy, AWARE (Suritsky & Hughes, 1993), teaches students to use teacher cues and to note key lecture ideas and other information in as complete detail as possible. Both strategies are taught using the eight-step instructional sequence detailed in chapter 2.

STEPS OF THE LINKS STRATEGY

The steps in the LINKS strategy are displayed in Figure 6.11. The first and second steps, *listen* and *identify verbal cues*, require students to listen carefully for cues the teacher uses. Teachers should provide cues to alert students that important information is about to be presented and therefore should be recorded in notes. Organizational and emphasis cues were discussed earlier in the chapter (and listed in Table 6.1). When students identify a cue, they should make a circle (referred to as a *link* or a *link for listening*) in the left margin of the paper. A link signals that notes should be written immediately following the cue. Drawing a link serves as a form of cognitive behavior modification to promote active listening for key lecture information. The link also serves as a measurable indicator to the teacher that students have recognized lecture cues even though they may have been unable to record the cued lecture idea completely.

Because students cannot possibly record all lecture ideas in their notes, they should *note key words* that follow each cue. Notes should be recorded using a telegraphic style. The following behaviors are suggested for writing telegraphic notes:

1. Write words, not complete sentences.
2. Abbreviate words.
3. Do not use any punctuation.
4. Draw a line through an error (do not erase notes).

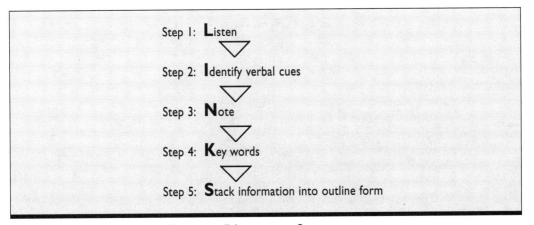

Step 1: **L**isten

Step 2: **I**dentify verbal cues

Step 3: **N**ote

Step 4: **K**ey words

Step 5: **S**tack information into outline form

FIGURE 6.11   STEPS OF THE LISTENING/NOTETAKING STRATEGY

5. Allow extra space to add more information.
6. Use synonyms.

The LINKS strategy requires students to use a simple two-column format for organizing notes. The left column contains main ideas, and the right column contains details. Each time a link is drawn, the student listens to the subsequent lecture information and decides if the lecture idea is a main idea or a detail. Then the student *stacks information into outline form* or records important lecture ideas in the appropriate column.

The LINKS strategy requires two practice phases. Figure 6.12 outlines a set of sample notes using the LINKS strategy and based on the accompanying lecture transcript.

STEPS OF THE AWARE STRATEGY

Similar to the LINKS strategy, the AWARE strategy teaches students to identify verbal cues and record the cued lecture ideas. Unlike LINKS, the AWARE strategy requires students to record some lecture information that the teacher does not cue. The goal is to record as much information as possible while making sure to record all cued lecture ideas fully. Figure 6.13 outlines the steps and substeps of the notetaking strategy.

The notetaking strategy requires skills that should be used prior to, during, and after the actual recording of notes. Subcomponents of the first step, *arrange to take notes*, focus on the preparation aspects of notetaking. Students have to be ready to pay attention and begin recording notes when the teacher begins lecturing. To accomplish this, students must arrive early or at least on time and have appropriate materials (e.g., pen/pencil, notebook) ready to use. If possible, students should sit near the front and center of the classroom to hear the lecture clearly and see any visuals on the chalkboard or wall screen. Finally, students should record the day's date in their notes to aid organization and provide a framework for review activities.

The second and third steps of the strategy, *write quickly* and *apply cues,* focus on important student behaviors during the lecture. Students should use a simple organizational system for writing notes. The notetaking strategy requires a simple system employing two levels of subordination, in which supporting details are indented below main ideas (discussed earlier). Although some researchers have suggested more complicated notetaking formats (e.g., traditional outline, three-column format), the simple indentation system is taught because the strategy includes a variety of other difficult notetaking skills that students are expected to master. After students learn the organizational system, they should be taught to abbreviate words. Abbreviations include symbols, standard abbreviations, initials for words used frequently in a given lecture, and some words written without vowels.

During the third step, *apply cues*, students listen for both accent and organizational cues by the teacher during the lecture, and they record the cued lecture ideas. Also, students should make a checkmark or asterisk in front of the cued lecture idea. Students need to prioritize the recording of cued information. For example, if students are recording a noncued lecture idea, when a lecture cue is stated, they should note one or two words about the noncued idea and then immediately record the cued lecture information. While reviewing their notes, students should read and study the cued (i.e., highlighted) lecture ideas first.

Lecture Transcript: Inventions

We all know that Alexander Graham Bell invented the telephone. And that we have Thomas Edison to thank for the lightbulb. We are surrounded by hundreds of equally important machines and gadgets. Someone had to invent them, probably after many hours of thought and hard work. Just who are these unknown inventors? I'm going to tell you about just a few of them right now.

One of them is Walter Hunt. You've probably never heard of him, have you? He was born in the United States in 1796. We have him to thank for inventing the safety pin in 1849. You may laugh at that, but just imagine how different your life would be without Walter Hunt's invention.

Another man who changed our way of life was Elisha Otis. That's E-l-i-s-h-a, Elisha, O-t-i-s, Otis. He invented the elevator in 1861. Without elevators, skyscrapers couldn't exist. After all, who would want to walk to the top of the Empire State Building?

It's interesting to note how essential some of these inventions are. We probably couldn't get along today without zippers, invented by W. L. Judson, J-u-d-s-o-n. Stores and businesses all have to have cash registers, invented by a man named Ritty, R-i-t-t-y. And almost every family has a sewing machine, invented by Elias Howe, E-l-i-a-s H-o-w-e.

Well, the point of all of this is that everything, even something as simple as a safety pin, is the product of someone's imagination. We have forgotten many of these people, but we really owe them a great deal for all the conveniences we have today. Just look around you and try to think what we would do without safety pins, bicycles, cash registers, or—heaven forbid—zippers!

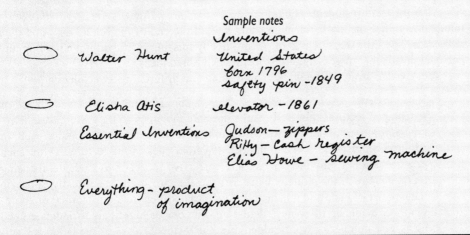

Sample notes

Inventions

Walter Hunt — United States / born 1796 / safety pin – 1849

Elisha Otis — elevator – 1861

Essential Inventions — Judson – zippers / Ritty – cash register / Elias Howe – sewing machine

Everything – product of imagination

FIGURE 6.12   SAMPLE NOTES USING LINKS

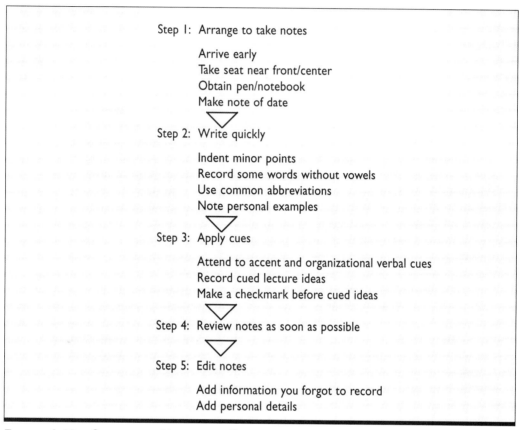

Step 1: Arrange to take notes

Arrive early
Take seat near front/center
Obtain pen/notebook
Make note of date

Step 2: Write quickly

Indent minor points
Record some words without vowels
Use common abbreviations
Note personal examples

Step 3: Apply cues

Attend to accent and organizational verbal cues
Record cued lecture ideas
Make a checkmark before cued ideas

Step 4: Review notes as soon as possible

Step 5: Edit notes

Add information you forgot to record
Add personal details

FIGURE 6.13   STEPS IN THE NOTETAKING STRATEGY

After the lecture students should review or *read the notes as soon as possible* (e.g., immediately after the class, during a study hall, at the end of the school day) and then *edit notes*. The Edit step focuses on filling in any missing information and noting any personal details that might trigger associations of noted ideas.

The AWARE strategy should be taught using two different practice phases.

1. Have students practice using the strategy while listening to brief audiotaped or videotaped lectures. For best results, prepare the tapes so the lectures are delivered at a rate of about 100 words per minute and last about 15 minutes each. In addition, intersperse a fixed number of verbal cues in the lectures. After each practice attempt, provide positive and corrective feedback to students, focusing on how many of the strategy behaviors the students used. Specifically, focus on the number of cued and noncued lecture ideas written in notes, number of abbreviations, evidence of some indentation, number of highlights to indicate cued ideas, and number of words added after the lecture. To assess the latter, ask students to edit notes with a different color pen.

2. After the initial practice phase, have students practice using the notetaking strategy in content-area classes. Obtain a model set of notes through a peer notetaker or from the content-area teacher. Evaluate notes using the same criteria as the initial practice phase. After each practice, provide positive and corrective feedback.

A study was conducted by Suritsky and Hughes (1993) to test the effectiveness of the AWARE strategy. The strategy was taught to nine college students with LD who were experiencing difficulty with a variety of notetaking skills. After mastering use of the strategy, the students recorded notes, in both simulated and real lecture classes, that were significantly more complete and contained more cued information.

SUMMARY

Notetaking is a time-honored practice in many secondary and postsecondary classrooms. In reality, good listening and notetaking skills are needed in many academic, social, and vocational situations. Many adolescents with LD have difficulties with some or all of the skills needed for successful notetaking and recall of lecture information later. Teachers can enhance students' notetaking success by providing appropriate notetaking accommodations, altering the lecture, providing instruction in notetaking skills, and teaching notetaking strategies to students.

REFERENCES

Aiken, E. G., Thomas, G. S., & Shennum, W. A. (1975). Memory for a lecture: Effects of notes, lecture rate, and informational density. *Journal of Educational Psychology, 67,* 430–444.

Anderson, T. H., & Armbruster, B. B. (1986). *The value of taking notes* (Reading Education Report No. 374). Champaign: University of Illinois at Urbana-Champaign, Center for the Study of Reading.

Beirne-Smith, M. (1989). A systematic approach for teaching notetaking skills to students with mild learning handicaps. *Academic Therapy, 24,* 425–437.

Bierne-Smith, M., & Deck, M. D. (1989). A survey of postsecondary programs for students with learning disabilities. *Journal of Learning Disabilities, 22,* 456–457.

Bireley, M. K., Landers, M. G., Vernooy, J. A., & Schlaerth, P. (1986). The Wright State University Program: Implications of the first decade. *Reading, Writing, and Learning Disabilities, 2,* 349–357.

Bos, C. S., & Vaughn, S. (1988). *Strategies for teaching students with learning and behavior problems.* Boston: Allyn & Bacon.

Bretzing, B. H., Kulhavy, R. W., & Caterino, L. C. (1987). Notetaking by junior high students. *Journal of Educational Psychology, 80,* 359–362.

Bryan, T. H., & Bryan, J. H. (1986). *Understanding learning disabilities* (3d ed.). Palo Alto, CA: Mayfield.

Burns, J. M., & Richgels, D. J. (1988). A critical evaluation of listening tests. *Academic Therapy, 24,* 153–163.

Bursuck, W. D., Rose, E., Cowen, S., & Yahaya, M. A. (1989). Nationwide survey of postsecondary education services for students with learning disabilities. *Exceptional Children, 56,* 236–245.

Carrier, C. A., Williams, M. D., & Dalgaard, B. R. (1988). College students' perceptions of notetaking and their relationship to selected learner characteristics and course achievement. *Research in Higher Education, 28,* 223–239.

Cowen, S. E. (1988). Coping strategies of university students with learning disabilities. *Journal of Learning Disabilities, 21,* 161–164, 188.

Craik, F. I., & Lockhart, R. S. (1972). Levels of processing: A framework for memory research. *Journal of Verbal Learning and Verbal Behavior, 11,* 671–684.

Deshler, D. D., Schumaker, J. B., Alley, G. R., Clark, F. L., & Warner, M. M. (1981). *LINKS: A listening/*

notetaking strategy. Unpublished manuscript, University of Kansas Institute for Research in Learning Disabilities.

DiVesta, F. D., & Gray, S. G. (1972). Listening and notetaking. *Journal of Educational Psychology, 65,* 321–325.

Einstein, G. O., Morris, J., & Smith, S. (1985). Notetaking, individual differences, and memory for lecture information. *Journal of Educational Psychology, 77,* 522–532.

Gajar, A. H. (1986). *Programming for the learning disabled: A program development and service delivery guide for university providers, diagnosticians, tutors, counselors, and learning disabled students.* Columbus, OH: AHSSPPE.

Greene, E. B. (1928). Lecture versus reading. *Genetic Psychology, 4,* 457–460.

Hall, R. J. (1980). Cognitive behavior modification and information processing skills of exceptional children. *Exceptional Child Quarterly, 1,* 9–16.

Hallahan, D. P., & Bryan, T. H. (1981). Learning disabilities. In J. M. Kauffman & D. P. Hallahan (Eds.), *Handbook of special education* (pp. 141–164). Englewood Cliffs, NJ: Prentice Hall.

Hallahan, D. P., & Reeve, R. E. (1980). Selective attention and distractibility. In B. K. Keogh (Ed.), *Advances in special education* (Vol. 1, pp. 141–181). Greenwich, CT: JAI Press.

Hartley, J. (1976). Handouts and student notetaking. *Programmed Learning and Educational Technology, 13,* 58–64.

Hartley, J., & Cameron, A. (1967). Some observations on the efficiency of lecturing. *Educational Review, 20,* 30–37.

Hartley, J., & Davies, I. K. (1978). Note-taking: A critical review. *Programmed Learning and Educational Technology, 15,* 207–224.

Hartley, J., & Fuller, H. (1971, August/September). The value of slides in lectures: An exploratory study. *Visual Education,* 39–41.

Hartley, J., & Marshall, S. (1974). On notes and notetaking. *Universities Quarterly, 4,* 225–235.

Horton, S. V., Lovitt, T. C., & Christensen, C. C. (1991). Notetaking from textbooks: Effects of a columnar format on three categories of secondary students. *Exceptionality, 2,* 19–40.

Howe, M. J. (1970). Note-taking strategy, review, and long-term retention of verbal information. *Journal of Educational Research, 63,* 285.

Hughes, C. A., Hendrickson, J. M., & Hudson, P. J. (1986). The pause procedure: Improving factual recall from lectures by low and high achieving middle school students. *International Journal of Instructional Media, 13,* 217–226.

Hughes, C. A., & Smith, J. O. (1990). Cognitive and academic performance of college students with learning disabilities: A synthesis of the literature. *Learning Disability Quarterly, 13,* 66–79.

Hughes , C. A., & Suritsky, S. K. (1993). Notetaking skills and strategies for students with learning disabilities. *Preventing School Failure, 38,* 7–11.

Hughes, C. A., & Suritsky, S. K. (1994). Notetaking skills of university students with and without learning disabilities. *Journal of Learning Disabilities, 27,* 20–24.

Hult, R. E., Cohn, S., & Potter, D. (1984). An analysis of student note-taking effectiveness and learning outcome in the college lecture setting. *Journal of Instructional Psychology, 11*(4), 175–181.

Keogh, B., & Margolis, T. (1976). Learn to labor and wait: Attentional problems of children with learning disorders. *Journal of Learning Disabilities, 9,* 276–286.

Kiewra, K. A. (1984). Implications for notetaking based on relationships between notetaking variables and achievement measures. *Reading Improvement, 21,* 145–149.

Kiewra, K. A. (1985a). Investigating notetaking and review: A depth of processing alternative. *Educational Psychologist, 20,* 23–32.

Kiewra, K. A. (1985b). Providing the instructor's notes: An effective addition to student notetaking. *Educational Psychologist, 20,* 33–39.

Kiewra, K. A. (1987). Notetaking and review: The research and its implications. *Instructional Science, 16,* 233–249.

Kiewra, K. A., & Fletcher, H. J. (1984). The relationship between levels of notetaking and achievement. *Human Learning, 3,* 273–280.

Knowlton, E. K. (1982). *Secondary teacher's expectations of learning disabled students* (Research Report No. 75). Lawrence: University of Kansas, Institute for Research in Learning Disabilities.

Ladas, H. (1980a). Notetaking on lectures: An information-processing approach. *Educational Psychologist, 15*, 44–53.

Ladas, H. (1980b). Summarizing research: A case study. *Review of Educational Research, 50*, 597–624.

Lazarus, B. D. (1988). Using guided notes to aid learning-disabled adolescents in secondary mainstream settings. *Pointer, 33*, 32–35.

Lazarus, B. D. (1991). Guided notes, review, and achievement of secondary students with learning disabilities in mainstream content courses. *Education and Treatment of Children, 14*, 112–127.

LeBauer, R. S. (1984). Using lecture transcripts in EAP lecture comprehension courses. *TESOL Quarterly, 18*(1), 41–54.

Lenz, B. K., Alley, G. R., & Schumaker, J. B. (1986). Activating the inactive learner: Advance organizers in the secondary content classroom. *Learning Disability Quarterly, 10*, 53–67.

Lerner, J. (1993). *Learning disabilities: Theories, diagnosis, and teaching strategies* (6th ed.). Dallas: Houghton Mifflin.

Link, D. B. (1980). *Essential learning skills and the low-achieving student at the secondary level: A rating of the importance of 24 academic abilities.* Unpublished master's thesis, University of Kansas, Lawrence.

Locke, E. A. (1977). An empirical study of lecture notetaking among college students. *Journal of Educational Research, 71*, 93–99.

Maddox, H., & Hoole, E. (1975). Performance decrement in the lecture. *Educational Review, 28*, 17–30.

Mandlebaum, L. H., & Wilson, R. (1989). Teaching listening skills in the special education classroom. *Academic Therapy, 24*, 449–458.

Maqsud, M. (1980). Effects of personal lecture notes and teacher notes on recall of university students. *British Journal of Educational Psychology, 50*, 289–294.

McGuire, J. M., Norlander, K. A., & Shaw, S. F. (1990). Postsecondary education for students with learning disabilities: Forecasting challenges for the future. *Learning Disability Focus, 5*(2), 69–74.

Moran, M. R. (1981). *A comparison of formal features of written language of learning disabled, low-achieving, and achieving secondary students* (Research Report No. 34). Lawrence: University of Kansas, Institute for Research in Learning Disabilities.

Palmatier, R. A., & Bennett, J. M. (1974). Notetaking habits of college students. *Journal of Reading, 18*, 215–218.

Pauk, W. (1974). *How to study in college.* Boston: Houghton Mifflin.

Peck, K. L., & Hannafin, M. J. (1983). The effects of notetaking pretraining on the recording of notes and retention of aural instruction. *Journal of Educational Research, 77*, 100–107.

Peper, R. J., & Mayer, R. E. (1978). Notetaking as a generative activity. *Journal of Educational Psychology, 70*, 514–522.

Peper, R. J., & Mayer, R. E. (1986). Generative effects of notetaking during science lectures. *Journal of Educational Psychology, 78*, 34–38.

Peters, D. L. (1972). Effects of notetaking and rate of presentation on short-term objective test performance. *Journal of Educational Psychology, 63*, 276–280.

Putnam, M. L., Deshler, D. D., & Schumaker, J. S. (1993). The investigation of setting demands: A missing link in learning strategy instruction. In L. S. Meltzer (Ed.), *Strategy assessment and instruction for students with learning disabilities* (pp. 325–354). Austin, TX: Pro-Ed.

Reid, D. K. (1988). *Teaching the learning disabled: A cognitive developmental approach.* Boston: Allyn & Bacon.

Richards, A. (1985). College composition: Recognizing the learning disabled writer. *Journal of Basic Writing, 4*(2), 68–79.

Robinson, S. M., Braxdale, C. T., & Colson, S. E. (1985). Preparing dysfunctional learners to enter junior high school: A transitional curriculum. *Focus on Exceptional Children, 18*(4), 1–12.

Rowe, M. B. (1976). The pausing principle: Two invitations to inquiry. *Research on College Science Teaching, 5*, 258–259.

Rowe, M. B. (1980). Pausing principles and their effects on reasoning in science. *New Directions in Community Colleges, 31*, 27–34.

Rowe, M. B. (1983). Getting chemistry off the killer course list. *Journal of Chemical Education, 60*, 954–956.

Saski, J., Swicegood, P., & Carter, J. (1983). Notetaking formats for learning disabled adolescents. *Learning Disability Quarterly, 6*, 265–272.

Schumaker, J. B., & Deshler, D. D. (1984). Setting demand variables: A major factor in program planning for the learning disabled adolescent. *Topics in Learning and Language Disorders, 4*(2), 22–40.

Schumaker, J. B., Sheldon-Wildgen, J. A., & Sherman, J. A. (1980). *An observational study of the academic and social behaviors of learning disabled adolescents in the regular classroom* (Research Report No. 22). Lawrence: University of Kansas, Institute for Research in Learning Disabilities.

Shaw, S. F., & Norlander, K. A. (1986). The special educator's role in training personnel to provide assistance to college students with learning disabilities. *Teacher Education and Special Education, 9*, 77–81.

Smith, P. L., & Tompkins, G. E. (1988). Structured notetaking: A new strategy for content area readers. *Journal of Reading, 32*, 46–53.

Suritsky, S. K. (1990). *Effects of verbal cues training on the quality of notes and immediate and delayed recall of learning disabled and non-disabled college students*. Unpublished manuscript, Pennsylvania State University, University Park.

Suritsky, S. K. (1992). Notetaking difficulties and approaches reported by university students with learning disabilities. *Journal of Postsecondary Education and Disability, 10*, 3–10.

Suritsky, S. K., & Hughes, C. A. (1993). *Notetaking strategy training for college students with learning disabilities*. Unpublished manuscript, Pennsylvania State University, University Park.

Swanson, H. L. (1985). Assessing learning disabled children's intellectual performance: An information processing perspective. In K. D. Gadow (Ed.), *Advances in learning and behavioral disabilities* (Vol. 4, pp. 225–272). Greenwich, CT: JAI Press.

Torgesen, J. K. (1977). The role of non-specific factors in the task performance of learning disabled children: A theoretical assessment. *Journal of Learning Disabilities, 10*, 27–34.

Torgesen, J. K., & Houck, D. G. (1980). Processing deficiencies of learning disabled children who perform poorly on the digit span test. *Journal of Educational Psychology, 72*, 141–160.

Vogel, S. A. (1982). On developing LD college programs. *Journal of Learning Disabilities, 15*, 518–528.

Vogel, S. A. (1985). Learning disabled college student: Identification, assessment, and outcomes. In D. D. Drake & C. K. Leong (Eds.), *Understanding learning disabilities: International and multidisciplinary views* (pp. 179–203). New York: Plenum Press.

Wallace, G., Cohen, S. B., & Polloway, E. A. (1987). *Language arts*. Austin, TX: Pro-Ed.

Westendorf, D. K., Cape, E. L., & Skrtic, T. M. (1982). *A naturalistic study of postsecondary setting demands*. Unpublished manuscript, University of Kansas, Lawrence.

Whyte, L. A. (1984). Characteristics of learning disabilities persisting into adulthood. *Alberta Journal of Educational Research, 30*, 14–25.

Wiens, J. (1983). Metacognition and the adolescent passive learner. *Journal of Learning Disabilities, 16*, 144–149.

Wilkinson, A., Stratta, L., & Dudley, P. (1974). *The quality of listening*. London: Macmillan Education.

7

Perspectives on Mathematics Instruction

SUSAN PETERSON MILLER

QUESTIONS TO KEEP IN MIND

- What math demands typically exist in secondary and out-of-school settings?

- What characteristics do secondary students display related to mathematics?

- Why should we consider setting demands and student characteristics together before making instructional decisions?

- Why do informal assessment procedures tend to be more valuable to teachers than formal assessment procedures?

- What issues have to be considered when selecting an appropriate mathematics curriculum?

- How does motivation influence math achievement?

- What instructional strategies are appropriate for teaching mathematics to adolescents with learning problems?

- What strategies promote generalization of acquired math skills?

ADVANCE ORGANIZER

Teaching mathematics to adolescents continues to be one of the most challenging tasks for today's educators. Fortunately, we have learned a great deal about mathematics instruction during the past 10 years. This new knowledge will help us become better math teachers, which undoubtedly will result in higher achievement by students.

In this chapter mathematical setting demands and the related student characteristics will be examined. Next, methodology designed to bridge the gap between these demands and student characteristics are explored. Specifically, the chapter focuses on curriculum, assessment, affective, and instructional issues. The goals are to:

- Discuss a variety of responses that have emerged as a result of poor math performance by secondary school students.
- Identify the mismatch between secondary school math demands and the typical characteristics of secondary students with learning disabilities.
- Identify the mismatch between out-of-school math demands and the characteristics of adolescents and young adults with learning disabilities.
- Present a model and make recommendations for developing or modifying an appropriate math curriculum.
- Describe formal and informal procedures for assessing the math performance of secondary students.
- Discuss the relationship between student motivation and learning mathematics.
- Identify strategies for increasing student motivation.
- Recognize effective instructional procedures for teaching mathematics to secondary students with learning disabilities.
- Target appropriate strategies to facilitate acquisition and generalization of math skills.

Figure 7.1 shows how the chapter has been organized.

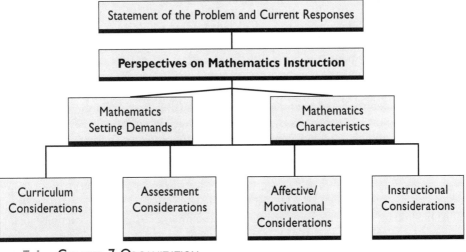

FIGURE 7.1 CHAPTER 7 ORGANIZATION

INTRODUCTION

The following case study describes how one teacher feels about teaching math to students with significant learning problems.

M s. Kay secretly hopes that none of her students will qualify for math assistance this year. If her students do qualify for these services, Ms. Kay hopes that some other special education teacher will want to teach the math. Ms. Kay would rather teach anything than math. She has these negative feelings because she had some negative experiences with math when she was a student. The thought of teaching math conjures up memories of lengthy practice sheets, impossible word problems, and frightening tests. Ms. Kay remembers one of her teacher's endearing comments: "I could explain this for 3 days and you still wouldn't understand it," or "That answer is about as useful as pockets in underwear." Even though these comments did not have malicious intent and were designed to evoke laughter, they communicated the subtle message of "You don't get this."

Fortunately, during our careers as teachers, many of us come to realize that it wasn't the math we despised but, instead, the way we were taught math. This realization is a major turning point for teachers who remember disliking math as a child.

Many students with learning problems have difficulty acquiring, retaining, and generalizing basic math skills (Kirby & Becker, 1988; Mattingly & Bott, 1990; Thornton & Toohey, 1985). Among students classified as having learning disabilities, lags in math achievement are as common as deficits in reading (McKinney & Feagans, 1980) even though more referrals for student evaluation are made on the basis of difficulties in reading and behavior (Garnett, 1987). Historically, math has been considered less vital than reading to adult success. More current opinions, however, dispute this viewpoint. Bartel (1990) stated that students with math deficiencies are just as disabled as individuals with reading problems. Johnson and Blalock (1986) studied adults with learning disabilities and found that these individuals were significantly more handicapped in daily life by math deficits than by poor reading.

Numerous investigators have begun to explore the scope of math difficulties in school-aged students. They have found that poor performance in mathematics extends beyond students identified as having learning problems (Engelmann, Carnine, & Steely, 1991). According to the National Assessment of Educational Progress, only 25% of fourth graders and 62% of eighth graders could solve five story problems (one of each operation and one requiring two operations) (Carpenter, Coburn, Reyes, & Wilson, 1976). Follow-up studies demonstrated that the performance of these students dropped further during subsequent years (Carpenter, Corbitt, Kepner, Lindquist, & Reyes, 1981). According to reports, 6% of students in the United States have serious deficits in arithmetic (Badian & Ghublikian, 1982), and only one third of seventh graders can add fractions such as 1/3 and 1/2 (Peck & Jencks, 1981). More recently, Dossey, Mullis, Lindquist, and Chambers (1988) reported that only half of 17-year-olds were able to cope with problems typically taught in junior high school. An estimated 50% of high school juniors and seniors master 8th-grade mathematics, and only 16% of 8th-grade students master the content in their math textbook (Anrig & LaPointe, 1989).

Specific investigations involving the math performance of students with learning problems further demonstrate the need for meaningful math instruction. Research suggests that math deficiencies of students with learning disabilities emerge in elementary school and continue throughout secondary school (Cawley & Miller, 1989; Mercer & Miller 1992b). Teachers of students with learning disabilities reported that two of three intermediate and secondary students had math deficits (McLeod & Armstrong, 1982). Moreover, 88% of students referred for learning disability services were one to three years below grade level in computation skills (Koppitz, 1971). Brenton and Gilmore (1976) reported that more than half of their students with learning disabilities were significantly below their arithmetic expectancy.

Warner, Alley, Schumaker, Deshler, and Clark (1980) found that students with learning disabilities show approximately 1 year of progress in math across grades 7 through 12. The progress of these students seems to reach a plateau after 7th grade. Cawley and Miller (1989) reported that math achievement levels at age 17 peak at grade equivalent standards of 5.8 for computation and 5.2 for applied problems. Cawley, Baker-Kroczynski, and Urban (1992) summarized recent research efforts and reported that students with learning problems may attain math proficiency at the 5th- to 6th-grade level. Thus, the combined efforts of numerous experts clearly suggest that many students in today's schools, including those with learning problems, have significant difficulty with mathematics. Empirical studies regarding these difficulties are substantial enough in number and degree to warrant serious educational response.

One response to the alarming statistics concerning poor student achievement in mathematics has been to increase the expectations or standards for student performance. Within the past 10 years most states have increased their graduation requirements in mathematics and have instituted minimum competency testing. In many cases students must pass these competency tests before receiving high school diplomas. Moreover, literature related to subject matter programming in general education classes reveals a trend toward higher standards by increasing the reading difficulty of school textbooks, including more problem solving, and introducing more rigorous requirements in secondary classrooms (Resnick & Resnick, 1985). Many states and school districts now include algebra as a graduation requirement for all students (Chambers, 1994). The phrase "algebra for all" is a frequently expressed goal in current math literature.

Another response to the poor math performance of many students has been a national call for reform in math education (National Council of Supervisors of Mathematics, 1988). The National Council of Teachers of Mathematics (NCTM) (1989) published math standards for various grade levels. These standards were designed to represent a national perspective regarding increased math requirements that will result in improved student performance. Unfortunately, as with several previous math reform movements (e.g., modern math, back-to-basics), the NCTM standards seem to lack research data to validate that instruction based on the proposed standards will be effective or efficient (Hofmeister, 1993; Mercer, Harris, & Miller, 1993; Rivera, 1993). Moreover, the standards seem to delineate broad goals rather than directly address the problem of low student performance in mathematics (Engelmann, Carnine, & Steely, 1991).

Thus, a large number of students who already have difficulty with math are faced with higher standards and expectations. To add to an already challenging scenario, this improved performance is now, more frequently than ever, expected to occur in general education classrooms. Many school districts are moving toward full or greater inclusion. Thus, students with disabilities are expected to master math content delivered in traditional formats, with traditional materials, in general education classrooms. The result of increasing curricular demands in mainstream classes is yet to be determined.

Perhaps another, more effective, response to improving the math performance of students is to carefully evaluate the curriculum and the specific instructional practices used to teach mathematics. Many authorities (Carnine, 1991; Cawley, Fitzmaurice-Hayes, & Shaw, 1988; Cawley, Miller, & School, 1987; Kelly, Gersten, & Carnine, 1990; Montague & Bos, 1986b; Scheid, 1990) have noted that poor or traditional instruction is a primary cause of math difficulties faced by many students with learning problems. This being the case, practitioners and researchers have to identify both *what* and *how* to teach in secondary math classrooms. A viable approach to making these important decisions is to:

- Examine the setting demands within which secondary students are expected to perform.
- Examine the students' characteristics.
- Design math curricula that bridge the gap between the demands and the characteristics.
- Identify validated instructional interventions that fit within the designed curricula.

The remainder of this chapter operationalizes this approach for designing mathematics instruction for secondary students with learning problems. Demands of secondary schools and out-of-school settings and the related characteristics of adolescents with math difficulties are presented. Following this discussion, curriculum and instructional strategies designed to bridge the gap between setting demands and student characteristics are covered.

SCHOOL DEMANDS IN MATHEMATICS AND RELATED STUDENT CHARACTERISTICS

To be successful in mathematics at the secondary level, students must meet many instructional and setting demands. Unfortunately, many secondary students with learning problems do not display the characteristics needed to meet these demands.

DEMAND #1: GAINING INFORMATION FROM MATH TEXTBOOKS

Most secondary schools use state-adopted mathematics textbooks. Some characteristics of the texts may hinder the academic progress of students with learning problems. Generally, these texts require a substantial amount of reading, and the type of reading is different from reading other content materials. Math texts frequently present material that is concise and densely packed with information that may be only peripherally related to preceding and subsequent sections in the text. Tables, symbols, and graphics integrated into the narrative require the reader to widen the visual span and sometimes skip a graphic to continue reading the text material (Hollander, 1988). Moreover, these books often use technical vocabulary that requires much abstract reasoning and the ability to retain and generalize skills over time.

Secondary students are expected to read text material and obtain information from a variety of graphics in their books. Reading text and graphics simultaneously in grade-level math books is challenging for students with disabilities. To add to this challenge, the readability level in many high school textbooks is not constant. Textbooks with readability levels higher than the student's grade placement are common (Schumaker & Deshler, 1984).

At the middle school level, math basals are used frequently to guide instruction. Basal programs typically include a sequential set of student math books, student workbooks, placement and achievement tests, and a teacher's manual. Research on these basal programs reflects several limitations that impact student performance negatively (Engelmann, Carnine, & Steely, 1991; Silbert & Carnine, 1990a, 1990b). Included among these limitations are:

- Provisions to ensure that students have mastered the necessary prerequisite skills often are marginal.
- The rate for introducing new concepts is too rapid.
- The presentation of strategies lacks coherence.
- Instructional activities lack clarity.
- The transition between initial teaching and independent working usually is inadequate.
- Content reviews are sparse.

Cawley, Miller, and School (1987) found that in secondary math classes more emphasis is placed on students' ability to solve textbook problems than on their ability to solve novel or life-based problems. This overreliance on textbook examples may contribute to the inadequate development of cognitive and metacognitive strategic behavior in mathematics.

Kameenui (1991) reported that textbooks dominate instruction in most secondary classrooms and actually become the de facto curriculum. In many classes the textbook structures or determines what the teacher teaches and thus replaces the teacher as decision maker. Despite the limitations of these materials, students are expected to use them and to perform successfully.

STUDENT CHARACTERISTICS RELATED TO TEXTBOOK USE

Estimates suggest that 85% of students with learning disabilities have specific reading disabilities (Hallahan, Kauffman, & Lloyd, 1985). Therefore, many students with learning disabilities have difficulty reading their math textbooks. They have further trouble comprehending vocabulary, understanding graphs, and reading tables. Language difficulties may inhibit their understanding of problem-solving activities and examples provided in the textbook. Moreover, students with disabilities frequently find that the information presented in the textbook is unfamiliar. Thus, conceptual problems arise. The combination of these characteristics inhibits students' acquisition of the math content and interferes with their ability to understand math word problems. Thus, the emphasis on textbook use in secondary settings actually may suppress a student's potential for math performance.

DEMAND #2: ACQUIRE BASIC SKILLS AND PASS MINIMUM COMPETENCY TESTS

Most states require that secondary students take minimum competency exams. In some states students must acquire certain basic skills and pass minimum competency tests as a requirement for promotion to the next grade or graduation from high school. The math section of these minimum competency exams contains information deemed appropriate for high school graduates to know so they can function successfully in society. Typically the tests require students to average numbers, perform whole-number operations, use measurement principles, calculate sales tax, use graphs to obtain information, figure store discounts, comparison shop, and use fractions, decimals, and percentages (Algozzine, O'Shea, Crews, & Stoddard, 1987).

STUDENT CHARACTERISTICS RELATED TO COMPETENCY TESTS

Students with learning disabilities frequently have difficulty taking tests. In one study more than 85% of the students with learning disabilities had significant problems in taking tests (Alley, Deshler, & Warner, 1979). Many secondary students with math disabilities have a history of failure and therefore feel insecure about their ability to succeed. Math anxiety and negative belief systems are common in these students.

Some students with disabilities also have fine-motor problems that affect their ability to write quickly and legibly. They may have trouble writing in small spaces, which frequently is a requirement of standardized testing.

A final aspect of student characteristics related to competency testing involves the math content itself. McLeod and Armstrong (1982) conducted an extensive survey of secondary learning disability teachers to determine the most common math deficit areas of their students. Included were division of whole numbers, basic operations involving fractions, decimals, percent, fraction terminology, multiplication of whole numbers, place value, measurement skills, and language of mathematics. These deficit areas clearly overlap with the skills typically included on the minimum competency tests.

Advocates of minimum competency testing frequently support modifications for students with learning disabilities, such as providing the student with more time and reading the questions to the student. In spite of these modifications, most students with learning disabilities fail minimum competency tests (Miller, 1993).

DEMAND #3: RETAIN PREVIOUS MATHEMATICAL LEARNING

The process of learning mathematics is gradual. At first students are taught basic concepts and foundation skills (addition, subtraction, multiplication, division). As they progress through the math curriculum, they are expected to apply math concepts and skills previously learned to new mathematical tasks. Math learning, then, is hierarchical. Each new skill builds on previous learning and gradually becomes more complex. Thus, memory is critical to success in math. Short-term, long-term, and sequential memory skills are needed for acquisition, maintenance, and retention of math skills.

STUDENT CHARACTERISTICS RELATED TO THE RETENTION OF MATH SKILLS

Many students with learning disabilities have memory deficits. Some students seem to understand the skills one day but do not remember them the next day, or the skills may decline between Friday and the following Monday. Research reports also indicate that students with disabilities regress in math performance over summer vacation (Tilley, Cox, & Stayrook, 1986).

One of the most common manifestations of memory problems in math is observed when students are expected to perform computations. Many students with learning problems have difficulty memorizing the basic math facts involved in addition, subtraction, multiplication, and division. Students who are unable to recall number facts quickly are at a distinct disadvantage in secondary math classrooms. These students must spend a lot of time and energy to solve higher-level math problems because they are slow with basic facts. Math skills other than computation also are affected by poor retention skills. For example, students have difficulty remembering newly acquired concepts, taking notes from the board or overhead projector, solving word problems, remembering geometric shapes and the number of angles in a geometric figure, remembering the steps involved in various algorithms, and performing math tasks that require visual sequencing.

DEMAND #4: DEMONSTRATE PROBLEM SOLVING ABILITY

Problem solving is rapidly assuming a larger role in both general and special education math curricula (Resnick, 1989). The National Council of Teachers of Mathematics (1989) identified problem solving as the top priority for math curriculum.

Most authorities (Cawley et al., 1987; Fleischner, Nuzum, & Marzola, 1987; Kameenui & Simmons, 1990) interpret problem solving within the context of math word problems. To be successful in math problem solving, students must acquire a mathematical knowledge base, apply acquired knowledge to new and unfamiliar situations, and engage actively in thinking processes (Mercer & Miller, 1992b). Moreover, students must analyze and interpret information as the basis for making decisions (Lerner, 1993), and they must develop appropriate strategies for attacking word problems systematically (Case & Harris, 1988; Mastropieri, Scruggs, & Shiah, 1991).

STUDENT CHARACTERISTICS RELATED TO PROBLEM SOLVING

Students with learning disabilities frequently have difficulty with problem solving (Miller & Mercer, 1993a). Cawley and Miller (1989) found that the problem-solving skills of 17-year-old students with learning disabilities peaked at the 5th-grade level. Research suggests that students with disabilities have trouble selecting relevant information, determining the correct operational processes to use, and evaluating the correctness of their answers (Lee & Hudson, 1981). These students have been described as passive learners who have difficulty selecting and applying task-appropriate strategies (Hutchinson, 1993; Mellard & Alley, 1981; Torgesen, 1982). Some speculate that students with learning disabilities often have a "production deficiency" that prohibits them from using strategic information in response to the same cues as the normal problem solver. Students with LD tend to rely on a trial-and-error approach to problem solving rather than content-specific strategies. They have difficulty discriminating between effective and ineffective problem-solving strategies (Montague, 1988).

Table 7.1 summarizes these secondary school demands and related student characteristics. When comparing the two, it is easy to understand why so many students with disabilities have difficulty in mathematics.

OUT-OF-SCHOOL DEMANDS IN MATHEMATICS AND RELATED STUDENT CHARACTERISTICS

When students with learning disabilities complete their secondary school experience, they are expected to make the transition into society and function as independent adults. In addition to mastering the demands of independent living, students are expected to enter employment settings or post-high school and college programs. Mathematics continues to play a significant role in each of these adult arenas.

USING MATH TO LIVE AS AN INDEPENDENT ADULT

Independent adults use math skills every day. Cooking requires measurement and time skills. Shopping requires an understanding of money conversion, making change, figuring sale prices, and managing a budget. Paying bills requires check-writing and banking skills. An important related skill is being able to balance a checkbook. Individuals involved in making home improvements use a variety of math skills including measuring, money skills, and fractions. Even sports and leisure activities involve math (e.g., keeping score in games such as bowling, scrabble, golf, or basketball, or planning quantities of food, eating utensils, and favors for a party). The need to acquire basic math skills for daily living activities is an obvious necessity.

USING MATH IN THE WORLD OF WORK

Although people generally agree that basic math skills are necessary to be successful in the world of work, little research has been done to indicate the specific math demands placed on students with disabilities who enter the workforce after completing school. An early investigation on this topic was based on a 34-item survey developed to obtain employers' perceptions of the importance of a variety of basic math skills and the extent to which these skills were required in the world of work. Of the 244 employers who completed the survey, 92% indicated that solving number problems was important in the

TABLE 7.1   MISMATCH BETWEEN SCHOOL SETTING DEMANDS AND STUDENT CHARACTERISTICS

Secondary School Math Demands	Characteristics of Students with LD
Use grade-level textbooks Tables, graphs, symbols, integrated into narrative text; technical vocabulary; readability levels uncontrolled; basal programs emphasize book completion	Poor reading skills; lack understanding of graphs, symbols, technical language; need extended practice; need time to achieve mastery; need reviews
Acquire basic skills and pass competency tests Addition, subtraction, multiplication, division; average, measure, calculate sales tax, figure store discounts, use graphs, fractions, decimals, percentages	Deficits in basic facts, fractions, decimals, percent, place value, measurement, math language; poor test takers, test anxiety, math anxiety
Retain previous math learning One skill builds on the next	Memory deficits
Demonstrate problem-solving ability Solve word problems	Passive learners; production deficiencies; lack strategies; difficulty deciding what information is important; problems with extraneous information

jobs they had available in their businesses for high school graduates. The employers indicated that adding, subtracting, multiplying, and dividing were the most important and most frequently used math skills in their businesses. More than half of the employers also indicated that computing hours on the job and solving decimal and percentage problems were important. Math skills viewed as less important because they were used rarely included solving problems using common weights, figuring perimeters and areas, solving problems using common measures, figuring simple interest, and problems using the metric system (Algozzine et al., 1987).

USING MATH IN POSTSECONDARY AND COLLEGE PROGRAMS

Postsecondary education (i.e., community college, vocational-technical training, 4-year college) is available to adults with disabilities who are able to meet the entrance requirements. Adequate math performance in high school or on entrance exams is part of the acceptance requirement at many of these institutions. Once admitted to a postsecondary educational program, math almost always is one part of the required curriculum. Many colleges do not alter the basic core math requirement even for students who have an identified learning disability.

Student Characteristics Related to Out-of-School Demands in Mathematics

The math challenges that students with disabilities encounter in secondary school settings do not disappear when these individuals leave school. For many students the learner characteristics and resulting math difficulties continue over their life span. Adults with learning disabilities report that difficulties in math impact their success or failure in postsecondary settings (Hughes & Smith, 1990). Young adults with learning disabilities are employed at a rate comparable to their peers without disabilities, but the type of employment differs. Individuals with learning disabilities are more apt to be employed in part-time jobs and jobs that pay less and have less status than jobs obtained by their peers (DeBettencourt, Zigmond, & Thornton, 1989; Sitlington & Frank, 1990; White, Schumaker, Warner, Alley, & Deshler, 1980). Coping with daily living and managing personal finances also are difficult for adults with disabilities (Lerner, 1993). The transition from secondary school to postschool social and economic independence is hard for many students, and students with disabilities in particular seem to need a lot of extra assistance at this point in their lives.

A summary of these out-of-school math demands and related adult characteristics is presented in Table 7.2. Review of these data explains why so many adults with disabilities continue to struggle with mathematics even beyond their high school experiences.

Mismatch Between Mathematics Setting Demands and Student Characteristics

Implications of the discrepancy between setting demands in mathematics and the related characteristics of secondary students and young adults with learning disabilities are extremely important. To be successful in secondary mathematics programs, students must gain information from math textbooks or basal math series, acquire basic math skills and pass competency tests, retain previously learned math skills, and demonstrate problem-solving skills. Yet, these students have difficulty reading and comprehending math textbooks, mastering basic math skills and passing tests, remembering previously learned skills, and solving word problems. The characteristics of these learners prevent success in secondary programs that are taught in traditional ways.

A similar pattern emerges when examining the math demands in postsecondary settings and the related characteristics of young adults with disabilities. To be successful in daily living, places of employment, and postsecondary educational settings, young adults must understand money concepts, basic addition, subtraction, multiplication, and division, basic measurement skills, percentages, and concepts involving time. Meanwhile, young adults who had difficulty with mathematics in high school continue to have problems with these skills in their postschool lives. These difficulties affect their ability to live independently, acquire and maintain meaningful employment, and succeed in training or college programs.

TABLE 7.2   MISMATCH BETWEEN OUT-OF-SCHOOL SETTING DEMANDS AND ADULT CHARACTERISTICS

Out-of-School Math Demands	Characteristics of Adults
Independent living 　　Measurement, time, money concepts, writing checks, balancing checkbook, keeping score during games	Lack basic math skills; have history of math failure
Employment 　　Addition, subtraction, multiplication, division, computing work hours, decimals, and percentages	Lack basic math skills
Postsecondary and college programs 　　Pass entrance exams; pass math courses	Poor test takers; lack needed prerequisite skills

This mismatch between math setting demands and characteristics of individuals with disabilities has to be addressed through appropriate curriculum design and effective instructional practices. Attention should be given to the gap between what skills students need to be successful and what skills they possess. Careful analysis of this gap will provide information regarding what to teach in math classes. After determining this, the next step is to examine the knowledge base of "best practices" in mathematics. This examination will assist in identifying *how* to teach the needed skills.

CURRICULUM CONSIDERATIONS

Decisions regarding appropriate math curriculum for secondary students with disabilities are sometimes difficult to make. These decisions, however, may make the difference between a student's success or failure in math endeavors. Thus, school personnel should consider carefully a variety of curricular issues.

TRADITIONAL MATHEMATICS CURRICULUM

Spiral math curricula are used commonly in today's schools. In spiral curricula many different math skills are introduced in a given school year. Once a designated skill has been presented briefly, the students move on to other skills. In subsequent years the same skills are presented again, supposedly in more depth. Although the intent is to increase the depth each year, in reality much time is spent reviewing and reteaching the same skills because students never really master the skills when they are first presented.

Analysis of a currently popular math series shows that 76% of the material in Grade 6, 80% in Grade 7, and 82% in Grade 8 consists of review (Engelmann, Carnine, & Steely, 1991). Superficial coverage of many different math skills does not lend itself to a genuine understanding of math concepts. This type of curriculum and instruction tends to be worksheet-driven, emphasizing "school compliance" behaviors rather than in-depth learning. Students do not "own" the material when it is presented in this manner. Thus, they lack the foundation skills needed for understanding higher-level math.

The second International Association for the Evaluation of Educational Achievement (1987) suggested that the main reason students perform poorly in math is the use of spiral curricula: "Content and goals linger from year to year so that curricula are driven by still unmastered mathematics content begun years before" (p. 9).

A related curricular problem that contributes to poor student performance is dependence on a fixed curriculum. In a fixed curriculum the content taught is driven by the textbook being used. Teachers feel subtle and not-so-subtle pressure to complete the textbook by the end of the year. The increasing number of rigid state and local math curricula that specify which math skills are to be presented by the end of the year in general education classes is magnifying the problem (Pieper & Deshler, 1985). This curricular approach promotes textbook-driven lectures and the assignment of textbook homework problems. The race to finish the book by the end of the year takes precedence over mastery learning. As with the spiral-curriculum approach, the fixed-curriculum approach frequently requires students to move on to new learning without mastering prerequisite skills.

The implications of these curricular approaches are obvious. Students with learning disabilities have different learning needs. Instructional modifications that are sensitive to the amount of time and practice needed for students with disabilities to reach mastery are critical to successful curriculum planning.

DEVELOPING AN APPROPRIATE MATH CURRICULUM

Curriculum development for secondary school mathematics is a challenging task. The determination of what to teach should be based on three interrelated variables: learner characteristics, secondary school setting demands, and anticipated postsecondary demands.

LEARNER CHARACTERISTICS

Characteristics of students with learning disabilities are reported in a variety of sources (Bley & Thornton, 1989; Lerner, 1993; Mercer, 1991). These characteristics have become more specific over the years as research endeavors have become more sophisticated. Careful consideration of learner characteristics is crucial to developing an appropriate and successful secondary math curriculum. Initial attention to learner characteristics will enhance the likelihood of designing an effective curriculum. Further, students' characteristics may change over time. Therefore, teachers have to consider and monitor students' attributes continually. Teachers must realize that even the best math curricula may have to be modified to meet the needs of certain students.

SECONDARY SCHOOL SETTING DEMANDS

Secondary school demands can be identified by directly observing math classes where the curriculum will be used. Observations in other content-area classes also may provide useful information because math frequently is integrated into other courses (e.g., science, home economics, physical education). Information also can be acquired by analyzing the scope and sequence of the required math courses and by examining competency tests that the students will be expected to pass.

ANTICIPATED POSTSECONDARY DEMANDS

Anticipated postsecondary demands seem to be more difficult to determine. Attention should be paid to employers and their stated needs regarding math performance of new employees. Evaluation of job requirements and school entrance requirements will assist in developing appropriate curricular programs. Recent emphasis on the need for transition plans for adolescents undoubtedly will help curriculum developers incorporate appropriate math skills in secondary programs. The Individuals with Disabilities Act requires that transition plans and services for adolescents with disabilities begin when the student is 16 years old and be included in the individualized education program (IEP). A natural outcome of this planning should be a curricular program that will allow the student to make the transition from school to postsecondary settings more successfully.

SELECTING CURRICULAR CONTENT

Current reform movements in math education are recommending that the content of the mathematics curriculum should change. Experts agree that computation skills are still an important component of the curriculum, but that the curriculum be extended beyond simply obtaining a correct written response to these basic facts. General consensus has been obtained among math educators regarding the need to teach concepts, critical thinking, operations, and real-life applications of mathematics (Mercer, 1991). The National Council of Supervisors of Mathematics (1988) identified 12 components of essential mathematics:

1. Problem solving
2. Communication of mathematical ideas
3. Mathematical reasoning
4. Application of mathematics to everyday situations
5. Alertness to the reasonableness of results
6. Estimation
7. Appropriate computational skills
8. Algebraic thinking
9. Measurement
10. Geometry
11. Statistics
12. Probability

Following identification of these 12 components, the National Council of Teachers of Mathematics (NCTM) released *Curriculum Evaluation Standards for School Mathematics* (Commission on Standards for School Mathematics of the NCTM, 1989). This document is widely known as "NCTM standards." The NCTM developed 40 curriculum standards to provide a framework for reforming school mathematics in the next decade. The standards identified for 9th- through 12th-grade students include:

1. Algebra
2. Functions
3. Geometry from a synthetic perspective
4. Geometry from an algebraic perspective
5. Trigonometry
6. Statistics
7. Probability
8. Discrete mathematics
9. Conceptual underpinnings of calculus
10. Mathematical structure

These standards supplement four general standards (mathematics as problem solving, communication, reasoning, and connections) that are promoted for all kindergarten through 12th-grade students.

To help prepare students for entrance into the general education mathematics programs, teachers should be aware of national reform movements. Many decisions remain, however, regarding the development of curriculum to prepare students with LD for these general education math classes. For example, should math instruction emphasize skills on the minimum competency exams? Should the students enroll in general education math classes and receive tutoring to assist in mastering that content? Should the students attend remedial math classes taught by special educators and then transition to general classes? Should the students attend compensatory classes taught by general educators? The answers to these questions are difficult to determine and frequently are made at an administrative or districtwide level. Regardless of how instruction is organized, teachers have to continue to develop and select math curriculum after carefully considering the characteristics and needs of the specific students in their classes.

Once teachers have analyzed student characteristics and needs, the appropriate content to teach will emerge. Specific skills needed for the students to be successful will become obvious. These skills then can be compared to the student's current level of functioning. Curriculum content that fills the gap between what the student knows and what he or she needs to know should be targeted for instruction. In that way, the content will be relevant to the student's goals and related setting demands. Table 7.3 extends the content presented in Tables 7.1 and 7.2 to illustrate the type of curricular decisions that may be made using this model of bridging the gap between student characteristics and setting demands or needs.

CURRICULUM DESIGN VARIABLES

After the needed content has been identified, several design variables should be taken into consideration when selecting, developing, or modifying an appropriate math curriculum. Among these variables a curriculum should provide examples, practice discriminating various types of problems, provide explicit instruction, separate confusing elements, and consider parsimony (see Figure 7.2). Attention to these variables in secondary mathematics curricula will enhance students' acquisition of new concepts and facilitate procedural competence.

TABLE 7.3   CURRICULAR DECISIONS TO MERGE SETTING DEMANDS AND STUDENT CHARACTERISTICS

Setting Demands	Student Characteristics	Curricular Decisions
In School		
Grade-level textbooks	Poor reading skills; lack understanding of graphs, symbols, technical language	Teach strategies for reading math texts; use supplemental materials; practice reading graphs
Acquire basic skills Pass competency tests	Deficits in basic facts; poor test-takers; test and math anxiety	Provide extensive practice in basic skills; reteach unmastered skills; provide test-taking strategies and anxiety-reducing techniques
Retain previous math learning	Memory deficits	Include daily review; conduct daily timings on basic skills; teach mnemonic devices
Demonstrate problem-solving ability	Passive learners; lack strategies; production deficiencies; difficulty deciding what information is important and what is extraneous	Teach strategies for attacking and solving word problems; provide relevant, functional practice
Out-of-School		
Independent living	Lack basic math skills; history of math failures	Teach basic living skills; emphasize functional math; use real-life simulations
Employment	Lack basic math skills	Teach basic skills; provide work setting requirements as rationale for learning
Postsecondary and college programs	Poor test-takers; lack prerequisite math skills	Teach test-taking strategies; teach to mastery; teach college preparatory content

PROVIDE EXAMPLES

When teaching new math skills or concepts, one of the most important things for teachers to do is to provide many examples. Research has validated the importance of providing a wide range of examples to illustrate each concept taught (Engelmann & Carnine, 1982; Engelmann, Carnine, & Steely, 1991; Kelly, Gersten, & Carnine, 1990; Woodward, 1991). If the teacher presents only a few examples, the students may form misconceptions that ultimately lead to error patterns. Moreover, a student is not likely to apply the skills in their other classes or outside of school if teachers provide only a few examples. In many cases presenting nonexamples is also helpful. Students' comprehension will

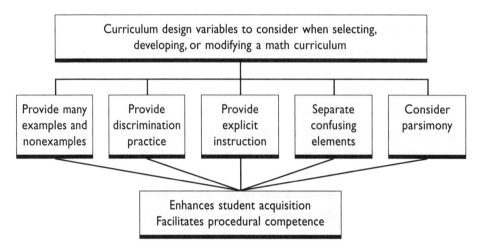

FIGURE 7.2 CURRICULUM DESIGN VARIABLES

increase when they understand what something is as well as what it is not.

PROVIDE PRACTICE IN DISCRIMINATING VARIOUS PROBLEM TYPES

Students with disabilities frequently have problems with discrimination. They commonly ignore the operational sign when computing answers to problems. Instead of subtracting, they add. Instead of multiplying, they add. Therefore, the instructional design should include distributed practice, in which problem sets are mixed. Skills and concepts previously learned should be reviewed throughout the curriculum and should serve as discrimination items for newer material.

After a skill has been taught in isolation, the students should have opportunities to demonstrate competence in the skill when it is imbedded within other problem types. Lessons that contain various problem types will facilitate students' ability to discriminate and generalize. Unfortunately, textbooks tend to present skills in massed practice formats. Problems of a single type are all presented at the same time. This reduces the amount of thinking the student has to do to solve the problems. This type of instruction without building in previously learned concepts is one explanation for math confusion and chronic error patterns of students with learning disabilities (Woodward, 1991). Figure 7.3 provides examples of single-problem practice, and Figure 7.4 shows examples of mixed practice.

PROVIDE EXPLICIT INSTRUCTION

Explicit math instruction is important for facilitating positive academic performance. Explicitness involves providing students with a rationale for learning the specific skill and discussing when and how they can use it. Explicitness also involves highly organized, step-by-step presentations for teaching the math content (Mercer & Miller, 1992b). Without explicit instruction, students may try to invent their own conceptual understandings. These understandings typically are not productive and can promote a sequence of error patterns. In short, explicit instruction helps prevent misunderstandings and errors and thus enables students' learning to be more effective and efficient.

All of these problems require double-digit subtraction without regrouping.

18	17	23	25	54	62
−12	−12	−10	−13	−12	−22

45	61	27	82	65	33
−21	−30	−26	−31	− 42	−21

12	25	37	43	78	95
−11	−14	−15	−32	− 65	−53

FIGURE 7.3   SINGLE-PROBLEM PRACTICE

This practice includes double-digit subtraction with regrouping, double-digit subtraction without regrouping, and double-digit subtraction involving single-digit numbers.

18	15	23	56	27	30
− 7	−10	−17	− 43	− 8	−15

19	23	57	63	92	19
−17	−12	−50	− 46	− 83	− 7

12	37	22	58	75	83
− 1	− 0	−22	−29	−25	−52

FIGURE 7.4   MIXED-PROBLEM PRACTICE

SEPARATE CONFUSING ELEMENTS

Several studies (Carnine, 1976, 1980; Kelly, Gersten, & Carnine, 1990) have documented the importance of separating confusing elements. Teaching confusing elements separately facilitates acquisition of the concept. For example, when teaching fractions, to use the words "bottom number" initially to refer to the denominator and introduce the term *denominator* later may be helpful. To prevent confusion, teachers can introduce the term *numerator* several lessons later. This approach seems to be more effective than introducing fractions and both new terms simultaneously (Kelly et al., 1990).

CONSIDER PARSIMONY

In curriculum development, parsimony refers to surveying the scope of instruction and then selecting the concepts and relationships between concepts that are *essential* to competent understanding. Identifying these essential components reduces time wasted on unnecessary tasks. For example, in teaching students about place value, instruction would begin with ones, tens, and hundreds, and gradually include thousands and ten thousands as the students are introduced to larger numbers involving these values.

Likewise, teachers probably would make the decision to teach place value using base 10 numbers, as that is the number system we use. The decision not to use base 4 or base 6 numbers would be considered parsimonious because the students will not be using base 4 or base 6 in the real world. Nor will students need to understand these bases for subsequent math skills taught in school. Concern for parsimony emerges mainly from the inevitable trade-off between the amount of material that the student is expected to cover and what realistically can be mastered within a fixed time (e.g., a school year) (Woodward, 1991).

A parsimonious approach links elements of knowledge so students can learn in a unified manner. When a curriculum is designed tightly and contains only essential instructional tasks, students realize quickly that what they learn at any given point in time must be retained because it will be used again when performing subsequent skills. Thus, students receive the message that each component of the curriculum is important. This message is quite different from the message obtained from spiral curriculum designs, in which concepts appear and disappear in a fleeting fashion throughout the student's school career (Woodward, 1991).

EFFECTS OF A QUALITY CURRICULUM

Individuals who design, evaluate, and adapt mathematics curricula must attend to the design variables described in the preceding section. The details of curriculum design impact student learning greatly. A carefully designed curriculum that includes research-based components will result in greater student achievement. Once the curriculum is determined, the teacher can focus on instructional planning to ensure that the students will gain maximum benefits from the teaching.

ASSESSMENT CONSIDERATIONS

The first task involved in planning mathematics instruction is to gather specific information about the student's current abilities and performance. This information may be obtained through formal and informal assessment procedures.

FORMAL ASSESSMENT PROCEDURES

Formal assessment procedures involve the administration of commercial tests to determine a student's current level of functioning in mathematics. The two major types of commercially produced assessment devices are achievement tests and diagnostic tests. Determining which to administer depends on the goals for assessment.

ACHIEVEMENT TESTS

Achievement tests are formal instruments that typically assess a range of skill domains (e.g., math, reading, and spelling) and result in a variety of derived scores (e.g., standard scores, percentiles, grade equivalents). These tests are norm-referenced and thus show how one student's score compares to other students' scores on which the test was standardized (Polloway & Patton, 1993).

Group achievement tests frequently are used in statewide and districtwide testing programs. All students or students in certain grades are tested according to a schedule. District personnel use the data obtained from these testing procedures to compare the students in their district to similar students nationwide. Included among the tests typically used for these purposes are the California Achievement Test (CAT) (California Test Bureau, 1985), the Metropolitan Achievement Test (MAT) (Prescott, Balow, Hogan, & Farr, 1984), and the Stanford Achievement Test (SAT) (Gardner, Rudman, Karlsen, & Merwin, 1982). Student data generated from these tests are insufficient for instructional planning.

Individual achievement tests are used commonly with students in special education and students who are being considered for special education services. These tests are administered individually rather than in large groups. School psychologists and special education teachers administer these tests to determine eligibility for services and current levels of academic functioning. Included among the tests typically used for these purposes are the Kaufman Test of Educational Achievement (K-TEA) (Kaufman & Kaufman, 1985), the Peabody Individual Achievement Test–Revised (PIAT-R) (Markwardt, 1989), the Wide Range Achievement Test–Revised (WRAT-R) (Jastak & Wilkinson, 1984), and the Woodcock-Johnson Psycho-Educational Battery–Revised (Woodcock & Johnson, 1989).

Mike is a new student at Azalea Middle School (a year-round school). He just arrived from a different state. His cumulative folder has not arrived yet. Mike's mom says he is in 7th grade and is 14 years old. She reports that he was in some special education and some general education classes at his old school. She can't remember which subjects were taught in the special education classes. Mike doesn't know which classes were special education classes either. He isn't happy about moving and says he doesn't care what classes he's put in because he isn't going to do the work anyway. He also says he hates year-round schools, even though he never has been in one before. Mike seems to have some serious attitude problems that will only get worse if he is placed inappropriately. Calls to the previous school have not been helpful. Mike's cumulative folder seems to be missing, and the teachers have left for summer break.

Mike's mom signed a permission form for Mike to be tested by the school psychologist at his new school to determine eligibility for special education services. After administering the Kaufman Test of Educational Achievement (brief form), the school psychologist reported that Mike earned a standard score of 70 in math, 95 in reading decoding, and 95 in spelling. The mean standard score for this test is 100. When these scores were compared to Mike's intelligence scores, it was determined that he had a math disability and should receive special education services in Ms. Juniper's math class.

DIAGNOSTIC TESTS

Diagnostic math tests are designed to assess specific academic areas in more detail than general achievement tests. These tests assist in determining a student's strengths and weaknesses. They also help identify specific problems that students are having in mathematics because they typically include a variety of skills via different subtests. Some diagnostic tests are norm-referenced, and others are criterion-referenced.

Diagnostic tests are appealing because of their potential diagnostic benefits. These tests, however, are not comprehensive enough to cover all math skills. Therefore, the examiner must determine the purpose for the assessment and then select the appropriate instrument to use. Included among the diagnostic tests used most frequently for mathematics are the Brigance Diagnostic Inventory of Essential Skills (Brigance, 1980), the Enright Diagnostic Inventory of Basic Arithmetic Skills (Enright, 1983), KeyMath–Revised: A Diagnostic Inventory of Essential Mathematics (Connolly, 1988), the Stanford Diagnostic Mathematics Test (Beatty, Madden, Gardner, & Karlsen, 1984), and the Test of Mathematical Abilities (Brown & McEntire, 1984).

The achievement and diagnostic tests just described contain only a limited number of samples for each specific subskill. Thus, they do not provide enough information to plan effective math instruction. Therefore, teachers must supplement these diagnostic data with informal assessment procedures.

Mike's achievement scores indicated that he had a math disability so he was placed in Ms. Juniper's special education math class. Ms. Juniper was planning to administer the Stanford Diagnostic Mathematics Test to her 7th-grade class to find out how her students were progressing and to help determine some IEP goals for the upcoming year. She included Mike in this group testing in hopes of obtaining some more information about his math problems. Knowing that he earned a 70 standard score on the Kaufman Test of Educational Achievement really didn't provide Ms. Juniper much useful information about teaching Mike.

Ms. Juniper administered the Brown Level of the Stanford Diagnostic Mathematics Test to her students. This test includes three subtests: Number System and Numeration, Computation, and Applications. Norm-referenced scores indicated that Mike was at the 50th percentile on the Number System and Numeration subtest, 25th percentile on Computation, and 20th percentile on Applications. Based on these findings, Ms. Juniper decided that Mike needed math instruction on Computation (i.e., primary facts and algorithms of addition, subtraction, multiplication, and division, as well as methods for solving simple and compound number sentences) and Application (i.e., applying basic math facts to solve word problems, measurement problems, and reading tables and graphs).

INFORMAL ASSESSMENT PROCEDURES

The informal assessment procedures used most commonly include teacher-constructed tests, math interviews, task analysis, analyzing error patterns, and curriculum-based assessment. These procedures can assist in both planning and monitoring math instruction.

TEACHER-CONSTRUCTED TESTS

Teachers may construct informal tests to assess students' achievement in a specific math skill or series of skills. A test item analysis of the achievement or diagnostic tests students have taken may be helpful. This analysis will help pinpoint skills to include on teacher-constructed tests. The test is tailored to individual student needs. Lerner (1993) suggested the following five-step sequence for developing teacher-made tests.

1. Select a skill or span of skills to be tested. (Math hierarchies in curriculum guides and textbooks may help in identifying appropriate skills to assess.)
2. Assemble sample test items. (If assessing a single skill, the test should contain at least 10 items. If assessing a span of skills, each skill included should have at least three test items. Easier items should be presented first. Subsequent test items should become gradually more difficult.) (See Figure 7.5.)
3. Have student take the informal test. (Decide what time limits will be placed on the test-takers.)
4. Score the test, and analyze the student's test responses. (Determine the student's knowledge and prerequisite skills. Analyze missed problems, and look for error patterns.)
5. Determine the criteria that will be used to judge whether the student knows the skill when the test is readministered.

Ms. Juniper decided to tackle Mike's difficulties with computation first and will integrate application level instruction once she has a better understanding of his computation skills. Ms. Juniper constructed a teacher-made test that spans several computation skills (Figure 7.5). She didn't expect Mike to have difficulty with addition, but she included addition problems so Mike would feel successful initially. She had noticed during class that when Mike thought something was going to be hard, he refused to begin the task. She didn't want him to give up on this test before he got started.

Mike's performance on the teacher-constructed test is seen in Figure 7.6. He did well with addition and subtraction problems. Multiplication obviously was difficult for him. He answered only one multiplication problem correctly (i.e., 3 × 1). Mike wasn't the first 7th-grade student who didn't know how to multiply, but Ms. Juniper couldn't help wondering how this had happened. Was Mike taught multiplication? Did he have a memory problem with basic facts? Was motivation the problem? Ms. Juniper decided that talking to Mike about this might yield some more useful information.

MATH INTERVIEWS

Math interviews can provide information that extends beyond paper-and-pencil tasks. In addition to figuring out what a student knows and does not know, the interviewer can focus on the student's thinking and determine if he or she is learning efficiently. The interviewer can determine what strategies the student uses when solving math problems.

The structure of math interviews will vary depending on the information to be obtained. Interviews are particularly helpful for determining how a student is thinking.

5	4	2	6	0
+ 3	+ 2	+ 2	+ 3	+ 9

7	9	8	5	8
+ 5	+ 3	+ 8	+ 6	+ 5

6	5	9	8	3
− 3	− 4	− 4	− 5	− 1

11	13	17	12	18
− 5	− 8	− 9	− 7	− 9

22	35	27	61	53
+13	+10	+11	+23	+12

26	37	63	57	65
+15	+29	+19	+23	+27

66	51	23	57	48
−23	− 40	−12	−32	−28

54	62	44	75	83
−29	−54	−28	− 47	−75

3	6	2	9	3
x 5	x 4	x 8	x 7	x 1

13	42	37	20	52
x 2	x 4	x 1	x 6	x 3

FIGURE 7.5   SAMPLE TEACHER-MADE TEST TO ASSESS A SPAN OF SKILLS

Introspection or retrospection may be used to assist in this process. *Introspection* involves having the student "think out loud" as he or she completes a math problem. *Retrospection* involves having the student complete the problem and then tell what he or she did (Ashlock, 1990). Both of these procedures can provide useful assessment information.

Math interviews also can be used to assess student attitudes toward mathematics. The assessment may involve direct questions (e.g., "What is your favorite thing about math?") or open-ended statements (e.g., "Math is very....") for the student to complete. When assessing attitudes, students must feel free to respond honestly. Teacher-student rapport is important to obtain valid information through the interview format.

To obtain information about specific math skills, the following questions may be appropriate:

5 + 3 **8**	4 + 2 **6**	2 + 2 **4**	6 + 3 **9**	0 + 9 **9**
7 + 5 **12**	9 + 3 **12**	8 + 8 **16**	5 + 6 **11**	8 + 5 **13**
6 − 3 **3**	5 − 4 **1**	9 − 4 **5**	8 − 5 **3**	3 − 1 **2**
11 − 5 **6**	13 − 8 **5**	17 − 9 **8**	12 − 7 **5**	18 − 9 **9**
22 +13 **35**	35 +10 **45**	27 +11 **38**	61 +23 **84**	53 +12 **65**
26 +15 **41**	37 +29 **66**	63 +19 **82**	57 +23 **80**	65 +27 **92**
66 −23 **43**	51 −40 **11**	23 −12 **11**	57 −32 **25**	48 −28 **20**
4̸54 −29 **25**	5̸62 −54 **8**	3̸44 −28 **16**	6̸7̸5 −47 **28**	7̸83 −75 **8**
3 × 5 **8**	6 × 4 **10**	2 × 8 **10**	9 × 7 **16**	3 × 1 **3**
13 × 2 **6**	42 × 4 **10**	37 × 1 **11**	20 × 6 **8**	52 × 3 **10**

FIGURE 7.6   COMPLETED TEACHER-MADE TEST ASSESSING A SPAN OF SKILLS

- Tell me how you would solve the problem.
- Solve this problem, and tell me what you're thinking as you complete each step.
- What is the first thing you need to do when solving a problem such as...?
- Pretend I'm your student, and teach me how to do this problem.
- How do you know this answer is correct?
- Tell me two possible ways to find the answer to this problem.
- Can you show me a faster way to solve this problem?
- What kind of picture could you draw to help solve this problem?
- How do you remember all the steps to perform to answer a problem like ...?

To obtain information about a student's attitude or feelings about math, the teacher can ask some of the following questions:

- What is your favorite thing about math?
- What is your least favorite thing about math?
- Why do you think you have to study math?
- Do you ever use math outside of school? If so, where?
- What is your favorite way to learn math?
- Do you like to work alone or with others?
- If you earn an A on your next math test, who would you like me to tell?
- What math skill do you think you need to work on?

During a math interview with Mike, Ms. Juniper asked him what he liked best about math. He said he liked addition and subtraction even though it was "baby math." He also said he liked "measuring stuff." Then Ms. Juniper asked Mike what he liked least about math. Without hesitation he said, "stupid times tables." Ms. Juniper probed further and found out that Mike had gone to four different schools in the 2nd grade, four different schools in the 3rd grade, and three different schools in the 4th grade. No wonder times tables were "stupid"! Mike most likely missed the basic instruction and the practice needed to master this skill.

Ms. Juniper told Mike that she had a great program that would teach him those times tables once and for all. She began talking about how much fun they would have and how this program would help him with other math skills as well. Mike listened with a slight glimmer of hope in his eyes.

Task Analysis and the Clinical Mathematics Interview (CMI)

Task analysis can be defined as "a sequence of evaluation activities that pinpoints the instructional problem and guides the teacher in planning an effective sequence of remedial tasks" (Wallace & Kauffman, 1986, p. 133). A thorough task analysis typically involves determining the sequential steps involved in learning the math skill. Specific behaviors needed to perform each step then are identified. Frequently a checklist that corresponds to the individual tasks required to perform a given math operation is used during this type of assessment. These lists sometimes are provided in commercial materials. If they are not readily available, teachers can develop their own. An example is provided in Figure 7.7.

Problem: Matt kept a record of the amount of time he spent on homework this week. What is the
average amount of time spent per night?

Mon.	30 min.
Tues.	45 min.
Wed.	20 min.
Thur.	30 min.
Fri.	35 min.

Student's Work:

Teacher's Checklist:
   1. Student adds the five entries.   ☐
   2. Student adds correctly.   ☐
   3. Student counts the number of entries to be averaged.   ☐
   4. Student counts correctly.   ☐
   5. Student divides number of entries into the sum of the entries. ☐
   6. Student divides correctly.   ☐

Teacher's Conclusions:

FIGURE 7.7   EXAMPLE OF TEACHER-MADE TASK ANALYSIS CHECKLIST

Cawley (1975, 1985) developed the Clinical Mathematics Interview (CMI), a functional and structured application of task analysis. The CMI is used as a diagnostic procedure that integrates (a) the content of the curriculum, (b) the modes of instruction, and (c) the algorithm or rule the student selects when attempting to solve the problem. When implementing the CMI, the student is given a computation test. After the student completes the test, the teacher scores the items and sorts them into sets of those solved correctly and those solved incorrectly. Next the teacher questions the student about the problems with incorrect answers. The questions are designed to explore the algorithms the student used. On a subsequent day, the missed problems are presented in an alternative mode, such as manipulating objects, solving the problem orally, using pictures or tallies, or recognizing the solution from a series of alternatives. These CMI procedures can contribute valuable information for planning instruction.

T he student who completed the work (averaging five numbers) illustrated in Figure 7.7 is named Jennie. When Jennie's teacher, Mr. Abernathy, realized that Jennie may not under stand how to divide, he constructed a teacher-made division test. The test contained three division fact problems (15 ÷ 3, 24 ÷ 6, and 9 ÷ 3); three problems involving single-digit num-bers divided into double-digit numbers with remainders (16 ÷ 3, 55 ÷ 7, and 63 ÷ 8); three problems involving single-digit numbers divided into three digit numbers without remainders (160 ÷ 5, 222 ÷ 2, and 190 ÷ 2); and three problems involving single-digit numbers divided into three-digit numbers with remainders (123 ÷ 6, 454 ÷ 3, and 723 ÷ 8). Jennie's performance on the division test confirmed what Mr. Abernathy had suspected after analyzing her attempt to average five numbers. Jennie successfully solved the basic division facts and the problems in-volving single digits divided into double-digit numbers with remainders. She missed all the problems involving three-digit problems.

After grading Jennie's test, Mr. Abernathy interviewed her. He asked her to tell him step-by-step how she obtained her answer for a couple of the three-digit problems she had missed. Jennie explained that for the problem 160 ÷ 5, she asked herself how many times does 5 go into 16 and got 3. Then she asked herself how many times does 5 go into 0 and got 0. Thus, her answer was 30. Mr. Abernathy realized quickly that Jennie was forgetting to multiply, sub-tract, and bring down the next number. He planned a lesson for the next day to review this type of division problem. After reteaching the skill, he provided Jennie with similar problems and asked her to identify the problems that she had solved correctly. Jennie now was able to discriminate between the correct algorithm and the error pattern she had demonstrated on the previous day. Mr. Abernathy told Jennie that he was happy with her work and that during their next lesson she would apply her new understanding to finding averages. Jennie knew she would get those word problems about averages correct now.

ANALYZING ERROR PATTERNS

Careful examination of students' answers to a set of math problems may reveal patterns in the types of errors they are making (see Error Patterns Q & A box). Once an error pattern has been identified, teachers can plan appropriate instruction to remedy the problem. Teachers who fail to recognize a math error pattern and instead assume that students are "careless" or simply "don't know their facts" actually promote the continuation of erro-neous procedures. Students will continue to practice the same errors if they are not iden-tified and corrected.

Several categories of computational errors have been noted. Among these are the following.

1. *Defective algorithm.* The student does not perform the operation appropriately; steps of the operation either are out of sequence or are performed incorrectly.
2. *Computational error.* The student applies the correct operation, but the response is based on an error in recalling basic number facts.
3. *Wrong operation.* The student responds to a problem by using an operation other than the one required to solve the problem.

Q & A

ERROR PATTERNS

Q: *Can you identify the error patterns made by these students?*

Terry
$$\begin{array}{r} 24 \\ \times\,2 \\ \hline 48 \end{array} \qquad \begin{array}{r} 61 \\ \times\,2 \\ \hline 122 \end{array} \qquad \begin{array}{r} \overset{2}{53} \\ \times\,7 \\ \hline 491 \end{array} \qquad \begin{array}{r} \overset{3}{65} \\ \times\,6 \\ \hline 540 \end{array}$$

Neil
$$\begin{array}{r} 33 \\ 2\overline{)66} \\ 6 \\ \hline 6 \\ \hline 6 \end{array} \qquad \begin{array}{r} 37 \\ 5\overline{)365} \\ 35 \\ \hline 15 \\ 15 \end{array} \qquad \begin{array}{r} 39 \\ 7\overline{)651} \\ 63 \\ \hline 21 \\ 21 \end{array} \qquad \begin{array}{r} 89 \\ 3\overline{)294} \\ 27 \\ \hline 24 \\ 24 \end{array}$$

Jerry

$$\frac{5}{3} \times \frac{2}{3} = \frac{5}{3} \times \frac{3}{2} = \frac{15}{6} \qquad\qquad \frac{1}{3} \times \frac{4}{5} = \frac{1}{3} \times \frac{5}{4} = \frac{5}{12}$$

$$\frac{3}{4} \times \frac{1}{2} = \frac{3}{4} \times \frac{2}{1} = \frac{6}{4} \qquad\qquad \frac{2}{3} \times \frac{3}{4} = \frac{2}{3} \times \frac{4}{3} = \frac{8}{9}$$

A: *Terry* adds the number associated with the crutch before multiplying the tens figure.

Neil records the first quotient figure in the ones column, and in the tens column he records the second digit he determines. He records the answer right to left.

Jerry uses the division procedure of inverting and multiplying.

---

4. *Place value problems.* The student knows the basic facts but is deficient in some aspect of place value concepts.
5. *Random response.* The student responses show no discernible relationship to the given problem.
6. *Poor writing skills.* The student makes errors as a result of illegible numbers or an inability to align problems correctly, or both.
7. *Inappropriate inversions.* The student displays reversals in some critical dimension of the operational procedure.
8. *Identity errors.* The student misreads 0 for 1.
9. *Zero errors.* The student solves problems with zero as if the zero were not there or as if the zero were 1.

A study examining the frequency of the various types of errors found that most student errors fall in four of these categories. (Tindal & Marston, 1990):

1. 38% of student errors were basic fact errors.
2. 22% of the errors involved place value.

3. 21% of the errors were the result of inappropriate inversions or reversals.
4. 18% resulted from using a defective algorithm.

CURRICULUM-BASED ASSESSMENT

Curriculum-based assessment is useful for measuring math learning and monitoring on-going progress. This approach to assessment provides an in-depth probe of specific math skills based on problems encountered in the classroom curriculum. When implementing curriculum-based assessment, teachers construct tests or probes that measure student progress on math skills that are part of the student's individualized education program objectives. For example, if a student's IEP objectives include memorizing the multiplication tables, the teacher might construct a probe sheet containing 60 multiplication facts. The student is given 1 minute to complete as many problems as possible on the probe. This sheet or alternate forms of the probe are administered regularly until the student demonstrates mastery (e.g., 40 problems correct with two or fewer errors). The results of each 1-minute timing can be graphed and the data used to determine whether the student is progressing adequately toward the predetermined objective or goal.

Polloway and Patton (1993) identified several advantages that accrue from curriculum-based assessment procedures:

1. The probes are designed to assess a specific skill.
2. The probes include enough problems to determine clearly whether the student can or cannot perform the skill.
3. If the teacher has any doubts about the test results, constructing a similar probe for the student is easy. The results of both probes then can be compared.
4. The accumulation of student data can guide instructional decision making. For example, if a student fails to improve on a particular probe, that is the teacher's cue to teach the skill in a different manner.

You may remember that Ms. Juniper determined, through a teacher-made test and math interview, that Mike needed instruction on the basic multiplication facts. Therefore, she began by teaching the concept of multiplication using poker chips and dominoes. She taught Mike that multiplication involves groups of objects. Thus, the problem 6 × 4 really means six groups of four objects. She used small paper plates to represent the groups and the poker chips and dominoes to represent the objects in each group. Once Mike understood what multiplication means and could demonstrate his knowledge using the manipulative devices, Ms. Juniper taught the same concepts using pictures of objects and tally marks.

After Mike demonstrated thorough understanding, Ms. Juniper began working on Mike's fluency in solving multiplication facts. She provided practice opportunities and encouraged Mike to begin memorizing the facts so he wouldn't have to use objects or tallies to determine the answers. Ms. Juniper decided to use curriculum-based assessment to monitor his progress. Ms. Juniper constructed an assessment sheet containing 60 multiplication facts (see Figure 7.8). Initially Ms. Juniper had Mike practice solving multiplication facts with one of his peers, using flashcards. At the end of the peer practice session, Ms. Juniper administered the assessment sheet. She gave Mike 1 minute to complete as many problems as he could in the order

8	0	1	3	1	8
× 7	× 6	× 9	× 6	× 1	× 8
3	4	2	6	1	7
× 2	× 5	× 7	× 6	× 0	× 5
3	8	6	2	7	0
× 7	× 4	× 7	× 2	× 1	× 9
2	8	9	3	5	4
× 9	× 8	× 4	× 3	× 3	× 7
2	6	8	6	7	5
× 1	× 3	× 5	× 4	× 0	× 2
7	2	3	7	3	4
× 7	× 7	× 1	× 5	× 4	× 1
5	3	7	8	6	3
× 1	× 2	× 4	× 1	× 2	× 7
6	8	5	6	7	8
× 3	× 1	× 0	× 8	× 9	× 0
5	8	7	8	8	7
× 6	× 5	× 5	× 9	× 4	× 6
7	8	6	8	9	6
× 8	× 6	× 9	× 3	× 5	× 4

FIGURE 7.8   SAMPLE CURRICULUM-BASED ASSESSMENT SHEET

they were presented. He was told that skipped problems would have to count as errors. After the minute, Ms. Juniper would score the assessment sheet to determine how many correct digits (not problems) and incorrect digits Mike had written. Mike then plotted his score on a graph. This allowed both Mike and Ms. Juniper to monitor his progress.

As you can see in Figure 7.9, Mike wasn't making much progress with the peer practice. Therefore, Ms. Juniper decided to try computer practice instead. Mike loved using the computer and began making rapid progress.

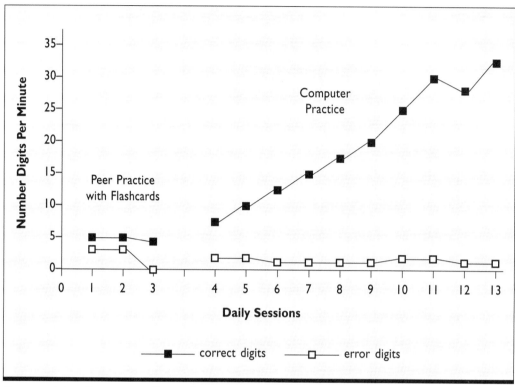

FIGURE 7.9   CURRICULUM-BASED PROGRESS CHART

AFFECTIVE AND MOTIVATIONAL CONSIDERATIONS

Once the math curriculum has been selected and assessment of student skills has been completed, the students' affective and motivational characteristics have to be considered. Knowledge of these characteristics will assist greatly in planning appropriate instructional techniques.

AFFECTIVE AND MOTIVATIONAL DEFICITS

In many instances students with learning difficulties in mathematics have a negative attitude toward acquiring the skills they need. These students sometimes develop mental blocks toward math instruction because of repeated failures throughout their school experience. Failure breeds insecurity and results in the "I can't do it" or "This is stupid" or "This is boring" attitude.

The term *learned helplessness* often is used to explain the poor motivation of adolescents with learning disabilities. This learned helplessness, or the inability of individuals to view their own behavior as having a positive effect on their schoolwork, may contribute to poor performance. Frequently students who get caught up in the learned helplessness cycle relate negative thought patterns to their academic work even when they are successful. For example, they may complete a math assignment successfully and still say things such as, "I can't do these problems" or "I just got lucky" or "The teacher graded these easy. He must have been in a good mood." These comments reflect a lack of confidence in performing math skills.

MATH ANXIETY

Some students with a poor attitude related to mathematics also develop math anxiety, an emotion-based reaction to mathematics that causes individuals to freeze when they confront math problems or have to take math exams. Fear of school failure is one of the causes of math anxiety. This anxiety makes learning new math skills difficult. It also impedes the student's ability to apply or generalize their math knowledge when taking tests (Slavin, 1991). Many students and adults with learning disabilities report that anxiety is a constant feeling that affects their ability to think clearly and causes them to avoid math tasks that may lead to failure.

AFFECTIVE AND MOTIVATIONAL GUIDELINES

The National Council of Teachers of Mathematics (1989) and the National Council of Supervisors of Mathematics (1988) both have stressed the importance of addressing the affective side of mathematics instruction. Research has shown that positive affect increases feelings of self-efficacy in secondary students with learning disabilities. Moreover, positive mood affect has a positive influence on adolescents' perceived self-control and willingness to take charge of their learning (Bryan & Bryan, 1991). Secondary students with learning disabilities clearly need carefully planned instruction to ensure success and promote positive attitudes toward mathematics. Guidelines for promoting positive attitudes toward math learning are discussed next.

ESTABLISH GOAL-SETTING PROCEDURES

Research supports the use of goal-setting in mediating human performance. Clear but challenging goals within the learner's reach and goals that incorporate feedback to the learners enhance student performance on math tasks (Bavelas & Lee, 1978; Fuchs, Bahr, & Rieth, 1989; Locke & Latham, 1990; Schunk, 1985). Also, secondary students who select their own goals perform better on math computation than students who are assigned goals (Fuchs, Bahr, & Rieth, 1989). Involving students in the goal-setting process seems to enhance the student's commitment to the goals and ultimately enhances the sense of accomplishment the student experiences upon achieving the goal. Certainly this process will help improve math motivation.

Another strategy for improving a student's motivation for learning mathematics is to relate current instruction to the student's future goals and interests. To do this, teachers must spend time discussing the importance of learning math skills to achieving both long- and short-term goals of the student. For example, if a student wants to own his own business, a rationale for understanding budgets and money usage can be made easily. If the student wants to be a carpenter, the importance of acquiring measurement skills can be emphasized. Involving the student in the rationale-building process is frequently helpful. In this way, the relevance of math instruction becomes more clear to students, and their motivation to learn increases.

teve, another student in Ms. Juniper's class, was working on building multiplication fluency. He understood what multiplication means but needed to solve the problems faster.
Ms. Juniper was using the same curriculum-based assessment sheet to monitor Steve's progress
as she was using with Mike. Remember the sheet with 60 problems? Steve's progress was slow.
One day when Steve answered a few more problems than the day before, he smiled and said,
"Hey, I'm getting better." Ms. Juniper decided that Steve may benefit from daily goal setting
because he liked the idea of beating his previous score. The next day, before starting the 1-
minute assessment sheet, Ms. Juniper sat down with Steve and said, "You know, Steve, I think
it's time for us to set some goals for this multiplication sheet. Remember yesterday when I
asked you to write the numbers 0 to 9 as many times as you could in 1 minute? That was so I
could see how fast you can write numbers. Well, you wrote 80 numbers in 1 minute! That's
pretty fast. We can use this writing rate to help us set a goal for your multiplication sheet.
What we do is take 75% of your writing rate and use that as your goal for the multiplication
sheet. Okay, 75% of 80 is 60. So 60 digits correct on your multiplication sheet would be a
reasonable goal. Why do you think our multiplication goal is less than 80?"

Steve replied, "'Cause it takes longer to think of the multiplication answer than it does to
just write a number."

"That's exactly right!" said Ms. Juniper. Then she continued, "So our overall goal is 60
digits correct in a minute. As soon as you reach your goal, we won't have to practice these
problems every day any more. You will be at mastery and won't need so much practice. Let's
see if we can come up with a reasonable goal for today. Let's look at your chart and see how
you did yesterday. How many digits did you get correct?"

"I got 25, and I didn't get any wrong," replied Steve.

"That's right. So, how many more digits do you think you can get today?" Steve thought
about it and said, "Well, maybe I could try to get four more today."

Ms. Juniper was pleased and said, "I think that's a great goal. Now let's look at your assessment sheet and figure out what problem you would have to get to have 29 digits correct."

Together Ms. Juniper and Steve counted digits and figured out where he would have to
get on the sheet to meet his goal. Steve drew a line, which they called his "goal line," on the
sheet to serve as a visual cue. This simple strategy turned out to be a great motivator for
Steve. He enjoyed figuring out a goal, marking the place and then trying to get to it. He reached
his goal most days and always exclaimed, "Hey, I did it. I beat my score!" Steve reached his goal
of 60 digits in 3 weeks. He certainly was proud!

STRUCTURE INSTRUCTION FOR SUCCESS

The affective characteristics of students with disabilities are influenced greatly by the
amount of success they have. Therefore, teachers have to structure math instruction so
students can succeed. Careful assessment of student skills assists in identifying appropriate math tasks to build on knowledge previously acquired. Task analysis also can assist in ensuring that instructional steps are small enough for the student to comprehend
and thus succeed.

Positive and efficient feedback also is important to students regarding their performance on various math skills. Teachers who provide basic and elaborated corrective feed-

back will enhance the achievement of students in their classes greatly (Gersten, Carnine, & Woodward, 1987; Kline, Schumaker, & Deshler, 1991; Robinson, DePascale, & Roberts, 1989). As students achieve, they feel successful and develop positive attitudes toward instruction (see Corrective Feedback Q and A box).

REDUCE MATH ANXIETY

To establish positive attitudes toward math, the teacher must attempt to reduce any math anxiety in a student. Lerner (1993) suggested several strategies, including the following:

1. *Use competition carefully.* Having students compete with themselves (as Steve did in the previous case study) rather than their peers may be more effective. When competition is part of the instructional program, be sure that students have the skills to compete with reasonable assurance that they will succeed.
2. *Provide clear directions.* Students need to understand what they are expected to do on math assignments. Check students' comprehension of the instructions by asking them to verbalize what they are supposed to do on a given task.
3. *Allow students enough time to complete their math assignments.* Consider giving some take-home tests.
4. *Reduce the pressure involved in taking tests.* Teach the students strategies for taking tests. Consider giving practice tests.

MOTIVATE STUDENTS VERBALLY

Communicating positive expectations to students is important. The teacher has to communicate the expectation and belief that success in math is probable. Likewise, verbal

Q & A

CORRECTIVE FEEDBACK

Q: *What is an effective way to provide corrective feedback?*
A: The following steps may be followed when providing students with feedback regarding their performance on math homework or classwork.

Step 1: Score the student's product for correct and incorrect responses.
Step 2: Analyze the student's errors to determine any consistent error pattern.
Step 3: Meet with the student to discuss his or her performance.
Step 4: Show the student which problems are correct and which are incorrect, and point out the error pattern if one exists.
Step 5: Show the student how to perform the task.
Step 6: Ask the student to practice the application.
Step 7: Close the feedback session with a positive statement about the student's performance and your expectations for the future. For example: "Matt, you've really done a good job listening and figuring out why these problems were incorrect. I'm sure the next time you solve problems like this, you'll remember to subtract to determine the remainders."

praise for effort and achievement in math is important. Moreover, teachers should attempt to help students realize that effort affects performance outcomes. This will help them realize that their behavior directly influences what happens to them and, consequently, they are in control of their own learning. Finally, teachers can motivate students verbally by modeling enthusiasm and a positive attitude toward math (Mercer & Miller, 1992b).

MAKE MATH INSTRUCTION FUN

Student motivation in math undoubtedly will increase if teachers introduce instructional procedures that are fun for the students. This means exploring topics of interest that involve students actively in the learning process. Computer-assisted instruction, brain teasers, and instructional games all help make math practice fun. Some students enjoy peer-tutoring opportunities or cooperative learning activities, or both. Observing student responses to a variety of math activities will help determine what they view as fun and meaningful. This information is useful in terms of planning appropriate instruction to promote positive attitudes toward mathematics.

INTEGRATE MATH INTO SUBJECT AREAS OF INTEREST TO THE STUDENTS

Studying math within the context of high-interest subjects is highly motivating to students. For example, a student who is interested in geography can learn math concepts within a geographical context. Included among the possible math activities related to geography are the following.

1. Determine total mileage between various places on a map.
2. Determine variations in time based on designated zones.
3. Establish a budget for various mock vacations.
4. Study average daily temperatures for various cities.
5. Project population growth within various countries.

Integrating math into other subject areas is advantageous particularly when the student views math negatively but values other parts of the school curriculum.

Figure 7.10 lists affective and motivational characteristics of students with math disabilities along with related treatment options. These lists are not all-inclusive. They provide preliminary information to help teachers think about the students in their classes. As time goes on, teachers will get to know students on a more personal level and will be able to assess educational interventions that are most appropriate for improving their motivation and willingness to learn mathematics.

INSTRUCTIONAL CONSIDERATIONS

Within the field of math education, two diverse instructional approaches have emerged: didactic and discovery. The *didactic approach* emphasizes teaching the basic skills first and then providing students with opportunities to apply these skills in problem-solving activities. The *discovery approach* encourages students to establish an understanding of the math process required to solve problems prior to formal instruction in the basic skills (Polloway & Patton, 1993). The discovery approach is less structured than the didactic

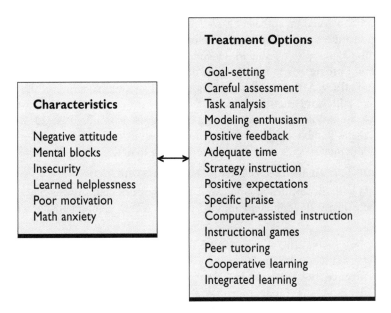

Characteristics	Treatment Options
Negative attitude	Goal-setting
Mental blocks	Careful assessment
Insecurity	Task analysis
Learned helplessness	Modeling enthusiasm
Poor motivation	Positive feedback
Math anxiety	Adequate time
	Strategy instruction
	Positive expectations
	Specific praise
	Computer-assisted instruction
	Instructional games
	Peer tutoring
	Cooperative learning
	Integrated learning

FIGURE 7.10   AFFECTIVE AND MOTIVATIONAL CHARACTERISTICS AND TREATMENT OPTIONS

approach and relies on students' being able to figure out things without much direct instruction. Teacher prompts and cues are minimized under the discovery approach. Although the discovery approach has a certain intuitive appeal, it may not be the best approach for students who need prompts, models, and concrete instruction to acquire new skills. Teachers must be careful when selecting instructional approaches for students with disabilities. Teachers have a professional obligation to select approaches that result in effective, efficient learning.

ACQUISITION GUIDELINES AND ISSUES

The acquisition stage of learning implies that the student has little or no knowledge of the skill or concept to be taught (Rivera & Bryant, 1992). Thus, instruction must be thorough and well organized. Teachers must plan lessons systematically to ensure that students understand the new content. Effective instructional procedures designed to facilitate the acquisition of math skills and concepts have been identified and validated in recent years. A number of these procedures is presented in the following pages.

TEACH FOR UNDERSTANDING

During the acquisition stage of computational or problem-solving skills, students should be instructed in a way that ensures understanding. Many authorities (Heddens & Speer, 1992; Reisman, 1982; Underhill, Uprichard, & Heddens, 1980) believe that the concrete-representational-abstract (CRA) sequence is an excellent means of teaching students to understand math concepts, operations, and applications. Recent research has validated the opinions of these authorities (Miller, Mercer, & Dillon, 1992; Peterson, Mercer, & O'Shea, 1988).

Initial instruction, at the *concrete level*, utilizes manipulative devices. Students learn to demonstrate the skill or concept using objects from their environment (e.g., cubes, poker chips, place value sticks). Once a student masters the skill at the concrete level, instruction progresses to the *representational level* and tasks involving pictures of objects and tallies. After the student demonstrates an understanding of the skill using pictures and tallies, instruction progresses to the *abstract level*, at which the student learns to solve the problems without objects or pictures or tallies. Instead the problems are solved using numbers only. Providing instruction using the CRA sequence ensures that the student understands the math concepts prior to determining the correct answer.

PROVIDE TEACHER-DIRECTED SYSTEMATIC INSTRUCTION

Students with disabilities respond well to teacher-directed lessons that follow a logical sequence. The following steps may be used to create comprehensive, success-oriented lessons:

1. *Provide an advance organizer.* The purpose of the advance organizer is to prepare students for the lesson that is about to take place. An effective advance organizer connects the current lesson to previous learning, identifies the skill the students are about to learn, shows the students the materials that will be used in the lesson, and provides a rationale for learning the math skill that will be taught.

2. *Describe and demonstrate the skill.* After the advance organizer has been presented, the skill is described and demonstrated. While demonstrating the skill, the teacher verbalizes thoughts that occur while solving the problem. Thus, students observe mechanical steps involved in determining the answer and hear thoughts that facilitate the process.

3. *Have students model the skill.* After the teacher has demonstrated several examples of the new skill, students are given an opportunity to model what they observed and heard. The teacher should be present when this modeling is done so student errors can be detected and corrected immediately. Remediation is easier at this point in the lesson and becomes more difficult if students practice their errors before receiving the corrective feedback.

4. *Provide practice.* When acquiring new skills, students must have ample opportunities for practice. The initial practice should be guided. Students need feedback regarding their initial practice attempts. At this point in the lesson, the teacher praises effort and encourages students to take risks. Incorrect answers are viewed as an opportunity to learn. If, however, a student has a great deal of difficulty with guided practice, the teacher demonstrates the skill again and gives the student additional opportunities to model.

   Once guided practice is successful, students are given independent practice to demonstrate their knowledge of the skill without any assistance. This independent practice can be used to assess whether a student is ready to move on to subsequent lessons involving the same skill and ultimately whether the student is ready to progress to a new skill.

5. *Provide feedback.* At the conclusion of each lesson, or at least prior to starting a new lesson, students receive feedback regarding their performance. Included in this feedback is verbal praise about the things the student did well, identification

of error patterns or incorrect answers, modeling or reteaching confusing concepts, and a positive statement regarding future attempts with the skill.

This systematic approach to teaching math lessons can be used regardless of the skill being taught and regardless of whether the teaching involves concrete, representational, or abstract-level understanding.

Teach Students a Variety of Math Strategies

Students who are successful in mathematics seem to self-generate strategies that assist them in solving problems. Students with math disabilities seem to lack the ability to design their own strategies spontaneously. These students have been characterized as passive learners, who have difficulty selecting and applying task-appropriate strategies to complete their math work (Mellard & Alley, 1981; Torgesen, 1982). Instead, they seem to rely on lengthy trial-and-error approaches to solve math problems. In many cases this is neither effective nor efficient.

Thus, a critical component of math instruction for students with disabilities is strategy instruction. Within the context of mathematics, strategies may be defined as "general skills or abilities that can be learned, are useful for a variety of problems, may be used singly or in combinations to solve a single problem, and give the individual the tools with which to begin or continue productive work on a problem" (Meiring, 1980, p. 7). Stated another way, a learning strategy is an individual's approach to a task; it includes how the person thinks and acts when planning, executing, and evaluating performance on a task and its outcomes (Ellis, Deshler, Lenz, Schumaker, & Clark, 1991). When implementing strategy instruction for mathematics, teachers should be aware of several issues (Montague, 1988).

1. *Be aware of individual students' cognitive characteristics*. When planning strategy instruction, teachers must realize that students will have a variety of strategic preferences. Strategies can be individualized to accommodate these preferences. For example, when solving word problems, some students prefer to read the problem aloud; others comprehend more through silent reading. Some students respond well to visual depictions of the story on paper; others form mental images. Some students do better if they underline relevant information and cross out unneeded information to reduce the stimuli field. Perhaps a reasonable approach to assessing what strategies work for a given student is to teach several different strategies and then monitor student performance to see which are most beneficial. Eventually students who have been taught a number of strategies begin to adapt and create their own strategies.

2. *Be aware of students' behavioral characteristics including motivation and self-esteem*. To accomplish instructional goals, teachers have to be aware of students' levels of motivation and self-esteem. The relationship between self-esteem and achievement must be acknowledged. Certainly students who learn to use strategies that help them succeed in mathematics will feel better about themselves and their abilities.

3. *Individualize instruction*. As teachers progress with strategy instruction, they will come to realize that certain strategies are more salient than others for different

students. Initially, strategy instruction should be structured for the students, but as the strategies are internalized, students can take a more active role in selecting and adapting appropriate strategies for various tasks.

4. *Teach for generalization.* Special and general education teachers both should participate in generalizing math strategies. A major purpose for teaching students to use strategies is to enable students to solve a variety of problems in a variety of settings under a variety of conditions.

Many instructional techniques are available to facilitate strategy instruction with secondary students who have math disabilities. Among these are teaching basic rules and axioms, using mnemonic devices, teaching step-by-step procedures, implementing self-monitoring, and teaching word problems using a graduated word problem sequence. These strategies are discussed in the following pages.

TEACH BASIC RULES AND AXIOMS   Teaching rules that apply to a variety of math operations can assist students in acquiring basic skills. For example, when teaching secondary students the basic multiplication facts, it usually can be assumed that the students have attempted to memorize the facts in the past. Memorization is difficult for many students with disabilities. Some of these students respond positively to learning a few rules that they then can apply to many problems. The following multiplication rules are applicable.

- Any number times 0 is 0.
- Any number times 1 is the number.
- Any number times 2 is double the number.
- Any number times 5 is counting by fives.

Teaching students with disabilities basic math axioms also is helpful. The most commonly used axioms follow with relevant examples.

1. *Commutative property of addition.* The order of the numbers added together does not change the answer.

$$a + b = b + a$$
$$5 + 3 = 3 + 5$$

2. *Commutative property of multiplication.* The order of the numbers being multiplied does not change the answer.

$$a \times b = b \times a$$
$$4 \times 3 = 3 \times 4$$

Students should be taught that no commutative property for subtraction or division exists.

3. *Associative property of addition.* When adding several numbers, the grouping arrangement does not change the answer.

$$(a + b) + c = a + (b + c)$$
$$(3 + 2) + 1 = 3 + (2 + 1)$$

4. *Associative property of multiplication.* When multiplying several numbers, the grouping arrangement does not change the answer.

$$(a \times b) \times c = a \times (b \times c)$$
$$(4 \times 2) \times 3 = 4 \times (2 \times 3)$$

Again, the students should be taught that no associative property exists for subtraction or division.

5. *Distributive property of multiplication over addition*. The product of a number and a sum can be expressed as a sum of two products.

$$a \times (b + c) = (a \times b) + (a \times c)$$
$$4 \times (20 + 4) = (4 \times 20) + (4 \times 4)$$

6. *Inverse operations*. The operation "undoes" what another operation does; the operation is opposite in its effect (e.g., addition and subtraction; multiplication and division).

$a + b = c$	$c - a = b$	or	$c - b = a$
$6 + 2 = 8$	$8 - 6 = 2$	or	$8 - 2 = 6$
$a \times b = c$	$c \div a = b$	or	$c \div b = a$
$4 \times 2 = 8$	$8 \div 4 = 2$	or	$8 \div 2 = 4$

Rules and axioms should be taught when students are learning applicable content. Thus, the students can put the axioms to use immediately.

Use Mnemonic Devices Bellezza (1981) defined mnemonic techniques as systematic procedures for enhancing learning and memory. They are learning strategies that can be used to improve initial acquisition and later recall of information. According to Scruggs and Mastropieri (1990), mnemonics have been used for years, but only recently have researchers begun investigating their effectiveness with students who have learning difficulties. To date, several studies have validated the benefits of mnemonic instruction (Mastropieri & Scruggs, 1989; Pressley, Levin, & Delaney, 1982; Scruggs & Mastropieri, 1989).

Acronyms are the most familiar type of mnemonic device used in mathematics. An acronym is a word formed from the initial letters of other words. Thus, they sometimes are referred to as "first-letter mnemonics." In mathematics acronyms frequently are used to help students remember the steps involved in solving a problem.

When teaching a math skill using the concrete-representational-abstract sequence, discussed earlier in this chapter, mnemonic devices can help facilitate the transition from representational instruction to abstract instruction. The transition from using pictures or tallies to using only numbers is difficult for many students with disabilities. They seem to need the additional support that mnemonic devices can provide. The SOLVE and DRAW mnemonic devices both were created with this in mind. These two strategies cue students to answer math facts from memory, if possible, and to use previously learned strategies (e.g., drawing tallies) to determine the answers to any problems not yet committed to memory (Miller & Mercer, 1993b). The mnemonic device SOLVE stands for the following steps for computing basic facts:

1. **S** ee the sign.
2. **O** bserve and answer (if unable to answer, keep going).
3. **L** ook and draw.
4. **V** erify your answer.
5. **E** nter your answer.

The mnemonic DRAW stands for the following steps for computing basic facts:

1. **D** iscover the sign.
2. **R** ead the problem.
3. **A** nswer or draw and check.
4. **W** rite the answer.

DRAW is used throughout the Strategic Math Series Program, with extensive validation to support its implementation with students who have difficulty with basic math facts (Mercer & Miller, 1992b, 1993; Miller & Mercer, 1991a, 1991b).

Mnemonic devices also have been used to help students solve word problems. Mnemonics created especially for this purpose are FAST DRAW (Mercer & Miller, 1992b) and SIGNS (Watanabe, 1991). FAST DRAW is an appropriate strategy to teach students who learned DRAW previously.

The steps of FAST are:

1. **F** ind what you're solving for.
2. **A** sk yourself, "What are the parts of the problem?"
3. **S** et up the numbers.
4. **T** ie down the sign.

This portion of the mnemonic device is used to interpret the word problem and figure out what numerical problem has to be solved. Then the student proceeds to solve the computation problem using the steps of DRAW.

The mnemonic device SIGNS stands for the following steps:

1. **S** urvey question.
2. **I** dentify key words and labels.
3. **G** raphically draw problem.
4. **N** ote type of operation(s) needed.
5. **S** olve and check problem.

For mnemonic instruction to be effective, teachers must allocate instructional time to demonstrate how the strategy works and the students must have ample time to practice using the mnemonic device. Mnemonic devices should be selected to meet students' specific needs. Students must understand the vocabulary used in the mnemonic steps, and the steps should be kept to a minimum. If taught properly, mnemonic devices can assist students with memory problems and can facilitate independent learning.

TEACH STEP-BY-STEP PROCEDURES FOR SOLVING PROBLEMS Montague and Bos (1986a) demonstrated the effectiveness of teaching adolescents steps to complete when solving math word problems. Their eight-step strategy was designed to enable students to read, understand, carry out, and check math word problems encountered in the general math curriculum at the secondary level. The eight steps in their strategy are:

1. *Read the problem aloud*. The students read the problem and receive help with any unknown words.
2. *Paraphrase the problem aloud*. The students state the important information and repeat the question aloud.

3. *Visualize.* The students draw a representation of the problem.
4. *State the problem.* The students complete these statements aloud: "I have....I want to find...." They also underline the important information.
5. *Hypothesize.* The students complete these statements aloud: "If I...then..."
6. *Estimate.* The students estimate what the answer will be.
7. *Calculate.* The students compute the answer.
8. *Self-check.* The students refer to the problem and check each step.

This strategy had positive effects on both skill acquisition and generalization to more difficult word problems during a research study designed to determine its effectiveness (Montague & Bos, 1986a). More recently, Montague, Applegate, and Marquard (1993) reduced these steps to seven, omitting number 4 ("State the problem"), but added a "say-ask-check" procedure to each of the remaining steps. Again, positive results were obtained; students improved in mathematical problem-solving performance on two different measures of one-, two-, and three-step word problems and also compared well with a normally achieving peer group.

IMPLEMENT SELF-MONITORING   A common concern of teachers of students with learning disabilities is that students have difficulty working independently. This frequently leads to uncompleted assignments and thus poor math grades. Self-monitoring strategies represent a viable intervention to improve students' work habits and increase their productivity in math class.

Self-monitoring, the ability to regulate one's own behavior, has been implemented successfully with students with disabilities through a variety of techniques including self-recording, self-evaluation, and self-reinforcement (Dunlap & Dunlap, 1989; Hughes, Ruhl, & Peterson, 1988; Shapiro, 1989). In *self-recording* students count and make formal notes of their own behaviors. In *self-evaluation* students make a quality-based judgment about their work. In *self-reinforcement* students select and administer their own rewards based on their performance.

These self-monitoring procedures seem to be beneficial particularly for students with learning disabilities because of the ongoing instructional cues that tend to produce specific response strategies and self-initiated responding (Kneedler & Hallahan, 1981). For example, checklists can be devised that cue students to use specific strategies to solve math problems. As each step of the strategy is used, the student checks it off (i.e., self-records). These checklists help students respond consistently and accurately and can be developed to assist in either computation or problem-solving tasks. Figure 7.11 presents sample self-monitoring forms.

TEACH WORD PROBLEMS USING A GRADUATED WORD PROBLEM SEQUENCE   Historically, word problems in mathematics have been challenging for students with learning disabilities. Cawley and Miller (1989) found that the problem-solving skills of 17-year-olds with learning disabilities peaked at the 5th-grade level. Likewise, Lee and Hudson (1981) reported that adolescents with learning disabilities had significantly more difficulty completing math word problems than their nondisabled peers. Students with learning disabilities have trouble selecting relevant information and determining the correct operational processes to obtain the answer. These students also have a higher rate of refusing to solve the problems, and they have significant difficulty evaluating the cor-

Independent Work Chart

	Self-Recording		Self-Evaluation
	# Problems Completed	# Problems Correct	Overall Rating*
Monday			
Tuesday			
Wednesday			
Thursday			
Friday			
		Total Weekly Points	

*1 = Need improvement
2 = Good performance
3 = Outstanding performance
12–15 Total Points = Self-reinforcement opportunity

Self-Recording Checklist for Subtraction Facts

1. Read the problem ☐
2. Draw tallies ☐
3. Cross out tallies ☐
4. Count how many are left ☐
5. Write answer ☐
6. Check your work ☐

FIGURE 7.11   SELF-MONITORING FORMS

rectness of their answers. Word problems with extraneous information are especially challenging for students with disabilities (Blankenship & Lovitt, 1976).

Current research on problem-solving approaches indicates that teachers have to instruct students to attack word problems in a systematic and strategic manner (Case & Harris, 1988; Mastropieri, Scruggs, & Shiah, 1991; Watanabe, 1991). A recently developed instructional strategy facilitates the acquisition of problem-solving skills by using a graduated word problem sequence (Miller & Mercer, 1993a).

At first the word problems contain just a few words. After the students demonstrate an ability to solve these problems, word problems involving sentences are presented, and finally the student progresses to the more traditional paragraph problems. Initially the paragraph problems do not contain any extraneous information. After students achieve mastery with these problems, they learn to solve problems that contain extraneous information. After identifying the extraneous information, students are taught to cross it out and focus on the information needed to solve the problem. The last component of the word problem sequence is to have students make up their own word problems. Validation data strongly support the use of this strategy for solving addition, subtraction, multiplication, and division word problems (Mercer & Miller, 1993; Miller & Mercer 1992b). The stages in this graduated sequence are identified in Figure 7.12.

Let's assume that you have just finished teaching one of your students how to complete single-digit subtraction facts using manipulative devices and pictures of objects. The student has mastered the skill at both the concrete and the representational levels, so you are going to transition to abstract-level instruction. Now the student will begin solving these problems without using counters, pictures, or tallies. You also decide to integrate subtraction word problems into your abstract level instruction. How could you apply the graduated word problem sequence to your subtraction instruction? Table 7.4 illustrates sample word problems that could be used in six sequential abstract-level lessons.

DIVERSIFY INSTRUCTION

When teaching mathematics for skill acquisition, the teacher has to keep in mind that individual differences among students will necessitate a variety of instructional techniques. Moreover, math instruction that is always presented the same way may become boring to the students. Teachers who diversify their instruction are more likely to have motivated students who are willing to take risks while learning new material. The following pages describe some of the options available for diversifying math instruction.

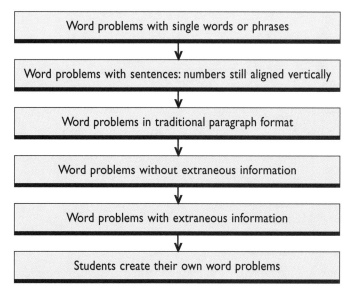

FIGURE 7.12   GRADUATED WORD PROBLEM SEQUENCE

TABLE 7.4   GRADUATED WORD PROBLEM SEQUENCE—SAMPLE PROBLEMS

Level of Instruction	Lesson #	Sample Problem
Abstract	1	7 apples − 6 apples apples
Abstract	2	8 pieces of candy − 8 pieces of candy sold are left
Abstract (#s aligned)	3	Jennie had 4 pens. She lost 2 of them. She has ____ pens left.
Abstract (no extraneous)	4	Jill checked out 5 books from the library. She has read 1 book. How many more does she have to read?
Abstract (extraneous)	5	Luis had 8 sheets of paper. Tom had 6 frogs. Luis gave his 8 sheets of paper to Sylvia. How many sheets of paper does Luis have left?
Abstract	6	Students are taught to make up their own word problems that will use the operation being taught (e.g., subtraction).

INTERACTIVE UNIT MODEL   Cawley et al. (1976) developed the interactive unit model to provide a method for programming instructional variation into math lessons. The model focuses on the interaction of teacher, student, and skill area. The teacher can provide instruction by:

- manipulating something
- displaying something
- saying something
- writing something.

The student can respond by:

- manipulating something
- identifying something
- saying something
- writing something.

The various combinations of teacher action and student response provide 16 ways to diversify instruction (Polloway & Patton, 1993). Teachers can experiment with the different instructional combinations to find what works best with their students.

INSTRUCTIONAL ARRANGEMENTS   Another method for diversifying instruction is to use a variety of instructional arrangements within the classroom setting. Among the possibilities are large-group formats in which the teacher provides direct instruction to the whole class, small-group formats such as cooperative learning (Sutton, 1992), pairs of individuals such as peer tutoring arrangements or one-to-one instruction and feedback, and, finally, opportunities for students to interact with educational materials or technology can be provided. Effective teachers recognize the benefits of each of these arrangements and make appropriate decisions regarding their use on a daily basis. Using more than one teaching arrangement keeps the classroom alive and tends to meet the individual needs of more students.

CALCULATORS IN THE CLASSROOM   The National Council of Teachers of Mathematics (1989) supports the use of calculators in mathematics classes across grade levels. Calculators can be useful in developing understanding of place value, relationships among numbers, operations, decimals, changing fractions to decimals, and percentages, as well as for making mathematical estimates and checking answers. Calculators are appropriate for lessons that aim to teach mathematics reasoning rather than calculation (Lerner, 1993; Mercer, 1991). The NCTM recommends that calculators be used to:

- concentrate on the problem-solving process rather than on the associated calculations
- gain access to mathematics beyond the students' level of computational skills
- explore, develop, and reinforce concepts
- experiment with math ideas and discover patterns
- perform the tedious computations that arise when working with real data in problem-solving situations.

Calculators can be used to motivate math performance. Many students enjoy hands-on devices. Care should be taken, however, when selecting appropriate calculators for classroom use. They should be selected with the grade of the student and the purpose of their use in mind (Bitter & Hatfield, 1991). For students with disabilities, calculators should have buttons that are easy to manipulate and display screens that are easy to read.

COMPUTER-ASSISTED INSTRUCTION   Another option for diversifying math instruction is to incorporate the use of computers. Computer-assisted instruction is particularly beneficial to students with disabilities because it can individualize, provide feedback, and provide repetition. Moreover, it elicits a high level of motivation from many students (Bahr & Rieth, 1990). Computer software provides opportunities for extensive drill-and-practice in a variety of math skills.

Simulation software programs also are available. Simulations are "micro worlds" that model real-world situations on the computer screen. Math-related programs are available that allow students to run a business, calculate profits and losses, and estimate inventories (Marshall, 1990). Problem-solving programs also are available to supplement classroom mathematics programs.

The National Council of Teachers of Mathematics (1989) strongly supports the use of computers in math instruction. The NCTM advocates the use of computers as tools to assist in the discovery of math concepts. The NCTM also sees computers as instructional aids that can help with the transition from concrete to abstract levels of understanding in math. Programming languages, spreadsheets, data analysis, and graphical analysis all can add depth to secondary mathematics programs.

Even though computer-assisted instruction offers many advantages, careful planning is needed before using this technology with students. Of the thousands of software programs that have been developed, not all of these programs represent quality work. Before integrating math software programs into the curriculum, teachers must evaluate the products they plan to use. Some questions to ask while previewing software are:

- Does this program relate to specific math objectives?
- Are the directions easy to understand?
- Are the screen displays appealing and easy to see and understand?
- Does the program offer flexibility?
- Can the program's response time be controlled?
- Will the program maintain students' interest?
- How many students can use the program at the same time?
- How many practice opportunities are provided?
- How is student performance monitored?
- What happens when a student answers a problem incorrectly?
- Is this program appropriate for students in the acquisition stage of learning, or is it more appropriate for students who need to build fluency?

For teachers who are just beginning to use math software or do not have the time to review various programs extensively, other resources are available. Professional journals (e.g., *Teacher, Technology & Learning, Electronic Learning*) sometimes provide software reviews and listings of software appropriate for specific skills or units of instruction. Other colleagues (e.g., media specialists, computer teachers, math teachers) also can be helpful. These resources can aid particularly in identifying poorly designed software, which can save a lot of time.

VIDEODISC INSTRUCTION   Videodisc instruction is an alternative to traditional computer-assisted instruction. Videodiscs have tremendous information-storage capabilities and enhanced graphic abilities. The pictures or images on videodisc can include segments of videotape, film clips, still pictures, or slides. Narration that eliminates the need for written text is also possible. This technology has been used successfully to supplement math instruction primarily in the areas of fractions, decimals, and word problems. Initial research has shown that adolescents with learning problems can use videodisc technology to solve complex, meaningful mathematics problems and can transfer these skills to other real-world tasks (Bottge & Hasselbring, 1993; Masters, Mori, & Mori, 1993). Thus, this technology seems to have positive implications for both acquisition and generalization of math learning. As videodisc accessibility continues to expand, well developed products undoubtedly will find their way into the classroom.

GENERALIZATION GUIDELINES AND ISSUES

The preceding suggestions to teach for understanding, provide teacher-directed systematic instruction, teach students a variety of math strategies, and diversify instruction will enhance the likelihood of successful acquisition of math skills by secondary students with learning disabilities. These recommendations are applicable regardless of the specific curricular content selected (e.g., functional math skills, problem solving, basic academic math skills). Skill acquisition is, however, only one component of the instructional process. Of equal importance is the generalization of acquired math skills.

Generalization refers to the student's ability to perform the targeted math skills in different, nontraining conditions (i.e., across subjects, settings, people, behaviors, or time) without arranging the exact same events in the new condition that were present in the training condition. If students are taught to count money in a math class, will they be able to count money at home, on the job, or in a grocery store? Can the students apply their math learning in the real world?

Typically, students with disabilities have a difficult time generalizing math skills. Lack of teacher attention to generalization has contributed to this problem. Research has documented that generalization must be taught before, during, and after instruction (Ellis, Lenz, and Sabornie, 1987a, 1987b). Mercer and Miller (1992b) made the following suggestions for promoting generalization prior to, during, and after instruction.

1. Before teaching a new math skill, conduct class discussions that include a rationale for learning the skill. Assist students in identifying where they will be able to use the skill outside of the classroom.
2. Involve students in setting challenging but attainable goals for learning the new material.
3. Develop student motivation to learn the skill.
4. Provide students with a variety of examples and experiences throughout the instructional process.
5. Remind students regularly of the rationale for learning the skill.
6. Teach math skills to a mastery level.
7. Encourage students to create meaningful math problems related to new knowledge.
8. Provide opportunities for students to practice the skill in their daily lives, and encourage them to generalize.

Although programming instruction for generalization takes some time, that time is well spent. A primary goal for math instruction is to prepare students to meet the math demands in their postsecondary settings. Teaching students to generalize is critical to meeting this goal.

Figure 7.13 summarizes the major instructional considerations related to skill acquisition and generalization. Acquisition and generalization must be integrated when providing math instruction.

SUMMARY

Teaching students with learning disabilities to acquire and generalize mathematics skills continues to be challenging. Fortunately, much more attention has been given to this content area over the past decade. Experimental studies have provided new knowledge regarding the assessment and teaching of secondary mathematics. Today's teachers are

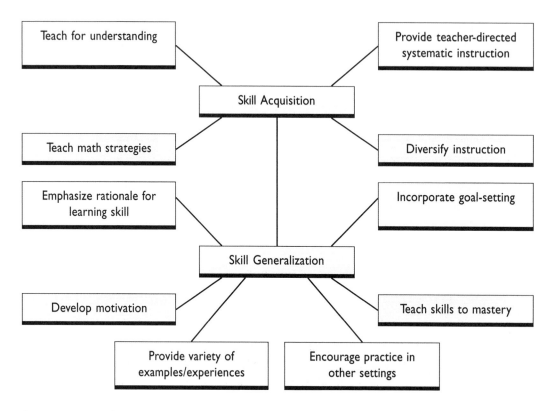

FIGURE 7.13 INSTRUCTIONAL CONSIDERATIONS

assimilating the new knowledge and implementing appropriate teaching strategies in their classroom settings. Educators must continue refining validated teaching techniques. Improvements in instructional math processes undoubtedly will increase academic achievement while students are in school and will enhance the likelihood of their continued success outside of school.

REFERENCES

Algozzine, B., O'Shea, D. J., Crews, W. B., & Stoddard, K. (1987). Analysis of mathematics competence of learning disabled adolescents. *Journal of Special Education, 21*(2), 97–107.

Alley, G. R., Deshler, D. D., & Warner, M. M. (1979). Identification and learning disabled adolescents: A Bayesian approach. *Learning Disability Quarterly, 2*(2), 76–83.

Anrig, G. R., & LaPointe, A. E. (1989). What we know about what students don't know. *Educational Leadership, 47*(3), 4–9.

Ashlock, R. B. (1990). *Error patterns in computation: A semiprogrammed approach* (5th ed.). New York: Macmillan.

Badian, N. A., & Ghublikian, M. (1982). The personal-social characteristics of children with poor mathematical computation skills. *Journal of Learning Disabilities, 16*, 154–157.

Bahr, C. M., & Rieth, H. J. (1990). The effects of instructional computer games and drill and practice software on learning disabled students' mathematics achievement. *Computers in the Schools, 6*, 87–101.

Bartel, N. R. (1990). Problems in mathematics achievement. In D. D. Hammill & N. R. Bartel, *Teaching students with learning and behavior problems* (5th ed., pp. 289–343). Austin, TX: Pro-Ed.

Bavelas, J. B., & Lee, E. S. (1978). Effects of goal level in performance: A trade-off of quantity and quality. *Canadian Journal of Psychology, 32*, 219–240.

Beatty, L. S., Madden, R., Gardner, E. F., & Karlsen, B. (1984). *Stanford Diagnostic Mathematics Test* (3rd ed.). San Antonio, TX: Psychological Corporation.

Bellezza, F. S. (1981). Mnemonic devices: Classification, characteristics, and criteria. *Review of Educational Research, 51*, 247–275.

Bitter, G. G., & Hatfield, M. M. (1991, January). Here's a math-teaching strategy that's calculated to work. *Executive Educator,* pp. 19–21.

Blankenship, C. S., & Lovitt, T. C. (1976). Story problems: Merely confusing or downright befuddling? *Journal for Research in Mathematics Education, 7*(5), 290–298.

Bley, N. S., & Thornton, C. A. (1989). *Teaching mathematics to the learning disabled.* Austin, TX: Pro-Ed.

Bottge, B. A., & Hasselbring, T. S. (1993). A comparison of two approaches for teaching complex, authentic mathematics problems to adolescents in remedial math classes. *Exceptional Children, 59*, 556–566.

Brenton, B. W., & Gilmore, D. (1976). An operational definition of learning disabilities (cognitive domain) using WISC full scale IQ and Peabody Individual Achievement Test Scores. *Psychology in the Schools. 13*, 427–432.

Brigance, A. H. (1980). *Brigance diagnostic inventory of essential skills.* North Billerica, MA: Curriculum Associates.

Brown, V. L., & McEntire, E. (1984). *Test of mathematical abilities.* Austin, TX: Pro-Ed.

Bryan, T., and Bryan, J. (1991). Positive mood and math performance. *Journal of Learning Disabilities, 24*, 490–495.

California Test Bureau. *California Achievement Tests.* (1985). Monterey, CA: McGraw-Hill.

Carpenter, T. P., Coburn, T. G., Reyes, R. E., & Wilson, J. W. (1976). Notes from the national assessment: Problem solving. *Mathematics Teacher, 32*, 389–393.

Carpenter, T. P., Corbitt, M. K., Kepner, H. S., Jr., Lindquist, M. M., & Reyes, R. E. (1981). *Results from the second mathematics assessment of the national assessment of educational progress.* Reston, VA: National Council of Teachers of Mathematics.

Carnine, D. (1976). Similar sound separation and cumulative introduction in learning letter-sound correspondences. *Journal of Educational Research, 69*, 368–372.

Carnine, D. (1980). Two letter discrimination sequences: High-confusion alternatives first versus low-confusion alternatives first. *Journal of Reading Behavior, 12*(1), 41–47.

Carnine, D. (1991). Curricular interventions for teaching higher order thinking to all students: Introduction to the special series. *Journal of Learning Disabilities, 24*, 261–269.

Case, L. P., & Harris, K. R. (1988, April). *Self-instructional strategy training: Improving mathematical problem solving skills of learning disabled students.* Paper presented at annual meeting of American Educational Research Association, New Orleans.

Cawley, J. (1975). *Math curricula for the secondary learning disabled student.* Paper presented at symposium on learning disabilities in secondary schools, Norristown, PA.

Cawley, J. (1985). *Secondary school mathematics for the learning disabled.* Rockville, MD: Aspen.

Cawley, J. F., Baker-Kroczynski, S., & Urban, A. (1992). Seeking excellence in mathematics education for students with mild disabilities. *Teaching Exceptional Children, 24*, 40–43.

Cawley, J., Fitzmaurice-Hayes, A., & Shaw, R. (1988). *Mathematics for the mildly handicapped—A guide to curriculum and instruction.* Boston: Allyn & Bacon.

Cawley, J. F., Goodstein, H. A., Fitzmaurice, A. M., Lepore, A., Sedlak R., & Althaus, V. (1976). *Project MATH.* Tulsa, OK: Educational Development Corp.

Cawley, J. F., & Miller, J. H. (1989). Cross-sectional comparisons of the mathematical performance of children with learning disabilities: Are we on the right track toward comprehensive programming? *Journal of Learning Disabilities, 22*, 250–259.

Cawley, J. F., Miller, J. H., & School, B. A. (1987). A brief inquiry of arithmetic word-problem solving among learning disabled secondary students. *Learning Disabilities Focus, 2*, 87–93.

Chambers, D. L. (1994). The right algebra for all. *Educational Leadership, 51*(6), 85-86.

Commission on Standards for School Mathematics of the National Council of Teachers of Mathematics. (1989). *Curriculum and evaluation standards for school mathematics.* Reston, VA: National Council of Teachers of Mathematics.

Connolly, A. J. (1988). *Key Math–Revised: A Diagnostic Inventory of Essential Mathematics.* Circle Pines, MN: American Guidance Service.

DeBettencourt, L. U., Zigmond, N., & Thornton, H. (1989). Follow-up of postsecondary-age rural learning disabled graduates and dropouts. *Exceptional Children, 56,* 40–49.

Dossey, J., Mullis, I., Lindquist, M., & Chambers, D. (1988). *The mathematics report card: Are we measuring up?* Princeton, NJ: Educational Testing Service.

Dunlap, L. K., & Dunlap, G. (1989). A self-monitoring package for teaching subtraction with regrouping to students with learning disabilities. *Journal of Applied Behavior Analysis, 22,* 309–314.

Ellis, E., Deshler, D., Lenz, K., Schumaker, J., & Clark, F. (1991). An instructional model for teaching learning strategies. *Focus on Exceptional Children, 23*(6), 1–23.

Ellis, E. S., Lenz, B. K., & Sabornie, E. J. (1987a). Generalization and adaptation of learning strategies to natural environments: Part 1. Critical agents. *Remedial and Special Education, 8*(1), 6–20.

Ellis, E. S., Lenz, B. K., & Sabornie, E. J. (1987b). Generalization and adaptation of learning strategies to natural environments: Part 2. Research into practice. *Remedial and Special Education, 8*(2), 6–23.

Engelmann, S., & Carnine, D. (1982). *Theory of instruction: Principles and applications.* New York: Irvington.

Engelmann, S., Carnine, D., & Steely, D. G. (1991). Making connections in mathematics. *Journal of Learning Disabilities, 24,* 292–303.

Enright, B. E. (1983). *Enright diagnostic inventory of basic arithmetic skills.* North Billerica, MA: Curriculum Associates.

Fleischner, J. E., Nuzum, M. B., & Marzola, E. S. (1987). Devising an instructional program to teach arithmetic problem-solving skills to students with learning disabilities. *Journal of Learning Disabilities, 20,* 214–217.

Fuchs, L. S., Bahr, C. M., & Rieth, H. J. (1989). Effects of goal structures and performance contingencies on the math performance of adolescents with learning disabilities. *Journal of Learning Disabilities, 22,* 554–560.

Gardner, E. F., Rudman, H. C., Karlsen, B., & Merwin, J. C. (1982). *Stanford Achievement Test.* San Antonio, TX: Psychological Corporation.

Garnett, K. (1987). Math learning disabilities: Teaching and learners. *Reading, Writing, and Learning Disabilities, 3,* 1–8.

Gersten, R., Carnine, D., & Woodward, J. (1987). Direct instruction research: The third decade. *Remedial and Special Education, 8*(6), 48–56.

Hallahan, D. P., Kauffman, J. M., & Lloyd, J. W. (1985). *Introduction to learning disabilities* (2d ed.). Englewood Cliffs, NJ: Prentice Hall.

Heddens, J. W., & Speer, W. R. (1992). *Today's mathematics* (7th ed.). New York: Macmillan.

Hofmeister, A. M. (1993). Elitism and reform in school mathematics. *Remedial and Special Education, 14*(6), 8–13.

Hollander, S. K. (1988). Teaching learning disabled students to read mathematics. *School Science and Mathematics, 88,* 509–515.

Hughes, C. A., Ruhl, K. L., & Peterson, S. K. (1988). Teaching self-management skills. *Teaching Exceptional Children, 20*(2), 70–73.

Hughes, C. A., & Smith, J. O. (1990). Cognitive and academic performance of college students with learning disabilities: A synthesis of literature. *Learning Disability Quarterly, 13,* 66–79.

Hutchinson, N. L. (1993). Effects of cognitive strategy instruction on algebra problem solving of adolescents with learning disabilities. *Learning Disability Quarterly, 16,* 34–63.

International Association for the Evaluation of Educational Achievement. (1987). *The underachieving of curriculum: Assessing U.S. school mathematics from an international perspective.* Urbana: University of Illinois.

Jastak, S. R., & Wilkinson, G. S. (1984). *The Wide Range Achievement Test–Revised.* Wilmington, DE: Jastak Associates.

Johnson, D., & Blalock, J. (1986). *Adults with learning disabilities: Clinical studies*. Orlando, FL: Grune & Stratton.

Kameenui, E. (1991). Toward a scientific pedagogy of learning disabilities: A sameness in the message. *Journal of Learning Disabilities, 24*, 364–372.

Kameenui, E. J., & Simmons, D. C. (1990). *Designing instructional strategies: The prevention of academic learning problems*. Columbus, OH: Merrill.

Kaufman, A. S., & Kaufman, N. L. (1985). *Kaufman Test of Educational Achievement*. Circle Pines, MN: American Guidance Service.

Kelly, B., Gersten, R., & Carnine, D. (1990). Student error patterns as a function of curriculum design: Teaching fractions to remedial high school students and high school students with learning disabilities. *Journal of Learning Disabilities, 1*, 23–29.

Kirby, J. R., & Becker, L. D. (1988). Cognitive components of learning problems in arithmetic. *Remedial and Special Education, 9*(5), 7–16.

Kline, F. M., Schumaker, J. B., & Deshler, D. D. (1991). Development and validation of feedback routines for instructing students with learning disabilities. *Learning Disability Quarterly, 14*, 191–207.

Kneedler, R. D., & Hallahan, D. P. (1981). Self-monitoring of on-task behavior with learning disabled children: Current studies and directions. *Exceptional Education Quarterly, 1*, 73–82.

Koppitz, E. M. (1971). *Children with learning disabilities: A five year follow-up study*. New York: Grune & Stratton.

Lee, W. M., & Hudson, F. G. (1981). *A comparison of verbal problem-solving in arithmetic of learning disabled and non-learning disabled seventh grade males* (Research Report No. 43). Lawrence: University of Kansas, Institute for Research in Learning Disabilities.

Lerner, J. (1993). *Learning disabilities: Theories, diagnosis, and teaching strategies* (6th ed). Boston: Houghton Mifflin.

Locke, E. A., & Latham, G. P. (1990). *A theory of goal setting and task performance*. Englewood Cliffs, NJ: Prentice Hall.

McKinney, J. D., & Feagans, L. (1980). *Learning disabilities in the classroom* (Final project report). Chapel Hill: University of North Carolina, Frank Porter Graham Child Development Center.

McLeod, T. M., & Armstrong, S. W. (1982). Learning disabilities in mathematics skill deficits and remedial approaches at the intermediate and secondary level. *Learning Disability Quarterly, 5*, 305–311.

Markwardt, F. C. (1989). *Peabody Individual Achievement Test–Revised*. Circle Pines, MN: American Guidance Service.

Marshall, G. (1990, July). A changing world requires changes in math instruction. *Executive Educator*, pp. 23–24.

Masters, L. F., Mori, B. A., Mori, A. A. (1993). *Teaching secondary students with mild learning and behavior problems*. Austin, TX: Pro-Ed.

Mastropieri, M. A., & Scruggs, T. E. (1989). Constructing more meaningful relationships: Mnemonic instruction for special populations. *Educational Psychology Review, 1*, 83–111.

Mastropieri, M. A., Scruggs, T. E., & Shiah, S. (1991). Mathematics instruction for learning disabled students: A review of research. *Learning Disabilities Research & Practice, 6*, 89–98.

Mattingly, J. C., & Bott, D. A. (1990). Teaching multiplication facts to students with learning problems. *Exceptional Children, 56*, 438–449.

Meiring, S. (1980). *Problem solving...A basic mathematics goal: 1. Becoming a better problem solver, 2. A resource for problem solving*. Columbus: Ohio Department of Education.

Mellard, D., & Alley, G. (1981). *Production deficiency vs. processing dysfunction: An experimental assessment of LD adolescents* (Research Paper No. 40). Lawrence: University of Kansas Institute for Research in Learning Disabilities.

Mercer, C. D. (1991). *Students with learning disabilities*. New York: Merrill.

Mercer, C. D., Harris, C., & Miller, S. P. (1993). Reforming reforms in mathematics. *Remedial and Special Education, 14*(6), 14–19.

Mercer, C. D., & Miller, S. P. (1992a). *Multiplication facts 0–81*. Lawrence, KS: Edge Enterprises.

Mercer, C. D., & Miller, S. P. (1992b). Teaching students with learning problems in math to acquire, understand, and apply basic math facts. *Remedial and Special Education, 13*(3), 19–35, 61.

Mercer, C. D., & Miller, S. P. (1993). *Division facts 0–81*. Lawrence, KS: Edge Enterprises.

Miller, K. (1983). *An analysis of the performance of LD students on the Kansas Minimal Competency Test.* Unpublished doctoral dissertation, University of Kansas, Lawrence.

Miller, S. P., & Mercer, C. D. (1991a). *Addition facts 0–9.* Lawrence, KS: Edge Enterprises.

Miller, S. P., & Mercer, C. D. (1991b). *Subtraction facts 0–9.* Lawrence, KS: Edge Enterprises.

Miller, S. P., & Mercer, C. D. (1993a). Using a graduated word problem sequence to promote problem-solving skills. *Learning Disabilities Research & Practice, 8,* 169–174.

Miller, S. P., & Mercer, C. D. (1993b). Using mnemonics to enhance the math performance of students with learning difficulties. *Intervention in School and Clinic, 29,* 78–82.

Miller, S. P., Mercer, C. D., & Dillon, A. S. (1992). CSA: Acquiring and retaining math skills. *Intervention in School and Clinic, 28,* 105–110.

Montague, M. (1988). Strategy instruction and mathematical problem solving. *Reading, Writing, and Learning Disabilities, 4,* 275–290.

Montague, M., Applegate, B., & Marquard, K. (1993). Cognitive strategy instruction and mathematical problem-solving performance of students with learning disabilities. *Learning Disabilities Research & Practice, 8,* 223–232.

Montague, M., & Bos, C. S. (1986a). The effect of cognitive strategy training on verbal math problem solving performance of learning disabled adolescents. *Journal of Learning Disabilities, 19*(1), 26–31.

Montague, M., & Bos, C., S. (1986b). Verbal mathematical problem solving and learning disabilities: A review. *Focus on Learning Problems in Mathematics, 8*(2), 7–21.

National Council of Supervisors of Mathematics. (1988). *Twelve components of essential mathematics.* Minneapolis: Author.

National Council of Teachers of Mathematics. (1989). *Curriculum and evaluation standards for school mathematics.* Reston, VA: Author.

Peck, D. M., & Jencks, S. M. (1981). Conceptual issues in the teaching and learning of fractions. *Journal of Research on Mathematics Education, 12*(15), 339–348.

Peterson, S. K., Mercer, C. D., & O'Shea, L. (1988). Teaching learning disabled students place value using the concrete to abstract sequence. *Learning Disabilities Research, 4*(1), 52–56.

Pieper, E., & Deshler, D. (1985). Intervention consideration in mathematics for the LD adolescent. *Focus on Learning Problems in Mathematics, 7*(1), 35–47.

Polloway, E. A., & Patton, J. R. (1993). *Strategies for teaching learners with special needs* (5th ed). New York: Merrill.

Prescott, G. A., Balow, I. H., Hogan, T. P., & Farr, R. (1984). *Metropolitan Achievement Tests.* San Antonio, TX: Psychological Corp.

Pressley, M., Levin, J., & Delaney, H. D. (1982). The mnemonic keyword method. *Review of Educational Research, 52,* 61–91.

Reisman, F. K. (1982). *A guide to the diagnostic teaching of arithmetic* (3d ed.). Columbus, OH: Merrill.

Resnick, L. (1989). Developing mathematical knowledge. *American Psychologist, 44,* 162–169.

Resnick, L., & Resnick, D. (1985). Standards, curriculum and performance: A historical perspective. *Educational Researcher, 14,* 5–20.

Rivera, D. M. (1993). Examining mathematics reform and the implications for students with mathematics disabilities. *Remedial and Special Education, 14*(6), 24–27.

Rivera, D. M., & Bryant, B. R. (1992). Mathematics instruction for students with special needs. *Intervention in School and Clinic, 28,* 71–86.

Robinson, S. L., DePascale, C., & Roberts, F. C. (1989). Computer-delivered feedback in group-based instruction: Effects for learning disabled students in mathematics. *Learning Disabilities Focus, 5*(1), 28–35.

Scheid, K. (1990). *Cognitive-based methods for teaching mathematics to students with learning problems.* Columbus, OH: LINC Resources.

Schumaker, J. B., & Deshler, D. D. (1984). Setting demand variables: A major factor in program planning for the LD adolescent. *Topics in Language Disorders, 4*(2), 22–40.

Schunk, D. H. (1985). Participation in goal setting: Effects on self-efficacy and skills of learning disabled children. *Journal of Special Education, 19,* 307–317.

Scruggs, T. E., & Mastropieri, M. A. (1989). Mnemonic instruction of learning disabled students: A field-based investigation. *Learning Disability Quarterly, 12,* 119–125.

Scruggs, T. E., & Mastropieri, M. A. (1990). Mnemonic instruction for students with learning disabilities: What it is and what it does. *Learning Disability Quarterly, 13*, 271–280.

Shapiro, E. S. (1989). Teaching self-management skills to learning disabled adolescents. *Learning Disability Quarterly, 12*, 275–287.

Silbert, J., & Carnine, D. (1990a). *Effective instruction in mathematics—The role of basal programs: A case study of fifth-grade fractions.* Unpublished manuscript, University of Oregon, Center for the Study of Improving Math Instruction, Eugene.

Silbert, J., & Carnine, D. (1990b). *The mathematics curriculum—Standards, textbooks, and pedagogy: A case study of fifth-grade division.* Unpublished manuscript, University of Oregon, Center for the Study of Improving Math Instruction, Eugene.

Sitlington, P. L., & Frank, A. R. (1990). Are adolescents with learning disabilities successfully crossing the bridge into adult life? *Learning Disability Quarterly, 13*, 97–111.

Slavin, R. (1991). *Educational psychology.* Englewood Cliffs, NJ: Prentice Hall.

Sutton, G. O. (1992). Cooperative learning works in mathematics. *Mathematics Teacher, 85*(1), 63–66.

Thornton, C. A., & Toohey, M. A. (1985). Basic math facts: Guidelines for teaching and learning. *Learning Disabilities Focus, 1*(1), 44–57.

Tilley, W., Cox, L. S., & Stayrook, N. (1986, Jan.). *An extended school year validation study* (Management Information Paper, Report No. 86-2). Seattle: Seattle Public Schools.

Tindal, G. A., & Marston, D. B. (1990). *Classroom-based assessment.* New York: Merrill.

Torgesen, J. (1982). The learning disabled child as an inactive learner: Educational implications. *Topics in Learning and Learning Disabilities, 2*, 45–52.

Underhill, R. G., Uprichard, A. E., & Heddens, J. W. (1980). *Diagnosing mathematical difficulties.* Columbus, OH: Merrill.

Wallace, G., & Kauffman, J. M. (1986). *Teaching children with learning and behavior problems.* New York: Merrill/Macmillan.

Warner, M., Alley, G., Schumaker, J., Deshler, D., & Clark, F. (1980). *An epidemiological study of learning disabled adolescents in secondary schools: Achievement and ability, socioeconomic status and school experiences* (Report No. 13). Lawrence: University of Kansas Institute for Research in Learning Disabilities.

Watanabe, A. (1991). *The effects of a mathematical word problem solving strategy: Own problem solving performance by middle school students with mild disabilities.* Unpublished doctoral dissertation, University of Florida, Gainesville.

White, W. J., Schumaker, J. B., Warner, M. M., Alley, G. R., & Deshler, D. D. (1980). *The current status of young adults identified as learning disabled during their school career* (Research Report No. 21). Lawrence: University of Kansas Institute for Research in Learning Disabilities.

Woodcock, R. W., & Johnson, M. B. (1989). *Woodcock-Johnson Psycho-Educational Battery–Revised.* Allen, TX: DLM.

Woodward, J. (1991). Procedural knowledge in mathematics: The role of the curriculum. *Journal of Learning Disabilities, 24*, 242–251.

Social Skills Strategy Instruction

DAVID SCANLON

QUESTIONS TO KEEP IN MIND

- When are a student's social skills a "problem?"

- Are students with learning disabilities more or less likely than their peers to have social skills problems? Why?

- What do learning disabilities have to do with problems with social skills?

- When I sense that a student is having a social skills problem, how can I be sure?

- How can I narrow down the problem so I can plan the most appropriate intervention?

- If a social skills problem is present, how should I intervene?

- What factors can contribute to social skills problems, and how can I address them?

ADVANCE ORGANIZER

When considering the strengths and weaknesses of adolescents with learning disabilities, areas that come to mind probably include reading proficiency, organizational skills, and cognitive processing. For some, however, we immediately think of their social awkwardness or inappropriateness. Students with LD sometimes stand out because they are so different from the others. They may have trouble making friends, not participate in discussions, speak in belligerent tones, be overly trusting, or generally act immature. These are the students who often have difficulty getting along with others and who may have trouble learning because their poor social skills get in the way.

The social skills of some adolescents with LD are detrimental to their full and successful participation in school, work, social circles, and family. How they interact socially during adolescence also has implications for their lives throughout adulthood. Research indicates that, though adolescents with LD generally interact* in ways that appear similar to their noneducationally disabled peers, they tend to be less adept at many social skills (e.g., Bell, Feraios, & Bryan, 1991; Oliva & La Greca, 1988). The peers that adolescents with LD resemble most closely socially are those who are at-risk academically and low-achieving (Deshler & Schumaker, 1983).

As students with LD become more involved in the mainstream, the challenge of interacting in socially appropriate ways becomes more complex. The mainstream presents new and varied settings with new social expectations. The demands as to how students with LD learn appropriate social skills also change. They are expected to be more independent in making social decisions. Also, peers in the mainstream may be less tolerant of inappropriate behavior than resource room peers. Whether faced with new challenges in the mainstream or not, one thing remains certain: Some adolescents with LD need help with their social skills.

INTRODUCTION

Success in school, on the job, and in other aspects of daily living depends on knowledge and skills related to completing tasks. Social skills knowledge is just as important as content knowledge and skills in getting along, learning, and completing tasks. Nevertheless, social skills are a commonly overlooked aspect of adolescents' success in school and daily living. IEP objectives and day-to-day priorities tend to be directed at academic outcomes. Appropriate social skills, however, are essential to students' motivation and ability to learn academic content and the process of learning (Wentzel, 1991).

Most adolescents have rough moments in terms of social interactions. For example, many are openly moody, use inappropriate language, and fight and rebel against adults. These adolescents are not necessarily considered to have serious social problems. Although their teachers and parents/guardians may get a few gray hairs, even adolescents

---

* Throughout this chapter references to how a student "interacts" are intended to include when a student appears *not* to interact (e.g., remaining silent when asked a question).

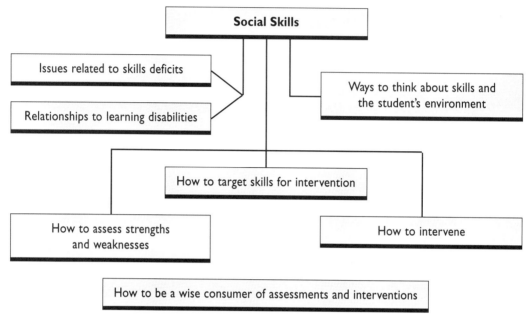

FIGURE 8.1   CHAPTER 8 ORGANIZATION

who are no strangers to trouble because of the ways they interact usually mature into adults with acceptable social skills.

Some adolescents, however, have social problems that interfere with their learning, and eventual quality of life. These students need to learn how to interact in more socially appropriate ways.

The organization of discussion in this chapter is shown in Figure 8.1.

THE IMPORTANCE OF SOCIAL SKILLS

The following scenario illustrates the importance of social skills.

Ms. Santos approaches a group of her science students who seem to be having trouble setting up their experiment. She says to one student "Althea, I know you know how to set this up correctly, I've watched you do it before. You need to help your group. Show the others how to do it."

As Ms. Santos walks away, Juanita grabs the rubber hose and clamp and says to Althea, "Keep your mouth shut, you kiss-up. I can do this. You'd probably blow us all up. Wouldn't she?"

Warren, who considers Althea to be one of his best friends, nervously agrees with Juanita. He tries to help Juanita figure out the experiment, doing his best not to even look at Althea. Althea's response is to sit silently and watch Juanita and Warren work.

In this situation all three students have used poor social skills. Clearly, Juanita has not been helpful to the other members of the group, nor has she accepted that they could be helpful. She may have wanted to figure out the lab herself or assumed that Althea and Warren were incapable of setting it up. Regardless of the reason, she inappropriately "negotiated" trying to do it herself. Degrading Althea and enlisting Warren was an uncalled-for response to the situation.

The scenario does not tell us how Warren felt about Juanita, but we do know that he and Althea are friends. Warren chose a path that was unsupportive of his friend. Appearing to be so fickle probably did not win him many good graces from Juanita either. Warren made poor decisions about friendship interactions and about participating as a member of a group. One could argue that he wisely prevented himself from suffering harsh treatment from Juanita. Although there may be some truth to that, his method resulted in other social problems. He actually seemed to be more of a "kiss-up" than Althea.

Finally, poor Althea, who could have responded in worse ways, did little to help her situation. She could have offered assistance to Juanita, spoken up to Juanita without stooping to her style of communication, and offered support to Warren that would encourage him to not abandon their friendship.

Any teacher with even 1 or 2 years of experience will report that plenty of students interact like Althea, Juanita, and Warren. Now imagine the consequences of these types of interactions in other settings such as when socializing with friends, interacting with family, in a potential problem situation with authorities, or in response to an employer's requests. That is how important social skills are in and out of school.

Poor social skills in school can be related to the following factors.

1. Limited opportunities to learn
2. Negative academic and social self-concept
3. Social isolation

For example, a student's not knowing how to ask for help in an appropriate way can lead to not asking a question at all or asking it in ways that lead the teacher and the student's peers to respond to how the question was asked instead of the content of the question. Poor social skills also can negatively color how others view the student. Teachers may find themselves spending more effort trying to "control" students with poor social skills than teaching those students (e.g., Juanita in the vignette). Results of studies involving school children with LD and their teachers have demonstrated that, although teachers interact with students with LD approximately as often as with other students, the interactions are more likely to be related to behavior management than to academic content (Bryan & Wheeler, 1972; Dorval, McKinney, & Feagans, 1982). Peers are less likely to risk working on an important project with someone who is uncooperative or with whom they find getting along difficult, and students seldom elect to interact with someone who is socially unpopular. Thus, the benefits of sharing one's own knowledge and learning from others are diminished for adolescents with poor social skills.

Students who have difficulty interacting in acceptable ways also are at-risk for developing a negative academic self-concept. As a result of negative social interaction in the classroom, students may develop self-fulfilling prophecies of social incompatibility and academic mediocrity (Mehring & Colson, 1990). For example, if Juanita routinely responds to requests for information in belligerent tones, she will not be tapped to share what she knows very often. If she is unaware of the effects of her behavior, she may perceive others' resistance to call on her as a sign that she has "dumb ideas." At a minimum, if she does not share her ideas, she will have little reason to develop faith in them (nor will she develop the skills to express them effectively).

Poor social skills also can contribute to being a social outcast. Appropriate socialization is tricky during adolescence, when students are establishing their own identity and making a transition into adulthood. Adolescents must deal with adult issues concerning their independence, responsibility, physical and sexual development, and changing societal pressures and expectations. During adolescence students undergo changes in social norms. The methods of social interaction to which they have been accustomed may no longer apply. For example, before adolescence, many children separate themselves by gender. By adolescence, students are expected to interact maturely with students of both genders in academic and social contexts.

In addition to changes in social norms over time, social norms also change with contexts. Sometimes what constitutes acceptable social behavior is context-specific. For example, adolescents are known to use every four-letter name in the book to address their friends in the cafeteria or hallways. When they are together in the classroom or at one another's homes, however, the norms must change. Students who navigate delicate context norms incorrectly may fall out of favor with others because they act counter to what is socially acceptable.

SOCIAL SKILLS AND THE ADOLESCENT WITH LEARNING DISABILITIES

Not all adolescents with poor social skills have a learning disability, nor do all adolescents with LD have poor social skills. Still, for some, social skills are a serious problem. Tanis Bryan and her colleagues are among those who have made major contributions to our knowledge of students with LD and their social interactions. Among the findings of their nearly two decades of research (primarily with children and early adolescents) are that students with LD often are poor at constructive communication. For example, they may have trouble asking questions and soliciting information needed to complete tasks; they also may have difficulty dissenting from others' opinions (Bryan, Donahue, & Pearl, 1981; Bryan & Pflaum, 1978; Bryan, Wheeler, Felcan, & Henek, 1976).

These same students may have difficulty interpreting social cues and judging their role in social situations properly. For example, 7th- and 8th-grade students with LD were found to be less likely than their nondisabled peers to recognize when characters in a story were making deceptive statements, even when they knew the statements to be false (Pearl, Bryan, Fallon, & Herzog, 1991). These students stand a good chance of being taken advantage of. In simple terms, they often lack good judgment. Responding to a survey on attitudes and knowledge about AIDS, high school students with LD were approximately as knowledgeable as their peers, but these same students reported they were less likely to assert control over personal behaviors they knew could lead to transmission of the HIV virus (Bell et al., 1991). In this instance, limited social skills literally could be fatal for the student and others with whom he or she has contact.

Interestingly, a student's failure to perform a certain social skill or apparent lack of social awareness is not always an indication of his or her not knowing what to do. True to the nature of some individuals with LD, a student may know how to perform a specific skill but choose not to. One of the factors that sometimes distinguishes a student with LD is poor decision making. This lack of sound judgment about what is best to do, or seeming inertia, indicates where social skills intervention is needed for the student.

In some instances the student not only can perform the skill well but also is well aware of when, how, and why to perform it (i.e., has all the information necessary to make a sound decision). For this student intervention has to center on the significance of performing the skill and strategies for actually performing it. This may include helping the student appreciate the active role he or she can take in daily interactions.

The poor social skills of adolescents with LD rarely are overlooked by those who interact with them. For example, Bryan et al. (1981) found that students with LD who used phrasing, tone, and gestures that other students with LD perceived as inappropriate were ignored more often than other participants in group activities. Bursuck (1989) asked peers and teachers of elementary mainstream classroom students with LD to rate the social status and interactions of students with LD. Peers and teachers both rated the students with LD as practicing more negative behaviors and fewer prosocial interactions than other students. Fewer friendships, peers being less willing to work with them on academic tasks, and teachers perceiving them as less desirable members of the class are all consequences of poor social skills for students with LD (Vaughn, 1985).

Given the need these students have for support to overcome their social difficulties and their areas of learning disability, low social status is particularly harmful. At a minimum these students would benefit from greater tolerance when they act inappropriately. Certainly they would benefit even more if they also were empowered by learning how to use appropriate social skills.

Many students with LD face the related problems of not being good at recognizing the appropriate social norms for a specific context and lacking the ability to select appropriate social skills for a given context. These are things their noneducationally disabled peers typically do better. For example, Oliva and La Greca (1988) asked 11- and 13-year-old boys to report their strategies and goals for responding to several social situations (e.g., what to do during free time on the first day at a new school). The students with LD generated goal responses that were less sophisticated than their nonLD peers. Their strategies, however, were more similar to those of their peers.

Pearl and Bryan (1994) asked adolescents with LD to explain how they would act if they were caught during several hypothetical misconduct situations. The adolescents with LD were more likely than nondisabled adolescents to suggest escaping as a response to being caught in inappropriate conduct.

Because many adolescents with LD fail to monitor and control their interactions appropriately in different situations, they are less likely than others to sense a social problem. Consequently, they will continue to interact inappropriately, even after others begin to avoid them or respond to them in other negative ways. If adolescents with LD do not recognize that they have a problem with their interactions, they likely will repeat their inappropriate interactions in the future. Interventions to improve the social skills of adolescents with LD and others' perceptions of them are necessary.

If a seemingly minor social skills problem (e.g., not selecting skills appropriate for a given context) goes unchecked long enough, the consequences can be anything but minor. We know already that peers and teachers may develop low opinions of the student, that the student may develop a low-concept, and that low regard in turn can lead to limited opportunities to interact and learn. When denied the skills and opportunities to interact more appropriately, socially inappropriate adolescents may become adults with the same social skills problems.

Assuming that one or two social problems are not important enough to warrant intervention can result in the adolescent continuing those inappropriate behaviors the rest of his or her life. Likewise, the teacher should not assume that peer pressure or a few negative consequences will spur the student to change. After all, he or she has made it to adolescence without learning how to do some things other adolescents have.

Indirect relationships may be present between social skills deficits and school failure, adolescent delinquency, and adult misconduct. In many instances disciplinary problems in school and the community are linked to inappropriate social interactions. In a study of 589 secondary school students with LD, Wagner (1990) found that those who had disciplinary problems, such as being suspended, fired, or arrested, were 16% more likely to receive one or more failing grades than those without disciplinary problems. Adolescents with LD are far more likely than their nondisabled peers to drop out of school (Wagner, 1990). Of the adolescents with LD who dropped out of school, 22% had disciplinary problems while in school (Wagner, 1991). Students with LD who dropped out perceive themselves as having had lower status among their peers than do students with LD who completed school (Seidel & Vaughn, 1991).

Although some school dropouts have higher self-esteem and sense of personal control once they are out of school (Wehlage & Rutter, 1986) and are economically and socially stable, the disadvantages of dropping out outweigh the advantages far more often. Typically, school dropouts have lower academic skills than school completors (Alexander, Natriello, & Pallas, 1985), which impairs their competitive worth in the job force and their quality of living. These individuals are twice as likely to be unemployed or earning as much as 12% to 18% less than those who complete high school (Levin, 1972; U.S. Bureau of the Census, 1983). Estimates as to how many individuals incarcerated in the United States have a learning handicap range from 28% (Rutherford, Nelson, & Wolford, 1985) to 42% (Morgan, 1979).

These figures do not mean that all adolescents with LD and social skills problems are likely to fail to complete school or to run afoul of the law. We do not know what percentage of all adolescents or adults with LD these figures represent. They may in fact be a small proportion of these populations. Adolescents with LD are no more likely to get in trouble with authorities than any other group of adolescents. Once in trouble, however, they are less likely than their peers to get themselves out of it. Students with LD have been found to be less competent than low-achieving and average-achieving peers at interpreting social situations and generating and selecting appropriate responses (Tur-Kaspa & Bryan, 1994).

Think of students who, when caught with marijuana or alcohol, try to bluff their way out of it, or when caught as part of a group, focus their efforts on protecting the others while unduly incriminating themselves. Ineffective handling of such situations can heighten the severity of the consequences. This is the link between social skills and school failure, delinquency, and adult misconduct. Failure to select and enact appropriate social skills in a given situation can mushroom into suspension, adjudication, decreased mental health, and so on. Therefore, even more so than for peers with more appropriate social judgment and skills, the poor social skills of adolescents with LD can contribute to lifelong negative consequences.

Although not all students with LD experience the same social skills strengths and weaknesses in the same ways, the following summarizes the spectrum of possibilities:

1. No social skills problems
2. Poor constructive communication skills in:
   a. asking questions
   b. offering opinions
   c. interpreting social cues
   d. judging social roles
   e. deciding how to interact
3. Negative consequences:
   a. ignored by others
   b. judged to be less desirable
   c. limited opportunities to learn new ways to interact
   d. inappropriate social decisions
   e. undesirable quality of living

RELATIONSHIP BETWEEN LEARNING DISABILITIES AND SOCIAL SKILLS

The social skills of adolescents with LD may be no better or worse than those of any other adolescent. Still, the social skills of some may contribute to or compound their learning disability. To understand fully the issues related to students with LD and social skills, consider the definition of learning disabilities. The federal definition accompanying the Education for All Handicapped Children Act of 1975, and its reauthorization as the Individuals with Disabilities in Education Act, makes no mention of social skills. Instead, the definition cites an imperfect ability to carry out specific psychological processes necessary for learning.

In 1981 the National Joint Committee on Learning Disabilities (NJCLD) (which included representatives of learning disabilities, communication disorders, and literacy advocacy groups) suggested that learning disabilities may "occur concomitantly with other handicapping conditions (e.g., ... social ... disturbance)" (Hammill, Leigh, McNutt,

& Larsen, 1981, p. 336). The NJCLD, however, did not intend this definition to include social skills as a criteria (Hammill, 1990). In 1987 the Interagency Committee on Learning Disabilities (composed of representatives from the Department of Health and Human Services and Department of Education) proposed a modified definition of learning disabilities. The Committee recommended that social skills deficits and peer rejection be included in the criteria for defining LD. Both of these alternative definitions sought recognition of the relationship between social skills and learning and the commonalty of poor social skills and peer rejection for students with LD.

Sometimes the relationship between learning and social skills is fairly obvious. For example, some students' acting-out behaviors are dramatic enough to lead to their being suspended from school. For many more students, however, acting out in class is just enough to keep them off-task, which means that they do not benefit from the lesson. The relationship of social skills and learning also can be less obvious. Recall that poor social skills can lead to a negative self-image and a negative view of the individual by others. Because of the negative image, others (students and teachers alike) may limit their interactions with the student, and the student may consider himself or herself as less intelligent. The end result is limited opportunities for the student to interact and learn.

Opponents of including social skills deficits and peer rejection in the definition of learning disabilities do not discount the evidence that some students with LD have inappropriate skills and experience rejection. Rather, these opponents believe that when they occur with individuals with LD, they are either coincidental to or a byproduct of the learning disability and are not a primary deficit. Coleman and Minnett (1993) offered two supporting rationales for this interpretation.

1. The social status of students with LD is comparable to that of students without LD. Students in both populations range from those who act in socially appropriate ways and enjoy peer acceptance to those who do not. Some students with LD are among the most socially appropriate students in your school.
2. A causal link between social skills and learning disabilities has not been established. Instead, low academic achievement, regardless of educational disability, is consistent with low social status. As we know, not all students with LD are poor achievers, and those who are may not be poor achievers across all areas of the curriculum.

Coleman and Minnett further suggested that the varied nature of the social skill deficits of students with LD does not differ from those of their noneducationally disabled peers with low social status. Although these are accurate characterizations of students with LD, many students with LD and others with low social status (typically at-risk and low-achieving students) are significantly different in how they learn and manage their social skills. Three distinctions highlight the relationship between learning disabilities and social skills. *First*, students with LD do not fully share the experiences of their mainstream peers. Many students with LD receive at least part of their education in pull-out programs or unique instructional situations within the regular classroom (e.g., being given less responsibility when studying along with their nondisabled peers, receiving individual attention from a paraprofessional). Thus, they have fewer opportunities to interact with and learn the social norms of regular education teachers and peers (e.g., Allington & McGill-Franzen, 1989).

Second, the learning needs of students with LD are distinct from those of their peers. Given competing demands on teachers, such as increasing the amount of content to cover (Wiggins, 1989) and expectations for improved student performance, providing the instructional support that students with LD require to learn the same skills as their mainstream classroom peers is a challenge. This type of instructional support may mean students learning an entire process in incremental stages, taking a longer time to achieve mastery, or using different modalities to respond. (The dilemma of needing special attention and suffering from special attention is a two-edged sword. Intelligently developed IEPs seem to be the best response.)

Third, students with LD differ from their peers by not self-monitoring their performance without being cued to do so, not readily altering their behaviors based on self-monitoring or cueing from others (such as the teacher), and having fewer alternative skills in their repertoire than average achieving peers (Torgesen, 1982; Wansart, 1990; Wong, 1980). The consequences of poor social skills can be severe for many students with LD. Thus, regardless of whether poor social skills belongs in the definition of LD, the predicament for students with LD who do have inappropriate social skills and suffer peer rejection may be worse than for their nondisabled peers.

ADDRESSING THE SOCIAL SKILLS NEEDS OF ADOLESCENTS WITH LD

Addressing the social skills needs of adolescents with LD (or any student) involves three stages: (a) assessing students' current social skills status, (b) targeting social skills to be encouraged, improved, or discouraged, and (c) implementing and evaluating an appropriate social skills intervention. These stages, depicted graphically in Figure 8.2, will be discussed in the remainder of this chapter.

ASSESSING SOCIAL SKILLS

Three methods are used commonly to assess social skills. All three are known as *sociometric measures*, or assessments of social interaction or status in a social group. Two of the methods—social skills ratings and social status nominations—may be completed while reflecting on the target student. The third method is direct observation of social interactions, which can include self-reports by students. These methods are shown in Figure 8.2.

SOCIAL SKILLS RATINGS

Using social skills ratings, teachers, peers, and others rate a targeted student's performance of skills associated with friendliness, ability to get along, general classroom skills, and the like. The scores on a rating scale indicate how well or poorly a student is performing the specific skills. Typically, a rating scale consists of a list of several social skills on which the rater will evaluate the targeted student. Using the scale, the rater

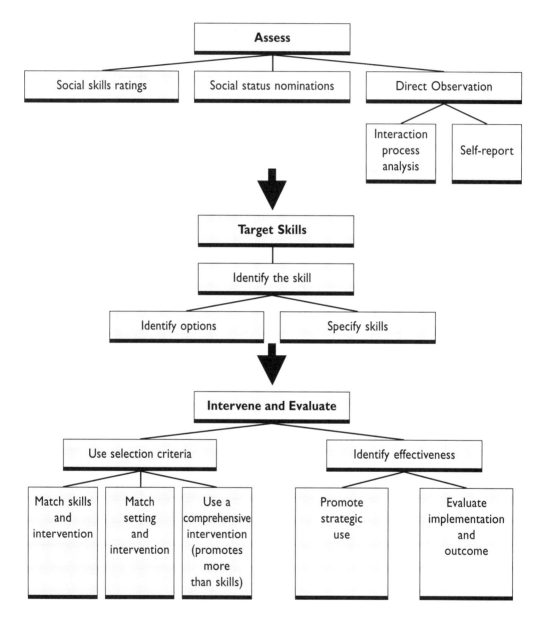

FIGURE 8.2   STAGES OF SOCIAL SKILLS INTERVENTIONS

assigns a score to how well the student performs (or resists performing) each skill. Scores the rater assigns are similar to grades. Common score ranges are: +, −; A, B, C, D, F; and 1-*not done*, 2-*poor*, 3-*strong*, 4-*excellent*. With ranges much broader than five, the significance of a difference between two scores is hard to distinguish (e.g., 6 versus 7 on a scale of 1 to 8).

Typically, each skill on a rating scale is scored individually. The score assigned for the performance of any one skill does not depend on the performance of any other skill. (If the score for one skill were to depend on how well the student performed the others, this would be a *ranking* of how well the student performed those skills. Usually we are concerned with how well the student performs certain skills, so a score showing how well these skills are done makes more sense than a score comparing one skill to another.)

Once the skills in question have been rated independent of each other, the teacher may want to compare the scores to help plan interventions. Over time the rating scale may be completed again, to chart whether the student is or is not progressing. A simplified version of a rating scale is a checklist.

Depending on the scale the teacher selects or creates, the skills may reflect social skills in general or those for a specific context. The Social Skills Rating System (SSRS) (Gresham & Elliott, 1991) is an example of a rating scale that can be used to assess similar social skills at school and home. Using this rating system, different raters score how well the student performs similar skills at school, at home, and in the community. Several rating scales and checklists appropriate for students with LD are:

- *Manual for the Child Behavior Checklist and Revised Child Behavior Profile*, by T. M. Achenback and C. S. Edelbrock (City, VT: Queen City Printers, 1983).
- *School Social Skills Rating Scale (S³ Rating Scale)* by L. Brown, D. Black, and J. Downs (East Aurora, NY: Slosson Educational Publishers, 1984).
- *Social Skills Rating System (SSRS)*, by F. M. Gresham and S. N. Elliott (Circle Pines, MN: American Guidance Service, 1991).
- *The Walker-McConnell Scale of Social Competence and School Adjustment,* by H. M. Walker and S. R. McConnell (Austin, TX: Pro-Ed, 1988).

Much of the research on the social status of students with LD uses social skills rating scales. Rating scales can provide a relative index of how any one social skill compares to others. By analyzing rating scales, teachers are able to identify specific social skills to target for intervention.

Ms. Santos thought Althea was not socializing enough with her peers during free time. The teacher used a social skills rating scale to evaluate Althea in three contexts: (a) when the whole classroom was involved in teacher-mediated discussions, (b) during small-group work in her class, and (c) when Althea and other students seated at the same cafeteria table were socializing during a study period (the situation that had sparked her interest). Because she was concerned with how often Althea participated as well as the quality of her participation, Ms. Santos used a rating scale that assessed Althea's (a) initiating and (b) responding to others' contributions, and (c) whether her contributions were well received or not. She completed the scale while observing Althea.

As might be expected, Ms. Santos found that Althea interacted differently in the three settings. As she had suspected, Althea seldom initiated contributions or responded to others in the cafeteria setting. Her contributions, however, were received similarly to how they were in the other two settings. Ms. Santos now was confident that Althea was not interacting in social situations with peers the same way she was in the other two contexts. Ms. Santos knew that she now had to figure out why this was the case and what, if anything, she should help Althea do about it.

SOCIAL STATUS NOMINATIONS

Nomination devices are used to identify the targeted student's social status. The targeted student is "nominated," or ranked, in comparison to others on social standing or use of social skills. Often nomination devices are used to gauge how well a student is liked compared to others. For example, students may nominate peers with whom they do and do not like to socialize. Teachers may nominate students they most and least like to have in their class. Nominators may be asked to identify approximately three students with whom they would most and least like to work or socialize, or who perform certain skills well or poorly. (Particularly in the elementary grades, students' choices may be limited to same-gender peers.) Figure 8.3 presents a sample nomination device.

An advantage of status nominations is that they identify the perceptions others hold of the student with LD in comparison to other students in the same setting. Using nominations, however, has three potential drawbacks.

Directions:

The following is a list of all students in your 3rd-period class. Please identify the three who are willing to volunteer most often to help classmates complete assignments. Then identify the three who are never willing to (or if all volunteer sometime, the three who are least likely to) volunteer to help classmates. If more than three students never volunteer, identify only those three you think are least willing to do so.

William B.	Tammy G.	Roger S.
Sandra B.	Buddy H.	Peter S.
Emillia C.	Janice J.	Jamaica T.
Roger D.	Jerry M.	Felicia T.
Caesar D.	Grace P.	Willie W.
Fred F.	Ruth R.	Sue Z.
Mark G.	Mary Ellen R.	

3 who volunteer most often

_____   _____   _____

3 who volunteer least often

_____   _____   _____

FIGURE 8.3   SAMPLE SOCIAL STATUS NOMINATION DEVICE (FOR TEACHERS)

1. Nominators may overlook a student simply because they do not think of him or her when completing the device. This problem can be avoided by providing a list of all students eligible for nomination.
2. Not being nominated as among either the top or bottom three leaves the teacher with no indication of the social standing of many students.
3. Nomination devices that ask for a ranking of all students tend to be completed arbitrarily unless the pool of nominees is small.

Try to rank your own friends according to their compatibility with you. Aside from one or two who are truly special friends and a few you barely tolerate, ranking the rest probably is difficult for you. In addition to these potential drawbacks, many parents/guardians and educators are concerned about the ethical and educational implications of asking students to nominate their peers. Completing a nomination form may cause students to contemplate their peers in ways they had not before. The consequences can include changed friendship and interaction patterns based on perceptions of status. The students rated as highly popular or rejected can suffer as a result of their peers' changed friendships and interactions. They can gain false friends or become socially isolated. Although we all separate ourselves into various social groupings, most parents/guardians do not want teachers to sanction their children's rank-ordering friendships.

Teachers and educational researchers concerned with social skills often use skill rating and status nomination devices they develop themselves. Developing nomination devices is particularly common because they seem to be such an easy thing to create. Teachers who develop their own devices should follow some simple guidelines.

1. *Closely follow the format of previously developed materials.*

There is little sense in "throwing out the baby with the bath water." If you know of assessments that work but, for whatever reason, do not want to use them, start from the framework of what made them successful. If the directions were particularly clear, word your directions similarly. If the ways in which skills were named made them obvious immediately to everyone using the assessment, use the same wordings whenever you can. Pay attention to factors such as how much space was allotted for writing and the overall layout on the page.

2. *Be precise.*

Precise assessment devices can avoid a lot of confusion and increase the value of the outcomes. Directions should be clear. Conceivably, your instructions could be asking for one thing and interpreted to mean another by those using the device. For example, if you ask students to nominate who they "most like to work with in a group," they may respond in terms of who is most fun instead of who is most helpful in the group. Also, asking teachers to rate how often Juanita uses polite language is not a good way to find out if she swears too much. You would be better off asking other teachers to rate how often she swears.

3. *Repeat and reword items.*

By listing two or three minor variations of the same skill on a rating scale, you will be able to check the consistency of the rater's responses. For example, if you want to know if a student is accepted or rejected by his or her peers, ask the raters to rate how well the targeted student is liked as well as how many friends he or she has and how close those friendships are. This will increase the likelihood that somewhat subjective ratings are accurate. If you find inconsistencies in responses, examine the item's wordings to determine if they tell you about nuances of the situation you had not considered before. Inconsistent answers also may indicate that you should go back to the drawing board and redevelop this part of the device.

In the case of nomination devices, these can be given on separate occasions. If a few weeks separate their administration, students likely will have forgotten their earlier answers and be forced to think all over again before responding. By repeating the use of the nomination device, responses that were colored by a bad day or unusual event can be uncovered.

4. *Be sure your materials are user-friendly.*

No matter whether students or adults are going to be using the materials you create, they should be materials that can be used with a minimum of confusion. Simple factors such as the quality of photocopy reproductions and readability level can influence how materials are used. Also, be considerate of the diverse backgrounds of potential users. Do not use gender-biased language or stereotypic depictions that may insult users or influence their assessments.

5. *Pilot-test materials before using them.*

To *pilot-test* means to conduct a trial run. You would not buy a car without test-driving it. The same should be true for using materials to evaluate a student's social standing. One good way to pilot-test materials is to use them. Try to evaluate some students other than the one about whom you are concerned. Try the materials more than once. Give them a real chance to shine or fail.

A second way to pilot-test materials is to give them to someone else to use. In this way you can find out whether others can make sense of what you created. Others also can point out biases you may have built into the device unwittingly. For example, they might find that all of the skills you include on a rating scale are negative.

The whole point of pilot-testing is to make sure that materials are appropriate before using them to help you make important decisions. If you find even small things about the measures to change, do so immediately. Do not assume you will remember to correct for them when interpreting your findings or that you will remember to explain them when sharing the materials with others.

Although teachers and researchers may use social rating and nomination devices they develop themselves, several published rating scales are used widely. The advantage of these scales is that the accuracy of what they measure is likely to have been checked carefully. For example, if a teacher wants to know who students think would be a good small-group leader, asking "Who is the group leader when you most enjoy working in groups?" could measure a different response than, "Who could do the best job of leading a group in which you work?" Published scales have usually been tested on large numbers of subjects, and potentially confounding items have been clarified. Published nomination devices are not as common because these devices are so easily constructed. You must be as precise as rating scale developers, however, when wording the instructions for nomination devices.

DIRECT OBSERVATION OF SOCIAL SKILLS

By using direct observations of social skills, the teacher, the student's peers, parents/ guardians, and the students themselves can keep track of social interactions. Specific skills can be watched for or general patterns can be observed. Generally the latter yields information of limited value to planning interventions. "Direct" does not necessarily mean charting social interactions as they happen. Depending on the complexity of the procedure, observers may sit and observe behaviors as they happen or observe an audiotape or videotape of a series of interactions. One advantage of direct observation is that actual occurrences of behaviors are recorded, which decreases the potential for other factors to influence what observers report. For example, factors such as gender, perceived sexual orientation, intelligence labels, and height have been found to influence some teachers' perceptions of students (American Association of University Women, 1992; Rofes, 1993/ 1994; Rosenthal & Jacobson, 1968; Wilson et al., 1986).

Teachers are no different from anyone else in having preconceived perceptions. Even an observer who is careful to keep biases in check can be guilty of homing in on the presence or absence of certain skills and ignoring other important skills. The focus of teachers tends to be on the student's learning performance and on managing the classroom. Given that teachers' attention is directed to these areas, they are apt to miss interactions in other areas. A disadvantage of direct observation systems is that they can be time-consuming. Particularly in a classroom where many students are vying for attention, to focus on a single student for any length of time without assistance can be difficult.

Typically, direct observation systems utilize some form of a checklist. The sociologist R. F. Bales developed an observation procedure that is slightly involved but is the basis for many used today. In his Interaction Process Analysis coding system (Bales, 1950, 1970), the observer records every interaction members of a group make during a predetermined period. Who initiated an interaction, with whom he or she interacted, and the type of interaction are noted. Figure 8.4 provides a sample interaction process analysis coding sheet. This type of system offers an excellent way to learn how to observe social interactions carefully, taking into account the context in which they occur.

Depending of the number of skills to be observed and the complexity of the learning tasks, students can be asked to observe themselves. This is both a time-saver for the teacher and a potential learning task for the student. One popular method of self-reporting involves the student's having a tape-recording on the desk that plays a beep at 3-minute intervals. Each time the student hears the beep, he or she records whether he or she was speaking using friendly tones, keeping hands to self, and so forth. The student does not have to record interactions at fixed intervals. If able to do so, the student could be asked simply to record every instance of a certain behavior. Record keeping can be as simple as scoring tally marks or noting the context each time the behavior is enacted.

When students can use these systems without detracting from their other activities they can use them to become acutely aware of ongoing social interactions. Some research has found that recording one's own behavior also can function as an intervention (Lloyd & Landrum, 1990). When students are aware of how they are interacting at a given time, they tend to increase their use of target skills. They do not even have to be

Students: *Althea* _____ _____ Date: *4/7* _____

Warren _____ _____ Situation: *Earth Science Lab*

Observer: *J. Giddes* _____

To complete the IPA coding sheet, write the first initial of each student who begins an interaction, followed by an arrow to the first initial of the student to whom the interaction is directed. Record each interaction in a separate column, in the order they occur.

Positive INSTRUMENTAL SKILLS								
shows solidarity	A→W,J							
shows tension release								
agrees								

EXPRESSIVE SKILLS								
gives suggestion		J→W						
gives opinion					W→J			
gives orientation								
asks for orientation								
asks for opinion					J→W			
asks for suggestion								

Negative INSTRUMENTAL SKILLS								
disagrees								
shows tension			W→J					
shows antagonism				A→W				

FIGURE 8.4   PARTIALLY COMPLETED INTERACTION PROCESS ANALYSIS CODING SHEET

Source: Based on *Interaction Process Analysis: A Method for the Study of Small Groups*, by R. F. Bales (Reading, MA: Addison-Wesley, 1950). For detailed instructions on scoring interactions using an IPA coding sheet see *The Sociology of Small Groups*, 2d edition, by T. M. Mills (Englewood Cliffs, NJ: Prentice Hall, 1984).

highly accurate self-observers for this method to have positive effects (Lloyd & Landrum, 1990).

Another way students may keep track of their own social interactions is to keep a daily journal. They may be asked to record reflections on use of a given skill during the day or how they handled specific situations. A journal is not an appropriate means to count instances of a specific skill, but it is a good way to track which instances stand out for students and to get some insight on how students reflect on their own social situation.

SELECTING A SOCIAL SKILLS ASSESSMENT METHOD

When making a choice among assessment methods, two factors should be considered:

1. Determine which can be used appropriately. For example, if you do not have the time to teach a student how to self-observe his or her own behavior and he or she is not quite sure of how to complete the recording sheet, the results you get from going ahead with this method probably will be misleading.
2. Select a method that assesses the social problem you suspected. Social status nominations, for example, might yield information such as whether peers do or do not like to work in a group with the targeted student but not which of the student's group interactions disturb them. In many instances you may want to use more than one assessment method so you get a complete picture of the significance of the suspected problem.

Ms. Santos used all three assessment methods to assess Warren's social interactions with teachers in the school. Each yielded a slightly different profile of the situation. The social skills rating indicated that Warren does have some inappropriate social skills during interactions with teachers. The social status nomination results (averaged from responses of several teachers) told her that other teachers like having Warren as a member of their class. Warren's self-report of his behavior did not indicate the problem clearly because the instances for recording his behaviors were too few to capture his periodic inappropriateness—falsely indicating that he was generally interacting appropriately. Further, Warren did not perceive anything to be wrong with his interactions.

Thus, the social skills rating was most helpful in capturing Warren's inappropriate social interactions with teachers, but the other two methods did yield some helpful information about how Warren and others perceive his interactions. Had Ms. Santos done a direct observation of Warren's interactions with teachers, information to help clarify differences in the results would have been forthcoming. The moral here is to select an assessment method or methods based on the user's ability to use it correctly and the likelihood that it will assess what the teacher is interested in.

CONSIDERATIONS FOR PREPARING TO USE ALL ASSESSMENT METHODS

To prepare to use any social skills assessment, two rules of thumb should be followed. First, those responsible for evaluating social skills must agree in advance as to the definition of the skills to be assessed and the method for assessing them. Because a social skill is a behavior to be acted (or stopped) and observed, the definition should include an observable behavior and the context(s) in which it should be able to be observed. (This does not mean that social skills do not have a cognitive component.) In cases in which skills can be performed at different frequencies or levels of proficiencies, that should be stated in the definition, too. This type of definition is known as an operational definition. Figure 8.5 provides two sample operational definitions of social skills. To be sure the skill is defined appropriately, teachers should think back to the initial concern that caused them to think about a social skills problem. Is it consistent with the skill defined?

When speaking with teachers <u>in or out of class</u>, Warren will <u>not speak using hostile tones</u>.
    (context)   *(observable)*

Juanita will <u>swear</u> <u>no more than three times a period</u> <u>when speaking in the classroom</u>.
    (observable)   *(level)*   *(context)*

FIGURE 8.5   EXAMPLES OF SOCIAL SKILLS STATED OPERATIONALLY

The second rule of thumb is that assessors of social skills need to agree on examples and nonexamples of how specific skills look and sound. Developing examples and nonexamples is a way to review the operational definition to be certain it means the same thing to all parties. A nonexample is a skill that may seem to represent the skill in question but really does not. "This is the answer we should get, stupid" is a nonexample of giving a suggestion, even though it has some of the right qualities of that skill. To be most useful, the nonexamples developed should be behaviors that reasonably could be mistaken for the skill. Developing an operational definition and examples and nonexamples is important whether the teacher's intention is to encourage, change, or stop performance of the target skill.

CONSIDERATIONS FOR USING ALL SOCIAL SKILLS ASSESSMENT METHODS

When using any social skills assessment, two additional rules of thumb should be kept in mind. First, the student in question should be compared with at least two other students. The two additional students selected to be evaluated should be in the same social setting as the targeted student (e.g., same classroom, same period of day) and to some extent have a profile similar to the targeted student (e.g., age and gender). Remember, even though they have many characteristics in common, the student who eats lunch alone in the cafeteria and the student who stars in school plays may be very different in a number of important ways. The two others should be evaluated using the same assessment device and at approximately the same time as the targeted student. For example, Althea could be observed during English class on Monday and Wednesday, Warren could be observed on Tuesday and Thursday, and so on.

Comparing the social skills status of the targeted student with two other similar students will help to establish if the social skills strengths and weaknesses of the targeted student are truly unique. This also can help in reflecting on the relative importance of targeting certain social skills. The social skills problem may be found to be endemic to a number of students in the same setting. Or the teacher may realize that what was thought to be a problem is actually an acceptable norm among students (in which case the teacher may or may not want to address it for all students in the setting). The teacher also might discover that similar interactions by other students do not seem to be a problem.

Finally, the context in which social skills are assessed should be appropriate and consistent. When a targeted student's social interactions, are of concern, the concern typically is about interactions in specific settings. A student may seem to interact inappropriately in only one classroom or during unstructured time. The social skills of another student may be of concern in almost every context.

Warren seemingly speaks to teachers in hostile tones no matter who they are or where they are. Skills assessment should occur in whatever the settings the concern is identified. Checking the status of Warren's social skills in other contexts is not appropriate until several checks have been made to clearly establish a problem. Once a social skills problem has been identified by consistent assessment, varying the contexts of assessment is appropriate. This will establish the pervasiveness of the problem. A few contexts may be discovered in which Warren's impolite speech does not occur. For example, Warren may not be impolite in the class of a teacher he perceives to pay little attention to rules for conduct. This exception can provide valuable insight into his behaviors.

Figure 8.6 reiterates the rules of thumb for social skills assessments.

TARGETING SOCIAL SKILLS FOR INTERVENTION

Once a need for social skills improvement has been established, the specific skills to reinforce, introduce, or reduce must be identified. Identifying a social skills need is relatively easy. Targeting specific skills can be more difficult. When a teacher desires to change a student's social interactions, decisions must be highly specific as to the skills in question.

Although *Juanita will improve her courteousness during group work* is a reasonable objective, it means different things to different people. Specifically stating that *Juanita will provide criticism politely during group work* and *Juanita will wait her turn to speak during group work* is more likely to lead to desired outcomes. Juanita will not have to guess what the target skills are, and Ms. Santos will be better able to identify appropriate and inappropriate instances of the skills.

When *preparing to use* social skills assessments:

1. Agree on skill definitions
   - no assumed shared understandings
   - name and operationally define skill(s)
2. Develop examples and nonexamples

When *using* all social skills assessments:

1. Compare the target student to two other students
   - students similar to target student (not with the same perceived social skills problem)
   - students from same setting(s)
2. Use the assessment in appropriate contexts
   - first in the setting where the problem is suspected
   - then in other relevant settings

FIGURE 8.6   RULES OF THUMB FOR ALL SOCIAL SKILLS ASSESSMENTS

To help make decisions about specific target skills, teachers first have to think out the skill options. Bales (1950) identified 12 general skills that represent the various social interactions that may occur in small groups (refer back to Figure 8.4). These skills are far too general to serve as target skills. Nonetheless, they are helpful in narrowing the focus.

Juanita will improve her courteousness during group work, for example, should be narrowed to *Juanita has difficulty expressing disagreement appropriately.* After identifying a fairly narrow social skills area on which to work, the teacher may begin to reflect on what led specifically to identifying the skills area (e.g., *When working in small groups, Juanita does not provide criticism politely*).

Resources are available to assist teachers in targeting specific skills. The most convenient resources to aid in identifying appropriate target skills are published social skills assessment instruments and social skills instructional curricula. The specific skills they address tend to be those that have been identified as issues for other students and usually are amenable to interventions. Four useful assessment instruments are listed on page 381. Several published social skills curricula appropriate for adolescents are:

- *The ACCESS Program*, by H. Walker, B. Todis, D. Holmes, and G. Horton (Austin, TX: Pro-Ed).

■ *ASSET: A Social Skills Program for Adolescents*, by J. S. Hazel, J. B. Schumaker, J. A. Sherman, and J. Sheldon-Wildgen (Champaign, IL: Research Press, 1981).

■ *Cooperation in the Classroom*, by D. W. Johnson, R. Johnson, and E. Holubec (Edina, MN: Interaction Book Company, 1988).

■ *Improving Social Skills: A Guide for Teenagers, Young Adults and Parents*, by P. Cvach, N. Sturomski, L. Meyer, and L. Trivelli (McLean, VA: Learning Disabilities Project, Intestate Research Associates, 1989).

■ *LCCE: Life Centered Career Education*, by D. Brolin (Reston, VA: Council for Exceptional Children, 1989).

■ *Learning to Get Along*, by D. Jackson, N. Jackson, M. Bennett, D. Bynum, and E. Faryna (Champaign, IL: Research Press, 1991).

■ *Metacognitive Approach to Social Skills Training*, by J. Sheinker and A. Sheinker (Rockville, MD: Aspen, 1988).

■ *The Prepare Curriculum*, by A. Goldstein (Champaign, IL: Research Press, 1988).

■ *The SCORE Skills: Social Skills for Cooperative Groups*, by D. S. Vernon, J. B. Schumaker, and D. D. Deshler (Lawrence, KS: Edge Enterprises, 1993).

■ *Skillstreaming the Adolescent*, by A. P. Goldstein, R. P. Sprafkin, N. J. Gershaw, and P. Klein (Champaign, IL: Research Press, 1980).

■ Social Skills for Daily Living, by J. B. Schumaker, J. S. Hazel, and C. S. Pederson (Circle Pines, MN: American Guidance Service, 1988).

■ *Social Skills on the Job*, by Macro Systems (Circle Pines, MN: American Guidance Service, 1989).

Some of these materials have been developed specifically for adolescents with LD. Examples of social skills they address are use of free time, temper control (SSRS; Gresham & Elliott, 1991), giving feedback, negotiation (ASSET; Hazel, Schumaker, Sherman, & Sheldon-Wildgen, 1981), and cooperative group skills (The SCORE Skills; Vernon, Schumaker, & Deshler, 1993). Using these rating, nomination, and observation systems, teachers can chart certain skills when they suspect possible social problems.

In addition to published social skills assessments and curricula, education journals and teaching methods textbooks containing theory and research on social skills can be excellent sources of recent social skills information. One more excellent resource is teaching colleagues who have experience interacting with adolescents.

Of course, those who interact routinely with the targeted student should be able to identify the general area where skills enhancement is needed. Thus, parents/guardians, other teachers, counselors, employers, and peers all are potentially helpful resources. The targeted student also may be helpful in identifying skills needs. These individuals should be sure they have targeted specific skills appropriately and that they are not just assuming a new skill will do the job.

Which of the following two skills are appropriate for Juanita if the goal is to decrease her use of profanity in class: *Juanita will (a) use polite language when speaking with others in class,* or (b) *decrease her use of profane language by 90% when speaking in the classroom.* Although both (a) and (b) have the potential to lead to reduced profanity, only (b) targets specifically a reduction in profanity. Thus, if Ms. Santos is monitoring Juanita's language using option (a), she could accurately note increased use of "polite language" without properly attending to any change in the amount of profanity. Selecting an appropriate goal still can lead to a problem if the goal itself or the degree of success expected is unrealistic. For example, if Juanita uses profanity frequently, reducing her use of profanity by 50% to start might be more realistic. Consulting with others who know the student is a smart idea.

CRITERIA TO GUIDE SELECTION

Once specific skills have been targeted, the intervention (curriculum) used to promote the student's adoption of these skills has to be selected. A variety of interventions suitable for different purposes are available. Many effective social skills interventions are teacher-made. When professionally developed interventions have been used to help identify target skills, the same interventions can be used to teach the skills. Of course, teachers could institute an intervention that is not used in the assessment process but is designed to teach the same skills. Or interventions could be adapted for target skills different from those they specify. Because a number of options surround selection from among the many interventions available, specific criteria to make a choice will be helpful.

Schumaker, Pederson, Hazel, and Meyen (1983) identified five criteria to consider in selecting a social skills intervention. They based these criteria on their knowledge of strategic instruction for adolescents with LD. Overall, they suggested, good social skills interventions are those that can be used to encourage a student with LD to interact successfully and that provide opportunities to practice new skills to be learned. The five criteria are to select a curriculum that can be used to (a) promote social competence, (b) accommodate the learning characteristics of students with mild disabilities, (c) target skill deficits common with populations with mild disabilities, (d) provide training of the skills, including in situational contexts, and (e) incorporate teaching methodologies effective with students with mild disabilities. Figure 8.7 provides a detailed explanation of each criterion.

In addition to these five criteria, three issues should be considered when selecting an intervention: (a) compatibility of the social skills intervention and the targeted social skills, (b) reasonableness of the setting and the instructional/learning demands of the intervention, and (c) whether the intervention promotes more than just the student performing certain skills (e.g., Does the student learn how to be strategic about selecting and using appropriate social skills?).

COMPATIBILITY OF TARGET SKILLS AND SOCIAL SKILLS INTERVENTIONS

Not all social skills interventions are appropriate for teaching all social skills. Incompatibility of skills and interventions may stem from an intervention having been designed for a specific circumstance. For example, much of what a student learns using the Social Skills on the Job curriculum (MacroSystems Inc., 1989) can be generalized to other settings, such as the classroom. Given that other interventions not focusing specifically on work-related skills are available, however, using this one may be inefficient if improved skills in the classroom is the goal. Many social skills curricula seem readily adaptable to

1. Promote social competence.
   - enables the student to perform specific skills (in synchronization and with fluency) and enhances his or her motivation to use them to achieve social goals (e.g., make friends, persuade others).

2. Accommodate the learning characteristics of students with mild handicaps
   - capitalizes on common learning characteristics of groups with mild disabilities and provides materials and suggestions for adapting curriculum to meet distinct needs of each group
   - easily understood, using materials with low readability levels and minimal writing requirements
   - aids the student in identifying specific social cues and problem solving to select appropriate social skills
   - minimizes failure while learning social skills; includes providing reinforcement for success during learning
   - provides a strategy to facilitate skill learning
   - includes procedures to teach generalization of skills to natural situations as well as procedures for assessing generalization
   - promotes student's motivation to set and achieve social goals after learning a skill

3. Target skill deficits common with populations with mild handicaps.
   - Specific skill areas identified are:
     - –give and accept negative feedback
     - –give positive feedback
     - –negotiate
     - –problem-solve
     - –resist peer pressure
     - –participate in a job interview
     - –explain a problem
     - –initiate activities
     - –join in activities
     - –make friends
     - –ask questions
     - –make self-disclosing statements
     - –follow directions
     - –converse

4. Provide training of target skills, including in situational contexts.
   - teaches social skills as well as how to identify which situations call for a skill
   - teaches general classes of social skills instead of specific skills to respond to specific situations (e.g., universally appropriate skills for resisting peer pressure versus learning specific skills for each situation in which peer pressure might occur)

5. Incorporate teaching methodologies effective with students with mild handicaps.
   - uses models and examples to teach use of a skill
   - makes student aware of rationale for using a skill and recognizing appropriate situations
   - provides opportunity for student practice
   - guides generalization of the skill to beyond the setting where it is learned
   - includes a method for measuring the student's skill proficiency prior to learning the skill, during learning, and at mastery

FIGURE 8.7   CRITERIA FOR SOCIAL SKILLS CURRICULA EXPLAINED

Source: From "Social Skills Curricula for Mildly Handicapped Adolescents: A Review," by J. B. Schumaker, C. S. Pederson, J. S. Hazel, and E. L. Meyen, in *Focus on Exceptional Children, 16,* 1–16.

adding, eliminating, or altering the specific social skills they are designed to teach. But consumer beware! Unless the authors of the interventions state that modifications are appropriate, they may not be. Sometimes a minor variation in an intervention's procedures can jeopardize its effectiveness. A combination of common sense and experience using an intervention as specified should help the teacher know when modifications can be made safely.

Setting and Instructional Demands of the Intervention

Teachers have to evaluate whether the selected intervention is appropriate for the settings in which the student will be expected to learn and utilize the target skills. Settings appropriate for a given intervention may be as broad as almost any one-on-one, small-group, or whole-class situation, or they may be as specific as employer-employee interactions. Some interventions are intended to be taught and practiced across situational settings. For example, Life Centered Career Education (LCCE) (Brolin, 1993) is used to teach students to apply specific skills in the classroom, at home, and at work.

The instructional demands of social skills interventions also vary. Busy teachers have to be thoughtful about how much attention they realistically can devote to a specific intervention, given all of the other demands on their time. In the same sense, some interventions may require more of students than they are prepared for (e.g., self-generate several appropriate skills options). Of course, problems are for solving. Solutions such as team teaching and teaching students to become peer tutors are possible.

Comprehensiveness of the Intervention

As Schumaker et al. (1983) recommended, an effective social skills intervention is one that teachers can use to teach students how to make decisions about applying appropriate social skills across a variety of settings. Thus, the most worthwhile social skills interventions include promotion of strategic use of social skills. Strategic individuals are those with knowledge of how, when, and why to use a skill and the ability to monitor her/his performance of those operations (Cross & Paris, 1988; Ellis et al., 1991). A strategic user of social skills is more likely to use appropriate skills across situations than one who has learned only a few isolated skills. This is especially the case for students who have multiple social skills needs.

Not all social skills interventions are designed to promote being strategic. As with nearly any curriculum, a good teacher can expand upon these lessons to promote strategic application. Selecting an intervention already designed to promote strategic application, however, has some logical advantages. First is the time factor. Many teachers do not have the time required to plan adaptations, experiment with them, and carefully collect and evaluate data to test their success.

Second, well designed and tested curricula take the guesswork out of making adaptations. Teachers who set out to adapt an intervention to add a strategic component should have expertise in devising strategic applications. Even teachers who are experienced at modifying lessons to make them strategic will have to go through a process of trial-and-error before reaching the most efficient adaptations. This is time that the teacher and the student may not have. Few if any interventions are so perfected that they would not benefit from some teacher personalization. A distinction can be made, however, between the types of adaptations that are made routinely in teaching (e.g., individualized attention for those who need it, adapting a rote learning lesson to a discovery learning lesson) and those required to transform the purpose of a previously developed instructional procedure into a strategy-oriented purpose.

INTERVENTION CHOICES

The types of social skills interventions appropriate for adolescents with LD can be categorized in a number of different ways. A general but useful way to do this begins with separating suggestions for activities with no supporting instructions or materials from interventions that include instructional guidelines and intervention materials. The former require more effort on the teacher's part to ensure methodological rigor. Conversely, the latter can require lengthy preparation or training on the teacher's part. Each of these categories can be broken down further by separating those used simply to promote demonstrating a target skill from those to promote the student's strategic application of a target skill.

Depending on the nature of the social skills problem, an intervention chosen to improve the situation may be quick and easy to implement or it may consist of a more extensive curriculum. When the social skills problem is isolated or minor (e.g., a student using insulting phrasing when asking for assistance), a simple and quick intervention may be appropriate. On the other hand, when the student has several social skills problems or the problem is complex (e.g., a student's wanting to make friends but not sure how to initiate interactions), a more comprehensive approach will be appropriate. Naturally, a quick and easy intervention is preferable. Selecting the most appropriate intervention can be only partially guided by what teachers think they can reasonably manage, however. Using an intervention simply because it is appealing may well be effective only in the short run.

SUGGESTIONS FOR ACTIVITIES

The following are several useful methods for teaching social skills. The first three are effective primarily as methods to make the student aware of the social skills situation.

PROMOTE STUDENT AWARENESS   This first intervention seldom is sufficient to bring about change in inappropriate behaviors by itself. It is, however, an initial step for most other interventions. In the case of a highly motivated student capable of initiating and monitoring her or his own changes in behavior, promoting awareness of the problem behavior may be enough. But that is expecting a lot from a student who is practicing a behavior inappropriate enough to warrant intervention in the first place. At any rate, the student's awareness of the problem is essential to comprehensive intervention.

To promote student awareness, the teacher first informs the student that a social skills problem exists. In a one-on-one conversation the teacher specifies what the problem skill is and identifies its negative consequences. The goal here is to make the student aware of the problem. Just informing the student of the problem will not guarantee that he or she will understand it. Thus, the teacher asks the student to articulate the problem behavior and its consequences. When doing this, the teacher asks the student to cite real examples and to go into detail in explaining them.

The teacher continues by asking the student to relate any insights into why he or she engages in the problem behavior and also to think of some appropriate alternatives. (Knowing that a problem exists but not knowing what to do about it is seldom useful.) Many students with LD have little knowledge as to why they act as they do and are unsure of alternative ways to behave. Nonetheless, the purpose of asking the student is to determine if he or she has some good ideas on which to build. The teacher might find that the problem goes much deeper than initially thought (e.g., a student may act out toward peers during class time in reaction to being taunted in the hallway by other peers). If the student is unable to identify the problem and its consequences himself or herself, chances are good that he or she will not be able to generate a positive change in behavior. Teachers should proceed to a more thorough intervention.

SELF-MONITORING   Three forms of self-monitoring—interviews, journal keeping, and record keeping of one's own behaviors—are popular.

Interviews work primarily as a method for probing students' awareness. Interviews, too, may be used to help students devise alternative behaviors. In interviews the teacher asks the students questions concerning whether they are aware of their behavior, why it is a problem, if they have any ideas as to why they engage in the behavior, whether the students desire to change the behavior, and what are possible alternatives as well as how to accomplish this. As with other methods of promoting student awareness, merely helping a student become aware of the problem is seldom sufficient for change. Interviews to accompany other interventions are useful to monitor progress and help the student participate in devising and monitoring the intervention process.

Journal keeping is similar to interviews in that it is primarily a method of raising student awareness. It, too, becomes more powerful when done in conjunction with another intervention. In journal keeping the student keeps notes on his or her social interactions and how the intervention is progressing. Keeping a journal causes students to reflect on their behavior, something many students with LD will not do readily otherwise. The students may be asked to record what skill they performed or how accurately they performed the skill or to reflect on the skill and how the intervention is going. The teacher may want to give students specific prompts to respond to (e.g., *"Who are you with?" "Did you perform the new skill?" "How did others respond to the new skill?" "How did you remember to perform the skill?"*). Popular options include students' making note whenever they perform the newly learned skill, or at predetermined times, or once or twice a day. A student can carry a small notebook with his or her other books and slip it into a purse or back pocket so it will be handy when needed.

One slightly more involved approach to journal keeping is to give the student a beeper (not allowed in many schools and community venues) and instruct the student to make a journal entry whenever he or she is beeped. Beeps may be sent at random, or at fixed intervals, or at times of the day when the teacher suspects the new behavior might be needed (e.g., at the end of hall-passing time). This is an effective way to prompt the student to make journal entries throughout the day and so produce an accurate cross-section of social interactions during the day. Teachers and others who interact with the student also may keep journals as a resource for comparison. These journals will help the teacher reflect on how well the intervention is going.

Record keeping of one's own behaviors is similar to journal keeping. The student uses a tally sheet to keep track of incidents of performing a targeted behavior. If the student is aware of his or her behaviors and is likely to remember to record occurrences, the teacher may simply instruct him or her to make a hashmark (or note the time) whenever the behavior is performed. A drawback, however, is that many students do not always remember to keep a record or the behavior may occur at inconvenient times to record it.

A tally sheet can be affixed to desktops or a notebook cover. Like journal keeping, this method is more likely to be effective if students are prompted to keep records themselves. A popular method is to make a tape recording that emits a beep at fixed intervals. Each time the beep sounds, the student notes how often he or she used the behavior since the last beep. The record can be kept on graph paper or transferred periodically onto a graph to depict changes over time.

An obvious problem is that the beep may distract others. Also, unless the student wears an earphone, the recording can be used only when the student is near a tape recorder. Still, it can be an effective method. It can contribute to changing behaviors (see Lloyd & Landrum, 1990). Further, instead of simply recording each instance of the desired skill, students could be asked to rate how well they performed the skill. The rating system should be simple (e.g., –, ~, +).

CONTRACTS/POSTED RULES   In contracts and posted rules, appropriate skills are identified and the student agrees to use them. These methods both begin by identifying the problem behavior, the student understanding why it is a problem, identifying an appropriate alternative behavior, and gaining the student's commitment to learn and use the new skill. Using a contract, the student, the teacher, and other involved parties (e.g. peers, other teachers, parents/guardians) sign the contract to signal commitment to the student using the new skill. At the teacher's discretion, the contract may include a statement of a reward for so-many instances of using the behavior. Generally, establishing a penalty for not using the behavior is less effective. When starting out, the student may gain so many penalties that he or she thinks that learning the skill is hopeless. We also know that reinforcements are far more effective in encouraging a behavior than are punishments.

A drawback to drawing a contract is that it is not a suitable way to remind the student to perform the new skill at times when the skill is called for. A partial solution to this drawback is to post classroom rules that call for performing the new skill. Still, students probably will not always review the poster when it is most needed as a reminder, but they will be more likely to contemplate it from time to time than they would a contract. If the rules are posted publicly, they should pertain to other students in the classroom as well. Many adolescents like to know the rules for acceptable behavior. Others, however, may consider having them posted as juvenile.

Despite their limitations, contracts and posted rules both can be effective when they are used in combination with more comprehensive interventions. In either case the student must understand the skills alluded to, including how and why they should be performed.

ROLE PLAYING   Role playing can help students become aware of their inappropriate behaviors. For example, a student may assume a peer's role and experience a peer using the inappropriate behavior toward him or her. Or the student can be asked to "play" two or three alternative behaviors and note their different effects on others.

Immediately following the role play the targeted student should describe what happened concerning the skill in question. This may be a one-on-one discussion, or it might involve other members of the group, depending on whether the teacher wants to have the targeted student hear others' perspectives. If awareness is the goal, students would do well to be aware of how their peers interpret the behavior. Also, when deciding between a one-to-one interaction or a group format, teachers should keep in mind in which situation the targeted student will likely be more reflective and forthcoming.

Role playing also can be an effective method of social skills intervention, provided that it is guided. Without guidelines as to how to interact and what to think about, role playing is reduced to an exploratory activity in which positive outcomes are not likely. Much like *promoting student awareness*, the student is left to his or her own devices. To be effective in helping a student adopt more appropriate social behaviors, the student should role play those desirable behaviors as a way to understand and practice them. Role playing the original problem behavior first can give the student a basis for comparison.

Appropriate guidelines for effective role playing include: (a) establishing clear objectives (e.g., learning two or three specific ways to respond to taunts and how to troubleshoot when they do not seem to work), (b) identifying roles to be played and how each role player should act (e.g., employing the desired skills), and (c) establishing what participants should think about and observe during the episode. Participation in role playing is far more effective than observation.

For learning about social skills, role playing should be at least partially scripted. Participants should be told specifically what to say and how to act. In this way behaviors and situations the teacher wants the students to experience will be more likely to come off as planned.

Warren is taunted in the hallways by being shoved. During role play, he should not be taunted by name-calling. Instead of giving Warren one more bad experience in the day, the teacher should give him some ideas on how he should respond. Because role-play participants are in effect acting, asking them to make up their responses to Warren's new behaviors, may be pointless. The teacher, however, may want Warren to come up with his own follow-through to their scripted responses. Further, if the initial results of Warren's new behaviors have the desired effect, he may be more encouraged to continue learning them.

Eventually Warren's responses to the taunts should be unscripted, as should the other participants' follow-through behaviors. This will give Warren practice at making decisions about when to perform his newly learned skills. In addition, Warren and the other students occasionally should switch roles so Warren will gain a firsthand perspective as to how his behaviors look and how others may feel in response to them.

PRAISE/REINFORCEMENT   Praise and reinforcement are not necessarily one and the same. Most of us respond positively to praise for our efforts. If students are told that they are trying hard or doing a good job, they will be more likely to continue exerting the effort. Praise and encouragement should be a part of any intervention.

For some students praise can be a reinforcer. In behavioral terms a *reinforcer* is the stimulus for a desired response (i.e., the new skill). Once the stimulus is received and associated with the response, the student will desire to perform the behavior so as to receive the stimulus again. Some students require something other than praise as a reinforcer, particularly as they learn a new skill.

A common reinforcer is tokens that may be added up and redeemed for something of value. Or the item of value may be given directly. Other commonly used reinforcers with adolescents include food items and frequently used school supplies. These tangible reinforcers are called extrinsic reinforcers.

The student must understand that the reinforcer will be awarded in exchange for performing the desired skill. Teachers should establish in advance whether the planned reinforcement is of interest to the student. If the skill is to be performed often, the reinforcer may be given after a certain preestablished number of performances (*interval reinforcement*) or every once and a while when the skill is performed (*random reinforcement*). Over time the tokens may be phased out and replaced with praise.

Ultimately, students should be taught to identify their own reinforcers, which include feeling good about performing the desired skill and taking notice of the beneficial outcome of performing the skill. These intangible reinforcers are called intrinsic reinforcers.

COOPERATIVE LEARNING AND SOCIAL SKILLS

Cooperative learning does not teach social skills. Rather, cooperative learning requires the use of appropriate social skills. Too often teachers have students work together in a group to create a joint product and expect that they will learn good social interaction skills in the process. First, this is not necessarily cooperative learning. To qualify as a cooperative learning group, the members must share a group goal, and some form of individual accountability must be present (Slavin, 1988). Second, although social skills may be learned in cooperative learning groups, they are not an unavoidable byproduct. Rather, students must learn how to behave in cooperative groups (Johnson & Johnson, 1986; Webb, 1989).

The teacher should decide what social skills will be involved. Among the great variety of cooperative learning methods, only a few are intended to be used to teach social skills. Typically, the skills students learn best during cooperative learning are those pertaining to their participation in the group. Other types of skills are better taught in more appropriate contexts.

Three approaches to teaching social skills for cooperative learning stand out as appropriate for adolescents. In the first method students use a T-chart (Johnson & Johnson, 1987) to name and define appropriate skills (see Table 8.1). On the left side of the "T" the skills are listed. How each skill looks and sounds is listed on the right side. To be most effective, the students should be involved in naming how performance of the skills looks and sounds. The teacher may want to identify some of the important skills in advance. Students in the group can generate others. Several skills important to cooperative learning groups are listed in Table 8.1.

In the second method, the *SCORE Skills* (Vernon et al., 1993), skills are taught to students as they work in cooperative groups. The skills learned are basic to cooperative group work and building a learning community. Instructional activities incorporate use of "scoreboards" similar to T-charts, on which the skills are named and example verbal-

TABLE 8.1   SAMPLE T-CHART FOR TEACHING SOCIAL SKILLS

Skill	Looks/Sounds Like
Contribute ideas	"I think..."
Request information	"What does that mean?"
Listen carefully	Don't be doing other things when someone is talking to you
Summarize	"So, what we decided was that..."
Encourage others to participate	"Tell us what you think."
Check for understanding	"Is this what you mean?" ..."Do you get it?"

izations/actions are paired. The instructional model used to teach these skills is the *strategies intervention model* (Ellis et al., 1991) developed at the University of Kansas. Students not only learn the skills but also how to be strategic users of those skills. Some of the materials used to teach this strategy are geared toward younger students, but teachers have modified them readily for adolescents.

A third method to encourage appropriate cooperative-group social skills is to use *scripted interactions*. Students are given specific statements to say, including questions to ask, sentence starters (e.g., "that's a good point; I'd like to add ..."), and sometimes specific roles to play in the group. In some cases scripts are used to prompt meaningful on-task conversation. In other instances scripts are provided for students to use as they encounter various scenarios (e.g., what to say instead of becoming belligerent when someone derides their contribution). Without a script to follow, some students will not make any contributions to the group.

Regardless of whether cooperative learning tasks are used to teach cooperative skills, they may be organized to promote use of appropriate skills. The *structural approach* (Kagan, 1989, 1990), for example, is a series of methods for structuring cooperative group activities to promote cooperative interactions. For example, to encourage all students to contribute, students must spend a poker chip to speak; students who use all of their chips must wait for others to finish theirs before being allotted more chips. Many of these techniques guide students on how and when to interact but do not directly address the content of their interactions. If that is a limitation for some students, the teacher may simply script their interactions.

A great variety of additional suggestions for social skills teaching activities is available. Some are published in textbooks and teacher's journals. Among the many excellent guides to some of these approaches are:

- *Strategies for Teaching Students with Learning and Behavior Problems,* 2d edition, by C. S. Bos and S. Vaughn (Boston: Allyn and Bacon, 1991).
- *Teaching Social Skills to Children,* by G. Cartledge and J. F. Milburn (New York: Pergamon Press, 1976).
- *Teaching Social Skills to Children and Youth,* by G. Cartledge and J. F. Milburn (Boston: Allyn and Bacon, 1995).

Many more intervention ideas are the products of trial-and-error experiences that teachers can learn about only by visiting with other teachers. Teachers' options are expanded even further if the teacher considers interventions not designed specifically for adolescents with LD, with the intent of adapting them.

Self-developed intervention materials should adhere to the same guidelines as those used for developing teacher-made assessment devices (i.e., closely follow the format of previously developed materials, be precise, repeat and reword items (or, in this case, find multiple ways for the student to learn and practice the target skills), be sure the materials are user-friendly, and pilot-test materials before using them).

INTERVENTIONS WITH GUIDELINES AND MATERIALS

A great number of options also are available from among interventions that are fully developed instructional routines complete with materials. These usually are published materials. Brief descriptions of several published interventions appropriate for adolescents with LD follow:

- *ASSET: A Social Skills Program for Adolescents*
  - *Authors:* J. S. Hazel, J. B. Schumaker, J. A. Sherman, and J. Sheldon-Wildgen
  - *Publisher:* Research Press, 2612 N. Mattis Ave., Champaign, IL 61820
  - *Description:* Social skills are taught to groups of students. Students learn both verbal and nonverbal social skill behaviors. Skills include: give positive feedback, give negative feedback, accept negative feedback, resist peer pressure, problem-solve, negotiate, follow instructions, and converse. Activity formats include group discussions and hypothetical problem-solving situations. Materials include demonstration videotapes, skill sheets, and skills performance checklists for students to complete.
- *The SCORE Skills: Social Skills for Cooperative Groups*
  - *Authors:* D. S. Vernon, J. B. Schumaker, and D. D. Deshler
  - *Publisher:* Edge Enterprises, Box 1304, Lawrence, KS 66044 (913)749–1473
  - *Description:* Students learn five skills basic to participating effectively in cooperative learning groups: (a) share ideas, (b) compliment others, (c) offer help or encouragement, (d) recommend changes nicely, and (e) exercise self-control. Students learn a mnemonic device to help them recall the skill steps. The skills are modeled for the students, who then role-play them. Materials include activity sheets and role-play instructions. Overhead masters also are included.
- *Skillstreaming the Adolescent*
  - *Authors:* A. P. Goldstein, R. P. Sprafkin, N. J. Gershaw, and P. Klein
  - *Publisher:* Research Press, 2612 N. Mattis Ave., Champaign, IL 61820
  - *Description:* Skills are learned in *structured learning groups*. Skill areas addressed include beginning skills, advanced skills, skills for dealing with feelings, alternatives to aggression, and planning. Students learn how to apply the skills

via responding to hypothetical problem-solving situations. Role playing is included. A list of 50 social skills and structured learning checklists are provided.

■ *Social Skills for Daily Living*

Authors: J. B. Schumaker, J. S. Hazel, and C. S. Pederson

Publisher: American Guidance Service, Publishers' Building, Circle Pines, MN 55014

Description: Social skills are taught to individuals or groups. Skill areas include "body basics" (prerequisite to all other skills), conversation and friendship, getting along with others, and problem solving. The skills may be applied at school, at home, and on the job. Assessment materials are included to help determine where in the curriculum to start a student. Materials include comic books written at low reading levels to introduce the skills.

No matter what intervention is selected, it should not be conceptualized narrowly as only teaching new behaviors. An adequate intervention must be comprehensive. Therefore, efforts in addition to activities used to teach the target skill must be carried out. Even when a minor change in social interactions is sought, long-range and short-term goals for change should be established. Support for achieving the goals should extend beyond the activities designed to teach a skill.

For many students with LD, recognition of the student's social skills should be noted directly in the IEP. The social skills goals then can become part of the student's overall curriculum. In this way other teachers and school staff members can be included when addressing the student's social skills curriculum. Including statements concerning social skills on the IEP ensures that the student's unique social and learning needs are addressed throughout the school day.

The IEP should state guidelines as to when and how exceptions to the general school policies should be extended to the student with LD. To avoid later conflict, school administration and staff and parents/guardians should participate fully in formulating these guidelines. In some instances school district attorneys should be consulted. This recognition of a legitimate disability should not become an abuse of privilege. Students with LD will not benefit from special privileges that are unnecessary for their success in school.*

In addition to a comprehensive approach within the school, in some instances families, employers, and other social groups should participate in determining how they can contribute to the social skills intervention. For example, they can help monitor the student's skill use or review with the student situations for using the skill. Setting goals and ensuring that the student's environment is conducive to successful intervention are important. Still, the ultimate goal is change in skills performance. For this reason, an intervention that promotes change in skills is at the core of comprehensive efforts.

Choosing the social skills intervention most appropriate for an individual or as the only social curriculum for an entire classroom is difficult. The students with whom the curriculum will be used are individuals. Thus, their skills needs and learning needs vary. To make sure a curriculum is compatible with students' needs and a teacher's teaching strengths, several curricula should be reviewed before adopting one. Some publishers offer sample materials or trial-use periods. Published reviews of social skills materials

---

* When guidelines are in place for an educationally disabled student, they are not privileges if they respond legitimately to a disability.

also may prove helpful. Several published reviews are described in the appendix to this chapter. Other sources of information are library research, contact with assessment and intervention authors and publishers, and consultation with fellow teachers. Curricula can be expensive, so the choice should be made carefully.

EFFECTIVE SOCIAL SKILLS INTERVENTIONS

Teaching social skills effectively involves more than just getting a student to perform specific skills. To make a meaningful, long-term change in social interactions, the student also must be taught to be a strategic user of the skills. Published interventions specify how to teach skills, but the teacher has the responsibility to help the student become a strategic user of the skills. A strategic user of social skills (or any skill) has command of three specific types of knowledge (Cross & Paris, 1988):

1. *Procedural knowledge* is knowledge of how to perform a specific skill or set of skills.
2. *Declarative knowledge* is knowledge of why a specific skill works as it does— understanding the mechanisms of a specific skill (e.g., offering an opinion involves knowledge of when an opinion is appropriate, how to interject, and how to phrase an opinion for desired results). Declarative knowledge also includes knowledge of the task to which the skill is being applied such as procedures for participating on a reciprocal teaching team (Palincsar & Brown, 1984).
3. *Conditional knowledge* is understanding which situations use of a specific skill is appropriate.

The strategic individual combines and coordinates these three types of knowledge by means of executive control (Cross & Paris, 1988). *Executive control* is the ability to simultaneously apply procedural, declarative, and conditional knowledge and to monitor one's own performance of them. Thus, effective strategic-oriented social skills interventions are those used to teach the target skills as well as how to perform and monitor those skills. Ellis, Deshler, Lenz, Schumaker, and Clark (1991) suggested that these types of knowledge fit collectively into the knowledge domain of strategy teaching and learning. Teachers should want their students to effectively master the knowledge domain for the social skills they learn.

In addition to the knowledge domain, effective strategy teaching attends to the *motivational domain* (Ellis et al., 1991). The two aspects of strategy learning addressed in the motivational domain are the student's belief systems and self-motivation. To apply social skills strategies effectively, students must have positive beliefs about their ability to perform the skills and about the value of performing the skills. Self-motivation also is critical to the student's independent strategic use of social skills. Without motivation, students are unlikely to effectively learn and apply skills or strategies they are taught (Mehring & Colson, 1990). Positive coping and affirmation statements, realistic goal-setting, and self-reinforcement all contribute to self-motivation.

Any intervention must incorporate evaluation of implementation and outcomes. When implementing an intervention, teachers need to evaluate their own practices to be sure the intervention is being delivered as planned. Any modifications should be noted so they may be used again if they are successful, or else avoided. A good way to evaluate one's own teaching skills is to have a fellow teacher observe during the intervention. The teacher also should periodically review information describing the procedures, as a self-check.

The success a student has with an intervention should not be assumed. It, too, should be evaluated carefully. Most interventions have procedures that should be followed for assessing and charting progress in learning target skills. Sometimes, the assessment procedure used to identify the social skills problem can be readministered to check progress. Ideally, evaluations should occur periodically during teaching/learning of the skills, instead of waiting until the teacher assumes the intervention has been successful. This way, modifications in intervention procedures can be made as needed. Further, the student's charting of his or her own progress can be a strong incentive to continue.

SUMMARY AND PERSPECTIVES

Identifying and solving a social skills problem seem relatively easy to do. Working carefully to identify a social skills problem and an appropriate intervention, however, may confirm the old adage, "Things are not always as they first appear." When seeing a student with a social skills problem, teachers should not assume that they are seeing the true problem. Two important issues have to be considered: (a) the source of social skills problems and (b) their solutions.

THE SOURCE: PEOPLE WHO LIVE IN GLASS HOUSES

To be sure that the social skills problem resides with the adolescent with LD, the teacher has to be sure that the problem is not with the student's environment. For example, Warren may address a classmate using hostile tones during lessons because that classmate physically bullies him in the hallways and Warren cannot muster a better response. Interventions that change the targeted student but ignore the source of the problem may teach the student how to cope with a problem situation but allow the underlying problem to go unchecked. This would be a case of punishing the victim. Further, the student who truly needs assistance, the problem maker, would not have received it. (This is not to suggest that Warren should not learn to handle difficult situations. Bad things do sometimes happen to good people.)

Identifying the true source of a problem can be challenging. Teachers may find that they hold unwarranted bias toward a given student. Teachers might discover that their classroom is a difficult place for certain students to act in socially appropriate ways. For example, class members may have to compete against their classmates to succeed. Or, for any number of reasons, they may routinely ostracize students who make positive contributions.

Adolescence is a period during which youth struggle constantly to remain socially acceptable, sometimes at all costs. One of the easiest ways to deflect attention from one's own social awkwardness is to capitalize on another's. Students with LD who appear socially different from their peers are ready targets. Students with LD who think differently, express themselves differently, are treated differently in any way, or in the perception of other adolescents just seem "different" can be a source of irritation to students in the majority.

Special education students often are victims of intolerance. A student who attends a resource room, for example, may be labeled a "retard." This label can be an open invitation for harassment and ostracism. Although we do know that many students with LD are socially rejected and that some have social skills problems, a direct relationship between the two has not been clearly established (Bryan & Lee, 1990).

The social skills "problem" may be a symptom of a deeper problem than how well the student interacts. Social deficits may be rooted in the student's learning disability. For example, a student may be disruptive during oral reading activities because of frustration stemming from a reading difficulty. Or an adolescent with LD may not process information fast enough during classwide discussions to make contributions. This could be interpreted falsely as being socially withdrawn. The teacher's attempts to encourage the student to respond will not be successful if they do not address the student's processing abilities.

When a student has problems interacting in acceptable ways, the solution may incorporate a combination of skills training and sensitivity training for those around the student. The teacher also may manipulate situations that induce inappropriate behaviors. For example, if Juanita taunts Althea routinely until Althea makes an outburst in class, Ms. Santos can make sure that they do not work in the same group or sit near each other.

Solutions: Get to the Root of the Matter

Regardless of whether the source of the social skills problem is or is not "within" the targeted student, the teacher's identifying appropriate social skills and intervening to encourage their use may not be enough to change the student's sociability. Even when target behaviors are altered as planned and the improved social skills are sustained over a long time, the change may be only superficial. Typically, only the behaviors the teacher targets specifically are affected. Students' overall knowledge of what appropriate interactions are and how to monitor their own social skills may not be altered significantly. The result in these cases is some changes in behavior but little change in overall status.

As evidence of this, McIntosh, Vaughn, and Zaragoza (1991) reviewed 22 special intervention studies. In 14 of these, social skills had been taught successfully to children or adolescents. They found that despite positive changes in skills, the targeted students' acceptance by peers did not change significantly. Assuming appropriate skills were targeted, one purpose driving the social interventions was not met. The researchers found that social skills training in combination with attention to factors such as the amount of time allotted for the interventions to be effective and incorporation of simultaneous cognitive behavior modification or metacognitive components did make a difference in social acceptance. The interaction of several such factors seemed to contribute to the effectiveness of the interventions. Those factors included a greater number of contact hours and metacognitive practices such as modeling and mnemonic strategies for the practice of skills. As the McIntosh et al. (1991) research review indicates, the effectiveness of a social skills intervention has not occurred until an outcome beyond a mere change in the targeted student's behavior has been noted.

In some cases social inappropriateness may be a call for help. The student could be signaling a problem situation at home or in personal health. For these reasons teachers and other individuals who typically would be part of an IEP team should be consulted whenever a social skills intervention is being considered. When a decision is made to teach a targeted student new social skills, they should be taught in a way that promotes sustained change by means of the students' independent use of the skills.

REFERENCES

Alexander, K. L., Natriello, G., & Pallas, A. M. (1985). For whom the school bell tolls: The impact of dropping out on cognitive performance. *American Sociological Review, 50*, 409–420.

Allington, R. C., & McGill-Franzen, A. (1989). School responses to reading failure: Chapter One and special education students in grades 2, 4, & 8. *Elementary School Journal, 89*, 529–542.

American Association of University Women. (1992). *How schools shortchange girls. The AAUW report: A study of major findings on girls and education.* Washington, DC: AAUW Educational Fund, National Education Association.

Bales, R. F. (1950). *Interaction process analysis: A method for the study of small groups.* Reading, MA: Addison-Wesley.

Bales, R. F. (1970). *Personality and interpersonal behavior.* New York: Holt, Rienhardt, & Winston.

Bell, D., Feraios, A. J., & Bryan, T. (1991). Learning disabled adolescents' knowledge and attitudes about AIDS. *Learning Disabilities Research and Practice, 6*, 94–111.

Brolin, D. (1993). *LCCE: Life centered career education.* Reston, VA: Council for Exceptional Children.

Bryan, T., Donahue, M., & Pearl, R. (1981). Learning disabled children's peer interactions during a small-group problem-solving task. *Learning Disability Quarterly, 4*, 13–22.

Bryan, T., & Lee, J. (1990). Social skills training with learning disabled children and adolescents: The state of the art. In T. E. Scruggs & B. Y. L. Wong (Eds.), *Intervention research in learning disabilities* (pp. 263–270). New York: Springer-Verlag.

Bryan, T., & Pflaum, S. (1978). Social interactions of learning disabled children: A linguistic, social, and cognitive analysis. *Learning Disability Quarterly, 1*(3), 70–79.

Bryan, T., & Wheeler, R. (1972). Perceptions of learning disabled children: The eyes of the observer. *Journal of Learning Disabilities, 5*, 484–488.

Bryan, T., Wheeler, R., Felcan, J., & Henek, T. (1976). "Come on, dummy": An observational study of children's communications. Journal of Learning Disabilities, 9, 53–61.

Bursuck, W. (1989). A comparison of students with learning disabilities to low achieving and higher achieving students on three dimensions of social competence. *Journal of Learning Disabilities, 22*, 188–194.

Coleman, J. M., & Minnett, A. M. (1993). Learning disabilities and social competence: A social ecological perspective. *Exceptional Children, 58*, 234–246.

Cross, D. R., & Paris, S. G. (1988). Developmental and instructional analyses of children's metacognition and reading comprehension. *Journal of Educational Psychology, 80*, 131–142.

Deshler, D. D., & Schumaker, J. B. (1983). Social skills of learning disabled adolescents: Characteristics and intervention. *Topics in Learning and Learning Disabilities, 3*, 15–23.

Dorval, B., McKinney, J. D., & Feagans, L. (1982). Teacher interaction with learning disabled children and average achievers. *Journal of Pediatric Psychology, 7*, 317–330.

Ellis, E. S., Deshler, D. D., Lenz, B. K., Schumaker, J. B., & Clark, F. L. (1991). An instructional model for teaching learning strategies. *Focus on Exceptional Children, 23*, 1–24.

Gresham, F. M., & Elliott, S. N. (1991). *Social skills rating system (SSRS).* Circle Pines, MN: American Guidance Service.

Hammill, D. (1990). On defining learning disability: An emerging consensus. *Journal of Learning Disabilities, 23*, 74–84.

Hammill, D. D., Leigh, J. E., McNutt, G., & Larsen, S. C. (1981). A new definition of LD. *Learning Disability Quarterly, 4*, 336–342.

Hazel, J. S., Schumaker, J. B., Sherman, J. A., & Sheldon-Wildgen, J. (1981). *ASSET: A social skills program for adolescents*. Champaign, IL: Research Press.

Interagency Committee on Learning Disabilities (1987). *Learning disabilities: A report to Congress*. Washington, DC: Author.

Johnson, D. W., & Johnson, R. T. (1986). Mainstreaming and cooperative learning strategies. *Exceptional Children, 52*, 553–561.

Johnson, D. W., & Johnson, R. T. (1987). *Learning together and alone: Cooperative, competitive, and individualistic learning*. Englewood Cliffs, NJ: Prentice Hall.

Kagan, S. (1989, December). The structural approach to cooperative learning. *Educational Leadership, 41*, 9.

Kagan, S. (1990). *Cooperative learning resources for teachers, 1990 edition*. San Juan Capistrano, CA: Resources for Teachers.

Levin, H. M. (1972). *The cost to the nation of inadequate education*. Study prepared for Select Committee on Equal Educational Opportunity, U.S. Senate, Washington, DC: Government Printing Office.

Lloyd, J. W., & Landrum, T. J. (1990). Self-recording of attending to task: Treatment components and generalization of effects. In T. E. Scruggs and B. Y. L. Wong (Eds.), *Intervention research in learning disabilities* (pp. 235–262). New York: Springer-Verlag.

MacroSystems Inc. (1989). *Social skills on the job*. Circle Pines, MN: American Guidance Service.

McIntosh, R., Vaughn, S., & Zaragoza, N. (1991). A review of social interventions for students with learning disabilities. *Journal of Learning Disabilities, 24*, 451–458.

Mehring, T. A., & Colson, S. E. (1990). Motivation and mildly handicapped learners. *Focus on Exceptional Children, 22*(5), 1–14.

Morgan, D. J. (1979). Prevalence and types of handicapping conditions found in correctional institutions: A national survey. *Journal of Special Education, 13*, 283–295.

Oliva, A. H., & La Greca, A. M. (1988). Children with learning disabilities: Social goals and strategies. *Journal of Learning Disabilities, 21*, 301–306.

Palincsar, A. M., & Brown, A. (1984). Reciprocal teaching of comprehension fostering and comprehension monitoring. *Cognition and Instruction, 1*(2), 117–175.

Pearl, R., & Bryan, T. (1994). Getting caught in misconduct: Conceptions of adolescent with and without learning disabilities. *Journal of Learning Disabilities, 27*, 193–197.

Pearl, R., Bryan, T., Fallon, P., & Herzog, A. (1991). Learning disabled students' detection of deception. *Learning Disabilities Research and Practice, 6*, 12–16.

Rofes, E. E. (1993/1994). Making our schools safe for sissies. *High School Journal, 77*(1,2), 37–40.

Rosenthal, R., & Jacobson, L. (1968). *Pygmalion in the classroom: Teacher expectation and pupils' intellectual development*. New York: Holt, Rinehart & Winston.

Rutherford, R. B., Nelson, C. M., & Wolford, B. I. (1985). Special education in the most restrictive environment: Correctional/special education. *Journal of Special Education, 19*, 59–71.

Schumaker, J. B., Pederson, C. S., Hazel, J. S., & Meyen, E. L. (1983). Social skills curricula for mildly handicapped adolescents: A review. *Focus on Exceptional Children, 16*, 1–16.

Seidel, J. F., & Vaughn, S. (1991). Social alienation and the LD school dropout. *Learning Disabilities Research, 6*, 152–157.

Slavin, R. E. (1988). Cooperative learning and student achievement. *Educational Leadership, 46*, 31–33.

Torgesen, J. K. (1982). The learning disabled child as an inactive learner: Educational implications. *Topics in Learning and Learning Disabilities, 2*(1), 45–52.

Tur-Kaspa, H., & Bryan, T. (1994). Social information-processing skills of students with learning disabilities. *Learning Disabilities Research and Practice, 9*, 12–23.

Vaughn, S. (1985). Why teach social skills to learning disabled students? *Journal of Learning Disabilities, 18*, 588–591.

Vernon, D. S., Schumaker, J. B., & Deshler, D. D. (1993). *The SCORE Skills: Social skills for cooperative groups*. Lawrence, KS: Edge Enterprises.

Wagner, M. (1990). *The school programs and school performance of secondary students classified as learning disabled: Findings from the National Longitudinal Transition Study of Special Education Students*. Menlo Park, CA: SRI International.

Wagner, M. (1991). *Dropouts with disabilities: What do we know? What can we do?* Menlo Park, CA: SRI International.

Wansart, W. L. (1990). Learning to solve a problem: A microanalysis of the solution strategies of children with learning disabilities. *Journal of Learning Disabilities, 23*, 164–170.

Webb, N. M. (1989). Peer interaction and learning in small groups. *International Journal of Educational Research, 13*, 21–39.

Wehlage, G. G., & Rutter, R. (1986). Dropping out: How much do schools contribute to the problem? *Teachers College Record, 87*, 374–392.

Wentzel, K. R. (1991). Social competence at school: Relation between social responsibility and academic achievement. *Review of Educational Research, 61*, 1–24.

Wiggins, G. (1989). The futility of trying to teach everything of importance. *Educational Leadership, 47*(3), 44–59.

Wilson, D. M., Hammer, L. D., Duncan, P. M., Dornbusch, S. M., Ritter, P. L., Hintz, R. L., Gross, R. T., & Rosenfeld, R. G. (1986). Growth and intellectual development. *Pediatrics, 4*, 646–650.

Wong, B. Y. L. (1980). Activating the inactive learner: Use of questions/prompts to enhance comprehension and retention of implied information in learning disabled children. *Learning Disability Quarterly, 3*, 29–37.

APPENDIX PUBLISHED REVIEWS OF SOCIAL SKILLS MATERIALS

Alberg, J. (April, 1993). *A practitioner's guide to social skills instruction.* Paper presented at annual meeting of Council for Exceptional Children, San Antonio, TX.

- eight "representative" social skills programs
- K–12
- intended for special education populations

Carteledge, G., & Milburn, J. F. (1986). *Teaching social skills to children* (Appendix A). New York: Pergamon Press.

Carteledge, G., & Milburn, J. F. (1995). *Teaching social skills to children and youth.* Boston: Allyn and Bacon.

- nature of materials (curriculum kits, audiovisual, games)
- age level
- includes special education and non-special education geared materials
- Appendix B lists addresses of materials publishers

Schumaker, J. B., Pederson, C. S., Hazel, J. S., & Meyen, E. L. (1983). Social skills curricula for mildly handicapped adolescents: A review. *Focus on Exceptional Children, 16*, 1–16.

- target population
- format of materials
- ability and/or motivational components
- learning characteristics
- skills/topics addressed
- specific skills versus social situations approach
- teaching methodology

Vaughn, S., McIntosh, R., & Hogan, A. (1990). Why social skills training doesn't work: An alternative model. In T. Scruggs & B. Y. L. Wong (Eds.), *Intervention research in learning disabilities* (pp. 279–303). New York: Springer-Verlag.

- subjects
  - age
  - gender
  - LD classification
- procedures
  - subject selection
  - group size
  - time for intervention
  - individualization of training
  - regular class involvement
  - cognitive behavior modification
- measures
  - follow-ups after intervention
- results
  - generalization of skills to other settings

9

Strategic Instruction in the Content Areas

JANIS BULGREN AND KEITH LENZ

QUESTIONS TO KEEP IN MIND

■ What are the conditions of the secondary school setting that promote or inhibit teachers' ability to effectively teach content to all students?

■ What are the characteristics of planning for effective content-area instruction for adolescents with LD?

■ How can teachers compensate for a student's lack of effective and efficient strategies as they teach content?

■ How can teachers integrate instruction in learning strategies into content-area courses?

■ How can curriculum be adapted and modified to cue learning and compensate for poor learning strategy?

ADVANCE ORGANIZER

tudents with learning disabilities at the secondary school level can be helped to respond successfully to many challenges they face. For example, many students with learning disabilities benefit from instruction in strategies that help them acquire the content of the middle school and high school curriculum more successfully. As important as learning strategies are to students with learning disabilities, however, they are not the total answer, especially for students who approach secondary content classrooms with inadequate prior knowledge about a subject area. Students who know many strategies but have little background knowledge of the world may have difficulty relating new information to their limited knowledge base. This difficulty produces far-reaching effects because much knowledge of the world is gained from participating in the wide range of content-area classes in the secondary school curriculum. Therefore, while students are acquiring strategies for learning, they also must be acquiring domains of important content information.

Content-area competence can be gained in a number of different domains, generally associated with specific academic subjects including: social studies (e.g., American history, world history, civics, state history, sociology), science (e.g., health, physical science, biology, physics, chemistry) language arts (e.g., literature, speech, drama, foreign language), mathematics (e.g., consumer math, algebra, geometry, calculus), and vocational or industrial education (e.g., home economics, mechanics, business, agriculture). In addition, a variety of other instructional areas, such as in technology, physical education, music, and art may demand that students demonstrate content mastery. These domains comprise the content curriculum of the traditional middle and secondary school programs.

Who should be responsible for ensuring that students learn the critical content? Sometimes a support teacher, such as a special education teacher, assumes the role of the content teacher. In many cases, however, the support teacher does not have the content-area expertise to assume this role. In most instances the support teacher is more appropriately responsible for teaching students the strategies they need to meet the demands of school and out-of-school settings. As a result, the general classroom teacher is most likely the one who must assume responsibility for promoting student competence in the content areas. Thus, content-area teachers must understand how to select and present content-area information in ways that circumvent or compensate for the ineffective or inefficient strategies of their students and their lack of background knowledge.

In previous chapters the focus has been on how to teach students the strategies required to meet the demands of the secondary school setting. In this chapter the focus is on how secondary content-area teachers can instruct groups of students in ways that are more sensitive to individuals' learning needs. More specifically, this chapter is about:

- *understanding realities and issues of secondary schools*, including past practices in content-area instruction in special education classrooms; the current realities facing secondary teachers, including the issues related to teaching content in the secondary curriculum and the resulting implications for developing new models

for curriculum and instruction; current instructional practices in the general classroom; and the role of instructional mediation for all students in the general classroom.

- strategic methods for teachers to use in *planning for content* acquisition to ensure that students acquire the critical content offered through secondary-level
courses, units, and lessons.
- *approaches to teaching for content acquisition*, incorporating methods designed
to enhance content acquisition, that teachers can use to lead students to organize,
understand, recall, and apply the critical content of the secondary curriculum;
strategy integration into content classrooms; and curriculum revision related to
promoting content-area learning.

The organization of this chapter is found in Figure 9.1.

Instructional Issues in Secondary Schools

Past Practices in Content-Area Instruction in Special Education Classrooms

Content-area instruction often has been delivered by special education teachers in special education classes. *Special education class* is a term that represents the various types
of special education and remedial classes in which content-area instruction is provided.
The special education class setting traditionally has offered three types of content learning opportunities for low-achieving students.

1. A special education class might be offered in which the curriculum is different
   from the regular education curriculum; this is truly an alternative content approach.
2. The special education class could offer instruction covering the same or equivalent content as that covered in the regular curriculum, differing in the manner in
   which the content is delivered.
3. The special education class could provide tutoring for the student so the student
   can participate in and meet the demands of regular classroom coursework.

Each of these delivery approaches will be reviewed.

Alternative Content Delivery

In some parts of the country, separate content classes are provided only for students for
whom the content of the general curriculum is not appropriate (e.g., individuals with
severe and moderate disabilities). In other places, however, these courses are offered to
students with mild disabilities as an alternative to participating in the general content
class. The alternative courses often use adapted textbooks and limit the amount of content covered. These courses frequently are not comparable to the content-area courses
offered in the general curriculum. They provide a different content learning experience

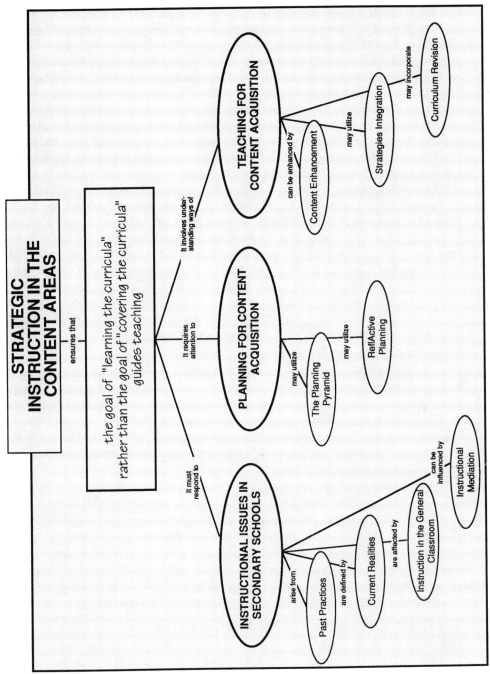

FIGURE 9.1   CHAPTER 9 ORGANIZATION

that may make the content easier to learn and more meaningful to students.

The alternative content approach is based on the concept of curriculum modification. *Curriculum,* as it is used here, is defined narrowly as the set of objectives or framework that defines what will be learned in conjunction with the written materials used to present the content. For many students who are significantly low-achieving (e.g. beginning readers, students with moderate disabilities), modification of the content curriculum to promote more appropriate and useful learning for these students can accomplish the intent of an appropriate education in a least restrictive environment. For many students with mild disabilities, those at-risk, low-achieving students, and marginal students (those having basic academic skills at a 4th-grade level or higher), this approach may not be an appropriate educational alternative.

The major criticism of the alternative approach has emerged from growing evidence of the insufficient background knowledge, scientific literacy, and cultural or social literacy of many low-achieving students. For example, Lenz (1984) found that a group of LD adolescents had significantly less background knowledge of social studies content than a peer group of adolescents judged to be normally achieving. This group of LD adolescents had a history of being in watered-down content classes or of being removed over the years from content-area classes for skill instruction. Yet, as these students moved into the secondary school setting, they were participating in the same content classrooms and operating under the same content classroom demands as students who had acquired adequate background knowledge in social studies content.

CONTENT-EQUIVALENT DELIVERY

Other parts of the country offer special education classes in which the content is equivalent to that covered in the general classroom. The content-equivalent approach involves total delivery of content by the special education teacher in a way that compensates for students' lack of basic skills, study skills, or strategies. This approach often involves audiotaping materials and using modified textbooks, expanded study guides and content outlines, alternative test formats, modified pacing, extended semesters, and so on.

TUTORIAL APPROACH

Elsewhere, the special education class course provides tutoring and review of content daily. In the tutorial approach another teacher is responsible for content delivery, and the special education teacher is responsible for providing short-term assistance in content areas in which the student is having difficulty or is failing. The special education teacher's major responsibility is to keep the student current in the general curriculum. Tutoring may be provided to students with or without specialized content-area courses. In some places the tutorial approach has been replaced by learning strategies instruction. In other instances no tutorial or other types of content-area support are provided.

THE DEBATE OVER INSTRUCTIONAL RESPONSIBILITIES

Discussion continues regarding who has the primary responsibility for teaching content to low-achieving students and how this should be accomplished. The increased attention to delivery of content to low-achieving students raises a number of issues related to implementation of the various methods for promoting content-area learning in the special education class setting.

First, some educators have questioned the ethical appropriateness (especially at the middle and high school levels) of support teachers delivering content in areas in which they are not certified and, in some cases, have never had a college course in that content area (e.g., Carlson, 1985). This practice has been questioned especially in states where special and regular diplomas are awarded differentially based on the type of courses that the student has taken and passed.

Second, the extent to which content learning is "watered-down" in the support setting is considered rarely in educational decision making. Therefore, we do not know whether sufficient content learning is occurring across the grades to prepare students to participate in future content-learning situations. This issue becomes especially relevant when students are removed from content-area classes for skill instruction or when content instruction is provided by a teacher who is not knowledgeable in that content area.

Finally, some educators argue that the main responsibility for educating the majority of children (including those with mild disabilities and other nonhandicapped but at-risk students) rests with the general classroom teacher and that all other teachers and staff should act as a support system or as team members in the learning process rather than being the primary provider of the student's education.

As the general education teacher assumes more responsibility for content-area instruction for students with learning disabilities, we should not be so naive as to believe that general classroom teachers can respond effectively to this challenge without support. A host of conditions affect how well teachers can respond to this challenge given the realities of the traditional secondary school setting.

CURRENT REALITIES IN SECONDARY SCHOOLS

Understanding the realities of teaching and learning in today's secondary school environment can help set the stage for discussing some of the methods for promoting content-area learning. The current realities of teaching in the secondary school setting include: (a) coverage of large amounts of content; (b) the complexity of content-area textbooks; (c) significant academic diversity among students; (d) limited academic interactions for students; (e) the practice of teaching primarily to achieving students; (f) limited time for planning and teaching; and (g) few opportunities for cooperative study, planning, or teaching among teachers. Some of the issues related to these classroom realities are discussed in this section, followed by some of the instructional implications for promoting content acquisition for students with learning disabilities as well as for many other students.

REALITY #1: PRESSURE TO COVER LARGE AMOUNTS OF CONTENT

ISSUES The amount of information that teachers feel pressured to cover is the biggest barrier to promoting meaningful learning for all students, regardless of their abilities or level of achievement. Secondary teachers see their primary role as "content experts" charged with delivering a considerable quantity of important information to students. To accomplish this, secondary content-area teachers commonly employ lecture as the primary vehicle of instruction (Goodlad, 1984; Putnam, Deshler & Schumaker, 1992; Moran, 1980). The result is often the presentation of great amounts of information, even though students often do not understand it.

To complicate matters, teachers constantly feel the pressure to teach more because of the information explosion in many content areas. Pat Cross of the University of California, Berkeley, Classroom Research Project captured the urgency that many teachers feel when she remarked, "If it weren't for students impeding our progress in our race to the end of the term, we certainly could be sure of covering the material. The question, however, is not whether we as teachers can get to the end of the text or the end of the term, but whether our students are with us on that journey" (personal communication, May 21, 1995).

Other authors echo these concerns. Newman (1988) has argued that "the addiction to coverage fosters the delusion that human beings are able to master everything worth knowing" (p. 346) and that this addiction "reinforces habits of mindlessness" (p. 346). In a similar vein the task force report of Project 2061 of the American Association for the Advancement of Science (1989) referred to the science and mathematics curriculum of secondary schools as "overstuffed but undernourished" (p. 14). In many ways we could describe the students who experience the coverage approach to instruction as also being "overstuffed and undernourished."

IMPLICATIONS   Many educators acknowledge the need to have a different perspective about what students really should understand as a result of participating in a course. In a sense these teachers are trying to step off the merry-go-round for a short time, take a look at the critical content and the strategies students must learn, and then focus on those outcomes. One approach for thinking differently about the amount of content to be learned in a course is captured by the phrase "less is more." As with many popularized phrases, this phrase must be explored in some depth rather than being taken at face value. In essence, educators must examine exactly what is meant by "less" and what is meant by "more."

As used here, "less" does not mean simply covering a smaller amount of content information. Rather, it means that teachers must consider carefully their courses and personal perspectives and ask critical questions such as: What is the important information that students should acquire before leaving the course? Which five or six key concepts will be used again and again in school and in life? What social skills will allow students to become interactive learners and problem solvers in school and in life? Which strategies for learning can students use in current courses and in a multitude of other situations? What level of understanding is needed to pursue subject areas later or to use that understanding in some other class? What motivates students to enjoy learning? The concept of "less" means devoting more attention to an in-depth and thorough understanding of fewer topics that are judged to be important and critical to learning and working. For the purpose of instructional decisions, "less" means "different" rather than "diminished."

What about the "more" in "less is more?" Again, "more" does not refer to additional knowledge of the same type that would have been delivered under a previous mindset that valued the delivery of large amounts of factual information. The word "more" also requires rethinking. Educators must ask themselves what students will learn, retain, and use. It most certainly will not be hundreds of individual, unrelated facts, although facts will be the necessary building blocks for new understandings. Instead, teachers need another set of critical questions, such as the following, to guide practice: Should students be able to compile a portfolio developed over the course that shows how their understanding has grown? Can the teacher see student growth as students become partners in learning, both with the teacher and with other students? Can students identify key concepts and show how each has been used at different points in the course? Do students know strategies for approaching novel tasks, asking questions that direct their thinking, making judgments, and arriving at conclusions?

The new perspective on content must include thinking more deeply about what is being taught, making careful decisions about content, and then teaching what is judged as critical. This view means abandoning our notion of "covering" the curriculum and replacing this with the idea of "learning" a critical curriculum based on depth of understanding, connectedness, organization, and application.

REALITY #2: COMPLEXITY OF CONTENT-AREA TEXTBOOKS

ISSUES Textbooks often are written with the expectation that students already are relatively expert at gaining information from textbooks. Many of these texts are written beyond the grade level of students, are poorly organized, and are written in an "unfriendly" or "inconsiderate" manner (Barba, Pang, & Santa Cruz, 1993; Hartman & Dyer, 1992; Konopak, 1988; Armbruster & Anderson, 1988). Of course, text features and approaches vary from publisher to publisher (Mastropieri & Scruggs, 1994), but, as a whole, U.S. textbooks are characterized by "encyclopedic" coverage with far less depth of coverage than in many other countries (Olson, 1994).

Even when textbooks are written in ways that "invite" learning, the sheer volume of information included in textbooks can be overwhelming for teachers and students alike, contributing to the overemphasis on coverage described earlier. Dempster (1993) pointed out that many texts are so packed with facts, names, and details that the real point of the lesson is often obscured. Taken together, the complexity of texts and the large amounts of information to be known about many subjects create a situation in which teachers have difficulty moving away from a coverage model.

IMPLICATIONS In response to the quality and expansiveness of textbooks, many teachers have become more aggressive in abandoning textbooks or using textbooks only as supplemental reference books. In some cases teachers are spending time helping students explore and select information from textbooks. More and more teachers are boldly skipping chapters and sections of texts and recreating the curriculum of the text. As teachers move away from structured texts, however, the need to impose some type of structure to help students organize and see the organization of information increases (Ciborowski, 1992). Teachers who shift from lecture-textbook instructional formats to lecture-discussion formats discover that they must find other ways to help students organize and structure what they are learning in the absence of the structure provided by a textbook.

REALITY #3: SIGNIFICANT ACADEMIC DIVERSITY

ISSUES The need to teach large amounts of information becomes considerably more challenging for content-area teachers when students with diverse perspectives and needs are combined in a single classroom. Because of the emphasis on learning content information from either lecture or written materials, content teachers have little time to devote to teaching students how to learn or to consider the background of students in planning how to present content. This is an area, however, in which many students with learning disabilities and other students considered at-risk for school failure need help to succeed in secondary content-area classes.

Although many secondary content-area teachers believe students need to acquire and use learning strategies, few secondary content teachers share the belief that they are responsible for teaching students these strategies (Lenz & Bulgren, 1994). Indeed, many secondary teachers believe that adaptations for students with learning disabilities are desirable but not feasible (Schumm & Vaughn, 1991). As a result, secondary content teachers may not feel comfortable making adaptations for individuals. Research has shown that general education classroom teachers often do not believe they have the necessary knowledge and skills to plan for inclusive teaching (Joint Committee on Teacher Planning for Students with Disabilities, 1995). Yet, teachers are aware of the diverse student abilities in their classes and the need to respond to this diversity.

Another complicating factor is that many teachers lack information about which students in a class have learning disabilities and which instructional techniques, activities, and materials have proven effective with these students. Given these realities, teachers often view the inclusion of groups of students of diverse abilities in their classrooms with mixed feelings.

Extending the challenge of responding to the diversity of their classes, many teachers argue that students with learning disabilities frequently are not the students who need the most attention in their classes (Joint Committee on Teacher Planning for Students with Disabilities, 1995). Often teachers report that students with disabilities have many more skills and abilities than students who have not received services from support classes. To these teachers the diversity of their classes, rather than the fact that students with learning disabilities require more specific types of accommodations, is a barrier to more inclusive educational practices. Actually, the likelihood that individuals with learning disabilities will receive special accommodations is low if a content-area teacher perceives that the needs of other students in the group will be unmet (Joint Committee on Teacher Planning for Students with Disabilities, 1995).

IMPLICATIONS   As teachers begin to respond to the diversity of their classes, changes must take place. First, teachers must begin to find instructional methods that are more sensitive to the individual's needs but that can be used effectively with the entire group of students. This means that teachers have to understand how to provide instructional leadership to guide students in the learning process when a variety of students in a class may not have the learning strategies necessary for acquiring the content.

Second, teachers will need to be prepared to know more about the diversity within their group of students. Lenz, Schumaker, and Deshler (1994) proposed a definition for significant academic diversity to capture the dimensions that have to be considered in teaching academically diverse classes:

> A class with significant academic diversity is characterized by students achieving in the average, above-average, and below-average range of academic performance as measured by teacher, school district, or state academic standards. This diversity in performance may be attributed to individual differences between teacher and students in learning needs, culture, gender, life experiences, abilities, skills, language proficiency, beliefs, goals, personal characteristics, orientations, or values.

This definition illustrates the types of differences that teachers identify among their students or between themselves and their students as they approach teaching. Kissam and Lenz (1994) came up with the acronym HALO (high achievers, average achievers, low achievers, and others) to describe this diversity. They argued that, in addition to the agreed-upon achieving groups, other students are present within or across these groups whom teachers do not think fit neatly into achievement-centered categories. For example, students may not learn because of cultural differences between them and their teachers. In addition, competing values and beliefs within the group may inhibit learning. At times students may be experiencing emotional stress within their lives because of family or peer problems or may be struggling with physical, sexual, or drug abuse.

Finally, students with disabilities may be included in any achievement category at different times. This diversity places greater pressure on teachers to teach content in ways that are sensitive to individual differences but are broad enough to be used with the group. The diversity encountered in many classes will require more thoughtful planning about the content and more class time to build good connections between the content and the students.

Most secondary teachers struggling with diversity in their classes respond by providing more opportunities for peer-assisted learning (Lenz, Schumaker, & Deshler, 1991). Peer-assisted learning may take the form of peer tutoring or cooperative learning group work. As peer-assisted learning is used to respond to diversity, more attention will have to be given to helping students learn social skills and attitudes for working with others who are different from themselves. This also will require additional planning and instructional time.

REALITY #4: LIMITED OPPORTUNITIES FOR ACADEMIC INTERACTIONS

ISSUES Interactions between teachers and students with learning disabilities are markedly different as students move from the elementary to the secondary level. At the secondary level students come in contact with a given teacher for shorter periods of the school day than at the elementary level, and the potential for a teacher to adjust instruction to meet individual needs, to provide additional assistance, or to make adaptations is far less (Schumaker & Deshler, 1988). This difference in school structure makes it more difficult for secondary content teachers to become familiar with the strengths and needs of all students, a factor that may be crucial for students with LD. In addition to total contact through the year, interactions within a single class period often are different from those at the elementary level.

Research provides further insights regarding student-teaching interactions within a given class period. In general, content teachers begin a class with specific plans regarding instruction and expectations about how activities and interactions will progress (Clark & Peterson, 1986). Once the complex flow of the class has begun, little time and energy are available to teachers to process the variety and quantity of information that emerges during classroom interactions (Clark & Peterson, 1986).

Many teachers recognize that this situation is not ideal. Researchers report positive results when teachers move out of their preplanned teaching routines (Morine-Dershimer, 1979). When this happens, the teacher can seize the "teachable moments" that give teachers opportunities to take advantage of chances to interact with students by explaining or clarifying a learning point (Shroyer, 1981). These types of opportunities for interactions, again, may be particularly critical for students with learning disabilities. These ideal moments may seldom occur, though, and students with learning disabilities often may not be the students involved in the interaction. Consequently, Brophy (1984) contended that the potential for improving teaching simply through more and better interactive decision making is limited because few teachers can interrupt the flow of lessons to think about alternatives. Therefore, Brophy (1984) emphasized the need for routinization of hierarchically organized sets of instructional principles so teachers can respond effectively to decision points that arise in the process of teaching.

IMPLICATIONS   A barrier to promoting the success of students with learning disabilities in the secondary school setting seems to rest with the quality and frequency of interactions between teachers and students. Some school districts have begun to experiment with ways of including students with disabilities in regular classroom settings without the support of special education personnel. Yet, to be successful, this inclusion must attend to the needs of students with disabilities. In instances where inclusion has been successful at the secondary school level, significant support services were provided to teachers and students that enhanced the quality of teacher-student interactions in learning. (Joint Committee on Teacher Planning for Students with Disabilities, 1995). These services focused on ensuring that:

— group instruction embedded prompts and teaching for all students to learn and use strategies.
— content-area learning was guided by routines that compensated for students' poor strategies and involved students in the learning process.
— additional support was made available by support-class teachers to help students learn and apply specific and general learning strategies.
— collaboration and teaming with a focus on enhanced student learning occurred frequently between special and regular education teachers.

REALITY #5: INSTRUCTION GEARED TO ACHIEVING STUDENTS

ISSUES   Secondary level content classrooms often focus on achieving students. In a study of teacher planning, Lenz and Bulgren (1994) found that most teachers plan for "B" students. Teachers reported that teaching to the "B" student allows them to challenge the "C" students while teaching at a high enough level to keep the "A" students motivated. The "D" and "F" students are expected to "get what they can." This response to planning and teaching often is the case even for teachers who have significant academic diversity among students in their classes.

As a result, the environment in many classrooms is one in which only some, but not all, students feel accepted, connected to what is going on in the classroom, and successful. This has been referred to as the "disconnected" classroom setting (Bulgren, Deshler, & Schumaker, 1993; Lenz, Marrs, Schumaker, & Deshler, 1993). In many "disconnected" classrooms the teacher's goal is simply to cover the content before the end of the school year, regardless of whether all students are learning.

IMPLICATIONS   Teaching to achieving students is highly reinforcing for a teacher because he or she can see results. To try to reach at-risk students is risky. To fail is not reinforcing. The process of planning and teaching, however, has to include more thinking about how teachers respond to students who are struggling with the content while maintaining the integrity of the curriculum for all students. Many teachers report that simply targeting and "studying" one or two students in both the low-achieving group and the high-achieving group over time has helped them shift their planning and teaching to meet the needs of low-achieving students while maintaining the motivation of high-achieving students.

Simply bringing the topic of planning and teaching on behalf of students with special needs to teacher planning meetings can broaden the scope of methods used in a class (Joint Committee on Teacher Planning for Students with Disabilities, 1995). Lenz, Bulgren, Deshler, Schumaker, and McKnight (1994) have documented how discussions between general classroom and support-class teachers regarding targeted high, average, and low-achieving students can affect the amount and types of accommodations that teachers will consider for their classes.

Students, too, have definite views regarding teachers' use of accommodations in content classrooms. In a student survey Vaughn, Schumm, and McIntosh (1991) found that, in general, students favor adaptations in instructional procedures, special assistance, and student groupings, but do not favor adaptations in assignments, tests, and textbooks. These views regarding teacher adaptations were found for both secondary and elementary students (Vaughn, Schumm, & Kouzekanani, 1993). Critically important to the underlying assumptions of this chapter is that the adaptations most students prefer are those that help promote learning. Students perceive teachers who make adaptations as better able to meet individual student needs, willing to provide extra help, and more caring and understanding of students. What adaptations, then, do students prefer? Adaptations that help all students learn! That concept is the subject of much of this chapter.

REALITY #6: LIMITED TIME FOR PLANNING AND TEACHING

ISSUES A further complicating factor for teachers who are challenged with reaching groups of students who have diverse learning abilities is limited planning and teaching time. What time is allotted to plan tends to be taken up with conferences, grading, and administrative tasks. As a result, for many secondary teachers, planning is done at times other than that scheduled (Lenz, Schumaker, & Deshler, 1991). This amount of planning time often is insufficient for developing new instructional techniques, activities, or materials that might help individual students or groups of students with special needs learn better in class. Given the demands of coverage and increased diversity, teachers simply do not have enough time to prepare for the demands they face. In addition, the amount of instructional time that teachers have available to interact with students in class is roughly the same as it was 50 years ago.

IMPLICATIONS Time is probably the biggest enemy of learning. There simply is not enough time to do what is required to do the best possible job. Given this reality, what can be done? First, adopting a "less is more" perspective in teaching content no longer becomes simply one option among many for teachers who are expected to be more responsive to the diversity of their classes. Currently, it is the best way to approach instruction responsibly. Second, teachers may need to redefine their instructional role by identifying how they are helping students learn to be independent explorers of the content. This means that teachers have to shift their self-view of "sage on the stage" to the image of "guide on the side."

REALITY #7: LIMITED OPPORTUNITIES FOR COLLEGIAL STUDY, PLANNING, OR TEACHING

ISSUES   Historically teachers have been isolated from other teachers as they teach. In the secondary school setting few opportunities exist to allow discourse on teaching and learning. Rarely do teachers share or discuss ways to reach "hard-to-teach" students. As a result, teachers may feel isolated and unstimulated. Frequently teachers are fearful of other teachers' views of their teaching (Johnson, 1990). As a result, ideas are not shared, and a spirit of community, or shared responsibility for solving some large educational dilemmas, is not cultivated. Finally, as new methods are introduced and inservice workshops are offered, implementation of potentially useful approaches often is abandoned because sufficient opportunities for support and problem solving are not made available (Showers, Joyce, & Bennett, 1987).

IMPLICATIONS   Even with new ways of thinking about content, teachers may feel alone as they attempt to make changes in how they teach. Support from general education teachers and special education teachers is one answer. Consultation and cooperation between regular and special education teachers can facilitate generalization of learning and processing for students and also provide support among teachers (Joint Committee on Teacher Planning for Students with Disabilities, 1995).

Another response is to draw upon ways of teaching that have been the expert domain of the special education teacher and to use those techniques more widely. What is it that special educators know, particularly about students with learning disabilities, that will help teachers approach the task of teaching content to all students, including those with learning disabilities and other students at-risk for school failure? The answer to this question is important because if techniques designed to enhance the content learning of students are to be widely used, these techniques must be suited to a wide range of students. Even if content sometimes is taught or supported by teachers in resource room settings, the techniques used in those settings must be the type adapted for the general classroom. Because of increased content demands, teachers' needs for consultation, and students' learning preferences, regular and special education teachers must work together.

INSTRUCTION IN THE GENERAL CLASSROOM

Although a number of efforts have been made within the general classroom setting to help low-achieving students be more successful in learning content, these efforts are not and cannot be the same as the approaches associated with content delivery in the special education class setting. Several conditions give rise to this circumstance:

1. The content parameters of the general curriculum usually cannot be altered.
2. Efforts to promote individual learning must not inhibit or detract from the learning of other students in the class, and to the maximum extent possible, should benefit all or the majority of students in the class.
3. The preparation, implementation, and evaluation of efforts and their results must be easily integrated in ongoing instructional efforts and time frames.

4. These efforts must be sufficiently powerful to influence the performance of low-achieving students in the context of the general classroom setting (Bulgren, Schumaker, & Deshler, 1988; Lenz, Alley, & Schumaker, 1987).

To incorporate these considerations, some research has been directed to teaching routines that teachers can use in general classrooms.

The concept of the *teaching routine* has emerged from efforts to apply general research on teacher thinking and effective instruction to the demands of teaching a variety of students considered at-risk for school failure. From the general research on teacher thinking and performance, a plausible picture of how teachers approach teaching has been proposed. Yinger (1977) indicated that teaching routines are sets of established procedures for students and teachers that control and coordinate sequences of behavior in the classroom. Clark and Peterson (1986) noted research suggesting that teachers establish these routines early, with few modifications or changes once they are established.

Examination of this instructional process has led educational researchers to begin to conceptualize the difference between effective and ineffective teachers. For example, effective teachers often are seen as those who identify and implement teaching routines that reduce student variability in learning and at the same time maximize individual achievement for all members of the class. Effective teachers also appear to monitor students' responses as the teaching routine is implemented, and if their performance is not appropriate, modify the routine or leave the routine to induce more appropriate learning.

Ineffective teachers, on the other hand, may not have developed powerful teaching routines or may be unable to break out of a set of routines once they have been initiated. The goal of the ineffective teacher is to "get through" the lesson, often ignoring or dismissing indications that some students are not learning (Joint Committee on Teacher Planning for Students with Disabilities, 1995).

This conceptualization of the teaching process provides a helpful framework for beginning to think about how instruction in the content areas can be enhanced for many low-achieving students. This approach allows us to acknowledge that most content teachers have a tremendous amount of information to process and act upon daily. As a result, most teachers do develop routines that help them survive on a day-to-day basis. When additional demands are placed on them to add to their instructional responsibilities, however—specifically the challenge to modify instruction for low-achieving students—the cost must be measured in terms of additional information-processing demands as well as time. Much like a full dinner plate that will overflow if additional food is added, the instructional demands placed on teachers are so great already that additional demands cannot be placed on them.

INSTRUCTIONAL MEDIATION FOR ALL STUDENTS IN THE GENERAL CLASSROOM

As deficiencies of content-area instruction in the special education class setting have become apparent, efforts have been made to include special education students, especially students with mild learning and behavior problems, in the general content classroom. These efforts have been accompanied by parallel efforts to infuse appropriate in-structural methods for students of diverse abilities into the general education setting. As a result of this trend, some educators have adopted a philosophy in which the role of the special education class teacher is to teach the student skills and strategies that will promote more effective and efficient learning while the role of the general content-area teacher is to present content in a manner that all students can understand and remember (Lenz, Clark, Deshler, & Schumaker, 1989). The assumptions regarding this role of the general content teacher must be understood in light of instructional mediation.

A critical issue in promoting the success of low-achieving students in content-area learning is the nature of the relationship between the learner and the teacher. Should the teacher take responsibility for mediating between the students' abilities and the to-be-learned material, or should the students be expected to learn to mediate between their abilities and the to-be-learned material? From these two alternative perspectives, methods for promoting student involvement in learning can be conceptualized as falling into one of two categories of cognitive mediators. Cognitive mediators are techniques a teaching agent (e.g., teacher, textbook, film) or a student utilizes to improve student learning. Cognitive mediators can be classified into two groups: externally generated mediators and internally generated mediators.

Externally generated mediators are the specific adaptations, modifications, or techniques a teaching agent uses to facilitate learning. These mediators are not under the learner's control, and their use depends on some external agent such a teacher, a peer, a textbook, or a computer. Much research on the improvement of teaching and student materials is based on the use of externally generated mediators. Two of the externally generated mediators that have been found to have facilitating effects on learning are inserting questions into the text (Kinder, 1992; Wager & Mory, 1992) and restructuring the text organization (Barba, Pang, & Santa Cruz, 1993; Hartman & Dyer, 1992; Konopak, 1988). The assumption is that externally generated mediators will induce the student to process information more efficiently by carefully using external stimuli or cues. The success of these mediators seems to depend on the ability of the teaching agent to incorporate mediators into the instructional process in a manner that will have a positive influence on learning. These may be thought of as teacher-mediated methods.

Internally generated mediators are the adaptations learners use to facilitate their own learning (e.g., learning strategies). The learner produces these mediators at his or her choice and convenience to meet specific learning needs. Internally generated mediation can be prompted through instruction in strategies the student can use to mediate learning independently using the cues the teaching agent provides. The assumption is that teaching students how to mediate their own learning through learning strategies will result in more efficient processing of information on an independent level. These may be thought of as student-mediated methods.

The power of an externally generated mediator may be conceptualized as the extent to which it promotes internally generated mediation by the student. That is, the most effective teaching methods and materials are those that promote the student's active learning through learning cues. The more limited a student's ability to mediate learning internally through appropriate cognitive strategies, the greater is the need for teaching agents to promote mediation externally through learning cues or to support a student's use of internal mediators.

The goal of intervention efforts based on teacher mediated methods is to deliver content information in a manner that takes into consideration the student's unique characteristics. Teacher-mediated methods encompass a wide variety of teaching procedures that vary only in the manner and context in which they are used. Whereas student-mediated interventions focus on changing the student, teacher-mediated interventions require teacher intervention. Therefore, the aim of teacher-mediated interventions is to identify how the teacher can mediate learning effectively to compensate for the student's inability to mediate learning independently.

A significant amount of space in this chapter is devoted to discussing the various procedures that can be used to enhance the delivery of content to low-achieving students through teacher-mediated methods. These procedures fall within the areas of both planning and teaching for content acquisition.

PLANNING FOR CONTENT ACQUISITION

Although most teachers have little time for teacher planning in their busy schedules, planning is vitally important when students of disparate abilities are included in the general education classroom. Promoting content-area learning requires devoting significant amounts of time to reflecting on the content and then taking action that will make a difference for students with learning disabilities. Teacher attention should be directed at selecting and teaching the critical content, creating a community in which the students are learning partners with the teacher, and committing to teaching techniques that reflect these principles.

Although most research on effective instruction traditionally has focused on what teachers actually do in the classroom, research on how teachers think about and approach instruction has been gaining momentum. For example, Clark and Peterson (1986) reviewed the research on teachers' thought processes, teachers' actions, and the observable effects of those actions in the classroom. Their survey of planning research reveals a growing awareness of the different types of teacher planning, the functions of planning, and the relationship between planning and the content of instruction. More recent research has provided new information about how teachers plan, particularly when the class is characterized by academic diversity (Joint Committee on Teacher Planning for Students with Disabilities, 1995).

THE PLANNING PYRAMID

The Planning Pyramid (Figure 9.2) was developed by Schumm, Vaughn, and Leavell (1994) to help secondary teachers make curricular decisions related to students with learning disabilities in the context of the broader group of students in a class. The planning process utilizes the Planning Pyramid to help teachers reflect on what to teach. In addition to this graphic device, a set of planning questions prompts teachers to think about different instructional areas.

The Planning Pyramid, which has three levels, encourages teachers to think about and represent the curriculum so as to provide opportunities for all students in the class to

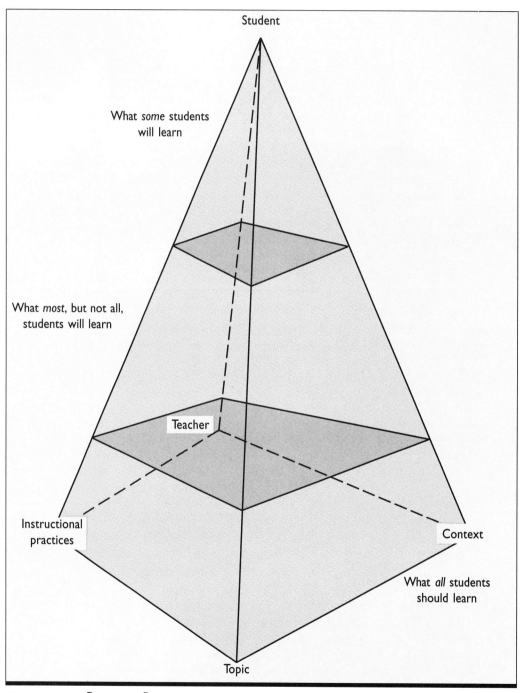

Student

What *some* students
will learn

What *most*, but not all,
students will learn

Teacher

Instructional
practices

Context

What *all* students
should learn

Topic

FIGURE 9.2   PLANNING PYRAMID

Source: *Planning for Academic Diversity in America's Classrooms: Windows on Reality, Research, Change and Practice*
(1995) by the Joint Committee on Teacher Planning for Students with Disabilities.

learn. Schumm, Vaughn, and Leavell (1994) developed planning forms for teachers to use as they plan instruction based on the Planning Pyramid. This form allows teachers to record target concepts, instructional strategies and adaptations, materials and resources, and evaluation procedures and other products. The first level, the base of the Planning Pyramid, represents the most important concepts to be taught. This level houses broad concepts and ideas that anchor the area to be taught. The guiding question here is: What do I want all students to learn?

The middle level of the Planning Pyramid is the level of information considered next most important for understanding the information. It includes additional concepts and information that support the concepts listed in the base of the Planning Pyramid. The guiding question here is: What do I want most of my students to learn?

The top level of the Planning Pyramid represents information that teachers consider to be of supplemental importance. It contains a list of information that the teacher expects only a few students in the class to learn. The guiding question here is: What information might some students learn? Schumm, Vaughn, and Leavell (1994) have cautioned teachers that the Planning Pyramid is to be used for placing content into levels of importance, not students into levels of achievement. Students with learning disabilities may be able to learn information categorized into any of the levels of the Planning Pyramid. The Planning Pyramid guides lessons at the unit and lesson levels.

PLANNING UNITS WITH THE PLANNING PYRAMID

The Planning Pyramid can be used to plan a unit of instruction. Schumm et al. (1994) presented the following orienting questions that can be used in a self-questioning process to guide teacher decision making about what concepts will be taught in a unit:

QUESTIONS PERTAINING TO THE TOPIC

- Is the material new or review?
- What prior knowledge do students have of this topic?
- How interesting is the topic to individual students?
- How many new concepts are introduced?
- How complex are the new concepts?
- How clearly are concepts presented in the textbook?
- How can I relate this material to previous instruction?
- When considering all topics I am responsible for covering this school year, how important is this topic in the overall curriculum?

QUESTIONS PERTAINING TO THE TEACHER

- Have I taught this material before?
- What prior knowledge do I have of this topic?
- How interesting is the topic to me?
- How much time do I have to plan for the unit and individual lessons?
- What resources do I have available to me for this unit?

QUESTIONS PERTAINING TO THE STUDENTS

- Will a language difference make a given concept difficult for a student to comprehend?

■ Will students with reading difficulties be able to function independently in learning the concepts from text?

■ Will a student with behavior or attention problems be able to concentrate on this material?

■ Will any students have high interest or prior knowledge of these concepts and be anxious to explore the topic in greater breadth or depth or share their knowledge with classmates?

■ Will the students have the vocabulary they need to understand the concepts to be taught?

■ What experiences have the students had that will relate to this concept?

■ Can this concept be related in some way to the cultural and linguistic backgrounds of the students?

A Unit Planning Form (Joint Committee on Teacher Planning for Students with Disabilities, 1995) can be developed to record the target concepts to be learned within the unit. Space should be provided for recording plans for (a) materials and resources; (b) instructional strategies and adaptations; and (c) evaluation procedures and other products (see Figure 9.3).

PLANNING LESSONS WITH THE PLANNING PYRAMID

The Planning Pyramid (Schumm et al., 1994) also can be used to plan lessons using a specific Lesson Planning Form (see Figure 9.4). The Lesson Planning Form helps teachers consider how teaching and planning will occur and is used to: (a) identify concepts to be taught, (b) consider the context of instruction (i.e., social aspects of the classroom), (c) identify most effective instructional practices, (d) structure an agenda for a lesson, (e) list material, (f) identify assignments, and (g) identify evaluation methods.

The lesson planning process associated with the Lesson Planning Form adds further details to what will be taught and how it will be taught by focusing on each lesson within the unit. The sequence presented below can be followed, and questions can be asked to develop a lesson plan on the Lesson Planning Form:

1. Concepts to be taught are identified based on the Planning Pyramid device by asking questions such as: What do I want all, most, and some of the students to learn as a result of this lesson?

2. The context of instruction is considered—social aspects of the classroom, the way the classroom is organized for instruction, and the school-based factors that affect the classroom environment. This information can be identified by asking the following questions:

   ■ How will class size affect my teaching of this concept?

   ■ How well do my students work in small groups or pairs? Which students need to work together?

   ■ What resources do I have to teach this topic?

   ■ What instructional practices can promote teaching, learning, and assessment most effectively?

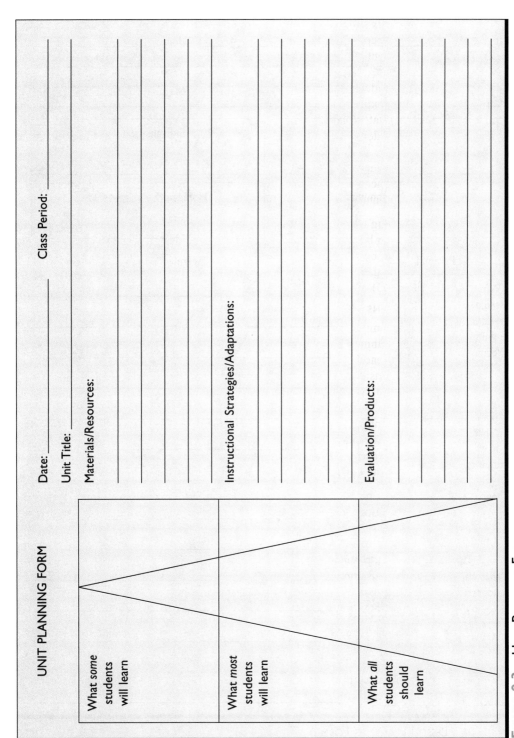

UNIT PLANNING FORM

Date: _____   Class Period: _____

Unit Title: _____

Materials/Resources:
_____
_____
_____
_____

Instructional Strategies/Adaptations:
_____
_____
_____
_____

Evaluation/Products:
_____
_____
_____
_____

What some students will learn

What most students will learn

What all students should learn

FIGURE 9.3   UNIT PLANNING FORM

Date: _____   Class Period: _____   Unit: _____

Lesson Objective(s): _____

_____

_____

Materials	Evaluation

In Class Assignments	Homework Assignments

Pyramid

Agenda

What
some
students
will
learn

What
most
students
will
learn

What *all*
students
should
learn

1 _____

_____

2 _____

_____

3 _____

_____

4 _____

_____

5 _____

_____

6 _____

_____

7 _____

_____

FIGURE 9.4   LESSON PLANNING FORM

The following questions can guide reflections:

- What methods will I use to motivate students and to set a purpose for learning?
- What grouping pattern is most appropriate?
- What instructional strategies can I implement to promote learning for all students?
- What instructional adaptations can I implement to assist individuals or subgroups of students?
- What learning strategies do my students know or need to learn that will help them master these concepts?
- What in-class and homework assignments are appropriate for this lesson?
- Do some assignments have to be adapted for children with special needs?
- How will I monitor student learning on an ongoing, informal basis?
- How will I assess student learning at the end of the lesson?
- How will I assess student learning of lesson material at the end of the unit?
- Are any holidays or special events likely to distract students or alter instructional time?

3. The lesson is synthesized by structuring an agenda for the lesson, listing materials to be gathered and used, identifying in-class and homework assignments, and identifying what method will be used to evaluate student learning.

REFLACTIVE PLANNING

Lenz and Bulgren (1994) have described planning that incorporates the principles of both reflection and action as ReflActive Planning.* ReflActive Planning has seven steps for general secondary content-area classroom teachers and their colleagues to use. The goal of ReflActive Planning is to plan group instruction that is more sensitive to individuals with special needs. Although the steps were developed with individuals with special needs in mind, a basic premise of ReflActive Planning is that every student needs to know certain important content information. Therefore, the goal of ReflActive Planning is to maintain the integrity of the content while enhancing it in ways that allow all students to learn better.

The seven steps of ReflActive Planning are organized in a logical sequence to prompt reflection for decision making in critical areas of student learning. Teachers are not expected to follow this sequence every time they plan. Rather, they are expected to use the seven steps to guide self-questioning and reflection in specific areas during planning and teaching. ReflActive Planning requires teachers to act on their planning by using graphic devices to share their plans explicitly with students. When teachers plan knowing that they will share their plans for the course, unit, or lesson with students, their planning becomes more learner-centered. This strategic planning is the basis for strategic teaching.

---

* The authors would like to thank Christopher Clark, Michigan State University, for describing teacher planning as "reflaction," from which the term "ReflActive planning" eventually emerged.

ReflActive Planning Process

When teachers used ReflActive Planning to plan courses, units, and lessons, they became more aware of the relative importance of different sets of information and the relationships expressed in their content. More time was spent helping students see the structure and organization of the content and teaching chunks of the content judged to be critical for other learning (Lenz, Deshler, Schumaker, Bulgren, et al., 1994; Lenz, Schumaker, Deshler, Boudah, et al., 1993; Lenz, Boudah, Schumaker, & Deshler, 1993). Independently, teachers began to adjust how they were teaching and evaluating student learning and performance.

Teachers are introduced to ReflActive Planning in three stages:

Stage 1   The seven steps involved in ReflActive Planning are described. The acronym SMARTER is used to help teachers remember the steps. The seven steps in SMARTER prompt the teacher to:

1. *Select* the critical content outcomes and develop a set of critical questions that all students should be able to answer by the end of instruction.
2. *Map* the organization of the critical content in a way that will show the structure of the content and will be meaningful to all students.
3. *Analyze* why the critical content might be difficult to learn based on:

amount	complexity
interest	student background
relevance	organization
abstractness	external conditions (e.g., interruptions)

4. *Reach* decisions about how the content will be taught and how the content might be enhanced during instruction to reduce potential learning difficulties through specific teaching devices, alternative teaching routines, instruction in learning strategies, or curriculum revisions.
5. *Teach* students about the enhancements in ways that will inform students about how to use the devices, routines, strategies, or curriculum revision, and explicitly guide students to become actively involved in exploring and using the enhancements to improve learning.
6. *Evaluate* mastery of the critical content and related processes for HALO (high-achievers, average-achievers, low-achievers, and others) (for a more complete discussion of HALO, see discussion elsewhere on the realities of academic diversity).
7. *Reevaluate* planning and teaching decisions for the next step in learning; the next step may be tomorrow's lesson, the next unit, or a revision for next year's course.

Stage 2   Teachers are asked to represent their planning decisions on a graphic device— for example, a map of the content illustrating the important content. Difficult but important relationships and ideas may be highlighted on the map. Questions that everyone should be able to answer are listed. Specific routines or learning strategies that will be used to promote learning are identified.

Stage 3 Teachers use the graphic device to launch instruction, organize information as instruction continues, and review learning at the end of instruction. Teachers use this graphic device to share with students their vision for an entire course, units within a course, and specific lessons.

A basic premise of ReflActive Planning is that every student needs to know a certain set of critical information. Students are expected to learn more than this set of critical information, of course, but ReflActive Planning focuses on reflecting on how to teach this more limited set of critical content really well. Teachers are asked to move away from simply covering a lot of information quickly and move toward more careful selection and instruction of critical information that opens the door for more learning.

The dimensions of ReflActive Planning emerged from numerous studies on course, unit, and lesson planning. In almost every instance, teachers who made the most changes on behalf of at-risk students were involved in working through the SMARTER steps and becoming more explicit about their plans with students (Joint Committee on Teacher Planning for Students with Disabilities, 1995). In addition, the use of these types of steps and processes of planning for more explicit instruction significantly enhanced communication between teachers.

The ReflActive Planning Process can be applied to course, unit, or lesson planning. Lenz and Bulgren (1994) reported that the largest changes in teacher planning occurred at the unit level. The number and quality of instructional accommodations observed, however, were the highest in classes in which planning changes had been achieved and integrated at all levels—course, unit, and lesson.

REFLACTIVE COURSE PLANNING ReflActive course planning involves using the SMARTER planning process to launch the course, maintain course themes throughout the course, and bring closure to the course. It also involves targeting certain students to guide reflection and instructional decisions throughout the course. When teachers used ReflActive course planning, they spent considerably more time introducing major course ideas, concepts, themes, and routines to students than teachers who did not use the routine.

The ReflActive Planning steps were used to help teachers reflect on course concepts and outcomes. To facilitate course planning, teachers:

— developed approximately 10 course questions representing the critical content that was the essence of the course.
— developed a course map representing the structure of the course content and how the content was to be covered and learned.
— identified what traditionally had made the course content difficult for students.
— identified routines and course "rituals" to be used throughout the course to help students learn the content of the course and to build a "learning community" in the classroom. Teachers considered a set of questions related to ensuring that students in their course felt they were part of a community of learners. These questions were raised as teachers developed course plans that were revisited throughout the year. The questions included the following:

  ▪ How can I nurture learners who are enrolled in this course to strengthen connections among them so they aid each other's learning?

■ How can I include everyone enrolled in the course in the learning process such that each person becomes an involved learner?

■ How can I determine the strengths and resources of each course participant and provide opportunities for each to contribute to the learning community?

■ How can I accommodate the limitations of course participants?

— translated their course planning decisions into graphic devices they used to "launch" the course (see Figure 9.5 and Figure 9.6). Teachers maintained course decisions and themes by revisiting course concepts, content, questions, routines and strategies, and classroom values at the beginning of each new unit.

— evaluated student perceptions of the course by how well students were able to answer the 10 course questions and developed ways for students to visibly see their progress in learning the content of the course.

— closed the course by evaluating the 10 course questions, discussing the quality of the community, and completing course content synthesis activities. Teachers committed to meeting regularly with colleagues to talk about the progress of individual students in attaining course content, progress in creating a learning community, and modification of course questions and routines.

The mind-set that teachers have about the inclusiveness of learning to be emphasized across an entire course will affect significantly how teachers respond to individuals with special needs in the context of the group. Development of a course planning routine to create a classroom "learning community" and to focus on major course themes significantly affects lesson and unit planning as well as how teachers attend to the needs of individuals in the context of the group.

REFLACTIVE UNIT PLANNING   ReflActive unit planning is used within the context of a course that has been developed using the course planning routine. When teachers were taught to use ReflActive unit planning, the way they presented content to students changed such that they became more explicit with students about what was to be learned, the relationships among chunks of content, and the activities to aid learning, and they frequently became more explicit in leading students in how to organize, understand, recall, and apply information (Lenz, Schumaker, Deshler, Boudah, et al., 1993). Understanding and retaining information by low-achieving students, students with learning disabilities, and average-achieving students improved substantially, as reflected in unit test scores and in scores on unit content maps and explanations of those maps. Figure 9.7 provides an example of a unit organizer.

In ReflActive unit planning a unit of instruction is defined as any chunk of content distinguished from a previous chunk of content through a closure activity (e.g., a test) or some kind of transition. To use the routine for a unit of content, teachers follow three stages:

Stage 1 Teachers use ReflActive Planning questions prompted by SMARTER to make instructional decisions about the unit of information. Planning decisions related to the unit are translated into a graphic device such as the unit organizer depicted in (Figure 9.7). The unit organizer: (a) contains a paraphrase of the unit topic, (b) shows how the unit relates to previous and future units, (c) de-

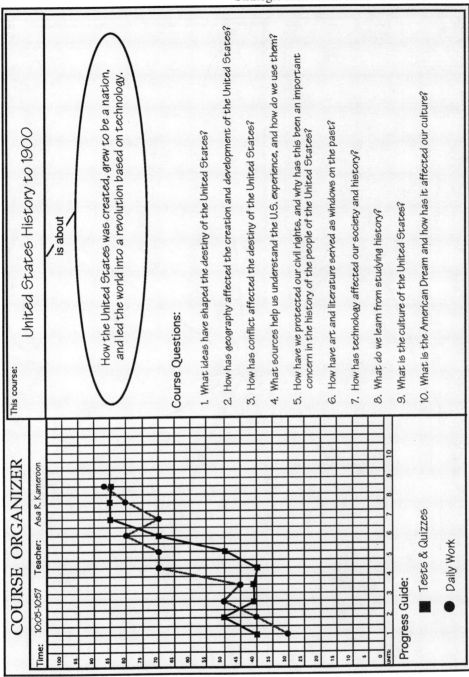

COURSE ORGANIZER

Time: 10:05–10:57 **Teacher:** Asa R. Kameroon

This course: United States History to 1900

is about

How the United States was created, grew to be a nation, and led the world into a revolution based on technology.

Course Questions:

1. What ideas have shaped the destiny of the United States?

2. How has geography affected the creation and development of the United States?

3. How has conflict affected the destiny of the United States?

4. What sources help us understand the U.S. experience, and how do we use them?

5. How have we protected our civil rights, and why has this been an important concern in the history of the people of the United States?

6. How have art and literature served as windows on the past?

7. How has technology affected our society and history?

8. What do we learn from studying history?

9. What is the culture of the United States?

10. What is the American Dream and how has it affected our culture?

Progress Guide:

■ Tests & Quizzes

● Daily Work

FIGURE **9.5** SAMPLE COURSE ORGANIZER

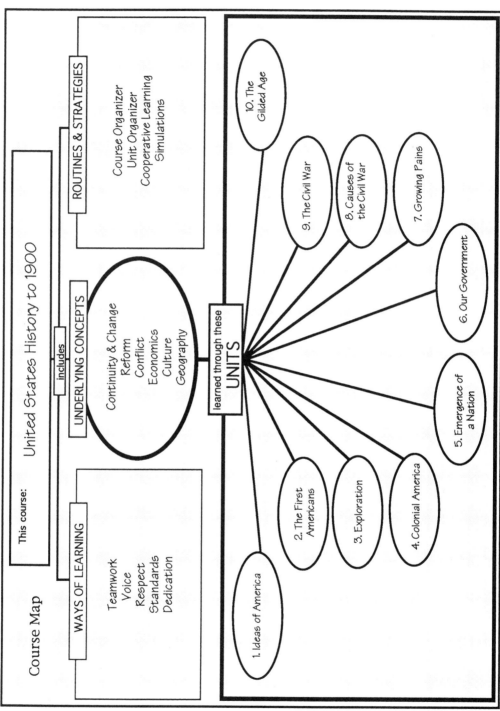

FIGURE 9.6   SAMPLE COURSE MAP

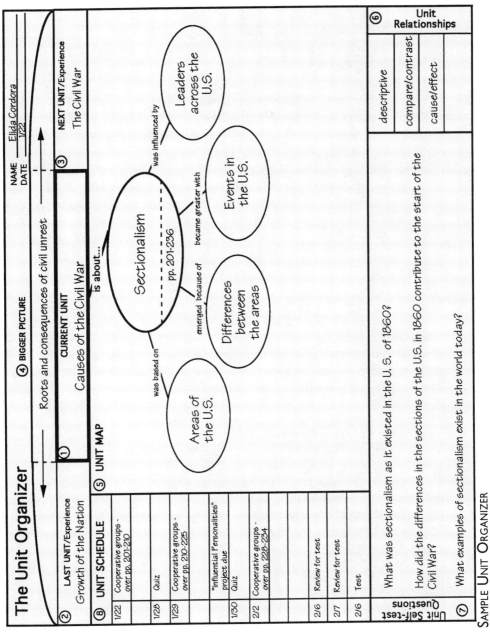

The Unit Organizer

NAME Elida Cordora
DATE 1/22

② LAST UNIT/Experience
Growth of the Nation

④ BIGGER PICTURE
Roots and consequences of civil unrest

③ NEXT UNIT/Experience
The Civil War

① CURRENT UNIT
Causes of the Civil War

⑤ UNIT MAP

is about...

Sectionalism
pp. 201-236

was influenced by → Leaders across the U.S.

became greater with → Events in the U.S.

emerged because of → Differences between the areas

was based on → Areas of the U.S.

⑥ Unit Relationships

| descriptive |
| compare/contrast |
| cause/effect |

⑧ UNIT SCHEDULE

1/22	Cooperative groups - over pp. 201-210
1/28	Quiz
1/29	Cooperative groups - over pp. 210-225
	"Influential Personalities" project due
1/30	Quiz
2/2	Cooperative groups - over pp. 228-234
2/6	Review for test
2/7	Review for test
2/6	Test

⑦ Unit Self-test Questions

What was sectionalism as it existed in the U. S. of 1860?

How did the differences in the sections of the U.S. in 1860 contribute to the start of the Civil War?

What examples of sectionalism exist in the world today?

FIGURE 9.7 SAMPLE UNIT ORGANIZER

picts the unit's organization in seven or fewer graphic parts, (d) shows the relationships among the parts, (e) provides labels for the relationships, (f) depicts a timeline of activities and assignments for the unit, and (g) has a space for critical questions to be addressed during the unit instruction. These will be referred to as *target questions*.

Stage 2 Teachers share unit organizer with students. They use an interactive process with students to share their plans for the unit using a graphic device. Students create their own graphic organizer for their notebooks. Students and teachers work together to generate a list of critical questions they want to be able to answer at the end of the unit.

Stage 3 This stage is implemented as the unit progresses and as it closes. The teacher and students revisit and expand on the unit organizer after it has been used to launch the course. Teachers show the organizer to students at the beginning of a lesson to review how far they have progressed and at the end of a lesson or section of a unit to review, to remind them of an assignment, refer to a critical question that can now be answered, or review for a test.

The process of "sharing" the unit plan seemed to be the most important part of the intervention (Lenz and Bulgren, 1994). Teachers reported that prior to using the planning process, they often had lost sight of the big picture of the unit and frequently became bogged down trying to cover masses of information. As a result, students had difficulty understanding relationships among the clusters of information presented. The teachers reported that construction of the unit organizer helped them focus their instruction and assessment activities and, as a result, students could understand important relationships. The teachers also reported that students' collaboration in constructing the routine and their freedom to modify the routine to suit their own needs without fear of being labeled uncooperative helped them use the routine successfully.

REFLACTIVE LESSON PLANNING   ReflActive lesson planning is used within the context of a unit that has been developed using the unit planning routine. The stages of ReflActive lesson planning are identical to the stages used for ReflActive unit planning. This is efficient because secondary teachers have little time for lesson planning (Lenz & Bulgren, 1994). Lesson planning often takes place in snatches of time (e.g., while driving the car, taking a shower, taking a walk). Thus, using the ReflActive planning process for lesson planning may not make much sense to teachers if it is not presented to them within the context of unit planning. Once teachers make the big decisions at the unit level, the smaller decisions at the lesson level fall into place easily. Teachers tend to use the whole ReflActive planning process, including full presentation of a lesson organizer (see Figure 9.8), for a particularly difficult lesson or series of lessons. SMARTER guides a reflective process, a graphic organizer of the lesson is constructed, the plan is shared with students, and the organizer is used to organize lesson progress and closure. As with the unit planning process, teachers reported that they like having the freedom to use as much or as little of the process as needed for a given course, unit, lesson, or given group of students.

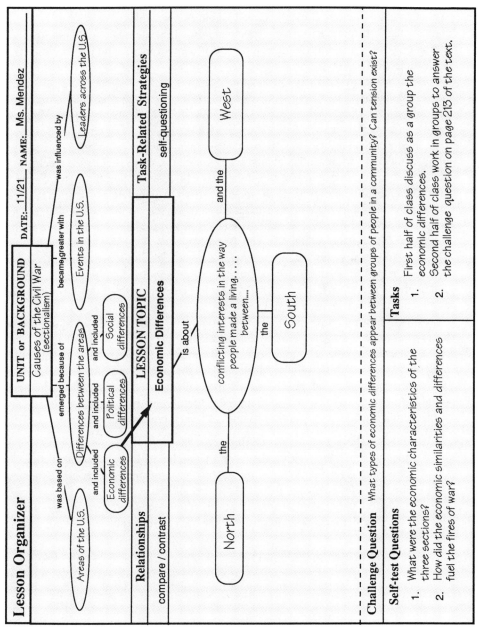

Lesson Organizer

UNIT or BACKGROUND   DATE: 11/21   NAME: Ms. Mendez

Causes of the Civil War
(sectionalism)

was based on → Differences between the areas → emerged because of → became greater with → was influenced by

Areas of the U.S.

and included → Economic differences

and included → Political differences

and included → Social differences

Events in the U.S.

Leaders across the U.S.

LESSON TOPIC

Economic Differences

Relationships   compare / contrast

Task-Related Strategies   self-questioning

is about

North — the → conflicting interests in the way people made a living..... between.... — and the → West

the → South

Challenge Question   What types of economic differences appear between groups of people in a community? Can tension exist?

Self-test Questions

1. What were the economic characteristics of the three sections?
2. How did the economic similarities and differences fuel the fires of war?

Tasks

1. First half of class discuss as a group the economic differences.
2. Second half of class work in groups to answer the challenge question on page 213 of the text.

FIGURE 9.8   SAMPLE LESSON ORGANIZER

CRITICAL ELEMENTS OF REFLACTIVE PLANNING

Although many elements of ReflActive Planning seem to have a positive effect in changing how teachers approach content-area planning, three elements stand out: (a) identification of target questions, (b) development of content maps, and (c) sharing the plans with students.

DEVELOPING THE CRITICAL QUESTIONS   Standing back and generating self-test questions that can be shared with students seems to help teachers link planning, teaching, and evaluation. The questions serve several purposes. *First*, generating these questions for a course, unit, or lesson helps a teacher sift through the vast amount of content and look for the critical information. In many ways the questions represent a practical means of reframing objectives. Unlike objectives, however, questions require the teacher to think about how he or she would like the student to talk about or talk through the content or task. Understanding the strategies a student is using to complete a task often requires the teacher and the student to converse about the student's approach to a task. Thinking about content in terms of questions can prepare teachers and students for this conversation.

Second, the questions often focus on the types of relationships embedded in the content. This helps direct students' attention to what is important about the content. *Third,* questions can help teachers and students monitor progress in learning. Regularly, the teacher and students can stop and ask, "Do I know the answer to this question yet?" *Fourth,* target questions can be used to guide self-testing and studying for tests.

Although formulating questions may be easy, forming a small set of questions that best represent the knowledge of an entire course, unit, or lesson is not as easy. In the case of generating 10 course questions, these questions may be formulated at the beginning of the year and reformulated, as needed, as the year progresses. This is one case in which the process is as valuable as the product. Of course, 10 is an arbitrary number and should be adapted to suit instructional needs; 3 or 13 may work just as well.

Formulating course questions provides at least three distinct benefits:

1. Once teachers have identified the target questions, they can present these questions to students. Writing them on a posterboard for permanent display in the classroom is useful. As a result, students have information about the themes and direction of the course in front of them at all times.
2. Students can be asked to answer the target questions at the beginning of the year. This provides a quick analysis about the background knowledge of all students in the class.
3. Students can be asked to answer the same questions at the end of the year. This gives an excellent indication of whether students have learned what was considered most important when it comes time to evaluate student acquisition of knowledge.

MAPPING CONTENT   Once a teacher has decided what is critical about a chunk of content, he or she draws a graphic organizer to make the structure or organization of the content explicit. In the maps developed for the course, unit, and lesson maps, the visual contained a paraphrase of the main idea or theme of the course, unit, or lesson and illustrated the organization of the content. For courses, the map may represent the order in which units of the course will be presented. For maps of units, teachers were asked to construct seven or fewer graphic parts representing major topics or ideas in the unit, show the connection between the parts using lines or arrows, and then label those connecting lines in the unit map to make the relationships explicit. Lesson maps were created using the guidelines for unit maps. In general, the maps that seemed to have the greatest impact on teachers and students incorporated a linear depiction of what was to be learned. For this reason, the traditional "webbing" commonly used for brainstorming was discouraged.

Mapping the content provides teachers with an opportunity to provide explicit information to students about the relationships between and among pieces of information. Many students, particularly students with learning disabilities, have difficulty seeing these relationships for themselves. Providing an explicit map of relationships is valuable especially for these students. It also is valuable for teachers because it reminds them of decisions about the structure of the course, unit, or lesson and what is most important to teach. Creating a content map has the added advantage of providing other teachers who may interact with a student an efficient overview of the content material and the important relationships to be mastered.

SHARING PLANS When teachers plan knowing that their plans will be shared with students, teachers become more careful and explicit about what they want to communicate to students. Essentially, teachers must shift their planning conversations away from trying to describe to another adult what they are going to do and move toward trying to communicate with their students. When this happens, they must think through the relationships and connections. The most difficult aspect of developing the content maps described earlier is creating the line labels that indicate how pieces of information are connected. Teachers seem to know the relationships but have not developed a vocabulary that allows them to describe relationships adequately to students who do not see the content connections automatically.

TEACHING FOR CONTENT ACQUISITION

Various instructional approaches have been investigated in an attempt to respond to the challenges associated with content demands of the general secondary classroom, the diverse abilities of students in these classes, teachers' instructional preferences, and limited planning time. Teaching for content acquisition in the regular content classrooms can be accomplished through: (a) content enhancement, (b) integration of strategies into content instruction, and (c) curriculum revision methods. Taken together, these represent varying levels of strategic approaches to teaching for content acquisition.

Strategic teaching is a form of instruction in which the teacher compensates for students' lack of strategies and models and guides students in learning how to learn. For the teacher, strategic teaching in the content areas is accomplished by informing students of the routines that are to be used and then explicitly modeling and guiding students through these routines in ways that show them how to learn the content. The goals involved in using these teaching routines are to: (a) compensate for students' inefficient or ineffective strategies, (b) prompt students to learn, develop, and use learning strategies associated with understanding and using the content, (c) incorporate modeling in how to use learning strategies in content areas so students see how strategies can be applied, and (d) allow the teacher to communicate that strategic approaches to learning the content are valued in the content-area curriculum. Enhancing content through devices, routines, and procedures that make information more learnable is an important element in strategic teaching.

CONTENT ENHANCEMENT

Research on the characteristics and development of teaching routines has been organized under an approach to content-area instruction called *content enhancement* (e.g., Bulgren, Schumaker, & Deshler, 1988; Lenz, Alley, & Schumaker, 1987; Lenz, Bulgren, & Hudson, 1990; Schumaker, Deshler, & McKnight, 1989). Lenz and Bulgren (1995) defined "content enhancement" as a way of teaching an academically diverse group of students that:

— meets both group and individual needs.
— maintains the integrity of the content.
— selects critical features of the content and transforms them in a manner that promotes learning.
— carries out instruction in partnership with students.

Content enhancement is based on a set of principles and has specific components. These are discussed next.

PRINCIPLES OF CONTENT ENHANCEMENT

Instructional techniques that fit the definition of content enhancement are based on principles that can guide teachers in how to teach students of varying ability to acquire content information. These principles, which form the foundation for the content enhancement process, emerged from research findings that cut across the areas of curriculum, instruction, educational psychology, and special education. These principles can guide teacher thinking, planning, and teaching in the content areas and define the teacher's role as professional, content expert, mediator of student understanding, and partner in the learning process.

INSTRUCTIONAL LEADERSHIP   Teachers who engage in content enhancement are professionals who are adept at organizing material and interacting with students in a manner that facilitates the processing of information. For example, Turnure (1985, 1986). has suggested that the teacher is the central organizer of various dimensions of the teaching process, all of which interact. These dimensions consist of: (a) the learner's characteristics (e.g., skills, knowledge, attitudes); (b) the learning activities (e.g., attention, discrimination, rehearsal); (c) the nature of the criterion task (e.g., recognition, recall, transfer); (d) the nature of the materials (e.g., sequencing, structure, appearance, difficulty), and (e) the instructional agent (e.g., how the teacher describes, questions, sequences instruction, or models instruction.)

Therefore, how a teacher approaches the organization of these various dimensions, achieves balance among these dimensions, and responds to new demands and procedures related to these dimensions is an important part of the instructional process. This perspective is supported by a number of educators and has been reinforced by a report from the National Institute of Education (1975) regarding the importance of research on teachers' thought processes as a means of understanding and improving the process of teaching. This report pointed out that any innovations related to the context, practices, and technology of teaching were of necessity mediated through teachers' minds and motives. Therefore, how a teacher processes information and approaches the teaching process probably is as important as understanding how a student approaches the learning process.

EXPERT INSTRUCTION   In content enhancement, because teachers are the experts, or should be the experts, in both content and content relationships, they are responsible for determining how to compensate for the inadequate or confusing presentation of knowledge. Content enhancement should promote instruction consistent with three major principles of expert instruction.

First, the teacher must become aware of the relationship between the various types of information the student must learn and how this information can best be presented. This awareness includes the presentation of important concepts, delivery of background knowledge, discussion of textbook formats, descriptions of methods or processes, explanation of facts or themes, exploration and discovery of information or ideas, and promotion of generalization of information to other areas.

Second, teachers must be aware of the problems that many students have in processing information. For example, the teacher must determine if a student has a limited set of background experiences, difficulties in understanding key conceptual information, unfamiliarity with processes or methods of inquiry, difficulties with the written word or textual formats, or an inability to generalize a specific skill from one area to another.

Third, teachers must be aware of ways to make information more meaningful to the student. These methods could include verbal expansions, verbal and concrete illustrations, graphics, or extended interactive routines that have been explained to students. Obviously, great responsibility is placed on the teacher, as expert, to become the primary "learning situation organizer."

FUNCTIONAL CONSTRUCTIVISM   In general, the assumptions underlying content enhancement are compatible with a view of instruction known variously as intentionalist, constructivist, or cognitivist. This approach to instruction emphasizes the learner's internal constructive processes (Armento, 1986; Mayer, 1987; Gagné, 1985). Researchers using this approach believe that human behavior must be studied not in isolation but, rather, in relation to thoughts, intentions, and affect. Teachers and students alike are seen as active constructors of meaning. As a result, the teacher engaged in enhancing content for learning must make predictions about how students will or will not be able to construct meaning from the information and then facilitate the learning process through classroom interactions and activities.

In content enhancement the ideas underlying constructivism are assumed to be tempered with the knowledge that the teacher as instructional leader brings to the learning situation. Ultimately the teacher is responsible for planning, monitoring, and mediating instruction. This understanding pervades various approaches to teaching in which the teacher is the learning mediator who monitors student comprehension and approaches the acquisition of strategies, at least initially, as a joint responsibility shared by the teacher and the students (Palincsar, Ransom, & Derber, 1988–89). To do this, the teacher devises ways that students can construct knowledge, but the learning situation always is under the watchful and expert eye of the teacher, who can direct learning and insert prompts, as needed, to help the student, always monitoring and adjusting to allow for learning.

The combination of ideas underlying constructivism and teacher mediation of student learning places content enhancement within the paradigm of functionalism (Lenz & Mercer, 1993). This paradigm is based on the assumption that learning depends on the individual within an ever-changing context. Depending on previous knowledge and skills, the student may need to have learning broken into parts. At other times the student may need to engage in active discussion to understand and assimilate new knowledge into an existing knowledge base.

The goal is to help students use strategies flexibly as they become good information processors. This can be facilitated by molding and maintaining an instructional framework for interactive learning that has been described by Borkowski and Muthukrishna (1992) as guided and direct, as well as transactional and constructive.

LEARNING PARTNERSHIP   A particularly important assumption in content enhancement is that students will be involved with the teacher in the learning process in a *learning partnership* (Bulgren, Schumaker & Deshler, 1993). Teachers involve students in learning partnerships in a variety of ways, depending on their background and repertoire of strategic approaches to learning. The teacher recognizes that the students who do possess learning strategies have a way to approach a learning task that guides their personal thinking and action and is a way to reflect on outcomes and to self-monitor actions. The teacher as "expert" also recognizes when students *do not* possess learning strategies, that is, when they are not learning independently in efficient and effective ways.

The teacher's goal is to facilitate explicitly the active construction of meaning and development of the learning partnership. This is important particularly for students with learning disabilities, who often do not recognize the usefulness or even the existence of innovative teaching practices when the teacher uses them (Lenz, Alley, & Schumaker, 1987). If this is not occurring, the teacher has ways to compensate for students' lack of learning strategies. This is the use of explicit teaching that can guide students in learning and learning partnerships.

COMPONENTS OF CONTENT ENHANCEMENT

Three components in content enhancement make it effective for all students, including students with learning disabilities: (a) devices, (b) routines, and (c) procedures associated with strategic teaching. *First*, teaching devices are instructional tools teachers use to enhance learning. They enable teachers to focus on specific points, make learning explicit, prompt elaboration on a point, and make ideas and relationships concrete. *Second*, teaching routines are instructional procedures designed to involve students in constructing or using the device and processing the information the device targets. This helps students learn the content and the thinking processes that can be generalized to other areas. *Third*, procedures associated with strategic teaching involve informing students about use of the devices and routines, teaching content explicitly with the devices and routines, and arranging for student interaction and involvement in the learning process. Components of content enhancement are presented in this section along with examples of instructional techniques that promote content enhancement.

DEVICES   A teaching device is an instructional technique or a tactic designed to achieve a singular goal in promoting learning. It is associated with facilitating organization and understanding, recalling, and applying information. Examples of teaching devices are a story illustrating a central point, an analogy linking familiar information to new information, a study guide to help students explore and test their knowledge about a chunk of information, and tables or diagrams used to clarify organization or understanding of information. A teaching device usually covers a small segment of a lesson and often is embedded in a teaching routine. For example, within a larger teaching routine designed to teach a broad concept, a device might be embedded to help students recall a list of features salient to the concept.

Teaching devices are used when specific elements of a lesson seem to present learning demands for the student that require more manipulation than the teacher predicts the student can handle effectively or efficiently. According to Schumaker, Deshler, and McKnight (1989), teaching devices are used to: (a) make abstract information more concrete, (b) connect new knowledge with familiar knowledge, (c) enable students who cannot spell well to take useful notes, (d) highlight relationships and organizational structures within the information to be presented, and (e) draw unmotivated learners' attention to the information.

The list of teaching devices in Figure 9.9 is presented in grid form to indicate both the type of device and the mode of presentation. Different types of devices are used to organize, promote understanding of, describe, demonstrate, or foster storage and recall of critical information. Modes of presentation include those that are presented verbally or structured visually.

Verbal devices a teacher may use during presentations include summaries, organizational cues, analogies, stories, role plays, and acronyms. Verbal devices are inserted in presentations to enhance meaning. A number of researchers have investigated the effects of using teaching devices with students who have learning disabilities. Some research has been done on the verbal cues teachers use and the effects of these cues on notetaking. Verbal cues signal the organization of information in an oral presentation. For example, students can be taught learning strategies to listen to the lecture, identify verbal cues, note key words, and order the information into an outline form (Scanlon, Schumaker, & Deshler, in prep). Once students learn to identify the cues a teacher uses to emphasize critical information, they can become more adept at identifying and learning the content. Visual devices to enhance presentations may be used in conjunction with verbal devices but are designed to promote greater comprehension by drawing students' attention to important points through focused observation. Visual devices used in presentations include graphic organizers, diagrams, tables, outlines, webs, models, films, demonstrations, and visual images to promote recall.

Teaching devices that have been used to denote the organization of information and might be presented visually to students include:

- Graphics consisting of diagrams with parts of the pictures or labels missing (Bergerud, Lovitt, & Horton, 1988)
- Study guides prepared with questions concerning main concepts and vocabulary

Mode: presentation

Type: used to	Verbal	Visual
Organize (arrange information in meaningful structures)	Summarization Chunking Advance Organizer Post Organizer Verbal Cues about organization	Outline Web Hierarchical graphic organizer Table Grid Flowchart
Promote Understanding (clarify words or concepts)	Analogy Comparison Synonym Metaphor Antonym Simile Example	Symbol Concrete Object Picture Model Diagram
Describe (tell a story)	Current Events Past Events Fictional Story Hypothetical Scenario Personal Story	Film Filmstrip Video
Demonstrate (show through action)	Role Play Dramatic Portrayal	Physical gesture or movement Movable Objects Demonstration
Promote Recall	Acronyms Keywords	Visual images Sketches

FIGURE 9.9   TEACHING DEVICES

words from the assigned passage (Bergerud, Lovitt, & Horton, 1988)

■ Charts and diagrams (Lovitt, Stein, & Rudsit, 1985)

■ Teacher-supplemented textbook adaptations such as vocabulary practice sheets and framed outlines (Lovitt, Rudsit, Jenkins, Pious, & Benedetti, 1985)

■ Outline/overviews prior to student reading of the text (Darch & Gersten, 1986)

■ Structuring information on a topic into categories using a free-form graphic or web. An example of this structuring of categories of information is semantic mapping (Anders & Bos, 1984; Johnson & Pearson, 1984). This approach is similar to concept webbing (Lenz & Bulgren, 1995).

■ Charts in the form of a grid to display relationships between words and concepts (Johnson, Toms-Bronowski, & Pittelman, 1982). This type of device has also been referred to as a relationship chart (Bos & Anders, 1987), semantic feature analysis (Johnson & Pearson, 1984), and a concept analysis table (Lenz & Bulgren, 1995).

While research continues to develop regarding how teaching devices are used to promote learning, many students, particularly those with learning disabilities or others at risk for school failure, clearly do not understand the point of using the devices. In some cases, students were found not to be aware that teachers were doing anything different when teachers incorporated devices into their teaching repertoire (Lenz et al. 1987). Therefore, teachers constantly must be aware of the need to bridge the gap between teacher use of a device and student awareness of its use and importance.

Teaching devices must be developed carefully and presented explicitly. If students are to benefit from the use of a device, they need to be informed about its purpose and usefulness, about when a device is being used in class, and about the role they are expected to play in the learning process associated with the device. This means that a teaching device must "grow up" to become a *teaching routine*. This occurs when the device is presented in conjunction with steps in a routine linking the underlying cognitive processes with the elements of each device and when the teacher presents the information explicitly in a sequence or pattern that the students can recognize. The students are included in a partnership of learning in which their thoughts and questions are valued and they take part of the responsibility for thinking and learning.

In sum, then, devices are conceptualized as a form of externally-generated mediators a teacher uses to facilitate learning. In the final analysis, the power of an externally generated mediator is determined by the extent to which it promotes internally generated mediation by the student. This occurs optimally when the teaching devices are embedded in a teaching routine that contains cues regarding expectations for student participation, guidance in how to use the device, and a review of the information learned, as well as how learning was achieved. Several teaching devices, including the visual devices presented in Figures 9.5 through 9.8 and Figures 9.10 through 9.12, have been used in association with teaching routines and strategic teaching procedures. Discussion related to these teaching devices that have "grown up" to become teaching routines are presented in the next section.

ROUTINES   A teaching routine is a set of integrated instructional procedures revolving around a specific teaching device designed to promote broad learning goals associated with the full spectrum of information acquisition, storage, and expression/demonstration of content information. A routine usually guides the delivery of large chunks of information in a lesson and may even be the focus of an entire instructional period. The purpose of a teaching routine is to structure instruction so that potential learning difficulties are anticipated and addressed.

These routines can focus on: (a) organization routines in which the student is made aware of the organizational elements of content information, and any preliminary information that will facilitate awareness of the content to be presented; (b) understanding routines in which the student is guided to deeper understanding of concepts and relationships between and among concepts; (c) recall enhancement routines through which the student is guided to identify important information and be able to recall the information when needed; and (d) application enhancement routines in which the teacher shifts the control of learning to students and sets up conditions in which students can demonstrate their competence with the information.

Attention to the organization of information has emerged primarily from research in cognitive psychology in the area of organizers. Interest in organizers centered initially on *advance organizers* (Ausubel, 1963; Ausubel, Novak, & Hanesian, 1968). Ausubel et al. (1968) described the advance organizer as a tool to provide ideational scaffolding for the incorporation and retention of more detailed and differentiated material. Research on the advance organizer has indicated that it is most likely to promote learning when students do not have the background knowledge for a particular task, do not make the connection between prior knowledge and the to-be-learned information, and do not make the connections between relationships in the to-be-learned information.

Although research on the use of advance organizers indicates that they can promote learning with low-achieving students, applications with individuals who have learning disabilities and other low achieving students indicate that many at-risk students: (a) do not recognize advance organizers independently when teachers use them (Lenz, Alley, & Schumaker 1987), (b) do not use lesson organizers independently to promote learning during a lesson (Scanlon, Schumaker, & Deshler, in press), and (c) usually can benefit from their use only when organizers are made explicit prior to, during, and after a lesson (Bulgren, Schumaker, & Deshler, 1988; Lenz, Alley, & Schumaker, 1987; Scanlon, Schumaker, & Deshler, in press). The key to making the organizer work to enhance learning seems to be related to the extent to which learners learn about the presence and use of organizers to enhance learning and are prompted by the teacher to become involved actively in using organizers (Lenz et al., 1987).

Lenz (1984) identified 12 types of organizer statements that could be used singularly or in combination as advance organizers, lesson organizers, or post organizers. These categories of organizers are:

1. Informing the student of the purpose of the organizer
2. Clarifying the actions that the teacher is to take
3. Clarifying the actions the student is to take
4. Identifying the topic of the learning task
5. Identifying subtopics related to the learning task
6. Providing background information
7. Stating the concepts to be learned
8. Clarifying the concepts to be learned
9. Motivating students through the presentation of rationales and examples
10. Introducing or repeating new terms or words
11. Providing an organizational framework for the learning task
12. Stating the outcomes desired as a result of engaging in the learning activity.

Routines to promote organization have been developed to teach a lesson, unit, chapter and course. In this development process, many of the devices used in the planning process "grew up" to become teaching routines that can be used to explicitly teach students about the organization of a lesson, chapter, unit, or course.

The *lesson organizer routine* (Lenz, Marrs, Schumaker, & Deshler, 1993) is built around a visual device, called the *lesson organizer*, that is shared with the students. The device is used to: (a) provide information about the lesson topic, (b) paraphrase the lesson topic into words the students can understand easily, (c) inform students about the relationship in the lesson content, (d) specify the strategies students can use to gain, store, or express information in the lesson, (e) show graphically how the lesson is related to the unit in which it is contained, (f) depict graphically how the lesson content is organized, and (g) provide questions for the students to test themselves as they review the content of the lesson.

A set of procedures for the lesson organizer guides the teacher in how to use the lesson organizer. The teacher uses the lesson organizer to share lesson goals, review critical background knowledge related to the lesson, help students see how the new information is connected to information previously learned, and describe and map the main concepts in the lesson and the relationships among them. In addition, the teacher uses the lesson organizer to link the content of the lesson to students' background knowledge. The teacher does this through stories, examples, and analogies. Finally, the teacher uses the lesson organizer to explore the critical content questions that students should be able to answer at the end of the lesson and then specifies tasks and expectations associated with the lesson (refer to Figure 9.8).

A *chapter survey routine* was developed to prepare students to process information from a text using a strategy with the acronym TRIMS (Schumaker, Deshler, & McKnight, 1989). TRIMS stands for title, relationship, introduction, main parts, and summary. The elements covered by TRIMS are used to prepare for a lesson and guide the teacher through a process that helps him or her analyze a textbook for useful organizers and cues embedded within the text. If these organizers are not present in the text, the teacher can use the TRIMS process as a guide to enhance the "inconsiderate" text.

A key part of TRIMS involves identifying common idea relationship structures and the signal words associated with these relationship structures. The organizational patterns or relationship structures are, in essence, advance organizers for the reading assignment. If the teacher and students become more aware of these structures, they will understand the text more readily. Common idea relationship structures and words that signal those structures include: (a) simple listing, (b) comparison/contrast, (c) temporal sequence, (d) cause/effect, (e) problem/solution, (f) general/specific, and (g) related concept or category. These structures are organized on a worksheet teaching device, and the teacher uses specific procedures to help students do a TRIMS of the chapter.

The *unit organizer routine* (Lenz, with Bulgren, Schumaker, Deshler, & Boudah, 1994) is built around a visual device, called the unit organizer, (see Figure 9.7), that is shared with students and contains: (a) information about the relationship between the various units in the course, (b) the unit visual, used to highlight the big ideas, themes, and sections of the unit, (c) the unit schedule, used to list assignments, topics, tasks, and activities that students can expect in the unit and the projected dates these will occur, (d) unit relationships to indicate how information should be manipulated, (e) unit self-test questions representing the most important learning in the chapter, and (f) an expanded unit visual to allow teacher and students to add information to each of the parts.

A set of instructional procedures guides the teacher in how to use the unit organizer. The teacher provides the name and focus of the unit, anchors the unit topic to prior knowledge by providing an analogy or "grabber," reviews previous learning, constructs a clear unit organizer, labels links between and among information represented on the unit organizer, explains time requirements, tasks, and learning targets, explains the daily use of the unit organizer, states expectations and rationales, and checks for understanding of the unit organizer. The teacher provides explicit instruction about how the unit organizer will be used routinely to monitor progress and guide class discussions.

The *course organizer routine* (Lenz, Deshler, Schumaker, Bulgren, et al., 1994) is built around a visual device, called the course organizer, that displays information about: (a) the target questions for the course, (b) important course projects or experiences, (c) the key course concepts, (d) a course map of the units to be covered, (e) a list of ways that the class will work on creating a learning community, (f) a list of the ways that learning and behavior will be managed, and (g) a list of the strategies that will be used and reinforced as students learn the content.

Teachers use the course organizer to launch the course at the beginning of the year. As the year progresses, teachers use the course organizer to remind students about where they are in the course and about course concepts and questions. Teachers provide explicit instruction to students about the parts of the course organizer and inform students that they should keep the two-page course organizer in their notebooks. Students are told how the course organizer will be used routinely to monitor progress and guide class discussions on relationships between units (see Figures 9.5 and 9.6).

In addition to organization of information, routines can be used to promote a more thorough understanding of information. Understanding difficult but important concepts and relationships has to involve higher-order processing strategies. Whereas the anticipated outcome of an organization routine is to become aware and ready to learn, the aim of the understanding process is to acquire new information by integrating the new information with prior knowledge. Therefore, as the teacher moves from orientation to understanding, the teacher shifts the emphasis of the lesson from reviewing and predicting to integrating and storing.

Based on current research and theoretical proposals in cognitive psychology (e.g., Gagné, 1985; Mayer, 1987), the learner's role in the process of understanding content requires: (a) receiving the content that is to be learned, (b) recognizing and organizing the relationships in the content, (c) retrieving knowledge already known that is related to the new content, (d) deciding the relevance of the prior knowledge and either deciding that the new information must be learned or need not be learned, (e) translating the content into networks of prior knowledge, and (f) making conclusions based on the integration of prior knowledge with new information. Therefore, if the student has difficulty processing information at any point, the teacher must begin to prompt understanding through specific pedagogy. Similar to the decision-making process that might be part of the orientation process, teachers again must rely on their knowledge of the variables surrounding the to-be-learned information as well as information about the students (Borkowski & Muthukrishna, 1992).

The types of demands related to promoting understanding of content area information minimally include: (a) learning concepts; (b) applying or generalizing learned concepts to novel situations; (c) comparing and contrasting concepts; (d) learning rules and propositions (which specify the relationship between concepts); (e) learning and integrating main ideas and details; (f) learning procedures, processes, or sequences of actions; (g) learning cause-and-effect relationships; and (h) exploring problems, making judgments, and arriving at solutions. Therefore, the teacher's role is to determine if one of these content learning demands is present (induced by either the text or the learning objectives and goals), organize and manipulate the content in a manner that highlights the demands of the content, and promote content acquisition in a manner consistent with learning goals.

Research and commentaries in the area of concept teaching provide the foundation for developing methods that help students understand critical information (Bruner, Goodnow, & Austin, 1956; Gagné, 1965; Ausubel, Novak, & Hanesian , 1968; Klausmeier & Associates, 1979; Klausmeier & Ripple, 1971; Merrill & Tennyson, 1977). Components such as the following all have been utilized in various ways in developing methods to enhance the understanding of content: (a) the attributes, properties, or characteristics by which things are placed in a specific category; (b) the rules by which these attributes are joined in a concept class; (c) the hierarchical patterns of superordinate, coordinate, and subordinate concepts into which a concept fits; and (d) the instances or examples of a concept.

The teaching of concepts has been emphasized widely when developing classroom materials. Specifically, it has been applied to science (Voelker, 1972) and social studies (Martorella, 1972), two important content areas. Furthermore, Taba's (1971) teaching model for concept attainment incorporates these components, and Becker, Engelmann, and Thomas (1971) used these components in developing a programmed learning text. An important component among the many that promote understanding for students with learning disabilities in the content classroom is explicit instruction to inform and remind students about the structure of teaching and instructional materials used in the classroom. The routines presented below as examples of understanding routines focus on how the teacher can promote the understanding of a single class of items, of similarities and differences between concepts, or of relationships between concepts.

The *concept mastery routine* (Bulgren, Deshler, & Schumaker, 1993) is built around a visual device, called the concept diagram, that allows the teacher to display information related to a key concept and to work with students to analyze and understand the concept. Graphic forms on the concept diagram aid in displaying complex and abstract information that can lead to in-depth understanding of a critical concept. The concept diagram device is used to display information about: (a) the name of the targeted concept, (b) the overall or supraordinate category or class into which the targeted concept fits, (c) key words or important information associated with the targeted concept, (d) characteristics (qualities, traits, or attributes) that set examples of the targeted concept apart from examples of all other concepts, (e) examples and nonexamples of the concept, (f) a working space in which instances that are not yet identified as examples or nonexamples of the concept can be analyzed to determine if they fit within the definition of the targeted concept, and (g) the definition of the targeted concept.

Teachers follow a specific set of instructional steps that make up the teaching routine to help students use the concept diagram to explore a concept. The teacher gives the name of a targeted concept to the students, ascertains that students understand the larger concept group into which the targeted concept fits, and explores with the students key words or important information that students already know about the targeted concept. Then the teacher works interactively with students to identify characteristics that always must be present, may be present, or never can be present in examples of the concept, practice thinking about a new item that may or may not be an example of the targeted concept, construct a good definition of the concept, and review both the knowledge about the concept and the process involved in using the concept diagram. An example of a completed concept diagram is provided in Figure 9.10.

The *concept anchoring routine* (Bulgren, Schumaker & Deshler, 1994a) is built around a visual device, called the concept anchoring table, that allows the teacher to display information about a difficult new concept by developing an analogy to a familiar concept that shares critical characteristics with the new concept as shown in Figure 9.11. Graphic forms on the concept anchoring table display information about: (a) the name of the new concept, (b) the name of the known concept that will be used to develop the analogy, (c) information that the students know about the known concept that will be used to create the analogy, (d) characteristics of the known concept, (e) characteristics of the new concept, (f) an explanation of how each characteristic listed for the new concept and the known concept are similar and allow development of the analogy, and (g) a way for students to convey their understanding of the new concept.

Instructional procedures that have been developed for the concept anchoring routine guide the teacher in how to use the concept anchoring table with students. The teacher names the new concept for students, names the known concept for students, explores with the students key words or important information that students already know about the known concept, elicits or provides characteristics of the new concept that parallel those targeted in the known concept, works with the students to elicit or provides understanding that the shared characteristics can fit into larger groups of characteristics that allow development of the analogy, and to state, in a way the teacher selects, their understanding of the new concept or how the known concept and the new concept are related. Figure 9.11 provides a sample anchoring table.

The *concept comparison routine* (Bulgren with Lenz, Deshler, & Schumaker, in press) is built around a visual device, called the *concept comparison table*, that allows a teacher to display information about two or more concepts or topics through an analysis of the characteristics the concepts share. As shown in Figure 9.12, graphic shapes on the concept comparison table display information about: (a) the names of two or more concepts, (b) the name of the larger concept group into which the concepts fit, (c) characteristics each of the concepts possess, (d) identification of the characteristics in each that are alike, (e) identification of the characteristics in each that are different, (f) identification of the larger categories that describe how the characteristics are alike, (g) identification of the larger categories that describe how the characteristics are different, and (h) a summary statement about how the concepts are alike and different.

Specific procedures for the comparison routine guide the teacher in how to use the comparison table to compare selected concepts. The teacher provides the name of the concepts to the students, explores the characteristics of each, determines interactively with the students which characteristics are alike and which are different, elicits or provides the categories that describe how the characteristics are alike or different, and works with the students to discuss their understanding of the similarities and differences of the concepts and the process involved in developing the comparison table. Similar devices and routines can be developed to help students understand other relationships such as identifying causes and effects or considering both sides of an issue.

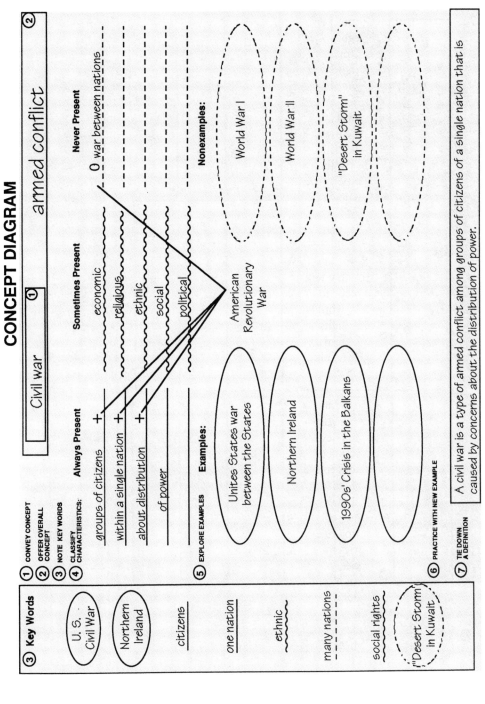

FIGURE 9.10 SAMPLES CONCEPT DIAGRAM

Anchoring Table

Name: _____ Date: _____

Unit: _____

① New Concept

Federalism in the U.S.A.

② Known Concept

Decision making in your school

③ Known Information

teachers

administrators

rules

penalties

not sure if powers are written down

teachers make assignments

administrators expel

④ Characteristics of Known Concept

Decisions are made by administrators & teachers.

Rules, written or understood, tell how power is divided.

Some powers belong to administrators (expel).

Some powers belong to teachers (give assignments).

Some powers belong to both (make rules, set penalties).

⑤ Characteristics of New Concept

Decisions are made by state & national govts.

Rules, based on Constitution, tell how power is divided.

Some powers belong to national govt (war, money).

Some powers belong to states (education, marriage, gambling).

Some powers belong to both (tax, punish crimes).

⑥ Characteristics Shared

2 groups are involved.

Rules tell how power is divided.

Some powers belong to one group.

Some powers belong to the other group.

Some powers belong to both groups.

⑦ Understanding of the New Concept: Federalism in the U.S.A. is a form of government in which decisions are made by both state and national govts. Rules to decide how power is divided are based on the Constitution. Some powers (e.g., make war, coin money) belong to the national govt. Other powers (e.g., education, marriage, gambling) belong to the states. Some powers (e.g., tax, punish crimes) belong to both.

ANCHORS Linking Steps	1. Announce the New Concept	2. Name Known Concept	3. Collect Known Information	4. Highlight Characteristics of Known Concept	5. Observe Characteristics of New Concept	6. Reveal Characteristics Shared	7. State Understanding of New Concept

FIGURE 9.11 SAMPLE ANCHORING TABLE

Comparison Table

2 overall concept
Economic conditions during the U.S. Civil War

| **concept** Southern economic conditions | **1 concept** Northern economic conditions |

3 Review characteristics

adequate food produced	adequate food produced
inefficient food distribution	efficient food distribution
few railroads	extensive, efficient railroads
limited industries	existing, prosperous industries

4 Same Characteristics

adequate food produced

6   Categories: Same

food production

5   Different Characteristics

7 Categories: Different

inefficient food distribution	efficient food distribution	food availability
few railroads	extensive, efficient railroads	transportation
limited industries	existing, prosperous industries	industry

8 Extension: What were the powers of each to raise and support armies?

9 Summarize understanding:

The economics of the North and South in the Civil War were similar because both produced adequate amounts of food. They were different because the North was superior in terms of availability of food, transportation systems, and industry.

FIGURE 9.12   SAMPLE COMPARISON TABLE

In addition to organizing and understanding information, secondary content class demands include the need for students to store and recall information.

The <u>recall enhancement routine</u> (Bulgren, Schumaker, & Deshler, 1994b) is built around a series of steps that involve cueing students that targeted information is important and that they should take notes, telling students about the type of mnemonic device that will help them remember the targeted information, presenting the information in conjunction with a selected mnemonic device, and reviewing the information and the device to assure understanding. Bulgren et al. provided a menu of mnemonic devices, including mental imagery devices, the keyword device, acronyms, and rhymes, for the teacher.

Creating devices for remembering depends upon a teacher's awareness of various devices that are available and may involve both extensive planning or spontaneous use. Among the many possible devices for remembering, with a multitude of variations, are the following:

1. *Mental imagery device.* Bellezza (1982) described various mental pictures and connections that facilitate memory.
2. *Keyword device.* Pressley, Levin, and McDaniel (1987) indicated that the most common version of the keyword method involves constructing interactive visual images. To do this, the learner generates an image of the definition referent as it interacts with a keyword. The keyword is a familiar concrete word that resembles a salient part of the unfamiliar vocabulary word. Mastropieri and Scruggs (1989) and Scruggs and Mastropieri (1990a; 1990b) have done significant research on keyword devices.
3. *Rhyming device.* Bellezza (1981) noted that at times information can be remembered by putting it into the form of a rhyme. Some rhymes have become part of almost every schoolchild's repertoire. These include rhymes designed to remember dates ("In 1492 Columbus sailed the ocean blue"). In classes in which the students are particularly receptive to this technique, the teacher could encourage construction of rhymes designed with the help of class members.
4. *Method of loci device.* Bellezza (1981) pointed out that students of rhetoric in ancient Greece and Rome commonly used the method of loci, which means "method of places." The method of loci involves memorizing a series of locations from one place to another and then associating items to be remembered in a sequence with each of those locations. Places where this method might be employed include the route from home to school and movement to various places within the school building or even within the classroom itself.
5. *FIRST-letter mnemonic device.* Nagel, Schumaker, and Deshler (1986) devised a FIRST-letter mnemonic strategy for students with learning disabilities and other low achievers. For this type of strategy, the student first must organize a list of words that must be remembered and write the first letter of each word. These letters then are analyzed to determine if they can be used to form a word.

Various other authors have presented reviews and discussions about a variety of techniques similar to those discussed here. These discussions or reviews include:

■ *Enhancements.* Hudson, Lignugaris-Kraft, and Miller (1993) identified seven types of content enhancements and provided research regarding advance organizers, visual displays, study guides, mnemonic devices, audio recordings, computer-assisted instruction, and peer-mediated instruction.

■ *Visual depictions.* Crank and Bulgren (1993) presented common structural components of visual depictions and examples of a variety of structures including central and hierarchical structures, directional structures, and comparative structures. These are used to express time, continuity, steps in a process, cycles, event chains, sequences cued by arrows, single concepts, and comparative structures.

■ *Mnemonic instructional devices.* Scruggs and Mastropieri (1990b) described the concept of mnemonic instruction, various types of mnemonic strategies, and how mnemonic instruction interacts with the specific learning characteristics of students with learning disabilities.

In addition to organizing, understanding, and recalling information, students in secondary content classes need to <u>apply</u> information in assignments or assessments. Teaching routines can be developed and used to lead students to more successful completion of assignments. The following examples of routines demonstrate how assigning work can be enhanced through more effective teaching routines.

The *quality assignment completion routine* (Rademacher, Deshler, & Schumaker, in press) is a routine for planning high-quality assignments. It has a planning phase, an explanation phase, and an evaluation phase. Each is interactive in nature, and each contains methods and procedures designed for teachers to use as they guide students to complete the tasks assigned. These phases are constituted as follows:

Planning Phase	1. Prepare a meaningful assignment based on a well-defined instructional objective.
	2. Link planning decisions to student motivation.
	3. Arrange clear directions.
	4. Note the time and details for the task-evaluation phase.
Explanation Phase	1. Activate the assignment completion process.
	2. State clear directions.
	3. Stop for students to react.
	4. Investigate student understanding.
	5. Guarantee work time and offering help.
	6. Note the due date, quality work expectations, and offer help.
Evaluation Phase	1. Analyze student satisfaction with the assignment, effort, and prompts.
	2. Analyze whether the completed assignment was done promptly, arranged neatly, finished completely, and edited for clarity.

The *project completion routine* utilizes a *project completion guide* (Lenz, Ehren, & Smiley, 1991) for goal setting and goal actualization. The goal setting component involves task evaluation and the generation of topics and specification of goals. A goal actualization component involves plan identification, plan expansion, consideration of demands, and self-monitoring.

At least seven major steps are required in teaching students to improve assignment completion using a goal attainment approach.

1. The teacher must identify the types of assignments that he or she requires for the expression of content mastery.
2. The teacher then must monitor student performance on the various assignments over time. At least three of each type of assignment should be collected and graded.
3. The teacher should present the evaluation information to students individually or as a group. If done as a group, the teacher should present averages of group performance to the class and private reports of individual performance to each student.
4. The teacher should assist students in setting goals related to improving grades on specific types of assignments and improving the rate of assignment completion.
5. For each goal the teacher should assist students in identifying specific problems or areas of difficulty and then develop plans to improve assignments.
6. The teacher and the student both monitor performance toward achieving these goals. The teacher should provide feedback on the types of problems that students are experiencing.
7. As goals are achieved, the teacher should help students set new goals and monitor progress. The teacher should explicitly draw student attention to improvement in grades that are related to improvements in assignment completion and management.

Research on the effects of students working together indicates that peers can facilitate content learning. *Peer-assisted assignment completion* is included in routines associated with teacher-mediated routines because, to be most successful, the teacher must arrange, direct, and monitor carefully the activities associated with peer interaction. Procedures related to promoting peer tutoring, student learning teams, and cooperative learning have been developed to guide teachers in promoting successful learning through these types of arrangements. The goal is to transfer the mediational responsibilities of learning from the teacher to a student's peer or peer group. Each student also assumes mediational responsibilities to participate in the group activity in a specified capacity.

To promote settings that facilitate these mediational responsibilities on the students' part, the teacher has to be aware of certain prerequisites and principles associated with cooperative learning. Certain cognitive prerequisites seem to be necessary for a student to respond appropriately to any type of goal structure, including a cooperative goal structure (Johnson, 1974).

1. The student must be aware that they are members of a group and that each member has a role in the group.
2. The student must be able to identify and respond to others' actions and performance.
3. A student must be aware of the goals of cooperation and interdependence and how attaining these goals can affect the performance of all group members.

The following set of procedures is a synthesis of procedures described by a number of researchers (e.g., Aronson, 1978; Delquadri, Greenwood, Whorton, Carta, & Hall, 1986; Jenkins & Jenkins, 1985; Johnson & Johnson, 1975; Slavin, 1983; Slavin, Leavey, & Madden, 1982). These procedures have been used to initiate and promote peer-assisted instruction combined with content enhancement guidelines designed to stimulate the activation process.

Preparation for peer-assisted assignment completion consists of the following steps:

1. Identify critical learning demands.
2. Develop appropriate assignments.
3. Determine the type of peer assistance required.
4. Develop procedures and materials related to task completion.
5. Identify evaluation, feedback, and reinforcement structures.
6. Identify peer groupings and pairings.
7. Develop a concrete implementation plan.
8. Identify and address prerequisites.

Another prerequisite to peer-assisted instruction involves students' social skills. Many low-achieving students do not know how to participate cooperatively in a group and may not be committed to the group's success. Therefore, specific social skills related to the group process may have to be presented. These skills might include accepting criticism, interrupting appropriately, asking a question, answering a question, asking for help, negotiating, and so on. Many of these skills are covered in the Social Skills for Daily Living curriculum (Schumaker, Hazel & Pederson, 1988).

STRATEGIC TEACHING Although the devices and routines that have been discussed are the heart of the content enhancement process, a key aspect of the effectiveness of these devices and routines is their successful implementation with students. Across the various studies on the content learning of low-achieving students, the aspects of the instructional process that are most related to improvement of student performance have centered on the extent to which students were informed of and involved in the enhancement process and could see the benefits of the enhancements on their performance. As a result, a true partnership must exist in which student and teacher know their individual roles as well as the roles of others in the class. In the process the teacher must take an active role in involving the student in the learning process, and the student must be an informed and involved participant.

The teacher is not merely a "presenter" of content information to those best able to assimilate that information. The teacher also is a "facilitator" who informs students of teaching techniques, clarifies expectations of students as partners in the learning process, and holds the students accountable for their role in the learning process. In short, strategic teaching, the final component in content enhancement, unites the teacher and students in a learning partnership by providing informed, explicit, and interactive instruction.

1. *Provide informed instruction.* Informed instruction means telling students about the teaching routines they will use. The students must be taught to identify the various teaching devices and the associated teaching routines so they can attend to and be aware

of the importance of the content presented. Teaching students about teaching routines is similar to teaching students a strategy. The teacher must address eight instructional stages:

a. Inform students of how content has been presented previously and what their level of performance has been.

b. Describe the routine to the students and explain the expectations regarding use of the device to improve learning—that initially the teacher will take responsibility for leading students through the routine but students must begin to assume some of the responsibility for enhancing learning.

c. Model how the routine will be used and how students should respond. Model how students will be cued to use the routine, show how students will participate in developing or implementing the routine, and demonstrate how understanding will be monitored to see if the routine is paying off. Teachers gradually begin to prompt students to participate in the model.

d. Question students about what each part of the routine means to ensure that students know how to use the routine to facilitate learning. If forms such as study guides, graphics, illustrators, or concept diagrams are being used, make sure that students understand each part of the form. Verbal rehearsal of the routine as a class or in groups is an excellent activity to encourage memorization of how the routine will be used.

e. As soon as possible after the routine has been presented, begin using the routine as much as possible. Initially slow down delivery of the routine and focus on its most important parts. The student should be able to see that the routine is helping him or her to learn. If the student does not see this relationship, he or she likely will not continue to attend to its use or choose to become involved in the enhancement process.

f. As students start to recognize specific routines and begin to use them to their advantage, increase the number of routines and include more difficult content elements. Monitor and maintain the success rate of students using a routine and mastering the content.

g. As the teacher and the student master implementation of each routine, the cueing and informing process can become less explicit (e.g., students expect the advance organizer and are ready for it every day). The goal is for the student to develop expectations about certain teaching routines and devices and identify and use these instructional enhancements automatically.

h. Gradually add and integrate other types of routines into the teaching process while maintaining routines that have been implemented already.

2. *Promote explicit instruction.* A process called the *Cue-Do-Review* sequence represents many of the elements of explicit instruction required for students to benefit from content enhancements and is used in the following way:

a. To further engage students in learning, *cue* the students about important content, ways the teacher will enhance learning, and expectations regarding attention, notetaking, and participation.

b. Teach (*do*) the content using the device and the linking steps.

   c. *Review* both the content information and the process involved in the teaching routine.

Taken together, this explicit instruction is referred to as the "Cue-Do-Review" sequence.

   3. *Promote interactive instruction.* Although the focus of the content enhancement process is on planning how to predict and compensate for unsuccessful learning in the content areas, teachers must be prepared to abandon specific routines and devices if they do not work and replace them with alternative learning activities. The ability to decide to abandon a plan and generate a new routine during the lesson to respond to student failure successfully makes the teaching process dynamic. Therefore, a critical assumption in content enhancement is that both unplanned and planned routines and devices are needed to promote maximum learning. As such, the teacher should use the routines and devices as planned but also must be flexible enough to digress from specific plans and add other routines and devices as indicated by student needs.

If new routines are required to respond to teaching needs, the following steps will guide teachers in this process:

1. Select an instructional device.
2. Develop a set of steps that can be used to link the content in the device to the student.
3. Inform students about the device and routine by teaching them how to recognize the device and how it should be used.
4. *Cue* students each time the device is used.
5. *Do* the routine on a regular basis in a flexible and creative manner that builds a learning partnership with students.
6. *Review* the information included in the device to check understanding and use of the device.
7. Prompt students to think about the strategies they are using when they use the routine.

These steps guide the development of new routines that are demanded by the teaching situation as analyzed by the teacher.

Regardless of whether the routines used are researched or newly developed by the teacher in response to student needs, certain assumptions regarding responsibilities and procedures must be met in content enhancement:

1. The content teacher is responsible for presenting information that will promote student understanding and remembering of content for low-achieving students.
2. The process of planning, teaching, and evaluating for learning should be based on careful consideration of the information-processing demands placed on the teacher and the student alike.
3. Enhancements, consisting of carefully planned instructional routines and devices, should be utilized to enhance the delivery of content information.
4. The teacher must inform students of the enhancements to be used in the delivery of information.

5. The teacher must cue students when specific enhancements are being used to promote learning.
6. The teacher must purposely implement the enhancement in a partnership with students.
7. The teacher should induce both himself or herself and the students to reflect on the enhancement and to evaluate its roles in learning and whether it has been an effective teaching/learning experience.

In addition to understanding specific research regarding content enhancement, an understanding of an even wider range of pedagogical approaches is useful to teachers in content classrooms with students of diverse abilities. The teaching routines presented here to illustrate the content enhancement process are representative of a variety of models of teaching that have potential for helping educators design instruction to help students achieve various objectives.

Joyce and Weil (1986) described several models of teaching that are of particular interest to teachers who are considering ways to teach content so students with varying academic backgrounds all can benefit from instruction. Joyce and Weil subsumed specific models under families of models such as the "information processing family." In this family Joyce and Weil included the concept attainment model, the inductive thinking model, inquiry training, advance organizers, memorization, the developing intellect model, and the scientific inquiry model. Of equal interest are representatives of other model "families" described by Joyce and Weil (1982), including the personal family, the social family, and the behavioral systems family. Presenting this wide array of models, these authors contended that all the models can be used to develop instruction to help a variety of students learn.

Joyce and Weil (1986) also contended that models can be combined to attack multifaceted educational problems and that it would be a mistake to assume that because one model has been shown to be effective, it should be used exclusively. The goal for all teachers, then, is to develop a repertoire of instructional techniques that can be selected where appropriate and combined when the combination would produce a more powerful instructional technique. Knowledge of a wide range of instructional techniques and the ability to adapt and adjust them according to student needs is crucial to meeting the needs of students of diverse abilities, skills, and background knowledge.

STRATEGY INTEGRATION APPROACHES

In addition to content enhancement and other models that focus on how content might be enhanced for students, alternative models of instruction have been developed to promote content acquisition. Some approaches—called strategy-integration approaches—weave strategies into content-area learning. In these, the teacher teaches strategies at the same time as the subject-area content is being taught.

STRATEGIES INTERVENTION MODEL (SIM)

In strategies integration approaches the teacher leads the students to use strategies as they learn content information. All learning can be facilitated if students know a wide range of learning strategies and also know where they are to be used and how to use them in various settings. If strategies are to be incorporated successfully into general classroom instruction, teachers likely will have to think about learning strategies as they plan, as they teach, and as they focus on student needs. As such, learning strategies may well be integrated into content instruction.

Some of the learning strategies interventions developed by the staff at the University of Kansas Center for Research on Learning have been field-tested in content classrooms. The learning strategies that general education teachers have used in the context of group instruction include the paraphrasing strategy (designed to teach students how to rephrase content information in their own words) (Schumaker, Denton, & Deshler, 1984), the ORDER strategy (designed to teach students how to represent common presentational structures found in texts and lectures) (Scanlon, Schumaker, & Deshler, in press), and some of the strategies embedded within teaching routines such as the recall enhancement routine (e.g., Bulgren, Schumaker & Deshler, 1994b).

Preliminary research from these studies suggests that students' acquisition of learning strategies in general classrooms will be accomplished only by providing explicit instruction in learning strategies and incorporating discussion and use of learning strategies into daily instructional tasks. Instruction has to be ongoing and intensive enough to respond to the needs of all students. Some students probably will need individual help and extra time to master the strategy.

INTEGRATED STRATEGIES INSTRUCTION

Ellis (1993) presented the integrative strategy instruction (ISI) potential model for teaching content-area subjects to adolescents with learning disabilities. This model is targeted at teaching students how to be strategic learners within the context of teaching content-area subjects. The assumption is that teachers will combine teacher-mediated instructional routines for teaching content with task-specific strategies for teaching cognitive processing. In general, four components guide the use of this model:

1. *Orienting*, which involves demonstrating how the strategy being used helps students learn.
2. *Framing*, in which the teacher demonstrates how the strategy is used in a learning task.
3. *Applying*, in which the student uses the strategy independently.
4. *Extending*, in which students are taught to use the strategy in other areas.

The ISI model assumes that teachers will match content instructional routines with task-specific strategies to activate student learning. Ellis also made suggestions regarding the use and monitoring of the strategies, direct instruction, dialectical instruction, peer-mediated learning opportunities, and integration of resource instruction and content-area class instruction. Ellis stressed that this model is a "potential" model because components of his model did not appear in the context of a formal research study.

STRATEGIC TEACHING AND LEARNING

Jones, Palincsar, Ogle, and Carr (1987) discussed an approach called strategic teaching. In a text devoted to the teacher's role as strategist, they discussed how teachers go about making decisions regarding the "what," "how," and "when" of teaching and learning. They provided a vision of the teacher's role in strategic teaching as a manager and an instructional leader, a model and a mediator of learning who demonstrates how to think about a task, apply strategies, and problem-solve in novel situations.

Further, the teacher is seen as a mediator who interacts with the students and the learning environment to help students learn to be independent, strategic learners through guidance and coaching. Therefore, the teacher's role is twofold: (a) to determine which strategies students need to learn content and (b) to help students learn to use those strategies. Contributors to their text illustrate strategic teaching in the content areas of science (Anderson, 1987), social studies (Alvermann, 1987), mathematics (Lindquist, 1987), and literature (Beach, 1987).

PROCESS-BASED INSTRUCTION (PBI) MODEL

According to Ashman and Conway (1989), the development of process-based instruction (PBI) reflects concerns for two types of demands on students—to develop (a) information-processing competence and (b) curriculum knowledge and skills in the classroom. Keys to the success of PBI instruction are the application of information-processing theory and concepts in classroom activities and content, identification of students for whom instruction is appropriate for the academic task based on different types of student learners, transfer of ownership of plans and types of strategies from the teacher to the student, and the explicit division between consolidation within the task cluster and generalization. This is to be accomplished in the five phases of assessment, orientation, strategy development, intratask transfer, and consolidation and generalization.

CURRICULUM REVISION APPROACHES

Another group of approaches emphasizes curriculum revision. Curriculum-revision approaches advocate modifying the structure of texts or materials, adding elements to texts or materials, supplementing texts, or offering materials in the form of audio or video devices. Various researchers have considered how instructional materials can be constructed in ways that help teachers deliver instruction in a variety of subject areas. Many of these researchers have taken into consideration recommendations that focus on students with learning disabilities. The following describes some approaches directed at various aspects of the curriculum as mediators of learning

EDUCATIONAL TOOLS—TEXTS, SOFTWARE, ACTIVITIES

Carnine presented design considerations for educational tools such as texts, software, and activities developed by the National Center to Improve the Tools of Educators, based on review of instructional research in a variety of disciplines. He discussed how educational tools can be designed, selected, and used to accommodate the needs of diverse groups of students as they study knowledge and reasoning in science (Grossen, Carnine, Romance, & Vitale, in press) and math (Carnine, Dixon & Silbert, in press) In general, Carnine argued for the construction of curriculum that can help students understand important concepts and strategies. This approach has been put into practice in a social studies textbook by Carnine, Crawford, Harniss, and Hallenbeck (1995).

In science, Carnine argued, such educational tools should focus on "big ideas" of science, those that represent critical scientific ideas and principles. These tools also should have powerful explanatory and predictive power, motivate the development of significant questions, and be applicable to many situations. He also argued that materials should be developed to teach strategies for science inquiry and component concepts using visual maps to model the strategies, confront common misconceptions, and provide relevant learning experiences in a scaffolded manner. He presented parallel suggestions for the development of math texts and materials.

In the field of social studies, Carnine, Miller, Bean, and Zigmond (in prep.) provided suggestions for teachers to improve instructional tools for teaching social studies to diverse learners by organizing information by big ideas such as important facts, concepts, or principles that enable learners to organize and interrelate information. The problem-solution-effect structure common in social studies is an example of a big idea. They also suggested teaching strategies, scaffolding, or providing temporary assistance along the path to self-regulated learning and effectively reviewing big ideas.

TEXTS

Carnine and Kameenui (1992) edited a text designed to promote higher-order thinking through a curriculum designed around the concept of "sameness." Although the audience for this book is the mainstream classroom, the editors argued that this type of curriculum can benefit a full spectrum of students. They suggested that the optimal way to develop and organize curriculum to accommodate atypical learners also may be an ideal way to teach higher-order thinking to general education students. The several chapters in their book are based on the assumption that higher-order thinking involves the integration of concepts, rules, strategies, schemata, systems, heuristics, algorithms, and so forth. The editors argued that the process underlying these concepts, rules, and strategies is noting sameness. Chapters deal with specific areas such as science, social studies, spelling, math, and writing, in addition to problem solving and transfer, higher-order thinking, and implications for students with learning problems.

MULTIPLE OPTION CURRICULUM

Cawley (1994) noted that the scientific community defined a curriculum model as that specifying domains to be covered and the curriculum as that specifying details such as the nature of the materials and sequence of topics. Cawley discussed the multiple option curriculum (MOC) model represented by Science for All Children (SAC) developed by Cawley, Miller, Sentman, and Bennett (1993), which gives teachers various options by which to organize the curricula to include many different levels when needed. This model suggests that all teachers have all grade levels of materials at their disposal.

In practice, the teacher is able to use activities from one grade level to provide the necessary background for students to participate in activities at a higher level or adapt to individual needs. The MOC consists of teaching guides which the teacher uses flexibly, rather than textbooks. For the secondary level the MOC model ideally provides the teachers a range of materials that can reach every student in the classroom.

THEMES

Cawley (1994) suggested an alternative curriculum framework using themes as curriculum organizers. While acknowledging the lack of experimental data on the effectiveness of themes in teaching students in classrooms, Cawley suggested this as an area for strong consideration. First, themes such as "change" can integrate major principles from physical, life, and earth sciences. Second, many states have described important themes in content areas, and some publishers have incorporated these into their programs. He argued that the activities by which students learn about themes in an area provide both depth and breadth of a comprehensive curriculum. He suggested that the thematic approach could restructure our current views of learning and teaching.

MODELS

Woodward (1994) emphasized using models in the curriculum revision process in science. He argued that teaching science through models requires curriculum developers to examine course content carefully to identify critical information, make assumptions explicit, and suggest applications. This is supported by Mayer (1989), who also indicated that models improve students' understanding of science, especially when explanations and illustrations of the models are well constructed.

Mayer defined a conceptual model as words or diagrams intended to be used to help learners build mental models of the system being studied. He noted that a conceptual model highlights the major objects and actions in a system, as well as the causal relations among them. Research by Mayer and Gallini (1990) supports this approach.

ACTIVITIES

Mastropieri and Scruggs (1994) suggested an activity-driven, inquiry-based, thematic approach to science education. Conducting research to compare an activities-oriented curriculum with traditional textbook-based approaches, they reported that, although little research is available in this area, there is enough to suggest that appropriately implemented activities-oriented approaches may facilitate science learning for students with learning disabilities better than textbook-oriented approaches. An activities-based approach may require peer mediation, special education support, inquiry instruction, specific coaching, cooperative learning, and activity-specific adaptations (Scruggs, Mastropieri, Bakken, & Brigham, 1993).

At another level some teaching devices have been incorporated into existing curriculum materials to enhance comprehension. It is important to be aware of materials already developed, tested, and used. Teachers can make use of content enhancement devices by drawing student attention to them during instruction and showing students how to use them. Some of the devices that already are part of textbooks include:

- *Textbooks to enhance organization*. To enhance students' ability to perceive text organization, some textbook publishers have begun to insert various organizers such as semantic maps, webs, and matrices (Schumm & Strickler, 1993).
- *Computer simulation to promote understanding*. To enhance understanding, computer simulations have been developed to promote student learning of information contained in a unit of health. The instruction focused not only on factual-level knowledge but also on higher cognitive skills when compared to structured teaching (Woodward, Carnine, & Gersten, 1988).
- *Computer simulation to promote reasoning skills*. Students' ability relative to drawing conclusions and criticizing syllogistic arguments has been enhanced through computer-assisted instruction (Collins & Carnine, 1988).

- *Audio-assisted instruction.* Audio-tutorial science lessons have been developed to help students in grades 1 and 2 learn concepts (Novak & Musonda, 1991).
- *Videodisc instruction.* Secondary teachers of students with learning disabilities reported positive results from and acceptance of videodisc instruction (Woodward & Gersten, 1992).

SUMMARY AND PERSPECTIVES

In planning for content-area learning, teachers must take into consideration some of the current realities of the secondary school setting. Secondary school courses tend to cover large amounts of information, and the textbooks selected to convey the content often are not well organized. In addition, secondary courses frequently address students with diverse academic abilities. Time for academic interactions frequently is limited, however, and instruction is apt to be geared for achieving students rather than students with learning disabilities.

In this already complex setting, teachers have limited time to plan and teach and few opportunities for collegial study, planning, or teaching. Furthermore, as a result of concerns raised about how students with mild disabilities have received content instruction in the past, more of these students are placed into general classrooms so they can benefit from instruction by content experts.

As a result, researchers have begun to explore what goes on in the general education classroom and have turned their attention to how instruction can be mediated so all students can learn better. This sets the stage for developing planning and teaching routines that can facilitate content acquisition. Planning for content acquisition can be enhanced by adhering to principles centering on how teachers think about instruction in diverse classes, that is, *teacher reflection,* and also how best to instruct in these diverse classes, by explicit *teacher action.* Teacher reflection and teacher action alike can be enhanced by giving attention to planning procedures such as those found in the Planning Pyramid and ReflActive Planning. Teaching for content acquisition can be enhanced by using content enhancements, integrating learning strategies into content instruction, and using revised curriculum designed to help students learn.

A shift to this way of thinking requires a new perspective about instruction. In this age of information explosion, teachers must reflect carefully on what is important and will have long-term usefulness for students. Then teachers must reflect on the best ways to teach this information. Sometimes decisions are going to be "best bet" decisions. Therefore, teachers have to be ready to revisit decisions and confirm or change their plans. Teachers must know whether students have the strategies to learn the content or whether they must compensate for students' poor strategies in the way they translate the content for them. The decisions teachers make about which teaching routines and curriculum resources to use and how well they use them will define how effectively teachers respond to the challenge of planning and teaching in the content classroom so all students benefit from instruction.

This shift also requires a new perspective about goals for students. An important goal is that all students become strategic learners capable of processing information creatively and effectively. Because information that students require to function in the world is growing at a rapid rate, today's students must learn "how to learn" so they can be independent learners and performers in school and after they leave school. No longer can students succeed with a repertoire of facts that teachers "give" them. The demands placed on students now graduating from secondary schools require a new way of learning and teaching that allows students to have understandings about the world and ways of thinking that will allow them to integrate new and different information they will encounter. Only this will prepare students to become fully functioning members of a rapidly changing and increasingly complex society.

REFERENCES

Alvermann, D. (1987). Strategic teaching in social studies. In B. F. Jones, A. S. Palincsar, D. S., Ogle, & E. G. Carr (Eds.), *Strategic teaching and learning: Cognitive instruction in the content areas* (pp. 92–110). Alexandria, VA: ASCD.

Anders, P. L., & Bos, C. S. (1984). In the beginning: Vocabulary instruction in content classrooms. *Topics in Learning and Learning Disabilities, 3*(4), 53–65.

Anderson, C. W. (1987). Strategic teaching in science. In B. F. Jones, A. S. Palincsar, D. S. Ogle, & E. G. Carr (Eds.), *Strategic teaching and learning: Cognitive instruction in the content areas* (pp. 73–91). Alexandria, VA: ASCD.

American Association for the Advancement of Science. (1989). *Science for all Americans: A project 2061 report on literacy goals in science, mathematics and technology.*

Armbruster, B. B. (1990). *Reading and questioning in content area lessons* (Technical Report No. 502). University of Illinois, Urbana: Center for the Study of Reading.

Armbruster, B. B., & Anderson, T. H. (1988). On selecting "considerate content area textbooks." *Remedial and Special Education, 9*(1), 47–52.

Ashman, A. F., & Conway, R. N. F. (1989). *Cognitive strategies for special education.* New York: Routledge.

Armento, B. J. (1986). Research on teaching social studies. In M. C. Wittrock (Eds.), *Handbook of research on teaching* (3d ed.). pp. 942–952. New York: Macmillan.

Aronson, E. (1978). *The jigsaw classroom.* Beverly Hills, CA: Sage.

Ausubel, D. P. (1963). *The psychology of meaningful verbal learning.* New York: Grune & Stratton.

Ausubel, D. P., Novak, J. D., & Hanesian, H. (1968). *Educational psychology: A cognitive view* (2d ed.). New York: Holt, Rinehart, & Winston.

Barba, R. H., Pang, V. O., & Santa Cruz, R. (1993). User-friendly text. *The Science Teacher, 60*(5), 14.

Beach, R. (1987). Strategic teaching in literature. In B. F. Jones, A. S. Palincsar, D. S. Ogle, & E. G. Carr (Eds.), *Strategic teaching and learning: Cognitive instruction in the content areas* (pp. 135–159). Alexandria, VA: ASCD.

Becker, W. C., Englemann, S., & Thomas, D. R. (1971). *Teaching: A course in applied psychology.* Chicago: Science Research Associates.

Bellezza, F. S. (1981). Mnemonic devices: Classification, characteristics, and criteria. *Review of Educational Research, 51*(2), 247–275.

Bellezza, F. S. (1982). *Improve your memory skills.* Englewood Cliffs, NJ: Prentice Hall.

Bergerud, D., Lovitt, T. C., & Horton, S. (1988). The effectiveness of textbook adaptations in life science for high school students with learning disabilities. *Journal of Learning Disabilities, 21*(2), 70–76.

Borkowski, J. G. & Muthukrishna, N. (1992). Moving metacognition into the classroom: "Working models" and effective strategy teaching. In M. Pressley, K. R. Harris, & J. T. Guthrie (Eds.), *Promoting Academic Competence and Literacy in School* (pp. 477–501). San Diego, CA: Academic Press.

Bos, C. S., & Anders, P. L. (1987). Semantic feature analysis: An interactive teaching strategy for facilitating learning from text. *Learning Disability Focus, 3*(1), 55–59.

Brophy, J. E. (1984). The teacher as thinker: Implementing instruction. In Duffy, G. G., Roehler, L., & Mason,

J. (Eds.), *Comprehension instruction: Perspectives and suggestions*. New York: Longman.

Bruner, J. S., Goodnow, J. J., & Austin, G. A. (1956). *The study of thinking*. New York: John Wiley & Sons.

Bulgren, J. with Lenz, B. K., Deshler, D. D., & Schumaker, J. B. (in press). *The content enhancement series: The concept comparison routine*. Lawrence, KS: Edge Enterprises.

Bulgren, J. A., Schumaker, J. B., & Deshler, D. D. (1988). Effectiveness of a concept teaching routine in enhancing the performance of LD students in secondary-level mainstream classes. *Learning Disability Quarterly, 11*, 3–17.

Bulgren, J. A., Deshler, D. D., & Schumaker, J. B. (1993). *The content enhancement series: The concept mastery routine*. Lawrence, KS: Edge Enterprises.

Bulgren, J. A., Shumaker, J. B., & Deshler, D. D. (1994a). *The content enhancement series: The concept anchoring routine*. Lawrence, KS: Edge Enterprises.

Bulgren, J. A., Schumaker, J. B., & Deshler, D. D. (1994b). The effects of a recall enhancement routine on the test performance of secondary students with and without learning disabilities. *Learning Disabilities Research and Practice, 9*(1), 2–11.

Carlson, S. A. (1985). The ethical appropriateness of subject-matter tutoring for learning disabled adolescents. *Learning Disability Quarterly, 8*, 310–314.

Carnine, D., Crawford, D., Harniss, M., & Hollenbeck, K. (1995). *Understanding U.S. history: Vol. 1. Through the Civil War*. Eugene, OR: Considerate Publishing.

Carnine, D., Dixon, J. R. C., & Silberts, J. (in press). Mathematics: Educational tools for diverse learners. In E. Kameenui, D. Carnine, & R. C. Dixon (Eds.), *Effective strategies for accommodating students with diverse learning and curricular needs*. Columbus, OH: Merrill.

Carnine, D. & Kameenui, E. J., Eds. (1992). *Higher order thinking: Designing curriculum for mainstreamed students*. Austin, TX: Pro-Ed.

Carnine, D., Miller, S., Bean R., & Zigmond, N. (in press). Social studies: Educational tools for diverse learners. In E. Kameenui, D. Carnine, & R. C. Dixon, Eds., *Effective strategies for accommodating students with diverse learning and curricular needs*. Columbus, OH: Merrill.

Cawley, J. F. (1994). Science for students with disabilities. *Remedial and Special Education, 15*(2), 67–71.

Carwey, J., Miller, J., Sentman, J. R., & Bennett, S. (1993). *Science for all children (SAC)*. Buffalo: State University of New York at Buffalo.

Ciborowski, J. (1992). *Textbooks and the students who can't read them*. Boston: Brookline Books.

Clark, C. M., & Peterson, P. L. (1986). Research on teaching social studies. In M. C. Wittrock (Ed.), *Handbook of research on Teaching*, (3d ed.). New York: Macmillan

Collins M., & Carnine, D. (1988). Evaluating the field test revision process by comparing two versions of a reasoning skills CAE program. *Journal of Learning Disabilities 21*(6), 375–379.

Crank, J. N., & Bulgren, J. A. (1993). Visual depictions as information organizers for enhancing achievement of students with learning disabilities. *Learning Disabilities Research & Practice, 3*, 140–147.

Darch, C., & Gersten, R. (1986). Direction-setting activities in reading comprehension: A Comparison of two approaches. *Learning Disabilities Quarterly, 9*, 235–243.

Delquadri, J., Greenwood, C. R., Whorton, D., Carta, J. J., & Hall, R. V. (1986). Classwide peer tutoring. *Exceptional Children, 6*(52), 535–542.

Dempster, F. N. (1993). Exposing our students to less should help them learn more. *Phi Delta Kappan, 14*(6), 433–437.

Ellis, E. S. (1993). Integrative strategy Instruction: A potential model for teaching content area subjects to adolescents with learning disabilities. *Journal of Learning Disabilities, 26*(6), 358–383.

Gagné, R. M. (1965). *The conditions of learning*. New York: Holt, Rinehart & Winston.

Gagné, E. D. (1985). *The cognitive psychology of school learning*. Boston: Little, Brown.

Goodlad, J. L. (1984). *A place called school*. New York: McGraw Hill.

Grossen, B., Carnine, D., Romance, N., & Vitale, M. (in press). Teaching science to diverse learners. In E. Kameenui, D. Carnine, & R. C. Dixon (Eds.), *Effective strategies for accommodating students with diverse learning and curricular needs*. Columbus, OH: Merrill.

Hartman, D. K., & Dyer, P. A. (1992). *An existential description of reading methods and materials in the content areas*. Urbana, IL: Center for the Study of Reading.

Hudson, P., Lignugaris-Kraft, B., & Miller, T. (1993). Using content enhancements to improve the performance of adolescents with learning disabilities in content classes. *Learning Disabilities Research & Practice,*

8(2), 106–126.

Jenkins, J., & Jenkins, L. (1985). Peer tutoring in elementary and secondary programs. *Focus on Exceptional Children, 17*(6), 1–12.

Johnson, D. D., Toms-Bronowski, S., & Pittelman, S. D. (1982). *An investigation of the effectiveness of semantic mapping and semantic feature analysis with intermediate grade level children (Program Report 83–3)*. Madison: University of Wisconsin, Center for Education Research.

Johnson, D. W. (1974). Instructional goal structure: Cooperative, competitive, or individualistic. *Review of Educational Research, 44*(2), 213–240.

Johnson, D. W., & Johnson, R. T. (1975). *Learning together and alone*. Englewood Cliffs, NJ: Prentice Hall.

Johnson, D. D. & Pearson, P. D. (1984). *Teaching reading vocabulary* (2d ed). New York: Holt, Rinehart & Winston.

Johnson, S. M. (1990). *Teachers at work: Achieving success in our schools*. New York: Basic Books

Joint Committee on Teacher Planning for Students with Disabilities. (1995). *Planning for academic diversity in America's classrooms: Windows on reality, research, change, and practice*. Lawrence: University of Kansas Center for Research on Learning.

Jones, B. F., Palincsar, A. S., Ogle, D. S., & Carr, E. G. (1987). *Strategic teaching and learning: Cognitive instruction in the content areas*. Alexandria, VA: ASCD in cooperation with North Central Regional Educational Laboratory.

Joyce, B. & Weil, M. (1986). *Models of teaching* (3d ed). Englewood Cliffs, NJ: Prentice Hall.

Kinder, D. (1992). An evaluation of history textbooks. *Journal of Special Education, 25*(4), 472–491.

Kissam, B., & Lenz, B. K., Eds. (1994). *Pedagogies for diversity in secondary schools: A preservice curriculum*. Lawrence: University of Kansas.

Klausmeier, H. J., & Associates (1979). *Cognitive learning and development: Information-processing and Piagetian perspectives*. Cambridge, MA: Ballinger Publishing.

Klausmeier, H. J., & Ripple (1971). *Learning and human abilities: Educational psychology*. New York: Harper & Row.

Konopak, B. C. (1988). Eight graders' vocabulary learning from inconsiderate and considerate text. *Reading Research and Instruction, 27*(4), 1–14.

Lenz, B. K. (1984). *The effect of advance organizers on the learning and retention of learning disabled adolescents within the context of a cooperative planning model*. Final research report submitted to the U.S. Department of Education, Special Education Services.

Lenz, B. K., Alley, G. R., & Schumaker, J. B. (1987). Activating the inactive learner: Advance organizers in the secondary content classroom. *Learning Disability Quarterly, 10*(1), 53–67.

Lenz, B. K., Boudah, D., Schumaker, J., and Deshler, D. (1993). *The lesson planning routine: A guide for inclusive lesson planning* (Research Report). Lawrence: University of Kansas Center for Research on Learning.

Lenz, B. K., & Bulgren, J. A. (1994). *ReflActive planning: Planning for diversity in secondary schools* (Research Report). Lawrence: University of Kansas Center for Research on Learning.

Lenz, B. K., & Bulgren, J. A. (1995). Promoting learning in content classes. In P. A. Cegelka & W. H. Berdine (Eds.), *Effective instruction for students with learning problems*, 385–417. Needham Heights, MA: Allyn & Bacon.

Lenz, B. K., Bulgren, J. A., & Hudson, P. (1990). Content enhancement: A model for promoting the acquisition of content by individuals with learning disabilities. In T. E. Scruggs & B. L. Y. Wong (Eds.), *Intervention research in learning disabilities* (122–165). New York: Springer-Verlag.

Lenz, B. K., with Bulgren, J. A., Schumaker, J. B., Deshler, D. D., & Boudah, D. J. (1994). *The content enhancement series: The unit organizer routine*. Lawrence, KS: Edge Enterprises.

Lenz, B. K., Clark F. C., Deshler, D. D., Schumaker, J. B. (1989). *The strategies instructional approach: A training package*. Lawrence: University of Kansas, Institute for Research in Learning Disabilities.

Lenz, B. K., Deshler, D. D., Schumaker, J. B., Bulgren, J., Kissam, B., Vance, M., Roth, J., and McKnight, M. (1994). *The course planning routine: A guide for inclusive course planning*. (Research Report). Lawrence: University of Kansas Center for Research on Learning.

Lenz, B. K., Ehren, B. J., & Smiley, L. R. (1991). A goal attainment approach to improve completion of project-type assignments by learning disabled adolescents. *Focus on Learning Disabilities, 6,* 166–176.

Lenz, B. K., Marrs, R. W., Schumaker, J. B., & Deshler, D. D. (1993). *The content enhancement series: The lesson organizer routine.* Lawrence, KS: Edge Enterprises.

Lenz, B. K., & Mercer, C. D. (1992). Cognitive approaches to teaching. In C. D. Mercer (Ed.), *Students with learning disabilities* (4th ed.) (pp. 268–309). New York: Macmillan.

Lenz, B. K., Schumaker, J. B., & Deshler, D. D. (1991). *Planning in the face of academic diversity: Whose questions should we be answering?* Paper presented at American Educational Research Association Conference, Chicago.

Lenz, B. K., Schumaker, J. B., & Deshler (1994) The preservice teacher training project: An inclusive teaching model. *Stratenotes,* U(6). Lawrence: University of Kansas Center for Research on Learning Disabilities.

Lenz, B. K., Schumaker, J. B., Deshler, D. D., Boudah, D. J., Vance, M., Kissam, B., Bulgren, J., & Roth, J. (1993). *The unit planning routine: A guide for inclusive planning* (Research Report). Lawrence: University of Kansas Center for Research on Learning.

Levin, J. R. (1988). Elaboration-based learning strategies: Powerful theory = Powerful application. *Contemporary Educational Psychology,* (13).

Lindquist, M. M. (1987). Strategic teaching in mathematics. In B. F. Jones, A. S. Palincsar, D. S., Ogle, & E. G. Carr (Eds.), *Strategic teaching and learning: Cognitive instruction in the content areas* (pp. 111–134). Alexandria, VA: ASCD in cooperation with North Central Regional Educational Laboratory.

Lovitt, T., Rudsit, J., Jenkins, J., Pious, C., & Benedetti, D. (1985). Two methods of adaptive science materials for learning disabled and regular seventh graders. *Learning Disability Quarterly, 8,* 275–285.

Lovitt, T. C., Stein, M., & Rudsit, J. (1985). *The use of visual spatial displays to teach science facts to learning disabled middle school students.* Unpublished manuscript, Experimental Education Unit, University of Washington, Seattle.

Martorella, P. H. (1972). Teaching concepts. In J. M. Cooper (Ed.), *Classroom teaching skills* (2d ed). Lexington, MA: D. C. Heath.

Mastropieri, M. A., & Scruggs, T. E. (1988). Increasing LD students' content area learning: Research implementation. *Learning Disabilities Research, 4,* 17–25.

Mastropieri, M. A., & Scruggs, T. E. (1989). Mnemonic social studies instruction: classroom applications. *Remedial and Special Education, 10*(3), 40–46.

Mastropieri, M. A., & Scruggs, T. E. (1994). Text versus hands-on science curriculum. *Remedial and Special Education, 15*(2), 72–85.

Mayer, R. E. (1987). *Educational psychology: A cognitive approach.* Boston: Little, Brown.

Mayer, R. E. (1989). Models for understanding. *Review of Educational Research, 59*(1), 43–64.

Mayer, R. E., & Gallini, J. (1990). When is an illustration worth ten thousand words? *Journal of Educational Psychology, 82,* 715–726.

Merrill, M. D., & Tennyson, R. D. (1977). *Teaching concepts: An instructional design guide.* Englewood Cliffs, NJ: Educational Technology.

Moran, M. R. (1980). *An investigation of the demands on oral language skills of learning disabled students in secondary classrooms.* (Research Report #1). Lawrence: University of Kansas Institute for Research on Learning Disabilities.

Morine-Dershimer, G. (1979). *Teacher plan and classroom reality: The South Bay study. Part 4* (Research Series No. 60). East Lansing: Michigan State University, Institute for Research on Teaching.

Nagel, D. R., Schumaker, J. B., & Deshler, D. D. (1986). *The learning strategies curriculum: The FIRST-letter mnemonic strategy.* Lawrence, KS: Edge Enterprises.

National Institute of Education. (1975). *Teaching as clinical information processing* (Report of Panel 6, National Conference on Studies in Teaching). Washington, DC: National Institute of Education.

Newman, F. M. (1988). Can depth replace coverage in the high school curriculum? *Phi Delta Kappan, 69*(5), 345–348.

Novak, J. D., & Musonda, D. (1991). A twelve-year longitudinal study of science concept learning. *American Educational Research Journal, 28*(1), 117–153.

Olson, L. (1994). International math and science study finds U.S. covers more in less depth. *Effective School Practices, 14*(3), 43.

Palincsar, A. S., Ransom, K., & Derber, S. (December 1988/January 1989). Collaborative research and development of reciprocal teaching. *Educational Leadership,* 37–40.

Pressley, M., Levin, J. R., & McDaniel, M. A. (1987). Remembering versus inferring what a word means: Mnemonic and contextual approaches. In M. G. McKeown & M. E. Curtis (Eds.), *The nature of vocabulary acquisition*. Hillsdale, NJ: Lawrence Erlbaum Associates.

Putnam, M. L., Deshler, D. D., & Schumaker, J. B. (1992). The investigation of setting demands: A missing link in learning strategies instruction. In L. J. Meltzer (Ed.), *Strategy assessment and instruction for students with learning disabilities: From theory to practice*. Austin, TX: Pro-Ed.

Rademacher, J. A., Deshler, D. D., & Schumaker, J. B. (in press). The development and validation of a classroom assignment routine for inclusive settings. *Learning Disability Quarterly*.

Scanlon, D., Schumaker, J. B., & Deshler, D. D. (in prep.). *The learning strategies curriculum: A listening and notetaking strategy*. Lawrence, KS: Edge Enterprises.

Scanlon, D., Deshler, D. D., & Schumaker, J. B. (in press). Can a strategy be taught and learned in secondary inclusive classrooms? *Learning Disabilities Research and Practice*.

Schumaker, J. B., Denton, P. H., & Deshler, D. D. (1984). *Learning strategies curriculum: The paraphrasing strategy*. Lawrence: University of Kansas.

Schumaker, J. B., & Deshler, D. D. (1988). Implementing the regular education initiative in secondary schools: A different ball game. *Journal of Learning Disabilities, 21*(1), 36–42.

Schumaker, J. B., Deshler, D. D., McKnight, P. (1989) *Teaching routines to enhance the mainstream performance of adolescents with learning disabilities*. Final report submitted to U.S. Department of Education, Special Education Services.

Schumaker, J. B. Hazel, J. S., & Pederson, C. S. (1988). *Social skills for daily living*. Circle Pines, MN: American Guidance Service.

Schumm, J. S., & Strickler (1991). Guidelines for adapting content area textbooks: Keeping teachers and students content. *Intervention in School and Clinic, 27*(2), 79–84.

Schumm, J. S., Vaughn, S., & Leavell, A. G. (1994). Planning pyramid: A framework for planning for diverse student needs during content area instruction. *Reading Teacher, 47*(8).

Schumm, J. S., Vaughn, S., & Saumell, L. (1992). What teachers do when the textbook is tough: Students speak out. *Journal of Reading Behavior, 24*(4), 481–503.

Scruggs, T. E., & Mastropieri, M. A. (1990a). The case for mnemonic instruction: From laboratory research to classroom applications. *The Journal of Special Education, 23*, 7–29.

Scruggs, T. E., & Mastropieri, M. A. (1990b). Mnemonic instruction for students with learning disabilities: What it is and what it does. *Learning Disability Quarterly, 13*, 271–280.

Scruggs, T. E., Mastropieri, M. A., Bakken, J. P., & Brigham, F. J. (1993). Reading vs. doing: The relative efforts of textbook-based and inquiry-oriented approaches to science education in special education classrooms. *Journal of Special Education, 27*, 1–15.

Showers, B., Joyce, B., & Bennett, B. (1987). Synthesis of research on staff development: A framework for future study and a state-of-the art analysis. *Educational Leadership 45*(3), 77–87.

Shroyer, J. C. (1981). *Critical moments in the teaching of mathematics: What makes teaching difficult?* Unpublished doctoral dissertation, Michigan State University, East Lansing.

Slavin, R. E. (1983). *Cooperative learning*. New York: Longman.

Slavin, R. E., Leavey, M., & Madden, N. A. (1982). Effects of student teams and individualized instruction on student mathematics achievement, attitudes, and behaviors. Paper presented at annual convention of American Education Research Association, New York.

Taba, H. (1971). *A teacher's handbook to elementary social studies* (2d ed.) Reading, MA: Addison-Wesley.

Turnure, J. E. (1985). Communication and cues in the functional cognition of the mentally retarded. In N. R. Ellis, & N. W. Bray (Eds.), *International review of research in mental retardation*. New York: Academic Press.

Turnure, J. E. (1986). Instruction and cognitive development: Coordinating communication and cues. *Exceptional Children, 53*(2), 109–117.

Vaughn, S., Schumm, J. S., & Kouzekanani, K. (1993). What do students with learning disabilities think when their general education teachers make adaptations? *Journal of Learning Disabilities, 26*(8), 545–555.

Vaughn, S., Schumm, J. S., & McIntosh, R. (1991, April). *Teacher adaptations: What students think*. Paper presented at meeting of American Educational Research Association, Chicago.

Vaughn, S., Schumm, J. S., Kouzekanani, K. (1993). What do students with learning disabilities think when their general education teachers make adaptations? *Journal of Learning Disabilities, 26*(8), 545–555.

Voelker, A. (1972). Concept learning in the science curriculum, K–12: Issues and approaches. In P. H. Martorella (Ed.). *Concept Learning: Designs for Instruction*. Scranton, PA: Intext.

Wager, W., & Mory, E. (1992). *Feedback questions and information processing—Putting it all together*. Proceedings of Selected Research and Development Presentation at convention of Association for Educational Communication and Technology.

Woodward, J., Carnine, D., & Gersten, R. (1988). Teaching problem solving through computer simulations. *American Educational Research Journal, 25*(1), 72–86.

Woodward, J. (1994). The role of models in secondary science instruction. *Remedial and Special Education, 15*(2), 94–104.

Woodward, J., & Gersten, R. (1992). Innovative technology for secondary students with learning disabilities. *Exceptional Children, 58*(5), 407–420.

Yinger, R. J. (1977). *A study of teaching planning: Description development using ethnographic and information processing*. Unpublished doctoral dissertation, Michigan State University, Institute for Research on Teaching.

10

Strategies for Transition to Postsecondary Educational Settings

DARYL MELLARD

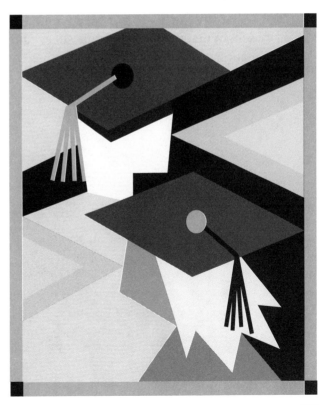

QUESTIONS TO KEEP IN MIND

▪ What value is attached to preparing students for postsecondary educational opportunities?

▪ What programmatic goals are set for high school LD services, as well as for individual students, that enhance the transition and success of students in postsecondary educational settings?

▪ What portion of students' preparation in high school is directed toward postsecondary educational opportunities?

▪ What structures are provided within the special services and high school that support students' succeeding in a postsecondary educational setting?

ADVANCE ORGANIZER

Students with learning disabilities (LD) who struggle to complete high school might find the college experience particularly challenging. Imagine the feeling of dread as the student walks into that first college class. Rather than a *classroom* of *30* students, as in high school, *150* or *200* students filter into an *auditorium*. Compounding that shock, the *graduate teaching assistant* explains that this is her first teaching assignment. She further explains that, because so many students are enrolled and because she has no help grading papers, the course grade will depend on the results of *two comprehensive exams* covering the *lectures* and *450-page textbook*. In such a situation the student might mutter in bewilderment, "Gee, Toto, I don't think we're in Kansas anymore."

The high school experience is stressful for most students with LD. These stresses might contribute to the 35% to 50% dropout rates commonly reported in this population. The formal educational experience of most students with LD ends when they complete high school or leave without completing high school. The above scenario of the first college semester illustrates factors that discourage students from pursuing further education. In doing so, students with LD limit the immediate and long-term quality of their lives. The topic of this chapter is preparing high school students with LD for postsecondary educational alternatives. The postsecondary educational setting is an important contributor

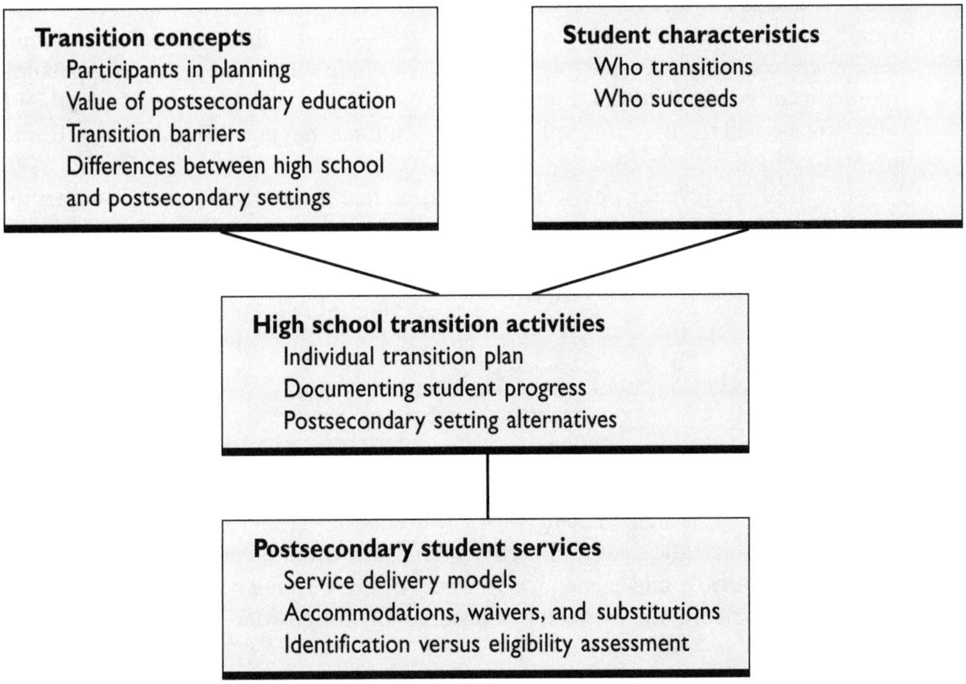

Transition concepts
  Participants in planning
  Value of postsecondary education
  Transition barriers
  Differences between high school
  and postsecondary settings

Student characteristics
  Who transitions
  Who succeeds

High school transition activities
  Individual transition plan
  Documenting student progress
  Postsecondary setting alternatives

Postsecondary student services
  Service delivery models
  Accommodations, waivers, and substitutions
  Identification versus eligibility assessment

FIGURE 10.1   CHAPTER 10 ORGANIZATION

to one's quality of life. The main focus among postsecondary alternatives will be offerings at community colleges, vocational technical schools, 4-year colleges, and universities. The encouragement, academic programming, and support system that high school teachers provide has a demonstrable influence on students' postsecondary choices and outcomes. This role prompts several questions. The chapter will help frame responses to these questions.

The goals for this chapter are consistent with common models of delivering services to students with disabilities in high school and postsecondary educational settings. In the broadest sense the goal is to help teachers and other service providers recognize their roles to ensure that students consider educational opportunities available once they complete their high school requirements and are prepared. More specifically, this chapter has four objectives:

- To assist teachers in preparing students for the academic and social demands of the postsecondary setting.
- To increase students' awareness of their options in postsecondary educational settings.
- To help teachers evaluate with their students the educational choices available.
- To describe the organization of student services in postsecondary settings.

The chapter first builds the case for why a larger portion of the LD population should value and utilize postsecondary educational opportunities. The case can be made quite simply that one's quality of life has many dimensions and that the level of educational attainment can contribute positively to those multiple dimensions. These opportunities do not occur by accident but, rather, require planning and preparation. Thus, the planning process and the need to involve many disciplines in repeated monitoring efforts are points of emphasis.

Our findings reveal a postsecondary setting that generally is quite a contrast to the secondary setting. The contrasts are in the available services, the role of the LD specialist, the legal protections, and the demands of the setting on the student. Figure 10.1 depicts the organization of this chapter.

MEANING OF TRANSITION

Recent surveys of future employment trends indicate that higher levels of academic functioning and postsecondary training degrees will be needed to compete successfully in the job market. Although students with LD are enrolling more frequently in programs leading to advanced degrees and certification, they often enter these programs poorly prepared emotionally and academically. Many of these young people desperately need a high school curriculum with greater emphasis on their transitional needs (Dowdy, Carter, & Smith, 1990, p. 346).

The concept of *transition* is important and comparatively new to special education service providers. Although employment goals have been part of most high school goals in the past, the structure for developing a plan toward that goal was variable prior to

1974. The requirement for an individualized education program (IEP) for each student receiving special education services provided a uniform structure and required setting long-term goals and short-term objectives as the benchmarks of progress. The IEP requirement was part of the legislation included in the Education for All Handicapped Children Act (EHA), Public Law 94–142, and its accompanying regulations. Through development of the IEP, the multidisciplinary team, including parents and students, could customize and plan curricular activities for individual students. This structure broadened the educational opportunities for students with disabilities.

In 1985 Will (1985) added a special emphasis for high school programs for students with disabilities, focusing on these students' transition to successful employment. Her definition of transition was "an outcome-oriented process encompassing a broad array of services and experiences leading to employment" (p. 1). The singular emphasis on employment as an outcome spurred further efforts to increase the quality of special education programs for a more broadly defined outcome.

Several other writers (e.g., Halpern, 1985; Wehman, Kregel, & Barcus, 1985) challenged the federal perspective as articulated by Will (1985). Halpern argued that the appropriate outcome target should be community adjustment and that employment is only one index of the level of that adjustment. Community integration may have been a new concern or target for student outcomes for many school districts (NICHCY, 1993, p. 13).

In federal legislation the term *transition services* means a coordinated set of activities for a student, designed within an outcome-oriented process that promotes movement from school to post-school activities, including postsecondary education, vocational training, integrated employment (including supported employment), continuing and adult education, adult services, independent living, and community participation (*Federal Register*, September 29, 1992). For the purposes of this chapter, the transition to postsecondary educational settings refers to the sequential process of students' completing secondary school requirements and planning and participating successfully in further formal educational activities in a degree or certification program. Postsecondary programs include community colleges, vocational and technical schools, and 4-year colleges and universities. Successful participation in these programs requires active long-range planning by students, their parents or guardians, and school staff. It is essential that students have a thorough understanding of the consequences and options for their postsecondary plans.

Completing the secondary school requirements does not always mean graduating with a high school diploma. For some students the best alternative is to pass high school equivalency examinations or the five areas of the General Educational Development (GED) exam. In working with the students, these alternatives to high school graduation should be considered carefully in light of the students' interests, motivation, and availability of program support. We need to realize that these alternatives to a traditional high school diploma may be the ticket for the student to access a postsecondary setting more quickly. Teachers do not want to advocate dropping out of school, but if students are headed out the door already, they should have an alternative. They need to know that there is no yellow brick road to an easy lifestyle but that the road can take them to a postsecondary setting in which they can pursue their educational goals.

PARTICIPANTS IN TRANSITION PLANNING

The planning process should involve the student's teachers and parents, the high school counselor, the vocational rehabilitation counselor, an admissions counselor to a postsecondary educational setting, and the student. Wehman, Kregel, and Barcus (1985) suggested adding to the team an adult service system representative and possibly an employer. The employer would be chosen to represent the perspectives of other employers and to describe the most important general characteristics that employers evaluate in hiring, retaining, and advancing their employees. Even if a student's initial interest may be to pursue additional education, the employer can be a resource to serve the student's eventual goal of employment that will support an independent lifestyle.

Transition planning is a student-centered activity that requires collaborative effort, and for the participants to share responsibilities (National Joint Committee on Learning Disabilities, 1994). Table 10.1 lists several of these key team members and their contributions to developing students' transition plans. What distinguishes this organization in transition planning is a broader representation of perspectives than that described by Wehman et al. (1985) or later by Rojewski (1989). Second, this listing was organized with an emphasis on students' continuing their formal education. Clark and Kolstoe (1990) included many of these same individuals in their discussion on planning students' transition to settings different from postsecondary educational settings. The various staff members are included to emphasize the importance of this transition planning. Although representatives of the school staff likely are part of the IEP team, other disciplines and settings have to be represented to add a broader perspective to the discussions. For example, vocational rehabilitation requires representation because this agency is infrequently associated with LD services (Osgood-Smith, 1992) but should have an expanded role in light of the agency's change in LD definition and policy.

We generally believe that students should contribute to the planning process. Students are not always willing participants, but including them at least as observers is important. Until recently few models have been offered for including students as active participants (Van Reusen & Bos, 1994). As the transition plan takes shape, though, they likely will see the value of reacting and offering their own suggestions for an effective plan. Their participation will heighten their motivation to achieve the agreed-upon goals. Also through their self-assessment, they can identify their strengths and weaknesses and set their priorities. They can describe the accommodations that work best for them to minimize their disability.

Kravets (1993b) developed several worksheets and self-assessments that are helpful in evaluating postsecondary educational options. Several features make her material particularly helpful. First, it includes sections relevant to the student's self-assessment as well as principles for evaluating colleges and the LD services available. In another section she outlines a four-step planning section of the tasks a student should complete in planning postsecondary options.

Davie (1987) provided an assessment that a teacher or a counselor might complete with a student to evaluate the student's level of independence and preparation for a postsecondary setting. Some of the questions in that assessment are:

TABLE 10.1 PARTICIPANTS AND THEIR ASSISTANCE TO STUDENTS WITH LD IN PLANNING
POSTSECONDARY EDUCATIONAL OPPORTUNITIES

Participants	**Assistance**
Special education staff	1. Products of completed coursework 2. Planning curricular adaptations to meet student's anticipated postsecondary needs 3. Documentation of student's disability and responses to instructional and test-taking accommodations 4. Comprehensive evaluations of student's knowledge, skills, and abilities in the areas of cognitive, academic, social, prevocational/vocational, and adaptive functioning 5. Arranging accommodations for any college entrance assessments used as a condition of entrance or matriculation 6. Guidance in developing the student's individual transition plan (ITP) beginning as early as age 14 7. Providing instruction in the learning strategies that will help the student meet the reading, notetaking, writing, and test-taking requirements of the postsecondary setting 8. Demonstrating sensitivity to the cultural and familial values influencing the student's and parent's decisions about educational goals and programming options
Parents or guardians	1. Assessment of the student's interests and motivation 2. Describing the available support system for the student to pursue postsecondary opportunities (e.g., transportation, housing, financial support) 3. Valuing the opportunities available through postsecondary educational settings 4. Keeping the records of comprehensive evaluations, IEPs, educational achievement documents and portfolio of class products 5. Insisting that their youngster organize all of their communications and documents from the postsecondary settings 6. Recognizing that parents are most frequently credited with students' success in education and jobs (e.g., Edgar, 1987; Dowdy, Carter, & Smith, 1990)
High school counselor	1. Ensuring that classroom and testing accommodations are appropriate to the student and documented 2. Assistance with identification and selection of appropriate postsecondary educational settings based on the student's interests and abilities and parent's concerns (e.g., transportation, expenses, housing, college size, and academic programs) 3. Assistance with the application process and arranging visits to alternative settings 4. Indicating the potential long-term value of completing additional formal educational opportunities

(continued)

Table 10.1 Continued

Participants	Assistance
	5. Academic counseling on appropriate coursework to prepare for post-secondary educational settings
	6. Liaison with Social Security Administration concerning establishing eligibility for Supplemental Security Insurance (SSI) and Social Security Disability Insurance (SSDI)
Employment representative	1. Description of employment setting demands
	2. Suggestions of educational/training experiences that would be valuable given student's expressed interests
	3. Identification of other community or business resources that would be valuable for student to explore
	4. Liaison with business and community resources
Vocational rehabilitation counselor	1. Information about vocational rehabilitation system's eligibility requirements and services
	2. Referral or assessment of student to determine qualifications for vocational rehabilitation services and support
	3. Assist in documentation of student's disability for admissions staff at postsecondary educational settings
	4. Ongoing follow-up to monitor and support student's progress
	5. Assessment of the student's career interests and vocational skills
Postsecondary setting admissions counselor	1. Assistance with admissions and enrollment process and timelines
	2. Serve as on-campus support for student and know other available support services
	3. Knowledge of course requirements and faculty dispositions toward accommodating student with LD
	4. Knowledge of documentation requirements for verifying student's disabilities and ensuring appropriate accommodations
	5. Liaison between high school setting and college setting for parents, teachers, and other involved agencies
	6. Knowledge of college's legal obligations to provide accommodations to student with disabilities under Section 504 of 1973 Rehabilitation Act (Public Law 93–112)
Student	1. Identify areas of career interest and levels of confidence for each
	2. Provide a self-assessment of views about various postsecondary options
	3. Describe academic areas of strengths and weaknesses, compensatory strategies, and learning preferences
	4. Describe the value of different accommodations

- How do you best learn something new? Is it easier when someone shows you how to do a task? Or do you prefer a slow, careful explanation?
- What kinds of places do you enjoy working in, and what are you good at doing that could lead to a meaningful job?
- Do you have good work habits?
- Are you on time with completing tasks and assignments?
- How well do you work with others of the same age? With others who are older?
- How are you going to handle the criticism that comes with high expectations from others such as a college instructor or employer?
- How do you manage your resources (e.g., energy, health, time, and money)?
- How many of the activities required for living independently do you manage on your own now? Those activities might include meal planning and preparation, doing laundry, paying bills, keeping a budget, and keeping materials organized.

The questions Davie (1987) developed are not intended as exhaustive but should provide a catalyst for discussions. They are best reviewed with the student or as a small-group activity with several students. Students need to be self-advocates—which at 16 to 18 years of age may be difficult but certainly should be encouraged. The educational environment and ITP- and IEP-related meetings provide some of the best training opportunities for students to develop their self-advocacy skills and gain a broader understanding of career and lifestyle issues they are confronting.

VALUE OF POSTSECONDARY EDUCATION

To most students with learning disabilities and, perhaps, their parents and guardians, the prospect of students continuing their education beyond the secondary level may seem foolhardy. After all, from their perspective, the most readily apparent manifestation of their learning disability is through classwork requirements. This disability was identified as such in a school setting, not in the church choir, the doctor's office, or a department store. The value attached to higher education, however, is no different for any student with or without disabilities.

Regardless of a person's attributes, quality of life is measured by the same scale. Therefore, an important consideration for students with disabilities is to realize that they face a greater imperative for developing their skills. That imperative exists because, regardless of the level of their success, they always will have to confront and consider the severity of their disability. Although the disability may exclude them from a few activities or career choices, it will influence their performance in any endeavor. This reality should be presented to the students and parents as part of their orientation to being a young adult or adolescent with disabilities. The student and his or her parents may have come to realize the effects in an educational setting, and that setting has had the most supportive environment. In comparison to the work environment, even the postsecondary setting is more accommodating.

In a number of studies young adults were asked about the quality of their lives since leaving high school. Quality of life was considered from several dimensions including their living situation, employment opportunities, and educational goals. Halpern (1993) suggested that three basic domains of outcomes are almost always worthy of assessment.

To understand a person's quality of life, one must examine the success achieved in three domains:

1. Physical and material well-being (including physical and mental health, food, clothing and lodging, financial security, and safety from harm)
2. Performance in a variety of adult roles
3. A sense of personal fulfillment (including happiness, satisfaction, and a sense of general well-being).

Halpern's second category of adult roles is much more encompassing and should be examined closely across several outcomes. Regarding various adult roles, Halpern identified eight areas of outcomes:

1. Mobility and community access (e.g., effectively using some form of transportation)
2. Vocation, career, and employment (e.g., having a job that reflects a career interest)
3. Leisure and recreation
4. Personal relationships and social networks (e.g., maintaining a network of friends)
5. Educational attainment (e.g., earning a high school diploma)
6. Spiritual fulfillment (e.g., participating in spiritual activities of choice)
7. Citizenship (e.g., voting)
8. Social responsibility (e.g., not breaking laws).

Why should these domains and areas of outcome be of concern to teachers, and, more important, to students? A person's quality of life can be examined in these domains. This model for quality of life provides teachers a framework for identifying a student's needs and planning appropriate postsecondary learning experiences. To help students consider their options for further education, teachers might want to provide students and their parents information about the research findings of the adult population with LD and of follow-up and follow-along studies. Halpern's framework was used to help organize the findings from these studies. This organization also would be useful in developing students' IEPs and ITPs, and the framework could be useful for students' self-assessment and goal setting. Two areas have been singled out here because they appeal to adolescents in particular: employment opportunities and financial earnings.

Adolescents seem especially prone to dismiss the value of education and have an overly optimistic view of their potential to live and work independently without education. The following list of authors and the publication dates of research articles came to a similar conclusion about employment outcomes for students with LD. These studies examined the employment pattern of students who were in high school and students who had graduated or left high school. The students who were no longer in school were followed for as long as 3 years after leaving school. Although some exceptions were reported, all of these 13 studies reported that the vast majority of students were employed in entry-level, base-wage positions and had low rates of advancement or improved positions. Examples of these kinds of jobs include laborers, sales clerks, food service workers, and the armed forces. The researchers include:

Cobb and Crump (1984)
Edgar (1987)
Fourqurean and LaCourt (1990)
Fourqurean, Meisgeier, Swank, and
  Williams (1991)
Haring, Lovett, and Smith (1990)
Malcolm, Polatajko, and Simons (1990)
Neubert, Tilson, and Ianacone (1989)

Scuccimarra and Speece (1990)
Shapiro and Lentz (1991)
Siegel and Gaylord-Ross (1991)
Siegel, Robert, Waxman, and
  Gaylord-Ross (1992)
Sitlington and Frank (1993)
Sitlington and Frank (1990)

The issue is not the value of any job over another. Employment is important for a number of reasons. Nevertheless, the positions obtained by individuals with LD most often offer little opportunity for advancement. Great competition from others in the workforce exists for these jobs, and continued education would open additional opportunities to other occupations, not limit them.

Other researchers have reported more positive outcomes for individuals with LD (Bruck, 1985, 1987; Adelman & Vogel, 1990), but these outcomes were for individuals who had attended more selective schools and received extensive interventions early in their education. The differences suggest that factors such as parental influence, educational attainment, and quality and length of interventions can make a difference, but these factors do not exist for the majority of students with LD. As the teacher and the other IEP team members work with these students and parents, the employment outcomes reported from follow-up and follow-along studies can be important in developing a sense of urgency to plan additional educational opportunities.

Another outcome for a student to consider is that jobs vary in potential earnings. As a simplistic example, a student who mows lawns in a northern state can expect to earn an income during a short growing season and, for at least that reason, a year-round job at minimum wage would provide greater earnings potential. A few lessons on the cost of living and lifestyle goals should have a sobering effect on the limits of a secondary education. For most students postsecondary education can be translated into better jobs and a higher quality of life.

Given the kinds of occupations described here, one might expect that earnings would be low. Studies examining the earnings of students with LD who left school early or had little postsecondary training or education have found consistently that more than half of the students were earning less than $5 an hour. A relatively easy lesson for students to do is a quick calculation of living expenses. One can see that $5 an hour provides a base wage but little beyond the minimums, and in some locations it would not meet the minimum requirements for affordable housing. In addition, a quick lesson about employee benefits likely would lead the student to conclude that entry-level jobs offer few benefits such as health or dental insurance, sick leave, vacation leave, maternity leave, or profit sharing. In six studies (Fourqurean, Meisgeier, Swank, & Williams, 1991; Neubert, Tilson, & Ianacone, 1989; Scuccimarra & Speece, 1990; Shapiro & Lentz, 1991; Siegel & Gaylord-Ross, 1991; Sitlington & Frank, 1990), few of the students received the described employee benefits. The vast majority of students had jobs without significant benefits.

Students should be able to figure out that jobs that pay near the minimum wage and offer few, if any, benefits do not represent the best opportunities. These earnings would place the student near the government's hypothetical poverty line. If those findings are not dismal enough, the real kicker is that almost three fourths of these students wind up living at home (Fourqurean & LaCourt, 1990). That should be frightening to the students and their parents alike. The parents are not likely to miss the significance of the discouraging statistics and, as a consequence, are likely to become quite involved in planning a successful transition. At this point astute teachers can extend the carrot of postsecondary educational opportunities. Teachers also should be aware of some of the factors that inhibit students' successful participation in postsecondary educational settings.

DIFFERENCES BETWEEN HIGH SCHOOL AND POSTSECONDARY SETTINGS

Ask a parent to name the biggest difference between high school and postsecondary settings, and the response might be that the college charges higher tuition! Although this may be true when comparing most 4-year colleges and universities with high schools, that financial difference is not so disparate in community college settings. The most significant differences, however, are more programmatic. The important differences concern the curriculum, instructional methods, and supportive services model.

The postsecondary setting offers the most significant opportunity for students to acquire the knowledge and skills for vocational attainment, which is tied to more positive outcomes, especially for students in vocational educational settings. High school can be seen as preparatory for the more specific postsecondary training. Kravets (1993a) outlined eight examples of differences between colleges and high schools, listed in Table 10.2.

The differences between high school and college are amplified by other changes that occur concurrently. For example, postsecondary settings for many students require leaving home. This can present significant challenges for students who have difficulty with the required social competencies (Mellard & Hazel, 1992; Putnam, 1984; Osgood-Smith, 1992). Brinckerhoff, Shaw, and McGuire (1992) and Dalke and Schmitt (1987) identified related areas of change including the decrease in contact among teachers and students, the increase in academic competition, the change in the students' support network because they are more independent, and a greater expectation that the students will achieve on their own.

NICHCY (1991) highlighted some of the significant differences between high school and postsecondary settings in terms of the available special education services. Among those differences is that the high school most likely is the last setting in which comprehensive services are available. These services included educational programming and other supports such as the entitlement to individualized education and psychological assessments, and a multidisciplinary team for planning and providing special educational and related services (e.g., speech and language therapy, occupational and physical thera-

TABLE 10.2   MAJOR DIFFERENCES BETWEEN HIGH SCHOOL AND COLLEGE

Areas	High School	College
Teacher-student contact	Teacher-student contact is closer and more frequent (5 days/week)	Instructor-student contact is more difficult and less frequent (1 to 3 times/week)
New status	Student establishes personal status in academic and social activity based on family-community factors	Student is in a new situation with little carryover of either family or community reputation
Counseling	Counseling by teachers or guidance counselors is personalized; guidance personnel are more easily available; parental contact is constant	Counseling is less valuable and must be sought by students; parental contact is much more difficult and limited
Dependence	Student is told what to do in most situations; follow-up on instructions is often the rule	Student is on his or her own; great self-discipline is required
Motivation	Student gets stimulation to achieve or participate from parents, teachers, and counselors	Student must supply his or her own motivation
Freedom	Student activity is established by school and community tradition and acceptance	Student has much more freedom; student must accept responsibility for his or her actions
Distractions	Distractions from school and community activity are present, but these are controlled partially by school and home	Many more distractions; many more temptations to neglect academic demands; many more opportunities to become involved in nonproductive activities
Value judgments	Student often makes value judgments based on parental values; many times value judgments are made for him or her	Student-student contact and instructor-student contact may lead to new value judgments arrived at without as many outside guidelines

Source: From *College and Post-secondary Options*, by M. Kravets, 1993, a presentation at the National Center for Learning Disabilities Educational Summit, Scottsdale, AZ.

pies, and adaptive physical education). Leaving high school creates a void that usually has been filled by the parents and family, as well as a carefully developed ITP and a high school program that provides follow-up to its graduates.

Teachers will want to point out to students and their parents that special education is different in postsecondary settings. It is replaced by some other organization such as student services, student assistance center, or disabled students' services. These differences are more than a name change. They reflect significant philosophical, legal, and practical changes.

In grades K–12 special education services are delivered through a federally legislated system that provides financial support to the states. In addition to the federal financial support, each state provides support for the added costs of services and for certifying instructional and support staff for students with disabilities. This federal support is not provided to any postsecondary setting. Similarly, in only a couple of settings is state support offered for higher education costs for students with disabilities. Philosophical differences influence these financial and support services offered to students after they leave high school. The high school special education staff might discuss how their services should be structured to ensure a smoother transition to postsecondary settings and follow-up of their school leavers. As part of planning the ITP, the students might be asked to identify the services they currently receive. For comparison, they could contact nearby postsecondary institutions and identify available services. This exercise will illuminate a different perspective on secondary and postsecondary services.

BARRIERS IN A POSTSECONDARY SETTING

The differences between high school and college can be challenging to many students. In addition, a number of factors have been identified that decrease the likelihood of a student's success in postsecondary settings. Prater and Minner (1986), Rosenthal (1986), and Putnam (1984) reviewed related literature regarding barriers. Among the barriers are three that are cited frequently: (a) the student's inappropriate, or lack of, preparation, (b) negative attitudes among faculty, and (c) lack of comprehensive support programs.

POSTSECONDARY PREPARATION

A student's preparation for college includes academic preparation and the ITP. Some of the common interventions in high schools may support a student in that setting but provide little support outside that setting (Mangrum & Strichart, 1988; Mellard & Clark, 1992). Examples of the "getting-by curriculum" include interventions that rely heavily on tutoring in the content areas, basic skills, work-study, and functional curriculum (Mellard & Clark, 1992). Students can complete their high school requirements through these intervention and curricular models, but have few of the skills required in higher education settings. Thus, students, teachers, and parents need to recognize the fundamental importance of the curricular and instructional decisions at the secondary level. The curricular decisions involve which coursework the student will complete.

The instructional decisions involve the methods used in providing the instruction. Instruction delivered through tutorial models may provide successful completion, but is that model the best for preparing the student for the level of independence expected at the collegiate level? Does the curriculum recognize the differences between high school and postsecondary settings and have options for students transitioning to the postsecondary setting?

In spite of the learning disability, students with LD need content instruction that will match their postsecondary plans. This need is no different than that for other students except that other students have access to the mainstream high school programs. Some of these course offerings may be unavailable or at a different level of academic rigor for the LD student. Students can wind up in basic skills courses that are not supportive of a postsecondary placement (Bursuck, Rose, Cowen, & Yahaya, 1989).

The best approach to this programmatic issue is through the content that gets included on the student's IEP and ITP. By identifying early in high school the range of postsecondary options the student would like to consider, the ITP and IEP can be developed accordingly. In the simplest plan the students would (a) identify the postsecondary settings they would like to consider, (b) review the entrance requirements to those settings, (c) review the kinds of secondary courses needed to meet those requirements and the high school's course requirements, and (d) match those requirements to the offerings at the secondary setting. The earlier this task is initiated, the greater flexibility the student will have in planning the high school curriculum. Any forward-thinking high school student interested in postsecondary education would follow the same strategy. The ITP team should serve as the catalyst that encourages the students' deliberations and supports their initiative.

When the instructional methods are considered, the ITP and IEP team again must consider students' postsecondary plans. These teams do not want to provide instruction that only ensures high school completion. They, too, need to have an informed vision of the setting demands a student will encounter in postsecondary settings and the available services. Experience is a valuable teacher. Guided experience with feedback is the needed teacher for these students with LD.

FACULTY ATTITUDES

Some observers have commented on the change of attitudes in instructional staff between primary grade level and elementary level to middle school, and on up through high school and postsecondary settings. The change is that a higher expectation is placed on the student to acquire the content and that the instructor is seen as presenter of that knowledge. The progression also corresponds to a decrease in teaching the tool skills for learning such as reading, arithmetic, and writing, and an increase in the student's independent application of those skills in learning the needed course content. At the college or university level in particular, scholarship and research interests dominate, and the setting is not viewed as a social service agency designed to accommodate all interested applicants. In some college settings these values are demonstrated in the admissions standards and student support services offered (Putnam, 1984; Rosenthal, 1986). For example, the more selective the admissions standards, the more specific and narrow is the college's perspective on the students it enrolls and graduates.

These different perspectives across the grade levels reveal a greater emphasis on maintaining the integrity of the academic program and on students' meeting degree requirements. The shift is not unwarranted on some accounts, but it also places greater burdens on the students. Students must work to meet the requirements of the degree, and those requirements are described clearly in terms of number and distribution of course credits. This standard for excellence means that all students should be treated equally. The requirements and treatments must be the same for all students. Equal treatment can be a handicap for students with disabilities. Their disabilities mean that they are not able to work on an equal footing with their nondisabled peers.

The alternative to equal treatment that at the same time can maintain the instructor's and institution's desired level of excellence is to provide equitable treatment (Lundeberg & Svien, 1988; Oliker, 1989). Equitable treatment emphasizes maintaining a high standard but providing accommodations that permit the student to meet course, department, and college requirements (Nelson, Dodd, & Smith, 1990; Vogel & Sattler, 1981).

SUPPORT PROGRAMS

Earlier the high school and postsecondary settings were differentiated on a number of dimensions. One of the most critical dimensions for the student with LD is the variation in support programs offered in the postsecondary setting. Provision of services is based on the individual institution. Rather than describing a continuum of services as required in the K–12 system, the postsecondary setting chooses its own model for services. This lack of uniformity could be a barrier to students because the opportunity for attending different postsecondary settings is limited by costs, distance from home, admissions requirements, career interests, campus size, and support groups. These issues are minimal in a high school setting. Yet, in planning a successful transition to a postsecondary setting, these issues must be considered carefully.

Variation in support programs and services has been well documented in a number of books and materials. These materials were designed to acquaint interested audiences with this range in services and to assist in choosing among the alternatives. Table 10.3 presents a partial listing of the many materials available for choosing postsecondary set-

TABLE 10.3   REFERENCE MATERIAL FOR LD SERVICES IN POSTSECONDARY SETTINGS

Date	Authors	Title
1985	R. Skyer and G. Skyer	*What Do You Do After High School?*
1985	C. T. Straughn and S. C. Colby	*Lovejoy's College Guide for the Learning Disabled*
1986	J. Slovak	*Bose Directory*
1988	C. T. Mangrum and S. S. Strichart	*College and the Learning Disabled Student*
1989	A. J. Sclafanai and M. J. Lynch	*College Guide for Students with Learning Disabilities, 1988–1989*
1992	Peterson's Guides	*Peterson's Guide to Colleges with Programs for Learning Disabled Students (4th edition, 1994)*
1993	M. Kravets and I. F. Wax	*K &W Guide to Colleges for the Learning Disabled*

tings. This listing is not exhaustive, and the selections have a particular emphasis. For example, the Kravets and Wax text does not include community college programs and emphasizes detailed information about colleges and universities. The high-tech solution also is available. MatchMaker (Alexander & Rolfe, 1992) computer software is for individuals who want a high-tech alternative to printed media and want to compare a student's interests with the services available in postsecondary settings. Depending on the amount of use the software might get and the availability of hardware, MatchMaker may be a good alternative to printed media. This software has yearly updates.

ADDITIONAL BARRIERS

In addition to the previous barriers discussed, several others contribute to making postsecondary transition difficult for students and the educational staff who want to assist with transition plans. One of these factors is the variation in the standards found in postsecondary settings for identifying and serving students with LD. No single characteristic is sufficient for identifying students with LD (Mellard & Deshler, 1984). At the extreme is a great variation in the kinds of information on which LD identification or eligibility for services is based. Unlike elementary through secondary schools, most postsecondary systems or even individual settings lack a uniform set of standards for making the determination of LD and appropriateness for services. Because no federal legislation such as PL 101–467, the Individuals with Disabilities Education Act of 1990, covers postsecondary settings and few state regulations have been developed, even greater variation is encountered than what is observed in school districts (Brinckerhoff, Shaw, & McGuire, 1992; Mellard, 1990). The important consequence is to realize that the individual program determines the services and requirements for accessing those services.

California's state university and community college systems are two exceptions to this trend with systemwide eligibility models (Chancellor's Office, 1988). In California community colleges the programs that provide services to students with LD are entitled to reimbursement from the state for the direct excess cost of providing those services. To ensure consistency across the 105 community colleges, the colleges have developed their own eligibility model (Mellard, 1990). Thus, the colleges have a financial incentive for having students meet their eligibility model. A benefit of this system is that it is recognized within the state's university system. Students who are judged eligible for services in the community colleges are eligible when they transfer to a 4-year program to continue their work toward a degree. This reciprocity is valuable to ensure a smooth transition between institutions.

As an enrichment activity, the teacher might contact five or so recent graduates from the program or include some students who exited early and arrange for them to visit the high school students. Have the students spend some time planning the questions they would like to ask the alumni. The questioning could be a one-on-one interview or a panel discussion with a moderator. The questions should address some changes the alumni have experienced since leaving high school. Alumni who have had a range of postsecondary experiences should be included to broaden the students' perspectives. Teachers also might want to include the students' parents. The discussion should be short and focused.

STUDENT CHARACTERISTICS

WHO TRANSITIONS

Not many students with LD attend a postsecondary school to continue their education (Fairweather & Shaver, 1991; Valdes, Williamson, & Wagner, 1990). The ratio is approximately three to one nondisabled to students with LD who attend a postsecondary school within a year after leaving high school. Our experience suggests that unless students with LD enter a postsecondary setting within the first year of leaving the secondary setting, the likelihood that they will participate later drops significantly.

Recent studies document that an increasing proportion of students with LD are attending postsecondary classes. The importance of this change is that colleges, community colleges, vocational and technical schools will become more sensitive to the needs of a more diverse population. As a consequence, the student should find services easier to access and more abundant. Also, programs likely will have more specific guidelines regarding eligibility for services.

The students with LD will demonstrate to colleges that LD cannot be characterized by a specific achievement disability and that accommodations must be tailored individually. From one perspective, no rules exist for the college to follow in learning to deal with the students with LD. Each student must be considered individually. This lesson likely was learned earlier in the K–12 system, as most of these students are products of that system.

Students with LD will not likely be alone as they attend a postsecondary setting. Several estimates suggest that LD represents one of the largest groups of students with disabilities on campus (CLD, 1993; Fairweather & Shaver, 1991). Fairweather and Shaver found that 17% of students with LD enrolled in some type of course in a postsecondary setting—8.5% in a vocational course, 6.8% in a 2-year course, and 1.8% in a 4-year course. The Council for Learning Disabilities (1993) reported that 9% of all students with LD were enrolled in 2-year or 4-year colleges. Elksnin and Elksnin (see chapter 11) reported that few students attend a 4-year college or university. They reported that fewer than 2% attended 4-year institutions, a value closer to Fairweather and Shaver's findings.

The staff and parents working with the student to prepare for postsecondary settings also should consider an important statistic regarding *when* these students participate. Results from several studies confirm that students who left school and participated in postsecondary educational opportunities did so within a year after leaving the secondary setting (Eagle, Fitzgerald, Gifford, Zuma, & MPR Associates, 1988; Jones, Sebring, Crawford, Spencer, & Butz, 1986a, 1986b). Therefore, the inclination to wait out a time before enrolling in a postsecondary program will decrease substantially the probability of reentering. Participation might be likened to a game of poker. Once a person is out of the betting, he or she is out for the rest of the hand. In this case, folding your hand likely will mean that the student will continue to hold those same losing cards. The best opportunity for participation comes with the support of parents and the high school team.

WHO SUCCEEDS

An important consideration is knowing which students are likely to be successful in the various postsecondary settings. Postsecondary educational opportunities are quite varied. Students have choices for colleges, universities, 2-year colleges, vocational and technical schools, and adult education. These choices must be considered carefully given the low completion rates. Approximately 30% of students with LD complete degrees successfully at community colleges and 4-year colleges and universities (Bursuck, Rose, Cowen, & Yahaya, 1989).

As the IEP and ITP are being developed in high school, realistic goal setting should take precedence. When considering alternative outcome goals, attention should be directed to narrowing the postsecondary settings to those that are most realistic for the student's skills and career interests. First, the high school's and state's graduation requirements must be considered. This first hurdle can be formidable, particularly as recent reforms in some states have increased the number of hours or credits required for graduation and implemented a minimum competency or exit testing program (Mellard & Clark, 1992). In light of these requirements, a student may elect to spend an extra year in high school to be better prepared and able to devote attention to more challenging content (CLD, 1993).

Miller, Snider, and Rzonca (1990) analyzed data from Iowa's follow-along and follow-up studies to learn which factors contributed to students' participation in postsecondary education. The assessed differences were in the areas of intellectual ability, reading, and math achievement, involvement in extracurricular activities, and access of community resources. In cognitive ability and achievement the differences were not too surprising. The brighter and more highly skilled students were more likely to participate. The assessed ability and achievement levels of students in postsecondary education, however, were below average. The intellectual ability level was a standard score of 96, and the grade-level equivalencies in reading and math were in the 7th-grade range. These low scores might encourage a large number of students to pursue a postsecondary education, albeit at one of the less selective choices of a community college or a vocational or technical school. That's encouraging because few students with LD are likely to achieve at a 12th-grade level and might needlessly rule out postsecondary educational options.

Our work with the California community college system provided an opportunity to describe numerous characteristics of students with LD in this postsecondary system. Approximately 1.2% of the students in the California community colleges are served as LD. A study completed in 1992 (Mellard, 1993) provided extensive details about the ability and achievement levels of students in the system. Students from 21 of California's 105 community colleges were tested. Table 10.4 summarizes selected test score information from our study. The test scores include the Full Scale IQ score from the Wechsler Adult Intelligence Scale–Revised (WAIS–R) (Wechsler, 1981), the Broad Cognitive score from the standard battery on the Woodcock–Johnson Psychoeducational Battery–Revised (WJ–R) (Woodcock & Johnson, 1989), and composite achievement test scores also from the WJ–R battery.

A variety of information could have been provided, but in the interest of parsimony, these few statistics were chosen. The tables include information about a students' group

TABLE 10.4   SELECTED TEST SCORE INFORMATION FROM CALIFORNIA COMMUNITY COLLEGES

Group	Count	Mean	Std Dev	Std Error	Min	Max	95% conf int
WAIS–R Full Scale IQ							
LD	156	92.1	11.9	.9	64.0	128.0	90.2 to 94.0
NLD	434	103.4	13.9	.6	72.0	148.0	102.0 to 104.7
AE/NC	15	97.7	11.9	3.0	69.0	114.0	91.0 to 104.3
WJ–R Broad Cognitive Standard Battery (Tests 1 to 7)							
LD	144	88.9	13.0	1.0	41.0	130.0	86.8 to 91.1
NLD	384	101.3	18.2	.9	46.0	151.0	99.5 to 103.2
AE/NC	13	92.1	13.4	3.7	69.0	130.0	84.0 to 100.2
WJ–R Basic Reading Skills Supplemental Battery Cluster							
LD	156	88.8	14.6	1.1	52.0	133.0	86.5 to 91.1
NLD	441	107.4	17.9	.8	48.0	160.0	105.7 to 109.1
AE/NC	14	86.4	15.8	4.2	65.0	121.0	77.2 to 95.5
WJ–R Reading Comprehension Supplemental Battery Cluster							
LD	151	88.5	12.4	1.0	54.0	129.0	86.5 to 90.5
NLD	425	100.3	16.7	.8	46.0	149.0	98.7 to 101.9
AE/NC	12	90.4	15.4	4.4	66.0	129.0	80.5 to 100.2
WJ–R Basic Writing Skills Supplemental Battery Cluster							
LD	148	83.2	10.8	.8	60.0	130.0	81.4 to 84.9
NLD	420	97.4	14.9	.7	60.0	154.0	95.9 to 98.8
AE/NC	12	81.3	14.0	4.0	70.0	120.0	72.4 to 90.2
WJ–R Written Expression Supplemental Battery Cluster							
LD	160	87.1	13.4	1.0	39.0	134.0	85.0 to 89.2
NLD	443	101.6	17.0	.8	53.0	151.0	100.0 to 103.2
AE/NC	13	80.2	15.5	4.3	39.0	97.0	70.8 to 89.6

membership as LD, nonlearning disabled (NLD), or enrolled in mostly adult education, non-credit classes. This latter group of approximately 15 students in adult education is a subset of the LD sample. This subset of adult education students was provided to have another contrast of student groups. The adult education group is not likely to be pursuing a college degree currently. Rather, they are participating for enrichment, retraining, or even to work on basic skills of the GED. For the different test scores, several numerical values are reported, including the number of students in the group (count), the mean score for the group, and several numbers that help describe the variation of scores within the group: the standard deviation (Std Dev), the standard error of the mean (Std Error), the minimum and maximum scores in the group (Min and Max), and the 95% confidence interval of the mean score (95% conf int).

These data confirmed several observations noted by Miller, Snider, and Rzonca (1990). In general, the mean level of performance on ability or aptitude and achievement measures was significantly lower for the students with LD than the general student population. The percentile rankings for these standard scores corresponded to approximately the 32nd percentile down to the 13th percentile. For the students without disabilities the mean scores were average and in a range of the 67th to the 42nd percentiles.

This information is important to teachers and potentially other IEP and ITP team members. As team members consider postsecondary options, these test scores might help members evaluate alternatives by comparing a student to two groups: (a) a student sample without disabilities and (b) a student sample with LD. Although selective colleges may have stringent requirements and be appropriate to higher-functioning students with LD (Adelman & Vogel, 1990; Shaywitz & Shaw, 1988), students with lower abilities have options as well. As can be observed in the pattern of scores, the achievement scores of students with LD are well below average, but that has not eliminated the community college option. With appropriate support services these students have achieved and through that experience improved their potential quality of life once they reach their educational goals.

Another indicator was participation in extracurricular activities in the school (Miller, Snider, & Rzonca, 1990). These activities were quite varied and allowed the students with specific learning disabilities to demonstrate their strengths, which surely also contributed to higher self-esteem. The activities cited were athletics, music, speech, drama, and debate.

The last area to demonstrate a difference was that the students also were involved in the community. They learned which resources were available and how to use them. Important resources include job training and placement services, vocational rehabilitation services, and adult education.

These areas also are dependent on family support and emphasis. The linkage between students' outcomes and family support is well documented and should be considered one of the most important resources for a student (Edgar, 1987; Kravets, 1993a; Oliker, 1989; Quinby, 1989; Spekman, Goldberg, & Herman, 1992). The school staff should encourage and foster this family resource.

The same themes are supported in the analysis of successful and unsuccessful young adults as described by Oliker (1989), Sitlington and Frank (1990), and Spekman, Goldberg, and Herman (1992). The latter authors noted several characteristics differentiating successful and unsuccessful adults. A realistic adaptation to life events was singled out as most important. This characteristic included self-awareness of strengths and weaknesses related to the learning disability, a proactive approach (meaning that they were involved in the world around them), and a willingness to persevere to their goals. This perseverance included a high level of emotional stability, ability to reduce personal stress, and coping strategies.

Another characteristic was goal-setting and goal-directed behaviors. These young adults had a vision of what they wanted to accomplish and willingness to reach the goal step-by-step. Oliker (1989) described this characteristic as motivation, which can be developed through home and school experiences. These experiences included students' participation in community and school activities. What these data seem to suggest is a significant paradox. Typically, students with LD are described as having few friends and limited social competence (Mellard & Hazel, 1992), yet these areas are exactly the ones that must be developed to increase students' likelihood of success in a postsecondary setting and quality of life as an adult in the community. This paradox should be understood as professionals and parents support the student and plan the IEP and ITP.

Yet another characteristic of students who are successful in postsecondary educational settings is related to the presence and use of effective support systems in their lives. This characteristic is similar to the findings of Miller et al. (1990) in their analysis. The role of "significant others" in their lives was important—if not from family members, then from mentoring relationships they developed with others in the community or school system. The support system seems to be critical to community integration and goal-setting behaviors discussed earlier.

HIGH SCHOOL TRANSITION ACTIVITIES

For a student to become successful in postsecondary settings, the high school program can contribute valuable opportunities. NICHCY (1991, 1993) outlined several of the areas that can smooth the transition. In addition, our work in the adult education, vocational-technical, and community college settings has provided insight in several areas that also become important to college planning for students with LD. The goals of a high school program to smooth a student's transition to college are the following:

1. *Developing students' effective study skills.* Effective study skills are critical, as the independence of college and the higher level of academic expectations place an increased burden on college students.

2. *Developing students' learning strategies.* The strategies are quite inclusive in improving students' ability to acquire meaning from written text and produce documents that demonstrate their knowledge of the content in a style that communicates the writers' intent.

3. *Arranging job try outs to allow students opportunities to evaluate different career and vocational options.* High school offers a great opportunity to inquire safely and test alternative vocational interests. Before rushing to the postsecondary setting, students can learn more about various career options that will help, not only in career plans but

also in selecting a setting that will provide the needed educational experiences.

4. *Arranging needed accommodations for college entrance exams and matriculation testing.* Students are entitled to assessments that do not penalize them for their specific learning disability. These accommodations include extended time, a reader, a scribe, a separate testing area, or shorter test sessions. The important point is for the students to learn which accommodations work best for them and gain the needed documentation to support their requests for the accommodations in standardized testing, and, later, college classes.

5. *Identifying colleges that provide educational programs relevant to career interests.* For any student seeking college admission, the planning should begin early in high school. For the student with LD the choice might be more difficult because of issues related to special admissions and ensuring that the needed support services are available. Matching the desired educational program and level of needed support services is an important step in college selection.

6. *Identifying the types of accommodations and support services that the student needs because of his or her disability.* The differences between a high school and a college are readily apparent. High school provides opportunities to learn what instructional and assessment accommodations work best. Postsecondary programs are likely to place more emphasis on providing the accommodations that the student used in general classes.

7. *Assistance in the application process.* Applying to colleges and for financial aid packages can be a daunting task. The sometimes bewildering application process and the waiting period could be part of the reason that few students with LD enter postsecondary education. Support in this area could lead to higher enrollments by students with LD.

8. *Assistance in preparing the documentation that the student can carry to the college.* The high school setting provides many protections and coordinated services that are greatly reduced, if not eliminated, once the student exits. Documentation of the history of the disability and effective interventions represents a valuable resource that can guide administrators and counselors in working effectively with students and reducing the apprehension and frustration they encounter in learning a new system. This documentation should include results of a recent comprehensive evaluation, a summary of previous evaluations, and, most important, information on the type and extent of services that have been provided. The typical IEP does not provide this information.

Cardarella (1989) provided one example of documentation that was helpful in postsecondary settings and vocational rehabilitation and was cited as a "best practice." The two- to three-page student reports describe progress to date. The organization included main headings in the student's academic areas (e.g., math and English, including reading and writing) and related areas influencing achievement such as learning style, successful modifications and intervention strategies, work-related skills, and last, concerns about the student. The documentation is an effective way to summarize information that other service providers would use.

A good plan for preparing this information is to collaborate with staff in postsecondary settings. That staff likely would welcome an extended discussion on the information and its format that is particularly helpful as they consider admissions questions, academic counseling, and appropriate classes, services, and accommodations. At the postsecondary setting this information might prove valuable in overcoming the reported negative attitudes held by some faculty members who confuse ADA (Americans with Disabilities Act) with the American Dairy Association or American Dental Association (e.g., Brinckerhoff, Shaw, & McGuire, 1992; Lundeberg & Svien, 1988; Nelson, Dodd, & Smith, 1990; Putnam, 1984; Shaywitz & Shaw, 1988).

A psychoeducational evaluation and an interview are important to more than half of the postsecondary personnel surveyed about LD eligibility procedures (Bursuck, Rose, Cowen, & Yahaya, 1989). The interview is likely the most common denominator of the LD assessment process used in a variety of settings and agencies. For this reason students should be familiar with both the process and the possible content of an intake procedure. In some instances students would be able to gather supporting documentation that could facilitate their answering the intake interview items.

The Appendix to this chapter presents an intake interview (Chancellor's Office, 1993), which is one example of information that college staffs use in judging students' eligibility. It might be used for practice in completing written materials and for interviews. The California intake interview is used at more than 105 campuses and is accepted in the California State University and University of California systems. In the community college system the interview might be administered in one of three ways: (a) personal interview, (b) written application followed by personal interview, or (c) computerized administration with a college staff member. As students progress through the postsecondary programs and occupational settings, they will realize that they have to be their own advocates, which requires accurate, effective communication skills. An interview is an important part of most employment applications and admissions to professional schools.

POSTSECONDARY STUDENT SERVICES

High school students should begin their evaluation of postsecondary settings early, certainly by their junior year. At that age several factors enter into the students' evaluation equation to calculate which is the best postsecondary setting for them. The students might ask if they should attend the program with: (a) the most rigorous academic program in their subject matter area of interest, (b) the program with the best services for students with LD, or (c) the program that is least expensive and closest to home. For students of this age, the answer probably is (d) the program with the most favorable gender ratio! On the other hand, if the quality of available LD services is a consideration, teachers might want to have some methods for helping the student evaluate those services.

Services in postsecondary settings take a variety of forms. One of the earlier organizations for services was described by Ugland and Duane (1976). Their model made available two ways of serving the needs of LD college students:

1. The student adapts to existing institutional standards with help from counseling, tutoring, and support services.
2. The institution adapts its basic teaching and program requirements to the student's learning style.

These two alternatives may be inclusive; however, the philosophy for serving students with disabilities, the available services, legal and judicial foundations for services, and faculty attitudes have changed from this formation.

Vogel's (1985) listing of characteristics of a model comprehensive college LD program is quite an extensive revision of Ugland and Duane's description. The 15 characteristics Vogel identified encompass an important perspective of services. These LD program characteristics are paraphrased below. They provide teachers and students with a frame of reference for weighing the merits of services available on different campuses.

1. Planning and staff development precede initiation of an LD program.
2. The administration is 100% supportive of the program and its goals.
3. An LD specialist has overall responsibility for the program.
4. Students with LD receive academic planning to ensure that they have a workable load.
5. The faculty is supportive of the LD program and its students.
6. The faculty is knowledgeable of legal requirements for accommodations and is supportive.
7. The staff includes trained assessment personnel who can complete psychoeducational evaluations and monitor student progress.
8. Students have an IEP and receive instruction in basic skills and compensatory techniques on a one-to-one basis.
9. Peer tutors provide support in coursework.
10. Accommodations (e.g., recorded textbooks, notetakers, readers, scribes) are available.
11. Modified examination procedures are accessible.
12. The LD staff and faculty communicate frequently.
13. Personal counseling, support groups, and peer advocates are available.
14. Career and life planning counseling is available.
15. Writing labs, math centers, language labs, study skills or learning centers are available and supported by a cooperative relationship between the LD specialists and the respective lab or center staffs.

From Vogel's listing the reader gets the distinct impression that a separate LD program exists for students. That model of a separate LD program is increasingly a rarity. What is more likely is an office or a program for students with disabilities. The program for students with disabilities serves *all* students with disabilities and may offer some services especially for students with LD.

SERVICE MODELS

Siperstein (1988) organized three types of service models in the postsecondary setting: (a) separate support services that augment regular college classwork; (b) services that center on a learning disability specialist and include tutoring, counseling, and advocacy; and (c) student services that are available to all students who identify themselves as having a disability. Vogel's description is similar to the (b) model described by Siperstein.

Kravets and Wax (1993) noted that no two postsecondary LD programs are alike but that similarities can be identified. In their review of college and university programs, they organized the available services into three categories. These have application for understanding services through any postsecondary setting and should be helpful in comparing alternative settings and matching settings to students' interests and needs. The three categories of programs are: (a) structured programs, (b) coordinated services, and (c) services.

STRUCTURED PROGRAMS

Colleges with *structured programs* offer the most comprehensive services for students with LD. The director and staff are certified in LD or related areas. The director is involved actively in the admission decision, and the criteria for admission often are more flexible than general admission requirements. Services are highly structured, and students are involved in developing plans to meet their specific learning styles and needs. Often students participating in structured programs sign a contract agreeing to participate actively in the program. The services usually carry an additional fee. High school students who have participated in a structured program or structured services in high school—such as a learning disabilities resource program, individualized or modified coursework, tutorial assistance, academic monitoring, notetakers, test accommodations, and skill classes—might benefit from exploring colleges with structured programs.

COORDINATED SERVICES

Coordinated services differ from structured programs in that the services are not as comprehensive. These services usually are provided by at least one certified LD specialist. The staff is knowledgeable and trained to provide assistance to students to develop strategies for their individual needs. The director of the program or services may be involved in the admission decision or in a position to assist students with an appeal if they are denied admission to the college. To receive these services generally requires specific documentation of the LD, and students are encouraged to self-identify prior to entry. Students voluntarily request accommodations or services in the coordinated services category, and specific skills courses or remedial classes may be available or required for students with LD who are admitted probationally or conditionally. High school students who may have enrolled in some modified courses, utilized test accommodations and required tutorial assistance but who typically requested services only as needed might benefit from exploring colleges with coordinated services or services.

SERVICES

Of the three categories, *services* is the least comprehensive. Colleges offering services usually provide assistance to all students. Most colleges require documentation of the disability if the student with LD is to receive accommodations. Staff and faculty support students with LD actively by providing basic services to meet the students' needs. Services are requested on a voluntary basis, and some limitations may be placed on the services available. Sometimes the small size of the student body enables the necessary personal attention to help students with LD succeed in college. High school students requiring minimum accommodations might benefit from and find comfort in knowing that services are available, knowing who the contact person is, and knowing that this person is sensitive to students with LD (Kravets & Wax, 1993, p. 1).

The student, parents, and teacher should be able to identify which of the three levels of services are most appropriate. The level of services the student needs also can vary with factors such as other support structures, difficulty of the field of study, the student's background preparation, anticipated academic course load and study requirements, and the negative influence of competing activities such as extracurricular activities and familial or job responsibilities. Students certainly should prepare their list of anticipated needed services and use that list as one guide in interviewing prospective institutions or reviewing their materials. The flyer for Mission College (Figure 10.2) provides an attractive presentation of the services that may be of interest to students with disabilities.

The following list of services from the California community colleges was developed as we worked with LD specialists there to identify a set of core services:

1. Individualized LD eligibility assessment
2. Academic counseling
3. Liaison with faculty members
4. Tutoring services

The purpose of the **DISABLED STUDENTS PROGRAM** is to help students with disabilities to carry out the requirements of their individual educational objectives with various combinations of assistance. *Services for Persons with a Disability* addresses itself to overcoming barriers caused by physical problems and/or learning difficulties and lack of college and community awareness.

Registration Priority	**Specialized Equipment**
Notetakers	**R.F.B. Liaison**
Interpreters	**Test-Taking Arrangements**
Tutoring	**Adaptive P.E.**
Special Classes	**LD Assessment**
Liaison with Faculty	**Speech/Language Assessment**
Community Liaison	

Other services may be available than those listed above, based on the students' individual situations and needs. Students who have physical or other disabilities which handicap them may be eligible for additional services through the state Department of Rehabilitation.

For more information call
(408) 748-2730   TDD (408) 727-9243

FIGURE 10.2 MISSION COLLEGE FLYER OF SERVICES, SANTA CLARA, CALIFORNIA

5. Vocational counseling
6. Special classes in LD
7. Personal counseling
8. Registration assistance
9. Liaison with campus and community agencies
10. Special materials and supplies
11. Special matriculation assistance
12. Job placement and development
13. Test-taking facilitation
14. Notetakers
15. Books on tape

This list reflects a range of academic, vocational, and personal services that fosters a smooth transition to a 2-year college program. The quality and organization of these services vary with the training and personality of the service providers and also institutional factors such as the college's perceived mission in postsecondary education. For example, colleges that emphasize later transfer to a 4-year setting have a different focus than settings with a vocational orientation.

As a class project students could develop a survey of postsecondary programs. The survey could elicit information regarding admissions standards, LD program eligibility standards, accommodations used frequently, grievance procedures, contact persons for services, enrollment numbers of students with LD, and gender ratios. The returned surveys could be organized into a notebook for future reference and updated as each year's class matriculates. The project not only would gather relevant information but also could stimulate interest in available postsecondary options. Two suggestions about this project are to: (a) do a little pilot test of the survey with a couple of college recruiters and parents of students; the parents can give some insight into the information they value in making a decision; and (b) survey a broad range of programs such as area vocational, technical programs, community colleges, proprietary colleges, professional schools, small, selective colleges, and public colleges and universities. Three journal articles that provide extensive reviews of the surveys they used in gathering information about the postsecondary services to students with LD are: Beirne-Smith and Deck (1989), Bursuck, Rose, Cowen, and Yahaya (1989), and Parks, Antonoff, Drake, Skiba, and Soberman (1987). Teachers might find their reviews helpful as resource material for similar activities undertaken with students.

On some campuses special courses are available to students with learning disabilities. Sierra College, for example, has a course titled "Learning Disabilities Orientation," which provides .5 units and is graded as credit/noncredit. The course is described as a 9-hour orientation to the college's LD program and assessment of learning strengths and weaknesses to determine eligibility for LD services using the step-by-step guidelines mandated by the California community college system. The assessment includes an intake interview (like the one in the Appendix), a perceptual assessment battery, and a combination of aptitude or intelligence testing and achievement battery. When a student is found to be eligible for LD services, the LD specialist works with the student to prepare an IEP. The current textbook for the class is Carol Wren and Laura Segal's (1985) treatment about college students with LD. Classes available through Diablo Valley College's Learning Skills Program in Pleasant Hill, California provide a number of class alternatives for students. The partial listing provided in Figure 10.3 indicates the range of available courses.

Why would a college, such as Sierra College and Diablo Valley College, offer a nontransfer course on LD assessment? Some students are required to maintain a minimum number of hours as a condition for receiving other services or as part of a work-study or loan program. Such an elective helps the student meet requirements for a mini-

---

Diablo Valley College Learning Skills Program

Learning Skills Program courses and services are provided for students enrolled at DVC who have a diagnosed learning disability or who are being assessed for learning disabilities.

COURSES FOR ADULTS WITH LEARNING DISABILITIES

Learning Skills 49: Assessment of Learning Disabilities (3 weeks, .5 units)

Analysis of learning strengths and weaknesses; determination of eligibility for services as a learning disabled adult according to California Community Colleges definition; strategies and follow-up suggestions for all students who take the course.

To be assessed for learning disabilities at DVC, students must be enrolled in at least one other academic or vocational course at the college.

Students who have learning problems that are determined *not* to be due to a learning disability will be referred to other support services to help them succeed with their chosen goals.

Learning Skills 51A: Learning Styles (3 weeks, .5 units)

A short-term course emphasizing helping the student to understand his/her learning disability through the use of discussion, films, articles, and textbooks. It includes learning to use accommodations, classes, and tutoring offered by the Learning Skills Program.

Learning Skills 51B: Create Your College Success (3 weeks, .5 units)

A short-term course emphasizing classroom behavior, interpersonal relationships, and working with instructors.

Learning Skills 51C: Introduction to Time Management and Goal Setting (3 weeks, .5 units)

A short-term course for students with learning disabilities emphasizing time management and goal setting. Time management will include getting the most out of your time, dealing with procrastination, and designing a time plan to fit your needs. Goal setting includes setting educational goals, career goals, and/or exploring alternatives to college.

FIGURE 10.3   SAMPLE LEARNING SKILLS PROGRAM

Source: Diablo Valley College, Pleasant Hill, California.

mum number of hours. More often than not, postsecondary institutions require a student to pay a fee or seek an independent evaluation for purposes of identification and eligibility. The fees for evaluations typically run from $200 to $1,000. This expense may be prohibitive. Thus, several advantages exist for the student. The college also benefits because the students are counted toward the program's enrollment, as a basis for funding. Through the program's weighted funding formula the enrollment can generate dollars. This option is the one way a college can recoup from the State some of the costs associated with individual psychoeducational evaluations.

ACCOMMODATIONS, SUBSTITUTIONS, AND WAIVERS

In comparison to secondary settings, student services in most postsecondary settings (a) vary even more extensively, (b) are not as well developed programmatically, and (c) are not multidisciplinary. In one review of postsecondary services and service delivery models, the authors concluded that programs were "stringing together" services with limited potential for fostering success (McGuire, Norlander, & Shaw, 1990). We have reviewed a number of legislative and legal differences between these two settings that influence student services. Unless those mandates change, the postsecondary setting will continue to be weighted toward advocacy and informational services rather than direct interventions.

Three topics are particularly important regardless of how the services are organized. Those three topics concern: (a) the academic related accommodations that you might expect, (b) the substitutions of curricular courses, and (c) the waiver of particular degree requirements. We probably would have grave concerns if students with LD, who were studying to be surgeons, were granted course waivers because they felt nauseous at the sight of blood. On the other hand, we would consider an oral exam permissible if the students' written expression was so poor that they could not communicate in a written form. We would want assurance that the deficit was not related to poor motor coordination or the students' ability to make accurate incisions or sew stitches. These issues of accommodations and course variances are important for a student's success and are also issues that the student and the transition team can consider along with postsecondary setting options.

Appropriate accommodations vary extensively but can be organized into four areas using a framework described by Nelson, Dodd, and Smith (1990): (a) instruction, (b) assignments, (c) examinations, and (d) special assistance. At issue is which accommodations are appropriate to the student and under what conditions they can be applied. Programs are not likely to provide a one-size-fits-all mentality to determine accommodations. Using accommodations in high school and documenting their use is important to building a history of the disability that will be of benefit to college admissions and their use in postsecondary classes. Documenting previous experience with a given accommodation should be persuasive to college faculty to allow a student to continue to use it as needed. The examples of notetaking and test-taking accommodations given in Figures 10.4, 10.5, 10.6, 10.7 illustrate documentation that supports a student's request for accommodation in other classes.

The accommodations in Table 10.5 are a representative sample of what a student, support staff, and faculty might want to consider. For a given class, an accommodation

Disabled Student Program
Notetaking Arrangements

In order for any student participating in the Disabled Student Program to use notetaking arrangements, the following steps <u>MUST</u> be taken.

1. Meet with your advisor, Carol Toppel, to discuss Support Services and receive approval.

2. Once notetaking arrangements are approved, DSP&S will notify your instructor(s).

3. Your instructor(s) is asked to recommend a student from class who would be willing to take the notes on NCR (carbonless) paper.

4. Privately you will be asked by your instructor(s) to see if you would mind their making a general announcement in class regarding your request. If you prefer not to disclose your name, other arrangements will be made.

5. After you meet with your notetaker, go to DSP&S in room S2-201 to fill out the necessary paperwork. Notetakers will be paid by the Disabled Students Program for their work.

6. The notetaker will receive NCR (carbonless) paper from DSP&S throughout the semester on which to take the notes. At the end of class, the notetaker will separate the NCR paper, give you a copy, and keep a copy.

7. You are responsible for getting the notes from the notetaker.

8. If a notetaker fails to fulfill his or her obligation or the notes are not clear, it is your responsibility to notify Carol.

TIPS FOR NOTETAKING

- Write down what the instructor puts on the board.
- Write down main ideas.
- Write down the details that support each main idea.
- Summarize the main ideas in your own words.

FIGURE 10.4   SAMPLE NOTETAKING ARRANGEMENTS

Source: Mission College, Santa Clara, California.

Disabled Student Program Test-Taking Arrangements

In order for any student participating in the Disabled Student Program to use test-taking arrangements, the following steps **MUST** be taken.

1. Meet with your advisor, Carol Toppel, to discuss Support Services and receive approval.

2. Once test-taking arrangements are approved, DSP&S staff will notify your instructor(s).

3. Two (2) weeks before **each** test, see DSP&S staff so arrangements can be made to pick up the test from your instructor.

4. Schedule an appointment with the secretary to take the test. Please come by in person or phone (408) 748-2730. Tell the secretary the following:

   ■ What day you want to take the test
   ■ What time
   ■ If you need help or simply need extra test-taking time

5. Any time you find you are unable to make your scheduled appointment, call (408) 748-2730 to reschedule.

6. You will be allowed up to a maximum of **double** the regular class time to take the test (i.e., if the class is allotted one (1) hour for the test, you will be given up to two (2) hours).

7. **YOU** are responsible for initiating this request for each test and making the necessary arrangements with the DSP&S staff.

8. Final exam requests **must be** made two (2) weeks before the scheduled final exam.

GOOD LUCK!

TIPS FOR TEST-TAKING

■ Get plenty of rest the night before.
■ Carefully read the entire question.
■ Remind yourself that you are well prepared.
■ Develop good study habits.

FIGURE 10.5   SAMPLE TEST-TAKING ARRANGEMENTS

Source: Mission College, Santa Clara, California.

FINALS

The following steps must be taken by all students using test-taking arrangements for finals.

1. **YOU** are responsible for initiating this request and making the necessary arrangements with the DSP staff.

2. Meet with DSP staff (2) weeks before your final(s) to schedule the time and day.

3. Discuss the type of support you will need the day of each final.

    For example, but not limited to:

    - reader
    - scribe (writer)
    - extra time

4. You will be allowed up to a maximum of double the regular class time depending on your instructor's guidelines for the final. Remember to allow for this when scheduling your appointment.

5. Each student will be issued a locker number and combination to store personal belongings. Only teacher-approved tools will be allowed for the final.

6. You are allowed to take breaks within the lab area only. If you need to use the restroom, you must notify a DSP staff person.

7. Due to the length of time, you are allowed to bring a drink and small snack (no meals).

8. Be sure to return your final to the DSP staff before leaving!

GOOD LUCK!

FIGURE 10.6   SAMPLE TEST-TAKING ARRANGEMENTS FOR FINALS

Source: Mission College, Santa Clara, California.

Student's Name _____ Semester/Year _____

Instructor _____ Ofc # _____ Ext. _____ Mailbox # _____

Course Title _____ Class Days/Hours _____

Instructor's Signature _____ Date _____

The above-named student is eligible for testing accommodations through the DSPS office. The exam will be proctored in the Assessment Center or at an alternative site deemed most appropriate given the nature of the course (i.e., Computer Lab for a computer test).

To help us maintain the security and integrity of your tests, please complete the following:

1. Method of test delivery:
   _____ I will send test to Ann Dadami
   _____ I will send test with student to Assessment Center in sealed envelope on day of test
   _____ I will send test to the Assessment Center

2. Exam Proctoring Checklist (the testing conditions that apply to your tests)
   _____ No notes allowed   _____ Notes allowed
   _____ CLOSED book   _____ OPEN book
   _____ NO calculator allowed   _____ Calculator allowed
   _____ NO dictionary   _____ Dictionary allowed
   _____ Scrap paper allowed   _____ All test materials must be returned
   _____ Blue book required   _____ Scantron required (specify form #) _____
   _____ Other (specify) _____
   _____

3. Length of time other students will have on tests _____

4. Will these conditions apply to all of your tests? _____ Yes   _____ No

5. Select preferred method of return:

   ☐ I'll pick it up from Assessment Center

   ☐ Deliver to my campus mailbox

   ☐ Deliver to my division mailbox

   ☐ Have student return to: (specify) _____

If you have any questions regarding completion of the Exam Proctoring Sheet, please call
_____ ext. _____.

Instructor Copy - white   Assessment Copy - yellow   DSPS Copy - pink

FIGURE 10.7   DISABLED STUDENT PROGRAMS AND SERVICES EXAM PROCTORING SHEET

Source: Diablo Valley College, Pleasant Hill, California.

TABLE 10.5   REPRESENTATIVE ACCOMMODATIONS

Types	Specific Accommodations
Instructional	1. Allow the student to tape-record classroom lectures. 2. Provide the student a copy of the instructor's lecture notes after the lecture.
Assignment	3. Extend deadlines for completing class projects, papers, and assignments. 4. Allow the student to complete alternative assignments. 5. Allow the student to do an extra-credit assignment when this option is not available to other students. 6. Provide the student with a detailed syllabus to give ample time to complete reading and writing assignments. 7. Allow the student to give oral presentations or tape-recorded assignments rather than complete written projects.
Examination	8. Allow the student to take an alternative form of the exams (e.g., multiple-choice versus essay or written responses rather than computer-scored response sheets). 9. Allow a proctor to rephrase test questions that are not clear to the student. 10. Allow the student extra time to complete tests. 11. Allow the student to dictate answers to a proctor. 12. Allow the student to respond orally to essay questions. 13. Analyze the process as well as the final solution (e.g., review the computations process as well as the student's answer). 14. Allow the student to use basic calculators during tests. 15. Allow misspellings, incorrect punctuation, and poor grammar without penalizing the student. 16. Allow the student to use a word processor, grammar checker, and spelling checker in preparing written responses.
Special assistance	17. Allow proofreaders to assist in correcting grammar and punctuation. 18. Allow proofreaders to assist in reconstructing the student's first draft of a written assignment. 19. Allow a proofreader to assist the student in substituting higher-level vocabulary for the original wording.

may not be appropriate and an alternative might be needed.

Course substitutions can be used in conjunction with accommodations. In a course substitution the student seeks to replace a course with an alternative that does not have the requirements or content that limited the student's ability to perform. Course substitutions are considered major decisions in that they are not decisions made by the individual instructor alone. Substitutions involve decisions at the departmental and institutional levels. As such, they require carefully developed justification. The postsecondary program should entail extensive discussion about the basis of the request, the legal and curricular documentation supporting the request, and an understanding of criteria on which to base the decision. A valid concern of the postsecondary program is that other students, for a variety of other reasons, might seek a substitution as well. The response should be carefully reasoned to preclude any action that later might be misconstrued as arbitrary.

Take the case of a college with a foreign language requirement and a student with a language deficit. A language course might be replaced with a course in computer language. Many might think computers are so foreign that the substitution is not compatible. Suffice it to say that replacing a Spanish or French foreign language competency with a Pascal, Cobol, or C computer language competency might be workable. The department likely will want to compare all of the intended outcomes of a language requirement with any from a proposed substitution. For that reason, the student seeking a substitution should understand the basis for the department's language requirement.

A second substitution might be considered for an individual with dyscalculia. If the person has problems with math calculations, the substitution might be to take a logic course in place of an algebra course. Both courses teach a system of thinking. Practically speaking, the substitution might work for individuals whose intended careers are oriented to areas with minimal mathematical requirements and who become skilled with computational prosthetics such as calculators.

A third option is a course waiver. This option is least likely because of the implication that the course or an equivalent is inappropriate to the major area of study. A waiver suggests that the major area of study can be defined without specific or closely related content.

IDENTIFICATION VERSUS ELIGIBILITY ASSESSMENT

Most students—most all of us, for that matter—find testing annoying at best, and a basis for great fear, indigestion, sleeplessness, and heightened anxiety. Because most of us like to avoid unpleasantness, understanding LD-related assessments might be useful. The distinction between identification and eligibility assessments sometimes is blurred and yet is important to distinguish. The outcomes from these two assessments are different. Students with a history of learning disability have been judged eligible for services and placement as described on the IEP. These decisions were made through referral, evaluation, and placement processes prescribed in federal (e.g., Public Laws 94–142 and 101–467) and state legislation and regulations and local school district plans.

Postsecondary settings do not have comparable legally binding mandates. No federal or state regulations describe the processes that the postsecondary system must follow to identify students with LD or determine whether students with LD should or should not receive special services. In addition, rarely do these postsecondary settings freely provide assessment services for diagnosing whether a student has a learning disability. Although assessment is readily available, significant costs can be associated with this service. Considering the emotional toll, time requirements, and related financial costs, the assessments should be as minimal as possible.

In the postsecondary setting the concern is less with identification and more with eligibility. In this setting the concern is whether the student's disability is serious enough to warrant services and, if so, to determine the appropriate services. This largely reflects the emphasis in federal legislation, Section 504 of the 1973 Rehabilitation Act. The problem that college staffs confront is that their students do not come from a single K–12 setting. The students don't matriculate through the grade levels as they do in a single school district wherein students pass along from one grade to the next and from one attendance center to the next center in a grade-based order (e.g., grade school to middle school to junior high to senior high school). Students enroll in postsecondary settings from a variety of school districts from a variety of states. Also, postsecondary settings are confronting a rise in the number of nontraditional students whose age and experience distinguish them from the traditional student who is more likely to begin college-related courses within a year or two after leaving high school. This lack of consistency in students' background experiences poses new challenges in the postsecondary setting and a great opportunity for high school special educators.

Postsecondary institutions enroll students with an LD diagnosis from a variety of programs including public school multidisciplinary teams, vocational rehabilitation programs, adult literacy programs, mental health services, medical centers, commercial learning centers, and private-practice physicians. The physician might be a neurologist, an optometrist, a chiropractor, or a pediatrician. Each of these service providers likely works from his or her own identification model and definition of learning disabilities. The definitions are tailored to the clients they serve, their financial support, and the services they provide. Therefore, postsecondary staffs would be wise not to compare one diagnostic model to another but, rather, approach the issue of whether sufficient documentation supports students' claims of disability and whether the disability is severe enough to distinguish them from the general student body and to warrant special services. This perspective allows the college to describe eligibility requirements for services. Students making the application should know who has the responsibility of making these decisions at the institution. One may be able to make the case that an LD specialist employed in a postsecondary setting would have a different view than a staff member in the admissions office.

Postsecondary institutions are particularly concerned with three aspects of verifying that students have disabilities. Any of the following would entitle a student to services as disabled:

1. The student has a diagnosis of a disability.
2. The student has a history of a disability.
3. The student has been treated as if he or she has a disability.

If any one of these conditions is met, the student likely will be eligible for services in the postsecondary setting. The teacher and the student need to recognize the emphasis these perspectives place on the student to clearly document information about the disability and the support services and accommodations that are warranted. Colleges are apt to be more concerned with maintaining their tradition of academic rigor and less with compromising their standards for excellence (Brinckerhoff, Shaw, & McGuire, 1992; West et al., 1993).

The collaborative team for an IEP and ITP has to differentiate among various assessments. One of the great services teachers can provide to students in transition consists of updated, appropriate assessments. The resulting information is important to postsecondary staffs as they make their eligibility decisions. In selecting assessments, several simple rules are useful:

1. Choose assessments that demonstrate students' disabilities and strengths. The postsecondary staff wants to provide appropriate services and accommodations. Students are not understood just by their weaknesses for which accommodations may be provided. Understanding students' strengths also helps in evaluating students' goals, degree interests, and course selections. For example, college coursework provides few tasks in which words have to be recognized in isolation but does require extensive reading of meaningfully connected prose. This suggests that information on a reading test that presents only words in isolation, such as the *Wide Range Achievement Test* Reading subtest (Jastak & Wilkinson, 1984) or the *Woodcock Reading Mastery Test* Word Identification subtest (Woodcock, 1987), is of limited value. A much better alternative would be something like the *Degrees of Reading Power* (Koslin, Koslin, Zeno, & Ivens, 1989) test. The task of reading words in isolation may be of diagnostic value in determining the student's phonetic processing, but the real task is in acquiring meaning in connected prose.

2. Include a normative comparison of a standard score and percentile rank. A student's portfolio of completed work or results of curriculum-based measurements can tell an important story about the student's success and level of skills and abilities. This story is incomplete without providing a broader context for understanding the student's achievement levels. The team members likely would feel uncomfortable in representing only the student's normative performance on the basis of a group-administered, standardized instrument. The individually administered test battery not only provides clinical information but also can be chosen to provide a better match of the student's strengths and weaknesses. For these reasons the standardized, normative measures should be included. The main concern should be with ensuring a smooth transition of the student from the secondary program to a host of other agencies with different agendas and eligibility requirements.

3. Don't put a lot of emphasis on the intellectual assessment. Tests of intellectual ability usually are administered as a matter of routine. Unless a significant pattern occurs in the scores or a shift in the score pattern is demonstrated across time, the only interest will be in having an index of the student's abilities as assessed on a standardized instrument. These scores should be interpreted as reflecting the lowest level of the student's abilities. The intellectual assessment might be thought of as reflecting the student's disabilities in composite scores, such as the Full Scale IQ or Extended Broad Cognitive Ability score. These scores set the minimum level of expected achievement. The staff should be especially interested in an estimate of the student's learning capacity in areas distinct from the disability. For that reason, patterns of scores may be of interest. The patterns should be interpreted in light of empirically demonstrated evidence that they are stable,

distinct, and have meaningful interpretations. An extensive folklore is attached to some traditional IQ scores that requires skepticism.

4. Think of the assessment in broad terms. School teams tend to focus on academic and aptitude assessments, and for good reason. For students of secondary school age, however, social competencies become particularly important. The differences we have highlighted between postsecondary and high school settings provide a rationale for this increased shift in emphasis to social competency, community integration, and adaptive behavior (Siperstein, 1988). Assessing social competence is more difficult. Try to include a number of instruments and reports from several individuals (e.g., teachers, the student, parents or guardians, and psychologists) to provide multiple perspectives on students' social competencies.

5. Encourage documentation about current instructional delivery methods and accommodations that work for the student. Documenting the instructional methods and current related goals for the student allows the postsecondary staff to assess more completely their potential suitability for the student in the new setting. This documentation includes information about what doesn't work or has not been successful with the student (e.g., success with the student completing work independently, success in the student's working with a same-age tutor, the student's awareness of academic strengths, the student's ability to self-monitor the accuracy of classwork and assignments, time management skills, and ability to organize work materials). The materials should be organized with consideration of who will be reviewing them. An admissions counselor will want a different level of details than an LD specialist.

SUMMARY

Should students with LD prepare for postsecondary options in high school? Without hesitation, the answer is "yes." At some point increased education may not improve one's quality of life. Even so, we might speculate that we lack sufficient evidence for students with LD to even guess what that point might be. Nevertheless, we can document clearly, from a library of follow-along and follow-up studies, that students currently are not often realizing any advantages from postsecondary education. Halpern (1993) likely would agree that most students with LD encounter a period of "purposeless unengagement" or, even worse, a period of self-denigrating or antisocial behavior. We argue that, though continued postsecondary education does not guarantee physical or material well-being, successful performance of adult roles, or personal fulfillment, a strong enough association exists that postsecondary alternatives should be considered and developed.

Can students make successful transitions to postsecondary settings? The answer is a qualified "yes." Based on the material we have presented, success depends on a lengthy list of considerations that influence the outcome. For that reason, the discussion of postsecondary options should begin early, include a variety of perspectives and information, and become the student's major research project during the early years of high school. As Halpern (1985) suggested, the objective and subjective indices of quality of life may have a closer relationship once more attention is given to student interests and preferences in developing transition plans.

The differences between the high school and postsecondary milieus are more than cosmetic. Postsecondary experiences have proven advantageous to some students and disadvantageous to other students. The postsecondary setting has its barriers that should be acknowledged and considered in evaluating alternative settings. Programmatic factors influencing the transition outcome include the organization of student services and how accommodations, substitutions, and waivers can be applied to students with LD to meet degree and setting requirements. A distinction has to be made between assessment outcomes: identification as LD and eligibility for LD services. From a student's perspective, the preeminent issue is having the disability and intervention strategies documented for the admissions office in the postsecondary setting.

Planning for the transition to postsecondary settings of students with LD may seem like a formidable hurdle to the high school staff. Yet, students' successful transition and quality of life are goals shared by a number of people. Students with LD, like all students, should receive opportunities for success in the postsecondary setting.

REFERENCES

Adelman, P. B., & Vogel, S. A. (1990). College graduates with learning disabilities—Employment attainment and career patterns. *Learning Disability Quarterly, 13*, 154–156.

Alexander, J., & Rolfe, J. (1992). *MatchMaker*. Evanston, IL: Keystone Group.

Beirne-Smith, M., & Deck, M. D. (1989). A survey of postsecondary programs for students with learning disabilities. *Journal of Learning Disabilities, 22*, 456–457.

Brinckerhoff, L. C., Shaw, S. F., & McGuire, J. M. (1992). Promoting access, accommodations, and independence for college students with learning disabilities. *Journal of Learning Disabilities, 25*, 417–429.

Bruck, M. (1985). The adult functioning of children with specific learning disabilities: A follow-up study. In L. Siegel (Ed.), *Advances in applied developmental psychology* (pp. 91–129). New York: Ablex.

Bruck, M. (1987). The adult outcomes of children with learning disabilities. *Annals of Dyslexia, 37*, 252–264.

Bursuck, B. D., Rose, E., Cowen, S., & Yahaya, M. A. (1989). Nationwide survey of postsecondary education services for students with learning disabilities. *Exceptional Children, 56*, 236–245.

Cardarella, J. High school teachers' summary of learning disabled graduates' strengths, weaknesses and learning styles. In Vocational Studies Center, *Successful vocational rehabilitation of persons with learning disabilities: Best practices* (pp. 237–243). Madison: University of Wisconsin.

Chancellor's Office. (1993). *Intake screening and eligibility record*. Sacramento: California Community Colleges, Disabled Students Program and Services.

Chancellor's Office. (1988). *Program development and management manual*. Sacramento: California Community Colleges, Disabled Students Program and Services.

Clark, G. M., & Kolstoe, O. P. (1990). *Career development and transition education for adolescents with disabilities*. Needham Heights, MA: Allyn & Bacon.

Cobb, R. M., & Crump, W. D. (1984). *Post-school status of young adults identified as learning disabled while enrolled in public schools: A comparison of those enrolled and not enrolled in learning disabilities programs*. University of Alabama, Department of Education. (ERIC Document Reproduction Service No. 253 029)

Council for Learning Disabilities. (1993). The college experience for students with learning disabilities. *Infosheet*, October.

Dalke, C., & Schmitt, S. (1987). Meeting the transition needs of college bound students with learning disabilities. *Journal of Learning Disabilities, 20*, 176–180.

Davie, A. R. (1987). *Young adults with learning disabilities and other special needs.* Washington, DC: Heath Resource Center.

Dowdy, C. A., Carter, J. K., & Smith, R. E. C. (1990). Differences in transitional needs of high school students with and without learning disabilities. *Journal of Learning Disabilities, 23*, 343–348.

Eagle, E., Fitzgerald, R., Gifford, A., Zuma, J., & MPR Associates. (1988). *A descriptive summary of 1980 high school sophomores: Six years later.* Washington, DC: U.S. Department of Education.

Edgar, E. (1987). Secondary programs in special education: Are many of them justifiable? *Exceptional Children, 53*, 555–561.

Fairweather, J. S., & Shaver, D. M. (1991). Making the transition to postsecondary education and training. *Exceptional Children, 57*, 264–270.

Fourqurean, J. M., & LaCourt, T. (1990). A follow-up of former special education students: A model for program evaluation. *Remedial and Special Education, 12*(1), 16–23.

Fourqurean, J. M., Meisgeier, C., Swank, P. R., & Williams, R. E. (1991). Correlates of postsecondary employment outcomes for young adults with learning disabilities. *Journal of Learning Disabilities, 24*, 400–405.

Halpern, A. S. (1985). Transition: A look at the foundations. *Exceptional Children, 51*, 479–486.

Halpern, A. S. (1993). Quality of life as a conceptual framework for evaluating transition outcomes. *Exceptional Children, 59*, 486–498.

Haring, K. A., Lovett, D. L., & Smith, D. D. (1990). A follow-up study of recent special education graduates of learning disabilities programs. *Journal of Learning Disabilities, 23*, 108–113.

Jastak, S., & Wilkenson, G. S. (1984). *Wide range achievement test–Revised.* Wilmington, DE: Jastak Associates.

Jones, C., Sebring, P., Crawford, I., Spencer, B., & Butz, M. (1986a). *High school and beyond: 1980 senior cohort second follow-up (1984).* Washington, DC: U.S. Department of Education.

Jones, C., Sebring, P., Crawford, I., Spencer, B., & Butz, M. (1986b). *High school and beyond: 1980 sophomore cohort second follow-up (1984).* Washington, DC: U.S. Department of Education.

Koslin, B. L., Koslin, S., Zeno, S. M., & Ivens, S. H. (1989). *Degrees of reading power.* Brewster, NY: Touchstone Applied Science Associates.

Kravets, M. (1993a, September). *College and post-secondary options.* Presentation at National Center for Learning Disabilities, Educational Summit, Scottsdale, AZ.

Kravets, M. (1993b). *The college planning handbook for students with learning differences.* Deerfield, IL: Deerfield High School.

Kravets, M., & Wax, I. F. (1993). *The K & W guide to colleges for the learning disabled.* New York: Harper Collins.

Lundeberg, M., & Svien, K. (1988). Developing faculty understanding of college students with learning disabilities. *Journal of Learning Disabilities, 21*, 299–300, 306.

Malcolm, C. B., Polatajko, H. J., & Simons, J. (1990). A descriptive study of adults with suspected learning disabilities. *Journal of Learning Disabilities, 23*, 518–520.

Mangrum, C. T., & Strichart, S. S. (1988). *College and the learning disabled student* (2d ed.). Orlando, FL: Grune & Stratton.

McGuire, J. M., Norlander, K. A., & Shaw, S. F. (1990). Postsecondary education for students with learning disabilities: Forecasting challenges for the future. *Learning Disabilities Focus, 5*, 69–74.

Mellard, D. F. (1990). The eligibility process: Identifying students with learning disabilities in the California community colleges. *Learning Disabilities Focus, 5*, 75–90.

Mellard, D. F. (1993). *Learning disabilities model development study technical report.* Sacramento: Chancellor's Office, California Community Colleges, Disabled Students Program and Services.

Mellard, D. F., & Clark, G. M. (1992). *National high school project: Vol. 2. A quantitative description of concepts and practices for students with disabilities.* Lawrence: University of Kansas. (ERIC Document Reproduction Service No. ED 355–685)

Mellard, D. F., & Deshler, D. D. (1984). Modeling the condition of learning disabilities on post-secondary populations. *Educational Psychologist, 19*, 188–197.

Mellard, D. F., & Hazel, J. S. (1992). Social competencies as a pathway to successful life transition. *Learning Disabilities Quarterly, 15*, 251–273.

Miller, R. J., Snider, D., & Rzonca, C. (1990). Variables related to the decision of young adults with learning disabilities to participate in postsecondary education. *Journal of Learning Disabilities, 23,* 349–354.

National Information Center for Children and Youth with Disabilities. (NICHCY). (1991, September). Options after high school for youth with disabilities. *Transition Summary, 7.*

National Information Center for Children and Youth with Disabilities. (NICHCY) (1993). Transition Services in the IEP. *Transition Summary, 3*(1).

National Joint Committee on Learning Disabilities. (1994). Secondary to postsecondary education transition planning for students with learning disabilities. *LDA Newsbriefs, 29*(2), 3–5.

Nelson, J. R., Dodd, J. M., & Smith, D. J. (1990). Faculty willingness to accommodate students with learning disabilities: A comparison among academic divisions. *Journal of Learning Disabilities, 23,* 185–189.

Neubert, D. A., Tilson, G. P., & Ianacone, R. N. (1989). Postsecondary transition needs and employment patterns of individuals with mild disabilities. *Exceptional Children, 55,* 494–500.

Oliker, N. (1989). Class privilege and the status of learning disabled students at selective institutions. *Latest Developments,* Fall, pp. 1–3. (Association of Handicapped Student Service Programs in Postsecondary Education, Columbus, OH)

Osgood-Smith, J. (1992). Falling through the cracks: Rehabilitation services for adults with learning disabilities. *Exceptional Children, 58,* 451–460.

Parks, A. W., Antonoff, S., Drake, C., Skiba, W. F., & Soberman, J. (1987). A survey of programs and services for learning disabled students in graduate and professional school. *Journal of Learning Disabilities, 20,* 154, 181–187.

Peterson's Guides. (1992). *Peterson's guide to colleges with programs for learning disabled students.* Princeton, NJ: Author.

Prater, G., & Minner, S. (1986). Factors inhibiting the performance of learning disabled students in postsecondary settings. *Reading, Writing, and Learning Disabilities, 2,* 273–277.

Putnam, M. L. (1984, January). Postsecondary education for learning disabled students: A review of the literature. *Journal of College Student Personnel,* pp. 68–75.

Quinby, S. E. (1989). A response to "Class Privilege and the Status of Learning Disabled Students at Selective Institutions." *Latest Developments,* Fall, pp. 1–3. (Association of Handicapped Student Service Programs in Postsecondary Education, Columbus, OH)

Rojewski, J. W. (1989). A rural based transition model for students with learning disabilities: A demonstration. *Journal of Learning Disabilities, 22,* 613–620.

Rosenthal, I. (1986). New directions for service delivery to learning disabled youth and young adults. *Learning Disabilities Focus, 2,* 55–61.

Sclafani, A. J., & Lynch, M. J. (1989). *College guide for students with learning disabilities 1988–1989.* Miller Place, NY: Laurel Publications.

Scuccimarra, D. J., & Speece, D. L. (1990). Employment outcomes and social integration of students with mild handicaps: The quality of life two years after high school. *Journal of Learning Disabilities, 23,* 518–520.

Shapiro, E. S., & Lentz, F. E. (1991). Vocational-technical programs: Follow-up of students with learning disabilities. *Exceptional Children, 58,* 47–59.

Shaywitz, S. E., & Shaw, R. (1988). The admissions process: An approach to selecting learning disabled students at the most selective colleges. *Learning Disabilities Focus, 3,* 81–86.

Siegel, S., & Gaylord-Ross, R. (1991). Factors associated with employment success among youths with learning disabilities. *Journal of Learning Disabilities, 24,* 40–47.

Siegel, S., Robert, M., Waxman, M., & Gaylord-Ross, R. (1992). A follow-along study of participants in a longitudinal transition program for youths with mild disabilities. *Exceptional Children, 58,* 346–356.

Siperstein, G. N. (1988). Students with learning disabilities in college: The need for a programmatic approach to critical transitions. *Journal of Learning Disabilities, 21,* 431–436.

Sitlington, P., & Frank, A. R. (1990). Are adolescents with learning disabilities successfully crossing the bridge into adult life? *Learning Disabilities Quarterly, 13,* 97–111.

Sitlington, P., & Frank, A. R. (1993). Dropouts with learning disabilities: What happens to them as young adults? *Learning Disabilities Research and Practice, 8*(4), 244–252.

Skyer, R., & Skyer, G. (1985). *What do you do after high school?* Rockway Park, NY: Skyer Consultation, Inc.

Slovak, J. (1986). *Bose directory*. Congress, NY: Bose Publishers.

Spekman, N. J., Goldberg, R. J., & Herman, K. L. (1992). Learning disabled children grow up: A search for factors related to success in the young adult years. *Learning Disabilities Research and Practice, 7*, 161–170.

Straughn, C. T., & Colby, S. C. (1985). *Lovejoy's college guide for the learning disabled*. New York: Monarch Press.

Ugland, R., & Duane, G. (1976). *Serving students with special learning disabilities in higher education—A demonstration project at three Minnesota community colleges*. Bloomington, MN: Normandale Community College. (ERIC Document Reproduction Service No. ED 135 434)

Valdes, K. A., Williamson, C. L., & Wagner, M. M. (1990). *The national longitudinal transition study of special education students, statistical almanac, volume 2: Youth categorized as learning disabled*. Palo Alto, CA: SRI International.

Van Reusen, A., & Bos, C. S. (1994). Facilitating student participation in individualized education programs through motivation strategy instruction. *Exceptional Children, 60*, 466–475.

Vogel, S. A. (1985). *The college student with a learning disability: A handbook for college LD students, admissions officers, faculty, and administrators*. Lake Forest, IL: Barat College.

Vogel, S. A., & Sattler, J. L. (1981). *The college student with a learning disability: A handbook for college and university admissions officers, faculty, and administration*. DeKalb: Illinois Council for Learning Disabilities.

Wechsler, D. (1981). *Wechsler adult intelligence scale–Revised*. New York: Psychological Corp.

Wehman, P., Kregel, J., & Barcus, J. M. (1985). From school to work: A transition model for handicapped students. *Exceptional Children, 52*, 25–37.

Will, M. (1985). *Transition: Linking disabled youth to a productive future*. OSERS News in Print, Washington, DC: U.S. Department of Education, Office of Special Education Services.

Woodcock, R. W. (1987). *Woodcock reading mastery tests–Revised*. Circle Pines, MN: American Guidance Service.

Woodcock, R. W., & Johnson, M. B. (1989). *Woodcock-Johnson psychoeducational battery–Revised*. Chicago: Riverside Publishing.

Wren, C., & Segal, L. (1985). *College students with learning disabilities: A student's perspective*. Chicago: DePaul University, Project Learning Strategies.

APPENDIX

SAMPLE INTAKE INTERVIEW

LEARNING DISABILITIES SERVICES

STUDENTS: The Chancellor's Office of the community college system is required by law to gather and maintain some student information. This information is the race, sex, age, and disability status of students requesting services through the learning disabilities program. The law also requires that conditions of participation provide equal opportunity for all students.

Providing this information is strictly voluntary for you. However, the college is required to complete each item since this form is the only means which the college has for this identification. For this reason, we ask your assistance in completing the form.

DESCRIPTIVE INFORMATION

Name (Print) _____ Date _____
Address _____ Home Phone _____
City _____ Zip _____
Work Phone_____ Can you be contacted at work?   Yes   No
Sex _____ Age _____ Date of Birth _____ Place of Birth _____
List name of person to notify in case of emergency:
Name _____ Relationship _____Phone _____
Address _____ City _____ Zip _____

1. How do you describe yourself and your mother/guardian? (Please check one for each category.)

	Self	Mother/Guardian		Self	Mother/Guardian
Alaskan Native	_____		Black, non-Hispanic	_____	
American Indian	_____				
_____			Hispanic		
Asian			Central American	_____	
Cambodian	_____		Mexican	_____	
Chinese	_____		South American	_____	
Filipino	_____		Other Hispanic	_____	
Japanese	_____				
Korean	_____		Middle Eastern	_____	
Laotian	_____				
Pacific Islander	_____		White/non-Hispanic	_____	
Vietnamese	_____		Other non-White	_____	
Other Asian	_____				
_____			Decline to state	_____	
_____			Unknown	_____	

REFERRAL INFORMATION

2. Who referred you to our program? _____
                                    (Name)   (Agency)
3. What are the reasons for your referral? _____
   _____

4. Are or were you a client of the Department of Rehabilitation?   Yes   No
   • If yes, please identify:
       a. What is your disability according to Dept. of Rehab.?_____
       _____
       b. Counselor's Name _____ Phone _____
       c. Address _____ City _____
       d. What is your rehabilitation plan? _____

5. Are or were you receiving services through
   _____DSP&S_____GAIN _____Workability _____Financial Aid
   _____EOPS _____SSDI _____Other Services _____None

FAMILY HISTORY

6. Does anyone in your family have a learning problem?　　　Yes　　　No
   • If yes, describe _____
   _____
   _____

7. Does anyone in your family have any other type of disability (e.g., physical, emotional, vision or hearing impairment)?　　　Yes　　　No
   • If yes, describe _____
   _____
   _____

8. Describe any family issues which you feel have affected your learning.
   _____
   _____
   _____

9. What are your current family responsibilities (e.g., children, parents, or extended family)?
   _____
   _____
   _____
   _____

WORK HISTORY

10. Are you currently employed?　　　Yes　　　No
    • If yes, please describe current employment:
      a. Where? _____
      b. Job duties? _____
      c. Number of hours per week? _____
      d. What is your weekly work schedule? _____
      e. How long have you had this job?　____Years ____Months ____Weeks

11. Describe any previous jobs, length of employment, and job duties. _____
    _____
    _____

HEALTH INFORMATION

12. Do you have vision problems?　　　Yes　　　No
    • If yes, describe: _____
    _____

13. Do you wear glasses or contact lenses?　　　Yes　　　No

14. Have you had an eye exam within the last two years?　　　Yes　　　No
    • If yes, when? _____

15. Do you have problems with hearing?   Yes   No
    • If yes, describe: _____

16. Did you have frequent ear infections or tubes in your ears?   Yes   No

17. Do you wear a hearing aid?   Yes   No

18. Have you had a hearing exam within the last five years?   Yes   No
    • If yes, when? _____

19. Do you have allergies or asthma?   Yes   No
    • If yes, please answer the following questions:
       a. Describe: _____
       _____
       b. How do the allergies, asthma, and medications influence your classwork?
       _____

20. Are you on any medication at the present time?   Yes   No
    • If yes, please give the name of the medication, dosage, and reason for taking.
       _____
       _____

21. Have you ever been on a long-term program of medication?   Yes   No
    • If yes, describe_____
       _____

22. Have you ever had difficulties with attention, concentration, or hyperactivity?_
    Yes   No
    • If yes, describe_____
       _____

23. Have you ever had a head injury?   Yes   No
    • If yes, specify when and describe: _____
       _____

24. Have you ever had seizures?   Yes   No
    • If yes, specify when and describe: _____

25. Have you ever had a neurological exam?   Yes   No
    • If yes, please answer the following questions:
       a. At what age? _____
       b. For what reason?_____

26. Have you ever had any serious injuries or illness (e.g., headaches, fever, etc.)?
    Yes   No

• If yes, specify when and please describe their impact on your education: ___

_____

27. Have you ever been hospitalized for emotional problems?   Yes   No
    • If yes, specify when and for how long: _____

28. Are or have you participated in individual or group counseling for emotional problems?   Yes   No

    • If yes, explain: _____
29. Do you have a history of substance abuse?   Yes   No
    If yes, explain: _____

30. Physician's Name_____ Phone_____
    Address_____City_____Zip _____

EDUCATIONAL INFORMATION

31. As far as you can recall, when did you first start having problems in school?
    _____Grade   _____Not applicable

32. Why do you think you have had problems in school? (Check all that apply.)
    ___Specific learning disability ___Tasks too difficult ___Physical handicap
    ___Home environment ___Lack of interest in school ___Limited ability
    ___Emotional problems ____Bad luck ___Poor attendance
    ___Economic disadvantage ___Other (specify): _____

33. Did you attend more than two elementary schools (K–6)?   Yes   No
    • If yes, explain: _____

34. Did you attend more than three schools in grades 7–12?   Yes   No
    • If yes, explain: _____

35. Were you retained in school, i.e., held back to repeat a grade(s)?   Yes   No
    • If yes, what grade(s) and why? _____

36. Were you ever tested for eligibility in special education prior to enrollment in college?   Yes   No
    • If yes, when and why? _____

37. Have you ever received special education services or been placed in remedial classes?   Yes   No
    ___Special Day Class ___Resource Program ___Remedial Class
    ___Speech and Language services ___Gifted ___Other
    • If yes, in what high school classes were you mainstreamed? _____

_____

38. What other school-related activities or issues influenced your achievement?
_____
_____

39. Did you drop out of school between kindergarten and 12th grade?   Yes   No
    • If yes, please answer the following questions:
       a. What grade(s)? _____
       b. For what reasons? _____

40. Are you a high school graduate?   Yes   No
    • If yes, list type of diploma, date received, and high school: _____
    _____
    • If no, did you complete a GED?   Yes   No
       If yes, when? _____

41. Have you attended any other postsecondary institution?   Yes   No
    • If yes, where? _____

42. For how many semesters/quarters have you attended college? _____

43. How many units have you earned? _____

44. In how many units (hours) are you currently enrolled? _____ Units (hours)

45. Are you required to take a certain number of units?   Yes   No
    • If yes, how many units and why? _____

46. Are you on academic probation?   Yes   No
    • If yes, why? _____

47. List all of your current classes. Describe any difficulties you are experiencing in each. How much time do you spend each week (including Saturday and Sunday) preparing for each of these classes?

Class	Describe Difficulties	Weekly Study Time
_____	_____	_____
_____	_____	_____
_____	_____	_____
_____	_____	_____
_____	_____	_____

48. Have you discussed your difficulties with the instructor?   Yes   No
    _____

49. In what type(s) of classes have you done well? _____

50. What are your goals for attending college? _____
    _____
    _____
    _____

    College Major_____ College Counselor _____

CULTURAL/LINGUISTIC HISTORY

51. Was English your first language?   Yes   No
    • If yes, STOP.
    • If no, please complete the remaining items.

52. Which language(s) do you speak at home?
    ___English
    ___English and some other languages (specify) _____
    ___Other languages only (specify) _____

53. Describe any learning difficulties you had in your first language. _____
    _____
    _____

54. At what age did you begin to learn English? _____

55. Describe any learning difficulties you had in learning English. _____
    _____
    _____

56. In what grade did you first enter the United States school system? _____

57. Have you taken English as a Second Language (ESL) or bilingual classes?
    Yes   No
    If yes, describe how well you did in these classes._____
    _____
    _____

STOP!
NOTES:
    _____
    _____
    _____
    _____
    _____
    _____
    _____
    _____

Source: Chancellor's Office, California Community Colleges, Disabled Students Programs and Services, *Intake Screening and Eligibility Record*, April 1, 1993.

11

Strategies for Transition to Employment Settings

LINDA K. ELKSNIN AND NICK ELKSNIN

QUESTIONS TO KEEP IN MIND

- What kinds of difficulties do adolescents with LD have which may affect their occupational success?

- What kinds of skills do employers value when assessing competence of employees?

- What are the demands of the vocational setting which may promote or inhibit success of adolescents with LD?

- How does recent legislation affect vocational programming for adolescents with LD?

- Why is it important for the special educator to understand the vocational education environment? How does this environment differ from the secondary academic environment?

- How can special educators and vocational educators more effectively collaborate to better meet the needs of adolescents with LD enrolled in vocational programs?

- How can assessment be conducted to develop effective vocational training?

- What types of career and vocational education curricula are available which can be used effectively with adolescents with LD?

- What are some of the challenges in designing programs for adolescents with LD who will directly enter the workforce?

A substantial body of research in cognitive science shows that providing students with real problems to solve in context is essential if they are to develop more complex modes of thinking and using knowledge in solving problems. This approach can also spur motivation to learn. The teaching of specific job skills, as in vocational education, thus offers manifold possibilities for presenting the kings of "cognitive apprenticeships" that have been suggested for helping students develop their thinking and their interest in learning.

Wirt, 1991

Graduates of vocational programs...must also demonstrate that they can work effectively in teams, find and solve complex problems, and rapidly absorb new information.

Aring, 1993

ADVANCE ORGANIZER

Students with LD are more likely than their nondisabled peers to drop out of school and to be underemployed and unemployed. The main reasons for employment problems are lack of interpersonal skills, lack of job-related academic skills, and lack of specific vocational skills (Okolo & Sitlington, 1986; Sitlington, 1986). Secondary academically focused programs need to be reexamined and restructured. Vocational education should be considered a viable option for many students. Two good reasons are:

1. Of adolescents with LD who graduate from high school, few go on to college.
2. Vocational education offers relevant training for students entering the world of work directly after high school.

Few students with LD go on to postsecondary training, yet our secondary special education programs often mirror the academically focused curriculum and instruction of the traditional American high school. In a national survey conducted by the American Council on Education, students with LD accounted for only 1.1% of all full-time, first-time entering college freshmen (Hippolitus, 1987). Wagner (1989) and her colleagues followed approximately 8,000 youths ages 13–23 with disabilities and reported that approximately 16% of students with LD entered postsecondary programs. Of these, 1.6% enrolled in 4-year colleges and universities, 4.9% in 2-year colleges, and 11.1% in vocational schools.

Programming decisions must be based upon realistic postgraduation goals. Most students who enter postsecondary training programs after high school graduation benefit from a more academically oriented curriculum. Students who enter the world of work immediately following high school need vocational training. Because graduation requirements differ for students enrolled in academic and vocational programs, students, with the assistance of teachers and counselors, must decide on their post-graduation goals early on so they will enter the appropriate educational program.

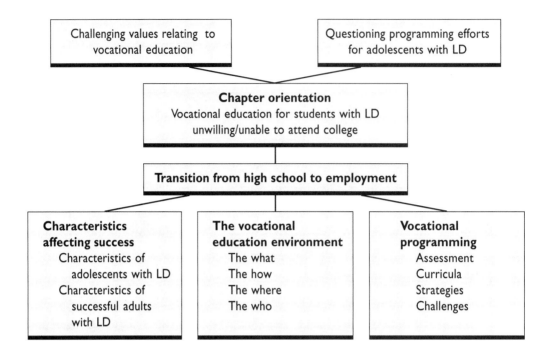

FIGURE 11.1 CHAPTER 11 ORGANIZATION

Consistent with provisions of the Individuals with Disabilities Act, adolescents with LD should participate in general education programs to the maximum extent appropriate. At the high school level general education programs include both academic and vocational programs. Successful completion of general education programs results in a high school diploma, giving students more postsecondary options, including entry-level employment, licensure, and participation in training programs such as apprenticeships.

Adhering to the organization of Figure 11.1, this chapter focuses upon ways in which teachers can help students enter and complete vocational education programs. Although program decisions must be made case-by-case, the severity of the learning disability generally will influence the type of vocational instruction an adolescent with LD will require. As shown in Figure 11.2, students with mild or moderate LD are more likely to be served in vocational programs with either indirect or direct special education services. These students will be prepared for entry-level competitive employment after completing all vocational program competencies. For example, the student may start his or her career as an automobile mechanic or as a bricklayer.

Some students require a simplified vocational education curriculum with direct special education services. These students complete *selected* vocational program competencies and will be prepared to be employed competitively in a related position. For example, the student may begin as a tire changer or as a bricklayer's helper.

Only students with the most severe disabilities require a differentiated vocational curriculum. These students also will require a higher level of support services in the

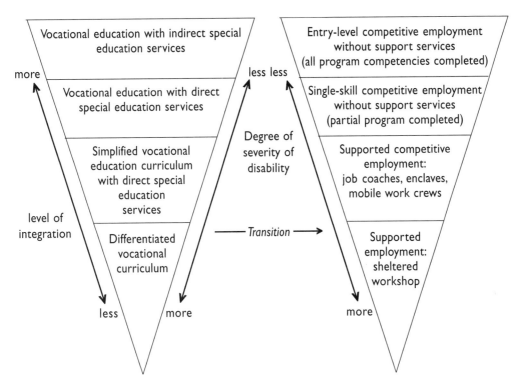

FIGURE 11.2   VOCATIONAL EDUCATION SERVICES AND OUTCOMES

workplace. Supported competitive employment is accomplished by providing job coaches or by placing employees in enclaves or mobile work crews. Job coaches or employment training specialists provide ongoing support to employees or teach skills onsite. *Enclaves* usually consist of six to eight individuals with disabilities working in occupational settings with nondisabled competitively employed workers. Supervision usually is provided on a long-term basis. *Mobile work crews* are teams of from four to six individuals with disabilities who perform service jobs in community settings under the direction of a work supervisor. Individuals who have the most severe disabilities are employed in *sheltered workshops*. The program needs of students with mild to moderate LD will be addressed in this chapter. Programs designed to integrate adolescents with more severe disabilities into the workforce are discussed in Bellamy, Rhodes, Mank, and Albin (1988), Moon, Inge, Wehman, Brooke, and Barcus (1990), and Wehman, Sale, and Parent (1992).

Results of follow-up and follow-along studies of students with LD are less than encouraging. As many as one third of our students with LD drop out of high school (Clark & Kolstoe, 1990; Wagner, 1989). The U.S. Department of Education reported that 42.9% of students with disabilities drop out of school, compared with 24.4% of the general population. More than 33% of students with LD drop out of school, the highest dropout rate of all disability groups with the exception of students who have emotional disturbance. Certain factors, such as multiple retentions, frequent absenteeism, expulsions/suspensions, poor academic performance, lack of parental support, substance abuse, social maladjustment, and lack of involvement in extracurricular activities, place a student at risk for dropping out. On the other hand, certain factors are associated with higher rates of school completion (Karpinski, Neubert, & Graham, 1992). *The Fourteenth Annual Report to Congress on the Implementation of the Individuals with Disabilities Act* (U.S. Department of Education, 1992) concluded that:

> Students who took occupational training in their most recent school year were significantly less likely to have dropped out of school.... Occupational vocational training was significantly related both to lower absenteeism and a lower probability of dropping out. (pp. 105, 106)

Education is a key component to economic growth, for individuals and nations alike. Even though high school graduates earn more than dropouts, graduates of vocational programs earn more than graduates who do not complete these programs.

Human capital theory assumes that economic growth of individuals and nations is dependent upon education. Considerable data support this view:

> It is hardly surprising that the well-educated have always been richer than the poorly educated. But the gap is getting steadily bigger. In 1980 a college-educated American ten years into his career earned 31% more than a contemporary who had finished only high school. By 1988 the earnings gap had yawned to 86%. (Woolridge, 1993)

In addition to level of education, evidence suggests that the type of education is related to economic return. Ghazalah (1991) reported that the mean income of graduates of high school vocational programs were 20% to 90% higher than that of students who graduated from general programs. Nations that desire to attain, regain, or maintain their economic edge have become more interested in educating individuals that belong to groups once considered undesirable, including individuals with disabilities. Vocational education offers students employment in higher paid jobs.

To develop and implement effective vocational and transition programs for students with LD, teachers first must increase their knowledge of the world of work. Business and industry in the United States is in the process of restructuring through downsizing and increased dependence upon technology. The demographics of the workforce have changed dramatically. According to 1989 data from the U.S. Bureau of the Census:

- ▪ The workforce is getting older.
- ▪ The workforce includes more women and minority workers than in the past.
- ▪ More immigrants are entering the workforce.

Fewer potential workers are available because of a declining birthrate, small reserve pool of trained workers, and increase in retirements with the graying of America (Meers, 1992). Consequently, employers are considering previously untapped labor pools, including individuals with disabilities, which is increasing the employment prospects for students with LD significantly.

The bad news for students with LD is that the ability to solve problems and participate in an even more complex, technologically based world are becoming essential employment skills:

> In 1965, a car mechanic needed to understand 5,000 pages of service manuals to fix any automobile on the road; today, he must be able to decipher 465,000 pages of technical text, the equivalent of 250 big-city telephone books. The secretary who once typed away at a manual typewriter must now master a word processor, a computer and telecommunications equipment. Even the cashier at the 7-Eleven store has to know how to sell money orders and do minor maintenance jobs on the Slurpee and Big Gulp machine. (Whitman, 1989, p. 46)

The need for these skills reflects radically changing employment demands. The United States is no longer a manufacturing power. The service industry accounts for the greatest number of actual and anticipated jobs in the country. Service jobs of the future will require skills in the areas of technology and telecommunications and the ability to use computers and automated equipment. These facts, coupled with the reality that the average American worker changes jobs six or seven times in his or her lifetime, suggest that adolescents with learning disabilities must learn to become independent problem solvers.

Employers highly value employees who can identify and solve problems independently. Employers of 438 large and 6,000 small businesses surveyed by the Committee for Economic Development ranked *knowing how to learn* as the most-needed skill for an employee to advance (Aring, 1993). Specific vocational skills were perceived as even less important than a high level of literacy, responsible attitudes toward work, the ability to communicate, and the capacity to learn. Whitman (1989) reported a need for literate employees who can reason, learn tasks independently, and deal skillfully with customers. Two U.S. Department of Labor Publications, *Learning a Living* (1992) and *What Work Requires of Schools* (1991), provide more information about employer demands.

Germany regards all education as vocational education because it leads to an occupation. Approximately 70% of German youth participate in apprenticeship programs because they believe they will obtain better jobs by learning in applied settings. About one third of German engineers enter apprenticeship programs prior to earning their engineering degrees. Americans, on the other hand, look upon vocational education as narrow training designed to prepare marginal students for manual, low-status work (Aring, 1993).

This chapter first examines characteristics of adolescents with LD that may affect their performance in vocational settings negatively. The demands of the vocational education setting are explored considering contextual variables such as history, legislation, curriculum, and instruction. Assessment issues relating to career and vocational education are discussed, along with career and vocational education curricula specifically developed for students with mild disabilities. Specific strategies that enable adolescents with LD to make a successful transition from high school to employment are examined. The chapter concludes with a discussion of issues and challenges involved in helping adolescents with LD make the transition to the world of work immediately following high school.

CHARACTERISTICS OF ADOLESCENTS WITH LD AFFECTING VOCATIONAL SUCCESS

Specifically, students with LD tend to:

— be passive rather than strategic learners.
— be hesitant to make a commitment to learn.
— avoid failure by bypassing tasks that are challenging.
— have difficulty establishing future goals.
— exhibit cognitive-processing deficits related to memory and metacognition.
— lack mastery of basic academic skills or lack ability to use these skills in problem-solving situations.
— use ineffective and inefficient learning/performance strategies.
— be poor social problem solvers.
— participate less than their peers in class and in social activities.
— have inappropriate stimulus control.

In addition, several characteristics have significant implications for students' transition to employment. These are discussed next.

LACK OF CAREER AWARENESS

Many adolescents with LD fail to develop realistic career goals, in part because of poorly developed problem-solving and goal-setting skills. Adolescents with LD often have difficulty assessing their own values, abilities, deficits, and interests needed to make decisions (Rosenthal, 1989). They also may lack basic career awareness because of schools' failure to provide career education during the early grades. The lack of awareness of realistic career options makes vocational training and career assessment difficult. It also suggests that teachers must provide students with career information and teach them strategies to make realistic career choices.

JOB-RELATED ACADEMIC SKILLS DEFICITS

By the time students with LD enter 9th grade, they are from 3 to 5 years below grade placement (Zigmond, 1990). These deficits tend to become more pronounced as they move through the high school grades. Deficits in basic academic skills in reading, mathematics, and written language not only hamper students' performance in content areas such as English, history, and science but also affect adversely students' performance in vocational programs that also have reading and writing demands. Students may be much more motivated to learn basic academic skills within a vocational context.

JOB-RELATED SOCIAL SKILLS DEFICITS

The well known social skills deficits of individuals with LD are discussed at length in chapter 11. Children with social skills deficits become even less socially skilled over time. Social skills influence employment significantly (L. Elksnin & N. Elksnin, 1995; N. Elksnin & L. Elksnin, 1991). Employer surveys indicate that interpersonal skills are even more highly valued than vocational or academic skills (Brown, 1976; Wilms, 1984). Some jobs require higher levels of social skill, and employers expect the employee with LD to come to the job prepared to interact appropriately with customers and co-workers. Many students will find employment in service industries that require higher-level social skills such as asking for assistance, responding to criticism, following directions, offering to help co-workers, providing information about the job, answering questions, greeting, conversing with others, using social amenities, and giving positive comments (Chadsey-Rusch, 1990).

CHARACTERISTICS OF SUCCESSFUL LD ADULTS

Although the deficits of people with LD are well known, less information is available regarding the characteristics of *successful* adults with learning disabilities. Identification of these characteristics will help teachers design programs that promote this development. Gerber, Ginsberg, and Reiff (1992) studied 46 highly successful and 25 moderately successful adults with LD. Success levels were determined by ranking each individual as high, moderate, or low for each of five criteria: income level, job classification, education level, prominence in one's field, and job satisfaction.

The overriding theme for these successful adults was *control* over one's life, accomplished through *internal decisions* and *external manifestations*. Internal decisions were related to a desire to get ahead, ability to set explicit goals, and ability to reframe or reinterpret the LD experience in a more productive way. External manifestations or behaviors included persistence, ability to seek out environments in which they could be successful, ability to use strategies to become successful, and surrounding themselves with supportive individuals. Results of Gerber's work and employer surveys suggest that teachers need to design programs that enable adolescents with LD to become independent and take control of their lives.

DEMANDS OF VOCATIONAL EDUCATION SETTINGS

If students with LD are to be integrated successfully in vocational education programs, teachers need to be more knowledgeable about vocational education. As a basis, we have to define the terms *career education, vocational education,* and *transition.*

DEFINING THE TERMS

Transition in the context of this chapter refers to the passage from high school to employment or postsecondary training. In a broader sense, transition means a passage from one stage to another, a series of events rather than a solitary event. For example, a student may make a transition to a vocational education program, from graduation to postsecondary training, and from training to work. As students with LD are not the most adaptable group, these multiple transition points present a unique set of challenges.

What is the relationship of career education and vocational education to transition? *Career education*, first described by Dr. Sidney Marland (1971) in his address to the National Advisory Council on Vocational Education, spans kindergarten through grade 12 and includes three components (Meers, 1992):

1. Vocational instruction to prepare the student for employment.
2. Instruction to prepare the student to live independently in the community.
3. Instruction to prepare the student to live independently at home.

The Division on Career Development of the Council for Exceptional Children defined career education as

> the totality of experiences through which one learns to live a meaningful, satisfying work life. Career education provides the opportunity for children to learn, in the least restrictive environment possible, the academic, daily living, personal-social, and occupational knowledges, and highest levels of economic, personal, and social fulfillment. The individual can obtain this fulfillment through work (both paid and unpaid) and in a variety of other social roles and personal life styles including pursuits as a student, citizen, volunteer, family member, and participant in meaningful leisure time activities. (CEC, 1978, p. 1)

Vocational education is part of career education and usually is implemented at the secondary or postsecondary levels. The American Vocational Association (1968) defined vocational education as

> education designed to develop skills, abilities, understanding, attitudes, work habits, and appreciations needed by workers to enter and make progress in employment on a useful and productive basis.

The goal of vocational education is the student's gainful employment. Both career and vocational education are essential if students with LD are to make a successful transition from high school to the real world.

BRIEF HISTORY OF VOCATIONAL EDUCATION

A brief history, outlined in Figure 11.3, will provide a context for understanding vocational education. In the United States vocational skills originally were developed through formal apprenticeships or informal passing of skills from father to son. The apprenticeship system began to decline as the Industrial Revolution created a large demand for unskilled labor, particularly women and young children. Not until the latter half of the nineteenth century were *industrial arts* taught in U.S. schools. Introduction of the Russian Manual Training System at the Philadelphia Centennial Exposition in 1876 formed the basis for most present-day vocational education trade programs. Craftsmen introduced tools and materials to students, who then completed exercises that had little to do with a completed product or article. Introduced from Sweden a decade later, the Sloyd System provided the foundation for modern industrial arts. Trained teachers rather than artisans taught students to make useful products with attention to neatness and accuracy.

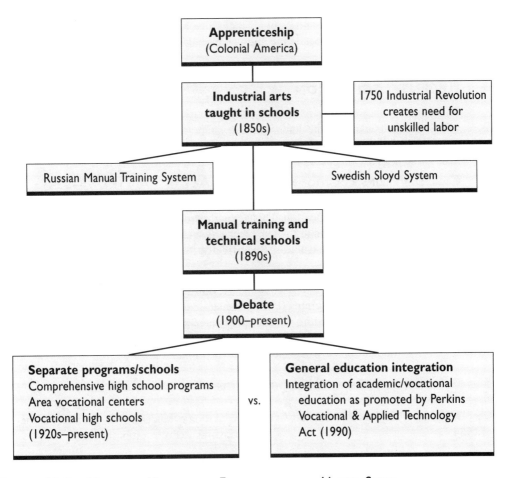

FIGURE 11.3   HISTORY OF VOCATIONAL EDUCATION IN THE UNITED STATES

The first manual training and technical schools in the United States were opened just prior to the beginning of the twentieth century. With the passage of laws outlawing child labor and requiring school attendance, many educators recognized the need to educate the "whole boy." (The "whole girl" received "on-the-job" training in the home.) This comprehensive education included vocational training.

From the turn of the century until the present, the merits of separate vocational programs in areas such as agriculture and trade and industry versus integration of vocational education into the general education curriculum have been debated. John Dewey was a strong proponent of the latter view. He believed that vocational education was essential to the well-being of *all* students. Dewey maintained that separate vocational education programs limited students and promoted educational dualism. From the 1920s through the 1960s and 1970s, however, the influence of the former position was felt through construction of vocational high schools and area vocational centers and establishment of separate vocational programs in comprehensive high schools. At present, the

Carl D. Perkins Vocational and Applied Technology Education Act Amendments (1990) support the integration of academic and vocational education as was once suggested by Dewey.

RECENT LEGISLATION

Since 1917 numerous laws have been passed to establish vocational rehabilitation services, train technicians for the defense industry, fund career education in the public schools, train unskilled youth and adults, and improve the employability of youth with disabilities. These laws are discussed below and outlined in Table 11.1.

CARL D. PERKINS VOCATIONAL EDUCATION ACT OF 1984 (PL 98–524)

A good way to think about the Perkins Act is that it did for vocational education what PL 94–142 did for general education. This act addresses the issues of vocational education of students with disabilities in the least restrictive environment and modification of vocational curriculum and instruction. Specifically, it requires the following:

1. *The student's individualized education program (IEP) must address vocational planning and programming.* Some school districts develop separate individualized vocational programs (IVP). A separate document is not required, and we see advantages to including vocational goals and objectives in the IEP. These advantages include promoting program support and continuity, as well as facilitating communication between special and vocational education.

TABLE 11.1   RECENT RELEVANT LEGISLATION AFFECTING VOCATIONAL EDUCATION

Carl D. Perkins Vocational Education Act of 1984	Education of students with disabilities in the least restrictive vocational setting
	Modification of vocational curriculum and instruction
Carl D. Perkins Vocational and Applied Technology Education Act Amendments of 1990	Integrates vocational and academic education
	Stresses development of thinking and learning skills
Education of the Handicapped Act Amendments of 1990	Vocational rehabilitation services designated as "related service"
	Defines transition services
	Requires transition services no later than age 16
Americans with Disabilities Act of 1990	Protects civil rights of persons with disabilities in private and public employment

2. *The student's vocational interests, abilities, and special needs must be assessed.* Many teachers of students with LD received training in assessment that was restricted to evaluation of academic achievement and student nonacademic behaviors. Few, therefore, are familiar with methods and procedures used to assess vocational interests and abilities. Some of these approaches are discussed later in this chapter.

3. V*ocational instruction, curriculum, equipment, and facilities must be adapted to meet the unique needs of the student with disabilities.* To meet this requirement, special and vocational educators have to collaborate. Typically, vocational educators are not trained to teach students with disabilities. In fact, many vocational educators are credentialed based upon their expertise in a trade rather than through completion of a teacher education program. Special educators need to work with vocational educators to assure that appropriate modifications and accommodations are made.

4. *The student with disabilities must be provided with counseling, guidance, and career development activities by professionally trained counselors.* Again, this requirement requires understanding by special educators of the role and function of vocational and guidance counselors along with a willingness to collaborate with these service providers.

5. *The student with disabilities must be provided with counseling services that will facilitate the successful transition from school to postschool employment.* Students will learn ways to make a successful transition from school to work through services including career and vocational counseling by special educators and counselors.

CARL D. PERKINS VOCATIONAL AND APPLIED TECHNOLOGY EDUCATION ACT AMENDMENTS OF 1990 (PL 101–392)

The Perkins Amendments shift vocational education from teaching specific job skills in separate vocational programs and schools to integrating vocational and academic education. Congruent with this shift is the emphasis on vocational education as a means of offering "cognitive apprenticeships" that develop students' thinking and interest in learning (Wirt, 1991). Consistent with the national restructuring movement, the Perkins Amendments give the local education agency greater flexibility and the opportunity to assume a leadership role in the reform of vocational education.

In addition, separate funding mechanisms were established for secondary and postsecondary vocational education. The amount of funds allocated to each level can be shifted, and in the future we may see relatively more funding of community and technical colleges and vocational/technical proprietary schools. Finally, the Perkins Reauthorization endorsed *TECH-PREP,* designed to prepare high school students who do not anticipate completing baccalaureate degrees to live and work in our technological society. We will discuss *TECH-PREP* in greater detail later in the chapter.

EDUCATION OF THE HANDICAPPED ACT AMENDMENTS OF 1990 (PL 101–476)

The amendments to PL 94–142 changed the name of the Education for All Handicapped Children Act to the Individuals with Disabilities Act, IDEA. IDEA added two new disability categories: autism and traumatic brain injury. Other changes were to designate social work services as a related service and to require that assistive technology services be specified within the individualized education program. Of particular relevance for teachers of adolescents with LD is the designation of vocational rehabilitation services, discussed later in this chapter, as a related service. IDEA defined transition services as

> a coordinated set of activities for a student, designed within an outcome-oriented process, that promotes movement from school to post-school activities, including post-secondary education, vocational training, integrated employment (including supported employment), continuing and adult education, adult services, independent living, or community preparation. (SS 300.18)

Coordinated activities include instruction, community experiences, development of employment and other postsecondary living objectives, instruction in daily living skills, and functional vocational evaluation. Transition services must be addressed in the IEPs of students ages 16 and older, although school districts are encouraged to address transition needs much earlier, as many students with LD leave school at age 16.

Q & A

INDIVIDUALIZED TRANSITION PLAN

Q: *My district requires that an individualized transition plan be written for each high school student with LD. Who is responsible for writing the ITP?*

A: First, IDEA requires that transition services be addressed in IEPs of students ages 16 and older. It does not require that a separate ITP be written. We recommend that transition goals be integrated within the student's IEP so services and programs do not become fragmented. Think of what has happened when we've opted to write separate speech and language IEPs for students with LD. In many cases there was little relationship between what occurred during speech and language therapy and the demands of the classroom and little collaboration between the classroom teacher and the speech and language clinician. When separate ITPs are written fragmented services tend to result. For some excellent strategies in how to integrate transition goals into the IEP, consider:

Integrating Transition Planning into the IEP Process, by L. L. West, S. Corbey, Boyer-Stephens, B. Jones, R. J. Miller, & M. Sarkees-Wircenski (Reston, VA: Council for Exceptional Children, 1992).

All individuals involved in delivering services should be involved in the process: school personnel who are preparing the student to make the transition from high school to work (special education teacher, vocational education teacher, guidance counselor, job coach, etc.) and community service personnel, private organization personnel, and employers who will receive the students when they exit high school. Parents and the student also must be involved in development of transition goals and objectives. This material has suggestions regarding how these individuals can develop collaborative working relationships.

AMERICANS WITH DISABILITIES ACT OF 1990 (PL 101–336)

The primary purpose of ADA is to protect the civil rights of individuals with disabilities in private employment, all areas of public services, public accommodations and transition, and telecommunications. Specifically, the act requires the following:

1. Employers with 15 or more employees cannot refuse to hire an otherwise qualified individual with a disability.
2. State and local governments cannot discriminate against an otherwise qualified individual with a disability.
3. Individuals with disabilities cannot be discriminated against by restaurants, hotels, and retail stores.
4. Buses, trains, and other forms of public transportation must be made accessible to persons with disabilities.
5. Persons with disabilities may not be excluded from public accommodations.
6. Telephone relay services used by persons with hearing disabilities must be offered.

UNDERSTANDING THE VOCATIONAL EDUCATION ENVIRONMENT

Vocational education is a totally different content area. The following discussion covers curricular and instructional issues relating to traditional vocational education programs. (See Table 11.2.) Although these programs are not designed specifically for adolescents with LD, we believe many students with LD should be fully integrated into vocational education with their nondisabled peers.

VOCATIONAL EDUCATION CURRICULUM: THE "WHAT"

The occupational areas that form the vocational education curricula are: agricultural education, business and office education, health occupations education, home economics education, industrial arts and technology education, and trades and industry education (Cobb & Neubert, 1992). Each vocational program area has a specific curriculum. Many states have adopted *competency-based vocational education curricula* (CBVE). CBVE consists of these components:

- Identification of realistic employment opportunities
- Identification of performance tasks
- Production of occupational inventories
- Analysis of occupational survey data
- Analysis of existing materials
- Development of required media and materials
- Development of lesson plans
- Field testing of media and materials
- Revision of media and materials
- Revision of task analysis

TABLE 11.2   VOCATIONAL EDUCATION ENVIRONMENT

What: The curriculum	Competency-Based Curricula (V–TECS) Occupation areas: agricultural education business and office education health occupations education home economics education industrial arts and technology education trades and industry education
Where: The physical setting	Area vocational centers Vocational high schools Comprehensive high schools General high schools
How: Delivery of curriculum	In-school instruction TECH-PREP (2+2, 4+2, 4+2+2) Out-of-school experience Cooperative work education Vocational student organizations AIASA, DECA, FBLA, PBL, FFA, FHA, HERO, HOSA, NPASO, OEA, VICA
Who: Roles and responsibilities	Special educator Employers Vocational educator Parents Guidance counselor Students Vocational rehabilitation counselor

A competency-based vocational curriculum format used by some states is the *Vocational-Technical Education Consortium of States* (V–TECS) curriculum. V–TECS produces catalogs and guides developed by vocational instructors and workers. Approximately 130 catalogs representing 250 job titles are offered with instructor guides available for each. Each catalog includes job performance standards, tasks, tools, and support materials. Materials may have to be supplemented or updated to make them relevant for a specific school district's vocational program offerings. Teachers of adolescents with LD can use V–TECS catalogs readily to develop IEP objectives. In Figures 11.4 and 11.5 Sarkees, Batsche, and McCage (1986) provide examples of how the V–TECS catalog can be used for this purpose. The annual goal for Janet is to demonstrate entry-level skills to be employed as an auto body repairer. The short-term objective, "Given a vehicle requiring headlamp alignment, the student will align the headlamp to meet state safety standards," will be accomplished by using the instructional methods and materials listed in the IEP. V–TECS materials also can help promote communication and understanding between special and vocational educators.

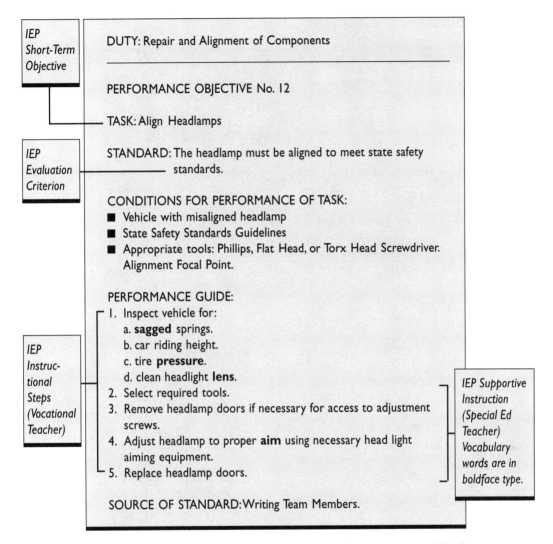

IEP
Short-Term
Objective

DUTY: Repair and Alignment of Components

PERFORMANCE OBJECTIVE No. 12

TASK: Align Headlamps

IEP
Evaluation
Criterion

STANDARD: The headlamp must be aligned to meet state safety
standards.

CONDITIONS FOR PERFORMANCE OF TASK:
■ Vehicle with misaligned headlamp
■ State Safety Standards Guidelines
■ Appropriate tools: Phillips, Flat Head, or Torx Head Screwdriver.
  Alignment Focal Point.

PERFORMANCE GUIDE:
1. Inspect vehicle for:
   a. **sagged** springs.
   b. car riding height.
   c. tire **pressure**.
   d. clean headlight **lens**.

IEP
Instruc-
tional
Steps
(Vocational
Teacher)

2. Select required tools.
3. Remove headlamp doors if necessary for access to adjustment
   screws.
4. Adjust headlamp to proper **aim** using necessary head light
   aiming equipment.
5. Replace headlamp doors.

IEP Supportive
Instruction
(Special Ed
Teacher)
Vocabulary
words are in
boldface type.

SOURCE OF STANDARD: Writing Team Members.

FIGURE 11.4 SAMPLE PAGE FROM V–TECS CATALOG AND CORRESPONDING IEP COMPONENTS

Source: "Nexus Between Competency-Based Education and Vocational Planning for Students with Handicapping Conditions: A Model," by M. Sarkees, C. Batsche, & R. McCage, 1986, *Career Development for Exceptional Individuals, 9*, p. 45. Used by permission.

OCCUPATIONAL INFORMATION RESOURCES

To better understand vocational curricula, teachers should be aware of available occupational information resources such as the *Dictionary of Occupational Titles, Guide for Occupational Exploration*, and the *Occupational Outlook Handbook*. These resources are useful when developing career awareness and career exploration activities, designing informal assessment instructions, and planning transition strategies. Used individually or together, these materials offer a comprehensive and standardized system of describing

INSTRUCTIONAL AREA: Auto Body Repairer

ANNUAL GOAL: Janet will demonstrate entry-level skills needed to be employed as Auto Body Repairer.

Instructional Objective	Instructional Methods, Media/ Material Title(s) Optional	EVALUATION OF INSTRUCTIONAL OBJECTIVES		PROGRESS		
		Tests, Materials, Evaluation Procedures To Be Used	Criteria of Successful Performance	Introduced	Developing	Employable
Given a vehicle requiring headlamp alignment, the student will align the headlamp to meet State Safety Standards.	1. Read the procedures with Janet prior to class and review new vocabulary. (Special Ed Teacher) 2. Read the State Safety Standards with Janet prior to class. (Special Ed Teacher) 3. Review list of required tools. (Special Ed Teacher) 4. Practice sheets for procedures, tools, and safety standards. (Special Ed Teacher) 5. Demonstration of headlamp alignment— performance guides 1–5. (Auto Body Teacher)	1. Vocabulary test of words within procedures and safety standards. 2. Performance test: Selection of required tools. 3. Headlamp to be aligned in vocational lab to meet criterion.	1. 90% accuracy on word recognition test. 2. Accuracy of tools selection. 3. Vocational teacher evaluation of headlamp alignment based on criterion in V–TECS catalog.			

FIGURE 11.5   SAMPLE IEP FORMAT USING V–TECS DATA

Source: "Nexus Between Competency-Based Education and Vocational Planning for Students with Handicapping Conditions: A Model," by M. Sarkees, C. Batsche, & R. McCage, 1986, *Career Development for Exceptional Individuals, 9,* p. 47. Used by permission.

jobs and the world of work, as well as a means of organizing information about the student's vocational interests, abilities, and aptitudes (Hursh & Kerns, 1988).

DICTIONARY OF OCCUPATIONAL TITLES (DOT)   Published by the U.S. Department of Labor (1977, 1986), the DOT describes more than 20,000 jobs in relation to people, data, and things according to physical demands, working conditions, and required worker aptitudes. The dictionary can be used to match student's skills with job requirements. Nine job categories are included in the DOT:

- Professional, technical, and managerial occupations
- Clerical and sales occupations
- Service occupations
- Agricultural, fishery, forestry, and related occupations
- Processing occupations
- Machine trades occupations
- Benchwork occupations
- Structural work occupations
- Miscellaneous occupations

GUIDE FOR OCCUPATIONAL EXPLORATION (GOE)   The GOE (Harrington & O'Shea, 1984) contains 12,000 occupations organized according to 12 interest areas: artistic, scientific, plants and animals, protective, mechanical, industrial, business detail, selling, accommodating, humanitarian, leading-influencing, and physical-performing. Interest areas are organized further into work groups and subgroups. When using the GOE, the Checklist of Occupational Clues is completed first. It examines one's interests, values, leisure activities, home activities, and school subjects. Responses are recorded on the Occupational Exploration Worksheet to identify work groups matched to these interests and abilities. After reading about those work groups in the guide, the person completes the Work Group Evaluation Chart to identify preferred occupations. Additional information about those occupations can be obtained through onsite visits, interviews, and further reading. The last step is to complete a plan of action outlining strategies to locate a job or obtain appropriate training for an occupation of interest.

OCCUPATIONAL OUTLOOK HANDBOOK (OOH)   Published every two years by the U.S. Department of Labor (1990–91), the OOH offers information about more than 850 occupations in 30 industries relative to the nature of work, training, qualifications, places of employment, opportunities for advancement, earning potential, and working conditions. The handbook is designed to be used for career exploration by adults, high school students, and college students.

DELIVERING THE VOCATIONAL EDUCATION CURRICULUM: THE "HOW"

In traditional vocational education programs occupational skills are taught through in-school instruction, out-of-school work experiences, and vocational student organizations (Cobb & Neubert, 1992). Students usually cannot enroll in a vocational program until their junior or senior year. Heavy reading and writing demands are placed on students even during in-school instruction.

The *out-of-school work experience* often involves *cooperative work education* (CWE), a capstone experience similar to student teaching. The student is placed with a cooperative employer who, along with the vocational instructor, provides on-the-job supervision and instruction. Approximately 1 million students in high schools and 2-year colleges enroll in CWEs each year.

Although high school students enrolled in college preparatory programs are encouraged to participate in relevant extracurricular activities, these activities are not required. In contrast, many vocational training programs require participation in *vocational student organizations (VSOs)*. The U.S. Department of Education recognizes nine VSOs:

- American Industrial Arts Student Association (AIASA)
- Distributive Education Clubs of America (DECA)
- Future Business Leaders of America (FBLA)
- Future Farmers of America (FFA)
- Future Homemakers of America (FHA)
- Health Occupations Students of America (HOSA)
- National Postsecondary Agriculture Student Organization (NPASO)
- Office Education Association (OEA)
- Vocational Industrial Clubs of America (VICA)

These organizations are regarded as "leadership clubs" that develop social, vocational, and fund-raising skills. They also foster personal growth and prepare the student to participate in civic and community affairs. Organizations often sponsor school-based enterprises (SBE), in which students provide goods or services to the community. Examples of SBEs are the establishment of an auto repair shop, a hair styling salon, a restaurant, a print shop, and an upholstery shop on campus and the sale of furniture, houses, or welded products on- and off-campus.

Like all of American education, vocational education currently is engaged in restructuring. An important component of the restructuring movement is TECH-PREP, a program designed to ensure that students who do *not* complete 4-year baccalaureate degree programs are equipped to live and work in a technological society. The Carl D. Perkins Vocational and Applied Technology Education Act defined TECH-PREP as

> an articulated program consisting of 2 years of secondary school preceding graduation and 2 years of higher education, or an apprenticeship program of at least 2 years following secondary instruction with a common core of required proficiency in mathematics, science, communications, and technologies designed to lead to an associate degree or certificate in a specific career field, such as engineering technology, applied science, mechanical, industrial, or practical art or trade or agriculture, health, business...and provides for effective employment placement activities or transfer of students to 4-year baccalaureate degree programs.

TECH-PREP is intended to be the centerpiece of the restructuring movement in vocational education. As indicated in the federal definition, the curriculum includes applied academics, technical skills, and information/communication skills. TECH-PREP uses a variety of models:

2 + 2	(2 years of high school courses and 2 years of postsecondary training)
4 + 2	(4 years of high school courses and 2 years of postsecondary training)
4 + 2 + 2	(4 years of high school courses and 2 years of technical college and 2 years at a baccalaureate degree-granting institution)

Additional information about TECH-PREP can be found in Brown, Asselin, Hoerner, Daines, and Clowes (1992).

Although popular in Europe, apprenticeship training is not used much in the United States (U.S. Department of Education, 1991). Estimates are that only about 300,000 individuals are enrolled in U.S. programs. Most are over the age of 18 and possess a high school diploma. Federal regulations must be followed for *registered apprenticeships*, including development of an organized training plan, completion of a minimum of 144 hours of classroom instruction, and completion of a minimum of 2,000 hours of on-the-job training under a written training agreement. However, 27 states do not rely on the Federal Bureau of Apprenticeships and Training in the Department of Labor to administer their apprenticeships, so standards vary from state-to-state.

THE PHYSICAL SETTING: THE "WHERE"

Vocational education typically is offered in four school environments. Students may attend *area vocational centers* for their vocational education and attend their home high schools for academic instruction. *Vocational high schools* offer both vocational and academic curricula. The vocational academy is a type of vocational high school that attempts to fully integrate vocational and academic instruction. The 100 or so academies in the United States share several characteristics, including the school-within-a-school organization wherein a group of students take a course sequence, vertical rather than horizontal segments of a thematic career area (i.e., health careers would consider physicians as well as paramedics), and the solicitation of active participation of area employers.

Approximately 30% of vocational education is offered in *comprehensive high schools*. These schools house five or more of the seven curricular areas within a traditional high school campus. *General high schools*, which may be located next to comprehensive high schools or vocational centers, offer fewer than five programs. Sixty percent of vocational education programs are housed in general high schools. We believe that students with LD should be integrated to the maximum extent appropriate into traditional vocational settings rather than being placed in special education vocational programs.

VOCATIONAL EDUCATION RESPONSIBILITY: THE "WHO"

To be an effective instructor of adolescents with LD, teachers have to be familiar with roles assumed by professionals representing several disciplines. In our minds, role definition presents a dilemma and a potential source of controversy. For example, are we responsible for teaching our students specific vocational skills? Is the vocational educator responsible for teaching job-related academic skills? In the discussion that follows, we provide some guidelines that we think will lead to higher levels of cooperation and collaboration and result in students' successful transition from school to work and independent living settings. Figure 11.6 depicts the interrelationships of the vocational education team.

SPECIAL EDUCATOR

Even though special educators lack vocational education *content area* expertise, they have several important roles to fulfill, including collaborating with vocational educators to identify appropriate instructional and curricular modifications and helping to imple-

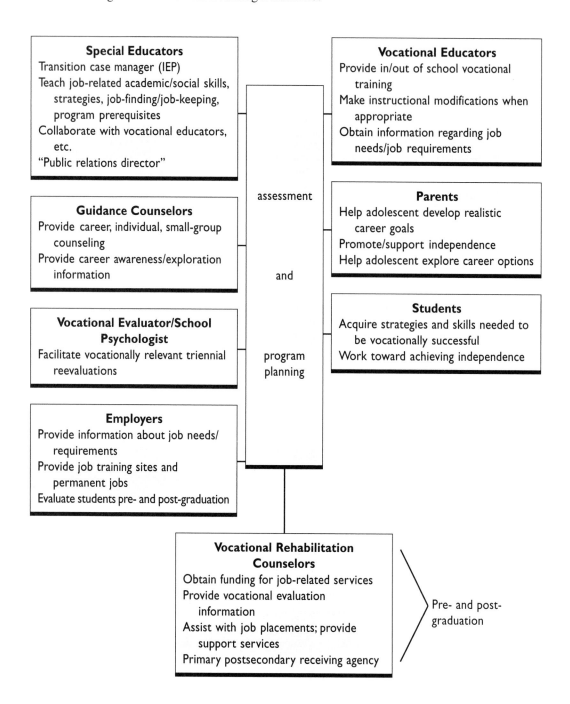

FIGURE 11.6   ROLES IN VOCATIONAL EDUCATION

ment these modifications. They can assist students by teaching them learning strategies that will make them better problem solvers, academic skills that are essential for the vocational program, and job-related social skills and job-seeking skills that will enable them to find and keep a job.

In addition, with the help of the school guidance counselor, special education teachers can provide students with career exploration opportunities. They also can serve as the case manager for transition. Finally, special educators should assume the role of public relations director and educate other professionals and members of the community regarding the abilities of students with LD.

VOCATIONAL EDUCATOR

Often the vocational educator does not have a baccalaureate degree but is credentialed based upon trade expertise and experience. In some states certification is handled separately from that of academic teacher certification. This means that the vocational educators are experts in their trade but may not have received formal teacher training, including coursework devoted to understanding students with disabilities. The vocational educator may need assistance from special educators in identifying appropriate areas of instructional or curricular modification. The vocational educator's primary responsibility is to provide specific vocational training and to locate training sites for students who desire postsecondary training. He or she also assists in developing the vocational and transition goals included in the student's IEP.

The vocational educator may regard adolescents with LD as less capable of being successful in vocational programs. Special educators need to recognize that students with LD must be prepared adequately to enter vocational education programs and acknowledge that these programs have prerequisites and place high demands on students once they matriculate. In addition, students may have to pass state licensure or qualifying exams to enter specific vocations such as cosmetology, health-related professions, and so forth.

GUIDANCE COUNSELOR

The school guidance counselor may conduct vocational and career assessment, provide career counseling, offer individual or small-group counseling, and assist the special educator in developing career awareness, exploration, and information activities. The counselor is an excellent resource regarding use of the occupational information resources which were discussed previously in this chapter.

SCHOOL PSYCHOLOGIST

The school psychologist promotes relevant evaluation by deemphasizing assessment for special education program eligibility and emphasizing career and vocational assessment. As the measurement expert, the school psychologist is an excellent resource to other school personnel regarding appropriate assessment instruments and practices.

EMPLOYERS

Employers provide job training sites and permanent jobs. Also, they are excellent sources of information about their needs and the requirements of specific jobs. Employers can help plan effective vocational and transition programs, and their evaluation of our students is the ultimate test of program effectiveness.

Q & A

VOCATIONAL EDUCATION

Q: *The vocational educators in my high school are reluctant to accept students with LD into their programs. What can I do to make them more accepting of my students?*

A: Full integration of adolescents with LD into vocational education programs depends on several factors. Does the student have the prerequisite academic and social skills needed to succeed in the program? Is the vocational educator willing and able to make instructional and curricular modifications when needed?

One way you can change attitudes is by making sure your students have the entry skills required by specific vocational programs. The best way to do this is to interview vocational educators, ask to see program competencies as outlined by V–TECS or the state department of education, and observe vocational classes. Ask the vocational educator what is expected the first day the student comes to class. For example, the metal shop teacher may expect all students to follow safety rules. Teach essential skills that the student lacks. In the case of safety rules, try to teach safety behavior in the vocational classroom. Provide the vocational educator with evidence (e.g., videotapes, permanent products) that the student has the required skills and behaviors.

The Carl D. Perkins Act requires that vocational curriculum and instruction be adapted to meet the needs of students with LD. From a practical standpoint, legislating attitudes usually is unsuccessful. Even so, you can help the vocational educator become more willing and able to make adaptations through collaborative consultation, defined by Idol, Paolucci-Whitcomb, and Nevin (1986) as "an interactive process that enables people with diverse expertise to generate creative solutions to mutually defined problems" (p. 1). Vocational educators have the content expertise but may lack pedagogical expertise, as many are not trained as teachers. Therefore, many vocational educators will be receptive to your ideas regarding modifying presentation and evaluation of content.

You may need to convince the vocational educator that students can learn information and demonstrate competence in many ways. For example, the vocational educator may have to be convinced that having the student demonstrate mastery of shop safety rules is an appropriate substitution for a satisfactory grade on a pencil-and-paper test. Vocational educators need to know that many students with LD are able to learn more effectively and efficiently through demonstration and modeling than through print.

An excellent resource you can use when identifying realistic instructional and curricular alternatives is the model developed by Laurie, Buchwach, Silverman, and Zigmond (1978). They ask you and the vocational education teacher to consider realistic *classroom organization, classroom management, presentation, practice,* and *testing alternatives.*

As you begin to place your students in programs, place your best students first. They will sell themselves!

PARENTS

Of course, parents participate in the IEP planning process. In addition, they can support their adolescent with LD in exploring career and employment options, as well as helping the student develop realistic career goals. By giving the adolescent with LD the chance to assume responsibility for school and home tasks, parents can help promote independence.

STUDENTS

The theme of this chapter and this book, for that matter, is promoting the independence of the adolescent with LD. These students need skills they can use to develop and reach their career goals. The strategies discussed here were selected because they enable adolescents to assume responsibility for decisions that will affect their transition to employment.

VOCATIONAL REHABILITATION COUNSELOR

Teachers of adolescents with LD must understand the role of the vocational rehabilitation counselor and services of the Department of Vocational Rehabilitation (DVR). The vocational rehabilitation counselor obtains funding for job-related services, provides vocational evaluation information, assists with job placements, provides support services, and advocates for the integration of persons with LD into community job settings (N. Elksnin & L. Elksnin, 1992). DVR offers an array of services, including academic support services, vocational training, educational and medical evaluations, medical treatment, and support services. Vocational rehabilitation, however, is an *eligibility* rather than an *entitlement program*. Students with LD are not eligible automatically for services once they leave school. Vocational rehabilitation has its own definition of LD and accompanying eligibility criteria. The agency defines persons with LD as "individuals who have a disorder on one or more of the psychological processes involved in understanding, perceiving, or expressing language or concepts (spoken or written)." To receive services, the individual with LD must meet three criteria.

1. Their psychological processing disorder is diagnosed by a licensed physician and/ or a licensed or certified psychologist who is skilled in the diagnosis and treatment of such disorders.
2. Their disorder results in a substantial handicap to employment.
3. There is a reasonable expectation that vocational rehabilitation services may benefit the individual in terms of employability.

Usually LD is diagnosed using the *Diagnostic and Statistical Manual of Mental Disorders–IV* (1994) as a learning disorder in the areas of reading, mathematics, and/or written expression.

Many eligible graduates never receive vocational rehabilitation services. More than one third of the young adults with LD who participated in a survey sponsored by the Learning Disabilities Association of America did not apply, nor did they know how to apply for services (Smith, 1992). Low rates of participation may stem from teachers' lack of awareness of vocational rehabilitation services, as well as definitional issues and funding priorities, which vary from state-to-state (Dowdy, Smith, & Nowell, 1992). In the future, vocational rehabilitation services may be more highly utilized, as they were designated as a related service under IDEA in 1990. DVR is the primary postsecondary agency for adults with LD.

VOCATIONAL PROGRAMMING

ASSESSMENT

The main purpose of vocational assessment, whether it is traditional or curriculum-based, is to effect a match between the student's abilities and vocational interests and an appropriate vocational training program. Because of the diverse content of vocational programs, assessment must result in an appropriate student-program match to avoid student failure or student dissatisfaction. Failure and dissatisfaction lead to "program hopping," which wastes the student's time. Most vocational programs take 2 years to complete, and changing programs is similar to changing college majors; the student loses time and credits. The career and vocational assessment requirements mandated by the Carl D. Perkins Act were designed to facilitate successful completion of programs and to eliminate "program hopping."

Few special educators receive training in career and vocational assessment. Vocational assessment data are used to make vocational program placement decisions and to assist students in making occupational choices. Here we provide a brief overview of traditional vocational assessment and curriculum-based vocational assessment. Although special educators may not be involved in the direct administration of instruments designed to assess vocational interests, aptitudes, and manual dexterity, we need to be familiar with the procedures used to assess students with LD. As professionals who are knowledgeable about formal and informal assessment, we are an excellent resource to vocational educators, guidance counselors, and vocational counselors.

TRADITIONAL VOCATIONAL ASSESSMENT

Traditional vocational assessment often is characterized as a *level system* (shown in Table 11.3) with the numbers of students receiving Level I assessment greatly outnumbering those requiring Level III assessment (Elksnin, 1992). *Level I assessment* is recommended for all students with LD. At this level test data relating to cognitive ability, achievement, and adaptive behavior are reviewed. *Level II assessment*, recommended for most students with LD, typically involves assessment of the student's *interests* and *aptitudes*. Students who are interested in entering 4-year colleges still should be evaluated, as interest and aptitude data are invaluable when assisting them in selecting institutions, majors, and formulating realistic long-term goals.

Interests have more influence over our career choices, but aptitudes determine how successful we will be in our chosen occupation. Assessment of aptitudes attempts to assess the *potential to learn*. Guidance and career counselors use aptitude test data when discussing job and training options with students. Some of the more commonly administered group aptitude tests are the *Differential Aptitude Test* (Bennett, Seashore, & Wehman, 1982), the *General Aptitude Test Battery* (U.S. Employment Service, 1982a), *Nonreading*

TABLE 11.3   LEVELS OF VOCATIONAL ASSESSMENT

Type	Method
Basic vocational assessment	
Level I	Medical examinations Informal teacher assessment Student records Special education test data Student and parent interviews Vocational counseling
Level II	Vocational aptitude test Vocational interest test
Comprehensive vocational assessment	All the above plus any or all of the following:
Level III	Vocational counseling (in depth) Dexterity and coordination tests Career and vocational exploration Work samples Behavior observations in a controlled work environment Job tryout Vocational classroom tryout

Source: *Educational assessment of learning problems: Testing for teaching* (2d ed.) (p. 409) by G. Wallace, S. C. Larsen, and L. K. Elksnin, 1992, Boston: Allyn & Bacon. Reprinted by permission.

Aptitude Test Battery (U.S. Employment Service, 1982b), and the *Armed Services Vocational Aptitude Battery* (Air Force Human Resources Lab, 1985) used by military recruiters. With the exception of the ASVAB, high reading demands may preclude use of these instruments with some students with severe LD (L. Elksnin & N. Elksnin, 1989).

Vocational interests begin to stabilize during the middle teen years, and interests remain more stable for females than males. Little information is available to determine if adolescents with LD exhibit a maturational lag in the development of interests, although this possibility has significant implications for career awareness and vocational training. Interests often are assessed using group-administered *verbal interest inventories* such as the *Occupational Interest Survey–Form DD* (Kuder & Diamond, 1985) and the *Self-Directed Search* (Holland, 1985).

In an effort to minimize the reading demands of these instruments, several *picture interest inventories* were developed, including the *Geist Picture Interest Inventory–Revised* (Geist, 1988), the *Reading-Free Vocational Interest Inventory–Revised* (Becker, 1988), and the *Wide-Range Interest Opinion Test* (Jastak & Jastak, 1979). The problem with many of these picture inventories, however, is that lower-level occupations typically are represented, although students with LD often are capable of employment in more challenging areas. A second problem may be limited occupational awareness, which may significantly restrict students' occupational interests. This second difficulty can be overcome by beginning career education early and providing students with LD with career exploration opportunities.

Comprehensive *Level III assessment* is reserved for those students with severe disabilities and is conducted only when we lack sufficient data to make vocational program placement decisions. Level III assessment may involve any of the procedures discussed next.

Work samples assess the student's performance on generic worker traits and potential for a job, occupational area, or training environment. A work sample does not necessarily have a counterpart in business or industry. *Commercial work samples* include the Jewish Employment and Vocational Services Work Sample System (Vocational Research Institute, 1976), the Talent Assessment Program (Nighswonger, 1981), and the VALPAR Component Work Sample Series (VALPAR International Corporation, 1981). These samples are expensive. For example, the complete set of 16 VALPAR work samples costs $25,000. In addition, commercial samples may not reflect training and employment opportunities in a school district or geographic region. An alternative to commercial samples are *teacher-made work samples*. With knowledge of task analysis and informal assessment, special educators can collaborate with vocational educators and develop their own work samples following these steps:

1. Examine training and employment options before selecting an area to sample.
2. Conduct an analysis of the job or training program.
3. Identify and sequence tasks of the job or training program.
4. Establish performance criteria.
5. Determine reliability and validity estimates.

A Work Sample Format is available from the Materials Development Center at the University of Wisconsin–Stout (Materials Development Center, 1977).

Other approaches used during Level III assessment include manual dexterity tests, job tryouts, and vocational classroom tryouts. Behavioral assessment in a controlled work environment may be conducted, along with *situational assessment*, which involves systematic observation of the student in a real or simulated work-related task. During this level of assessment, the student also should receive in-depth vocational counseling.

CURRICULUM-BASED VOCATIONAL ASSESSMENT (CBVA)

Special educators are familiar with curriculum-based academic assessment. CBVA evolved for the same reason—to make assessment more relevant to real task demands (Albright & Cobb, 1988). Traditional vocational assessment does not take into consideration local and regional training and employment options. Although IDEA theoretically requires that the individual needs of adolescents with LD be met, from a practical perspective the student likely will not receive vocational training in an area for which no program exists. Assessing the student to effect a match between abilities and interests and an occupation that is not available locally makes little sense. CBVA attempts to address these issues. In addition, it can be used throughout the student's vocational training program and transition to employment as well as a vehicle to promote collaboration between special and vocational educators.

Cobb (1983) described the CBVA process using the assessment paradigm outlined in Table 11.4. During screening, the multidisciplinary team determines the appropriate vocational training program based on examination of aptitude and interest testing data, as well as knowledge of the student. The team attempts to affect a match between student, services, and environment. Next, *placement* involves selecting an appropriate program or environment based upon formal assessment data, as well as providing the student with job-shadowing experiences, tours of vocational programs, and individual or small-group counseling.

During the *program planning* stage the team identifies discrepancies between the student's competencies and the demands of the vocational curriculum. Achievement is assessed using curriculum-referenced performance samples, curriculum-referenced math tests, cloze tests utilizing vocational education texts, and informal observation. *Assessment of student progress* is accomplished by conducting interviews with students, instructors, and employers; observing student performance, administering teacher-made tests, and evaluating course products. *Program evaluation* is conducted during the annual IEP review when the team reexamines the match between the student's interests and

TABLE 11.4   CURRICULUM-BASED VOCATIONAL ASSESSMENT

Stage	Assessment Activity
Screening	Aptitude testing data Interest testing data General knowledge of student
Placement	Formal assessment data Job shadowing Vocational program tours Counseling
Program Planning	Discrepancies between student's competencies and task demands
Assessment of Student Progress	Interviews Observation Teacher-made tests Course products
Program Evaluation	IEP review Determine match between student's interests and abilities and vocational curriculum and training

abilities and the vocational curriculum and training environment. The students should be involved actively at each step in the assessment. Mastering the *education planning strategy*, described later in this chapter, will enable students to become more actively involved in vocational decision making.

CAREER AND VOCATIONAL EDUCATION CURRICULA

Different models of transition have been proposed, beginning with Madeleine Will's Office of Special Education and Rehabilitation Services model in 1984. Feichtner (1989) described three school-to-work transition models: curriculum content, instructional stages, and support services models. We have added a fourth model, the futures-oriented curriculum model. These models are outlined in Table 11.5. With the exception of the futures-oriented curriculum model, these models were not designed specifically for adolescents with LD. In the sections that follow, we will discuss ways in which each model meets (and does not meet) the needs of students with LD.

CURRICULUM CONTENT MODELS

The goal of curriculum content models is to teach knowledge and skills needed for employment. Skills taught include basic academic skills, job-related social skills, occupa-

TABLE 11.5   CURRICULAR MODELS FOR STUDENTS WITH MILD DISABILITIES

Models	Features
Curriculum Content	Teaches occupational knowledge and skills ■ Brolin's Life-Centered Career Education model ■ Greenan's Generalizable Skills
Will's Support Services	Identifies level of support services needed to make successful transition from school to employment: ■ no special services ■ time-limited services ■ on-going services
Instructional Stages	Considers transition from school to work from a career development stages model ■ career awareness ■ career exploration ■ career preparation ■ career placement/implementation
Futures-Oriented Curriculum	Teaches skills that enable students to reach goals and objectives relating to current and anticipated environments

tional skills, and employability skills. Examples of curricula consistent with this model are Brolin's *Life-Centered Career Education (LCCE)* model (1989) and Greenan's (1987) *Generalizable Skills*.

One of the best known models of career education is *LCCE*, which includes three curricular areas supported by academic skills: daily living skills, occupational guidance and preparation, and personal-social skills. Each curricular area contains 22 competencies or goal areas that are met by acquiring 97 subcompetencies or objectives. For example, the "occupational guidance and preparation" area has six competencies:

1. Knowing and exploring occupational possibilities
2. Selecting and planning occupational choices
3. Exhibiting appropriate work habits and behavior
4. Seeking, securing, and maintaining employment
5. Exhibiting sufficient physical-manual skills
6. Obtaining specific occupational skills

The LCCE competencies appear as Figure 11.7.

Subcompetencies for "selecting and planning occupational choices" are:

- Make realistic occupational choices
- Identify requirements of appropriate and available jobs
- Identify occupational aptitudes
- Identify major occupational interests
- Identify major occupational needs

Brolin incorporates objectives, activities, and strategies, and suggested adult and peer roles when teaching each subcompetency. These suggestions for Competency 17, Subcompetency 75, appear in Figure 11.8.

The main advantage of LCCE for students with LD is that it emphasizes the need to infuse career education throughout the curriculum, across the grade levels. A primary reason for students' poor level of career awareness is that special education failed to provide career education during the early grades. The occupational guidance and preparation curriculum included in LCCE is appropriate for increasing students' career awareness. Because students with LD often have social skills deficits, the personal-social skills curriculum is useful in teaching general and job-specific social skills. The daily living skills curriculum may be appropriate only for students with severe LD. LCCE does not address specific occupational skills. Although academic skills support the three curriculum strands, Brolin does not address the issue of teaching job-related academic skills to older students.

Greenan (1987) defined a *generalizable skill* as a "cognitive, affective, or psychomotor trait (skill or skill area) that is basic to, necessary for success in, and transferable or common within and among vocational programs and occupations" (p. 275). By surveying vocational educators, Greenan (1983, 1986) and Greenan and Smith (1981) identified basic skills that generalize across secondary vocational training programs.

The generalizable skills curriculum has four general areas, each with several subcomponents.

Curriculum Area	Competency	Subcompetency: The student will be able to:	
DAILY LIVING SKILLS	1. Managing Personal Finances	1. Count money & make correct change	2. Make responsible expenditures
	2. Selecting & Managing a Household	7. Maintain home exterior/interior	8. Use basic appliances & tools
	3. Caring for Personal Needs	12. Demonstrate knowledge of physical fitness, nutrition & weight	13. Exhibit proper grooming & hygiene
	4. Raising Children & Meeting Marriage Responsibilities	17. Demonstrate physical care for raising children	18. Know psychological aspects of raising children
	5. Buying, Preparing & Consuming Food	20. Purchase food	21. Clean food preparation areas
	6. Buying & Caring for Clothing	26. Wash/clean clothing	27. Purchase clothing
	7. Exhibiting Responsible Citizenship	29. Demonstrate knowledge of civil rights & responsibilities	30. Know nature of local, state & federal governments
	8. Utilizing Recreational Facilities & Engaging in Leisure	33. Demonstrate knowledge of available community resources	34. Choose & plan activities
	9. Getting Around the Community	38. Demonstrate knowledge of traffic rules & safety	39. Demonstrate knowledge & use of various means of transportation
PERSONAL-SOCIAL SKILLS	10. Achieving Self-Awareness	42. Identify physical & psychological needs	43. Identify interests & abilities
	11. Acquiring Self-Confidence	46. Express feelings of self-worth	47. Describe others' perception of self
	12. Achieving Socially Responsible Behavior	51. Develop respect for the rights & properties of others	52. Recognize authority & follow instructions
	13. Maintain Good Interpersonal Skills	56. Demonstrate listening & responding skills	57. Establish & maintain close relationships
	14. Achieving Independence	59. Strive toward self-actualization	60. Demonstrate self-organization
	15. Making Adequate Decisions	62. Locate & utilize sources of assistance	63. Anticipate consequences
	16. Communicating with Others	67. Recognize & respond to emergency situations	68. Communicate with understanding
OCCUPATIONAL GUIDANCE AND PREPARATION	17. Knowing & Exploring Occupational Possibilities	70. Identify remunerative aspects of work	71. Locate sources of occupational & training information
	18. Selecting & Planning Occupational Choices	76. Make realistic occupational choices	77. Identify requirements of appropriate & available jobs
	19. Exhibiting Appropriate Work Habits & Behavior	81. Follow directions & observe regulations	82. Recognize importance of attendance & punctuality
	20. Seeking, Securing & Maintaining Employment	88. Search for a job	89. Apply for a job
	21. Exhibiting Sufficient Physical-Manual Skills	94. Demonstrate stamina & endurance	95. Demonstrate satisfactory balance & coordination
	22. Obtaining Specific Occupational Skills		

FIGURE 11.7   LIFE-CENTERED CAREER EDUCATION COMPETENCIES

3. Keep basic financial records	4. Calculate & pay taxes	5. Use credit responsibly	6. Use banking services	
9. Select adequate housing	10. Set up household	11. Maintain home grounds		
14. Dress appropriately	15. Demonstrate knowledge of common illness, prevention & treatment	16. Practice personal safety		
19. Demonstrate marriage responsibilities				
22. Store food	23. Prepare meals	24. Demonstrate appropriate eating habits	25. Plan/eat balanced meals	
28. Iron, mend & store clothing				
31. Demonstrate knowledge of the law & ability to follow the law	32. Demonstrate knowledge of citizen rights & responsibilities			
35. Demonstrate knowledge of the value of recreation	36. Engage in group & individual activities	37. Plan vacation time		
40. Find way around the community	41. Drive a car			
44. Identify emotions	45. Demonstrate knowledge of physical self			
48. Accept & give praise	49. Accept & give criticism	50. Develop confidence in oneself		
53. Demonstrate appropriate behavior in public places	54. Know important character traits	55. Recognize personal roles		
58. Make & maintain friendships				
61. Demonstrate awareness of how one's behavior affects others				
64. Develop & evaluate alternatives	65. Recognize nature of a problem	66. Develop goal seeking behavior		
69. Know subtleties of communication				
72. Identify personal values met through work	73. Identify societal values met through work	74. Classify jobs into occupational categories	75. Investigate local occupational & training opportunities	
78. Identify occupational aptitudes	79. Identify major occupational interests	80. Identify major occupational needs		
83. Recognize importance of supervision	84. Demonstrate knowledge of occupational safety	85. Work with others	86. Meet demands for quality work	87. Work at a satisfactory rate
90. Interview for a job	91. Know how to maintain post-school occupational adjustment	92. Demonstrate knowledge of competitive standards	93. Know how to adjust to changes in employment	
96. Demonstrate manual dexterity	97. Demonstrate sensory discrimination			
There are no specific subcompetencies as they depend on skill being taught.				

Source: *Life Centered Career Education: A Competency-Based Approach* (3d ed.) (pp. 10, 11), by D. E. Brolin, 1989, Reston, VA: Council for Exceptional Children. Used by permission

Domain: Occupational Guidance and Preparation
Competency: 17. Knowing and Exploring Occupational Possibilities
Subcompetency: 75. Investigate Local Occupational and Training Opportunities

Objectives	Activities/Strategies	Adult/Peer Roles
a. Select an occupational area and find local employers in the yellow pages.	■ Students use the newspaper help wanted ads to identify occupations that are of interest. ■ Students create a display on the bulletin board illustrating school and community sources of occupational information. ■ Students select an occupation, review the yellow pages under the occupational title or job required, review listing of employers, and select local employers.	■ Parents or peers help the student identify local sources of occupational information. ■ Representatives from each source discuss the kind of information they provide. ■ Business person discusses local occupational opportunities and industrial opportunities. ■ Employment service representative discusses job opportunities available locally and why these jobs are found in this location.
b. Collect and read help wanted ads in the occupational areas selected above.	■ Students clip help wanted ads from the newspaper regarding the local occupational areas selected, and bring them to class.	■ Parent and student review help wanted ads regarding occupations in local areas.
c. Utilize sources of employment information.	■ A local employer gives a demonstration on how to utilize each resource (e.g., who to talk to, what questions to ask, etc.). ■ Students discuss how they would acquire specific kinds of information. ■ Students identify the pros and cons of each source. ■ Students practice using sources to obtain specific information.	■ Employment service or rehabilitation counselor demonstrates how to obtain specific information from these agencies.
d. Local sources of employment information.	■ Students take a field trip to various sources of information. ■ Students record, in an occupational notebook, the kind of information available at each resource. ■ Students construct a display on a bulletin board identifying the kind of information available at each source.	■ Parents or peers help student locate various sources. ■ Peers accompany the student on trips to the various sources. ■ Employment service counselor discusses local sources of information on job opportunities. ■ Rehabilitation counselor discusses opportunities for training and employment.

FIGURE 11.8   SAMPLE LCCE SUBCOMPETENCIES

Source: Life Centered Career Education: A Competency-Based Approach (3d ed.) (pp. 107, 108), by D. E. Brolin, 1989, Reston, VA: Council for Exceptional Children. Used by permission.

1. Mathematics
   - whole numbers (5 skills)
   - fractions (4 skills)
   - decimals (6 skills)
   - percent (2 skills)
   - mixed operations (5 skills)
   - measurement and calculation (6 skills)
   - estimation (1 skill)
2. Communications
   - words and meanings (9 skills)
   - reading (8 skills)
   - writing (3 skills)
   - speaking (3 skills)
   - listening (4 skills)
3. Interpersonal relations
   - work behaviors (10 skills)
   - instructional and supervisory conversations (6 skills)
   - conversations (6 skills)
   - social conversations (4 skills)
4. Reasoning
   - verbal reasoning (16 skills)
   - problem solving (10 skills)
   - planning (14 skills)

Greenan's generalizable skills address areas of deficit common in adolescents with LD: job-related academic skills, job-related social skills, and general problem-solving skills. Academic domains in the curriculum include mathematics, reading, and writing. The job-related social skills identified by Greenan are skills that many students with LD lack. The reasoning skills portion of the curriculum teaches students verbal reasoning, problem solving, and planning skills, each of which has been identified as an area of deficit in adolescents with LD. Because Greenan's skills represent core skills in health; agriculture; business, marketing, and management; industrial education; and home economics, the special educator can address the needs of students enrolled in a variety of vocational programs.

INSTRUCTIONAL STAGES MODELS

Instructional stage models approach transition from a developmental perspective that assumes that transition from school to work progresses in stages. The career development stages are:

1. Career awareness from grades kindergarten through six.
2. Career exploration.
3. Career preparation.
4. Career placement or implementation.

The last three stages occur during the middle and high school years. LeConte (1987) presented an instructional stages model, Figure 11.9, in which job requirements and work

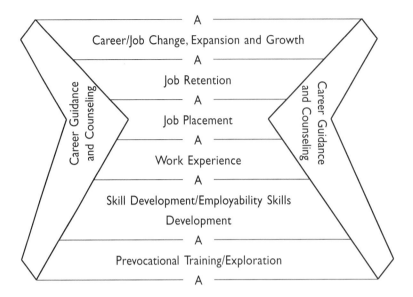

A is an assessment/transition decision point

FIGURE 11.9 LECONTE'S INSTRUCTIONAL STAGES MODEL OF TRANSITION

Source: School-to-Work Transition for At-Risk Youth (p. 18) by S. H. Feichtner, 1989, Columbus, OH: ERIC Clearing-house on Adult, Career, and Vocational Education, Center for Education and Training for Employment, Ohio State University. Used by permission.

patterns require lifelong decision making. LeConte's model considers multiple transition or decision points. The narrowing of the diagram represents the selection of occupational choices and career goals. The least amount of instructional support and preparation are required during job placement. The diagram again widens as the individual becomes aware of additional career opportunities following his or her first job.

A model rather than a curriculum, LeConte's paradigm integrates career and vocational education across the grade levels. An advantage of the model is that it recognizes the need for career education to begin early-on and thus lessens the probability that students with LD will enter high school lacking knowledge of career options.

SUPPORT SERVICES MODEL

Feichtner (1989) defined the support services model as including "planned activities designed to help meet specific academic, social-emotional, training, and daily living needs of the individual when the person requires assistance" (p. 19). One of the best known support services models is that proposed by Will (1984), former Secretary of the Office of Special Education and Rehabilitation Services (see Figure 11.10). Will recognized that, to make the transition from school to work, the students with disabilities (a) may not require special services, (b) may require special services such as vocational rehabilitation or postsecondary training for a time, or (c) may require ongoing services such as supported employment and lifelong mental health support.

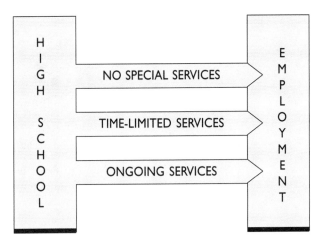

FIGURE 11.10   WILL'S SUPPORT SERVICE MODEL OF TRANSITION

Source: *School-to-Work Transition for At-Risk Youth* (p. 20) by S. H. Feichtner, 1989, Columbus, OH: ERIC Clearing-house on Adult, Career, and Vocational Education, Center for Education and Training for Employment, Ohio State University. Used be permission

The support services model addresses severity of disability. The model helps special educators and other service providers address the needs of students with LD across levels of severity as they make the transition from school to work. Some students with LD require time-limited services such as job coaches or work adjustment counselors, or assistance from agencies such as DVR as they enter the world of work. Students with severe LD may require ongoing services from DVR and long-term supervision as they work in enclaves or mobile work crews. Some students with LD will make the transition from school to employment without the need for support services. Will's model assists us in identifying the system of supports that students require in transition plans.

FUTURES-ORIENTED CURRICULUM MODEL

In addition to the models identified by Feichtner, we add a fourth, the futures-oriented curriculum (Schloss & Smith, 1990). An essential component of this model is the identification of goals and objectives to enable the student to succeed in current and anticipated environments. The student's strengths and weaknesses are assessed, and a record-keeping system is developed to monitor mastery of the objectives. In addition to emphasizing and remedying deficits related to essential skills, prosthetics are developed to enable the student to become less dependent on specific skills.

An advantage of this model is that it promotes maintenance and generalization by focusing on skills reinforced in the natural environment. A difficulty in implementing a futures-oriented curriculum lies in correctly identifying the anticipated environment. Table 11.6 lists the current and anticipated environments in which Jayne, a student with LD, will function.

After environments are identified, a skills checklist is developed similar to the list illustrated in Figure 11.11. Skills to be performed in the community are task-analyzed, and the student is assessed before, during, and after instruction. A system that documents the level of prompt (self-initiated, cue, verbal, modeling, physical assistance) re-

TABLE 11.6   FUTURES-ORIENTED MODEL OF TRANSITION FOR JAYNE

Current and anticipated environments in which Jayne will function:		
Setting	**Current**	**Anticipated By Age 20**
Residential	Home	Sharing an apartment
Vocational	Chores	Veterinary assistant
Transportation	School bus	Public transportation Bus Taxi Trains Planes
	Rides bike	Drives car
School	High school	Vocational training Community college
Leisure	Television VCR	Television VCR Camping Traveling
Consumer	All settings With escort	All settings Independently

Source: "A Futures-oriented Curriculum for Adolescents with Learning Disabilities, by P. J. Schloss and M. A. Smith, 1990, *Learning Disabilities, 1*(3), p. 132. (Reproduced with permission of the Learning Disabilities Association of America.)

quired for skill performance is used during assessment. What makes this model unique is that the student's needs come first, then curricular areas (math, reading, social studies, social skills, and so forth) are matched to skills—not the other way around.

The curriculum in the futures-oriented curriculum model is determined by the goals of the adolescent with LD, which makes this model attractive. The model can be used when developing vocational and transition IEP goals. A potential weakness of this model for students with LD is that many of them lack goal-identification and goal-setting skills and these skills may have to be taught before the student can become involved actively in the planning process.

STRATEGIES TO PROMOTE VOCATIONAL SUCCESS

Three strategies that promote decision making are: (a) the education planning strategy, designed to enable students to take control of their lives by participating in individualized education and vocational and transition planning meetings; (b) the community-based exploration guide, which assists adolescents with LD and their teachers and parents to plan transition activities; and (c) Job Clubs, a job-finding strategy.

EDUCATION PLANNING STRATEGY

The education planning strategy (Van Reusen, Bos, Schumaker, & Deshler, 1987) is a motivational tool students can use when attending IEP, IVP, and ITP meetings, career and vocational planning conferences, and so forth. Using the mnemonic device "I PLAN," the strategy consists of five steps.

Curricular Area(s)	Skill	(Identify Prompt Level)			
		Session Pre-test	Number	Follow-up Post-test	Test
Math/ Reading/ Social Studies/ Personal	I—Prepares to leave home A. Wears appropriate clothes B. Identifies destination C. Selects correct bus route D. Estimates time to leave E. Identifies and locates necessary money				
Math/ Motor/ Social Studies	II—Locates bus stop A. Leaves home on time B. Walks on sidewalk C. Crosses street D. Identifies bus stop area E. Walks to bus stop F. Waits at bus stop				

Reading/ Social Skills/ Motor/ Math	III—Boards bus
	A. Identifies bus as correct
	B. Waits for other passengers to disembark
	C. Waits turn to board bus
	D. Boards bus
	E. Greets driver by
	  1. Offering a greeting
	  2. Making a polite comment
	F. Identifies coins for fare
	G. Pays fare
	H. Locates seat
	I. Sits down				

Prompt Key SI–Self-Initiated C–Cue V–Verbal M–Modeling P–Physical Assistance					

FIGURE 11.11   FUTURES-ORIENTED CURRICULUM: PORTION OF SKILLS CHECKLIST

Source: "A Futures-Oriented Curriculum for Adolescents with Learning Disabilities," by P. J. Schloss and M. A. Smith, 1990, *Learning Disabilities, 1*(3), 133. (Reproduced with permission of the Learning Disabilities Association of America.)

STEP 1. Inventory strengths, weaknesses, goals, and learning choices. Students inventory their skills in the areas of reading, writing, math, study, social skills, and vocational skills using the form provided in Figure 11.12. Skill lists for each of these areas are provided to students to assist them in this effort. The list for vocational skills appears as Figure 11.13. Students formulate school, vocational, extracurricular, and future goals and identify the activities, materials, learning, and testing preferences that will enable them to meet these goals.

STEP 2. Provide inventory information to others at the meeting. During this step students learn when and how to provide information, use the inventory sheet to remember what to say, and make complete statements. In addition, students learn to use SHARE behaviors: Sit up straight, Have a pleasant tone of voice, Activate thinking by telling yourself to pay attention, participate, and compare ideas, Relax by not looking uptight and telling yourself to stay calm, and Engage in eye communication.

STEP 3. Listen and respond to others. Students learn to listen when someone asks a question or makes a statement and to respond by answering questions or adding information in a positive way. Information sheets are used to help students respond in a relevant manner. In addition to the SHARE behaviors, students actively listen, using appropriate body language, paraphrasing, and asking themselves questions. Finally, students are taught how to negotiate an agreement.

STEP 4. Ask questions during the meeting. Students learn when to ask questions—when they need information or they don't understand. They also learn how to ask questions, using "who," "what," "when," "where," "why," "which," or "how" to begin a question, asking complete questions, asking one question at a time, and using their SHARE behaviors.

STEP 5. Name your goals. During this last step students are taught to tell what they want to do and when they want to complete it at the end of the conference.

The authors of the educational planning strategy estimate that it takes from 4 to 6 hours to teach using a modification of the seven-step instructional sequence developed by Deshler and Schumaker (1986). We believe that I–PLAN offers students strategies they can use to become involved more actively in planning for the future.

COMMUNITY-BASED EXPLORATION GUIDE

The community-based exploration guide (CBEG) (Neubert & Foster, 1988a) is a five-step transition planning strategy that takes about 4 weeks to complete. It can be used several times for different transition situations. The CBEG was developed specifically to assist adolescents with LD to make a successful transition from high school to postsecondary training and employment settings. This strategy has the added advantage of promoting collaboration among teachers, parents, and students (N. Elksnin & L. Elksnin, 1990).

STEP 1. Develop an employability profile. Existing assessment data are used to provide information about a student's reading and math skills, expressed and tested vocational interests, dexterity, work habits, and learning style, as well as the student's overall strengths and weaknesses. During this step the student also lists three jobs or postsecondary options he or she would like to explore.

STEP 2. Identify areas to explore. Parents, teachers, and students use occupational information resources such as the Dictionary of Occupational Titles and the Worker Trait

INVENTORY SHEET

1. Strengths

Reading Skills:

_____
_____
_____
_____
_____
_____
_____

Writing Skills:

_____
_____
_____
_____
_____
_____
_____

Math Skills:

_____
_____
_____
_____
_____
_____
_____

Study Skills:

_____
_____
_____
_____
_____
_____
_____

Social Skills:

_____
_____
_____
_____
_____
_____
_____

Vocational Skills:

_____
_____
_____
_____
_____
_____
_____

2. Weaknesses to Improve

_____
_____
_____
_____
_____
_____
_____

_____
_____
_____
_____
_____
_____
_____

(continued)

FIGURE 11.12   INVENTORY SHEET FOR EDUCATIONAL PLANNING STRATEGY

Source: The Educational Planning Strategy (pp. 111–113) by A. K. Van Reusen, C. S. Bos, J. B. Schumaker, & D. D. Deshler, 1987, Lawrence, KS: EXCELL Enterprises. Used by permission.

3. Goals

School Goals:

Academic Goals:

_____
_____
_____
_____

Social Goals:

_____
_____
_____
_____

Vocational Goals:

_____
_____
_____
_____

Extracurricular Goals:

_____
_____
_____
_____

Future Goals:

_____
_____
_____
_____

4. Choices for Learning

Helpful Activities:

_____
_____
_____
_____

Helpful Materials:

_____
_____
_____
_____

Learning Preferences:

_____
_____
_____
_____

Testing Preferences:

_____
_____
_____
_____

FIGURE 11.12   CONTINUED

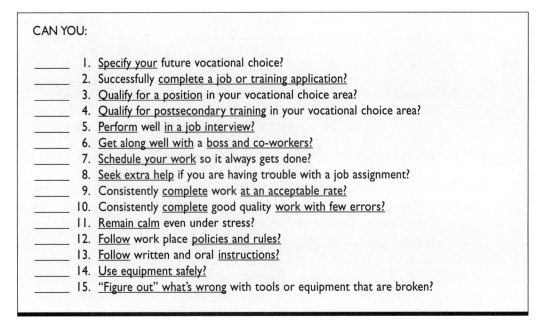

CAN YOU:

_____ 1. <u>Specify your</u> future vocational choice?
_____ 2. Successfully <u>complete a job or training application?</u>
_____ 3. <u>Qualify for a position</u> in your vocational choice area?
_____ 4. <u>Qualify for postsecondary training</u> in your vocational choice area?
_____ 5. <u>Perform</u> well <u>in a job interview?</u>
_____ 6. <u>Get along well with</u> a <u>boss and co-workers?</u>
_____ 7. <u>Schedule your work</u> so it always gets done?
_____ 8. <u>Seek extra help</u> if you are having trouble with a job assignment?
_____ 9. Consistently <u>complete</u> work <u>at an acceptable rate?</u>
_____ 10. Consistently <u>complete</u> good quality <u>work with few errors?</u>
_____ 11. <u>Remain calm</u> even under stress?
_____ 12. <u>Follow</u> work place <u>policies and rules?</u>
_____ 13. <u>Follow</u> written and oral <u>instructions?</u>
_____ 14. <u>Use equipment safely?</u>
_____ 15. <u>"Figure out" what's wrong</u> with tools or equipment that are broken?

FIGURE 11.13   EDUCATIONAL PLANNING STRATEGY

Sources: *The Educational Planning Strategy* (p. 119) by A. K. Van Reusen, C. S. Bos, J. B. Schumaker, & D. D. Deshler, 1987, Lawrence, KS: EXCELL Enterprises. Used by permission.

Group Guide (Appalachian Educational Laboratory, 1978) to explore occupational areas. In addition, the student selects a postsecondary training option of interest such as a 4-year college or university, community college, apprenticeship program, transition program, or vocational training program. At this point, even if the adolescent with LD expresses unrealistic career choices, parents and teachers provide support and encouragement.

STEP 3. Conduct community-based exploration activities. The student conducts an occupational or a postsecondary exploration, or both. Based upon areas of interest, the student identifies job site locations by talking with guidance counselors, friends, and parents, using the telephone book and employment agency references. The following information is obtained about occupational interests: types of jobs available; job duties; salary, benefits, and hours; advancement opportunities; and the application process. The student seeks out the following information about postsecondary training options: contact person, entrance requirements, cost, financial aid, program requirements, application process, and process for obtaining additional information such as a catalog or brochure.

STEP 4. Summarize. The student, parents, and teachers compare the student's profile developed during Step 1 with the job or training requirements identified during Step 3. If a reasonable match is found between the profile and the job or training program, the student proceeds to Step 5. In the case of a mismatch, the student goes back to Step 2 and selects other areas to explore.

STEP 5. Next steps. During the final step the student, parent, and teachers determine the types of strategies the student must use to reach training goals. These identified strategies become part of the IEP, ITP, or IVP. Neubert and Foster (1988b) recommend that these guidelines be used when developing a plan of action:

- Determine if relevant vocational training programs are offered in the school district.
- Contact appropriate personnel to determine if the student could become involved in a work-study program.
- Contact appropriate personnel to determine prerequisite requirements a student must meet to enter postsecondary training.
- Identify academic, social, and independent living skills the student has to have.
- Identify support systems the student will require to make a successful transition to employment or postsecondary training.

JOB CLUBS: A JOB-FINDING STRATEGY

Many students with LD lack the strategies required not only to select an occupation but also to find a job (N. Elksnin & L. Elksnin, 1988; L. Elksnin & N. Elksnin, 1991). Job Clubs offer an alternative conceptualization of job finding. The traditional paradigm of the employment process is as follows:

1. A job becomes available.
2. A job is advertised.
3. The prospective employer contacts the prospective employee.
4. The most qualified applicant obtains the job.

Nathan Azrin and his colleagues (Azrin & Besalel, 1980; Jones & Azrin, 1973) regard job finding as an exchange of social reinforcers rather than matching a worker's skills with an employer's job requirements. This alternative paradigm regards the employment process as an informal network that may be *more* dependent on factors unrelated to a worker's skills, such as ability to bond with the employer, than the applicant's training or skills. For example, Jones and Azrin (1973) found that individuals found out about more than two thirds of jobs from friends, acquaintances, and relatives.

The *Job Club* was developed by Azrin to teach the job seeker how to access the informal job information network. Rather than a solitary activity, job hunting becomes a social activity with the Job Club providing social support as well as expanding the job seeker's social network. Some evidence suggests that the Job Club is a more effective method of locating and securing employment than traditional employment counseling. In one study 93% of Job Club clients found jobs, compared to 60% of clients receiving vocational and career counseling (Azrin, Flores, & Kaplan, 1975).

The Job Club has eight major principles:

Principle 1.   Job-search skills are broken down into behaviorally defined steps.
Principle 2.   Job seeking is regarded as a full-time job, and the job seeker plans a structured job-seeking schedule.
Principle 3.   Job leads are obtained systematically through relatives and acquaintances. Job Club participants are taught how to use the telephone as the

primary contact for job leads, as well as how to gain access to more traditional job leads such as the yellow pages and the want ads.

Principle 4. Job seekers meet as a group, and members offer support and assistance to one another.

Principle 5. Job seekers learn to emphasize their personal characteristics through open letters of recommendation, resumes, and applications.

Principle 6. Job seekers learn to emphasize nonemployment-derived work skills.

Principle 7. Job seekers receive training and practice in traditional job-seeking skills such as interviewing, resume and letter writing, and filling out applications.

Principle 8. Job seekers keep progress charts, and data are used to evaluate performance and to determine if job-seeking behavior should change (L. Elksnin & N. Elksnin, 1991, p. 218).

The student first learns how to find job leads by developing lists of relatives, former co-workers, classmates and school acquaintances, friends and acquaintances, as well as newspaper help wanted ads and the telephone directory. The Reminder List of Friends and Acquaintances from Azrin and Besalel's *Job Counselor's Manual* appears as Figure 11.14. A similar format can be used to help the student keep track of job leads.

The student then learns *how to arrange interviews*. The Job Clubs model takes an aggressive approach to interviews. Rather than waiting to be called for an interview, the student learns how to approach the prospective employer by:

— writing a telephone script to ask for job leads.
— rehearsing telephone conversations with friends and relatives asking for job-finding assistance.
— prompting relatives and friends regarding potential job contacts by asking: "Are any companies expanding?" "Do you know someone at work who is leaving?" and so forth.
— making face-to-face contacts with friends, relatives, and acquaintances.
— contacting former employers.
— telephoning a prospective employer to obtain an interview using the following strategy:
   1. Introduce yourself.
   2. Ask for the name of the department head.
   3. Address the department head by name, and introduce yourself.
   4. Give your qualifications.
   5. Ask for interview.
   6. If he or she says no, ask for interview just in case opening occurs later.
   7. If he or she still says no, ask for other job leads.
   8. Ask for permission to use his or her name for leads.
   9. Ask for time to call back in case opening occurs.

Other steps in the job-finding process taught directly to students include time management and schedule planning, applying for the job, soliciting letters of recommendation, completing an application form, and interviewing. Students are taught to empha-

For each of the following activities, list the names of friends with whom you shared that activity at one time or another. They need not be your "best friend," as long as you know them well enough for them to remember you. Under each activity, list as many such acquaintances as you can, as long as they live or work in the general area where you would consider working.

People I have invited to my house, such as for parties or dinner: _____
_____   _____   _____
_____   _____   _____
_____   _____   _____

People who have invited me to their house: _____
_____   _____   _____
_____   _____   _____
_____   _____   _____

People who belong to a club with me: _____
_____   _____   _____
_____   _____   _____
_____   _____   _____

People I play or watch sports with: _____
_____   _____   _____
_____   _____   _____
_____   _____   _____

Roommates I've had: _____
_____   _____   _____
_____   _____   _____
_____   _____   _____

People I know from my neighborhood: _____
_____   _____   _____
_____   _____   _____
_____   _____   _____

People I have dated, double-dated with, or gone out with: _____
_____   _____   _____
_____   _____   _____
_____   _____   _____

People I send greeting cards to or receive them from: _____
_____   _____   _____
_____   _____   _____
_____   _____   _____

People who have the same hobby I do: _____
_____   _____   _____
_____   _____   _____
_____   _____   _____

People I've done a favor for or who did me a favor: _____
_____   _____   _____
_____   _____   _____
_____   _____   _____

People I've gone out with, such as to the movies, bowling, or card playing: _____
_____   _____   _____
_____   _____   _____
_____   _____   _____

People in my place of worship: _____
_____   _____   _____
_____   _____   _____

FIGURE 11.14   JOB CLUB MANUAL: REMINDER LIST OF FRIENDS AND ACQUAINTANCES

Source: Job Counselor's Manual: A Behavioral Approach to Vocational Counseling (pp. 156, 157) by N. H. Azrin and V. B. Besalel, 1980, Austin, TX: Pro-Ed. Used by permission.

size personal information relating to their backgrounds, special interests, hobbies, and families, as well as their educational achievements and employment skills, when applying for jobs. They also learn to solicit open letters of recommendation and how to ask reference people to address specific issues in their letters of support. Rather than regarding interviews as stressful and as vehicles only to secure a specific job, the student learns to approach the interview as predictable and as an opportunity to secure additional job leads and present information. Finally, the student becomes comfortable with the interview process by learning how to dress appropriately, anticipate questions, and preparing an information folder.

Azrin and Besalel's (1980) *Job Club Counselor's Manual* is designed for counselors working with adult populations; however it can be modified easily for use with adolescents with LD. In addition, the manual contains many useful forms that simplify the housekeeping involved in running a Job Club.

SUMMARY, ISSUES, AND CHALLENGES

Adolescents with LD often lack career awareness, have job-related academic skills deficits, and have job-related social skills deficits that may impede their successful transition from high school to work. Based upon the characteristics of successful adults with LD and employer and employment demands, secondary school programs should promote problem solving, decision making, and the ability to self-advocate.

NEED TO RETHINK SECONDARY SPECIAL EDUCATION PROGRAMMING

As students with LD entered secondary schools, special educators responded by developing and implementing secondary programs that grew out of elementary models. Consequently, program development failed to take into consideration where we would like students with LD to be when they exit school. In the future we will have to take a more outcome-based approach to secondary vocational programming. We will need to develop futures-oriented programs that enable students to reach their goals as well as meet the demands of vocational and employment settings. We also must acknowledge the need to create programs and provide instruction that will promote students' independence, as well as develop their ability to solve problems and make decisions.

The effect of learning strategies upon students' academic achievement has been well documented by Deshler and his colleagues at the University of Kansas, but application of these strategies to vocational curricula has received little attention. Many of the reading comprehension, notetaking, and test-taking strategies would seem equally applicable to vocational content. These strategies need not be limited to academic classes. Specific strategies should be designed for vocational classes. For example, Evers and Bursuck (1992) designed a self-questioning strategy to enable students to complete woodworking projects successfully. In addition, they modified generic strategies for use in vocational settings. For example, the original CANDO strategy (Ellis, Lenz, & Sabornie, 1987) was modified for technical class use:

C = Create a list of parts for the machine or piece of equipment.
A = Ask self if the list is complete.
N = Note if these parts contain smaller parts within.
D = Describe each part and how it relates to operation of the machine.
O = Overlearn the main parts and then the smaller parts.

RECOGNITION OF LACK OF ACCESS TO VOCATIONAL PROGRAMS

Despite passage of the Carl D. Perkins Act, many adolescents with LD are denied access to vocational programs (Cobb & Neubert, 1992). Lack of access may be traced to several factors. One reason may be a conflict between the goals of the special educator and those of the vocational educator. Special educators may focus on IEP objectives unrelated to skills required for vocational programs, or teach "academics for academics sake" rather than teaching these skills within a vocational context. Students' nonacademic behaviors may interfere with participation in vocational programs. Special educators must become familiar with vocational curricula and program requirements by collaborating more closely with vocational educators and also must convince vocational educators that information can be obtained in ways other than the printed word and ways to demonstrate competence other than paper-and-pencil tests.

Many students with LD have poor reading skills and learn to perform skills through modeling and coaching. Paper-and-pencil tests do not assess students' skill mastery adequately if the student's poor reading and writing skills get in the way. For example, a student may be able to repair a small motor, yet perform poorly on a paper-and-pencil test on small engine repair.

Students with LD also may be denied access to programs, even if they have appropriate academic skills and behavior, because the vocational education teacher's goals may be at odds with those of the special educator. We are interested in meeting the student's individual needs. Vocational educators are interested in high program completion rates and successful job placements. In some states programs are funded based upon the number of "completers" and the number of students placed in jobs successfully following training. Some vocational educators perceive students with LD as not being good risks for completion and placement. To change that perception, special educators have to produce qualified students and to change the perception by some vocational educators that students with LD are not capable.

NEED TO RETHINK VOCATIONAL PROGRAMMING

Special educators cannot continue to train students narrowly for specific jobs, as the average worker probably will be retrained an average of six times during his or her working career. Some jobs will not exist in the future. For example, programs that trained individuals to become keypunch operators have become obsolete. We must train our students to solve problems and make decisions. Cain and Taber (1987) addressed this need.

> Today's vocational education programs...tend to be overly preoccupied with academic instruction and student achievement. Further, the measurement of academic success is

Q & A

TRANSITION PLAN

Q: *My high school is in the process of developing a transition plan to help our students with LD make the transition from school to work. We're not sure how to start. Are any guidelines available?*

A: The most important thing to remember is that *transition* is a *process* of having students make a successful move from high school to employment or postsecondary training. Much of the work in the area of transition was begun by leaders in the field of mental retardation, and transition models for students with LD are still evolving. Between 1984 and 1990 the federal government funded 75 projects focusing on LD transition issues. After reviewing nine exemplary projects, Rojewski (1992) identified seven essential components:

1. Individualized planning.
2. Vocational preparation, to include systematic vocational assessment, job exploration, vocational counseling, and vocational skills training.
3. Academic remediation of academic deficits affecting vocational performance.
4. Vocational and academic counseling, which may include social support, social skills, instruction, and advocacy training.
5. Identification and coordination of support systems and services such as vocational rehabilitation and JTPA.
6. A structured job-seeking curriculum that includes activities such as interviewing, filling out applications, writing a resume, obtaining job leads, and so forth.
7. Follow-up and/or follow-along studies that determine program effectiveness and student support needs.

As you and your colleagues begin to develop your plan, consider these "best practices in transition" for students with LD. The list makes it clear that, to develop effective transition plans, cooperation among professionals representing a wide variety of disciplines (special education, vocational education, guidance, school psychology, vocational rehabilitation, etc.) must occur.

too often concerned with the memorization and mastery of subject matter and with test-taking performance skills. Problem-solving, decision-making, and critical thinking skills have tended to receive less emphasis in these programs even though these skills are of the utmost importance to achieving functional success as an adult. (p. 183)

NEED TO CHANGE ATTITUDES

For our students to participate more fully in vocational programs, teachers must attempt to change attitudes. Attitude change may have to begin at the personal level. Many teachers are covertly biased against vocational education. Increasing knowledge is a first step toward changing our attitudes. Acknowledging that many students with LD will be unable or unwilling to obtain postsecondary training after exiting high school will assist teachers in designing programs and adopting curricula that are better suited to these students' goals. In sum, perceptions of students with LD can be changed by: (a) providing information about LD, (b) appropriately preparing students based upon vocational program demands, (c) recommending students who are *qualified* for programs, and (d) helping vocational educators make appropriate curricular and instructional modifications.

Many employers have a limited understanding of LD and may be hesitant to employ students following vocational training. Although ADA is intended to eliminate employment discrimination toward people with disabilities, special educators can improve employers' attitudes by increasing their knowledge of LD and showing that students with LD can perform competently on the job. Interviewing employers to identify valued employee behavior will help special educators design relevant secondary programs.

Special educators also should work with parents to enable them to develop realistic career goals for their son or daughter with LD. If parents (and students) look upon vocational education unfavorably, they may consider it an inappropriate option for their child. Career education that begins during the primary grades and involves parents will foster the development of realistic goals.

Teacher Preparation Issues

Although strides have been made during the last decade to emphasize vocational education as part of secondary programming, many special education teacher preparation programs continue to be weighted in favor of elementary models. Educational assessment courses, for example, rarely address career and vocational issues and tend to be restricted to assessment of academic performance. Vocational educators rarely receive training in learning disabilities and general special education. At the preservice level, special education programs should include more formal coursework focusing on career and vocational education. At the inservice level, special educators can overcome a lack of knowledge about vocational education by collaborating with vocational educators. We need to ask ourselves continually, "What is the goal of programs for adolescents with LD?" What we say and what we teach must be congruent if we are to enable students with LD to make a successful transition to employment following high school.

References

Agran, M., Martin, J. E., & Mithaug, D. E. (1989). Achieving transition. *Teaching Exceptional Children, 22*(2), 4–7.

Albright, L., & Cobb, R. B. (1988). *Assessment of students with handicaps in vocational education: A curriculum-based approach*. Alexandria, VA: American Vocational Association.

Air Force Human Resources Lab. (1985, 1989). *Armed services vocational aptitude battery—Forms 14, 15, 16, 17*. San Antonio, TX: Brooks Air Force Base.

American Psychiatric Association. (1994). *Diagnostic and statistical manual of mental disorders–IV*. Washington, DC: Author.

American Vocational Association. (1968). *Definitions of terms in vocational, technical, practical arts education*. Washington, DC: Author.

Appalachian Educational Laboratory. (1978). *Worker trait group guide*. Bloomington, IL: McKnight.

Aring, M. K. (1993). What the 'V' word is costing America's economy. *Phi Delta Kappan, 74*, 396–404.

Azrin, N. H., & Besalel, V. B. (1980). *Job counselor's manual: A behavioral approach to vocational counseling*. Austin, TX: Pro-Ed.

Azrin, N. H., Flores, T., & Kaplan, S. J. (1975). Job-finding club: A group assisted program for obtaining employment. *Behavior Research and Therapy, 13*, 17–27.

Becker, R. L. (1988). *Reading-free vocational interest inventory–Revised*. Columbus, OH: Elbern Publications.

Bellamy, G. T., Rhodes, L. E., Mank, D. M., & Albin, J. M. (1988). *Supported employment: A community implementation guide*. Baltimore: Paul H. Brookes.

Bennett, G. K., Seashore, H. G., & Wesman, A. G. (1982). *Differential aptitude tests*. San Antonio, TX: Psychological Corp.

Brolin, D. E. (1989). *Life centered career education: A competency based approach* (3d ed.). Reston, VA: Council for Exceptional Children.

Brown, D. S., Gerber, P. J., & Dowdy, C. (1990). *Pathways to employment for people with learning disabilities*. Washington, DC: President's Committee on Employment of People with Disabilities.

Brown, K. W. (1976). What employers look for in job applicants. *Business Education Forum, 30*(7), 7.

Brown, J. M., Asselin, S. B., Hoerner, J. L., Daines, J., & Clowes, D. A. (1992). Should special needs learners have access to tech-prep programs? Examining tech-prep initiatives for special needs programming. *Journal for Vocational Special Needs Education, 14*(2, 3), 21–26.

Bursuck, W. D., & Rose, E. (1992). Community college options for students with mild disabilities. In Rusch, F. R., L. Destefano, J. Chadsey-Rusch, L. A. Phelps, & E. Szymanski (Eds.), *Transition for school to adult life: Models, linkages, and policy* (pp. 71–91). Sycamore, IL: Sycamore Publishing.

Cain, E. J., Jr., & Taber, F. M. (1987). *Educating disabled people for the 21st century*. Boston: Little, Brown.

Chadsey-Rusch, J. (1990). Teaching social skills on the job. In F. R. Rusch (Ed.), *Supported employment: Models, methods, and issues* (pp. 161–180). Sycamore, IL: Sycamore Publishing.

Clark, G. M., & Kolstoe, O. P. (1990). *Career development and transition education for adolescents with disabilities*. Boston: Allyn & Bacon.

Cobb, R. B. (1983). A curriculum-based approach to vocational assessment. *Teaching Exceptional Children, 15*, 216–219.

Cobb, R. B., & Neubert, D. A. (1992). Vocational educational models. In F. R. Rusch, L. Destefano, J. Chadsey-Rusch, L. A. Phelps, & E. Szymanski (Eds.), *Transition from school to adult life: Models, linkages, and policy* (pp. 93–113). Sycamore, IL: Sycamore Publishing.

Council for Exceptional Children. (1978). *Position paper on career education*. Reston, VA: Author.

Deshler, D. D., & Schumaker, J. B. (1986). Learning strategies: An instructional approach for low-achieving adolescents. *Exceptional Children, 52*, 583–590.

Dowdy, C. A., Smith, T. E. C., & Nowell, C. H. (1992). Learning disabilities and vocational rehabilitation. *Journal of Learning Disabilities, 25*, 442–447.

Elksnin, L. K. (1992). Career, vocational, and transition assessment. In G. Wallace, S. C. Larsen, & L. K. Elksnin, *Educational assessment of learning problems: Testing for teaching* (2d ed.) (pp. 402–458). Boston: Allyn & Bacon.

Elksnin, L. K., & Elksnin, N. (1989). Readability of vocational interest inventories: Implications for the vocational assessment of handicapped students. In G. F. Elrod (Ed.), *Career education for special needs individuals: Learning, earning, contributing* (pp. 41–51). Reston, VA: Council for Exceptional Children.

Elksnin, L. K., & Elksnin, N. (1990). Using collaborative consultation with parents to promote effective vocational programming. *Career Development for Exceptional Individuals, 13*, 135–142.

Elksnin, L. K., & Elksnin, N. (1991). The school counselor as job search facilitator: Increasing employment of handicapped students through Job Club. *School Counselor, 38*, 215–220.

Elksnin, L. K., & Elksnin, N. (1995). *Assessment and instruction of social skills*. San Diego: Singular Publishing.

Elksnin, N., & Elksnin, L. K. (1988). Improving job-seeking skills of adolescents with handicaps through job clubs. *Career Education for Exceptional Individuals, 11*, 118–125.

Elksnin, N., & Elksnin, L. K. (1991). Facilitating the vocational success of students with mild handicaps: The need for job-related social skills training. *Journal for Vocational Special Needs Education, 13*, 5–11.

Elksnin, N., & Elksnin, L. K. (1992). Life after high school: Promoting effective transition for the adolescent with learning disabilities (pp. 191–203). In F. R. Brown, E. Aylward, & B. K. Keogh (Eds.), *Diagnosis and management of learning disabilities: An inter-disciplinary/lifespan approach*. San Diego: Singular Press.

Ellis, E. S., Lenz, B. K., & Sabornie, E. J. (1987). Generalization and adaptation of learning strategies to natural environment: Part 1. Critical agents. *Remedial and Special Education, 8*, 6–20.

Evers, R., & Bursuck, W. (1992, October). *Creating successful students in vocational classes: How resource room teachers can help*. Paper presented at International Conference of Council for Learning Disabilities, Kansas City, MO.

Feichtner, S. H. (1989). *School-to-work transition for at-risk youth*. Columbus, OH: Ohio State University, ERIC Clearinghouse on Adult, Career, and Vocational Education, Center on Education and Training for Employment.

Gaylord-Ross, R. (Ed.). (1988). Vocational education for persons with handicaps. Mountain View, California: Mayfield Publishing.

Geist, H. (1988). *The Geist picture interest inventory, revised*. Los Angeles: Western Psychological Services.

Gerber, P. J., Ginsberg, R., & Reiff, H. B. (1992). Identifying alterable patterns in employment success for highly successful adults with learning disabilities. *Journal of Learning Disabilities, 25*, 475–487.

Ghazalah, I. A. (1991). *1979 vocational education graduates in 1986: A longitudinal study based on federal income tax data*. Athens: Ohio University.

Greenan, J. P. (1983). *Identification of generalizable skills in secondary vocational programs (executive summary)*. Urbana-Champaign: Illinois State Board of Education.

Greenan, J. P. (1986). Curriculum and assessment in generalizable skills instruction. *Journal for Vocational Special Needs Education, 9*(1), 3–10.

Greenan, J. P. (1987). Generalizable skills instruction. In G. D. Meers (Ed.), *Handbook of vocational special needs education* (2d ed., pp. 275–313). Rockville, MD: Aspen.

Greenan, J. P., & Smith, B. B. (1981). *Assessing the generalizable skills of postsecondary vocational students*. Minneapolis: University of Minnesota, Research and Development Center for Vocational Education.

Harrington, T. F., & O'Shea, A. J. (1984). *The guide for occupational exploration* (2d ed.). Circle Pines, MN: American Guidance Service.

Hippolitus, P. (1987). *College freshmen with disabilities: Preparing for employment*. Washington, DC: President's Committee on Employment of the Handicapped.

Holland, J. L. (1985). *The self-directed search*. Odessa, FL: Psychological Assessment Resources.

Hursh, N. C., & Kerns, A. F. (1988). *Vocational evaluation in special education*. Boston: Little, Brown.

Idol, L., Paolucci-Whitcomb, P., & Nevin, A. (1986). *Collaborative consultation*. Austin, TX: Pro-Ed.

Jastak, J. F., & Jastak, S. (1979). *Wide range interest-opinion test*. Wilmington, DE: Jastak Associates.

Jones, R. L., & Azrin, N. H. (1973). An experimental application of a social reinforcement approach to the problem of job-finding. *Journal of Applied Behavior Analysis, 6*, 345–353.

Karpinski, M. J., Neubert, D. A., & Graham, S. (1992). A follow-along study of postsecondary outcomes for graduates and dropouts with mild disabilities in a rural setting. *Journal of Learning Disabilities, 25*, 376–385.

Kranstover, L. L., Thurlow, M. L., & Bruininks, R. H. (1989). Special education graduates versus non-graduates: A longitudinal study of outcomes. *Career Development for Exceptional Individuals, 12*, 153–166.

Kuder, G. F., & Diamond, E. E. (1985). *Occupational interest inventory, Form DD*. Monterey, CA: CTB-McGraw Hill.

Laurie, T. E., Buchwach, L., Silverman, R., & Zigmond, N. (1978). Teaching secondary learning disabled students in the mainstream. *Learning Disability Quarterly, 1*(4), 62–72.

LeConte, P. (1987, October). *Vocational assessment for vocational education: A comprehensive model*. Paper presented at Fourth International Conference of Division of Career Development, Nashville, TN.

Marland, S. P. (1971). *Career education now*. Speech presented January 23 to convention of National Association of Secondary School Principals, Houston, TX.

Materials Development Center. (1977). *Work sample manual format*. Menomonie, WI: Author, University of Wisconsin-Stout.

Meers, G. D. (Ed.). (1987). *Handbook of vocational special needs education* (2d ed.). Rockville, MD: Aspen.

Meers, G. D. (1992). Getting ready for the next century. *Teaching Exceptional Children, 24*(4), 36–39.

Moon, M. S., Inge, K. J., Wehman, P., Brooke, V., & Barcus, J. M. (1990). *Helping persons with severe mental retardation get and keep employment*. Baltimore: Paul H. Brookes.

Neubert, D. A., & Foster, J. (1988a). *Community-based exploration guide.* Washington, DC: George Washington University Department of Teacher Preparation and Special Education.

Neubert, D. A., & Foster, J. (1988b). Learning disabled students make the transition. *Teaching Exceptional Children, 20*(3), 42–44.

Nighswonger, W. (1981). *Talent assessment program.* Jacksonville, FL: Talent Assessment.

O'Brien, J., & Stern, D. (1988). Economic issues in employing persons with disabilities. In R. Gaylord-Ross (Ed.), *Vocational education for persons with handicaps* (pp. 257–295). Mountain View, CA: Mayfield Publishing.

Okolo, C. M., & Sitlington, P. (1986). The role of special education in LD adolescents' transition from school to work. *Learning Disability Quarterly, 9,* 141–155.

Rojewski, J. W. (1992). Key components of model transition services for students with learning disabilities. *Learning Disability Quarterly, 15,* 135–150.

Rosenthal, I. (1989). Model transition programs for learning disabled high school and college students. *Rehabilitation Counseling Bulletin, 33*(1), 54–66.

Sarkees, M., Batsche, C., & McCage, R. (1986). Nexus between competency-based education and vocational planning for students with handicapping conditions: A model. *Career Development for Exceptional Individuals, 9,* 42–49.

Schloss, P. J., & Smith, M. A. (1990). A futures-oriented curriculum for adolescents with learning disabilities. *Learning Disabilities, 1*(3), 128–136.

Sitlington, P. L. (1986). *Transition, special needs, and vocational education.* Columbus: Ohio State University, National Center for Research in Vocational Education.

Smith, J. O. (1992). Falling through the cracks: Rehabilitation services for adults with learning disabilities. *Exceptional Children, 58,* 451–460.

U.S. Department of Education. (1991). *Combining school and work: Options in high schools and two-year colleges.* Washington, DC: Office of Vocational and Adult Education.

U.S. Department of Education. (1992). *Fourteenth annual report to Congress on the implementation of the Individuals with Disabilities Act.* Washington, DC: Division of Innovation and Development.

U.S. Department of Labor. (1977). *Dictionary of occupational titles* (4th ed.). Indianapolis: JIST Works.

U.S. Department of Labor. (1986). *Dictionary of occupational titles—fourth edition supplement.* Indianapolis: JIST Works.

U.S. Department of Labor. (1990–91). *Occupational outlook handbook.* Washington, DC: Government Printing Office.

U.S. Department of Labor. (1991, June). *What work requires of schools: A SCANS report for America 2000.* Washington, DC: Author.

U.S. Department of Labor. (1992, April). *Learning a living: A blueprint for high performance: A SCANS report for America 2000.* Washington, DC: Author.

U.S. Employment Service. (1982a). *General aptitude test battery.* Washington, DC: Government Printing Office.

U.S. Employment Service. (1982b). *Nonreading aptitude test battery.* Washington, DC: Government Printing Office.

VALPAR International Corporation. (1981). *Valpar component work sample system.* Tucson, AZ: Author.

Van Reusen, A. K., Bos, C. S., Schumaker, J. B., & Deshler, D. D. (1987). *The educational planning strategy.* Lawrence, KS: EXCELL Enterprises.

Vocational Research Institute. (1976). *Jewish employment and vocational services work sample system.* Philadelphia: Author.

Wagner, M. (1989, March). *The transition experiences of youth with disabilities: A report from the national longitudinal transition study.* Paper presented at meeting of Division for Research, Council for Exceptional Children, San Francisco.

Wallace, G., Larsen, S. C., & Elksnin, L. K. (1992). *Educational assessment of learning problems: Testing for teaching* (2d ed). Boston: Allyn & Bacon.

Wehman, P., & Kregel, J. (1988). Adult employment programs. In R. Gaylord-Ross (Ed.), *Vocational education for persons with handicaps* (pp. 205-233). Mountain View, CA: Mayfield Publishing.

Wehman, P., Sale, P., & Parent, W. (1992). *Supported employment: Strategies for integration of workers with disabilities.* Boston: Andover Medical Publishers.

West, L. L., Corbey, S., Boyer-Stephens, A., Jones, B., Miller, R. J., & Sarkees-Wircenski, M. (1992). *Integrating transition planning into the IEP process*. Reston, VA: Council for Exceptional Children.

Whitman, D. (1989, June). The forgotten half. *U.S. News & World Report*, pp. 45–53.

Will, M. (1984). *OSERS programming for the transition of youth with disabilities: Bridges from school to working life*. Washington, DC: Office of Special Education and Rehabilitative Services.

Wilms, W. W. (1984). Vocational education and job success: The employer's view. *Phi Delta Kappan, 65*, 347–350.

Wirt, J. G. (1991). A new federal law on vocational education: Will reform follow? *Phi Delta Kappan, 72*, 424–433.

Woolridge, A. (1993). Human capital around the world. *Effective school practices*, Winter, pp. 47–59.

Zigmond, N. (1990). Rethinking secondary school programs for students with learning disabilities. *Focus on Exceptional Children, 23*, 1–22.

12

Collaborative Teaming in the Secondary School

E. ANN KNACKENDOFFEL

QUESTIONS TO KEEP IN MIND

- What is collaborative teaming? Why is it important for a teacher of adolescents with learning disabilities?

- How can I bring along a person who resists my collaborative efforts?

- What is collaborative problem solving? When is it appropriate, and how can I use it in my role as a member of a collaborative team?

- What are some of the roles and responsibilities of key people involved in collaborative teaming?

- How can collaborative teaching be structured for different types of situations (e.g., students, classes, teachers)?

- Is conflict inevitable when I work with others? How can I avoid conflict, or should I even try?

ADVANCE ORGANIZER

Few "expert teachers" of adolescents with LD work alone. Actually these teachers intentionally design interventions for delivery by many professionals working together. That's because they know two heads are better than one—and several heads are better yet. The whole of the combined efforts then is greater than the sum of its parts. Professionals working together on behalf of adolescents with learning difficulties decrease the likelihood that those students will become "system casualties." Services for at-risk students often are most effective when teachers pool their expertise and creative energies (Dettmer, Thurston, & Dyck, 1993).

Collaborative teaming is integral to specialists in learning disabilities in a secondary setting. There are major concerns that secondary educators have when working with other professionals to deliver services to students with learning disabilities. These issues involve roles and responsibilities, how to facilitate partnership-building skills with other adults, the nuts and bolts of various collaborative teaching models such as cooperative teaching, and how to solve problems that arise in collaborative structures. Figure 12.1 shows how this chapter has been organized.

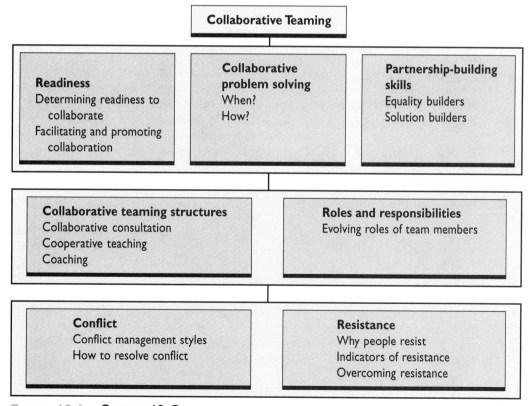

FIGURE 12.1   CHAPTER 12 ORGANIZATION

INTRODUCTION

Team or group approaches have long been a valued part of the special service professions and have become increasingly popular structures for addressing highly diverse issues in schools. The term *collaborative teaming* seems to embody this concept of working together. Knackendoffel, Robinson, Deshler, and Schumaker (1992) described collaborative teaming as an ongoing process whereby educators with different areas of expertise work together voluntarily to create solutions to problems that are impeding students' success, as well as to carefully monitor and refine those solutions. In short, the major goal of collaborative teaming is to improve services to students whose needs are not being met satisfactorily when professionals act alone rather than in concert with others.

The most productive collaborative relationships are characterized by mutual trust, respect, and open communication. Central to these relationships are the following beliefs:

1. All participants in the collaborative relationship must have equal status.
2. All educators can learn better ways to teach all students.
3. Educators should be involved continuously in creating and delivering instructional innovations.
4. Education improves when educators work together rather than in isolation. Effective collaborative relationships involve people who see themselves on the same side, working toward positive outcomes for students.

Collaborative teaming is a process rather than a specific service delivery model. For example, a general education teacher and a special education teacher may teach cooperatively in the same class setting with each taking on different instructional responsibilities depending on their individual strengths. In another teaming situation two teachers may get together regularly for cooperative planning purposes. In yet another scenario three special education teachers working in resource programs may team to coordinate group instruction and share students on their caseloads. In some schools, prereferral teams engage in collaborative teaming as they generate possible interventions for a student having difficulty in content classes.

Because collaborative teaming means people working together in a supportive and mutually beneficial relationship, its possibilities and different configurations are truly endless. This is not meant to imply that anything goes and can be passed off as teaming. Friend and Cook (1992) lamented that collaboration has become the buzzword of the 1990s and often is used carelessly to merely give the appearance of being in step with the latest educational innovations. The adolescents with whom we work are too important for us to simply go through the motions of collaboration to satisfy a school district's initiative or the latest educational trend. Friend and Cook (1992) identified what they refer to as *defining characteristics* of collaboration, which more fully explain what collaboration means. These are listed as follows:

1. *Collaboration is voluntary.* Education agencies can mandate administrative arrangements that require the staff to work in close proximity, but only the individuals involved can decide if their interactions will be truly collaborative.

2. *Collaboration requires parity among participants.* Each person's contribution to an interaction is valued equally, and each person has equal power in decision making. If one individual is perceived by others as having more power or more valuable knowledge or information, collaboration cannot occur.

3. *Collaboration is based on mutual goals.* To collaborate, professionals do not have to share many or all goals, just one that is specific and important enough to maintain their shared attention.

4. *Collaboration depends on shared responsibility for participation and decision making.* Equal participation in the decision making is important, but shared participation in task completion does not mean that tasks must be divided equally among involved individuals or that each must participate fully in all tasks. Participation in the activity often involves a convenient division of labor.

5. *Individuals who collaborate share their resources.* Each person engaged in a collaborative activity has resources to contribute that will be valuable for reaching the shared goal. The type of resources professionals have depends on their roles and the specific activity. Example resources include time and availability to carry out tasks, knowledge of a specialized technique, and access to other individuals or agencies that could assist in attaining the goal.

6. *Individuals who collaborate share accountability for outcomes.* Whether the results of collaboration are positive or negative, all the participating individuals are accountable for outcomes.

The term *emergent characteristics* of collaboration describes characteristics that must be present to some discernible degree at the outset of collaborative activity, and also emerge and grow when successful collaboration occurs. These are as follows:

1. *Individuals who collaborate value this interpersonal style.* Collaboration is difficult but rewarding. Individuals involved must believe that the results of their collaboration are likely to be more powerful and significant than the results of their individual efforts, or else they are unlikely to persevere. Typically, success leads to increased commitment to future collaboration.

2. *Professionals who collaborate trust one another.* Only after a period of time in which trust, and subsequently respect, are established can school professionals feel relatively secure in fully exploring collaborative relationships.

3. *A sense of community evolves from collaboration.* A sense of community is the perception that by interacting collaboratively, all participants' strengths can be maximized, their weaknesses can be minimized, and the result will be better for all. The willingness to work toward a common goal is accompanied by a decrease in concern about individual differences.

The benefits of collaboration do not come without risks. Collaboration is not accomplished easily, nor will teachers find it appropriate for every situation. Colleagues may not share one's enthusiasm. When collaborative efforts result in trusting relationships with colleagues and positive outcomes for students, however, the risks seem a small price to pay.

COLLABORATIVE TEAMING READINESS

If there is one obstacle to successful collaboration that will derail even the best developed plan, it is forcing collaboration between unwilling teachers. The decision to collaborate has to be made by the teachers who are involved and supported by the administration (Harris et al., 1987; Warner, 1990). The goal is always to move ahead in collaborative efforts. In your attempts to work with others, you will encounter various degrees of readiness to collaborate. Assessing where you are on the "relationship continuum" with the other person can help you choose realistic goals based on the colleague's level of readiness for collaborative teaming. In addition, this type of assessment can be useful in helping you determine how to best promote better relationships and move a colleague forward in your collaborative efforts.

If a relationship is nonexistent with the other party, the person may be hostile, indifferent, or apathetic, or this might be a person with whom no previous contact has existed. In any case the goal is to develop an amicable relationship with the person through social interaction or working together on committees or projects, sharing information or teaching ideas that might be of interest to the person. Lunching together or getting a cup of coffee after school provides other potential opportunities. This is not the time to push a specific agenda but, rather, to build a social relationship gradually with the person as a foundation for building a working relationship.

Sometimes only a social relationship exists with the other person (i.e., you might have social contact with the person but rarely engage in professional discussions). At this level the goal is to move into mutual discussion of work-related issues. For instance, when an opportunity arises, the colleague could be asked about some issue that the school board is debating or the colleague's opinion about the school's move to block scheduling could be solicited. The colleague might be asked about cooperative groupings or issues related to grading.

Often, what might be described as a "limited work relationship" exists. This can involve two types of people. One type asks for assistance but doesn't follow through. The second type discusses problems when they are brought up but seems unwilling to participate in finding solutions. It is important to attempt to determine why the person will not accept suggested solutions. Does the person feel alienated by the other person's attitude or behavior? Does the solution itself involve something with which the person feels uncomfortable? Once the underlying problem in the relationship has been discovered, the task is to develop strategies that will remove the problems and allow for more productive collaboration. If this fails, the problem may have to be reassessed and new solutions developed that will satisfy the other person's concerns.

In some cases, you may find that the person is willing to work with you as long as you initiate the contact but does not seem to recognize when to ask for assistance. The task at this stage is to work with the teacher in recognizing and identifying problems suitable for collaboration so the person will initiate future contacts. The person might be given a form such as the one in Figure 12.2 to indicate when assistance is needed.

When you are working with a colleague who initiates contact, identifies problems, and helps to develop and implement solutions, think about how this person can assist in

ASSISTANCE NEEDED

Teacher _____ Today's Date

Student _____

_____

Other _____

- [ ] There's a problem. Let's put our heads together.
- [ ] I need your help in the classroom.
- [ ] Develop alternative assignment or activity.
- [ ] Arrange cooperative learning groups & activities.
- [ ] Implement peer tutoring or peer partners.
- [ ] Produce alternative materials or locate resources.
- [ ] Develop a modified grading system.
- [ ] Create a study guide.
- [ ] Modify materials.
- [ ] Modify a test.
- [ ] Develop guided notes.

- [ ] Plan a lesson.
- [ ] Team teaching.
- [ ] Classroom management.
- [ ] Instructional strategies.

When? _____

Additional information:

_____

_____

_____

_____

FIGURE 12.2   ASSISTANCE REQUEST FORM

your efforts to develop better relationships with other teachers desired for the team but who may be at a lower level on the readiness scale. The teacher should be encouraged by being asked to work more closely with another staff member. This person's opinions should be solicited and respected.

Finally, after you have established a strong collaborative relationship with a colleague, you often find that the teacher not only seeks out assistance when needed but also becomes an active advocate of the teaming approach with other potential collaborative teachers. At this level the teacher believes strongly in your role, values your contribution, and is willing to help you expand to other settings. The collaborative relationship has become truly reciprocal.

Readiness to collaborate and team with one another is influenced by interactions. If a teacher is at a low level of readiness and is not progressing, the problem may reflect a lack of the other teacher's collaboration skills or may be the result of situational factors beyond the control of the other teacher. This may not be the other person's "fault." Some collaboration strategies are:

1. Treat others with respect. Demonstrate your respect for their ideas by really listening and letting them know they were heard.
2. Let others know that you appreciate their cooperation and value their expertise and knowledge.
3. Demonstrate through your actions that you deserve their trust.
4. Acknowledge the realities of the teacher's situation (large number of students, limited time, diverse student abilities, etc.).
5. Deemphasize your contribution to the collaborative process—"one-downmanship" (West, Idol, & Cannon, 1989).
6. Give others credit for their ideas and contributions.
7. Listen, listen, listen.
8. Use situational leadership; adjust your leadership style to the other person's needs (Idol, Paolucci-Whitcomb, & Nevin, 1986).
9. Use focusing statements to indicate that you not only have listened to your colleague's concerns but also are willing to incorporate them into the solution (Knackendoffel, Robinson, Deshler, & Schumaker, 1992) .
10. Communicate that the other teacher is free to accept or reject any recommendations.

COLLABORATIVE PROBLEM SOLVING

Nearly everything we do as learning disabilities specialists can be considered as some type of challenge or problem to be solved. At the heart of collaborative teaming is problem solving. Teachers engage in problem solving when they identify students, place them in programs, and decide on appropriate interventions. Teachers independently problem solve when they make decisions about scheduling or setting priorities in structuring a program. When the decision making is shared with others, problem solving becomes collaborative. Teachers engage in collaborative problem solving in team meetings and with individual colleagues to determine how to adapt instruction to meet students' needs.

Collaborative problem solving is fundamental to successful interactions with colleagues. And, though the steps to collaborative problem solving (Knackendoffel, Robinson, Deshler, & Schumaker, 1992) presented here may seem straightforward, their complexity lies in their skillful implementation (Cummings, Murray, & Martin, 1989). This involves a number of technical skills that are crucial to productive problem solving. The skills can be learned through practice. The relationship built with the other person determines, to a great extent, one's ability to problem-solve successfully.

Although the technical skills involved in problem solving are important, the way in which they are used and the tone and tenor of the meeting are equally important. A positive collaborative relationship must be developed across a series of problem-solving sessions. When a trusting or respectful relationship has been established using the partnership-building skills discussed in this chapter, the problem-solving process will help colleagues jointly structure an effective solution-finding session.

Before engaging in a full-blown problem-solving process like the one described here, the teacher has to determine if the problem-solving process is necessary. Sometimes a colleague simply may need to talk about a situation. In these cases the teacher's main responsibility is to be a good listener. Friend and Cook (1992) suggested asking oneself the following questions to determine whether undertaking collaborative problem solving is warranted:

1. Are the individuals who have responsibility and resources for addressing the problem committed to resolving it?
2. What might happen if nothing is done to resolve the problem?
3. Does the problem warrant the effort and resources that will be required to effect significant change?
4. Are adequate time and resources available to resolve the problem?

In some cases the answers to these questions might steer the teacher away from the problem-solving process. Perhaps the problem is beyond the control of the people who are interested in addressing it. Maybe some preliminary work on strengthening the relationship has to take place before approaching the problem with a colleague. On the other hand, the teacher may decide that collaborative problem solving does seem appropriate for the situation and it would be time well spent. Teachers who find themselves helping someone solve a problem must recognize that their role is to assist in solving the problem, not to solve the problem. This means helping the person: understand the problem situation, generate alternative solutions, evaluate each alternative solution, select the best solutions for the problem, implement the solution, evaluate the outcomes, and make adjustments as needed. Solving the problem for the other person shifts the whole tenor of the situation away from collaborative teaming. Avoiding behaviors that the other person would interpret as directing or controlling is critical.

If the colleague senses that the teacher is overly dominating, two scenarios are possible: (a) the person is likely to avoid similar interactions in the future or (b) may become dependent on the other teacher. Neither of these outcomes is desirable when the overall goal is for two parties to be working in collaboration on behalf of a student.

The problem-solving process—described only briefly here—is detailed in the manual developed by Knackendoffel, Robinson, Deshler, and Schumaker (1992) entitled, *Collaborative Problem Solving: A Step-by-Step Guide to Creating Educational Solutions*. The steps outlined in this process should enable a teacher to avoid prescribing a solution while helping the colleague participate actively in the problem-solving process. These steps structure the problem-solving sessions and transform them from advice giving to collegial or collaborative solution-finding exchanges.

The Problem-Solving Worksheet in Figure 12.3 can be used to facilitate problem-solving sessions. It serves as a reminder of the problem-solving steps and provides a structured guide for taking notes during the session. The problem-solving process involves a series of 13 steps that will enable teachers to avoid prescribing a solution while helping colleagues participate actively in the problem-solving process.

Step 1: *Define the problem*. A clear definition of the problem is critical to the remainder of the problem-solving process. Many people fail to arrive at effective solutions because they did not define the problem clearly. You want to arrive at one specific problem statement.

Step 2: *Gather specific information about the problem*. Gather as much information as possible to clarify the problem. Use active listening skills to get the other person to share information. The first two steps go hand-in-hand. You may need to gather information before coming up with a problem statement, or you may need to rewrite the problem statement after you have gathered additional information.

Step 3: *Explain problem-solving process, and state its usefulness*. Explain the process so your colleague has an overview of what is to follow. This may facilitate the process and prevent the potential problem of "shooting down" ideas during brainstorming, and thus stifling generation of further possible solutions (i.e., if your partner begins to tell you why a potential solution won't work during brainstorming phase of the process, you will be able to refer to the process that you agreed to follow and the importance of withholding judgment until all possible solutions are on the table for consideration).

Step 4: *Identify alternative solutions*. Use brainstorming to stimulate ideas. Finding a good solution is difficult and requires much thought. Initial solutions seldom are adequate. Begin by asking the other person for possible solutions. Offer your ideas in an open-ended fashion. All ideas should be treated with respect, and you should avoid negative or positive evaluation of any solution at this stage.

Step 5: *Summarize solutions*. When finished generating solutions, summarize all of the solutions you have written down and ask for any additional ideas before moving on.

Step 6: *Analyze possible consequences*. Go through the list of solutions one at a time, discussing possible consequences of each. Consider benefits, problems, practicality, time, and effort. Give each solution careful and serious consideration. Discuss possible consequences based on knowledge of best instructional practice. Don't write advantages and disadvantages on the Problem-Solving Worksheet. Just discuss them.

Step 7: *Rate each solution*. After analyzing consequences of all the solutions, review them one at a time, determine how satisfactory your colleague finds each solutions, and express your satisfaction with each solution. Combined Steps 6 and 7 so the pros and cons of each solution are fresh in your minds during the rating process (i.e.,

PROBLEM-SOLVING WORKSHEET

Problem-solving team members: Role:

  Mark Wilson   Science Teacher

  Linda Ryan   English Teacher

Student: Date:

Jason Roberts, Camra Stevens & Pete Hall   October 20

Step #1
  Problem:

> Jason, Camra and Pete are failing chapter tests.
> They need information from the textbook.

Step #2
  Details:

  Chapter test scores range from 40 to 50%. Tests mainly factual; given every other week; most information comes from textbooks. Students need to get information from tests. Some time to read in class; some outside reading needed.

Step #4   Step #7
Alternative solutions: Ratings:

Alternative solutions:	Exc.	Fair	Poor
1. Make study guides to go with chapters.	x		
2. Have students study in pairs.		x	
3. Tape record chapters.			x
4. Make special markings in selected textbooks.	x		
5. Have students read parts of chapters and share main ideas with other students.	x		
6. Schedule after-school study sessions.			x

Step #8
  Solution to be tried first:

  Give students a study guide and have them share information.

(continued)

FIGURE 12.3   COMPLETED PROBLEM-SOLVING WORKSHEET

Source: Adapted from *Collaborative Problem Solving: A Step-by-Step Guide to Creating Educational Solutions*, by E. A. Knackendoffel, S. M. Robinson, D. D. Deshler, & J. B. Schumaker, 1992, Lawrence, KS: Edge Enterprises. Copyright 1992 by Edge Enterprise. Adapted by permission.

Step #11

Implementation steps:	When	Who
1. Make up study guide for next chapter.	Thurs., 10/22	Mark
2. Make copies of study guide for all students.	Fri., 10/23	Mark
3. Assign chapter reading to all students.	Mon., 10/26	Mark
4. Have students hare information in class at 10:30.		Linda/ Mark
5. Continue sharing activity throughout unit.	10/28-11/8	Students/ Mark
6. Meet with Jason, Camra, & Pete and have them set goals.	10/26	Mark

Step #12

How will the plan be monitored?

Mark will give a copy of the study guide to Linda on Fri., 10/23; finalize plans for Tues., 10/27. On the afternoon of the 26th, Mark & Linda will discuss morning's activities; on 11/9 they'll meet to review test results.

What are the criteria for success?

Jason, Camra, and Pete to obtain a "C" grade on their chapter tests.

Step #13

Date and Time of Next Appointment: Tues., 10/27 and Mon., 11/9

FIGURE 12.3   CONTINUED

discuss advantages and disadvantages of first solution and then immediately rate that solution before moving on to discussion of second solution).

Step 8: *Select best solution*. Make mutual commitment to one solution. Give the list of rated solutions to your colleague, and ask which is the best one based on the ratings and your discussion of pros and cons and best instructional practice. You may choose to combine two closely rated and compatible solutions.

Step 9: *Determine satisfaction with chosen solution*. After selecting a solution, ask your colleague if he or she is satisfied with the selection. Don't make the mistake of trying to push a solution through persuasion. If the solution is not chosen freely, chances are that it will not be carried out. If none of the solutions is satisfactory, go back to generating more solutions.

Step 10: *State support for decision*. Show your support of the chosen solution. Your colleague needs to feel not only that you accept his or her choice, but also that you will be there to help implement the solution.

Step 11: *Develop plan of action*. Jointly specify tasks required to implement the chosen solution. Indicate who will be responsible for completing each task and a time frame for completion. This process gives you a clear plan of action and eliminates later questions concerning who is responsible for each step. It encourages accountability.

Step 12: *Develop monitoring system and specify criteria for success.* Include dates on which progress checks will be made and what is expected to be completed by those dates. Simple monitoring systems that require minimal time work best. Specify the criteria for success to avoid later misunderstandings and to be sure that both parties share the same expectations.

Step 13: *Schedule next appointment.* Schedule a follow-up appointment, and make a copy of the completed Problem-Solving Worksheet for your colleague. Along with encouraging action, follow-up sessions prevent the other person from feeling abandoned or alone in the struggle. The tone of the follow-up session should be one of reporting progress, encouragement, and fine-tuning the plan rather than checking-up on your colleague's progress.

Research on the collaborative problem-solving process (Knackendoffel, 1989) indicated that some general guidelines to ensure that the problem-solving process is effective. First, the problem-solving facilitator must insist on specificity. When confronted with a problem, people often make vague statements that do not specify what the student is doing that is inappropriate or what the student has to do to be successful in the setting where the problem is occurring.

The second guideline has to do with problem ownership. During field-testing of this process, LD teachers learning the process were quick to take ownership of problems. When discussing shared students with learning disabilities, the special education teacher seemed to feel responsible for solving any problems associated with that student. This does not foster collegial or collaborative management of the education of adolescents with learning disabilities.

The third guideline involves the brainstorming technique used in generating potential solutions. Both participants should refrain from immediately evaluating solutions as they are generated. Each solution is put on the table before evaluating its utility. For a number of reasons, this procedure is more effective than evaluating each solution as it is contributed. By making a list of potential solutions and evaluating them in relation to each other, personal attachments to and investments in certain solutions are minimized. This also eliminates problems that can arise when a person discounts every solution as it is mentioned by saying, "I don't think that will work" or "I've already tried that, and it doesn't work."

Finally, concrete plans are necessary. Often a solution is agreed upon, but without specific implementation and monitoring plans, it dies a quick death. Research on the change process shows clearly that people underestimate the amount of assistance and follow-up required to implement new ways of doing things (Fullan, 1982; Joyce, Bennett, & Rolheiser-Bennett, 1990). Plans stipulating who will implement certain parts of the solutions, when tasks are to be completed, and when and how progress will be evaluated are helpful to ensure that the solution is carried out.

The problem-solving worksheet is provided in Figure 12.3. It shows how a completed problem-solving worksheet might look and highlights the problem-solving steps with the corresponding parts of the worksheet.

PARTNERSHIP-BUILDING SKILLS

Most teachers spent little, if any, time in teacher preparation classes learning how to work with other adults. Yet teachers in today's schools rarely work in isolation. Increasingly, collaboration skills will be called upon as part of the teacher's daily job function. Strong interpersonal communication skills are as important to special education teachers as is knowledge of remedial and compensatory techniques. Beyond basic communication skills in areas such as active listening and effective questioning techniques, more subtle partnership-building skills can influence the long-term relationship between two professionals.

To take a professional relationship beyond the superficial level that often develops between teachers in the same building requires a commitment to build a long-term, productive, problem-solving partnership with the colleague.

Reaching the goal of a productive partnership is predicated upon a few basic principles. First, in a professional partnership the partners view themselves as being professionally equal and treat each other as professional equals. They respect and acknowledge each other's talents, skills, and expertise, and they value what the other person can bring to the partnership in terms of knowledge, ideas, skills, and perspective. Finally, they take care to protect the partner's feelings of competence and self-esteem (Knackendoffel, Robinson, Deshler, & Schumaker, 1992).

Partnership-building skills fall under two general categories: equality builders and solution builders. *Equality builders* are behaviors that enable the parties to be equals in their interactions. Special education teachers entering the domain of general education teachers easily fall into the role of an advice giver—or at least can be perceived that way. Offering advice is a natural reaction to a problem. Therefore, equality-building skills are particularly important during interactions that seem to invite advice giving. The goal is to give up a position of superiority. Instead, the special educator's statements should indicate that the colleague is an equal and has valued ideas and concerns. Examples are:

> "I'm glad you mentioned that concern. I hadn't thought of it from that perspective."

> "I really value this chance to work with you. I've seen that you put a great deal of care into what you do in the classroom."

> "You're the expert on your subject and this group of students, so I trust you to know best."

> "That must be a frustrating situation for you. I know it would be for me."

These statements convey the attitude of working together side-by-side. They also acknowledge the other teacher's expertise and show that the special educator can relate personally to what is being said while not using the situation as an opportunity to tell his or her own story.

Although some disagreement exists in almost any professional partnership, an accepting atmosphere can be established by avoiding criticizing, blaming, and disapproving statements and actions. Criticism only creates barriers between professionals and may ultimately sabotage a relationship. Sincere compliments and statements of appreciation also can facilitate partnership building. As a cautionary note, compliments sometimes create a feeling that the complimenting person is acting in a superior role or is trying to manipulate the person with false praise. Likewise, empathic statements, if used incorrectly, might be unproductive. For example, an empathic statement might be used as a lead to tell a story about one's own success in a similar situation. Some examples of what *not* to say are:

"I said from the beginning that I didn't think it would work."

"You know, you're one of the few people in this school who really know what teaching is all about."

"I know exactly how you feel. John Jones did something like that in my class last year, and I came up with the perfect way to handle the situation. Let me tell you what I did..."

"I know you're really angry at Kyle, and that's the reason you're having trouble thinking of solutions. You can't let your anger take over your logic."

Another set of partnership-building skills, *solution builders*, are needed when creating positive solutions with a colleague. Attempts to push a solution on the other person are likely to be rejected, either openly or surreptitiously, by the other party. Although the other party may state that the solution is acceptable, the opposite may be revealed in failure to carry through on responsibilities related to carrying out the solution. To arrive at mutually acceptable solutions, both partners must be convinced that the solution meets the needs of all parties involved. Personal investment in solutions and being right have no place in the collaborative problem-solving process.

Really listening to a colleague's concerns is important. Those concerns then can be incorporated into the chosen solution. An example is, "You're concerned about the message other students will receive if Paul doesn't seem to have to do as much as the other students. Let's see if we can find a solution that involves treating all students in a way they perceive as fair." By listening carefully and thinking about what this colleague is saying, the special education teacher can search for areas of agreement and communicate those areas of common ground: "Having a solution that requires Kathy to take responsibility for her work is something I can really support."

Immediately disagreeing with a colleague's suggestion focuses the discussion on the points that separate the two. If the colleague hears some agreement, he or she will feel affirmed and will be more willing to listen to the other's concerns and ideas. The words of the person offering an idea should show willingness to examine the solution and, if necessary, to discard or adjust it: "Here's an idea for us to consider. You've said that Bill doesn't believe he can succeed. What about a solution that includes making Bill aware of his poor beliefs about himself as a learner?" Whatever solution is chosen, ideally it should include instructional practices based on established learning principles. A good solution is based on what we know about best practice with at-risk students.

Diverting the discussion is one of the most common ways to switch a conversation from a colleague's concerns to a topic of one's own choice. Even if done unintentionally, such responses can communicate noninterest in the colleague's concerns. Another unfortunate tactic that teachers may be tempted to use when they don't agree with a colleague's solution is logical argument. Attempting to convince the other person by citing facts or logic without considering the emotional factors involved or clearly understanding the other party's concerns likely will fail. A logical argument presented at the wrong time can make the colleague defend his or her position more strongly. Rather than convincing the other person, it creates resistance, provokes defensiveness, and elicits counter-arguments and, thus, ultimately alienates the colleague.

Offering solutions to someone is a delicate matter. Solutions can be offered in ways that offend people. If the solution does not address the colleague's concerns adequately, he or she might feel that the other person was not truly listening. If the solution is offered in a way that indicates it is set in stone, the colleague may feel that the other person is acting in a superior role and not allowing any other say in the matter.

The partnership-building skills discussed here are not all-inclusive. They cover a few of the skills that are most critical when working with a colleague. Effective use of partnership-building skills and avoidance of the barriers does not happen overnight. Through self-examination and evaluation after each collaborative interaction, however, special educators should be able to improve their collaboration skills.

STRUCTURING COLLABORATIVE TEAMING ARRANGEMENTS

There probably are as many ways to arrange collaborative teaming structures as there are teams of teachers. Successful teams, however, do share common elements and avoid certain traps that can defeat even the best of intentions. Here we offer some personal insights and examples that have worked for other collaborating teachers. These starter techniques provide a basis for designing a personal blueprint for successful teaming.

COLLABORATIVE CONSULTATION

One service delivery approach known as *collaborative consultation* (Idol, Paolucci-Whitcomb, & Nevin, 1986) involves providing the general education content teacher with multidisciplinary planning support in an effort to improve the quality of instruction for LD students in their content classes. This approach engages the special educator in cooperative planning with the content teacher but not directly in actual program implementation. The general education teacher maintains primary responsibility for the delivery of instruction. This might be the option of choice when:

— the class contains only a few students with LD.
— targeted students can function relatively independently in the academic setting (because of the mild nature of their learning disability or success with previous intervention programs such as learning strategies).
— when general and special education teachers have been engaged in a cooperative

teaching arrangement for some time and think they are ready to phase out the direct service delivery program option.

— the special educator has limited time compounded by a large caseload.

Many special educators believe that collaboration means being in the classroom where the LD students are placed and being involved in cooperative teaching. Certainly this is one option, but it is not feasible, or even necessary in all situations. Teachers can collaborate with staff outside the cooperative teaching model in many ways. Through cooperative planning and collaboration, they can share information about students' learning strengths and weaknesses and possible teaching strategies and accommodations that might prove beneficial. A peer coaching technique might be used to share a teaching routine that the content teacher could implement in the class, or the special education teacher might do some demonstration teaching on a one-time or short-term basis to help the content teacher implement a new teaching technique in a class (Robinson & Knackendoffel, in prep.).

COOPERATIVE TEACHING

A special education teacher may be in a situation in which a large number of "high-need" students are enrolled in a class required for graduation. These two factors—the sheer number of students and their intense levels of needed educational services—may necessitate moving beyond collaborative consultation to a cooperative teaching model. *Cooperative teaching* (or co-teaching) is an approach in which general and special educators teach students jointly in educationally integrated settings (Bauwens, Hourcade, & Friend, 1989; Robinson & Knackendoffel, in prep.).

Cooperative teaching is a direct and complementary outgrowth of the collaborative consultation model described by Idol, Paolucci-Whitcomb, and Nevin (1986). Specifically, in cooperative teaching arrangements two or more educators (for our purpose, a general education teacher and a special education teacher) are present simultaneously in the content class and maintain joint responsibility for the instruction in the general education classroom. They have mutual ownership, pooled resources, and joint accountability. This approach has gained considerable popularity at the secondary level because it capitalizes on the specific and unique skills each professional brings to the classroom. General education teachers, as a group, are knowledgeable about curriculum and appropriate scope and sequence in traditional academic areas. They also know how to manage large groups of students for instruction. Special educators traditionally have been trained to target areas of difficulty within a curriculum and can analyze and adapt materials and strategies for instruction. Individualized instruction is almost second nature to most special educators.

Thus, the two professionals working together can bring a wealth of skills to the cooperative teaching arrangement. Each teacher's level of participation varies depending on the individual teachers' strengths and preferences, content being taught, and composition of students in the class.

Several different options are possible when arranging cooperative teaching. Three that will be discussed here are (a) team teaching, (b) supplemental learning activities, and (c) complementary instruction. Any of these approaches can be combined in a given situation and, therefore, should not be seen as mutually exclusive. Two teachers may start out using the supplemental learning activities model but after time feel comfortable enough with one another to engage in team teaching. Likewise, while team teaching, a teacher may discover the need to move into complementary instruction for a portion of the class period. Based on the skills and preferred styles of the teachers, they need to discover what will best accommodate the teaming situation. What works with one teacher with one group of students doesn't necessarily work in another classroom or with another teacher. Successful teaming means personalizing the approach for each situation.

TEAM TEACHING

Team teaching involves both the general educator and the special educator planning and teaching the academic subject content jointly to all students in the class. At various times, one teacher might assume primary responsibility for specific types of instruction or portions of the curriculum. For example, during a social science class, the special educator might introduce the lesson using an advance organizer and preteach key terms that will be used in the lecture and reading using direct instruction procedures. This might be followed by the general education teacher presenting a lesson on the causes of the Civil War.

When team teaching both teachers might share teaching responsibilities, shadow the other's teaching, or do a combination of both. Team teaching can be carried out in a number of ways. In practice, one teacher might be talking while the other is providing examples using an overhead transparency or chalkboard, or when preparing for instruction one teacher prepares the lecture while the other prepares study guides or cognitive maps to guide the instruction. Another example of team teaching is teachers' taking turns with lesson preparation to change the pacing and focus while the other monitors. Finally, one teacher can lecture to the class while the other provides examples to help clarify key points. Team teaching should not be confused with "turn-teaching" (I teach, you teach— back-and-forth). Team teaching can be described more accurately as teaching *in concert* with one another. It is more than merely going back and forth between two instructors who teach in the same classroom.

For team teaching to be most effective, thoughtful planning and coordination are important. When mapping out the lesson, the teachers can discuss places in the lesson where one teacher will model while the other speaks, or where one teacher will demonstrate while the other explains. Much of effective team teaching is also spontaneous and intuitive. If one teacher can try to see and hear the other teacher through the eyes and ears of the students, he or she might be able to determine if the pace is appropriate, when clarification is needed, or if recall can be facilitated by using a pause/discuss procedure (Ruhl, Hughes, & Schloss, 1987). Team teaching may be especially applicable at the secondary level when the LD specialist is certified in a specific content area where the cooperative teaching is occurring.

SUPPLEMENTAL LEARNING ACTIVITIES

Using the *supplemental learning activities* approach to cooperative teaching, general and special educators plan and deliver instruction together in the general education classroom. Under this arrangement the content teacher maintains primary responsibility for delivering the essential content, while the special education teacher is responsible for developing and implementing supplementary learning activities. These supplementary learning activities might include things such as cooperative learning (Johnson & Johnson, 1986; Rottier & Ogan, 1991; Slavin, 1986), peer tutoring (Jenkins & Jenkins, 1981; Miller, Kohler, Ezell, Hoel, & Strain, 1993), the pause/discuss procedure activity (Ruhl, Hughes, & Schloss, 1987), role plays, simulations, partner reading, numbered heads, learning games, center work, debates, and so on.

An example of a supplementary learning activity arrangement might look something like this. During cooperative planning two teachers agree that a certain skill in an English class should be taught to all students in their shared class. Together they determine which supplementary learning activities would be most appropriate for reinforcing the skill (e.g., peer tutoring, projects, cooperative learning). The English teacher then would introduce the content initially and the LD specialist would be responsible for the development and implementation of whatever supportive learning activities the two had agreed upon to reinforce the new content.

COMPLEMENTARY INSTRUCTION

One final example of a cooperative teaching structure that is particularly well suited for the secondary level is *complementary instruction*. Using this approach, the content teacher maintains primary responsibility for teaching the specific academic content while the special education teacher teaches the critical academic survival or learning skills necessary to acquire the content. These survival skills might include things such as notetaking, paraphrasing, outlining, memorizing, listening, and a host of learning strategies such as test taking, word identification, error monitoring, and so on.

Academic survival skills can be addressed with the entire class at the beginning of a lesson, throughout the presentation, or in a review at the conclusion of the lesson. If any students do not need this specialized complementary instruction, the content teacher could assign and monitor enrichment activities based on previously covered material while the remaining students are involved in the survival skills instruction. Besides deciding *when* during the period to instruct in survival skills, another consideration is *how often*? A teacher may prefer to provide academic survival skills instruction on a regularly scheduled basis (such as once a week, 3 days per week, or other schedule).

Complementary instruction differs from the supplemental learning activities approach in that in complementary instruction the content teacher takes responsibility for delivering the academic content (the "what" of learning) while the LD specialist in this case teaches the students "how to learn" (academic survival skills) or acquire the content. In contrast, with the supplemental learning activities approach the content teacher introduces the essential academic content of the lesson while the LD specialist develops supplementary activities to enrich the academic content, thereby aiding in the students' learning and retention of the information.

Complementary instruction traditionally has occurred in support class settings where the students with learning disabilities were pulled out for specialized instruction. One of the drawbacks of delivering specialized instruction in segregated special education settings is that students typically don't generalize newly acquired skills to the content class without deliberate efforts to teach for generalization. The benefit to the complementary instruction approach is that students are more likely to use the academic survival skills immediately and therefore see the need and benefit in learning the skills, thus increasing the motivation to learn and the probability of generalization.

Part of the appeal of cooperative teaching, besides the generalization issue, is that all students are more likely to receive appropriate educational programs, regardless of whether they meet the strict identification guidelines for a documented learning disability. Through cooperative teaching more individualized teaching becomes possible and each teacher is able to capitalize on his or her unique skills. Teachers using this arrangement have the added benefit of coaching one another so they begin to share the same language and a body of teaching information that will benefit them in a wide variety of teaching situations. Through cooperative teaching educators are able to minimize the need for more traditional special education pull-out programs when students have diagnosed learning disabilities (Bauwens, Hourcade, & Friend, 1989).

COACHING

One of the major misconceptions about teaching is that it is a relatively commonplace, easy-to-learn profession. In truth, planning for and carrying out instruction involves complex cognitive processes. Research shows that most teacher planning and decision making are on-line and spontaneous (Borko, Livingston, & Shavelson, 1990). Further, teachers tend to think in terms of activities, not objectives. To assist teachers in planning and adapting instruction for adolescents with learning disabilities, special educators have to understand the dynamics of this "on-the-spot" decision making. For most of us trained in special education, this represents a radical shift from the traditional short- and long-term objective model in which instructional planning is based on first specifying the objectives and then choosing carefully sequenced learning activities to meet these objectives.

This new body of research has clear implications for communication between special and general educators. Much of the emphasis has to be on assisting teachers with on-the-spot decisions regarding students with learning problems in the general education classroom. Communication has to be rooted in concrete images of more effective instructional practice—not so much in words as in concrete images (Gersten, 1990).

Aspects of the coaching model articulated by Joyce and Showers (1983) seem to be an excellent means of sharing this type of concrete, expert knowledge. *Coaching* is the process of giving teachers structured feedback about the instructional skills they used in a particular lesson (Cummings, 1985). Although some (e.g., Garmston, 1987) have made distinctions between different types of coaching (e.g., technical, collegial, and challenge coaching), the basic idea in a peer coaching situation is that teachers are engaged in instructing, training, and tutoring one another. Coaching typically involves numerous observations of classroom practice, followed by discussions (largely informal) of the observations. Often the person involved in coaching—in this case, the LD specialist—will model a teaching technique or strategy. Observations often center on a specific instructional practice with which the teacher is experimenting (Showers, 1985).

By its very nature coaching is concrete. It is rooted in the world of the classroom and the language of instruction, not the language of behavior management and psychopathology (Gersten, 1990). Those involved in coaching can model not only instructional techniques but also procedures for checking for student understanding during the lesson.

Coaches actually can model on-the-spot decision making. Sharing effective instructional methodologies is a process rather than a single act or event wherein a person merely tells another about a given teaching routine.

A major goal of collaboration with general education teachers should be to increase their expertise in working with students who have special learning needs in their classes. Coaching seems to have great potential for accomplishing this goal. When special educators share an instructional technique or strategy with a collaborating teacher, they must consider the complexity of the change process. To illustrate this point, consider when teachers have learned alternative teaching strategies through traditional theory/demonstration/practice staff development training designs. In studies in which half of the participants were assigned to "coaching" follow-up training programs while the remaining teachers were left on their own to implement the new teaching strategy, the coached teachers exceeded their uncoached comparison group in implementation of the new strategies by a dramatic margin. About 80% of the coached teachers transferred the new strategies to their active teaching repertoires, compared with about 10% of the uncoached teachers (Showers, 1990).

If colleagues are to adopt a new teaching strategy as part of their teaching repertoire, they must plan deliberately for this change process. Robinson and Knackendoffel (in prep.) suggested several key steps in the coaching process:

Step 1: Set stage for collaboration, and introduce teaching routine.
Step 2: Gain commitment to listen to teaching routine.
Step 3: Describe teaching routine.
Step 4: Model teaching routine.
Step 5: Gain commitment to try teaching routine.
Step 6: Offer assistance for initiating the routine.
Step 7: Collaborate on effectiveness of routine in content class.
Step 8: Provide for maintenance and adoption of teaching routine.

Systematic implementation of this process is designed to increase the likelihood that the new teaching routine will be adopted.

In many ways the process is analogous to an apprenticeship. Suggestions to colleagues should be clear, and they must be achievable (Rosenholtz, 1989). Often, in the role as the coach, modeling or demonstrating the alternative instructional strategy is appropriate. Quickly the learning teacher takes an active role in using the new technique while the coach assumes the role of facilitator, encouraging the teacher in implementing the teaching routine.

DEFINING ROLES AND RESPONSIBILITIES

Particularly in the infancy stage of setting up cooperative teaching programs, the special education teacher should choose to work with a person who has a similar philosophical orientation and teaching style. Down the road, with some experience and confidence, the special educator might be more adventuresome or take on the challenge of working with a teacher whose approach to teaching is much at variance.

The process should begin by selecting basic skill classes (e.g., English, Math) or required classes at the secondary level, such as American history, that all students must take to graduate. By choosing these classes, teachers will be able to reach the maximum number of targeted students. From the pool of teachers responsible for these classes, the choices can be narrowed by first thinking about the teachers who may be most open to collaboration. Teachers may be tempted to select teachers they think could benefit most from having a special education teacher in their classes (marginal teachers who are instructionally weak, teachers who are known for teaching only one way, or classes where LD students historically have had difficulty). Although the motive behind this plan may be good, the teacher runs the risk of failure. A better approach is to target strong teachers initially to engineer successful collaboration.

Once the class(es) and teachers targeted for the collaborative teaching model have been decided, the next step is to schedule students into the classes. When collaborative classes exist in a school, the temptation always is to overload these classes with high-risk students. Besides scheduling into the class students with identified learning disabilities, other students who may not have qualified for special education but nevertheless could benefit from this type of program may be placed there. Certainly this practice is well intentioned, but care must be taken not to upset the applecart. To maintain a balance and prevent the class from becoming a dumping ground or viewed as a special education class, a rule of thumb is to allow no more than 30%–50% of the composition to be learners with special needs (Nowacek, 1992). This includes the students identified for special education as well as others who have special learning needs.

Hand-scheduling is a must during this phase of preparation. It can be one of the most frustrating and difficult hurdles to overcome. Even though the class will have two teachers, collaborative classes should *not* be larger than average. In addition to scheduling students on the special educator's caseload into the collaborative class(es), these students also will have to be scheduled for resource or support classes when needed. Unfortunately, the more the teacher is involved in collaborative teaching, the less time is available for resource support, which presents yet another scheduling problem. With fewer options for scheduling students into the resource program, resource periods will become larger in terms of total number of students. This is not necessarily a negative factor, because teachers may discover that they can use the time in the support class more efficiently, as they will be working with these students throughout the day in their collaborative classes.

Also, teachers may find they can work with the other special education teachers in the school to staff a resource room more consistently throughout the day (i.e., instead of two special education teachers being scheduled in the resource room during one period, one of the teachers might run the support class and provide direct service while the other is involved in cooperative teaching or collaborative teaming activities). Figure 12.4 shows three examples of how special education teachers at three different secondary schools coordinated their schedules.

Sometime before the first day of class, the teacher should meet with the collaborating team members to discuss and plan the program. Some teachers spend up to a year preparing to work as a team and creating collaborative teaching structures. Others seem to be thrown together almost haphazardly and meet only a few times before starting the

Example #1: Middle School Special Education Teacher Schedules

Period	Teacher A	Teacher B
1	Collaborative teaming	Direct service
2	Direct service	Collaborative teaming
3	Plan with 7th grade teams	Direct service
4	Lunch and plan	Direct service
5	Collaborative teaming	Lunch and plan
6	Direct service	Plan with 8th grade teams
7	Direct service	Collaborative teaming

Example #2: Middle School Special Education Teacher Schedules

Period	Teacher A	Teacher B
1	Cooperative teaching (7 ENG)	Direct service
2	Direct service	Cooperative teaching (8 MATH)
3	Team plan/Collaborative teaming	Direct service
4	Lunch and plan	Direct service
5	Cooperative teaching (7 SS)	Lunch and plan
6	Direct service	Team plan/Collaborative teaming
7	Direct service	Cooperative teaching (8 ENG)

Example #3: High School Special Education Teacher Schedules

Period	Teacher A	Teacher B	Teacher C
1	Cooperative teaching (9 MATH)	Direct service	Direct service
2	Direct service	Cooperative teaching (9 ENG)	Direct service
3	Direct service	Cooperative teaching (9 ENG)	Collaborative teaming
4	Lunch and plan	Direct service	Lunch and plan
5	Cooperative teaching (9 SS)	Lunch and plan	Direct service
6	Collaborative teaming	Direct service	Cooperative teaching (9 SCI)
7	Direct service	Collaborative teaming	Cooperative teaching (9 MATH)

FIGURE 12.4 PROGRAM EXAMPLES

program. Regardless of the preparation time involved, teachers often feel at a loss about what to discuss about their individual roles in a collaborative class. When faced with the prospect of collaborative teaching, they might ask, "What will I do for a whole period in another teacher's classroom?" "What type of assistance can I provide, and how will I be received by the teacher and the students?"

First, teachers should throw out any preconceived notions about how things *should* be done in a collaborative class. The format of each collaborative class will be the result of the interaction between the collaborating teachers. Many teachers involved in collaborative teaching describe their role as "evolving" (Nowacek, 1992). They learn to "read" their team member by standing back and observing, waiting to see what they can do rather than coming in with their role and responsibilities chiseled in stone. Teachers must be willing to play the role of an aide at times, particularly in the beginning. To establish their contribution and role in the classroom, they might reflect on the needs and how they can best fit into those areas. Initially this may mean running off papers or typing a test. In the beginning suggestions should be offered tactfully. With time, the partner likely will not wait for suggestions but, instead, will actually solicit opinions and feedback from the partner—a perfect opportunity for coaching. This level of trust and respect does not happen overnight. Secondary teachers have a long history of working solo. Therefore, establishing a "comfort zone" will take time.

Even though the role of the teachers involved in collaborative teaching is an evolving one, that is not to say that time spent discussing possible roles and parameters of the program is not time well spent. This discussion might begin with each teacher answering these questions independently:

- How do you envision your role and the partner's role in the collaborative teaching model?
- What are the possible advantages of teaming?
- What are your fears?

After considering these questions, the answers should be discussed with one another. This will help highlight areas of agreement and difference so the process of negotiation of roles and responsibilities can begin and together the teachers will truly share the territory of the classroom. A format similar to the one provided in Figure 12.5 might be used to help structure and guide this process.

Another way a teacher might prepare for the collaborative class is to conduct a setting demands interview with the classroom teacher prior to working together and arrange to observe the class on one or more occasions. Formats suggested in *Assessing Classroom Demands* (Knackendoffel & Robinson, in prep.) and *The Instructional Environment Scale* (Ysseldyke & Christenson, 1993) might provide a structure for determining the demands of the content class. Teachers will want to gather information regarding the various teaching methods used (e.g., lecture, small-group instruction, cooperative learning), how students are evaluated, what type of tests are given, and what written products are required of the students, collect information about the textbook suitability for students who are reading below grade level, and determine the teacher's expectations regarding classroom management.

How do I envision my role in this collaborative situation? How do I envision my partner's role?

My Role	Partner's Role	
_____	_____	Lead teacher
_____	_____	Support teacher
_____	_____	Co-teacher
_____	_____	Sharing instructional strategies and techniques (peer coaching)
_____	_____	Modeling teaching routines and instructional strategies
_____	_____	Cooperative teaching
_____	_____	Joint planning
_____	_____	Determining course content
_____	_____	Grading responsibilities
_____	_____	Student supervision
_____	_____	_____
_____	_____	_____

RESPONSIBILITIES/ASSISTANCE:

My Role	Partner's Role	
_____	_____	Modifying tests
_____	_____	Developing alternative assessments
_____	_____	Developing student notes
_____	_____	Monitoring and assisting students during instruction and seatwork activities
_____	_____	Developing study guides and/or review sheets and exercise
_____	_____	Adapting the textbook and/or other readings
_____	_____	Developing alternative learning arrangements or groupings (peer tutors, coop. learning)
_____	_____	Adapting assignments
_____	_____	Developing a modified grading system
_____	_____	Classroom management
_____	_____	_____
_____	_____	_____

What are the possible advantages of us teaming together?

What are my fears about collaborative teaching?

(continued)

FIGURE 12.5   DETERMINING COLLABORATIVE ROLES AND RESPONSIBILITIES

Why would someone want me as a partner? (your strengths)

Instruction:

Personal:

Organization:

Misc.

Issues to discuss before entering into collaborative teaching arrangements:
- What will each teacher's responsibility be for students with special needs (instruction, seating, grouping, grading, assignments, etc.)?
- Grading (philosophy, who will do it, recording in grade book, modifications in grading system)
- Who will present the content?
- How will the planning take place?
- How will we handle various task completion issues (absences, missing homework, etc.)?
- How will we present our model to parents and students (i.e., Why are two teachers in this classroom?)?
- Discuss and agree on classroom routines.
- What type of behavior management system will be in place, and what will each of our roles be?

How will you evaluate and revise your model?
(Periodically both teachers should respond to these questions and discuss.)

What is going well?

What would you change?

FIGURE 12.5   CONTINUED

The special educator can learn more specific information by requesting certain materials (e.g., textbook, graded tests, and homework) to study after the interview is completed. For example, looking over a graded test may reveal how the teacher scores an essay question when a student knows the basic concept but has poor writing skills. This type of information usually is not extrapolated during the interview.

During one or more observations in the classroom, the special educator can observe the general class environment, witness the instructional presentation in action, observe student behaviors such as on- and off-task during class, and reflect on teacher behaviors regarding classroom management, provisions for feedback and reinforcement, and a host of other interactions between teachers and students. An example interview summary sheet and observation summary form are provided in Figures 12.6 and 12.7. After the observation(s), interview, and examination of materials, the setting demands information can be compiled, and the special educator should set up a time to meet with the content teacher to share the results. Initially the purpose of this meeting might be to have the content teacher confirm or dispute the special educator's findings so inaccurate information can be corrected.

If the summary depicts an accurate picture of the setting demands, the utility of this task becomes readily apparent. Many teachers report that the setting demands interview opens the door for discussions between the content teacher and the special educator about teaching methods, test modifications, adapting materials, and so on (Knackendoffel, 1989). It can be used as a springboard for future discussions about material modification and instructional grouping arrangements. This information also can help teachers better prepare students for meeting the demands of specific content classes.

UNDERSTANDING AND RESOLVING CONFLICT

One area that often causes anxiety is how to avoid conflict in the collaborative role. Traditionally, school professionals have disliked and avoided conflict. This was particularly the case when school culture emphasized isolation rather than collaboration. Increasingly, staff members in today's schools are expected to work together, which is bound to result in conflict sooner or later. Simply stated, conflict is any situation in which two or more people disagree about something. Conflict is unavoidable. Differences in opinions, values, and needs are part of our daily existence. Conflict is neither good nor bad (Schmuck, Runkel, Arends, & Arends, 1977). The judgment one makes about conflict is what determines whether it is perceived as having positive or negative outcomes.

As a response, one might remember the old saying, "When life gives you lemons, make lemonade!" Instead of wasting an inordinate amount of energy on avoiding conflict, the teacher might think of some of the potential positive outcomes that can emerge. Conflict may result in higher-quality decisions, as well as the involved parties' taking greater ownership in decisions. Another value of conflict is that it can prevent stagnation, stimulate interest and curiosity, and foster creativity (Bolton, 1979). Finally, more open, trusting relationships may emerge as a result of conflict. Confrontation is a necessary ingredient of organizational renewal.

When the causes of conflict and influencing factors are understood, teachers are

Summary of Setting Demands Interview			
Course	Grade	Semester/Year	Date
Teacher		School	Interviewer

TEACHING METHOD	PRESENTATION/LECTURE
STUDENT RESPONSE/PARTICIPATION	TEXTBOOK/SUPPLEMENTAL MATERIAL
TESTS	WRITTEN PRODUCTS/MAJOR PROJECTS
GRADES	CLASS MANAGEMENT

FIGURE 12.6   SUMMARY OF SETTING DEMANDS INTERVIEW

Summary of Setting Demands Observation

_____	_____	_____	_____
TEACHER	SUBJECT	GRADE	DATE

CLASS ENVIRONMENT: :# of students_____
Describe setting atmosphere:

Describe room arrangement:

INSTRUCTIONAL PRESENTATION:
Lessons/materials used:

Media used:

Group/individual instruction:

Describe activities/student involvement:

TEACHER BEHAVIORS:
Describe classroom management:

Describe teacher feedback/reinforcement:

Describe teacher/student interaction:

STUDENT BEHAVIORS:
Describe on-task/off-task behavior:

Describe student involvement activities:

FIGURE 12.7   SUMMARY OF SETTING DEMANDS OBSERVATION

better able to identify and manage conflict situations that arise in teaming efforts. The conflict experienced in the teacher's role is influenced significantly by the school's organization and administration. Factors such as the principal's leadership style and communication among various components of the organization affect the likelihood of conflict.

Personal characteristics of one's colleagues also can be a source of conflict. When people are in difficult conflict situations, many times they display a variety of negative behaviors such as verbal or physical aggression, reduced conversation, or walking away.

CONFLICT MANAGEMENT STYLES

Friend and Cook (1992) maintain that most people have a preferred conflict management style. Table 12.1 identifies five conflict management styles and the characteristics of each style. None of these styles is entirely positive or negative. Depending on the situation in which it is used, each has both merits and drawbacks.

COMPETITIVE STYLE

People who use the competitive style try to overpower the other person who is standing in their way. They focus on "winning" at the expense of the relationship. This style often is associated with power. At times a competitive style might be appropriate (e.g., when ethical issues are at stake). Usually, however, this style can seriously damage the collaborative relationship. This approach should be reserved for issues in which a person believes with the heart and soul.

AVOIDANCE STYLE

Individuals who use avoidance as a conflict management style turn away from conflict. On the outside they may give the impression that everything is fine, but just beneath the surface tension is building. Maybe a person refuses to discuss an issue or a group consciously avoids an underlying issue because it is "too hot to handle." In some situations this may be an appropriate response. When emotions are running high, the teacher may think it best to let people cool off before addressing the conflict. Avoidance also might be an appropriate strategy if time is lacking to address the problem. Or the issue may be inconsequential and not worth discussing. The danger with avoidance is that the issue sometimes is important and differences of opinion should be discussed and resolved. By avoiding the situation, the problem might actually worsen.

ACCOMMODATING STYLE

The accommodating person would rather give in than face a conflict situation. Many teachers of LD adolescents have operated with this style for years because they want to preserve positive relationships with colleagues. This might be an appropriate tactic if the issue is relatively unimportant, because the relationship certainly is an important consideration in successful collaboration. After time, however, this teacher may feel that he or she is *always* the one who is making concessions and eventually may begin to feel that others are taking advantage of him or her. This can damage the relationship in the long run. The bottom line is that an accommodating style is a useful tactic to explore for people who have a tendency to try to win every battle. It is inappropriate for those who feel resentful that colleagues don't respect their opinions or generally take advantage of their accommodating style.

TABLE 12.1   STYLES OF MANAGING CONFLICT AND THEIR CHARACTERISTICS

Style	What They Do
Competitive	pursue their goals try to get their way or win their position press their points by showing the other person the logic and benefits of their position assert their wishes
Avoidance	sometimes let others solve the problem try to avoid tension and unpleasantness are likely to postpone so they have time to think over an issue avoid controversial positions
Accommodating	focus on areas of agreement rather than issues that separate try to soothe feelings and preserve the relationship sometimes are willing to sacrifice their own wishes for the wishes of others work hard not to hurt others' feelings
Compromising	try to find a compromise are willing to give up some points in exchange for others are likely to propose a middle ground try to reach a fair agreement in which both parties gain and losses are equalized
Collaborating	attempt to deal with the concerns of all parties involved seek the help of others when working out a solution attempt to get all concerns and issues immediately out in the open share their ideas and also ask others for their ideas deal with problems head on attempt to work through differences

COMPROMISING STYLE

Some degree of negotiation will be necessary to function within a collaborative environment. Somewhere along the road, teachers may develop the notion that negotiation means compromise ("I give up something; you give up something"). This may result in a solution that is acceptable to all but that does not exactly meet the needs of anyone. Using a compromising style in conflict management is expedient and therefore may be called for when there is limited time to resolve the conflict. Compromise can have drawbacks if two competitive individuals, when in a conflict situation, decide to compromise. They may feel dissatisfied and conflict may surface at a later time. Friend and Cook (1992) described compromise as being more assertive and cooperative than the avoiding style but less so than the collaborating style.

COLLABORATIVE STYLE

A collaborative approach to conflict calls for high degrees of both assertiveness and co-operativeness. It often involves developing a completely new alternative to the conflict situation. It is a time-consuming process and can only happen when professionals learn about and come to trust one another. Therefore, like the other styles discussed, it may not be the most appropriate choice, or even an option, in all conflict situations.

SUGGESTIONS FOR RESOLVING CONFLICT

No simple formula can be applied to every conflict resolution situation encountered in collaboration. Probably the best overall technique is problem solving. Conflict management is merely a special example of the problem-solving process. The steps in problem-solving are as follows:

1. Identify and define the problem (conflict) using active listening to reduce anger or defensiveness in the other person.
2. Don't rush; take time to understand the other person's point of view.
3. Generate several alternative solutions, taking care not to evaluate until all possibilities are out on the table.
4. Evaluate the alternative solutions by examining flaws, barriers, difficulties in implementing, and so on. Make a decision.
5. Make a mutual commitment to one solution. Don't persuade or push a solution. If it is not freely chosen, it is unlikely to be carried out.

Clear communication is essential. Listeners should concentrate on *what* the speaker is saying and *how* it is being said. They need to understand the point of view of the person with whom they have a conflict. This will help in constructively resolving it. Paraphrasing important concepts helps clarify areas of uncertainty, and emphasizes them, and it lets the other person know that he or she is understood. Active listening can go a long way in diffusing some of the tension in a conflict situation.

Negotiation is another useful technique. Even though most people do not view themselves as negotiators, they probably engage in informal negotiations every day. During conflict situations the negotiation strategies have to be more conscious and deliberate. In their book *Getting to Yes*, Fisher and Ury (1981) identified four principles of negotiation that can be used in conflict situations.

1. Separate the person from the problem. Look beyond the surface of the conflict, and respond to the people issues. Preserving the relationship should be a top priority. Try to understand the other person's thinking by putting yourself in his or her shoes, and then try to make your proposals consistent with the other person's values.
2. Focus on interests, not positions. Behind opposing positions lie shared and compatible interests as well as the conflicting one. Identify interests by addressing the following:
   a. Ask why the other person wants what he or she wants.
   b. Ask "why not?" Think about his or her choice. Why doesn't he or she like your position? What interests stand in the way?

    c. Realize that each side has multiple interests. Look for compatible interests when searching for solutions.

    d. Recognize that the most powerful interests are basic human needs. Don't overlook the obvious (security, sense of belonging, recognition, control over one's life).

3. Once interests have been identified, invent options for mutual gain. Four obstacles that inhibit the generation of multiple options are:

    a. Premature judgment.

    b. Searching for a single answer.

    c. The assumption of a fixed pie (either/or).

    d. Thinking that "solving their problem is *their* problem."

    Invent creative options by:

    — separating the act of inventing options from the act of judging them.

    — developing many options.

    — searching for mutual gain (identifying shared interests).

4. Insist on using objective criteria to evaluate your decision. The key here is using fair standards.

MANAGING RESISTANCE

Resistance can be even more troubling than out-and-out conflict. With conflict situations, the disagreement is apparent, and one can choose whether to resolve it or not. Resistance is much more elusive. The words, actions, and even inaction of colleagues may be interpreted in many different ways.

WHY PEOPLE RESIST

Friend and Cook (1992) identified many causes for resistance. People often resist because of how they perceive the change or its outcomes. Change requires new ways of thinking. Doing so is difficult and induces feelings of awkwardness (Fullan, 1985). Basically, it evokes fear of the unknown. The perceptions actually may be inaccurate or the person may be reacting to partial information. Generally, the more ambiguity, the more likely the resistance.

    Colleagues also are likely to resist because of the personal impact of the change. For example, if the proposed change will alter their professional functioning or role, they may be afraid of failing. They may not feel comfortable in learning new skills or practices. These feelings of insecurity can be exacerbated when people think they lack the training or experience to carry out the new role. If the proposed change involves working with others and the person is accustomed to working more autonomously, that person's autonomy may be threatened.

    Sometimes people resist an idea based on the person who is suggesting it rather than any specific objection to the idea itself. They may have a different personal style or may not respect the individual because of past experiences. The resistance even could be based on the person's being new or not having established a trusting relationship with the person proposing the change. Imagine the potential for resistance evoked by a new staff member approaching a veteran teacher about co-teaching a class together.

Finally, sometimes people resist change for change's sake. They become comfortable in their role or wish to maintain the status quo. As a rule, organizations resist any type of change. Schools, like other organizations, seek to maintain some level of homeostasis.

INDICATORS OF RESISTANCE

Because resistance is much more elusive than conflict, how can people recognize it? Friend and Cook (1992) pointed out several ways in which resistance may be manifested. One particularly disturbing type of resistance is when people seem to support one's ideas by their verbal and nonverbal responses but then choose not to act on them. People often choose this response because agreeing overtly with the ideas and subsequently not acting upon them is easier than openly disagreeing with the person and possibly initiating conflict, or at least a lengthy discussion.

Another subtle type of resistance is when the other party procrastinates in one way or another—slow to implement the intervention, schedule a meeting, and so on. Certainly these delays can be legitimate, but if a pattern of delays emerges, it is likely an indicator of resistance.

At times people show their resistance by making comments such as:

- We've always done it this way.
- This is just the latest educational fad. I'm sure we'll be on to something else tomorrow.
- I don't see anything wrong with the way we're doing things now.

They are saying that they prefer to rely on past practice and are generally suspicious of change. A related approach is when the person refuses to take responsibility for rejecting the change. Instead, the colleague may defer to another group (e.g., parents, other teachers), an authority figure such as an administrator, or cite a policy or law that would prohibit the idea. Comments may include:

- The administration in this district has never been supportive of this type of service delivery.
- I think you'll be facing an uphill battle with most of the parents.
- Even if I agree, you'll never get the other teachers to go along with this idea.

Finally, one of the clearest indicators of resistance is when the person simply refuses an offer to participate. Of the indicators of resistance discussed thus far, this might be the preferred one, as it is not subtle and clearly conveys resistance. Knowing that resistance exists, the teacher can either acknowledge the appropriateness of the resistance or use strategies to overcome the resistance (discussed later).

WHEN TO ADDRESS RESISTANCE

When sensing resistance, the teacher must decide whether to address it or not. Friend and Cook (1992) suggested that the person examine if the resistance is appropriate, whether the effort to address it is warranted, and others' commitment to change.

When encountering resistance, the place to start is to consider the situation from the other person's point of view. Does the change place undue hardship on the person? Looking at the resistance through the eyes of the other party better prepares one to address the obstacles that stand in the way of implementation.

Another consideration is whether addressing the resistance is warranted. Sometimes the best response to resistance may be not to respond at all. In some situations the effort simply may not be worth it. For example, a teacher may lack the administrative backing to pursue an idea with a resistant staff. Or the teacher may be aware that personnel changes will be taking place at the end of the year, which will make the struggle a moot point.

Finally, the teacher should assess the other person's commitment to change. This will help gauge one's own commitment to change. Too, people are less likely to change if emotions are running high. Sometimes, letting an idea simmer in others' minds before readdressing with a highly resistant staff can be advantageous.

STRATEGIES FOR OVERCOMING RESISTANCE

Persuasion is one strategy that is available. Several resistance management strategies may be beneficial.

1. *Provide incentives/recognition.* Adults, not unlike students, have different needs at different times. If they are to be influenced their emotional and physical needs have to be met (DeBoer, 1986). The idea here is to reward the person for participating. This might include things that would reduce workloads, such as assistance with classroom chores (e.g., test grading, preparing study guides). All of us appreciate recognition. Exemplary programs can become model classrooms for others to observe.

2. *Provide modeling/observation time.* If the colleague can observe implementation of a new instructional procedure or visit another school where a similar program is being carried out, perhaps he or she will be more receptive to the change. Providing this opportunity to observe someone else removes some of the fear associated with the unknown. For example, a good way to alleviate a teacher's fear about a student who is to be mainstreamed into the class is to arrange an informal meeting with another teacher who has worked with the student successfully.

3. *Anchor change in familiarity.* People like to feel comfortable, and change generally makes us feel uncomfortable. Therefore, the change should be tied to others' knowledge and experience. Each of us has a certain tolerance for change. The key is to determine the other person's tolerance and propose ideas that fall within it. The information shared is not as important as *how* the information is perceived (Shelby, 1986). When proposing a new idea, frame the idea in familiar language, and ground the idea in the other person's value system. This requires some reflection before making the proposal so it can be "packaged" in a way that will make it acceptable to the other person.

4. *Address others' needs.* One approach that has proven effective when dealing with resistance is to identify the underlying needs of the other person and enable those needs to be addressed (Fisher & Ury, 1981). Although we all have our own unique needs, teachers often have needs in common such as the need to feel control over the immediate work setting (e.g., classroom, caseload, schedule), a need to be appreciated and acknowledged for their efforts on behalf of students, and a need for a high degree of structure in their

roles (Friend & Cook, 1992). To the extent that teachers can relate their proposals to the needs of others, the greater is the chance it will be accepted.

5. *Involve others in planning*. Regardless of the nature and scope of the change, teachers will meet much less resistance if they include others early in the planning process (Johnson & Johnson, 1987; Margolis & McGettigan, 1988). This early involvement allows them to address concerns as they arise and provides the colleagues with a sense of ownership and a personal investment in making the plan successful.

6. *Solicit feedback*. Much of the resistance encountered in the collaborative role can be alleviated by simply asking for input from those involved. For example, if you are working with a content teacher on accommodations for a student with a learning disability in a social science class, you might gather information in a setting demands interview (discussed earlier in this chapter) to determine what approaches seem most suited to the class. Once these accommodations have been implemented, the two of you should meet to discuss whether these have been successful. The feedback should be used to alter the plan and make it more effective. Again, this type of approach helps participating teachers feel more involved in the plan and fulfills their need to be appreciated and acknowledged for their efforts on behalf of students (Margolis & McGettigan, 1988).

7. *Stress voluntariness when resistance is present*. None of us likes to be told to do something whether we like it or not. When people sense they are being backed into a corner with few or no options, they are likely to dig in their heels and resist the proposed change. People like to have their input sought and feel their contribution is valued. When interacting with others concerning change, the teacher should convey clearly that they have a choice (West, Idol, & Cannon, 1989). A general principle for addressing resistance is to respect the rights of others to object to change and to encourage them to discuss their points of view.

Summary

Adolescents with learning disabilities are not educated in a vacuum. Successful programming for these students involves many school professionals working together to integrate their programs for the benefit of students with learning disabilities. Collaborative teaming probably can best be described as an attitude rather than a certain way of delivering services. Several options, such as collaborative consultation, cooperative teaching, and coaching, embody the collaborative teaming spirit. No one method can be prescribed for all situations. The special educator's role is to assess the current situation and create an individualized plan. An important part of this preparation is to define the roles and responsibilities of collaborating teachers to alleviate potential misunderstanding and capitalize on the skills and expertise of participating teachers.

One of the first steps to collaboration involves determining colleagues' readiness to collaborate. This informal assessment process will help avoid the pitfall of trying to force collaboration between unwilling parties. It also will assist in moving a relationship along the continuum of collaboration. Success when working with others stems largely from one's ability to communicate effectively and employ strategies to manage resistance. Building strong relationships with colleagues is important to collaborative efforts. Working effectively with other adults is just as important to the role of an LD specialist as knowing effective instructional strategies to use with students. Basic communication skills are prerequisite to collaboration but are not sufficient in and of themselves. Partnership-building skills facilitate the long-term professional relationship with colleagues. These skills go beyond the surface communication skills employed in our individual interactions.

The problem-solving technique described in this chapter can be applied in virtually every situation that includes students with LD. It provides a process and structure to guide problem-solving sessions. Teachers who have used this process report that the outcomes of their problem-solving sessions are more satisfying and productive (Knackendoffel, 1989). Understanding and resolving conflict and managing resistance to change is part of the problem-solving process.

REFERENCES

Bauwens, J., Hourcade, J. J., & Friend, M. (1989). Cooperative teaching: A model for general and special education integration. *Remedial and Special Education, 10*(2), 17–22.

Bolton, R. (1979). *People skills: How to assert yourself, listen to others, and resolve conflicts.* New York: Simon & Schuster.

Borko, H., Livingston, C., & Shavelson, R. J. (1990). Teachers' thinking about instruction. *Remedial and Special Education, 11*(6), 40–49, 53.

Cummings, C. (1985). *Peering in on peers: Coaching teachers.* Edmonds, WA: Teaching, Inc.

Cummings, A. L., Murray, H. G., & Martin, J. (1989). Protocol analysis of the social problem solving of teachers. *American Educational Research Journal, 26,* 25–43.

DeBoer, A. (1986). *The art of consulting.* Chicago: Arcturus Books.

Dettmer, P., Thurston, L. P., & Dyck, N. (1993). *Consultation, collaboration, and teamwork for students with special needs.* Boston: Allyn & Bacon.

Fisher, R., & Ury, W. (1981). *Getting to yes.* Boston: Houghton Mifflin.

Friend, M., & Cook, L. (1992). *Interactions: Collaboration skills for school professionals.* New York: Longman.

Fullan, M. (1982). *The meaning of educational change.* New York: Teachers College Press.

Fullan, M. (1985). Change processes and strategies at the local level. *Elementary School Journal, 85*(3), 391–420.

Garmston, R. J. (1987). How administrators support peer coaching. *Educational Leadership, 44*(5), 18–26.

Gersten, R. (1990). Enemies real and imagined: Implications of "teachers' thinking about instruction" for collaboration between special and general education. *Remedial and Special Education, 11*(6), 50–53.

Harris, K. C., Harvey, P., Garcia, L., Innes, D., Lynn, P., Munoz, D., Sexton, K., & Stoica, R. (1987). Meeting the needs of special high school students in regular education classrooms. *Teacher Education and Special Education, 10*(4), 143-152.

Idol, L., Paolucci-Whitcomb, P., & Nevin, A. (1986). *Collaborative consultation.* Austin, TX: Pro-Ed.

Jenkins, J. R., & Jenkins, L. M. (1981). *Cross age and peer tutoring: Help for children with learning problems.* Reston, VA: Council for Exceptional Children.

Johnson, D. W., & Johnson, F. P. (1987). *Joining together: Group theory and group skills* (3d ed.). Englewood Cliffs, NJ: Prentice Hall.

Johnson, D. W., & Johnson, R. T. (1986). Mainstreaming and cooperative learning strategies. *Exceptional Children, 52,* 553–561.

Joyce, B., with Bennett, B., & Rolheiser-Bennett, C. (1990). The self-educating teacher: Empowering teachers through research. In B. Joyce (Ed.), *Changing school culture through staff development* (pp. 26–40). Alexandria, VA: Association for Supervision and Curriculum Development.

Joyce, B., & Showers, B. (1983). *Power in staff development through research on training.* Alexandria, VA: Association for Supervision and Curriculum Development.

Knackendoffel, E. A. (1989). *Development and validation of a set of teaming strategies for enhancing collaboration between secondary resource and content teachers.* Unpublished doctoral dissertation, University of Kansas, Lawrence.

Knackendoffel, E. A., & Robinson, S. M. (in prep.). *Assessing classroom demands.* Lawrence, KS: Edge Enterprises.

Knackendoffel, E. A., Robinson, S. M., Deshler, D. D., & Schumaker, J. B. (1992). *Collaborative problem solving: A step-by-step guide to creating educational solutions.* Lawrence, KS: Edge Enterprises.

Margolis, H., & McGettigan, J. (1988). Managing resistance to instructional modifications in mainstreamed environments. *Remedial and Special Education, 9*(4), 15–21.

Miller, L. J., Kohler, F. W., Ezell, H., Hoel, K., & Strain, P. S. (1993). Winning with peer tutoring: A teachers' guide. *Preventing School Failure, 37*(3), 14–18.

Nowacek, E. J. (1992). Professionals talk about teaching together: Interviews with five collaborating teachers. *Intervention in School and Clinic, 27*(5), 262–276.

Rosenholtz, S. J. (1989). Workplace conditions that affect teacher quality and commitment: Implications for teacher induction programs. *Elementary School Journal, 89,* 421–439.

Robinson, S. M., & Knackendoffel, E. A. (in prep.). *Developing collaborative programs: Promoting professional development and change.* Lawrence, KS: Edge Enterprises.

Rottier, J., & Ogan, B. J. (1991). *Cooperative learning in middle-level schools.* Washington, DC: National Education Association.

Ruhl, K. L., Hughes, C. A., & Schloss, P. J. (1987). Using the pause procedure to enhance lecture recall. *Teacher Education and Special Education, 10*(1), 14–18.

Schmuck, R. A., Runkel, P. J., Arends, J. H., & Arends, R. I. (1977). *The second handbook of organization development in schools.* Palo Alto, CA: Mayfield.

Shelby, A. N. (1986). The theoretical bases of persuasion: A critical introduction. *Journal of Business Communication, 23,* 5–27.

Showers, B. (1985). Teachers coaching teachers. *Educational Leadership, 42*(7), 43–48.

Showers, B. (1990). Aiming for superior classroom instruction for all children: A comprehensive staff development model. *Remedial and Special Education, 11*(3), 50–53.

Slavin, R. E. (1986). *Using student teaming learning* (3d ed.). Baltimore: Johns Hopkins University.

Warner, S. (1990). Research into practice: Collaboration and consultation in action. *LD Forum, 16*(2), 16–17.

West, J. F., Idol, L., & Cannon, G. (1989). *Collaboration in the schools.* Austin, TX: Pro-Ed.

Ysseldyke, J. E., & Christenson, S. L. (1993). *The instructional environment system–II: A system to identify a student's instructional needs.* Longmont, CO: Sopris West.

Author Index

Subject Index